VICTIM POLICIES AND CRIMINAL JUSTICE ON THE ROAD TO RESTORATIVE JUSTICE

A collection of essays in honour of Tony Peters

VICTIM POLICIES AND CRIMINAL JUSTICE ON THE ROAD TO RESTORATIVE JUSTICE

A collection of essays in honour of Tony Peters

E. Fattah & S. Parmentier (eds.)

Leuven University Press
2001

Published with the support of the K.U.Leuven Commissie voor Publicaties

Blijde Inkomststraat 5, B-3000 Leuven (Belgium)

ISBN 90 5867 181 X

D/2001/1869/95

Cover: W. Platteborze

Illustration cover : Made by the artist C. Orrico, the statues on the cover of this book represent Don Quijote and Sancho Panza, two legendary figures created by Don Miguel de Cervantes and very dear to Tony Peters. Reproducing his own words, they have introduced him to the classics of world literature and to the magic world of Spain and of Latin America. With hindsight, the academic career of Tony Peters can be characterised as combining the best of both figures: the critical attitude and discipline of the knight, and the pragmatism and *joie de vivre* of his servant.

TABLE OF CONTENTS

PART II: ON REFORMING CRIMINAL JUSTICE

PART III: ON DEVELOPING RESTORATIVE JUSTICE

INTRODUCTION

E. Fattah & S. Parmentier

On October 1st, 2001, Tony Peters retired as a professor of criminology at the Katholieke Universiteit Leuven, after 35 years of intensive academic activity. During his long tenure, he has had a considerable impact and has left an unmistakable print on many: students, colleagues, researchers, professionals, criminal justice practitioners, and policy makers alike. They all admired his personal qualities and his amazing ability to make the link between criminological theory and praxis.

A quick overview of his curriculum reveals a varied and distinguished career in teaching and research. Born in 1941, Tony Peters studied sociology and criminology at the K.U. Leuven in the late 1950s and early 1960s. He became one of the first assistants of the new School for Criminology, which was founded within the frame of the Faculty of Law in 1969, right after the division of the University of Leuven in a Dutch-speaking and a French-speaking entity. Over the years, the School (now Department of Criminology) has grown considerably to its current size of nearly 50 staff members, who study a wide variety of criminological topics from an interdisciplinary perspective, thus making it one of the major centres of criminological research in Europe. Tony Peters completed his Ph.D. in Criminology in 1976, with a study on the unequal living conditions of the detainees in Leuven central prison. It was one of the first empirical and critical studies of the Belgian prison system, and it marked the beginning of his long-standing interest in penology and prison matters, which lasted for nearly two decades. At the end of the 1980s, Tony Peters turned his attention to victims and victim issues, again through empirical research about the phenomenon of victimisation and about policy developments in this field. By doing so, he introduced in Belgium the discipline of victimology, as an integral part of criminology. This interest in "the reverse side of crime" led him and his Research Group on Penology and Victimology in the early 1990s to explore the newly emerging paradigm of restorative justice, as a third way between retributive and rehabilitative justice. Since that time, he has been actively researching and promoting this third way, whereby offenders and victims are confronted with one another with the objective of finding an acceptable solution to their common problem and of restoring their relationship, an approach which can be used in a variety of settings within and outside the criminal justice system.

In the course of his long career, Tony Peters developed a worldwide network of academic contacts. He was a visiting professor at the universities of Edinburgh, Montréal, Las Palmas, and the Universidad del Pais Vasco. He stood at the cradle in the early 1990s of exchanges of students and teachers in criminology within the European Union in the framework of the ERASMUS programme. Building on these enriching experiences, he and Ezzat Fattah took the initiative in 1996 to establish a Euro-Canadian exchange programme on Victimization, Mediation, and Restorative Justice, together with a number of European and Canadian universities. Tony Peters also inspired the establishment of a Master's programme in European Criminology at the K.U.Leuven and still acts as its first director.

Given the wide experience of Tony Peters in criminological theory, practice, and policy, it was not surprising that when the news of his impending retirement became known, many of his national and international colleagues expressed a desire to see a collection of essays published in his honour, and readily agreed to personally contribute to that collection. We are both fortunate and honoured to have been entrusted with the task of putting this collection together and preparing it for publication.

This collection contains 22 previously unpublished papers that were written specifically for this volume. We wish to take this opportunity to express our sincere thanks to all those whose contributions appear in this text and also to those who expressed a keen interest in contributing but were unable to do so because of work pressures and time constraints.

Although contributions of this kind inevitably result in a more or less heterogeneous group of essays, we were able to organize the 22 papers into three sections under the following headings: Part I is entitled *On Promoting Victim Policies*; Part II *On Reforming Criminal Justice*; and Part III *On Developing Restorative Justice*. All three areas are ones to which Tony Peters has made a significant contribution and for which he is known as an international authority. During his long and productive academic career Tony Peters led many struggles for criminal justice reform. He was a leading figure in the movement to recognize crime victims' plight and to reaffirm their rights. In Belgium, he spearheaded the early initiatives in restorative justice and became one of its outspoken proponents nationally and internationally. There is no doubt that these three major topics and the various developments and reforms that are addressed in the papers will dominate the thinking about, and the practice of, criminal justice in the years to come. Thus, in addition to paying homage to a congenial friend and an illustrious colleague, we hope that this book will appeal and prove useful to all those who have an interest in victims issues, in criminal justice reform, and last but not least, in the promising paradigm of restorative justice.

In working our way through the editorial process, we have received the precious assistance of Anita Van Cleynenbreugel of the Law and Society

Institute at the K.U. Leuven, who has typed and retyped the incoming manuscripts with great care and tremendous diligence. Hilde Lens and Beatrice Van Eeghem of Leuven University Press have been very helpful in supporting the proposal for the present book and in promoting it on a national and international scale. To all of them, we like to express our sincere thanks.

May we end by saying that this is not the only volume that will honour Tony Peters on the occasion of his retirement. Colleagues in his native Belgium and the neighbouring Netherlands have contributed to another volume produced in his mother language under the title *Herstelrecht tussen toekomst en verleden* (Restorative Justice Between the Future and the Past), also published by Leuven University Press, under the editorship of Lieven Dupont & Frank Hutsebaut.

PART I

ON PROMOTING VICTIM POLICIES

VICTIMIZING THE HELPLESS. ASSAULTING CHILDREN AS A CORRECTIVE MEASURE

Ezzat A. Fattah

"It is very difficult for people to believe the simple fact that every persecutor was once a victim."

Alice Miller[1]

"In the earliest stage of life, it is possible for a child to forget about the extreme acts of cruelty he or she has endured and to idealize their perpetrator. But the nature of the subsequent enactment reveals that the whole history of early persecution was stored up somewhere: the drama now unfolds in front of the spectators with an amazing resemblance to the original situation but under another guise: in the reenactment, the child who was once persecuted now becomes the persecutor."

Alice Miller[2]

Preamble

On September 10, 1996, the news agency Reuter reported that the European Commission of Human Rights has agreed to take up the case of a 12-year-old British boy seeking to overturn British laws allowing his parents to spank him. The boy's stepfather beat him with a cane when he was nine and his lawyers were contesting British laws sanctioning 'reasonable chastisement' of children. Reuter viewed the decision as a first step paving the way toward a possible ruling by the European Court of Human Rights banning any type of beating of children in Britain, a ruling that would eventually bring Britain into line with other European countries that had already banned corporal punishment of children.

1 A. MILLER (1990) *For Your Own Good: Hidden Cruelty in Child-Rearing and the Roots of Violence,* 249. New York: Farrar, Straus, Giroux.

2 MILLER, *o.c.*, 145.

Two years later the European Court of Human Rights ruled unanimously (23/09/1998) that "*beating with garden cane applied with considerable force on more than one occasion reaches level of severity prohibited by Article 3 of the United Nations Convention on the Rights of the Child*".[3] In addition to the reference to Article 3, the Court also referred to Articles 19 and 37 of the same Convention.

Article 19 stipulates that:

"1. States Parties shall take all appropriate legislative, administrative, social and educational measures to protect the child from all forms of physical or mental violence, injury or abuse, neglect or negligent treatment, maltreatment or exploitation, including sexual abuse, while in the care of parent(s), legal guardian(s) or any other person who has the care of the child."

Introduction

In recent years the issue of child abuse has become an area of serious concern. Not infrequently, the physical and sexual abuse of children is even portrayed as a major social problem of staggering proportions. And yet the criminal codes in many countries continue to allow the use of physical violence against children as a corrective measure. For example, section 43 of the Canadian Criminal Code stipulates that "every schoolteacher, parent or person standing in the place of a parent is justified in using force by way of correction toward a pupil or child, as the case may be, who is under his care, if the force does not exceed what is reasonable under the circumstances". Surprisingly, what is "reasonable" seems to be left to the personal discretion and individual interpretation of each parent or schoolteacher!

Attempts to repeal Section 43 have failed despite overwhelming evidence that the vast majority of cases, which are later diagnosed and classified as child abuse, are in fact cases of physical punishment gone too far, too awry, or too amiss. Actually, the demarcation line between what is reasonable corporal punishment and what is physical abuse is quite blurred, as is the dividing line between 'spanking" and "beating". To quote Alice Miller[4]:

"*Although people tend to make a distinction between "spanking" and "beating" a child, considering the former a less severe measure than the latter, the line between the two is a tenuous one.*"

---

3 E.Ct.H.R., *A. v. The United Kingdom*; Appl. 25599/94. European Court on Human Rights, *Reports of Judgments and Decisions*, 1998-VI, 90, 2692-2718.

4 MILLER, *o.c.*

Miller then relates a report she heard on an American radio station. The news item was about a man –a member of a Christian fundamentalist sect in West Virginia– who "spanked" his son for two hours. The little boy died as a result. Miller points out that even when a spanking is a gentler form of physical violence, the psychic pain and humiliation and the need to repress those feelings are the same as in the case of more severe punishment and lead to the same negative consequences.

Parents who constantly complain about how violent society is, and who want to curb their children's exposure to violence in the media, particularly TV, see nothing wrong in subjecting their children to physical violence! What could have a stronger impact on children's personality and behavior: watching violence on television or experiencing violence themselves? Seeing cartoon characters being kicked on the screen or seeing their siblings being spanked, beaten or battered?

Parents whose sense of fairness would be deeply offended if they happened to see a confrontation between two parties of unequal strength, parents who would bitterly complain if their child was hit by an older or stronger boy in school, see nothing wrong in using physical force themselves against helpless and defenseless little creatures who cannot protect themselves or hit back at their tormentor! They see nothing wrong in applying not only the force of their hands but also that of a cane, a rod, a strap, or a wooden spoon.

The paradoxes of spanking are many. The more the spanking occurs, the less feared it is and the more ineffective it becomes as a means of changing the child's behavior. Quite often, the spanking results in defiance. The disapproved behavior is repeated in a deliberate attempt to provoke the parent, or to see what the parent's response this time will be. This leads to what could be described as the vicious cycle of spanking and misbehavior. McCord[5] reports that punishments tend to increase the attraction of activities punished. She also suggests that although severe penalties may force compliance in specific instances, the behavior being punished is actually more likely to occur at a time or place when opportunities for detection are reduced.

---

5 J. McCord (1991) Questioning the Value of Punishment, 38(2) *Social Problems* 167-179.

1. The Manifest Reluctance to do Away with a Medieval Practice

Opposition to corporal punishment of children has markedly increased in many European countries. There is a growing acceptance and endorsement of the view that a child is an autonomous individual whose physical inviolability must be respected and guaranteed. This has led to the complete banning of all corporal punishment and other ill-treatment of children in countries such as Sweden in 1979 and Finland in 1984.[6] Two years later it was banned in Denmark, followed by Norway in 1987 and Austria in 1989.[7] More recently, it was banned in Cyprus (1994), Denmark (1997), Latvia (1998), Croatia (1999), and Germany (2000).

In fact, as early as 1969, the Finnish Penal Code section permitting corporal punishment of a child (that is the equivalent to section 43 of the Canadian Criminal Code) was repealed. But because the simple removal of the section was not uniformly interpreted to be a total ban on corporal punishment, the working group in charge of drafting the new legislation stated in no uncertain terms that "the child shall be raised in such a way that he receives understanding, safety, and affection. The child shall not be oppressed, corporally punished, or ill-treated in any way".[8] This wording is similar to the one used in the Swedish Parenthood and Guardianship Code of 1979 which stipulates that "A child shall not be exposed to corporal punishment or any form of ill-treatment".[9]

The rise of religious fundamentalism, the shift to the right, the popular perception that the youth of today are lawless, lack discipline or that society is becoming too lax, have thwarted attempts to ban the cruel and destructive practice of corporal punishment of children. In fact, there are reasons to believe that approval of harsh rearing practices, or what Alice Miller[10] calls the "poisonous pedagogy", remains widespread in many societies. The reasons are not difficult to comprehend. Miller points to one of the reasons. She writes: [11]

"The conviction that parents are always right and that every act of cruelty, whether conscious or unconscious, is an expression of their love

---

6 M. KORPILAHTI (1989) Child Abuse and the Courts: Finnish and Swedish Experiences, in: E.A. FATTAH (ed.), *The Plight of Crime Victims in Modern Society*. London: Macmillan.

7 Repeal 43 Committee (1994) *Brief to Minister of Justice, Solicitor General and Others*. Toronto, Canada, April 1994.

8 KORPILAHTI, *o.c.*

9 *Ibid.*, 216.

10 MILLER, *o.c.*

11 *Ibid.*, 5.

is so deeply rooted in human beings because it is based on the process of internalization that takes place during the first months of life – in other words, during the period preceding separation from the primary care-giver."

While the popular myth of universal and eternal parental love may have been acceptable centuries ago, it is surely not acceptable today when homicide statistics show that the majority of children murdered in Canada and the United States are killed by their parents!

Attempts to reason with parents who use harsh and cruel rearing practices, and to inform them of the serious negative consequences of corporal punishment on the child's development and behaviour, fall, more often than not, on deaf ears. The prevailing attitude among parents and their typical response is that "this is my child and nobody is going to tell me or teach me how to discipline them or how to bring them up".

Many people view corporal punishment of children as a parental right and are, therefore, extremely reluctant to relinquish the power (and the threatening authority) that this perceived right places in their hands. Whether they believe that it is a divine right bestowed upon them by the bible, or a secular right bestowed upon them by the criminal code, is of little importance.

Another reason for the popularity of corporal punishment as a rearing practice is the inability of most parents to conceive of other means of disciplining or correcting the misbehavior of their children. This inability, usually expressed in the often heard desperate utterance "I talked to him but he never listens", is very similar to the public's inability to conceive of means other than punishment to deal with those who violate the law or cause injury or harm to others.

One of the manifest failures of Canadian society, a society that professes a high level of intolerance to violence and crime, is the failure to provide adequate training in child rearing to prospective parents. Parents, particularly young ones, are ill prepared for the most difficult task in their lives: bringing up children. In a highly regulated society where people need approved training and authorized license to become plumbers, electricians, car mechanics, etc., they are not required to receive any training to become parents. It is not surprising therefore that most parents have a very limited repertoire of techniques to use in the event they need to deal with the child's disobedience or unruly behaviour. As a result they tend to employ the same methods their parents used with them, thus perpetuating the cycle of violence and abuse.

2. The Rationalizations and Neutralizations

In the eyes of the well-intentioned parents, who are generally unaware that by hitting or beating their offspring they are trying to satisfy their own psychological needs, the use of corporal punishment is an acceptable, justified, and highly desirable practice. Rationalizations and neutralizations are used to convince one self and others that the violence done to the child, the pain inflicted on him/her, is not reprehensible but commendable. The rationalizations are indispensable because they enable the parents to do irreparable harm to the child's body and psyche while maintaining a clear conscience and without losing any sleep over their actions.

Undoubtedly, the most popular of all rationalizations is that corporal punishment is "in the best interest of the child". The title that Alice Miller chose for her scathing indictment of violent and cruel child-rearing practices is revealing. The book's title is *For Your Own Good*, which is the most common excuse used by parents to justify the willful use of violence against, and the deliberate infliction of pain upon, their children. In the book, Miller explains how along with corporal punishment, a whole gamut of ingenious measures are applied, measures which are difficult for the child to comprehend and which for that very reason often have devastating effects in later life, and all is done with the pretext that they are "for the child's own good".

It is interesting to see how the justifications used by society for punishing offenders and law-violators become an integral part of the rationalization vocabulary used by hitting, beating and spanking parents. Who has not heard parents excusing their violent and cruel behavior towards their children with the justification that he/she "deserves a good hard spanking" for having done this or that, or for having behaved in such or such a manner?

Another popular rationalization is the deterrence excuse: "this will teach him/her a lesson, they will not do this again". Actually, the parent knows full well that past spanking has neither taught the child a lesson, nor prevented the undesirable behavior from being repeated. Still, the use of such rationalization makes the use of force appear necessary, warranted and applied for a seemingly utilitarian purpose.

Such rationalizations and justifications, as popular as they may be, do not mask the real motives behind the use of corporal punishment and the psychological needs the parent is trying to meet by using violence against the child. The justification vocabulary cannot hide the fact that corporal punishment is applied not for the child's welfare but to satisfy the parents' need to assert their authority, to exercise their power,[12] to alleviate their anger and frustration and to relieve their tension.

Many of the psychological theories meant to explain violence and aggression provide important clues to the understanding of parents' spanking/beating behavior and to the real motives behind it. Beating the child, an accessible, helpless, defenseless, and easy target, a victim who cannot strike back, has a magical cathartic effect. It assuages the parent's anger and rage; it abates the stress and frustration from which they are suffering. Corporal punishment with its potential for damaging the child for life, provides a welcome outlet for the parent's pent-up emotions and exercises a calming and soothing effect on their feelings of helplessness and frustration. In Miller's words:[13]

> *"Since tormenting one's children is a legitimate part of child-rearing, this provides the most obvious outlet for bottled-up aggression...Because an aggressive response to emotional and physical abuse is forbidden by parents in almost all religions, this outlet is the only one available."*

3. The Negative Consequences of Corporal Punishment

The negative consequences of corporal punishment are too many to enumerate and some are more obvious than others. It is certain that physical punishment, regardless of what form it takes, does not promote love but hate, does not promote affection but rejection, does not promote tenderness but anger and hostility. Could there be any doubt that violence against children is one of the major sources, perhaps the main source, of infantile hatred? Is it reasonable to assume that the violent environment created by physical punishment is a breeding ground for hatred?

The anger, the hostility, the frustration resulting from being spanked, beaten, caned, must be temporarily suppressed because the child cannot fight back, cannot attack the tormentor. Such suppressed, pent-up emotions need to find an outlet, a way of being discharged. One has to wonder whether the cruel crimes committed in adolescence or adulthood are acts by which victimized and brutalized individuals are avenging, years or decades later, traumata suffered in early childhood.

If revenge and retaliation are "normal" reactions or responses to victimization, and the strong popularity of punishment of offenders (and the death penalty) seem to suggest they are, one has to wonder about the

12 *Ibid.*
13 *Ibid.*

retaliatory and vengeful responses to acts of violence suffered in childhood at the hands of cruel or abusive parents. In what way do the victims (the children) try to satisfy those vengeful sentiments? In what form and against whom do those emotions find their outlet?

Is there a relationship between being subjected to physical punishment in childhood and delinquent, criminal or violent behavior in adolescence or adulthood? In other words, does corporal punishment turn child victims into adult victimizers?

First, an attempt will be made to answer this question by reviewing research findings on the topic. Secondly, some of the mechanisms that might be responsible for such transformation and role reversal will be presented.

4. Some Research Findings on the Effects of Corporal Punishment

4.1. Punishment of Children

The evidence pointing to a positive relationship between being subjected to violence in childhood and becoming a perpetrator of violence later on is simply too overwhelming to be ignored.[14] Three types of data are available: anecdotal, clinical and statistical.

---

14 A. BUTTON (1973) Some Antecedents of Felonious and Delinquent Behavior, 2(3)(Fall) *Journal of Clinical Child Psychology* 35-7; A. BANDURA & R.H. WALTERS (1959) *Adolescent Aggression*. New York: Ronald Press; A. MAURER (1974) Corporal Punishment, 29 *American Psychologist* 614-26; J.H. PFOUTS et al. (1981) Deviant Behaviors of Child Victims and Bystanders in Violent Families, in: R.J. HUNNER & Y.E. WALKER (eds.), *Exploring the Relationship Between Child Abuse and Delinquency*, 79-96. Montclair: Allanheld, Osmun; J. GARBARINO (1981) Child Abuse and Juvenile Delinquency: The Development Impact of Social Isolation, in: HUNNER & WALKER, *o.c.*, 115-127; R.J. BENTLEY (1981) Child Abuse, Cross-Cultural Childrearing Practices and Juvenile Delinquency: A Synthesis, in: HUNNER & WALKER, *o.c.*, 128-44; A.H. GREEN (1981) Child Abuse and the Etiology of Violent Delinquent Behavior, In HUNNER & WALKER, *o.c.*, 152-160; R.W. WEINBACH (1981) Theoretical Linkages Between Child Abuse and Juvenile Delinquency, in: HUNNER & WALKER, *o.c.*, 161-166; J. ALFARO (1981) Report on the relationship between child abuse and neglect and later socially deviant behavior, in: HUNNER & WALKER, *o.c.*, 175-219; C.M. MOUZAKITIS (1981) An Inquiry Into the Problem of Child Abuse and Juvenile Delinquency, in: HUNNER & WALKER, *o.c.*, 220-32; S.C. WICK (1981) Child Abuse as Causation of Juvenile Delinquency in Central Texas, in: HUNNER & WALKER, *o.c.*, 233-39; F.B. RAYMOND, (1981) The Influence of Child Abuse on Psychosexual and Psychosocial Development and Implications for Delinquency, in: HUNNER & WALKER, *o.c.*, 240-251.

4.2. Anecdotal Data

Many are familiar with what has been described as the cycle of violence and abuse: beaten and abused children who later on become cruel and abusive parents. They may use violence not only against their own children but also against their partners, as well as their elderly parents and grandparents. Few have not heard of battered wives who end up killing their tormentors, and it is now common knowledge that many rapists and child molesters have been sexually molested when they were young. Nothing of this is new, it has been known for a very long time and is behind the popular saying "violence breeds violence" or "violence begets violence".

Anne Rule,[15] former policewoman turned novelist and true crime author, affirms that every "sadistic sociopath" killer she has ever written about had suffered abuse in early childhood, under the age of five: abandonment, physical abuse, sexual abuse, humiliation, rejection.

4.3. Clinical/Experimental Data

Psychiatrists were among the first to draw attention to the link between corporal punishment, abuse and neglect, and subsequent criminal and violent behavior. Almost four decades ago, psychiatrist C.G. Curtis[16] suggested that abused or neglected children might *"become tomorrow's murderers and perpetrators of other crimes of violence, if they survive"*.

As early as 1951, Hartogs pointed to the extremely high incidence of victimization among the sex offenders he examined.[17] Although he does not seem to have used a non-criminal control group, but only compared sex offenders to non-sex offenders, he reported that no less than 92 percent of the former had been frequently and severely beaten by their father or mother or both parents. Among non-sex offenders, the percentage of those with an early history of beating by parents was 62 percent. According to Hartogs, most of the sex offenders were whipped with razor straps, sewing machine straps, electric cords, broom sticks and iron bars and were occasionally tied to a chair or a bed by their father or mother for the purpose of beating. Some were frequently kicked against the head, abdomen or legs or otherwise

---

15 A. RULE (1991) *If You Really Loved Me*. N.Y.: Pocket Books.

16 C.G. CURTIS (1963) Violence Breeds Violence – Perhaps? (April) *American Journal of Psychiatry* 120.

17 P. HARTOGS (1951) Discipline in the Eearly Life of Sex-Delinquents and Sex-Criminals, (March 9) *Nervous Child* 167-73.

physically tortured by their parents. Milder forms of punishment like withdrawal of food, liberty, money, sports, friends, were concurrently used by the parents who did not make use of any other form of discipline or authority. In two cases, mothers undressed their children completely before beating them. In one case, the father used to knock out his son, whenever he felt like punishing him.[18] Psychologists[19] have reported for many years that severe pain elicits a vicious aggressive attack in practically every animal species. And psychological and behavioral studies on humans[20] have shown that severe parental punishment (SPP) is definitely a precursor of aggression in humans. Welsh[21] suggests that the level of expressed delinquent aggression, particularly in males, is a function of the severity of parental punishment to which they were subjected. He further suggests that since severe parental punishment (SPP) is highly related to aggression, known abused children are likely to have one of the highest probabilities of becoming delinquent of all societal subgroups. Welsh's findings are in accord with those of several other studies all of which report that the aggressiveness of the child is related to the severity of punishment imposed by the parents.[22] More recently, Murray Straus[23] reached identical conclusions.

In his excellent analysis of physical punishment of children, Philip Greven[24] insists that it is at the root of the aggression and violence that pervade American society and that it is responsible for the American obsession with defense and warfare. Greven offers convincing evidence showing that physical punishment of children consistently appears as one of the major influences shaping subsequent aggressiveness and delinquency of

---

18 *Ibid.*, 167-8.

19 For ex., N.H. AZRIN (1967) Pain and Aggression, 1 *Psychology Today* 27-33.

20 R.S. WELSH (1976) Severe Parental Punishment and Delinquency: A Developmental Theory, (Spring) *Journal of Clinical Child Psychology* 17-21.

21 *Ibid.*

22 R.R. SEARS, E.E. MACCOBY and H. LEVIN (1957) *Patterns of Child Rearing*. Evanston, Illinois: Row, Petersen; BANDURA & WALTERS, *o.c.*; W. MCCORD, J. MCCORD & A. HOWARD (1961) Familial correlates of aggression in non-delinquent male children, 62 *J. Abnorm. Soc. Psychol.* 79-93; L.D. ERON, L.O. WALDER, R. TOIGO and M.M. LEFKOWITZ (1963) Social class, parental punishment for aggression, and child aggression, 34 *Child Development* 849-67.

23 M.A. STRAUS (1994) *Beating the Devil out of Them: Corporal Punishment in American Families*. New York: Lexington Books.

24 P. GREVEN (1990) *Spare the Child: The Religious Roots of Punishment and the Psychological Impact of Physical Abuse*. N.Y.: Alfred A. Knopf.

males. He quotes research by Slaby and Roedell,[25] among others, showing that *"one of the most reliable predictors of children's level of aggression is the heavy use by parents of harsh punitive discipline and physical punishment"*.[26] Greven affirms that the infliction of pain through physical punishments is one of the primary causes of subsequent aggression, anger, and hostility, which often take the form of delinquency and criminality. He writes:

> *"The overwhelming evidence now available from scholarship on the roots of delinquency and crime suggests that corporal punishment – the application of the rod and other implements of discipline – is a major factor in the generation of the rage, aggression, and impulses for revenge that fuel the emotions, fantasies, and actions of individuals, mostly male, who become active delinquents or criminals."*[27]

4.3. Statistical/Longitudinal Data

To see whether a link exists between being beaten, abused or neglected as a child and later delinquent and criminal behavior, researchers have conducted retrospective and prospective studies, tracing delinquents backwards or abused children forward. Prospective studies follow up individuals who had been abused or neglected as children earlier in their lives to find out the incidence of later delinquency.[28] Retrospective studies on the other hand, identify a sample of delinquent youth and then use a reverse records check to determine the incidence of abuse or neglect in the delinquent's background.[29]

If the findings of these studies are to be summarized in a nutshell, we may say that the general finding of prospective studies is somewhat reassuring while the general finding of retrospective studies is rather alarming. Prospective studies tend to show that the majority of those who are abused as children do not become persistent delinquents or hardened criminals. Retrospective studies on the other hand suggest that a large

---

25 R.G. SLABY & W.C. ROEDELL (1982) The Development and Regulation of Aggression in Young Children, in: J. WORELL (ed.), *Psychological Development in the Elementary Years*, 97-149. N.Y.: Academic Press.

26 GREVEN, *o.c.*, 194.

27 GREVEN, *o.c.*, 197.

28 C.S. WIDOM (1990) Childhood Victimization: Risk Factor for Delinquency, in: M.E. COLTEN & S. GORE (eds.), *Adolescent Stress – Causes and Consequences*, 201-222. New York: Aldine de Gruyter.

29 *Ibid.*

number of serious delinquents and violent criminals had suffered various forms of victimization, sometimes quite early in life.

The fact that not all children who are beaten, abused, spanked later become adult victimizers does not by any means negate or contradict the existence of a causal link between the victimization and the subsequent offending. As Straus[30] points out: *"Two thirds of those who smoke a pack of cigarettes a day or more do not die of lung cancer or other smoking related disease. Yet we do not take that as invalidating the theory that smoking causes lung cancer".*

McCord[31] cites three longitudinal studies that compared children whose parents depended on physical punishments with those whose parents did not, one in Finland,[32] the second in Great Britain,[33] and the third in the United States.[34] All three studies found that those whose parents used harsh physical punishments had greater probabilities for subsequently committing serious crimes. In another longitudinal study of victims of child abuse, McCord[35] concluded that violence tends to increase the probability that victims will commit serious crime.

Another study worth mentioning is one conducted by Cathy S. Widom[36] who has done extensive research on the link between child abuse, neglect, and violent criminal behavior. Using a prospective cohorts design, official criminal histories for a large sample of substantiated and validated cases of physical and sexual abuse and neglect from the years 1967 through 1971 (n=908) were compared with histories of a matched control group (n=667) of individuals with no official record of abuse or neglect. Abused and neglected subjects had higher rates of having an adult criminal record than controls and a larger number of arrests as an adult. Based on a logit analysis, a model using four explanatory variables (age, sex, race, and abuse/neglect status) provided a good fit. In comparison with controls, abused and

---

30 M.A. STRAUS (1991) New Theory and Old Canards about Family Violence Research, 38(2) *Social Problems* 180-97.

31 MCCORD, *o.c.*, 167-79.

32 L. PULKKINEN (1983) Search for Alternatives to Aggression in Finland, in: A.P. GOLDSTEIN & M.H. SEGALL (eds.), *Aggression in Global Perspective*, 104-144. Elmsford, N.Y.: Pergamon Press.

33 D.P. FARRINGTON (1978) The Family Background of Aggressive Youths, in: L.A. HERSER, M. BERGER & D. SHAFFER (eds.), *Aggression and Anti-Social Behavior in Childhood and Adolescence*, 73-93. Oxford: Pergamon Press.

34 J. MCCORD (1988) Parental Behavior in the Cycle of Aggression, 51 *Psychiatry* 14-23.

35 J. McCord (1983) A Forty Year Perspective on effects of Child Abuse and Neglect, 7 *Child Abuse and Neglect* 265-270.

36 C.S. WIDOM (1989) Child Abuse, Neglect, and Violent Criminal Behavior, 27(2)(May) *Criminology* 251-271.

neglected subjects also had a higher frequency of arrests for violent offenses as adults; however, this was due primarily to significantly more adult violent offenses by abused males.

Widom concludes that childhood victimization has demonstrable long-term consequences for adult criminal behavior and that early child abuse and neglect also have demonstrated long-term consequences for violent criminal behavior. The fact that abused females were more likely than control females to have an arrest as an adult led Widom to suggest that experiencing early child abuse or neglect has a substantial impact even on individuals with little likelihood of engaging in officially recorded criminal behavior.

5. The Mechanisms of Victim-Victimizer Transformation

The mechanisms by which a beaten, abused or victimized child is transformed into an adult victimizer are many. Brutalization, retaliation, desensitization, learning, imitation, transference, identification with the aggressor, are all processes that are useful in understanding and explaining this curious metamorphosis.

In a study of dangerous violent offenders, Athens[37] analyzed the brutalization process that shaped the subjects' personality and later behavior. He describes the brutalization process as one wherein people undergo "course and cruel treatment at the hands of others that produces a lasting and dramatic impact upon the subsequent course of their lives".

The most popular explanations for the cycle of violence stress the role of social learning, imitation, role modeling and adoption of norms. The basic tenet of these explanations is that children learn by example. Experiencing violence, being hit, beaten or spanked, as well as watching others being hit, beaten or spanked will teach the child that the use of violence and physical force is O.K., that it is legitimate, appropriate and acceptable as a mode of conflict resolution or for dealing with certain undesirable behaviors or situations.

The processes of learning and imitation are summarized in an eloquent manner by Alice Miller[38] as follows:

> *"When children are trained, they learn how to train others in turn. Children who are lectured to, learn how to lecture; if they are admonished, they learn how to admonish; if scolded, they learn how to scold; if ridiculed, they learn how to ridicule; if humiliated, they learn*

---

37 L.H. ATHENS (1989) *The Creation of Dangerous Violent Criminals.* London: Routledge.

38 MILLER, *o.c.*

how to humiliate; if their psyche is killed, they will learn how to kill – the only question is who will be killed: oneself, others or both."

Joan McCord[39] affirms that violence does seem to beget violence. She, however, challenges the argument that violence begets violence through acceptance of family (sub-cultural) norms of violence. This is because she found neglect, rejection, and physical abuse result in similarly high rates of crime. She offers as an alternative explanation what she calls *"a norm of self-interest"*. This norm, rather than a norm of violence, she believes, underlies the education shared by those who are rejected, neglected, and abused and it is the norm of self-interest that leads to violence in some circumstances.

Retaliation, though usually absent as an explanation in most writings on the topic, is undoubtedly an important mechanism in role reversal. In cases of vengeance, reprisal, getting even, paying back, settling of accounts, the victimization suffered is a direct contributor to the ensuing aggression, the sine qua non for it. Victimized children who are unable to get even with their violent parents will direct their retaliatory action to their siblings, other children or even animals. Later on, their retaliation will take the form of aggression against others.

Greven maintains that the violation of the child's body and soul by painful punishments generates the anger and the rage that later foster violence against the self and others.[40] That rage, he asserts, is the most common and continuous source for the destructive and aggressive impulses felt, imagined and acted on. According to Greven, physical punishments, particularly severe ones, further inhibit the development of empathy in later life. He affirms that one of their most enduring consequences is the stifling of empathy and compassion for oneself and others. This process, as described by Greven, is strikingly similar to the brutalization process described by Athens.[41]

Another related process is the process of desensitization to violence and aggression. Desensitization is often mentioned in the context of violence in the media when it is maintained that children's frequent exposure to violence in the comics, movies or on television desensitizes them to violence.[42] If this is true, then experiencing and/or witnessing violence in the household are

---

39 McCord (1991), *o.c.*

40 Greven, *o.c.*

41 Athens, *o.c.*

42 V.B. Cline, R.G. Croft & S. Courrier (1973) Desensitization of children to television violence, 27 *Journal of Personality and Social Psychology* 360-65; Thomas et al. (1977) Desensitization to portrayals of real life aggression as a function of exposure to television violence, 35 *Journal of Personality and Social Psychology* 450-458.

bound to have a desensitizing effect. This results not only in the lowering of inhibitions towards the use of violence, but also in reducing the perpetrator's awareness of the pain and suffering that the violence is causing the victim.

Moreover, violence can have a crippling effect on the child's affect and emotional development. It can stifle all tender emotions. Three decades ago, Dr. Karl Menninger,[43] a distinguished American psychiatrist, affirmed, on the basis of abundant clinical experience, that where a child has been exposed early in his life to episodes of physical violence, whether he himself is the victim or is the witness, he will often later demonstrate similar outbursts of uncontrollable rage and violence of his own. He explained that:

> *"Aggression becomes an easy outlet through which the child's frustrations and tensions flow, not just because of a simple matter of learning that can be just as simply unlearned, not just because he is imitating a bad behavior model and can be taught to imitate something more constructive, but because these traumatic experiences have overwhelmed him. His own emotional development is too immature to withstand the crippling inner effect of outer violence. Something happens to the child's character, to his sense of reality, to the development of his controls against impulses that may not later be changed easily but which may lead to reactions that in turn provoke more reactions – one or more of which may be "criminal".*[44]

Another mechanism that might help explain the transformation of victimized children into teenage or adult victimizers is the psychoanalytic concept of "identification with the aggressor". Identification with the aggressor has been used to explain a wide variety of phenomena from the behavior of inmates in Nazi concentration camps to the Stockholm Syndrome. It refers to children's identification with a punitive parent-figure and their incorporation of his or her aggressive qualities.

Aggressive behavior of victimized children has also been attributed to transference, a mechanism through which emotions relating to repressed experiences in childhood are reproduced.

Conclusion

A review of available research on the effects of physical punishment of children yields strong and convincing evidence of a positive link between corporal punishment (and other forms of victimization) and the violent,

---

43 K. MENNINGER (1968) *The Crime of Punishment*. New York: The Viking Press.
44 *Ibid.*, 215.

aggressive and delinquent behavior of the child in later years. Explanations for this transformation from victim to victimizer have come from various disciplines: psychiatry, psychology, sociology, criminology and victimology.

At a time when there is growing concern about child abuse, about violence and aggression, about delinquency and crime, it is only logical that everything should be done to change the conditions, the attitudes, the practices and the behaviors that are at the origin of these problems or that contribute to their occurrence.

Repealing criminal code sections sanctioning the use of physical force against children is only one very modest step in the right direction, but is far from being enough. It simply conveys a message that the use of physical force and violence as a means of disciplining children is no longer acceptable. But much more is needed if society is genuinely committed to protecting the physical integrity of children and to preventing them from developing into brutal, violent and ruthless victimizers. Everything should be done to change the prevailing rod mentality. The popular neutralizations and justifications that allow parents to falsely maintain that spanking children is done for their own good need to be denounced. Through education and training parents (and prospective parents) can be discouraged from using their helpless, defenseless children as targets for the letting out of their own pent-up tensions and aggression, or as instruments to alleviate their rage, anger or frustration. The law has to affirm the inviolability of the child. And as a society concerned about violence we have to condemn its use in all contexts, all settings and all circumstances, and in particular against the most vulnerable and most helpless members of society: the children.

References

Alfaro, J. (1981) Report on the relationship between child abuse and neglect and later socially deviant behavior, in: R.J. Hunner and Y.E. Walker (eds.), *Exploring the Relationships Between Child Abuse and Delinquency*, 175-219. Montclair, N.J.: Allanheld, Osmun.

Athens, L.H. (1989) *The Creation of Dangerous Violent Criminals*. London: Routledge.

Azrin, N.H. (1967) Pain and Aggression, 1 *Psychology Today* 27-33.

Bandura, A, and Walters, R.H. (1959) *Adolescent Aggression*. New York: Ronald Press.

Bentley, R.J. (1981) Child Abuse, Cross-Cultural Childrearing Practices and Juvenile Delinquency: A Synthesis, in: R.J. Hunner and Y.E. Walker (eds.), *Exploring the Relationship Between Child Abuse and Delinquency*, 128-44. Montclair: Allanheld, Osmun.

Button, A. (1973) Some Antecedents of Felonious and Delinquent Behavior, 2(3)(Fall) *Journal of Clinical Child Psychology* 35-7.

Cline, V.B., Croft, R.G. and Courrier, S. (1973) Desensitization of children to television violence, 27 *Journal of Personality and Social Psychology* 360-65.

Curtis, G. (1963) Violence Breeds Violence – Perhaps? (April) *American Journal of Psychiatry* 120.

Eron, L.D., Walder, L.O., Toigo, R. and Lefkowitz, M.M. (1963) Social class, parental punishment for aggression, and child aggression, 34 *Child Development* 849-67.

Farrington, D.P. (1978) The Family Background of Aggressive Youths, in: L.A. Herser, M. Berger and D. Shaffer (eds.), *Aggression and Anti-Social Behavior in Childhood and Adolescence*, 73-93. Oxford: Pergamon Press.

Fattah, E.A. (1994) *The Interchangeable Roles of Victim and Victimizer*. Helsinki: HEUNI.

Garbarino, J. (1981) Child Abuse and Juvenile Delinquency: The Development Impact of Social Isolation, in: R.J. Hunner and Y.E. Walker (eds.), *Exploring the Relationship Between Child Abuse and Delinquency*, 115-127. Montclair: Allanheld, Osmun.

Green, A.H. (1981) Child Abuse and the Etiology of Violent Delinquent Behavior, in: R.J. Hunner and Y.E. Walker (eds.), *Exploring the Relationship Between Child Abuse and Delinquency*, 152-160. Montclair: Allanheld, Osmun.

Greven, P. (1910) *Spare the Child: The Religious Roots of Punishment and the Psychological Impact of Physical Abuse*. N.Y.: Alfred A. Knopf.

Hartogs, P. (1951) Discipline in the Early Life of Sex-Delinquents and Sex-Criminals, (March 9) *Nervous Child* 167-73.

Korpilahti, M. (1989) Child Abuse and the Courts: Finnish and Swedish Experiences, in: E.A. Fattah (ed.), *The Plight of Crime Victims in Modern Society*. London: Macmillan.

Maurer, A. (1974) Corporal Punishment, 29 *American Psychologist* 614-26.

McCord, J. (1983) A Forty Years Perspective on effects of Child Abuse and Neglect, 7 *Child Abuse and Neglect* 265-270.

McCord, J. (1988) Parental Behavior in the Cycle of Aggression, 51 *Psychiatry* 14-23.

McCord, J. (1991) Questioning the Value of Punishment, 38(2) *Social Problems* 167-79.

McCord, W., McCord, J., and Howard, A. (1961) Familial correlates of aggression in non-delinquent male children, 62 *J. Abnorm. Soc. Psychol.* 79-93.

Menninger, K. (1968) *The Crime of Punishment*. New York: The Viking Press.

Miller, A. (1990) *For Your Own Good: Hidden Cruelty in Child-Rearing and the Roots of Violence*. New York: Farrar, Straus, Giroux.

Moore, D.W., and M.A. Straus (1987) *Violence of Parents Toward their Children: New Hampshire*. Durham, N.H.: Family Research laboratory. University of New Hampshire.

Mouzakitis, C.M. (1981) An Inquiry Into the Problem of Child Abuse and Juvenile Delinquency, in: R.J. Hunner and Y.E. Walker (eds.), *Exploring the Relationship Between Child Abuse and Delinquency*, 220-32. Montclair: Allanheld, Osmun.

Pfouts, J.H. et al. (1981) Deviant Behaviors of Child Victims and Bystanders in Violent Families, in: R.J. Hunner and Y.E. Walker (eds.), *Exploring the Relationship Between Child Abuse and Delinquency* 79-96. Montclair: Allanheld, Osmun.

Pulkkinen, L. (1983) Search for Alternatives to Aggression in Finland, in: A.P. Goldstein and M.H. Segall (eds.), *Aggression in Global Perspective,* 104-144. Elmsford, N.Y.: Pergamon Press.

Raymond, F.B. (1981) The Influence of Child Abuse on Psychosexual and Psychosocial Development and Implications for Delinquency, in: R.J. Hunner and Y.E. Walker (eds.), *Exploring the Relationship Between Child Abuse and Delinquency,* 240-251. Montclair: Allanheld, Osmun.

Repeal 43 Committee (1994) *Brief to Minister of Justice, Solicitor General and Others*. Toronto, Canada, April 1994.

Rule, Ann (1991) *If You Really Loved Me*. N.Y.: Pocket Books.

Sears, R.R., Maccoby, E.E., and Levin, H. (1957) *Patterns of Child Rearing*. Evanston, Illinois: Row, Petersen.

Slaby, R.G., and W.C. Roedell (1982) The Development and Regulation of Aggression in Young Children, in: J. Worell (ed.), *Psychological Development in the Elementary Years,* 97-149. N.Y.: Academic Press.

Straus, M.A. (1991) Discipline and Deviance: Physical Punishment of Children and Violence and Other Crime in Adulthood, 38(2) *Social Problems* 133-53.

Straus, M.A. (1991) New Theory and Old Canards about Family Violence Research, 38(2) *Social Problems* 180-97.

Straus, M.A. (1994) *Beating the Devil out of Them: Corporal Punishment in American Families*. New York: Lexington Books.

Thomas et al. (1977) Desensitization to portrayals of real life aggression as a function of exposure to television violence, 35 *Journal of Personality and Social Psychology* 450-458.
Weinbach, R.W. et al. (1981) Theoretical Linkages Between Child Abuse and Juvenile Delinquency, in: R.J. Hunner and Y.E. Walker (eds.), *Exploring the Relationship Between Child Abuse and Delinquency,* 161-166. Montclair: Allanheld, Osmun.
Welsh, R.S. (1976) Severe Parental Punishment and Delinquency: A Developmental Theory, (Spring) *Journal of Clinical Child Psychology* 17-21.
Wick, S.C. (1981) Child Abuse as Causation of Juvenile Delinquency in Central Texas, in: R.J. Hunner and Y.E. Walker (eds.), *Exploring the Relationship Between Child Abuse and Delinquency*, 233-39. Montclair: Allanheld, Osmun.
Widom, C.S. (1989) Child Abuse, Neglect, and Violent Criminal Behavior, 27(2)(May) *Criminology* 251-271.
Widom, C.S. (1990) Childhood Victimization: Risk Factor for Delinquency, in: M.E. Colten and S. Gore (eds.), *Adolescent Stress – Causes and Consequences,* 201-222. New York: Aldine de Gruyter.

THE STATUS OF VICTIMS OF CRIME IN SOUTH AFRICA: DEVELOPMENTS SINCE 1994

Beaty Naudé

Introduction

The first multiracial democratic elections on 27 April 1994 brought about significant socio-political, economic and legal transformation in South Africa. Prior to this the rights and needs of crime victims received very little attention from the old apartheid regime resulting in them being neglected by the criminal justice system while limited support services for victims of crime were mostly rendered by non-governmental organisations. Dissatisfaction with South Africa's crime rate coupled with low reporting and conviction rates has resulted in a renewed focus on the rights and needs of crime victims and their treatment in the criminal justice system. This paper will critically focus on the status of crime victims since 1994.

1. Violence in South Africa

South Africa is a severely traumatised nation as a result of the violence perpetrated during the apartheid era (a system of racial and cultural discrimination) and the liberation struggle which intensified after the 1976 Soweto youth uprising when 140 school pupils were killed by the police.

African youth were increasingly drawn into political violence and according to Gibson[1] they were socialised to find violence completely acceptable, and human life cheap. Innocent civilians were killed in brutal terrorist attacks while in black townships civilians, suspected of being collaborators and those who preferred not to participate in various boycott activities, were often brutally assaulted or publicly executed by the necklacing method (placing a burning tyre doused with an inflammable liquid around the victim's neck and then setting it alight). Both the civilians, who witnessed these brutalities, and the young activists, who committed these atrocities, were emotionally blunted and scarred. Young white males over the age of sixteen who were forced to do compulsory military service in the defence force to fight against fellow South Africans were equally scarred with no proper debriefing when the peace accord was brokered.

1 K. GIBSON (1991) Home, no place to hide, *The Star Newspaper*, Johannesburg, 2.

They were disinformed about the liberation fighters which distorted their perceptions and beliefs of fellow South Africans. Parents whose children were killed or maimed in the struggle and who were kept in the dark about the brutality of the war were also disillusioned and emotionally scarred. Police brutality was rife and many so-called enemies of the state were killed in the most brutal and inhumane manner by police death squads sanctioned by the state as was testified in numerous cases heard at the Truth and Reconciliation Commission hearings. Members of some liberation armies robbed banks and cash in transit vehicles killing indiscriminately during the attack to obtain funding for the liberation struggle. Many of these disaffected fighters continue with this violent lifestyle and execute their crimes with military precision. As a result of the economic boycott against South Africa, business and government officials were encouraged to circumvent sanctions by smuggling arms and commercial goods needed by the country. This blurred the dividing line between socially acceptable and criminal behaviour and contributed to high rates of corruption and poor business ethics.

This created disrespect for law and order and a culture of violence enmeshing many people which is currently compounded by the difficulty of adjusting to the new social policy of integration and a high unemployment rate which is officially given as 21.7%,[2] while the expanded unemployment rate is 36%. It is further estimated that as many as 60% of school leavers are currently unemployed. Contrary to developed countries, 44% of the South African population of 40.5 million is under the age of 19. The legacy of apartheid further created huge racial disparities and black South Africans are the most disadvantaged in terms of education, income and housing while new affirmative action employment policies discriminate against whites resulting in bitterness and disillusionment among some members of the population.

2. Violent crime rates in South Africa

South Africa's murder rate is exceptionally high when compared to that of other countries in the southern African region as is evident from police recorded murder statistics.

---

2 Republic of South Africa, Statistics SA (2001) (www.statssa.gov.za).

Table 1: Murder ratios in southern Africa per 100 000 of the population[3]

Country	Ratios
Malawi (1997/98)	4.3
Mauritius (including attempted murder) (1998)	3.3
South Africa (1998)	37.6
Zimbabwe (1998)	7.4
Botswana (1998)	11.4
Lesotho	n/a
Swaziland (1997)	25.1
Namibia (1998)	17.9
Zambia	n/a

Overall violence involving a weapon (firearms, knives, pangas) is high in the region but more so in South Africa as is evident from the international victim crime surveys conducted in the main southern African cities by the author and fellow researchers in collaboration with the UN Interregional Crime and Justice Research Institute (UNICRI) in Italy since 1996. This is the first independent crime data using the same questionnaire and research methodology which makes it possible to compare crime rates in southern Africa.

Table 2: Weapons used in selected violent crimes in southern Africa (%) [4]

Country	Robbery	Assault	Sexual assault
South Africa	73.3	62.9	37.1
Zimbabwe	51.0	19.8	9.7
Botswana	28.5	39.9	11.7
Swaziland	46.0	11.6	36.0
Lesotho	43.9	46.1	20.6
Namibia	44.0	38.2	31.3
Zambia	38.8	50.0	75.0

3 J.H. PRINSLOO & C.M.B. NAUDÉ (1999) *The impact of crime on economic development in southern Africa*, unpublished Research report, 85. Pretoria: University of South Africa, Institute for Criminological Sciences.

4 *Ibid.*, 84.

There is further ongoing political violence in South Africa, particularly in the provinces of KwaZulu-Natal and the Eastern Cape, and violence in the black taxi industry where commercial competition between the various taxi associations for ranks and routes have resulted in numerous killings of taxi operators and their passengers. The minibus taxi industry developed in the late seventies as a result of poor bus and train transportation for black people who were obliged by apartheid legislation to live outside white urban areas far from their places of work and they currently serve 65% of the commuter market. Alcohol related violence is also a cause for concern and a recent study by the SA Medical Research Council found that alcohol played a role in 75% of homicides involving a weapon. More than half of the 6 859 murders investigated by the Council were committed with guns and a third with sharp objects such as knives and pangas and the most vulnerable age groups were the youth and young adults aged between 15 and 44.

The smuggling of firearms is an enormous problem in southern Africa as a result of the many liberation wars and internal conflicts in the region and it is estimated that as many as eight million illegal firearms are in circulation in South Africa alone.[5] Violence against women is also very prevalent and research by Jewkes, Penn-Kekana, Levin, Ratsaka & Schrieber[6] confirms that one in four South African women are abused in their life time.

It is, however, of interest to note that South Africa's victimisation rates over one year for conventional crimes are not that exceptional when compared to the crime rates of other countries in the southern African region who participated in the international victims of crime surveys since 1996.

---

5 V. GAMBA (1999) *Small arms proliferation in Southern Africa: An overview*, ISS Monograph Series 33, 6. Pretoria: ISS.

6 R. JEWKES, L. PENN-KEKANA, J. LEVIN, M. RATSAKA & M. SCHRIEBER (1999) *Violence against women in three South African Provinces*, Research report, 10. Pretoria: CERSA (Women's Health), Medical Research Council.

Sexual Offences Court was also established in March 1993 in the Regional Magistrate's Court in Wynberg, Cape Town to protect victims from secondary victimisation during the court proceedings. A private waiting room was available to complainants, two full-time prosecutors were assigned to the court and five magistrates presided in the court on a rotation basis.[11]

There was no State Compensation Fund to assist victims of crime except for the State President's Fund for Victims of Terrorism which was established on 20 May 1983 during the height of the liberation struggle.

From the above it is evident that support services for victims of crime and violence in South Africa were limited in their scope and reach, fragmented, unco-ordinated, mostly reactive and ineffective.[12] Services were further mostly Euro-centric without making provision for cultural and language diversity. Most services were focussed on rape and child sexual abuse cases while the needs of other types of crime victims were ignored.

4. Developments since 1994

4.1. The Bill of Rights in the new Constitution

Precolonial African societies mostly focussed on the victim of crime rather than the offender emphasising reconciliation and restitution to restore the harm caused by crime,[13] whereas modern Western criminal justice systems mostly focus on the rights of the accused. South African law also followed this trend as it is mainly based on Roman-Dutch law although extensively modified by English law and certain influences from Europe.[14] It is therefore not surprising that the Bill of Rights in the new Constitution (Act 108 of 1996), adopted on 8 May 1996, granted numerous rights to arrested, detained and accused persons such as the right to remain silent, not to be compelled to make any confession, the right to legal assistance, the right to a fair trial, to be presumed innocent and to challenge evidence while granting no rights to crime victims. Past unjust discriminatory laws, particularly in the case of political activists, to which many of the newly elected members of government were subjected probably

---

11 S. STANTON & M. LOCHRENBERG (1995) Victims of Justice, Indicator South Africa,(2) Winter, *Crime and Conflict*, 13-16, 14.

12 South African Law Commission (1997) *Sentencing restorative justice (Compensation for victims of crime and victim empowerment)*, Issue paper 7, Project 82, 34. Pretoria: SA Law Commission.

13 N. NSEREKO (1992) Victims of crime and their right, in: M. MUSHANGA (ed.), *Criminology*, 21. Rome: UNICRI.

14 C.R. SNYMAN (1997) *Criminal law*, 14. Durban: Butterworths.

contributed to the concern to extensively protect the rights of arrested persons. Yet the insensitivity to crime victims is difficult to comprehend as the new Constitution is very enlightened and, for example, also protects the rights of homosexual people. The author, who was then the president of the Criminological Society of South Africa, submitted a proposal to Mr Cyril Ramophosa, chairman of the Constitutional Commission, when the Constitution was made available for comments, to enshrine the following victim rights in the final Constitution:

- the right to be treated with dignity and respect by the criminal justice system
- the right to protection, assistance and treatment
- the right to information with regard to the criminal proceedings
- the right to restitution and compensation
- the right to bring to the court's attention the harm suffered as a result of the crime by means of a crime impact statement

A victims' charter setting out the rights of crime victims.

A copy of a research report setting out a proposed model for South Africa to deal more effectively with the rights and needs of crime victims in terms of international trends was also offered to the commission.[15] It is not clear why the commission decided not to enshrine the rights of victims in the Constitution.

4.2. The National Crime Prevention Strategy

The National Crime Prevention Strategy (NCPS),[16] which was adopted in May 1996 was the first official move from an offender-based criminal justice system to a victim-centered criminal justice approach. The Victim Empowerment and Support Programme (VEP) is one of the key programmes flowing from the NCPS and its main aim is the development of interventions and modifications in the criminal justice process to empower victims by "*addressing the negative effects of criminal activity on victims, through programmes which mediate these effects and provide support and skills to address them.*
Providing a meaningful role for the victim in the criminal justice process.
Making the criminal justice system more sensitive and service oriented towards victims.
Enhancing the accessibility of the criminal justice system to victims".[17]

15 See: NAUDÉ (1995) *o.c.*

16 Republic of South Africa, Inter-departmental Working Group of the Departments of Correctional Services, Intelligence, Justice, Safety and Security and Welfare (1996) *National Crime Prevention Strategy*, 66. Pretoria: Govt. Printer.

17 *Ibid.*, 65.

The NCPS further argued that victim empowerment can make an important contribution to crime prevention as crime is a social issue rather than a security issue and that a more restorative justice approach will prevent repeat victimisation as a large proportion of crime is the result of repeat victimisation within close-knit social groupings. This is confirmed by the findings of the first National Victims of Crime Survey in South Africa,[18] which found that 80% of assault incidents and 75% of sexual offences were committed by a spouse/partner, relative or other acquaintance. The survey further found that repeat victimisation was high in South Africa[19] as 45% of sexual assault victims and 36% of assault victims reported that they were the victims of two or more offences during 1997.

It is not clear why the drafters of the NCPS decided on the term victim empowerment to describe basic services to which all victims should be entitled. This is perhaps due to the fact that the term empowerment was a popular political slogan at the time as one of the main aims of the liberation struggle was the empowerment of the disempowered black population. It is debatable whether the provision of basic services to crime victims can really be described as empowering them and it may even create unrealistic expectations among some unsophisticated victims. Nel and Kruger also seem to have difficulty in defining this term as they indicate that victim empowerment *"firstly implies a certain philosophy, method or technique of handling victims in which it is accepted that, rather than being dependent on the expertise and assistance of a professional or someone else, all people have certain skills and competencies which, when facilitated appropriately, can come to the fore to assist individuals to help themselves or to cope better with an incident of victimisation".*[20] They then further describe victim empowerment as a specific approach by service providers (state and private) to delivering the service they were put in place to deliver in the first instance and to do it with the client's needs in mind which will then lead to a more efficient and user-friendly criminal justice system and 'empowerment' and 'support' of the victim flows from this.[21] In my view the term victim empowerment is just as inappropriate as the term survivor which is often favoured when referring to victims. I personally prefer the term victors of crime rather than victim or survivor as it has a far more positive connotation.

It would appear as if the main aim of the government was the prevention of crime and repeat victimisation while the rights and needs of crime victims were of secondary concern. The NCPS was extensively reviewed in 1999 setting a

---

18 M. ORKIN (1998) *Victims of crime survey*, 49. Pretoria: Statistics SA.
19 *Ibid.*, 43.
20 NEL & KRUGER, *o.c.*, 97.
21 *Ibid.*

number of priorities following an audit of its projects in 1998. However, the office of the NCPS, which was based at the Ministry of Safety and Security, has now been terminated although the NCPS remains government's official crime policy and, according to an official in the Department of Justice, the principles and approaches of *"the NCPS are now considered to be a philosophy that must be followed by all government departments in all spheres of activity that may have a bearing on crime prevention"*. The NCPS as a structure has been replaced by the Integrated Justice System in the Department of Justice which is financially supported by Business Against Crime (BAC). Although a number of criticisms were levelled at the NCPS,[22] it should have been expanded, as a national crime prevention strategy which is regularly reviewed and evaluated, is an important measure in the fight against crime and to alleviate public fears about crime.

4.3. The Victim Empowerment Programme (VEP)

According to their 2000 status report, the vision of the VEP is to provide a caring and supportive service to victims of crime that is accessible, timeous and thorough, thus contributing to a sense of empowerment and an environment conducive to peaceful communities. The programme is currently co-ordinated and implemented by the Department of Social Development (previously Welfare) with an inter-departmental and inter-sectoral Victim Empowerment Management Team which comprises the Departments of Social Development, Health, Correctional Services, Justice, Education, the South African Police Services, provincial co-ordinators and some non-governmental organisations providing victim services. According to the VEP effective victim empowerment means services that are

- available, accessible, thorough and professional;
- rendered in an empowering, respectful and supportive manner;
- co-ordinated and integrated effectively;
- efficient in providing all the necessary information on available services to victims;
- efficient in providing information on the progress of relevant criminal investigation and information on the procedures and processes to victims.[23]

The VEP Business Plan is a very ambitious plan focussing on some 46 projects with specific target dates ending in 2001.[24] The following national

22 C.M.B. NAUDÉ (2000) The South African National Crime Prevention Strategy: A critique, 13 (2) *Acta Criminologicae,* 1-10.

23 South African Law Commission (2001) *A compensation scheme for victims of crime in South Africa*, Project 82, 21. Pretoria: SA Law Commission.

projects have to date been developed which have no doubt improved the services to crime victims[25]:

- guidelines for voluntarism in victim empowerment;
- expansion and/or duplication of a one-stop services project including domestic violence projects;
- research and co-ordination;
- undertaking victim crime surveys;
- programmes which prevent and respond to violence against women;
- programmes for perpetrators of violence;
- programmes for establishing shelters for abused women and children;
- training social workers and lay-counsellers in the implementation of the Domestic Violence Act;
- developing a resource directory on domestic violence for referral purposes;
- programmes which prevent and respond to rape and sexual offences;
- integration of victim-empowerment, economic and HIV/Aids programme; and
- establishing trauma response units.

Partnerships with private organisations are also emphasised and at provincial level the Department of Social Development is funding various NGOs and CBOs that are implementing victim programmes although there are complaints from some organisations that they have trouble accessing these funds even when services have been implemented in terms of a business plan approved by the VEP Management Team. In some of the nine provinces Project Managers have been appointed to oversee the functioning of state funded projects and to date 66 VEP projects have been established at provincial level, the majority of which operates on a 24 hour one-stop service centre. A range of services are rendered by trained professional and/or voluntary staff and each of the 66 projects reaches at least twenty victims per month, resulting in a total of 1 320 victims per month (15 320 annually) having access to these services. The first national victims of crime survey was conducted in 1998 by Statistics South Africa which provided valuable information on the nature and prevalence of victimisation, where the crime occurred and by whom it was committed. Various VEP training programmes for service providers such as social workers, the police and health care practitioners have also been conducted.[26]

The VEP has also recently compiled a list of service providers that deal with issues pertaining to violence against women in collaboration with the National

---

24 L. CAMERER & S. KOTZE (1998) (eds.), *Special report on victim empowerment in South Africa*, 125 ff. Pretoria: Halfway House, ISS.

25 South African Law Commission (2001) *o.c.*, 21.

26 *Ibid.*, 22ff.

Network on Violence Against Women and the Centre for the Study of Violence and Reconciliation in Johannesburg. The organisations included in the audit counsel and advise women on issues such as domestic violence, sexual abuse and harassment and maintenance while some also run shelters. The distribution per province is as follows:

Table 4: List of service providers dealing with issues pertaining to violence against women in South Africa[27]

Eastern Cape	25	
Western Cape	48	
Northern Cape	10	
KwaZulu-Natal	36	
Free State	15	
Gauteng	76	
Mpumalanga	13	
North West	10	
Northern Province	8	(Total 241)

The majority of the projects funded by the VEP are, however, based in urban, peri-urban and semi-rural areas while the outlying rural areas still remain under-serviced.[28] Services are furthermore mostly focussed on violence against women and children while services to victims of other crime types remain limited. According to the same SA Law Commission Report,[29] most of these services are at a level of basic psychological first aid which may be sufficient for the majority of victims while research indicates that a small percentage of victims exposed to violence may develop post-traumatic stress disorder, which requires more specialised intervention. There is concern about the psychological harm to victims who cannot afford privately funded specialized trauma services. A further concern is the fact that no evaluation criteria have been put in place to evaluate the standard and efficacy of existing services. The report further found that there is evidence of an improvement of services to crime victims in certain areas although few have been properly evaluated and that there is still a significant gap between policy-making and implementation. Co-operation between the various departments and other service sectors is also

27 South African Law Commission (2001) *o.c.*
28 *Ibid.*, 24.
29 *Ibid.*, 24.

problematic and the provision of services is further undermined by a lack of resources which contributes to inconsistencies in the number of services available to crime victims in terms of type of service and area with the rural areas being significantly under serviced.

4.4. The SA Police Services (SAPS)

The 1998 White Paper on Safety and Security, shifts the emphasis of policing to crime investigation, visible policing and improved services to victims of crime and stresses that law enforcement (policing) and crime prevention should be integrated while partnerships with business and civil society are promoted. It is obvious that police services to victims of crime need to be improved as the third international victims of crime survey conducted in the Johannesburg area in 2000 by the author and her fellow reseachers found that 55.7% of victims expressed dissatisfaction with the manner in which the police dealt with their case while only 44% of all crimes were reported to the police by the victims. It is further of significance to note that 72.6% of the victims expressed the view that private security officers did a good job combating crime in their area while only 45.7% expressed this view with regard to the police. Police brutality is still a problem as the Independent Complaints Directorate investigated 172 deaths in police custody and 315 deaths as a result of police action for the period April 2000 to March 2001. The total number of complaints against the police increased from 1 999 in 1997/98 to 4 380 in 1999/2000 - an increase of 119%. The murder of police officers is also high in terms of international standards: 1325 police officers were killed during the period January 1994 and June 1999.[30]

Three-day training programmes to sensitise police officers to treat crime victims with dignity and respect are currently in progress and to date approximately 10 000 police officers have received the basic training course which deals with topics such as interpersonal and communication skills, how to recognise and deal with trauma and victim rights and needs. This is part of a three-year programme to train all South Africa's 102 354 police officers. It is debatable whether such short courses can really inculcate a caring and empathetic treatment of victims and it can even be argued that it may trivialise the rights and needs of crime victims although it is a good starting point. It should form a comprehensive part of the general police training course. The National Directory of Services on Violence Against Women have also been distributed to police stations to use as a source to enable the police to refer

30 Criminal Justice Monitor (2001) *Nedbank ISS Crime Index 1*, 22-24.

victims for assistance when required. There are also currently 87 Child Protection and Sexual Offence Units countrywide.

A draft Victim Empowerment Policy Framework and Guidelines have recently been compiled setting out the department's philosophy regarding the treatment of victims by the police, the roles and responsibilities of members of the SAPS with regard to victim empowerment as well as guidelines for the implementation and evaluation of victim empowerment programmes at local level in collaboration with local Community Police Forums. The importance of private waiting rooms for victims of rape is emphasised as well as the establishment of victim support centres and the training and supervision of volunteers. The department is also currently conducting an audit to determine which police stations are providing services to crime victims in terms of the policy guidelines. Financial constraints seem to be the biggest obstacle in improving services to victims of crime and the SA Law Commission[31] recently expressed concern that a lack of resources such as a shortage of vehicles to investigate crimes and a lack of private interviewing rooms for police and social workers in many areas can increase levels of secondary victimisation.

4.5. The Department of Justice

A draft Charter of Victims' Rights has just been completed in collaboration with all the departments involved in the VEP which has been submitted to the public for comments at a three-day workshop in September 2001. The charter is based on internationally recognised basic principles of victim rights. It is divided into four sections and section one deals with the rights and standards of service to which a victim is entitled. The second section explains the processes in the criminal justice system while part three gives an outline of the rights and services a victim can expect during the criminal justice process. Section four outlines the complaints procedure and includes an address list of service providers.

The following rights are set out in the charter:

- the right to be treated with fairness, dignity and privacy
- the right to offer information
- the right to receive information
- the right to protection
- the right to compensation
- the right to restitution
- the right to assistance.

---

31 South African Law Commission (2001) *o.c.*, 24.

The charter will be implemented in two phases. Phase one is the administrative implementation which will commence as soon as the relevant Ministeries have approved the charter, while phase two entails the legislative implementation which will take effect as soon as the South African Law Commission has completed an investigation into the legislation that may have to be amended to bring it in line with the rights set out in the charter.

The department further plans to develop a comprehensive policy statement on victim empowerment. As far as victims are concerned audits have been undertaken to determine the standard of general service delivery in the courts (1999), services available to victims of domestic violence (1999), the issuing of protection orders for the purposes of implementing the Domestic Violence Act (2000) and an audit of the status of victim support services is in progress through the distribution of the Accountability Framework to all Magistrate Offices. A new audit of the available victim support services in the courts will be done via the accountability framework in September/November 2001. Support services to victim of crimes in the courts seem problematic as a number of private victim support agencies have indicated that they experience difficulty with some courts. Community initiatives are utilised to render services to crime victims in many courts.

Better case-management at the pre-trial stage has resulted in less delays and victims are also supplied with information brochures setting out their rights, responsibilities and the law. Victims also receive trauma counselling and are assisted with the completion of family violence interdicts.

The bail system has also been improved to prevent dangerous repeat offenders from being released on bail which may compromise the safety of the victim and other witnesses. The pre-trial services project is currently operating at three magistrate courts (Mitchell's Plain, Johannesburg and Durban).

Citizen's Advice Desks were established in Durban, Pretoria and Johannesburg in 1999/2000 and it has now been decided to implement two desks in each province. The aim of these desks is to incorporate and expand community participation in the administration of justice, as they will be the first points of contact for the public. Information and general advice will be provided to court users, as well as information regarding the court system, the administration of justice and people's rights. Some courts have also set up a witness friend to assist witnesses with issues such as directing them to the correct courts and to provide support to them.

Separate waiting rooms must also be established for all victims of violence, with a particular focus on women and children. Child friendly rooms, which include warm painted walls with pictures and toys are also being incorporated with the asistance of community volunteers. The department is also continuously providing pamphlets, brochures, videos and posters in these areas.

Closed circuit televisions and one-way mirrors have been installed in approximately 180 courts countrywide to protect witnesses under the age of 18 years and to prevent the emotional stress of testifying in open court in the presence of the accused.

Specialised courts dealing with sexual offences have been set up in the Western Cape province during 1993. Similar courts have since been set up in seven other courts countrywide and areas which do not presently have specialised courts have specialist personnel to handle sexual offences. A National Task Team was established to oversee the extension of the Sexual Offences Courts and their objectives are to obtain donor funding to extend the project, to draft a blueprint for sexual offences courts, to co-ordinate and ensure participation among all roleplayers and to co-ordinate specialised training of court officials. Family courts, which have jurisdiction in all family related matters including domestic violence, have been established in Cape Town, Port Elizabeth, Johannesburg and Lebowakgomo.

The training and education of service providers is also a priority. Training is, for example, provided to court personnel working in the Sexual Offences Courts in terms of the Guidelines on the Handling of Victims of Sexual Offences since 1997 as well as training of service providers on the new Domestic Violence Act. The Justice College is also training court officials in the Gauteng area on issues regarding domestic violence and restorative justice. They have also integrated a training programme for service providers on violence against women.

Public awareness and outreach programmes are also regarded as a priority and a toll free women's help line for crisis counselling and information was established in 1999. Information videos and brochures dealing with specific victim and crime issues are available to help educate the public and workshops with NGOs are also regularly held to discuss any problems they may encounter with the services delivered by the department.

National Policy Guidelines on Victims of Sexual Offences were developed in 1998 which are available to service providers to prevent secondary victimisation in the criminal justice system which will be reviewed in 2001. Guidelines for the Prosecutorial Services are also currently being developed by the Office of the National Directorate of Public Prosecutions to develop a coherent and uniform formulation of prosecutorial guidelines in the Department of Justice.

A number of important Acts were passed by Parliament dealing with victims of specific crimes. In terms of the new Domestic Violence Act (Act 116 of

1998), physical, sexual, emotional and economic abuse constitutes violence. The new act now also covers people who share the same residence, are co-habiting, dating, engaged or in a customary relationship and a woman who has been abused can apply for a protection order. The police must also assist her to get to a hospital, to obtain counselling and to find alternative accommodation in a safe house or shelter. Due to a lack of resources the police, however, have difficulty in providing this service and a recent study by the Gender Advocacy Project in the Cape found that only about 40% of interdicts against abusive spouses were granted in the areas sampled 32. A waiting period of as much as six weeks before some cases are heard because of court congestion increases the woman's vulnerability. Although the woman's physical abuse was stopped by the interdict, it often resulted in increased emotional abuse by the partners. The Organised Crime Amendment Act (Act 121 of 1998) makes provision for the Asset Forfeiture Unit to seize the assets of people who had obtained these assets by means of criminal activities. This money will be paid into the Criminal Asset Recovery Fund and some of it will be used to fund organisations which provide services and assistance to crime victims. The Criminal Law Amendment Act (Act 105 of 1997) which came into effect in 1998 obliges courts to impose mandatory minimum sentences of 15, 20 and 25 years imprisonment for a first, second and third conviction in the case of serious crimes such as murder, rape and robbery, unless substantial and compelling reasons are provided by the accused to warrant a departure from the guidelines. These longer prison sentences will in time substantially reduce the risk of criminal victimisation for all civilians although the act is severely criticised by the judiciary who also apply it inconsistently. The Draft Sentencing Framework Bill 2000 has extensively reviewed sentencing procedures in South Africa and also makes provision for victim impact statements (which should rather be termed crime impact statements) to be submitted to the court to bring to the court's attention the harm suffered by the victim as a result of the crime. The Draft Child Justice Bill 2000 also makes provision for the introduction of restorative justice sentencing options such as family conferences and victim-offender-mediation in which the victim will play a more substantial role.

4.6. The Department of Health

It was unfortunately not possible to obtain a comprehensive overview about the services provided to victims by the Department of Health. No information could be obtained about the number of hospitals and clinics which provide separate

---

32 C. TERREBLANCHE (2001) 'Gaps' in Domestic Violence Act leave women vulnerable, 4. *The Pretoria News*, 30 July 2001.

trauma units for rape victims but the Department of Health representative on the VEP working committee stated that they provide a national service to all hospitals which request it and that they were recently instrumental in assisting three hospitals in rural areas (Umtata, Nelspruit and Port Shepstone) with the opening of trauma units for rape victims. Approximately 500 health care workers were also trained to provide a better and more humane service to crime victims.

The department is, however, criticised for its refusal to provide anti-retroviral drugs free of charge to rape victims to prevent the development of HIV/Aids due to financial constraints of the health budget. Effectively this means a death sentence for rape victims who cannot privately afford these drugs. According to UNAIDS approximately 12.9% of the adult South African population is HIV/Aids positive and testing at public sector antenatal clinics indicates that HIV is more prevalent among African women.[33] A 2000 survey of 16 548 pregnant women who attended antenatal clinics found that 24.5% tested positive for HIV.[34]

The well-known Johannesburg journalist, Charlene Smith, who was raped by a stranger who forced his way into her home on the night of 1 April 1999, singled out the hospital where she went for treatment as well as the department's refusal to provide her with anti-retroviral drugs as the most traumatic of her experiences with the criminal justice system. Her inhumane treatment by the health care workers received wide publication in the media.

4.7. Crime Victims' Fund

The South African Law Commission[35] estimates that a fully fledged compensation scheme for victims of violent crime could cost as much as R2.3 billion (R8 is US$1) per year which is not viable in the short-term. They recommend that a short-term pilot targeted compensation be implemented for certain types of victims as specified in the guidelines:

Compensation for rape victims by 2002 to assist them medically and to ensure that they receive appropriate social and psychological support. An amount of R2 000 is proposed.

Compensation for crime victims disabled due to crime by 2003 to help them purchase mechanical devices such as artificial limbs, wheelchairs or to make

33 Republic of South Africa, Statistics SA, *o.c.*, 37.

34 *The Pretoria News*, 25 March 2001.

35 South African Law Commission (2001) *Sentencing (A compensation scheme for victims of crime in South Africa),* Discussion paper 97, 202. Pretoria: SA Law Commission.

changes to their homes to cope with their disabilities. An amount of R5000 is proposed.

Compensation for the dependents of indigent murder victims by 2004. A minimum payment of R5 000 to R15 000 is proposed (increased to take into account inflation rates between now and the time of the development of the scheme).

It is further recommended that the pilot schemes be supported by legislation and that the Crime Victims' Fund be financed by:

- state allocations through the budget process over the next four years
- a dedicated tax on firearm ownership and ammunition purchases, as well as alcohol purchases as research indicates that firearms and alcohol abuse play a major role in the majority of serious violent crimes.
- a special levy payable by all offenders, regardless of the crime punished
- funds raised from voluntary third parties such as corporate donations.

This method of funding is suggested as many offenders are poor and conviction rates are low.

It was further recommended that Police and Hospital Trauma Units improve their record keeping to ensure that they are able to meet the requirements of the Crime Victims' Fund as not all victims of violence will be entitled to compensation.

Research by Schönteich[36] confirms that prosecution and conviction rates in South Africa are low. In 1998 only 46% of murder cases, 44.9% of rape cases and 38.2% of serious assault cases were sent to the prosecutor for a decision to prosecute while the conviction rates were as follows: murder 15.7%, rape 8.9% and serious assault 12.6%.

5. Victim services provided by private organisations

As was indicated previously by the VEP audit, 241 organisations provide various services to crime victims in South Africa. It is not possible to discuss the activities of each organisation individually and only one national and one local service will be highlighted by way of example. Business Against Crime (BAC) which was established in 1996 in response to then President Mandela's request for the private sector to partner the South African government in its fight against crime is the most active national organisation. They are involved in a number of crime combating projects in partnership with the government. Since 1998 they have facilitated the establishment of 67 victim support schemes

36 M. SCHÖNTEICH (1999) Lack of conviction: Prosecution's poor performance, *Nedcor ISS Crime Index* 2.

in Gauteng and eleven in Mpumalanga. These schemes are currently assisting nearly 4 000 victims per month (48 000 annually) and as a result of the success of these schemes, BAC is now investigating the feasibility of extending the project to police stations situated in high crime areas in all the provinces. Their Community Based Victim Support Project is in partnership with the SAPS Service Delivery Improvement Programme (SDIP) and is based on the effective utilisation of SAPS knowledge, community experience and business skills and resources to design and implement local solutions to local crime and service delivery problems. The BAC Victim Support Scheme entails the establishment of community based volunteer networks linked to their local Community Police Forum and police station. They have also developed a Community Based Victim Support Programme to help victim support schemes being established and also publish a number of information brochures informing victims of their rights as well as information directories to obtain services.

Inter Trauma Nexus renders a comprehensive service with the aid of trained volunteers working in more than 18 teams in the Pretoria area. Their main aim is to create and maintain a multi-professional support network by recruiting psychologists, social workers, legal advisers, church leaders, business advisors and volunteers from the community to support victims of crime and victims of other types of trauma. Most of their services are, however, provided to victims of crime and crime related trauma. More than 8 000 people received support on a short-term basis in 2000 while 1 235 people received long-term support counselling. The largest portion of these people were effected by sexual violations, such as rape, sodomy, indecent assault or attempts thereto. Problems in families and domestic violence made up nearly 20% of cases. Other problems involved car hijacking, robbery and the abuse of drugs. All voluntary supporters and professionals receive in house training on basic crisis handling and helping models and volunteers can specialise in specific areas of support in terms of their own skills and interest. They operate in Gauteng mostly from police stations and at business premises in exchange for victim support to these institutions. Funding is obtained from individual donors and training fees.

It is evident that private organisations render the majority of victim support services in South Africa and that most provide psychological support to victims of sexual and domestic violence on a short-term basis as was indicated in the SA Law Commission Report.[37] The criticism that was levelled at the VEP projects basically also apply in the case of private services in that it is limited to certain crimes, mostly concentrated in the urban and peri-urban reas and that the standard of these services are not properly evaluated. The Johannesburg

37 South African Law Commission (2001) *A compensation scheme for victims of crime in South Africa, o.c.*, 24.

2000 victims of crime survey found that only 10% victims of sexual assaults and 8.7% of assault victims made use of the services of a victim support agency while 49.3% and 57.6% respectively, expressed the view that the services of such agencies would have been useful indicating that victim support services are used on a very small scale. It would seem as if many victims attain self-healing with the help and support of loved ones in the light of the fact that a fairly large percentage of victims did not seem to regard specialised victim support services as helpful. Yet it is equally true that many crime victims still do not receive help as was evident from a recent court case in Cape Town where a twelve year old rape victim reported that she had not received any psychological treatment but that attempts were being made to obtain some help for her.[38] It is equally important to conduct a survey among victims of crime to determine their exact needs. Many victims have an immediate need of assistance to repair damaged property and other practical help such as transport to report the crime to the police which is not always provided by victim support services.

Conclusion

South Africa has no doubt made enormous progress in expanding services to crime victims and the government has certainly become much more geared to the rights and needs of crime victims which has resulted in a number of policy documents and training programmes being developed for service providers in the criminal justice system. Structures such as the VEP have also been put in place to oversee the countrywide implementation of victim support services on a more equitable basis in all areas. However victim services are still lacking in many rural areas and most of the existing services are focussed on victims of domestic violence and child abuse. These services are further not evaluated in terms of standards and victim needs. Many victim rights are still paper rights at this stage but hopefully this will soon be rectified and the rights be accorded proper status in policy and in legislation although criticism has been levelled at the government for being slow in implementing policy. This is confirmed by the slow progress being made with the payment of reparation to victims of human rights abuses from 1960 to May 1994 as recommended by the Truth and Reconciliation Commission in their 1998 report. Although R600 million was made available by the government in 1998, only R32 million has to date been paid out [39]. The government is also inclined to abandon important projects. A

38 *The Pretoria News*, 2 August 2001.

39 South African Law Commission (2001) *A compensation scheme for victims of crime in*

case in point is the second national victims of crime survey due in 2001 which will not be conducted in the near future due to a lack of funds.

References

L. Camerer & S. Kotze (1998) (eds.), *Special report on victim empowerment in South Africa*. Pretoria: Halfway House, ISS.

Criminal Justice Monitor (2001) *Nedbank ISS Crime Index 1.*

V. Gamba (1999) *Small arms proliferation in Southern Africa: An overview*, ISS Monograph Series 33. Pretoria: ISS.

K. Gibson (1991) Home, no place to hide, *The Star Newspaper,* Johannesburg.

R. Jewkes, L. Penn-Kekana, J. Levin, M. Ratsaka, M. & M. Schrieber (1999) *Violence against women in three South African Provinces*, Research report. Pretoria: CERSA (Women's Health), Medical Research Council.

C.M.B. Naudé (1995) *An international perspective on victim participation in the criminal justice process with specific reference to victim impact statements*, Research report. Pretoria: University of South Africa, Department of Criminology.

C.M.B. Naudé (2000) The South African National Crime Prevention Strategy: A critique, 13(2) *Acta Criminologicae,* 1-10.

J. Nel & J. Kruger (1999) *From policy to practice: Exploring victim empowerment initiatives in South Africa*, 9. Pretoria: CSIR Report;

N. Nsereko (1992) Victims of crime and their right, in: M. Mushanga (ed.), *Criminology*. Rome: UNICRI.

M. Orkin (1998) *Victims of crime survey*. Pretoria: Statistics SA.

J.H. Prinsloo & C.M.B. Naudé (1999) *The impact of crime on economic development in southern Africa,* unpublished Research report, 85. Pretoria: University of South Africa, Institute for Criminological Sciences.

J.H. Prinsloo & C.M.B. Naudé (2001) *Criminal victimisation in southern Africa: The unique status of the ICVS*. Paper delivered at the Cross-National Comparative Crime Victimisation Workshop, 21-24 June 2001, NSCR, Leiden, The Netherlands, pages 1-20.

Republic of South Africa, Department of Welfare, Working Group on Crime Related Matters (1994) *White Paper on Social Welfare*. Pretoria: Govt. Printer.

Republic of South Africa, Inter-departmental working group of the Departments of Correctional Services, Intelligence, Justice, Safety and

---

South Africa, o.c., 37.

Security and Welfare (1996) *National Crime Prevention Strategy*. Pretoria: Govt. Printer.
Republic of South Africa, Central Statistical Services (now Statistics SA) (1998) *Women and men in South Africa*. Pretoria: Govt. Printer.
C.R. Snyman (1997) *Criminal law*. Durban: Butterworths.
M. Schönteich (1999) Lack of conviction: Prosecution's poor performance, *Nedcor ISS Crime Index* 2.
South African Law Commission (1997) *Sentencing restorative justice (Compensation for victims of crime and victim empowerment)*, Issue paper 7, Project 82. Pretoria: SA Law Commission.
South African Law Commission (2001) *A compensation scheme for victims of crime in South Africa*, Project 82. Pretoria: SA Law Commission.
South African Law Commission (2001) *Sentencing (A compensation scheme for victims of crime in South Africa),* Discussion paper 97. Pretoria: SA Law Commission.
S. Stanton & M. Lochrenberg (1995) Victims of Justice, Indicator South Africa, (2) Winter *Crime and Conflict* 13-16.
C. Terreblanche (2001) 'Gaps' in Domestic Violence Act leave women vulnerable, 4. *The Pretoria News*, 30 July 2001.

THE POSITION OF VICTIMS AND VICTIM SUPPORT IN THE NEW SPANISH JUVENILE CRIMINAL LAW

José Luis de la Cuesta

Introduction

In the final decade of the last century, important changes took place in the justice system in Spain concerning the treatment of young and juvenile offenders.[1] The new legislation has gradually introduced a combined system of tutelary, penal and social aspects.

The participation of victims in proceedings established for the prosecution of criminal offences committed by minors has been a controversial matter for a long time. Successive juvenile criminal laws have gradually expanded the legal position of victims, and the possibilities for reparation and victim support services.

This article gives an overview of these developments, primarily from a legal angle, and offers some critical reflections.

1. The new Spanish Juvenile Criminal Law

The previous tutelary legislation (of 1948) was declared unconstitutional (by STC 14 February 1991) and the new Act 4/1992 provisionally set up a hybrid model, consisting of tutelary, penal and social aspects. The new model -applicable to offenders between 12 and 16 years of age- was first and foremost based on the principle of concern for the minor.[2] This principle, which was considered the main criterion to govern any intervention, essentially came down to the minor's education and social reintegration needs, and did not include punishment nor repression. Consequently, the new juvenile process paved the way for the implantation of different means of distraction in the Anglo-Saxon line of *diversion*, making it possible to close proceedings without imposing any measures, in view of certain circumstances: the severity of the crime, the circumstances and characteristics of the minor, the absence of violence or intimidation, or

1 J.L. De La Cuesta (1999) El abandono del sistema tutelar: evolución del derecho español en materia de protección y de tratamiento de los menores delincuentes y en peligro, 37(1/2) *Annales Internationales de Criminologie* 101 ff.

the minor's efforts to make amends with the victim. It also envisaged referring minors who had committed non-serious acts (which did not involve violence or intimidation) to the social services, either directly or with a warning.

The Act also introduced technical teams, as insistently requested by the authors,[3] formed by a psychologist, a social assistant and an educator. The "overriding role"[4] of the team was to issue a report for the Public Prosecutor and the Judge about the psychological, the pedagogical and the family situation of the minor and his background, in order to make it easier to take more relevant decisions concerning the minor's education and his social reintegration.

As regards sanctions, new measures, not in the least imaginative[5] or novel,[6] took the form of educational interventions lasting up to a maximum of two years. The principle of flexibility in choosing, deciding and applying measures and reserving internment as a last resort were the main characteristics of the Act concerning this matter.

It is clear that the development of this new Juvenile Criminal Law was decisively influenced by the approval of a new Spanish Penal Code in 1995. In fact, the new Penal Code raised the initial age limit for the application of its provisions to 18 years, and referred any prosecutions of minors of that age to the Act regulating the penal liability of minors, thus maintaining the system introduced in 1992 and temporarily in force.

January 2000 witnessed another major legislative change. That month was promulgated the new Act regulating the penal liability of minors (Act 5/2000), which entered into force one year after its publication in the State Official Gazette (*Boletín Oficial del Estado*) on 13th January 2000. Although this new Act adopts the majority of changes that had been introduced in 1992, an overriding transformation in the treatment of juvenile delinquency has undoubtedly taken place.

---

2 J.R. Palacio Sanchez Izquierdo (2000) El principio del superior interés del menor, *Surgam*, 466-467, 55 ff.

3 A. Beristain (1995) Prólogo, in: J. Urra Portillo (1995) *Menores, la transformación de la realidad, Ley Orgánica 4/1992*, XIV. Madrid.

4 Urra Portillo, *o.c.*, 8.

5 M.P. Manzana Laguardia (1992) Notas acerca del Proyecto de Ley sobre Reforma urgente del procedimiento de Menores, 571 *Revista General de Derecho* 2543 ff., 2543.

6 J.C. Lopez Caballero (1994) La Legislación reformadora de menores en España y Brasil: un análisis comparativo, 4 *Revista de Derecho Penal y Criminología* 491 ff., 548.

The Act clearly refers to the minor's "penal" liability, in other words penal liability in the formal sense, that is governed by parameters similar to those for adult liability. The liability of minors, however, is also different from that of adults with regard to its consequences, as it must lead to a non-punitive reaction, which is materially educational. Penal liability can be demanded for people aged between 14 and 18 years, the new age limits established by Juvenile penal law (art. 1). The Act distinguishes between minors (14-18 years) and young people (over 18 years of age). Furthermore, an additional distinction is made amongst minors, between those who are 14-16 years old and those over 16 years of age, who may be subjected to longer-lasting measures of internment (even for up to 8-10 years, followed by probation, in the case of very serious crimes or terrorist acts, respectively). Reaching the adult age does not, however, put a end to the execution of such measures, which are pursued until the proposed objectives have been reached (art. 15). From the age of 23, youngsters are referred to one of the centres mentioned in the General Penitentiary Act (*Ley Orgánica General Penitenciaria*).

As an exception to the rule, youngsters over 18 and under 21 years of age may also be tried by means of juvenile jurisdiction (art. 4), providing that the crime was not serious and did not involve violence or intimidation towards people or jeopardize human life or physical integrity, that the subject has not been found guilty of committing criminal acts by way of a binding judicial decision since reaching the age of 18, and that their circumstances and the degree of maturity recommend following this procedure, especially if it is suggested by the technical team in its report. However, this possibility has still not come into force and it is temporarily suspended.

The juvenile process is fully approved with regard to all matters concerning the presumption of innocence and the rights of the defence, which leaves open interesting possibilities for exercising the "regulated" opportunity[7] in proceedings. The Public Prosecutor's participation is intense, both in the investigation of the facts and in the institution of the proceedings. He must also ensure that juvenile rights are respected and watch over minors' interests (art. 6). The Public Prosecutor cannot take decisions that restrict the fundamental rights of minors; this is the exclusive

7 F. BUENO ARUS (1997) El Anteproyecto de Ley Orgánica reguladora de la Justicia de Menores elaborado por el Ministerio de Justicia, 11 *Eguzkilore. Cuaderno del Instituto Vasco de Criminología* 159 ff., 164.

competence of the Juvenile Judge, at the request of the Public Prosecutor, and by justified ruling (art.23-3).

The Act of 2000 includes a whole list of measures (art. 7)[8] and regulates their application and execution, based on the principle of legality (art. 43) and under the control of the Juvenile Judge. When imposing a measure, the facts and their legal qualification must be taken into account, but the minor's age, his family and social circumstances, his personality and interest are more important aspects for consideration (art. 7.3). The execution of measures is the competence of Autonomous Communities and here, the principle of proximity applies: the minor must be sent to the most suitable centre near his home, unless agreed otherwise by the Juvenile Judge in the interest of the minor.

Internment is divided into two phases: internment in the centre itself, and probation (art. 7.2). Internment in a closed centre is only applied in the case of intentional crimes with violence or intimidation, or a serious risk to human life or physical integrity (art. 9.2ª).

The maximum duration of measures for criminal acts is two years, 100 hours of community service and 8 weekend stays (art. 9.3ª). Those over 16 years of age may be subjected to measures lasting up to 5 years, depending on the violence of the acts, on the threat or serious risk to human life or physical integrity, and on the fact whether the individual has educational needs that justify extending the measure.[9] In extremely serious cases (and repeated offences are always considered to be extremely serious) the judge may impose a measure of internment in a closed centre for one to five years and, then, probation for another five years; in these cases, the modification or suppression of the measure cannot be pronounced until after the first year of the effective execution of the measure of internment (art. 9.5ª).

Despite the above, for very serious crimes (homicide, murder, rape and qualified sexual assaults, terrorism and, in general, crimes punished by the Penal Code with penalties of over fifteen years' imprisonment), the duration

---

8 Internment in a closed centre, in a semi-open centre, in an open centre; therapeutic internment; outpatient treatment; attendance at a day centre; weekend stays; probation with intensive supervision; simple probation; living with a family or educational group; community services; carrying out socio-educational tasks; warning; deprival of motorcycle or motor vehicle driving licence, of the right to obtain them, or of administrative permits for hunting or fishing or the use of any type of weapon; absolute disqualification (this last measure, introduced by the reform brought about by Act 7/2000, of 22 December, concerns terrorism)

9 In these circumstances, community service may reach up to 200 hours and weekend stays up to 16 weekends (art. 9.4ª).

of internment is longer. In such cases, it may reach up to four years (five, for terrorist acts) for those under 16 years of age, and eight years (ten, for terrorist acts) for those over 16 years of age (Act 7/2000, of 22 December), followed by probation, and in cases of terrorism, by an additional absolute disqualification (four to fifteen years).

There has been a need and a demand for this new Act for a long time. A positive aspect of the text lies in its integral nature: it regulates all aspects of the intervention regarding juvenile delinquents, not only the proceedings and the measures, but also the principles to be applied, the execution of the sanctions and the civil liability.

Many points are worth commenting on. Let us just briefly say that despite the great effort to make the educational model compatible with the sanctioning model and the guaranteeing model, looking to make solutions more flexible and to favour non-intervention, we are faced with outlooks and ideologies that are not always compatible. Moreover, it is based on the fundamental principle of greater concern for the minor; this continues to be, however, an ambiguous concept -concerning the minor's personal development, his educational needs, his social reintegration-, the content of which has not been sufficiently developed. The Act makes an important distinction between two age brackets (14-15; 16-17); but the difference of treatment is sometimes too great. With regard to those over 18 years of age, I believe that the best solution is to refer them to the adult magistrate, authorising the latter to apply juvenile legislation for matters concerning measures to be taken, and for the possibilities of avoiding or suspending proceedings. Under the new Act, juvenile proceedings are too similar to adult proceedings, even though there are large differences. In principle, possibilities open to *diversion* should be considered to be sufficient. The Public Prosecutor still has to perform an excessively wide range of functions and faculties. The regulation of *preventive measures* is too restrictive and the period of precautionary internment can be, in practice, too long. Conferring the prosecution of minors under the age of 18 accused of terrorist acts to the National Court of Justice (*Audiencia Nacional*) (brought in by Act 7/2000) breaks the proximity principle and merely copies the system applied to adults. Moreover, greater emphasis should have been placed on communication between the *technical team* and the Juvenile Judge. The measures, in view of their regulation, should be considered more as genuine juvenile penalties,[10] or in other words as "punitive sanctions".[11] Even though there is a broad list of measures, there is a lack of more imaginative solutions that could perhaps be put into practice through socio-educational programmes. I believe that the duration of the interventions anticipated for extremely serious cases and, above all, for very serious crimes and terrorist acts is excessive.

In my view, many aspects of the new system require further regulative development, but this is generally not envisaged: to this aim, the Act refers to Autonomous Community regulations. Given the importance of the issues which need to be developed, these regulations should ideally be approved by autonomous legislative assemblies, with respect for the minimal rules generally established in adult legislation.

2. The victim's position in the new Juvenile Penal System

The participation of victims in proceedings established for the prosecution of criminal offences committed by minors has been a controversial matter for a long time.

In the tutelary system, the victim's participation was generally excluded. Victims, however, were allowed to bring civil actions and to contest certain rulings. Several authors have discussed this issue, thereby affirming the "peculiarity" of the procedural position of victims.[12]

---

10 J. CEREZO MIR (2000) (2ª ed.), *Derecho Penal. Parte general*, 106. Madrid: Lecciones; X. ETXEBARRIA ZARRABETTIA (2001) Aspectos sustantivos. Edad. Medidas. Contenido. Prescripción. Concursos. Régimen Transitorio, 7 ff, 32, in : Consejo Vasco de la Abogacía (ed.), *Ley Orgánica 5/2000 de Responsabilidad Penal de los Menores*. Bilbao: Consejo Vasco de la Abogacía; O. GARCIA PEREZ (2000) La evolución del sistema de justicia penal juvenil. La Ley de Responsabilidad Penal del Menor de 2000 a la luz de las directrices internacionales, 32 *Actualidad Penal* 682 ff., 686; against: B. FEIJOO SANCHEZ (2001) Sobre el contenido y la evolución del Derecho Penal español tras la LO 5/2000 y la LO 7/2000, 4 *Revista Jurídica*, Universidad Autónoma de Madrid, 9 ff.

11 I. SANCHEZ GARCIA DE PAZ. (2000) La nueva ley reguladora de la responsabilidad penal del menor, 33 *Actualidad Penal* 699 ff., 719.

12 M.J. CORONADO BUITRAGO (1993) La singular posición de la víctima en la justicia de menores, in: Consejo General del Poder Judicial (ed.), *La Victimología*, 397ff., 397. Madrid: CGPJ; J. LAMO RUBIO (1999) La víctima en el actual proceso de menores: presencias y ausencias, núm 4897 *La Ley* 1 ff.; L. RODRIGUEZ SOL (1996) El Fiscal y la protección de las víctimas en el proceso de menores, núm. 1750 *Boletín de Información del Ministerio de Justicia* 137 ff., 137.

The urgent reform of 1992 did not change this position: it prevented victims from participating in the new juvenile process; at the same time, it maintained the victim's right to contest certain rulings (art. 46 Regulations). However, the victim's position was in some way reinforced through their taking part in the framework of possibilities open to avoid proceedings and to suspend the verdict (because of reparation or a promise of reparation) (arts. 15.1 and 16.3, Act 4/1992).

2.1. The inexistence of actions by private persons

In line with the previous legislation, also the new Act 5/2000, in regulating the penal liability of minors, excludes "the actions by private persons" (art. 25). The Explanatory Report (*Exposición de Motivos*) (II, 8) clearly mentions that victims cannot bring private actions, nor can citizens in general bring public actions. Of course, this does not prevent victims or citizens in general from reporting punishable acts, which they obviously must do if they have knowledge of them; likewise, the Public Prosecutor must notify the initiation of proceedings to those who reported the crime (art. 16.2).

One of the reasons traditionally put forward against private persons bringing actions in the framework of juvenile justice was the fact that minors could not be held liable or imputable. This argument is difficult to maintain in the new Spanish system of juvenile offenders, because the new system is based on the provisions of art. 19 Penal Code,[13] and clearly refers to the penal liability of minors. Moreover, the principle of juvenile liability is upheld in the section dealing with the commission of punishable acts and the absence of any of the circumstances of exemption or extinction of the criminal responsibility envisaged by the Penal Code for adults (art. 5). Thus, there are enough reasons for affirming that the age limit of 18 years envisaged by art. 19 of the Penal Code is not a reason for non-imputability,[14] but a personal limit to the application of the adult Code. Consequently, it must be concluded that in Spanish Law the age limit for penal imputability ("*irrefutable presumption of irresponsibility*"[15]) is fixed at 14 years of age (art. 3) and that, between 14 and 18 years of age, the penal imputability that

---

13 J. CUELLO CONTRERAS (2000) *El nuevo derecho penal de menores*, 49. Madrid: Civitas.

14 Against: FEIJOO SANCHEZ, *o.c.*, 24 s.

15 SANCHEZ GARCIA DE PAZ, *o.c.*, 706.

may occur is not full, but can at least be considered as semi-imputability[16] or reduced imputability[17]

Along with the non-imputability of juvenile offenders, another argument usually serves in favour of the procedural exclusion of victims, namely the fact that the retributive content of the interventions directed at juvenile offenders is scarce or even null. Indeed, the new system is based on the fundamental principle of "greater concern for the minor", which entails their education and social reintegration. However, excluding all possibilities of participation on the part of the victim may lead to undesirable *"situations of defencelessness"*.[18] In order to avoid such situations, victims should be given opportunities to participate, not concerning the measures to be taken, but at least in proving the facts and the liability of the minor.[19]

In any case, it is clear that the "monopoly of penal action" by the Prosecution Service in Act 5/2000 not only serves to ensure that priority is given to educational goals, but also to guarantee *"the maintenance of the principle of opportunity so often stated in the regulations examined"*.[20]

2.2. The possibility of victims participating in criminal proceedings

The inexistence of actions on the part of private persons in juvenile proceedings does not prevent victims from exceptionally being allowed to participate in both the institution of proceedings and the hearings, but not in the execution of measures.[21] However, this only occurs on limited occasions -as a *"mere aid"*[22]- and for certain crimes.

In fact, art. 25 grants victims the permission to appear in the proceedings for acts where all of the following circumstances coincide:

- they involve serious or less serious criminal offences;

---

16 *Ibid.*, 715.

17 GARCIA PEREZ, *o.c.*, 683 ff.

18 R. VENTURA FACI. & V. PELAEZ PEREZ (2000) *Ley Orgánica 5/2000 de 12 de enero reguladora de la responsabilidad penal de los menores*. Comentarios y jurisprudencia, 124. Madrid: Colex.

19 J.L. DE LA CUESTA ARZAMENDI (2001) Responsabilidad civil. Procedimiento. Incoación. Efectos, in: Consejo Vasco de la Abogacía, *o.c.*, 175 ff., 179.

20 G. LANDROVE DIAZ (2001) *Derecho Penal de Menores*, 293. Valencia: Tirant lo Blanch.

21 A. MAESO VENTUREIRA (2001) Procedimiento. Incoacción. Competencia objetiva, territorial y funcional. Partes. Instrucción. Sentencia. Recursos, in: Consejo Vasco de la Abogacía, *o.c.*, 67 ff., 75.

22 G. LANDROVE DIAZ (1998) *La moderna victimología*, 294. Valencia: Tirant lo Blanch.

- they are committed by people over the age of 16;
- violence or intimidation was inflicted on people, or human life or physical integrity was jeopardised.

Although extensive,[23] this participation is not a full participation as a party, but it is limited by the very same contents of article 25. Those who appear in proceedings are granted the following faculties:

- to witness the proceedings and to be notified of investigations that are requested and that have been agreed to;
- to propose, perform and evaluate evidence (in both the institution of proceedings and the hearing) concerning the crime and its circumstances; however, evidence regarding the psychological, educational, family and social situation of the minor is excluded; also, identity parade evidence may be rejected if the acting body does not consider it to be essential for the verification of the acts or the minor's participation in them;
- to draw up the allegations which they consider appropriate on the basis of new pieces of evidence and concerning facts that are proven, and the minor's participation in them, with the exclusion of any measures envisaged;
- to reiterate their claim before the Juvenile Court, should the Public Prosecutor refuse the victim's presence in the institution of proceedings (5 days);
- to reiterate the claim to produce pieces of evidence refused by the Public Prosecutor, in the brief of allegations or during the hearing phase;
- to lodge a reform appeal against judicial decrees and rulings (3 days) and an appeal against the judicial decree that resolves any conflicting views on the ruling;
- to lodge an appeal against the sentence which is passed; this appeal can only be based on legally valued causes: the Court's incompetence, the inadequacy of the proceedings, a violation of the essential guarantees of the trial, leading to the victim's defencelessness or the lack of consideration of essential pieces of evidence for the qualification of the facts; victims cannot lodge an appeal in cassation for the unification of doctrine.

Furthermore, art. 35 states that victims that have presented themselves may attend the hearing. At this moment, the victims will give their opinion on the production of new pieces of evidence and will be heard in relation to proven evidence and the participation of the minor. In view of the

---

23 GARCIA PEREZ, *o.c.*, 694.

foregoing, it is surprising that art. 37, when regulating the organisation of the hearing, does not contemplate the victim's participation and only orders the Public Prosecutor, the minor's lawyer, the minor himself and the technical team to be heard. However, in no way can this omission be an obstacle to the victim's participation in conformity with arts. 25 and 34[24]

2.3. Reconciliation and/or reparation

Another aspect which can also be considered as an exception to the principle of the non-participation of victims in juvenile proceedings, is the important position they occupy in dismissing the case. This may result from reconciliation or reparation (art. 19), and is a manifestation of the *"principle of regulated opportunity in the interest of the minor"* [25] as recognised by Spanish Juvenile Criminal Law.

There are two legally approved possibilities for avoiding trial:

- abstention from starting proceedings on the part of the Prosecution Service; and
- dismissal of the case because of reconciliation or reparation between the minor and the victim.

The first, the abstention from starting proceedings on the part of the Public Prosecutor, is envisaged for those acts which constitute misdemeanours or less serious crimes,[26] which do not involve violence or intimidation, and whenever the minor has not committed similar acts in the past (art. 18). However, this does not put an end to negotiations on civil liability and the Public Prosecutor must inform the juvenile social service, in order to take the necessary measures of protection.[27] Furthermore, in less serious crimes and misdemeanours, the Public Prosecutor is authorised to desist from continuing with the proceedings which have already started, should there be reconciliation between the minor and the victim or reparation (or a promise of reparation) of the harm caused (art. 19). In these cases, the Public Prosecutor must bear in mind the severity of the acts (in

---

24 J.N. MARTI SANCHEZ (2001) Protección de la víctima y responsabilidad civil en la ley penal de los menores, 4 *Actualidad Penal* 65 ff., 82.

25 J.R. PALACIO SANCHEZ IZQUIERDO (2001) La abogacía en la ley penal. Turno de oficio, in Consejo Vasco de la Abogacía, *o.c.*, 199 ff., 204.

26 In Spanish law, less serious crimes are generally those punished with less serious penalties; in general, in the case of imprisonment, those lasting six months to three years (art. 33.3, a) PC).

27 Critically: LANDROVE DIAZ (2001) *o.c.*, 287.

particular, the lack of violence or intimidation) and the circumstances of the minor; the technical team acts as a mediator.

Here, the position of the victim is fundamental. Art. 19.2 of the Act strictly provides that "reconciliation has occurred when the minor recognises the harm caused and apologises to the victim and the latter accepts his apologies". Reparation is legally considered as "the undertaking assumed by the minor with the victim to perform certain deeds in the interest of the latter or the community and their effective completion". Reparation touches upon the framework of "penal liability"[28] and must not be confused with the obligations to give, to do or not to do in the area of civil liability. It should be clear that the good intentions of the minor to reconcile or to repair are not enough. The victim must accept the apologies, in the case of reconciliation,[29] or accept the promise of reparation made by the minor.[30] The doctrine, however, considers that this acceptance does not necessarily have to be explicitly stated; not refusing or not denying to accept is enough.[31] Furthermore, reparation may also constitute compliance with the educational measures proposed by the technical team in its report. Obviously, in order for reconciliation and reparation to produce the desired effects they must be carried out effectively. Only then (unless reparation has not been possible because of reasons not attributable to the minor's will) can the Public Prosecutor consider the order completed and can he ask the judge to dismiss the case. In the event of non-compliance with the reparation or educational activity, the proceedings continue (art. 19.5).

It is important not to confuse reconciliation and reparation with civil liability. As indicated in art. 19.3, the latter is not necessarily affected by reconciliation or by the promise of reparation by way of certain activities in favour of the victim or the community. On the contrary, if the victim does not renounce, he may claim civil liability by following the procedure established in the Act itself (arts. 61 ff.). Moreover, other agreements may be made in the framework of liability *"which may consist of promising not*

---

28 M. RICHARD GONZALEZ (2000) El nuevo proceso de menores, *La Ley*, 28 junio, 1 ff., 4.

29 Critically: M.C. GOMEZ RIVERO (2001) Algunos aspectos de la Ley Orgánica 5/2000, de 12 de enero, reguladora de la responsabilidad penal del menor, 10 *Actualidad Penal* 163 ff., 168.

30 If the victim is under-age or incapable, his legal representative must accept the promise, with the Juvenile Judge's approval (art. 19.6).

31 MARTI SANCHEZ, *o.c.*, 77.

to bring a civil liability action envisaged in article 64, such as subordinating the complaint to the minor not carrying out certain deeds".[32]

3. Civil responsibility "Ex Delicto"

The definitive exclusion of public actions on the part of private persons does not at all affect any claim for civil liability, which is regulated in Title VIII of Act 5/2000 (arts. 61-64).[33]

3.1. The "separate procedure"

Private persons can, in fact, bring their civil actions before the Juvenile Judge, in a way completely separate to criminal proceedings, by means of a procedure regulated in art. 64 and this may even occur when the Public Prosecutor desists from starting or continuing proceedings.[34] As in adult criminal law, victims may also reserve to claim this civil liability before a civil jurisdiction (art. 109.2 Penal Code), or they may present themselves at the separate procedure at any time if it has been opened by the Public Prosecutor.

This procedure has a *"special and hitherto unheard-of legal nature"*:[35] it is independent of public action and it is hard to qualify as a civil process. This procedure is opened when the Public Prosecutor informs the Court of the start of investigations or proceedings (art. 64.1). Both the Juvenile Judge and the Public Prosecutor must, in fact, inform the possible victims of this and they have a period of one month (art. 61.1) to bring a civil action (art. 64.1).

Once the victims and possible civilly liable people have presented themselves, contentious proceedings are initiated which do not require the participation of a lawyer,[36] and which may only conclude when the main prosecution is over.[37] In fact, art. 64.8 provides that the civil sentence -that

---

32 *Ibid.*, 80 ff.

33 De La Cuesta Arzamendi, *o.c.*, 175 ff..

34 J.A. Toro Peña (2000) La responsabilidad civil en la Ley Orgánica 5/2000, in Encuentro La Ley Orgánica Reguladora de la Responsabilidad Penal de los Menores, Consejo General del Poder Judicial, Fiscalía General del Estado y Comunidades Autónomas, Madrid 18-20 octubre 2000, 12.

35 Ventura Faci & Pelaez Perez, *o.c.*, 212.

36 Critically: Richard Gonzalez, *o.c.*, 1688.

37 Ventura Faci & Pelaez Perez, *o.c.*, 216 ff.

can be appealed before the Provincial Court of Justice (*Audiencia Provincial*)- must be pronounced once the juvenile proceedings are over (art. 64.8).

This sentence, however, does not definitely resolve the matter, as surprisingly [38], and very critically,[39] art. 64.10 saves "the parties' right to instigate an ordinary judgement on the sentence", even though in this trial "the facts that the Juvenile Judge esteemed worthy" are considered to be proven, "as is the minor's participation". It is also interesting to note that in the framework of the separate procedure, no possible precautionary measures assuring civil liability are contemplated; in any case, these would have to be orchestrated through the supplementary application of the Code of Criminal Procedure (*Ley de enjuiciamiento Criminal*).

3.2. The content of civil responsibility: restitution, reparation and compensation

The content and the extent of civil liability derived from offences committed by minors is identical to that which is established in the Penal Code for the civil responsibility of adult delinquents, referred to in art. 62 of the Act.

The origin of civil liability lies in "the execution of an act described by law as a crime or misdemeanour", as a consequence of which a series of "injuries and losses" (art. 109, 1 PC)[40] are brought about. In accordance with art. 110 PC, civil liability is mainly manifested in three different ways:[41]

- restitution;
- reparation of damages; and
- compensation of material and moral losses.

---

38 DOLZ LAGO, M.J. (2000) La nueva responsabilidad penal del menor (Comentarios a la Ley Orgánica 5/2000, de 12 de enero), *Revista General del Derecho* 249.

39 LANDROVE DIAZ (2001) *o.c.*, 383.

40 See also Civil Liability Act and Insurance of Motor vehicle movement, modified by Act 30/1995 of 8 November, Private insurance supervision, Act 50/1980 of 8 October, Insurance Contract, Act 35/1995 of 11 December, Aid and assistance to victims of violent crimes and sexual offences, Act 32/1999 of 8 October, Solidarity with victims of terrorism.

41 Even though they are not mentioned in Act 5/2000, they also include the civil liability of procedural expenses (art. 123), in other words, "the fees and indemnities brought about in legal proceedings" and "always the fees of private prosecution in crimes which can only be tried at the request of a party" (art. 124). (VENTURA FACI & PELÁEZ PÉREZ, *o.c.*, 209).

Restitution occurs in cases of dispossession, and consists in giving the item or property back to its legitimate owner or possessor. As far as possible, the same item must be returned in its original condition at the time of dispossession, paying for any deterioration or damage it has suffered (art. 111.1). It is the duty of the judge or the court to determine the importance of this deterioration or this damage, which must be assumed by the person who caused it or, failing this, by the civilly liable person, even when it was not caused intentionally. The item must be given back even if it has been legally acquired by a third party, unless the latter acquired it "in the manner and with the requirements established by law making it irrecoverable" (art. 111.1). However, if as a result of restitution the third party in good faith considers himself to be deprived of the item he legally acquired, he may appeal against the corresponding party and likewise claim compensation from the "person civilly liable for the crime or misdemeanour" (art. 111.1).

Reparation concerns cases of loss, destruction or damage of property liable to patrimonial or affective valuation. There are many possible ways of reparation: obligations to give, obligations to do, obligations not to do. Whatever the case, determining what reparation consists of is a legal competence and must be carried out bearing in mind "the nature of the damage and the offender's personal and patrimonial circumstances" (art. 112). It is also the responsibility of judges and courts to decide the course of action to be taken should the debtor blamefully not fulfil his obligations and, in particular, their substitution by compensation of injuries and losses "taking as a basis the value of the last thing to disappear or of the service which was lastly rendered impossible"(art. 1135 II CC).[42] The judges and courts also decide if the offender must carry out the reparation or if the reparation must be done at his expense (art. 112 PC).

As regards the compensation of material and moral losses, art. 113 PC includes not only those of "the victim", but also those which may have been suffered by "his relatives or third parties". It is difficult to determine or prove what moral losses are and one sector of the doctrine leaves out so-called "purely moral losses", which would not strictly have economic repercussions and would not be legible for compensation unless specifically regulated, as in the Civil Protection Act on the right to honour, to personal and family privacy and to one's own image. However, art. 113 PC does not

42 TORO PEÑA, *o.c.*,10.

make this distinction and thus opts for the compensation of all moral losses.[43]

Even when criteria approved by legal and regulative norms are used (for example Act 30/1995, concerning insurance), judges and courts have full competence to determine the amount of reparation and compensation -which are first priority pecuniary duties (art. 126)- and they can moderate the amount in view of the victim's contribution "to causing the damage or loss suffered through his behaviour" (art. 114 PC). They may also divide up payment of pecuniary obligations -in view of the victim's needs- if the person who is civilly liable is not wealthy enough to pay them all at once (art. 125).

3.3. Civilly liable persons

Apart from the odd additional regulation included in Act 5/2000, juvenile criminal legislation is no different from the adult Penal Code as far as civilly liable people are concerned.

The perpetrator or accomplice minor is, primarily, the civilly liable person for the injuries and losses brought about by the criminal act, when he is declared criminally liable for the acts committed (art. 116.1 PC and 1000 LECrim). If various people are involved in committing the crime or misdemeanour,[44] they are civilly liable in accordance with the share which respectively corresponds to them (art. 116.1 PC). The minor will also be civilly liable despite there being a cause of exemption from criminal liability because of the presence of psychic alterations or anomalies, complete intoxication, alterations in perception, state of necessity or insuperable fear (art. 118 PC). In such cases, other people may equally and directly have to assume civil (and not criminal) liability, such as:

- parents, guardians or keepers -legal or de facto- of the person of unsound mind or of whoever suffers alterations in perception, should they have acted blamefully or negligently;
- people who have benefited from taking advantage of the state of necessity; or
- whoever caused the insuperable fear.

---

43 DE LA CUESTA ARZAMENDI, *o.c.*, 190.

44 The civil liability of perpetrators and accomplices is direct and jointly shared by categories and subsidiary in relation to quotas established for other civilly liable people (art. 116.2 PC).

Anyone who lucratively participates in a crime or misdemeanour is likewise civilly liable to the extent of his participation (art. 122 PC).

In order to address "victims' interests and needs" (Explanatory Report) Act 5/2000 deals directly with civil liability which may involve parents, guardians, protectors and legal or de facto keepers of minors under the age of 18 who commit criminal offences. Art. 61.3 confirms their direct civil liability (in that order) with regard to the injuries and losses caused by the minor and considers them to be jointly liable together with the minor.

According to the majority of authors we are faced with going one step further in the civil liability of parents, guardians, protectors and keepers becoming more objective. This is comparable with the growing insistence for them to seriously assume their duties to watch over minors subjected to their authority, guardianship, safekeeping or custody. Traditionally founded on "culpa in vigilando", art. 1903 CC had gradually inverted the weight of evidence and this liability became quasi-objective and only avoidable if the parents, guardians, etc. were capable of proving "that they had used all the diligence of a good parent to prevent the damage". However, from Act 5/2000 on, and in order to face up to the widespread insolvency of minors under the age of 18,[45] attempts were made to establish *"joint, direct and objective civil liability"*,[46] regardless of whether the duties of vigilance were met or not. This liability is based on *"the content of relations"*[47] between parents, guardians, keepers or protectors and the minor and can be modulated by juvenile judges in the event of parents and others not favouring "the minor's behaviour with fraud or serious negligence" (art. 61.3).

I personally understand that art. 61.3 still leaves a small possibility for parents and others for not being regarded as civilly liable, in a purely objective sense: the alternative to fraud or to serious negligence is not just the accidental case, but also non-serious negligence or blame, which I believe should both be present anyway for the affirmation of joint civil liability contemplated by art. 61.3.[48]

---

45 A. Martinez Serrano (1998) El tratamiento de la responsabilidad civil en la Ley de Justicia Juvenil, In *Estudios Jurídicos*, 444. Madrid: Ministerio Fiscal, VII.

46 Landrove Diaz (2001) *o.c.*, 371.

47 Marti Sanchez (2001) *o.c.*, 73.

48 De La Cuesta Arzamendi (2001) *o.c.*, 184; see, however, Landrove (2001) *o.c.*, 373; Vaquer Aloy (2001) La responsabilidad civil en la Ley Orgánica de responsabilidad penal de los menores: una propuesta de interpretación, in *La Ley*, 12 enero, 1 ff., 1.

Art. 63, Act 5/2000 also contemplates the civil liability of *insurers*, which according to art. 117 PC, are "directly civilly liable up to the limit of legally established or conventionally agreed compensation, without prejudice to its repetition against the corresponding party".

Subsidiary civilly liable people are governed in Juvenile Criminal Law by art. 120 PC. For lack of those who are criminally responsible for the crimes or misdemeanours, this article considers these to be parents or guardians of people over the age of 18 who are subjected to their paternal authority or guardianship and who live with them, and natural or legal entities for crimes committed using their media, in their establishments (if they benefit from the infringement of police regulations or similar regulations), by their employees or salespeople in the performance of their duties or services or at the occasion of their salespeople, representatives or authorised people using their vehicles which are liable to jeopardise third parties.

Finally, Act 5/2000 deals with claims for civil liability to the Public Administration (*Administración Pública)*, which are possible in view of Art. 121 PC. Claims must be made directly to the Governments Services (art. 61.4, in relation to art. 145 of the Act on the Legal System of Government Services and Common Administrative Procedure (*Ley de Régimen Jurídico de las Administraciones Públicas y del Procedimiento Administrativo Común*)). This is a subsidiary liability, that does not require proof of guilt or negligence and that may be directed against the functionaries themselves (art. 9.4 Act on the Judiciary (*Ley Orgánica del Poder Judicial*) in relation to Act 4/99). Whatever the case, the contents of art. 61.4 in no way prevent civil liability action from being brought by means of the separate procedure.[49] In this case the juvenile judge would examine the claims made against the Public Administration.

4. Institutional Victim Support

Obviously, the generally established institutional victim support system also applies to victims of criminal offences committed by minors. This system, however, has only really been developed in the late 1990s. Of course, the State compensation system for (bodily) damages caused by terrorism began

49 As correctly pointed out by TORO PEÑA, *o.c.*, 28.

to take shape in 1979,[50] and during the 1980s victim support centres began to be set up through Autonomous Communities.[51] However, it was only in 1995, almost at the same time as the approval of the new Penal Code, that Act 35/1995 of 11 December was promulgated. In a somewhat "ambiguous"[52] and even "unfortunate"[53] way, it was called the Act for the provision of aid and assistance to victims of violent crimes and sexual offences (*Ley de ayuda y asistencia a las víctimas de delitos violentos y contra la libertad sexual*).

4.1. Public funds

Act 35/1995, of 11 December and its complementary provisions, contemplates a series of public funds for victims of (intentional) violent crimes and sexual offences, the applicability of which in Juvenile Criminal Law is explicitly recognised by art. 61.4, Act 5/2000.

These funds try to show the state's solidarity with victims of intentional violent crimes and sexual offences committed in Spain from 13th December 1995. They are directed at covering death and disabilities caused by physical or mental injury or damage originated by crime, and also the costs of therapeutic treatment chosen by the victim in cases of damage to mental health caused by sexual offences. The funds are not compatible with receiving compensations established by the sentence (art. 5)[54] nor can they exceed their amount (art. 6).

Direct and indirect victims of the aforementioned offences are beneficiaries of these funds. They must be Spanish or EU nationals, people who normally reside in Spain or nationals of those States which give similar reciprocal treatment to Spanish persons who are victims of crime in their territory (art. 2.1). Applications have to be submitted to the Ministry of

---

50 De La Cuesta Arzamendi (1988) La reparación de la víctima en el derecho penal español, in: A. Beristain Ipiña (dir.), *Las víctima del delito,* 137ff. Bilbao.

51 The promulgation in 1994 of Act 19/1994, of 23 December, concerning the protection of witnesses and expert witnesses in criminal proceedings, established victim-witness protection measures during the institution of proceedings and prosecution.

52 Landrove Diaz (2001) *o.c.*, 118.

53 Gonzalez Vidosa, F.(2001) *¿Qué es la ayuda a la víctima?*, 7. Barcelona: Atelier.

54 Or with those which he is entitled to from private insurance or the Social Security; only funds derived from injury or damage causing the victim's permanent disability or death are considered to be compatible with "any public allowance that the beneficiary has the right to receive" (art. 5.3).

Economic Affairs in a period of one year from the moment that the crime has been committed.[55]

Funds will only be granted if the crime is reported beforehand, and that it has been proved that the crime existed and that it has a causality relationship with the death, the injury or damage to the health, by means of a binding judicial decision that concludes criminal proceedings. However, the victim or his beneficiaries may be granted provisional financial aid (for up to 80% of the anticipated maximum amount) if they are left in a precarious economic situation (art. 10). The Ministry's decisions can be contested before the National Committee for Aid and Assistance to Victims of Violent Crimes and Sexual Offences (*Comisión nacional de Ayuda y Asistencia a las Víctimas de Crimes violentos y contra la Libertad Sexual*) created by art. 11 of the Act.

Once financial aid has been granted, the State acquires (art. 13) the rights of the victim or the beneficiary "against the person civilly liable for the criminal act" up to the limit of the total amount of the financial aid (provisional or definitive) granted.

In short, Act 35/1995 is a quite "restrictive" act, that limits itself to basically covering *"certain situations of precariousness and helplessness, in cases where serious injuries or death have been suffered"*.[56] At this moment, an evaluation of the applications for financial aid is not satisfactory,[57] in view of the limited number of administrative cases handled.

4.2. Victim support

Along with public funds, Act 35/1995 dedicates the contents of its II chapter (arts. 15 and 16) to victim support, which is presented as a *"different concept"*[58] to financial aid.

Firstly, it explains the information duties of the police, the Public Prosecutor, the judges and magistrates towards victims, who must be kept informed about:

- developments which occur during the investigations (unless this may jeopardise the outcome), the criminal proceedings and the verdict;

---

55 The period is interrupted when criminal proceedings begin and resumed when binding judicial decision is passed (art. 7).

56 GONZALEZ VIDOSA (2001) *o.c.*, 79.

57 ZARAGOZA AGUADO, J.A. (2000) La víctima y su protección asistencial en el Derecho español, *Estudios jurídicos*, 295 ff., 307. Ministerio fiscal, II.

58 LANDROVE DIAZ (1998) *o.c.*, 124.

- the possibilities of obtaining the restitution and reparation of damages through criminal proceedings; and,
- in the case of victims of violent and sexual crimes, the possibility of applying for the funds envisaged in Act 35/1995 and the procedure for doing so.

It stipulates that victims must always be interrogated "with respect for their personal situation, their rights and their dignity" and the Public Prosecutor is entrusted with protecting the victim against all undesirable publicity, which may even entail applying for the criminal proceedings to be held behind closed doors.

Art. 16 concerns victim support centres, which must be implanted in the "headquarters of Courts and Tribunals or in all Public Prosecutor Offices where they are required", either directly by the Ministry of Justice or through agreements with Autonomous Communities or Local Corporations.

In fact, victim support centres in Spain go back to the middle of the 1980s, when in view of "state neglect" and based on the example of the centre created in Valencia by the Autonomous Government, some Autonomous Communities and Town Councils began to set up these centres or services. The functions of these centres are to provide victims with information and direct counselling (even in reporting crimes or constituting the accusation in proceedings), to handle resources available for "mitigating the situation of victimisation", and also to collaborate with the criminal justice administration system, as a whole.[59]

The State's main bodies did not very effectively apply this aspect of Act 35/1995 either, and it was not until 1999 that the state structure of victim support centres came into function[60]

4.3. Victims of terrorism

Even though the purpose of Act 35/1995 was *"to gradually homogenise the legal funding system for victims of all crimes"*,[61] assistance to victims of terrorism has continued to lie in the hands of the Ministry of the Interior.

---

59 GONZALEZ VIDOSA, *o.c.*, 32 ff.; also DE LA CUESTA, GONZALEZ VIDOSA & JORGE MESAS (1998) The treatment of victims of crimes and offences in the Spanish system of justice, in: E. FATTAH & T. PETERS (eds.), *Support for crime victims in a comparative perspective. A collection of essays dedicated to the memory of Prof. Frederic McClintock*, 69ff. Leuven: Leuven University Press.

60 ZARAGOZA AGUADO, *o.c.*, 305.

61 *Ibid.*, 300.

These victims are still given support by means of a separate system, which is compatible with civil liability compensations and broader, both in matters of the protection covered and of the financial aid quantities and the forms of indemnity. Alongside state regulations there are also autonomous regulations that establish complementary funds for cases not generally contemplated[62]

State regulations on the assistance to victims of terrorism are currently determined by the following texts:

- Regulations on the provision of funds and compensations to victims of terrorist acts (*Reglamento de ayudas y resarcimientos a las víctimas de delitos de terrorismo*), approved by the Royal Decree 1211/1997, of 18 July (modified by RD 1734/1998, of 31 July);
- Act 32/1999, of 8 October, on solidarity with victims of terrorism; and
- Regulations on the application of this Act, approved by RD 1912/1999, of 17 December.

As regards terrorism, the State not only assumes the indemnity of damages and the provision of certain funds, but also the payment of special economic compensations. Both physical and psychical damages (and treatment costs), and material damage to usual housing, commercial and industrial establishments and private or transportation vehicles can be compensated. The ordinary funds envisaged are: study funds; psychological and psycho-pedagogical assistance; and funds for support and programmes of defence associations for victims of terrorism. There are also special funds for the coverage of personal and family situations of special need which are unattended or insufficiently covered by ordinary funds (art. 41 Regulations).

Special economic compensations were introduced by the Act on solidarity with victims of terrorism.[63] Only physical or physico-physical damages (not material and/or moral ones) suffered by victims of acts between the 1st January 1968 and the 9th October 1999 can be compensated. If their right to compensation is not recognised by a binding judicial decision (art. 2 Act), the criteria given in the Act's annex are applied.[64]

---

62 These exist in the Autonomous Communities of the Basque Country, Navarra and Madrid.

63 See also the Royal Decree of 23 January 1998 on the procedure and criteria for assigning funds to victims of terrorism derived from profits obtained in the National Lottery draw on 18 October 1997; see: LANDROVE DÍAZ (1998) *o.c.*, 155 ff.

64 Funds for exemption from academic fees and for financing medical treatments, prostheses and surgical operations not covered by another public or private system are also included (art. 7 Act).

Compensations -which could be applied for during a six month period from the moment the Act came into force- are compatible with other allowances, funds, compensations or indemnifications which are legally recognised, even by the legislation on funds to victims of terrorism (art. 6.5 Act).

The list of beneficiaries of compensation, funds and indemnifications concerning terrorism is broader than the list of beneficiaries for violent crimes and sexual offences. It is within the competence of the Ministry of the Interior to decide on the incoming applications. These decisions, with regards compensation and funds, may be contested before the National Committee for Aid and Assistance to Victims of Violent Crimes and Sexual Offences.

References

Beristain, A. (1995) Prólogo, in: Urra Portillo, J. (1995) *Menores, la transformación de la realidad, Ley Orgánica* 4/1992. Madrid.

Bueno Arús, F. (1997) El Anteproyecto de Ley Orgánica reguladora de la Justicia de Menores elaborado por el Ministerio de Justicia, 11 *Eguzkilore. Cuaderno del Instituto Vasco de Criminología* 159 ff.

Cerezo Mir, J. (2000) (2ª ed*), Derecho Penal. Parte general*. Madrid: Lecciones.

Consejo Vasco de la Abogacía (2001) (ed.), *La Ley Orgánica 5/2000 de Responsabilidad Penal de los Menores*. Bilbao: Consejo Vasco de la Abogacía.

Coronado Buitrago, M.J. (1993) La singular posición de la víctima en la justicia de menores, in: Consejo General Del Podar Judicial (ed.), *La Victimología*, 397 ff. Madrid.

Cuello Contreras, J. (2000) *El nuevo derecho penal de menores*. Madrid: Civitas.

de la Cuesta Arzamendi (1988) La reparación de la víctima en el derecho penal español, in: A. Beristain Ipiña (dir.), *Las víctima del delito,* 137 ff. Bilbao.

de la Cuesta J.L., F. Gonzalez Vidosa & J. Mesas (1998) The treatment of victimas of crimes and offences in the Spanish system of justice, in: E. Fattah & T. Peters (eds.), *Support for crime victims in a comparative perspective. A collection of essays dedicated to the memory of Prof. Frederic McClintock,* 69ff. Leuven: Leuven University Press.

de la Cuesta Arzamendi, J.L. (2001) Responsabilidad civil. Procedimiento. Incoación. Efectos, in: Consejo Vasco de la Abogacía, *o.c.*, 175 ff., 179.

de la Cuesta, J.L. (1999) El abandono del sistema tutelar: evolución del derecho español en materia de protección y de tratamiento de los menores delincuentes y en peligro, 37(1/2) *Annales Internationales de Criminologie* 101 ff.

Dolz Lago, M.J. (2000) La nueva responsabilidad penal del menor (Comentarios a la Ley Orgánica 5/2000, de 12 de enero), *Revista General del Derecho* 249.

Etxebarria Zarrabeitia, X. (2001) Aspectos sustantivos. Edad. Medidas. Contenido. Prescripción. Concursos. Régimen Transitorio, in: Consejo Vasco de la Abogacía (ed.), *La Ley Orgánica 5/2000 de Responsabilidad Penal de los Menores*, 7 ff. Bilbao: Consejo Vasco de la Abogacía.

Feijoo Sánchez, B. (2001) Sobre el contenido y la evolución del Derecho Penal español tras la LO 5/2000 y la LO 7/2000, 4 *Revista Jurídica*, Universidad Autónoma de Madrid, 9 ff.

García Pérez, O. (2000) La evolución del sistema de justicia penal juvenil. La Ley de Responsabilidad Penal del Menor de 2000 a la luz de las directrices internacionales, 32 *Actualidad Penal* 682 ff., 686.

Gómez Rivero, M.C. (2001) Algunos aspectos de la Ley Orgánica 5/2000, de 12 de enero, reguladora de la responsabilidad penal del menor, 10 *Actualidad Penal*, 163 ff.

González Vidosa, F. (2001) *¿Qué es la ayuda a la víctima?* Barcelona: Atelier.

Lamo Rubio, J. (1999) La víctima en el actual proceso de menores: presencias y ausencias, *La Ley*, núm. 4897, 1 ff.

Landrove Díaz, G. (1998) *La moderna victimología*. Valencia: Tirant lo Blanch.

Landrove Díaz, G. (2001) *Derecho Penal de Menores*. Valencia: Tirant lo Blanch.

López Caballero, J.C. (1994) La Legislación reformadora de menores en España u Brasil: un análisis comparativo, 4 *Revista de Derecho Penal y Criminología* 491 ff.

Maeso Ventureira, A. (2001) Procedimiento. Incoacción. Competencia objetiva, territorial y funcional. Partes. Instrucción. Sentencia. Recursos, in: Consejo Vasco de la Abogacía (ed.), *La Ley Orgánica* 5/2000 de Responsabilidad Penal de los Menores, 67ff. Bilbao: Consejo Vasco de la Abogacía.

Manzana Laguardia, M.P. (1992) Notas acerca del Proyecto de Ley sobre Reforma urgente del procedimiento de Menores, 571 *Revista General de Derecho* 2543 ff.

Martí Sánchez, J.N. (2001) Protección de la víctima y responsabilidad civil en la ley penal de los menores, 4 *Actualidad Penal*, 65 ff.

Martínez Serrano, A. (1998) El tratamiento de la responsabilidad civil en la Ley de Justicia Juvenil, *Estudios Jurídicos*. Madrid: Ministerio Fiscal, VII.

Palacio Sánchez Izquierdo, J.R. (2000) El principio del superior interés del menor, *Surgam* 466-467, 55 ff.

Palacio Sánchez Izquierdo, J.R. (2001) La abogacía en la ley penal. Turno de oficio, in: Consejo Vasco de la Abogacía (ed.), *La Ley Orgánica* 5/2000 de Responsabilidad Penal de los Menores, 199ff. Bilbao: Consejo Vasco de la Abogacía.

Richard González, M. (2000) El nuevo proceso de menores, *La Ley*, 28 junio, 1 ff.

Rodríguez Sol, L. (1996) El Fiscal y la protección de las víctimas en el proceso de menores, *Boletín de Información del Ministerio de Justicia*, núm. 1750, 137 ff.

Sánchez García de Paz, I. (2000) La nueva ley reguladora de la responsabilidad penal del menor, 33 *Actualidad Penal* 699 ff.

Toro Peña, J.A. (2000) La responsabilidad civil en la Ley Orgánica 5/2000, in: *Encuentro* "La Ley Orgánica Reguladora de la Responsabilidad Penal de los Menores", Consejo General del Poder Judicial, Fiscalía General del Estado y Comunidades Autónomas, Madrid, 18-20 octubre 2000.

Urra Portillo, J. (1995) *Menores, la transformación de la realidad, Ley Orgánica 4/1992*. Madrid.

Vaquer Aloy (2001) La responsabilidad civil en la Ley Orgánica de responsabilidad penal de los menores: una propuesta de interpretación, *La Ley*, 12 enero, 1 ff.

Ventura Faci, R. & Peláez Pérez, V. (2000) *Ley Orgánica 5/2000 de 12 de enero reguladora de la responsabilidad penal de los menores. Comentarios y jurisprudencia*. Madrid: Colex.

Zaragoza Aguado, J.A. (2000) La víctima y su protección asistencial en el Derecho español, *Estudios jurídicos*. Ministerio fiscal, II, 295 ff.

PUBLIC DAMAGE FUNDS. EUROPEAN DEVELOPMENTS AND SOME COMPARATIVE OBSERVATIONS

Marc Groenhuijsen

It is a distinct pleasure and a privilege to have an opportunity to contribute to a book in the honour of Tony Peters. I have known him for many years, and during this period of time my admiration for his academic achievements has increased steadily. His writings demonstrate traditional scholarship, going hand in hand with a strong commitment to humanitarian values. For Tony Peters, the rule of law is not to be taken for granted. Legal institutions are to be scrutinized with a constantly critical eye. For quite a long time, this attitude did not make Tony Peters a happy professional researcher. The criminal justice system he was studying so intensely typically malfunctioned in an appalling way. It obviously did not serve the interests it is supposed to protect. The system could easily be proven to be manifestly unfair to its main clients, victims of crime and offenders alike. This only changed with the ascent of the concept of restorative justice. The idea -or ideal- of restorative justice opened up completely new horizons for criminologists and penologists. The non-repressive and non-retributive nature of this new paradigm[1] held the promise of finally contributing to substantive justice in the aftermath of crime. Hence, during the last decade and a half, promoting restorative justice became one of the academic aspirations of Tony Peters.

Introduction

It is with this background in mind that I have selected the topic for my contribution to the book written in his honor. It is about public damage funds. These funds have been established by national governments in order to pay compensation to crime victims in cases where no other means of redress is available. In the subsequent sections of this paper I will examine the nature and the legal status of public damage funds. It will be demonstrated that these

1 Tony Peters and myself have been arguing for a long time about the question whether restorative justice does or does not constitute a new paradigm in the true sense of the word. He feels that is the case, I disagree strongly. It is easy to appreciate one another when sharing the same views; however, mutual respect deepens when there is fundamental disagreement on important issues which can be discussed in a friendly and constructive atmosphere.

funds genuinely are resources of last resort. It is generally taken for granted that criminal law in itself only enters the picture when all alternative remedies have failed. Hence the common designation of criminal law as an *ultimum remedium*. But when this label corresponds to reality, than this is *a fortiori* the case with the availability of public damage funds. Their existence can easily be characterized as a *plus quam ultimum remedium*. And they are unique in another sense also. As far as I can see, provisions on damage funds constitute the sole statutory mechanism outside the criminal justice system where the legal position of crime victims is categorically determined. These characteristics by themselves justify specific attention directed to public damage funds. On top of that, however, it should be noted that State compensation is one of the criminal justice-related subjects that have been dealt with on a supra-national level. All of this leads to the following questions to be addressed in the following sections. What is the background and the content of international legal documents governing national State compensation schemes? How have the international guidelines been incorporated in some noteworthy domestic legal systems and how are these national schemes operated in actual practice? Can examples of best practice be identified and in what way could they be emulated in other jurisdictions? I am convinced this type of questions commands the attention of Tony Peters. They directly affect the well-being of a vulnerable category of citizens -the victims of crimes which (more often than not) have not been successfully investigated by the government- and they concern the crossroads between normative legal discourse on the one hand and empirical research on the other.

1. Legislative initiatives on the European level

The first important document to be mentioned here is the European Convention on the Compensation of Victims of Violent Crime, which was agreed upon by member States of the Council of Europe in 1983. The objective of this Convention is to define and prescribe minimum standards which have to be observed by national governments. The standards are based on the principles of equity and social solidarity. The focal provisions of the Convention can be summarised as follows.

Compensation is to be paid by the State on whose territory the crime was committed to subjects of countries who have signed the convention and to subjects of any Council of Europe member State who has permanent residence in the country where the crime took place (art. 3). Compensation at least covers loss of income, hospital and other medical expenses, funeral costs and -for dependents of deceased victims- the cost of life sustenance (art. 4). The restrictive or limited nature of this first convention is evidenced by the conditions that may be incorporated by the member States in their domestic legislation. They are allowed to stipulate a threshold (minimum) sum of money and a maximum for each payment (art. 5). They can set a time limit for claims (art. 6) and they are allowed to refuse or diminish a claim in the light of the financial means at the disposal of the victim (art. 7). Refusal or reduction is also possible because of the conduct of the victim prior to, during or after the crime, or in connection with previous involvement with organized crime (art. 8). The principle of subsidiarity is further witnessed by the provision that payments from any other source (the offender, private insurance or social security) must be deducted from state compensation (art. 9). It is remarkable that the Convention states as a 'basic principle' that the signatory states will take steps in order to ensure that information about public damage funds be available to potential applicants (art. 11). Apparently the drafters of the Convention anticipated serious problems in this respect. Unfortunately, the two decades that have since elapsed have done little to ease their concerns.

So, the Council of Europe took the lead in setting standards on State compensation. The European Union has traditionally been a legal entity where it is much more difficult to accomplish binding agreements in matters related to national criminal justice systems. As far as the topic under consideration is concerned, in December of 1998 the first breakthrough was achieved in the Vienese Plan of Action by the European Council and Commission concerning the execution of the Treaty of Amsterdam.[2] The decisive conceptual legal innovation in this document is constituted by a broader definition of the quintessential term 'freedom'.

The Treaty of Amsterdam (...) opens the way to giving 'freedom' a meaning beyond free movement of people across internal borders. It is also freedom to live in a law-abiding environment in the knowledge that public authorities are using everything in their individual and collective power (...) to combat and contain those who seek to deny or abuse that freedom.' In connection with the issue of State compensation a prudent first step is then taken in the 51st (and final!) priority set in the Action Plan: "address the question of victim support by making a comparative survey of victim compensation schemes and assess the feasibility of taking action within the Union".

Since that time developments have taken place at rather high speed. In July

2 Action Plan of the Council and the Commission on how best to implement the provisions of the Treaty of Amsterdam on an Area of Freedom, Security and Justice (OJ C19/1 23.1.99) adopted on 3.12.1998.

1999 the European Commission issued a 'communication' to a number of EU institutions on the legal position of crime victims in the Union.[3] In this document, the Commission first notes that not all member States have yet ratified the Council of Europe Convention and implores the members concerned to do so forthwith. Next, the Commission observes that existing domestic legislation reveals major differences between the various States, for instance when it concerns the required nationhood of potential applicants of a public damage fund. The Commission reminds all authorities of the famous verdict of the Court of Justice in the *Cowan case*, prohibiting the limitation of State compensation schemes to the scope of their own nationals, thus excluding residents of other EU countries. In this judgement it was held equally illegal to restrict applications to those 'nationals or countries that have entered into a reciprocal agreement with that state'. Accordingly, the Commission recommends to consider a number of important changes in national legislation. It is stated as a priority that compensation should be awarded as soon as possible after the crime occurred, when necessary by means of up front interim-payments. On top of that, the government should actually assist the victim in the process of debt collection from the offender. And finally, the member States must intensify mutual cooperation in order to improve claims for compensation abroad by allowing these claims to be filed in the home country of the victim.

The first concrete results were achieved during the meeting of the European Council in October 1999 at Tampere. The heads of government agreed to the following conclusion[4]: "Having regard to the Commission's Communication,[5] minimum standards should be drawn up on the protection of the victims of crime, in particular on crime victims' access to justice and on their rights to compensation for damages, including legal costs. In addition, national programmes should be set up to finance measures, public and non-governmental, for assistance to and protection of victims." This carefully crafted conclusion at first sight looks rather restrained and is therefore apparently not overly impressive. Upon closer inspection, though, the deeper meaning of this conclusion is that it has subsequently been interpreted as a *mandate* for deeper involvement in various victim-related issues. This is evidenced by the progress made during a follow up-meeting in October 2000 in

3 *Crime Victims in the European Union. Reflections on Standards and Action*, Communication to the European Parliament, the Council, and the Economic and Social Committee, Brussels July 14, 1999, COM (1999) 349.

4 Conclusions of the Presidency, European Council in Tampere, October 15-16, 1999, SN 200/99, conclusion 32.

5 This is a reference to the *Communication* mentioned in footnote 3 above.

Umea in Sweden.[6] During this meeting more focus was given to the direction in which change in Europe might take shape. The principle of subsidiarity retains its prominent status - the perpetrator carries the primary as well as the ultimate responsibility for the crime.[7] On a European level it is generally considered to be a reasonable eligibility requirement that the crime must be reported to the police.[8] In order to increase the number of legitimate claims coming to the attention of the authorities, it is stipulated that the victim ought to have the choice between filing the application in the country of the *locus delicti* or in his home country. In cases where only the former option is available, authorities of the home country must be prepared to give assistance in filing the application. Another idea which surfaced is that better use should be made of the *network* of national State compensation schemes in order to increase the number of applications resulting from cross border victimization. And it was stressed that priority must be given to the dissemination of *information* to victims about compensation opportunities, which is deemed to be a prime responsibility of the police force. And finally it was decided that more work should be devoted to establishing common minimum standards for compensation. As far as material damages are concerned the Council of Europe Convention is still regarded as a benchmark: compensation must be provided for hospital and other medical costs, for loss of income and for personal properties. Regarding moral damages, however, there is a conspicuous degree of uncertainty at the European level. The optimum conclusion in this respect was that "there was agreement that further work was necessary to define the concept of moral damages, after which further consideration should be given to the possible inclusion of such damages in the minimum standards". The official report of the meeting at Umea concludes with the statement that "the future ambition could be to fulfill the mandate given at Tampere, by proposing binding legislation at Union-level".

We have not reached that stage yet. In the Framework decision of the European Council dated 15 March 2001 on the status of the victim in criminal procedures,[9] the issue of State compensation is carefully treated with benign neglect. The preamble of this document recalls the previously stated intention

---

6 I refer to the document entitled *The Umea Expert Meeting on Compensation to Crime Victims in the European Union*, Umea, Sweden, October 23-24, 2000.

7 The principle of subsidiarity has also been recognized on a global level, e.g. in the United Nations *Declaration on the Basic Principles of Justice for Victims of Crime and Abuse of Power* (1985). From an Australian perspective: I. FRECKELTON (2001) *Criminal Injuries Compensation: Law, Practice and Policy*. Sydney: Law Book Company.

8 This requirement is, however, optional. It is, for instance, not part of Dutch law.

9 2001/220/JHA.

to conduct a comparative survey of State compensation schemes. And it is specifically mentioned that the provisions of the framework decision are not confined to attending to the victims' interests under criminal proceedings proper: they explicitly also cover certain measures to assist victims before or after criminal proceedings which might mitigate the effects of the crime. But that is it. Contrary to earlier drafts of the framework decision,[10] there is not a single article in it dealing with the matter of State compensation. The "ambition to fulfill the mandate given at Tampere" is still a promise or an aspiration in dire need of substantive follow up-action.

2. National compensation schemes and their implementation

The preceding account of developments at a European level is illuminating in more than one sense. It is striking that the principle of subsidiarity is the unquestioned starting point and constant frame of reference. State compensation only enters the equation in the most serious cases and when no alternative remedies are available. On the other hand, however, it is remarkable that quite a bit of debate within European institutions is about under serving of eligible victims. Many people qualifying for compensation just do not apply for it, and this is a cause for widespread concern. Finally, it can be concluded that the involvement of 'Europe' has been inspired and accelerated by the specific problems caused by cross border victimization. This is easily understandable in the light of the standards determining the 'competency' of the European Union. Conversely it makes sense that the debate on compensation in the international arena also provoked national authorities to ponder the legal situation of their own citizens. It would clearly be inexplainable to pay attention to the needs of victims of foreign origin without providing at least the same type of care to local victims.

Carrying these observations in mind we now turn our attention to some of the European jurisdictions operating State compensation schemes.

---

10 I myself have played a modest part in the preparatory stages leading up to the adoption of the framework decision. During the negotiations it became evident that quite a few member States are reluctant to accept the idea of binding legislation at the Union level because they are afraid of possible financial implications. This sealed the fate of dealing with the topic in the framework decision.

2.1. England, Scotland and Wales

In England, Scotland and Wales[11] a State compensation fund has been in operation since 1964. It is this fund which has repeatedly been presented to the rest of the world as an example to be imitated. This begs the question whether this reputation is well-deserved. In 1996 the new Criminal Injuries Compensation Act (CICA) 1995 came into force. The present discourse is restricted to this latest legislative Act and its application in daily practice.

Payments according to this scheme are not to be regarded as corollaries of liability in the legal sense of the word. Instead, the transfer of money is to be considered as 'expressions of public sympathy and support for innocent victims'. An eligibility requirement is that there is a case of an intentional violent crime (including arsony and poisoning). It is interesting to note that compensation can also be awarded when the injury was incurred while apprehending a criminal, while trying to prevent crime and when assisting police activities in this respect.[12] The relevant statute contains a specific provision concerning the notoriously difficult subject of domestic violence. Compensation can only be claimed when the perpetrator is criminally prosecuted and when the claimant and the perpetrator are no longer living in the same household. Furthermore, the violence has to be reported as a crime to the police. Conversely, State compensation in general does not depend on the arrest or conviction of the perpetrator. The claim has to be filed within two years of the time of the crime committed.

From a comparative point of view, the scheme is relatively generous. For this reason, I quote the entire list of damages that can be compensated.[13]
For personal injury, the scheme contains three possible components:

- the tariff of injuries,[14] which fixes a standard amount of compensation according to the type of injury. There are some 380 injury descriptions ranked against 25 levels of award between £1,000 and £250.000 (the values having been drawn by reference to awards made under the former common law damages scheme)
- actual net loss of earnings or earning capacity, which excludes the first 28 weeks of loss but can run in cases of severe injury for the remainder of the

11 It must be noted that Northern Ireland has its own Scheme.

12 I leave aside the typically English provisions dealing with railroad offenses.

13 E.g. CICA's Third Report (2000) *Annual report 1998/99*, 7. Edinburgh: The Stationery Office.

14 The fundamental difference with the system before 1996 is that awards for the non-financial elements -principally pain and suffering- are fixed according to a tariff of injuries.

victim's working life and may include ultimate pension loss

- the cost of medical or other care, which, subject to incapacity exceeding 28 weeks, can be assessed from the date of injury for the remainder of the victim's natural life.

In claims following homicide, the components are:

- a standard amount of £5,000 for each qualifying claimant (or £10,000 if there is only one claimant)
- dependency on the deceased's income, running until he/she would have reached normal retirement[15]
- funeral expenses.

The subsidiary nature of the compensation scheme is also in the United Kingdom manifested by a number of eligibility requirements. There is the requirement that the crime has been reported to the police and the obligation to assist the police in their investigation of the case. Naturally, the victim has to cooperate with the CICA in the procedure leading up to a decision on the claim. It is of singular importance that the conduct of the victim prior to, during or after the incident can constitute grounds to reduce or to refuse the claim for compensation. Simply speaking, this consideration is tantamount to an assessment of the level of co-responsibility on the part of the victim. Particularly remarkable is the fact that payment from the fund can be adversely affected by the character of the applicant as this is shown by his own criminal record. The relevant provisions far exceed the exclusion of payments in cases of internal feuds within criminal gangs. The British legislation is based on the view that "a person who has committed criminal offenses has probably caused distress and loss and injury to other persons, and has certainly caused considerable expense to society by reason of court appearances and the cost of supervising sentences ...". On the basis of this rationale another extensive tariff list was drawn up, indicating which prior convictions lead to 'penalty points' (ranging from 0% to 100%).

As far as procedure is concerned, the first item of note is the wide discretionary power of the 'claims officer'. He has the authority to extend the period in which the claim can be filed and he is responsible for the investigation on the legitimacy of the claim. The procedure allows for the possibility of interim payments, up to 50% of the amounts indicated by the applicable tariff. The final decision by the claims officer is taken on the

15 A rather special component is: loss to a child under 18 of a deceased parent's services, made up of a standard amount of £2,000 a year until age 18, plus the actual costs incurred, again running to age 18, in replacing that parent's services, whether by the surviving parent giving up or reducing employment so as to provide the care, or by engaging paid help, or by a combination of measures.

evidentiary criterion of the 'balance of probabilities'. Usually, compensation is awarded as a one-time lump sum. Interestingly, the claims officer has the power to issue directions as to the way the money is to be managed. When the compensation involves a very large amount, there is the possibility of an annual, inflation-proof and tax-free payment, a method which can be particularly beneficial to dependents of homicide victims. If the applicant disagrees with the decision of the claims officer, he can ask for a review by a more senior officer of the CICA. When the result of that review is still unsatisfactory, he can appeal to the Criminal Injuries Compensation Appeals Panel (CICAP), an institution which is completely independent from the CICA.

Because of space constraints only the most basic facts can be reported here about the way the legal provisions are applied in daily practice. After the introduction of the new Act the period of 1996-1997 has to be considered as a trial year, when the competent authorities still had to get used to changed circumstances.[16]

In 1997-1998 a decision was taken on 80,000 claims. The number of cases in stock slightly decreased to 104,000 cases. In nearly 58,000 instances the decision was favourable, benefiting some 31,500 victims. Total amount paid out was £80 million, averaging over £2,500 per victim. The highest individual award was £190,000. The expenditures on administering the fund were some £19 million. The average duration of the procedure leading up to payments was 6 to 8 months. The most frequently obtaining grounds for refusing a claim were: the damage was below the threshold level of £1,000, the victim cooperated insufficiently in bringing the offender to justice, lack of evidence of a violent crime, co-responsibility of the victim for the crime having occurred, and prior criminal conviction of the applicant (accounting for over 90% of the refusals).

The next year, 1998-1999, shows a slightly upward curve. The unfinished case-load was again somewhat diminished to a level of 103,000 cases; the average period needed to take a decision remained the same at 6 of 8 month (60%). 85,000 cases were dealt with, leading to 75,000 positive outcomes and awards to some 40,000 applicants who received a grant total of £107 million. The highest amount of compensation in a single case equaled the legal maximum of £500,000. Administrative costs of running the program remained at the level of £18,5 million. The grounds for refusing claims did not change much, with the exception that the number of applications for amounts below the threshold dropped significantly.

The most recent numbers I have been able to trace are about the year 1999-

16 The following data are drawn from the annual reports of the CICA.

2000. The number of files on the shelf went back to some 87,000. A decision was taken on 76,000 claims, with compensation awarded to 46,000 victims. It is estimated that this figure corresponds to 10-25% of all victims of violent crime who would have met all eligibility requirements. The sum total of awards was £108 million. Over 50% of the applications were processed within 6 months. After 12 months a final decision was taken in 85% of all the claims filed.

2.2. Germany

The German Act on State Compensation (the *Opferentschädigungsgesetz*) came into force in 1976.[17] The ideological background of this Act is the consideration that when the government is unable to prevent serious violent crime, the least it can do is to take care of the victims of these transgressions. The principle of social justice requires the State to intervene when the fate of innocent citizens in great distress is at stake. In the light of this *ratio legis* it follows that property crime and traffic offenses are kept outside of the scope of State compensation.

As far as the relevant criminal conduct is concerned, it must be noted that intentional poisoning is included in the terms of reference, as well as causing danger -either intentionally or by negligence- by means of intrinsically hazardous goods.

The nature of damages that can be compensated is not clearly defined. The Act refers to 'medical or scientific consequences' of the crime, resulting in a claim on the government "to supply care by corresponding application of the Bundesversorgungsgsetz" (an Act on social security). Physical damage (injuries) is meant to also include damage to objects like glasses or artificial teeth. The reference to the 'Versorgungsgesetz' indicates that it is more common in Germany than elsewhere to award *periodical payments*: in 1997, for instance, some 7000 victims were entitled to this type of pension. There is no compensation for pain and suffering.

The German compensation scheme is also based on the principle of subsidiarity. Other sources of redress are given priority (insurance, social security, restitution by offenders) and an award from the State compensation fund is means tested. And finally the subsidiary nature of the scheme is also evidenced by some of the eligibility requirements. Equity dictates that

---

17 The Act was later on changed in 1984 and in 1993. The first period of its operation is described and discussed from a comparative point of view by U. WEINTRAUD (1980) *Staatliche Entschädigung für Opfer von Gewalttaten in Grossbritannien und der Bundesrepublik Deutschland*. Baden-Baden: Nomos Verlagsgesellschaft.

compensation is not awarded in cases of inappropriate conduct by the victim. An example of this is when the victim fails to contribute adequately to police investigations or to the prosecutor preparing charges. An award can equally be refused when the damage resulted from political controversies to which the victim was a party. The same principle obtains when the victim is -or has been- involved in organized crime, unless he can prove that the damages he suffered are completely unrelated to this involvement.

Empirical data on the application of the State Compensation Act are scarce and hard to retrieve. The numbers I have been able to find nevertheless indicate that expenditures under the Act have over the years consistently and substantially increased. In 1980 the total amount of compensation paid to victims was 7,5 million DM, rising to 27 million DM in 1985, over 42 million DM in 1990, nearly 97 million DM in 1995, and -after the most recent changes in the legal provisions- over 190 million DM in 1998.

2.3. Belgium

The establishment of the Belgium State Compensation Fund dates back to the middle 1980s. Here, as elsewhere, the idea on which the scheme is founded is collective solidarity among citizens of a single nation. Any award is governed by equity: there is never any right to compensation based on liability of the State. The fund is resourced by the ministry of Justice on the one hand and by a so-called 'victim-tax' on the other: this is a surcharge of 5 BF levied on any person sentenced in a criminal court.

A condition to receive support from the State is that an intentional violent crime was committed on Belgian soil. Direct victims and dependents of homicide victims qualify to make an application to the scheme. A rather special category of victims who are eligible is constituted by those who voluntarily assisted the law enforcement officers in clearing up the crime (art. 42). There is a separate provision requiring the decision makers to take into account 'relationships between the victim and the perpetrator'. This special clause is designed with an eye to not completely excluding innocent victims of domestic violence.

The Belgians make a distinction between main compensation, interim payments (in very urgent circumstances) and additional compensation (after the main payment has taken place and new circumstances have surfaced). Main compensation equals the amount of the actual damages incurred by the victim, with a deduction of 10,000 BF in every case and a ceiling of 2,5 million BF. Relevant damages have to concern loss of income, medical expenses and physical disablements. For dependents of homicide victims the focus clearly is on sustenance costs. Compensation for pain and suffering is excluded as a general rule. However there is a caveat here. According to the applicable regulations the assessment of physical disabilities caused by the crime opens up an opportunity to pay compensation for moral damage and physical or mental hardship during the period of illness, even when these hardships have not affected the economic activity or circumstances of the victim. Dependents and next of kin of homicide victims cannot claim moral damages.

In Belgium, the subsidiary nature of the scheme is exemplified by the relatively large number of cases in which an award is refused on the ground of favorable financial circumstances of the victim. And like in the countries we have reviewed before, all other possible means of redress (insurance, restitution by offenders) take precedence over State compensation. When the offender is known, it is even an eligibility requirement for the victim to constitute himself as a civil claimant during the criminal proceedings.

In as far as empirical data are available, they show that the use being made of the scheme has been extended over the years. In 1987 the sum total of awards reached the modest level of 1 million BF, which increased to nearly 13 million BF in 1991. A further hike was achieved to 32 million BF in 1993. In terms of eligibility requirements it stands out that many applications were refused on the ground of absence of a pressing financial need and by reason of failure to constitute oneself as a civil claimant during the criminal trial. In 1994-1995 the total amount of State compensation was 50 million BF; in 1996 is reached 60 million BF and in 1997 it slightly depressed to 52 million BF. Only in the past couple of years a rapid -even an explosive- increase in the volume of awards took place. In 1998 the fund encompassed 95 million BF, in 1999 it totaled 168 million BF, which had further risen to 254 million BF in 2000.[18] The spectacular blossoming of State compensation in the past three years can be attributed to several factors. Firstly the notorious Dutroux case has increased public awareness of the difficult position of many crime victims. And the resulting increased level of sensitivity has lifted the veil of denial that for a long time prevented the opportunity of open discussions about criminal victimization. In this new climate it is easier for victims to step forward and claim their rights, including the right to State compensation. Secondly, a legislative initiative that came into force in 1997 has been instrumental in bringing about improvements. The accessibility of the fund was facilitated, the

18 The increase in the volume of awards was naturally matched by a similar trend in the number of applications (1997: 391; 1998: 873; 1999: 715; 2000: 740) and the number of decisions rendered (1997: 125; 1998: 192; 1999: 530; 2000: 732). See: Commissie voor Hulp aan Slachtoffers (forthcoming) *Verslag van de werkzaamheden 2000-2001*. Brussel: Commissie voor Hulp aan Slachtoffers.

administrative capacity of the fund was enlarged (from 2 chambers to 6), close relatives of deceased victims were allowed more room to file claims and payments for moral damages were expanded. And finally, these statutory innovations were seconded by several policy measures taken by the Belgian government (including a large publicity campaign) aimed at increasing public knowledge about the existence and accessibility of the fund.

2.4. Other countries

There are many other European countries operating State compensation schemes. It is -for obvious reasons- impossible to account for all of these in the present contribution. It will just have to suffice to list some details about other countries which confirm the above mentioned main features of standing State compensation schemes throughout Europe.

On the one hand only Finland and France offer opportunities for State compensation in cases of property crime. Conversely, only Italy and Greece do not have any institution resembling the basic function of State Compensation Funds described in the previous sections. This state of affairs only underlines that the perspective resembled by the Council of Europe Convention of 1983 has been generally accepted in its main components in virtually all countries in Europe.[19]

Final remarks and conclusions

What lessons can be drawn from the developments described and analyzed in the preceding sections? The first element that needs to be highlighted concerns the *ratio legis* of State compensation schemes. In all the countries we have reviewed it became evident that the state does not accept liability for the crime committed against the victim. Awards from a compensation fund are based on the idea of social justice and collective solidarity. This also accounts for the subsidiary nature of State compensation. Awards are only granted in the most serious cases and on the basis of equity. The notion of 'equity' is not without its own problems. In several countries, this criterion effectively forces the authorities to scrutinise the behavior of the victim prior to, during or after the crime. For the victim, this procedure might easily evoke the image of a world

19 Of all the EU countries, only Italy, Austria, Ireland and Spain have not yet signed the Convention. Belgium, Greece and Portugal have signed but not yet ratified the Convention.

turned upside down: as if not the perpetrator, but the victim is the one who has to justify his conduct. Furthermore, in some countries the standard of 'equity' is taken as a ground to exclude victims who themselves have criminal records. As we have seen, England -for instance- goes as far as to impose mandatory reductions on awards to victims who have prior convictions. In this respect Germany employs a more sophisticated system, by allowing full compensation when it can be demonstrated that the intentional violent crime was in no way connected to the victims prior involvement with organized crime. In Belgium it is not uncommon to use the criterion of 'equity' in a way that leads to reduced awards when the victims life style and general demeanor is not impeccable and, inversely, grant higher sums of compensation when the victim is one of commendable reputation. This shows that the somewhat feeble *ratio legis* underlying State compensation schemes might in actual practice lead to distinctions between 'classes' of victims who are more or less worthy of financial protection by the state. I very much doubt whether this kind of moral differentiations is consistent with the general ideas that inspired the Council of Europe to adopt the Convention in 1983.

A second point that needs to be highlighted is that victims of crime in general do not spontaneously tend to ask for help, neither for emotional support, nor for financial assistance. From a policy point of view, this means that it is by definition insufficient to set up a State compensation scheme and then expect the victims to find a way to contact the system. This is confirmed by experience throughout Europe. In all the jurisdictions under consideration only a relatively small fraction of those eligible actually apply for an award. This is not likely to change by the mere passing of time. The international trend clearly shows an increasing number of victims finding their way to the compensation schemes. The background of this development is formed by policy measures aimed at improving public knowledge about the existence and scope of these funds, as well as establishing better referral channels involving the police and non-governmental victim support units. The Belgium accomplishments in recent years can serve as an example of best practice in this respect. It is also extremely important to pay attention to the *proportion* of applications that is *refused.* Denying a claim is tantamount to not meeting existing expectations. It is common knowledge that this can easily lead to secondary victimisation. From this point of view it is disconcerting that in the countries I have examined over 50% of the applications do not lead to an award by the compensation fund.

A few more examples of best practice can be inferred from the preceding sections. In terms of eligibility requirements the British and Belgian experiences indicate how important it is to have special provisions for the victims of domestic violence. If there are no statutory safeguards to protect their interests, this singularly vulnerable category of victims is likely to be underserved by State compensation schemes. As far as the *level* of awards is concerned, the British tariff-system proves to be valuable. I would like to emphasize that this is partly due to the fact that the values of the tariffs have originally been drawn by reference to awards made under the former *common law* damages scheme. Experience in other countries -like The Netherlands- shows that there will be widespread disillusionment with the fund when awards for (moral) damages by the compensation fund are systematically at a lower level than similar claims would yield when filed against an opponent in a civil court. The specific *way* in which the award is paid can also be of extreme importance. The British and German examples of offering a possibility for annual (periodical) payments turn out to be beneficial in many instances. And for a long time it has been recognized that interim payments before the fund makes its final decision are quite nearly a necessity. The Belgian option of also offering *additional* payments -in the light of changed circumstances after the main compensation has been awarded- is also a rare yet fruitful option.

Finally, a State compensation scheme cannot be operated in a responsible way without paying attention to solid *communication* with its main clients. As always, information is of paramount importance. The victim needs to know what is going on and why. He needs to understand rules and procedures. He needs explanation of opportunities and limitations of the scheme. And if by chance the outcome is unfavourable, there is an additional reason for being careful. The least that government officials ought to do in cases like that, is to explain the reasons why the victim could not be compensated for his losses. In today's actual practice, though, this very basic requirement is still not met in quite a few jurisdictions.

ÉVOLUTION DE LA LÉGISLATION ET DES POLITIQUES CONCERNANT LES BESOINS DES VICTIMES D'ACTES CRIMINELS DANS LE SYSTÈME CORRECTIONNEL DU CANADA

Arlène Gaudreault

Depuis 17 ans, je suis impliquée dans diverses initiatives visant la promotion des droits des victimes d'actes criminels au Québec et au Canada. Dans ce parcours, Tony Peters est l'une des personnes qui m'a le plus influencée. En 1994, nous avons eu l'occasion de partager l'enseignement du cours de victimologie dans le programme de maîtrise de l'École de criminologie à l'Université de Montréal. Au cours des dernières années, nous avons entretenu une étroite collaboration dans le cadre du programme d'échanges pour les étudiants de la Communauté européenne et du Canada, lequel portait sur la victimisation, la justice réparatrice et la médiation. Tous ces contacts m'ont permis d'apprécier sa rigueur intellectuelle et l'ampleur de ses connaissances. Je l'ai souvent envié pour sa capacité d'abattre tant de travail. Il me semblait infatiguable ! Il reste pour moi un modèle et un inspirateur dans l'engagement que je poursuis. En choisissant le thème de la place des victimes dans le système correctionnel canadien, j'ai voulu approfondir un champ d'intérêt que nous partageons: le développement et l'amélioration des pratiques qui s'inscrivent dans le courant de la victimologie de l'action.

Introduction

Le Canada est reconnu comme l'un des chefs de file relativement au développement des initiatives en faveur des victimes. Il fut l'un des premiers pays à adopter une *Loi sur l'indemnisation des victimes d'actes criminels* (1972), posant ainsi un geste humanitaire à leur endroit. Au milieu des années 1970, les premiers services d'aide aux femmes violentées émergent sous la poussée des féministes et des organisations communautaires. La décennie 80 va représenter une étape charnière dans la reconnaissance des droits des victimes. En 1983, le Rapport du Groupe d'étude fédéral-provincial canadien *Une justice pour les victimes d'actes criminels* donne le ton et formule 79 recommandations visant à améliorer leur situation. À la même période, le Canada participe activement à l'élaboration de la Déclaration de principes fondamentaux de justice relatifs aux victimes de la criminalité et aux victimes d'abus de pouvoir de l'Organisation des Nations

Unies (1985). Dans cette foulée, il adopte un Énoncé de principes fondamentaux pour les victimes d'actes criminels (1988) et, par la suite, toutes les provinces canadiennes se dotent d'une *Loi sur l'aide aux victimes d'actes criminels*.

Comme dans bien d'autres pays, nos premières réformes visent à améliorer l'expérience des victimes devant les tribunaux et l'accès à des programmes d'aide dans la communauté.[1] Leurs besoins et leurs préoccupations au moment de l'exécution de la peine et de la mise en liberté du délinquant sont pendant longtemps laissés pour compte. Il faudra attendre la fin des années 1980 pour que, s'inspirant de ce qui se fait déjà aux États-Unis, le Canada amorce une réflexion sur les droits des victimes à cette étape du processus pénal et que l'on songe à introduire des changements.

Cet article situe d'abord les attentes et les perceptions des victimes face au système correctionnel. Il reflète ensuite l'évolution de la législation canadienne en matière de libération conditionnelle et des politiques correctionnelles ayant permis de redonner une plus grande place aux victimes et ce, au cours des deux dernières décennies. Il en retrace les principaux jalons et s'attarde plus particulièrement sur certaines dispositions de la *Loi sur le système correctionnel et la mise en liberté sous condition* (1992) laquelle a donné le coup d'envoi à toute une série de nouvelles mesures. Enfin, à la lumière des nombreuses études et consultations menées au Canada depuis plus de vingt ans, il jette un regard critique sur les réponses apportées aux revendications des victimes et sur les défis à relever.

Pour mieux comprendre la teneur des différentes initiatives présentées dans le cadre de cet article, il importe de souligner que, dans le système de justice pénale canadien, les compétences sont partagées entre deux paliers de gouvernement. Les instances fédérales possèdent la compétence quant à l'adoption des lois, du droit et de la procédure criminelle alors que l'administration de la justice, y compris l'application des lois, est du ressort des provinces et territoires.

La Commission nationale des libérations conditionnelles (CNLC) peut prendre des décisions touchant la mise en liberté sous condition de tous les délinquants condamnés à une peine de 2 ans ou plus et des délinquants qui purgent une peine de durée moindre dans les territoires et les provinces, sauf celles qui ont leur propre commission de libération conditionnelle (Québec, Ontario, Colombie-Britannique). Quant au Service correctionnel du Canada

---

1 A. GAUDREAULT (1996) Les premiers centres d'aide aux victimes d'actes criminels: lorsque la mémoire refait surface, in: J. COITEUX, P. CAMPEAU, M. CLARKSON, M.M. COUSINEAU (Sous la dir.), *Question d'équité. L'aide aux victimes d'actes criminels*, 181-203. Montréal: Association québécoise Plaidoyer-Victimes.

(SCC), il assure la garde des délinquants pendant leur période d'incarcération et leur surveillance lors des programmes de libération dans la communauté. Ces deux organismes sont sous la juridiction du gouvernement fédéral et, de même que la Gendarmerie Royale du Canada, ils relèvent de l'autorité du ministère du Solliciteur général du Canada.

1. La perception des victimes à l'endroit du système correctionnel

Au cours des dernières années, plusieurs recherches et enquêtes de victimisation ont confirmé l'opinion négative d'un grand nombre de citoyens face à l'appareil pénal et les critiques ont été encore plus sévères à l'endroit du système carcéral et des libérations conditionnelles.[2]

Le système correctionnel représente un univers complexe dont, très souvent, les victimes ne comprennent pas les multiples rouages. Il est régi par de nombreuses règles et décisions qui, à leurs yeux, permettent aux délinquants de retrouver trop rapidement leur liberté et de bénéficier de privilèges qui ne tiennent pas compte de leurs préoccupations, de l'intérêt public ou de l'intention du juge lorsqu'il a fixé la durée de la peine.

Du point de vue des victimes, le personnel des services correctionnels ou des libérations conditionnelles n'évalue pas les délinquants en fonction du tort causé mais en s'appuyant plutôt sur des principes abstraits et complètement détachés de la réalité de leur comportement. Les libérations hâtives, les échecs et les récidives en libération conditionnelle, le "confort" des conditions en détention: ces images, largement entretenues par les médias, alimentent leur sentiment de méfiance. Cette perception négative du traitement que réserve le système de justice pénale aux criminels peut prolonger le traumatisme lié à l'infraction et compromettre, voire retarder leur processus de guérison.

Les rapports entre les victimes et le système correctionnel sont également teintés par leurs expériences et leurs contacts antérieurs avec la police et les tribunaux. Très souvent, elles n'ont pas reçu le soutien qu'elles requéraient ou n'ont pas été entendues. Elles ont été laissées à l'écart des

2 M. Baril, S. Durand, MM. Cousineau, S. Gravel (1984) *Mais nous, les témoins... Une étude exploratoire des besoins des témoins au Palais de justice de Montréal*, Collection Victimes d'actes criminels, document de travail no. 10, Ottawa: ministère de la Justice; J. Shapland, J. Wilmore & P. Duff (1981) *The Victim in the Criminal Justice System*, Final report to the Home Office. Oxford: Center for Criminological Research; G.W. Skogan (1998) *Victim Survey at Century's End*, in: J. Van Dijk, E. Van Kaam, J. Wemmers (eds.), *Caring for Crime Victims, Selected Proceedings of the 9th International Symposium on Victimology*, 41-53. N.Y: Criminal Justice Press; Statistiques Canada, Centre canadien de la statistique (1998) *Juristat*, vol. 18, no. 9, juin 1998.

décisions et n'ont pu obtenir réparation. Bon nombre ont le sentiment d'avoir été revictimisées.[3] Elles ont refoulé des sentiments de colère et de frustration qui, bien des années plus tard, refont surface au moment de la libération conditionnelle.

Elles estiment qu'il appartient aux divers éléments du système de justice pénale d'apporter des réponses qui reconnaissent que des torts leur ont été causés. Cette préoccupation est tout aussi importante au moment de la mise en liberté sous condition du délinquant que lors de l'imposition de la sentence. Plusieurs victimes, particulièrement celles qui ont perdu un être cher ou subi de graves préjudices, tiennent à ce que l'auteur du délit soit confronté aux conséquences de son geste. Lorsque ce dernier reconnaît sa responsabilité, elles peuvent mettre plus facilement un terme à leurs souffrances et tourner la page.

Les victimes ne souscrivent pas toutes aux valeurs et aux pratiques des organismes correctionnels lesquelles sont surtout axées sur la réinsertion sociale des délinquants. Bon nombre veulent que justice soit faite et s'attendent à ce qu'on s'assure du châtiment et de la punition des délinquants.

En fait, pour les victimes, le système correctionnel est source de nombreuses insatisfactions. Dès le milieu des années 1970, il est pris à partie par le mouvement féministe et par les organismes qui se portent à la défense des droits des victimes. Si les changements tardent à venir, progressivement, de nouvelles mesures vont contribuer à rétablir ce difficile équilibre entre leurs intérêts et ceux des délinquants.

2. Un premier branle-bas

En 1899, le Parlement canadien adoptait la *Loi concernant la libération conditionnelle des détenus*. Au cours du dernier siècle, la législation en matière de libération conditionnelle a été révisée et modifiée à plusieurs reprises. Cependant, ce n'est qu'à partir des années 1980 qu'on met davantage l'accent sur la prévention du crime, sur les victimes et sur la protection de la société.[4]

En 1984, le ministère du Solliciteur général du Canada s'engage dans une importante révision de la philosophie correctionnelle et amorce, du même coup, une réflexion critique sur la réponse des services correctionnels aux

---

3 A. GAUDREAULT (2001) *La victimisation secondaire*, in : D. JOLIVET, G. LOPEZ., S. TZITZIS (dir.), *Dictionnaire critique des sciences criminelles*. Paris: Dalloz. (À paraître).

4 Commission nationale des libérations conditionnelles (1998) *La libération conditionnelle: Pour la sécurité du public*. Ottawa: Ministre des Travaux publics et Services gouvernementaux Canada.

besoins des victimes. Dans un premier document de travail, *La victime et le système correctionnel,*[5] (1987), le Ministère reconnaît qu'il faut prendre des mesures pour répondre aux aspirations raisonnables et légitimes des victimes.

En 1987, un comité de la Chambre des Communes se penche également sur les besoins des victimes au stade de l'exécution de la peine. Des travaux de ce comité émerge le Rapport Daubney, *Des responsabilités à assumer* (1988),[6] lequel recommande qu'elles soient informées de la date d'audience en libération conditionnelle et de la mise en liberté du détenu. Il fait valoir qu'elles peuvent jouer un rôle dans le processus décisionnel en soumettant à la CNLC une copie de la déclaration de la victime au tribunal qu'elles ont produite avant le prononcé de la sentence. Il passe néanmoins sous silence le fait que cette disposition vient à peine d'être adoptée dans le *Code criminel* et, qu'à toutes fins pratiques, peu d'entre elles peuvent s'en prévaloir. Il ne souscrit pas à leur participation aux audiences, soit comme parties soit comme témoins, car cela risquerait de ralentir et d'alourdir la prise de décision mais aussi de "rouvrir des blessures et rallumer des passions guéries et éteintes". En fait, les recommandations de ce Rapport sont plutôt frileuses !

En 1989, la CNLC décide d'aller de l'avant et elle se dote d'une *Politique sur l'intervention auprès des victimes* afin de leur accorder la possibilité de communiquer ou d'obtenir sur demande certains renseignements et, malgré l'avis du Rapport Daubney, d'assister aux audiences comme observateurs. L'année suivante, dans le cadre de la réforme du droit pénal, le Solliciteur général du Canada et le ministre de la Justice déposent un autre rapport, *Vers une réforme : détermination de la peine, affaires correctionnelles et mise en liberté* sous condition. Ce document endosse en majeure partie la Politique de la CNLC qui, entretemps, a fait l'objet d'une consultation auprès des victimes et des organismes qui les représentent.[7] En 1991, le Solliciteur général dépose le projet de loi C-36, *Loi sur le système correctionnel et la mise en liberté sous condition* (LSCMLC). Après étude à la Chambre des Communes, la Loi sera promulguée en 1992.

---

5 Solliciteur général Canada. Secrétariat du ministère (1987) *La victime et le système correctionnel*, Document de travail no. 4. Canada.

6 D. DAUBNEY (1988) *Des responsabilités à assumer,* Rapport du Comité permanent de la justice et du solliciteur général sur la détermination de la peine, la mise en liberté sous condition et d'autres aspects du système correctionnel. Ottawa: Approvisionnements et Services Canada.

7 Commission nationale des libérations conditionnelles (1990) *Victimes et la Commission nationale des libérations conditionnelles.* Document de travail. Canada.

3. La réforme de 1992 : un coup de barre important

3.1. La possibilité de recevoir des informations

Lors de l'adoption de la *Loi sur le système correctionnel et la mise en liberté sous condition* (LSCMLC), pour la première fois, le législateur incorpore la définition de ce qu'est une victime et il précise les personnes qui peuvent avoir accès à des renseignements. En plus des victimes directes, cette définition englobe les membres de la famille, les conjoints et, lorsque la victime est un enfant ou qu'elle est incapable, les tuteurs ou les soignants. La Loi établit cependant une distinction très nette entre ce que les victimes doivent ou peuvent recevoir et elle comporte des réserves qui limitent l'accès à l'information.

Elle reconnaît, tout d'abord, que les victimes ont le droit de recevoir des informations de base sur le délinquant et sur les dates d'admissibilité et d'examen applicables aux permissions de sortir ou à la libération conditionnelle. L'accès à ce type de renseignements porte très peu atteinte à la vie privée du délinquant puisqu'ils sont de notoriété publique et qu'ils n'ont aucun caractère confidentiel du point de vue juridique.[8] Il s'agit davantage d'un geste de courtoisie afin de réduire les angoisses de la victime.[9]

Par ailleurs, le SCC et la CNLC, s'ils le jugent approprié, peuvent fournir d'autres informations telles que les dates et les conditions des programmes de mise en liberté, la destination du détenu lors de sa libération. Cependant, chaque demande doit être examinée afin de déterminer si l'intérêt de la victime l'emporte sur l'atteinte à la vie privée du délinquant. Le cas échéant, elle sera refusée. Le SCC et la CNLC disposent donc d'un pouvoir discrétionnaire non négligeable pour donner accès ou non à ces renseignements et, dans les faits, ces dispositions représentent plus un privilège qu'un droit au sens strict.

Les nouvelles mesures prévoient encore que les victimes peuvent faire une demande écrite pour avoir accès au *Registre des décisions*, leur permettant ainsi de connaître les critères sur lesquels la CNLC s'est appuyée lors de l'étude de la mise en liberté du détenu. Ce registre peut comprendre également des commentaires sur le délinquant, sa participation à des programmes et son projet de sortie.

---

8 A. GAUDREAULT (2000) *Les victimes et la libération conditionnelle: un lien à définir*, 16e Conférence annuelle de l'Association internationale des responsables des libération conditionnelle (APAI), Ottawa. (Texte inédit).

9 Solliciteur général Canada, Secrétariat du Ministère (1987) *La victime et le système correctionnel. Révision du droit correctionnel.* Document du travail no. 4. Canada.

3.2. Transmettre des informations et pouvoir influencer les décisions

Toutes les consultations entreprises à la fin des années 1980 ont permis de rappeler que la CNLC doit tenir compte de toutes les informations pertinentes, notamment celles transmises par les victimes, car elles peuvent aider à évaluer la nature et les conséquences du crime, le risque de récidive, la propension du délinquant à commettre un crime violent en liberté, les conditions à lui imposer et son projet de sortie.[10] Ces renseignements sont d'autant plus importants lorsque le délinquant est un membre de la famille de la victime ou s'il doit retourner vivre dans son entourage à sa sortie de prison.[11]

En accordant aux victimes la possibilité de transmettre des informations par écrit sur l'impact du crime ou sur leurs craintes par rapport à la libération éventuelle du délinquant, on répond à leur désir de pouvoir influencer les décisions. En contrepartie, le SCC et la CNLC ont l'obligation légale de partager au délinquant tous les renseignements pris en considération dans l'évaluation du risque. C'est donc une arme à double tranchant pour les victimes, particulièrement pour celles qui craignent de se retrouver en présence de l'agresseur ou de subir ses représailles. On peut comprendre dès lors que certaines vont hésiter, voire refuser de communiquer des informations surtout lorsque leur sécurité ou celle de leurs proches est en cause.

3.3. Assister aux audiences

Au Canada, la CNLC doit tenir une audience avec le détenu avant de prendre la décision de lui refuser ou de lui octroyer une mise en liberté sous condition. Cette rencontre se tient dans un établissement pénitentiaire. Elle lui donne l'occasion de faire valoir son point de vue, de communiquer des renseignements et de présenter son projet de sortie. Le détenu peut être accompagné d'un assistant (ami, parent ou avocat) qui peut le conseiller et parler en sa faveur.

Avant 1992, la présence des victimes aux audiences de libération conditionnelle n'était pas permise et elle pas été acceptée d'emblée. On

---

10 Commission nationale des libérations conditionnelles (1992) *Initiatives à l'intention des victimes*, Canada.

11 D. BELISLE, S. LACROIX, J.M. TRUDEAU, Y. GAUDREAU (2000) *Interaction de la Commission nationale des libérations conditionnelles avec les victimes.* Communication présentée au Xe Symposium international de victimologie, Montréal, août 2000.

craignait surtout qu'elle perturbe le fonctionnement des audiences, nuise à la réinsertion du délinquant et ravive les souffrances liées au crime. Nonobstant ces réserves et s'appuyant sur l'obligation de rendre compte et de transparence, le législateur donne aux victimes le droit d'assister aux audiences mais sans y participer ou intervenir de quelque façon que ce soit.[12] Le statut d'observateur leur est accordé en tenant compte de certains critères: le bon déroulement de l'audience, la protection des tiers, les intérêts du détenu et la sécurité de l'établissement. Privées du droit de parole, on leur offre en retour la possibilité d'exprimer leur opinion sur ce qu'elles y ont entendu, en écrivant à la Commission.

Ce statut d'observateur qui les confine à regarder et à écouter, ne répond qu'en partie aux besoins exprimés par les victimes. Mais, à tout le moins, il leur permet de recevoir des informations de la part du détenu ou des services correctionnels qui, autrement, n'auraient pas été accessibles. Il les aide également à mieux comprendre les décisions de la CNLC et à voir comment les diverses instances s'acquittent de leurs obligations. C'est une première brèche!

Depuis la mise en vigueur de la LSCMLC, de plus en plus de personnes ayant subi des dommages moraux ou corporels suite à la perpétration d'un crime se sont adressées à la CNLC. Dans la seule période du 1er avril 1999 au 31 mars 2000, 11,177 contacts ont été établis par téléphone ou par correspondance avec des victimes. Dans près de 50% des cas, elles ont demandé à être informées des décisions prises par la Commission. En grande majorité, il s'agissait de victimes d'infractions de nature sexuelle (51 %), d'autres crimes violents (44 %) ou non violents (5%). La CNLC a transmis 3,219 copies du Registre des décisions. Enfin, 791 personnes se sont prévalues du droit d'assister aux audiences; près de la moitié d'entre elles (41 %) avaient subi un crime.[13]

4. Le temps des bilans et des changements

Au cours de la dernière décennie, la LSCMLC a été examinée à plusieurs reprises afin d'en revoir les modalités d'application et de déterminer si des améliorations devaient être apportées, notamment en ce qui a trait aux questions concernant les victimes. À chaque fois, c'est l'occasion de mener des audiences et des consultations auprès d'un vaste éventail de groupes et personnes intéressés par le processus correctionnel, partout à travers le

12 Commission nationale des libérations conditionnelles (1992) *Initiatives à l'intention des victimes*. Canada.

13 BELISLE et al., *o.c.*

Canada. Plusieurs publications reflètent l'évolution de ces travaux et discussions.[14]

Il est intéressant de jeter un regard sur la position des victimes et sur leurs revendications, à la lumière de ces multiples consultations. L'analyse fait d'abord ressortir que les messages des victimes restent constants et qu'elles se rallient à certains consensus.[15] Le déséquilibre entre leurs droits et ceux des accusés, l'insuffisance des ressources pour leur venir en aide et le traitement qui leur est réservé dans le système de justice pénale : ces questions font encore l'objet de vigoureuses récriminations et elles sont sources de frustration même si les victimes reconnaissent que des progrès ont été réalisés.

En ce qui a trait aux dispositions de la loi et aux politiques internes de la CNLC et du SCC, elles réclament de nombreux changements. Que veulent-elles au juste? Les victimes souhaitent d'abord être traitées avec respect et dignité, que leurs intérêts soient pris en considération dans les différentes opérations et décisions de chacun des éléments du système de justice pénale, y compris lors de l'exécution de la peine.[16]

Le besoin d'information reste prioritaire. Elles mettent l'accent sur l'importance de recevoir plus de renseignements au sujet du délinquant : sa participation dans les programmes, son comportement et ses transferts en établissement, les nouvelles accusations dont il a fait l'objet pendant son incarcération ou pendant sa surveillance dans la collectivité. Elles jugent

---

14 Chambre des Communes Canada (1998) *Les droits des victimes -Participer sans entraver*. Rapport du Comité permanent de la justice et des droits de la personne, Canada. Chambre des Communes Canada (2000) *En constante évolution: la Loi sur le système correctionnel et la mise en liberté sous condition*. Rapport du Sous-Comité sur la Loi sur le système correctionnel et la mise en liberté sous condition, Comité permanent de la justice et des droits de la personne, Canada; Solliciteur général Canada; Secrétariat du Ministère (1987) *La victime et le système correctionnel*. Révision du droit correctionnel. Document du travail no. 4, Canada ; Solliciteur général du Canada (1990) *Vers une réforme Les affaires correctionnelles et la mise en liberté sous condition*. Ottawa: Ministre des Approvisionnements et Services Canada ; Solliciteur général du Canada (1998) *Pour une société juste, paisible et sûre. La loi sur le système correctionnel et la mise en liberté sous condition. Cinq ans plus tard. Document de consultation*. Ministre des Travaux publics et Services gouvernementaux Canada ; Solliciteur général du Canada (2000) *En constante évolution: la Loi sur le système correctionnel et la mise en liberté sous condition*. Réponse au Rapport du Sous-comité sur la Loi sur le système correctionnel et la mise en liberté sous condition du Comité permanent de la justice et des droits de la personne, Canada; Solliciteur général du Canada (2001) *Consultations régionales des victimes du crime. Points saillants et messages clés*, Canada; Commission nationale des libérations conditionnelles (1990) *Victimes et la Commission nationale des libérations conditionnelles: un document de travail*, Canada; Commission nationale des libérations conditionnelles (1992) *Initiatives à l'intention des victimes*, Canada.

15 Solliciteur général du Canada (2001) *o.c.*

16 Service correctionnel canadien (1995) *Victimes d'actes criminels et Service correctionnl,* Document inédit.

que le législateur doit aller plus loin face à la divulgation de ces renseignements qui sont nécessaires pour mieux connaître le cheminement du délinquant et ses efforts pour se réadapter. Obtenir plus de détails leur permet de mieux comprendre les motifs des décisions du SCC ou de la CNLC mais aussi d'influencer ceux qu'elles désapprouvent. De plus, elles considèrent que les mécanismes visant à transmettre l'information doivent être nettement améliorés à tous les niveaux.

Ce besoin de savoir est surtout motivé par des raisons de sécurité et non par un désir de vengeance.[17] La condamnation ou l'emprisonnement n'entraîne pas une rupture systématique ou définitive des liens entre la victime et l'agresseur. Beaucoup d'entre elles, en particulier les victimes de délits de violence, ont peur d'être revictimisées ou de se retrouver en contact avec l'auteur du délit lorsqu'il aura purgé sa peine. Si le délinquant doit un jour ou l'autre réintégrer la société et s'il peut bénéficier d'une remise en liberté avant la fin de la sentence, elles n'en considèrent pas moins que la remise en liberté doit être assortie de restrictions ou de conditions plus strictes leur garantissant une meilleure protection ainsi que celle de leur famille et de la collectivité.

Elles veulent aussi qu'on protège davantage leur vie privée. Plusieurs victimes expriment leur désaccord avec le fait que l'on partage avec le détenu leur déclaration sur l'impact du crime et leurs représentations devant la CNLC. "Tout lui est dévoilé, alors qu'on nous divulgue tout à la miette!".[18] Elles craignent que le délinquant, puisqu'il connaît leurs "états d'âme", se saisira de l'occasion pour mieux paraître devant les commissaires et pour exprimer de faux remords. À leur avis, cela lui donne des armes pour manipuler.

Elles souhaitent aussi faire peser leurs préoccupations dans la balance et obtenir un droit de parole aux audiences. C'est une source d'irritation que de rester dans leur coin alors que le détenu défile les progrès accomplis sans qu'on leur permette de dire tout le mal qui a été fait.[19] Pouvoir réfuter les propos du délinquant, formuler des commentaires sur les conditions de mise en liberté, s'adresser à la CNLC au moment de leur choix lors des audiences, s'exprimer à huis clos parce qu'il est menaçant de dévoiler ses peurs et ses émotions devant le délinquant: leurs revendications vont beaucoup plus loin que ce que prévoit le cadre législatif actuel.

---

17 Solliciteur général du Canada (2001) *o.c.*

18 *Ibid.*

19 Service correctionnel canadien (1995) *Victimes d'actes criminels et Service correctionnel,* Document inédit.

En définitive, elles réclament un droit de parole réel, des conditions qui assurent leur sécurité, le soutien dans leurs démarches lorsqu'elles décident d'assister aux audiences et d'y produire une déclaration.

5. L'étape des réajustements

En novembre 2000, le Solliciteur général du Canada réaffirmait que la législation actuelle ne répond pas à toutes les demandes exprimées par les victimes et qu'elle devait être modifiée. Il entérinait alors les propositions d'un comité parlementaire à l'effet qu'on devrait s'orienter vers les mesures suivantes: permettre aux victimes de présenter aux audiences des libérations conditionnelles une déclaration mise à jour des répercussions du crime soit en personne ou soit par enregistrement audio ou vidéo; leur transmettre les enregistrements sonores des audiences de la CNLC si elles ne peuvent assister aux audiences; obliger le SCC à les informer des évasions, des transferts et des autorisations lors des programmes de mise en liberté surveillée; créer un bureau des plaintes et d'information des victimes.[20]

Depuis juillet 2001, les politiques de la CNLC ont été modifiées afin de donner aux victimes la possibilité de faire une déclaration verbale sur les répercussions du crime, sur leurs préoccupations quant à leur sécurité et sur les raisons pour lesquelles elles estiment que le délinquant présente un risque. Quant aux autres propositions, elles sont encore à l'étude. Même si elles ont reçu un accueil plutôt favorable, l'examen de la réforme de la LSCMLC n'a pas encore été soumis au Parlement canadien.

Conclusion

Le Canada est considéré comme l'un des pays les plus progressistes dans le domaine correctionnel. Les changements législatifs et les politiques en faveur des victimes des dernières années sont susceptibles de favoriser un meilleur accès à la justice et d'accroître leur compréhension du système correctionnel. Ils permettent d'actualiser davantage les objectifs formulés dans l'Énoncé de mission du SCC et de la CNLC afin d'assurer la protection du public, de promouvoir la transparence et l'obligation de rendre compte

20 Chambre des Communes Canada (2000) *En constante évolution: la Loi sur le système correctionnel et la mise en liberté sous condition*. Rapport du Sous-Comité sur la Loi sur le système correctionnel et la mise en liberté sous condition, Comité permanent de la justice et des droits de la personne. Canada.

lors de la prise de décision en matière de liberté sous condition.[21] Ils représentent une autre avancée dans la campagne que les victimes ont menée pour faire reconnaître leurs droits à cette étape du processus pénal.

Malgré les progrès accomplis, il existe encore d'importantes barrières pour rétablir la confiance du public et la crédibilité des différents acteurs qui oeuvrent au sein de la commission des libérations conditionnelles et des services correctionnels.

Trop souvent encore, les victimes doivent se débrouiller pour avoir accès aux informations. De plus, leur "droit de savoir" est limité et sans cesse confronté au pouvoir discrétionnaire des instances correctionnelles. Soupesé avec le droit du délinquant à la vie privée, il passe difficilement le test. Cette remarque formulée par un proche d'une victime d'homicide lors d'une réunion de consultation reflète bien ce que ressentent plusieurs victimes : "Les criminels font de notre vie privée, une vie publique. Mais ils veulent qu'on fasse de leur vie publique, une vie privée".[22]

A moult reprises, les victimes ont réclamé le droit de prendre part plus activement au processus correctionnel. "Nommer le mal qui a été fait", "cesser d'être des figurants", "avoir leur mot à dire" : la déclaration verbale des victimes aux audiences est un pas en avant mais elle ne répond pas à toutes leurs requêtes. Il faut rappeler qu'à cette étape, les décisions sont prises surtout en fonction du danger que représente le délinquant s'il est remis en liberté. Si les conséquences du crime et les traumatismes sont des éléments dont il faut tenir compte dans le processus décisionnel, ils n'en représentent pas moins un facteur parmi d'autres. Dans quelle mesure vont-ils peser dans l'évaluation et la gestion du risque? La question mérite d'autant plus d'être posée que les recherches sur la déclaration de la victime au tribunal démontrent que cette dernière a finalement eu peu d'impact sur les décisions des juges au moment de rendre sentence.[23] Se retrouver en présence du délinquant, dans un contexte intimidant, devoir y déballer ses émotions et surtout être capable de les "gérer" : tout cela en vaut-il la peine

---

21 Solliciteur général du Canada (1998) *Pour une société juste, paisible et sûre. La loi sur le système correctionnel et la mise en liberté sous condition. Cinq ans plus tard*, Document de consultation. Ministre des Travaux publics et Services gouvernementaux Canada.

22 Solliciteur général du Canada (2001) *Consultations régionales des victimes du crime*, *o.c.*, Canada.

23 L. SEBBA (1996) *Third Parties. Victimes and the Criminal Justice System*. Ohio State University Press; K. ROACH (1999) *Due Process and Victim's Rights: The New Law and Politics of Criminal Justice*, University of Toronto Press; A. YOUNG (2001) *Summary of the Report on the "Role of the Victim in the Criminal Process: A Literature Review"*. Ottawa: Ministère de la Justice du Canada.

au bout du compte? Certes, il faudra évaluer ces nouvelles mesures afin d'en juger l'efficacité.

Au cours des dernières années, le SCC et la CNLC ont mis en place diverses politiques et procédures afin d'assurer un suivi rigoureux aux demandes des victimes.[24] Des coordonnateurs aux victimes ont été désignés dans tous les établissements pénitentiaires et les bureaux régionaux de la CNLC afin de leur prodiguer l'information, de les accueillir et les accompagner dans leurs démarches lors des audiences de la libération conditionnelle. Au Québec, depuis 1995, des sessions de formation permettent de mieux outiller et de soutenir les intervenants du système correctionnel dans leur nouveau rôle. Tous ces efforts méritent d'être soulignés. Ils ont sans doute contribué à faire en sorte que les victimes soient mieux entendues et davantage traitées avec le respect qui leur est dû.

Mais, en même temps, ces changements ont bouleversé les façons de faire. Désormais, dans l'évaluation du risque ou la surveillance des contrevenants, les intervenants du système correctionnel ne peuvent plus ignorer les préoccupations des victimes. S'ouvrir à la réalité des victimes a enrichi la façon dont ils s'acquittent de leur travail mais elle a créé de nouvelles obligations. Cela ne s'est pas fait sans heurt et sans une nécessaire adaptation. Conflits de rôle, perte d'objectivité, impuissance devant la détresse émotionnelle de certaines victimes, stress occasionné par la présence des observateurs aux audiences : les malaises sont perceptibles.[25] Même s'ils ne sont pas insensibles aux traumatismes des victimes, plusieurs intervenants estiment qu'il ne leur appartient pas de leur offrir un soutien "qui a une connotation thérapeutique" et qu'il faut s'en remettre davantage aux services dans la communauté pour leur venir en aide. Il faut s'attendre à d'autres réajustements dès lors que les dernières propositions vont accroître les contacts avec les victimes et générer de nouvelles demandes.

Manifestement, le système correctionnel ne répond qu'en partie aux attentes et inquiétudes des victimes d'actes criminels. Individualiser les réponses, faire preuve d'une compréhension plus nuancée de leurs besoins, leur épargner de nouvelles souffrances: autant de défis qui l'attendent. L'avenir nous dira s'il a été en mesure de les relever !

La reconnaissance des droits des victimes s'inscrit dans un long et difficile cheminement. Comme le montrent les récents développements dans

---

24 G. THIBEAULT, J.M. LAVOIE, G. PETIT-CLAIR, J.M. TRUDEAU, D. BÉLISLE. Y. GAUDREAU (1996) *La place des victimes au Service correctionnel du Canada et à la Commission nationale des libérations conditionnelles*, 105-108. Actes du colloque 7 et 8 novembre 1996 : Victimes d'actes criminels: de l'impuissance vers l'autonomie..., Montréal: Association québécoise Plaidoyer-Victimes.

25 Service correctionnel canadien (1995) *Victimes d'actes criminels et Service correctionnel*, Document inédit; THIBEAULT et al., *o.c.*

le domaine correctionnel canadien et ailleurs, ces droits ne leur sont accordés, la plupart du temps, qu'avec prudence et parcimonie.

Références

Baril, M., Durand, S., Cousineau, M.M., Gravel, S. (1984) *Mais nous, les témoins... Une étude exploratoire des besoins des témoins au Palais de justice de Montréal.* Collection Victimes d'actes criminels, document de travail no. 10, Ottawa: ministère de la Justice.

Belisle, D., Lacroix, S., Trudeau, J.M., Gaudreau, Y. (2000) *Interaction de la Commission nationale des libérations conditionnelles avec les victimes.* Communication présentée au Xe Symposium international de victimologie, Montréal, août 2000.

Chambre des Communes Canada (1998) *Les droits des victimes -Participer sans entraver.* Rapport du Comité permanent de la justice et des droits de la personne, Canada.

Chambre des Communes Canada (2000) *En constante évolution: la Loi sur le système correctionnel et la mise en liberté sous condition.* Rapport du Sous-Comité sur la Loi sur le système correctionnel et la mise en liberté sous condition, Comité permanent de la justice et des droits de la personne, Canada.

Commission nationale des libérations conditionnelles (1990) *Victimes et la Commission nationale des libérations conditionnelles.* Document de travail, Canada.

Commission nationale des libérations conditionnelles (1992) *Initiatives à l'intention des victimes*, Canada.

Commission nationale des libérations conditionnelles (1998) *La libération conditionnelle: Pour la sécurité du public.* Ottawa: Ministre des Travaux publics et Services gouvernementaux Canada.

Daubney, D. (1988) *Des responsabilités à assumer.* Rapport du Comité permanent de la justice et du solliciteur général sur la détermination de la peine, la mise en liberté sous condition et d'autres aspects du système correctionnel. Ottawa: Approvisionnements et Services Canada.

Gaudreault, A. (1996) *Les premiers centres d'aide aux victimes d'actes criminels : lorsque la mémoire refait surface*, in: Coiteux, J., Campeau, P., Clarkson, M., Cousineau, M.M. (Sous la dir.), *Question d'équité. L'aide aux victimes d'actes criminels,* 181-203. Montréal: Association québécoise Plaidoyer-Victimes.

Gaudreault, A. (2000) (ed.), L'aide aux victimes d'actes criminels au Canada et au Québec: esquisse d'un parcours, in: École nationale de la

magistrature, *Oeuvre de justice et Victimes*. Paris: Ed. L'Harmattan. (À paraître).
Gaudreault, A. (2000) *Les victimes et la libération conditionnelle: un lien à définir*, 16e Conférence annuelle de l'Association internationale des responsables des libération conditionnelle (APAI). Ottawa. (Texte inédit).
Gaudreault, A. (2001) *La victimisation secondaire*. in: Jolivet, D., Lopez., G., Tzitzis, S. (dir.), *Dictionnaire critique des sciences criminelles*. Paris: Dalloz. (À paraître)
Groupe d'étude fédéral-provincial canadien Sur la justice pour les victimes d'actes criminels (1983) Ottawa: Ministre des approvisionnements et Services Canada.
Roach, K. (1999) *Due Process and Victim's Rights: The New Law and Politics of Criminal Justice*. University of Toronto Press.
Sebba, L. (1996) *Third Parties. Victimes and the Criminal Justice System*. Ohio State University Press.
Service correctionnel canadien (1995) *Victimes d'actes criminels et Service correctionnel*. Document inédit.
Shapland, J., Wilmore, J. and Duff. P. (1981) *The Victim in the Criminal Justice System*, Final report to Home Office. Oxford: Center for Criminological Research.
Skogan, G.W. (1998) Victim Survey at Century's End; in: Van Dijk, J., Van Kaam, E., Wemmers, J. (eds.), *Caring for Crime Victims, Selected Proceedings of the 9th International Symposium on Victimology*, 41-53. N.Y: Criminal Justice Press.
Solliciteur général Canada, Secrétariat du Ministère (1987) *La victime et le système correctionnel. Révision du droit correctionnel*. Document du travail no. 4. Canada.
Solliciteur général du Canada (1990) *Vers une réforme Les affaires correctionnelles et la mise en liberté sous condition*. Ottawa: Ministre des Approvisionnements et Services Canada.
Solliciteur général du Canada (1998) *Pour une société juste, paisible et sûre. La loi sur le système correctionnel et la mise en liberté sous condition. Cinq ans plus tard. Document de consultation*. Ministre des Travaux publics et Services gouvernementaux Canada.
Solliciteur général du Canada (2000) *En constante évolution : la Loi sur le système correctionnel et la mise en liberté sous condition*. Réponse au Rapport du Sous-comité sur la Loi sur le système correctionnel et la mise en liberté sous condition du Comité permanent de la justice et des droits de la personne. Canada.

Solliciteur général du Canada (2001) *Consultations régionales des victimes du crime. Points saillants et messages clés*. Canada.
Statistiques Canada, Centre canadien de la statistique, *Juristat*, vol. 18, no.9, juin 1998.
Thibeault, G., Lavoie, J.M., Petit-Clair. G., Trudeau, J.M., Bélisle. D., Gaudreau, Y. (1996) *La place des victimes au Service correctionnel du Canada et à la Commission nationale des libérations conditionnelles*, Actes du colloque 7 et 8 novembre 1996: Victimes d'actes criminels : de l'impuissance vers l'autonomie..., 105-108. Montréal: Association québécoise Plaidoyer-Victimes.
Young, A. (2001) *Summary of the Report on the "Role of the Victim in the Criminal Process: A Literature Review"*. Ottawa: Ministère de la Justice du Canada.

L'INDEMNISATION DES VICTIMES D'INFRACTIONS PÉNALES DANS LE DROIT FRANÇAIS

Georges Picca

Introduction

Longtemps absente des codes et des audiences des tribunaux, la victime est aujourd'hui devenue un acteur à part entière d'une justice pénale qui se veut davantage "restorative"[1] que répressive. Il en résulte un langage nouveau, parfois surprenant pour le non-spécialiste mais qui nourrit une doctrine active et de nombreux colloques: victimologie, victimisation, victimation....[2]

Dans un discours criminologique, deux fois centenaire et, partant en quête de renouvellement on pourrait penser que la victime a ainsi supplanté le délinquant comme sujet principal d'intérêt. Cependant la réalité ne saurait se limiter à une telle apparence. D'une part, cette renaissance de la victime dans le champ pénal, puise ses sources bien au-delà de la seule criminologie. D'autre part ce nouveau rôle concédé à la victime est désormais consacré dans nombre de systèmes juridiques nationaux. Il se concrétise généralement par l'aide ou l'indemnisation de la victime. En outre la plupart des pays développés ont inclus dans leurs recherches statistiques sur la criminalité des enquêtes dites de victimisation en vue d'évaluer l'importance de l'insécurité dans la population, due à la délinquance.

---

1 Centrée sur la victime et l'auteur de l'infraction cette nouvelle conception de la fonction de justice pénale est dite "restorative" (anglais) (restaurative ou réparatrice en français) dans la mesure où elle met l'accent sur la solution du conflit crée par le délit en tentant de le résoudre par l'intermédiaire d'une médiation entre victime et auteur du délit, afin d'éviter l'intervention du parquet et de la justice pénale. (voir notamment sur cette question T. PETERS & I. AERTSEN (1995) Restorative Justice. In search of new avenues in judicial dealing with crime, in: C. FIJNAUT, J. GOETHALS, T. PETERS & L. WALGRAVE (eds.), *Changes in Society, crime and criminal justice in Europe,* vol. I, 311-342. Antwerpen: Kluwer.

2 La victimologie est une courant d'opinion et de recherche, qui s'est développé à partir de la criminologie, mettant l'accent sur le rôle de la victime dans le processus criminel. Voir: E. FATTAH (1967) Vers une typologie criminologique des victimes, *Revue internationale de politique criminelle* 162-170; D. SZABO (1981) La victimologie et la politique criminelle, *Revue internationale de criminologie et de police technique* 343. Victimisation ou victimation, sont des mots destinés à rendre compte sur le plan statistique de l'importance du nombre de victimes.

Enfin ce nouvel intérêt pour la victime a également favorisé une institution nouvelle, aujourd'hui en plein essor: la procédure de médiation.[3]

Celle-ci consiste à rechercher grâce à l'intervention d'un tiers médiateur, une solution librement négociée entre victime et délinquant au conflit né d'une infraction. Elle constitue ainsi une troisième voie entre la poursuite pénale et le classement sans suite du dossier. En cas d'entente entre la victime et l'auteur d'infraction le parquet s'engage à ne pas poursuivre le délinquant.

1. Reconnaissance de la victime

Les origines de cette reconnaissance sociale de la victime sont diverses et, au premier chef, la place considérable occupée par les victimes dans la représentation contemporaine des médias. De la Shoah au terrorisme quotidien, en passant par les catastrophes naturelles (tremblements de terre, inondations) et industrielles (Tchernobyl, Bhopal), l'image d'une victimation de masse s'est imposée avec insistance par la voie des médias, au voyeurisme certes mais aussi, à la compassion universelle et anonyme.

Un second fait social a contribué à favoriser, en France, notamment, ce nouvel intérêt pour les victimes et plus particulièrement celles de la délinquance. C'est une certaine inefficacité de la justice pénale dans la poursuite et la sanction des délinquants, inefficacité due à une saturation des parquets et des services de police, face à l'accroissement de la criminalité. Faute de pouvoir punir le délinquant l'État favorise l'indemnisation de la victime, c'est ce qu'on a pu qualifier de "victimophilie".[4]

On peut en effet être tenté de voir là un certain échec de la justice publique substituée, dans tout État moderne, à la vengeance privée. De même la reconnaissance sociale de la victime risque d'être perçue, à certains égards, comme une résurgence de la vengeance privée ou, tout au moins, d'une compensation pécuniaire qui, dans l'histoire du droit pénal continental en a été une variante.[5] On ne peut cependant voir dans ce nouveau rôle conféré à la victime un simple retour à la vengeance privée par opposition à

---

3 Voir T. PETERS (1996) La peine considérée dans une perspective de réparation, *Revue internationale de criminologie et police technique*, n° 1, 3-29.

4 Voir notamment dans R. GASSIN (1995) (4ème édit.) *Criminologie*. Paris: Dalloz; et sur le plan de la responsabilité civile *"Notre système juridique donne l'impression que la victime est la personne la plus importante du monde"*, cité par Ph. MALAURIE (1999) *Droit civil. Les obligations*, vol. 1. Paris: Ed. Cujas.

5 Sur l'évolution historique du droit pénal, voir: J. PRADEL (2001) *Droit pénal général*. Paris: Éd. Cujas.

la justice publique. Ce serait méconnaître l'importance de la diversité des actions existantes, qu'elles soient l'œuvre de l'État ou d'associations privées, qui ont contribué, par la même, à élaborer un véritable statut social de la victime.

Les réalisations dans ce domaine se sont multipliées dans différents États. Mais on doit également prendre en compte les initiatives internationales qui les ont accompagnées ou précédées. Plusieurs textes internationaux ont reconnu l'aide aux victimes dans ses principes généraux parmi lesquels la Déclaration des principes fondamentaux de justice relatifs aux victimes de la criminalité et aux victimes d'abus de pouvoir des Nations Unies de 1985 et les Recommandations du Conseil de l'Europe sur la participation du public à la politique criminelle, sur la position de la victime dans le cadre du droit et de la procédure pénale, et sur l'assistance aux victimes et la prévention de la victimisation.

La qualification juridique et la notion de victime demeure néanmoins encore incertaine. Aux termes de la Déclaration de 1985 "on entend par *"victimes"* des personnes qui, individuellement ou collectivement, ont subi un préjudice, notamment une atteinte à leur intégrité physique ou mentale, une souffrance morale, une perte matérielle ou une atteinte grave à leurs droits fondamentaux en raison d'actes ou d'omissions qui enfreignent les lois pénales en vigueur dans un État membre, y compris celles qui proscrivent les abus criminels de droits." Par suite, "une personne peut être considérée comme victime dans le cadre de la présente déclaration, que l'auteur soit ou non identifié, arrêté, poursuivi ou déclaré coupable, et quels que soient les liens de parenté avec la victime. Le terme victime inclut aussi, le cas échéant, la famille proche ou les personnes à charge de la victime directe et les personnes qui ont subi un préjudice en intervenant pour venir en aide aux victimes en détresse ou pour empêcher la victimation".

L'application de la Convention européenne des droits de l'homme n'offre pas davantage de précisions dans ce domaine. En revanche les États membres de Union européenne sont convenus récemment (15 mars 2001) des critères de protection des victimes, d'accès à la justice et aux services d'aide aux victimes qui devraient s'appliquer aux législations nationales.[6] Ces critères prennent en compte les progrès accomplis depuis les années 80 dans la reconnaissance des droits des victimes. Les victimes d'infractions, y compris les personnes étrangères, doivent être respectées et entendues, orientées vers des services ou organismes d'aide aux victimes et recevoir des

6 Déclaration-Cadre, le 15 mars 2001, relative au statut des victimes dans le cadre de procédures pénales, *J.O.C.E.*, 22 mars 2001, L 82-1.

informations sur les procédures pénales, les mesures de protection et les nécessités d'indemnisation.

En principe il n'existe cependant pas de définition juridique de la "victime" autres que celles citées plus haut. C'est également le cas dans le droit positif français. La notion de victime à laquelle se référent à la fois le Code de procédure pénale et le Code pénal ne correspond pas à un concept juridique ou à une qualification pénale précise mais, est pris dans le sens que lui est généralement réservé par le langage courant.

Historiquement et dans une interprétation sociologique, la victime (latin: victima) est la personne offerte en sacrifice aux divinités; elle assure une fonction d'apaisement du trouble provoqué par la violation criminelle de la norme sociale.

L'histoire du droit pénal nous enseigne que la place et le rôle de la victime ont évolué avec le passage progressif dans les sociétés modernes du système de la vengeance privée, en usage dans les sociétés premières, à celui de la justice publique. Dans cette dernière étape la vengeance privée est abolie au profit de peines légalement définies et prononcées par la justice publique. Seul subsiste, sous la forme de l'action civile, le droit pour la victime de réclamer réparation préjudice subi, aux cotés du parquet: c'est la distinction procédurale entre l'action publique et l'action civile, réservée à la victime qui a subi un préjudice du fait de l'infraction.

La victime, ainsi limitée à un cadre juridique déterminé, était devenue un protagoniste de second plan dans le procès pénal. On assiste, par suite, aujourd'hui à l'attribution à celle-ci d'un nouveau rôle dans le fonctionnement de la justice pénale.

Cette évolution ne trouve pas uniquement sa source dans un souci de compassion et de justice. Elle s'inscrit également dans une perspective plus générale, de limitation du domaine de la justice publique au profit d'une certaine recherche de "privatisation" de la fonction de justice. C'est aussi la manifestation du souci de régler un certain nombre de conflits plus ou moins graves par une voie civile négociée plutôt que par la voie pénale traditionnelle. A cet égard il faut souligner l'importance, après la médiation, du courant de dépénalisation, décriminalisation, voire de contestation globale ou partielle du système pénal.[7]

---

7 L. HULSMAN (1982) *Peines perdues, le système pénal en question*, vol. 1. Paris: Édit. Le Centurion; L. HULSMAN (1984) *Fondements et enjeux de la théorie de l'abolition du système pénal*, vol. 1, 297-317. Bruxelles: Editions de l'Université de Bruxelles; voir également: Conseil de l'Europe (1980) *La décriminalisation*. Strasbourg: Conseil de l'Europe; J. VERIN (1974) Une politique criminelle de non-intervention, *Rev. Sciences Criminelles* 401-405.

2. Indemnisation des victimes

Le système français d'indemnisation des victimes a commencé à s'appliquer aux victimes d'actes de terrorisme (loi du 9 septembre 1986), puis aux victimes d'infractions pénales en général (loi du 6 juillet 1990). La notion de victime n'est donc pas limitée, à l'origine, à un cadre strictement pénal, elle s'étend également aux victimes d'évènements exceptionnels. Les procédures qui sont ici évoquées visent néanmoins principalement les victimes d'infractions pénales.

Toute personne ayant subi un préjudice résultant de faits volontaires ou non, présentant le caractère matériel d'une infraction, peut obtenir réparation intégrale des dommages qui résultent des atteintes à la personne. Cela suppose que la victime est de nationalité française ou bien, si les faits ont été commis sur le territoire national, la victime doit appartenir à un État membre de la Communauté européenne (art. 706,3 du Code de Procédure Pénale). Cela suppose également que la victime n'a pas commis de faute.

Le dommage, pour donner lieu à indemnisation, doit consister, d'abord en des faits ayant entraîné la mort, une incapacité permanente ou une incapacité totale de travail personnel égale ou supérieure à un mois (ce qui correspond aux infractions d'homicide volontaire ou non, aux coups mortels, aux violences et aux blessures par imprudence). Le même article vise ensuite les faits d'agressions sexuelles (viols et autres agressions) et les faits d'atteinte sexuelle sur mineur.

Dans ce cadre, il est prévu "la réparation des dommages qui résultent des atteintes à la personne". Cette expression inclut le préjudice moral et même esthétique, et évidemment le préjudice économique né de la diminution des revenus professionnels. Mais elle exclut les dommages qui ne résultent pas d'une atteinte à la personne. En outre, le dommage doit résulter de "faits volontaires ou non qui présentent le caractère matériel d'une infraction".

Il existe également une seconde hypothèse (art. 706,14 du Code de Procédure Pénale) visant des dommages dont le préjudice se limite à une incapacité inférieure à un mois et la victime étant dans une situation matérielle ou psychologique grave. Dans ce cas l'indemnisation a un caractère subsidiaire: elle n'entre en jeu que si la victime se trouve dans une situation économique difficile, c'est-à-dire ne dispose que d'un plafond de ressources fixé par la loi.

L'intérêt du régime d'indemnisation réside également dans sa procédure. L'indemnité est versée par un organe unique appelé "Fonds de garantie des victimes des actes de terrorisme et d'autres infractions". Cet organe est alimenté par un prélèvement annuel sur tous les contrats d'assurances de biens conclus en France. Ce n'est donc pas l'État qui assure le financement. Dans d'autres systèmes juridiques nationaux les fonds d'indemnisation peuvent être alimentés par différentes sources (versement d'amendes, saisie des biens des délinquants etc.)

Il est à noter que la décision sur l'indemnisation peut prendre deux formes: si les victimes d'actes terroristes doivent s'adresser au Fonds de garantie, les autres doivent saisir la Commission d'indemnisation des victimes (CIVI) qui existe auprès de chaque tribunal de grande instance. Elle doit être saisie par la victime dans les trois ans à compter de l'infraction. S'agissant du contenu de la décision sur l'indemnité, la victime ne peut en obtenir une que si elle ne peut pas être indemnisée à un autre titre.

Une loi du 15 juin 2000 a enfin renforcé les droits des victimes. Il est désormais reconnu un rôle essentiel aux associations d'aide en leur attribuant une existence légale, consacrant une pratique établie. Le procureur de la République pourra désormais faire appel à une association d'aide aux victimes conventionnée pour porter aide à une victime.

Au 1er janvier 2001, l'Institut national d'aide aux victimes groupait 147 services d'aide et 138 associations. Cet Institut National d'Aide aux Victimes et Médiation (INAVEM) a en outre édité un recueil des textes internationaux relatifs à l'aide aux victimes.

3. Victimisation et réparation dans la société contemporaine

La reconnaissance d'un droit à réparation en faveur des victimes doit être considérée comme un acquis humain et social.[8] Mais au-delà de cette simple constatation se pose une interrogation plus fondamentale qui ne concerne pas seulement les victimes d'infractions. Doit-on reconnaître à toutes les victimes d'évènements imprévisibles une créance sur la société ?

La question est actuelle dans la mesure où la vie moderne a créé de nouveaux risques, sans pour autant que puisse être établie une faute au sens juridique et que soit toujours clairement identifiée une responsabilité. Ainsi à côté du système civil de l'assurance privée, le droit français a t'il déjà institué une réparation spécifique des dommages subis par les victimes d'accidents de la circulation ou de la chasse, au moyen d'un Fonds de garantie assez proche du Fonds d'indemnisation des victimes d'infractions pénales. Les problèmes suscités par les victimes de transfusion de sang contaminé ont

---

8 T. PETERS (2000) Victimisation, médiation et pratiques orientées vers la réparation, 38 *Annales Internationales de Criminologie* 135-175.

également contribué à poser à nouveau la question de l'indemnisation des victimes d'un dommage sans responsable direct identifié.

Ainsi se dessine un droit de la responsabilité visant à faire peser la réparation des dommages causés par des évènements, qui par leur ampleur et leur imprévisibilité ne peuvent relever de l'assurance privée, par la collectivité nationale sans identification d'une faute prouvée. C'est une forme de socialisation des risques, satisfaisante pour les victimes mais qui témoigne aussi, au niveau des principes, d'un déclin de la notion même de responsabilité fondée sur la faute, que celle-ci soit réparée par l'individu ou par l'État suivant sa nature.

Longtemps les victimes d'infractions pénales, limitées par l'action civile, pouvaient demeurer sans indemnisation lorsque l'auteur du délit contre lequel elles avaient exercé leur action était insolvable, était en fuite ou était inconnu. C'était par hypothèse choquant et, c'est précisément afin de pallier cette situation qu'est intervenu le système actuel. Il est né -on l'a vu- à propos de victimes d'attentats terroristes ce qui justifiait la mise en jeu d'une responsabilité de l'État s'agissant d'un trouble grave et imprévisible à l'ordre public. C'est fort de ce précédent et, sous une revendication de victimes, que le mouvement en leur faveur s'est développé.

On doit toutefois souligner que la charge financière de cette indemnisation est répartie sur l'ensemble de la collectivité nationale et non juridiquement prise en charge par l'État, son financement étant assuré par un prélèvement sur tous les contrats d'assurance.

La réparation du préjudice subi par la victime trouve cependant son fondement dans le risque que l'activité criminelle a fait courir à la victime à laquelle on ne peut reprocher, par hypothèse, aucune faute. Or ce risque est né d'un mauvais fonctionnement des services de police et de justice et, plus généralement de la politique criminelle qui doit assurer l'ordre public et la sécurité des individus et des biens.

Dès lors si indemniser les victimes apparaît comme un progrès humain, fonder une politique criminelle sur une telle réparation reviendrait à méconnaître la vocation naturelle de la politique criminelle qui est de prévenir les risques nés de la délinquance avant d'en réparer les dommages. Dans la mesure où cette forme de sanction réparatrice, que doit être l'indemnisation de la victime ne peut être mise à la charge de l'auteur du délit, le recours à l'État se justifie, à raison du mauvais fonctionnement d'un service public celui de la politique et de la justice.

La compassion ne doit pas en effet remplacer la rigueur de la justice.

DE LA RECONNAISSANCE DES DROITS DES VICTIMES À LA JUSTICE RESTAURATIVE

Robert Cario

Introduction

La victimologie et l'aide aux victimes ont connu un essor remarquable au cours des vingt dernières années. Sous l'impulsion de législations étrangères pionnières[1] et de textes internationaux ou régionaux novateurs,[2] la victime commence à reconquérir sa place au centre du conflit d'origine pénale qui l'atteint, de manière totalement illégitime, dans sa personne, son honneur, ses biens ou dans celle et ceux d'un être proche. Le carcan dirigiste dans lequel l'Etat l'a enfermée durant de longs siècles,[3] pour donner libre cours à son jaloux monopole de répression puis de réhabilitation de l'infracteur, commence à exploser sous la pression des revendications victimologiques aujourd'hui (re)connues comme scientifiquement fondées et humainement justifiées.

La situation observable en France est, de ces points de vue, assez encourageante. C'est autour des années 80 que les premières préoccupations législatives et réglementaires apparaissent (Loi sur l'indemnisation des victimes en 1977, Circulaire de 1983 sur la protection des victimes et le renforcement de leurs droits, principalement), aiguillonnées par les Services

---

1 Les premières législations nationales spécifiques aux victimes ont vu le jour dans les années 1960, dans le registre principalement indemnitaire: en Nouvelle Zélande (1963), Grande Bretagne (1964), Etats-Unis (la Californie ouvrant la voie en 1965), Canada (1967), Autriche (1972), Finlande (1973), République Fédérale d'Allemagne (1976), Suède (1978).

2 Convention Européenne du 24 novembre 1983 relative au dédommagement des victimes d'infractions violentes; Résolution 40/34 adoptée le 11 déc. 1985 par l'Assemblée Générale de l'O.N.U. portant *Déclaration des principes fondamentaux de justice relatifs aux victimes de la criminalité et aux victimes d'abus de pouvoir*; Recommandations du Conseil de l'Europe: R(85)11 sur *La position de la victime dans le cadre du droit pénal et de la procédure pénale*; Recommandation R(87)21 sur *L'assistance aux victimes et la prévention de la victimisation*, Recommandation R(99)19 sur *La médiation pénale*, Recommandation R(00)20 sur *Le rôle de l'intervention psychosociale précoce dans la prévention des comportements criminels* (http://cm.coe.org); V. Déclaration-Cadre, le 15 mars 2001, relative au statut des victimes dans le cadre de procédures pénales, *J.O.C.E.*, 22 mars 2001, L 82-1 (http://www.europa.eu.int/eur-lex).

3 V. not. J.P. ALLINNE, in: R. CARIO & D. SALAS (2001) *Œuvre de justice et victimes*. Paris: Ed. L'Harmattan, Coll. Sciences criminelles.

d'Aide aux victimes naissants, fédérés dès 1986 au sein de l'Institut National d'Aide aux Victimes et de Médiation (INAVEM), lequel s'est depuis constitué en Forum avec des partenaires, aux missions équivalentes, de quinze pays européens.

En ce sens, de nombreux textes ont intégré en droit interne de multiples dispositions destinées à assurer l'indemnisation intégrale des victimes, par la création, unique à ce jour, du Fonds de Garantie des Victimes d'Attentats et d'autres Infractions (FGTI).[4] Bien plus, toute victime ayant subi un préjudice résultant de faits volontaires ou non qui présentent le caractère matériel d'une infraction peut saisir la Commission d'indemnisation des victimes d'infractions (CIVI) indépendamment de toutes poursuites pénales.[5] A l'heure de la pénalisation inflationniste des comportements humains, il s'agit-là d'un moyen, certes ambigu, de décriminalisation de fait. Néanmoins, il est apparu, au travers de recherches féministes essentielles, que la réparation indemnitaire pour être nécessaire apparaît insuffisante, tant les conséquences psychologiques et sociales de l'infraction perturbent, parfois durablement, le vécu quotidien des personnes victimisées. Sans compter que nombre d'entre elles demeurent inconnues des autorités judiciaires comme des services sanitaires et sociaux. Les avancées de la victimologie de l'action ont surtout permis de mettre en évidence l'ampleur des dommages causés à la victime et la nécessité impérieuse de leur venir en aide le plus tôt et le plus massivement possible, dans le cadre d'une démarche globale et intégrée. Constats et propositions des Associations de victimes le confirment tragiquement, aussi bien au cas de victimisations individuelles[6] que collectives.[7]

Pour autant, en France pour le moins, ce n'est que depuis 1998 que le paysage normatif a réellement changé. La première politique pénale raisonnée à l'égard des victimes provient finalement de la Circulaire du 13

---

4 http://fgti.fr . Ce fonds est alimenté par un prélèvement obligatoire de 22 francs sur les 60 millions de contrats d'assurance de biens.

5 V. art. 706-3 *Code de Procédure Penale (C.P.P.).*

6 V. not. A. BOULAY (2001) Réflexions sur la place des victimes dans le système judiciaire par des parents d'enfants assassinés, in: CARIO & SALAS, *o.c.*, 129-144; Http://apev.org.

7 V. not. Etude épidémiologique des conséquences sanitaires des attentats (ESCAT), *In Paroles de victimes*, 2001-12/14 ; (Http://www.sos-attentats.org) ; V. également, C. LIENHARD (2001) Catastrophes et droits des victimes, in: CARIO & SALAS, *o.c.*, 145-165 ; V. *Journal des accidents et des catastrophes*, Centre Européen de Recherche sur le Droit des Accidents Collectifs et des Catastrophes, Colmar/UHA (Http://www.iutcolmar.uha.fr/cerdacc).

juillet 1998,[8] fortement inspirée par celle du 25 juillet 1983[9] qui n'a guère reçu d'application concrète soutenue. La première politique publique d'aide aux victimes est esquissée par le Rapport Lienemann remis le 29 mars 1999 au Premier Ministre,[10] dans la veine du Rapport Milliez de 1982.[11] Le droit des victimes est ainsi en cours d'élaboration et la reconnaissance des droits individuels des victimes en cours d'acquisition. La Loi du 15 juin 2000 renforçant la protection de la présomption d'innocence et les droits des victimes (adoptée le 30 mai après d'âpres discussions parlementaires et dans l'indifférence médiatique quasi généralisée relativement aux victimes), consolide un peu plus le statut légal des victimes d'infractions.[12]

Sans préjuger de l'application concrète effective de tous ces textes (problématique du manque oblige ![13]), on peut considérer que la victime n'est plus tout à fait « l'oubliée » du procès pénal. Mais cette reconnaissance ne sera consolidée vraiment que par l'affirmation formelle et solennelle des droits fondamentaux qui s'attachent au statut de victime, lequel constitue, lorsque les faits victimels surviennent, le socle autour duquel s'organisent la régulation du conflit et les prises en charge (1). Un tel statut, inévitable dans un premier temps, ne peut cependant être que provisoire, le temps de la résorption des traumatismes : sa cristallisation, comme c'est actuellement le cas, est un obstacle sérieux à la restauration sociale de la victime, finalité de l'intervention socio-judiciaire. La justice restaurative, si chère à Tony Peters en l'honneur de qui sont rédigées ces quelques réflexions, semble être la voie de l'espoir de voir enfin pris en compte le crime dans son endroit comme dans son envers,[14] en toute dignité, humanité et solidarité (2).

---

8 *Circ.* NORJUS 9800177C relative à la politique pénale d'aide aux victimes d'infractions pénales, *B.O.M.J.*, 1998-71, 4-37.

9 *Circ.* 83-21-F1, *B.O.M.J.* 20 sept. 1983, 11 et s.

10 V. M.N. LIENEMANN (1999) *Pour une nouvelle politique publique d'aide aux victimes.* Paris: La Documentation française; M.N. LIENEMANN (1988) *Vers une politique publique d'aide aux victimes*, multigraph. INAVEM; A. BERNARD & R. CARIO (2001) *Les politiques publiques interministérielles d'aide aux victimes.* Paris: Ed. L'Harmattan, Coll. Sciences criminelles.

11 P. MILLIEZ (1982) (Dir), *Rapport de la Commission d'étude et de proposition dans le domaine de l'aide aux victimes*, multigraph., Min. Justice.

12 Sur tous ces aspects, V. not. R. CARIO (2001) (2è éd.), *Victimologie. De l'effraction du lien intersubjectif à la restauration sociale.* Paris: Ed. L'Harmattan, Coll. Traité de Sciences criminelles.

13 Circulaire du 27 janvier 2000, relative au bilan d'application de la Circulaire du 13 juillet 1998 relative à la politique pénale d'aide aux victimes, in: R. CARIO (2001) *Victimologie. Les textes essentiels*, vol. 2-2, 123-130. Paris: Ed. L'Harmattan, Coll. Traité de Sciences criminelles.

14 V. M. BARIL (1984) *L'envers du crime*, multigraph. Montréal: Centre International de Criminologie Comparée, Coll. Cahiers de Recherches Criminologiques.

1. La conquête des droits des victimes

La complexité des victimisations comme celle des dispositifs destinés à les prévenir, les arrêter et les réparer, rendent d'autant plus nécessaire la protection effective des droits propres de la victime, également acquis à ses ayants-droits et à ses proches. La difficulté principale de leur plein exercice provient aujourd'hui encore de l'absence de globalisation de la réponse socio-judiciaire à leur égard, les victimes étant morcelées par les multiples intervenants au procès pénal. De tels droits doivent être inscrits dans un procès équitable respectueux de la « *la dignité attachée à la qualité morale de la personne humaine* ».[15] Reconnue publiquement par la mise en mouvement du processus pénal, la victime se trouve alors restaurée dans l'estime de soi. A la condition que les intervenants soient d'authentiques professionnels de l'aide aux victimes, rompus aux techniques de leur discipline, mais également formés aux sciences humaines et à la criminologie (au sens large incluant la victimologie), préparés au partage des connaissances transdisciplinaires. Or le constat est actuellement simple: « trop souvent encore les victimes se retrouvent seules, sans écoute et soutien, pour affronter les difficultés personnelles et les difficultés de procédure auxquelles elles sont confrontées ».[16] Comment, dans ces conditions, la victime peut-elle faire respecter ses droits à la reconnaissance (1.1), à l'accompagnement (1.2) et à la réparation (1.3)?

1.1. Droits à la reconnaissance

Reconnaître, c'est considérer la personne de la victime. Or, par le crime éprouvé, la victime est projetée dans l'abîme que cette catastrophe intersubjective a creusé. La « re-co-naissance » apparaît bien alors comme la seule manière de restaurer le lien social, de permettre à la victime de réintégrer le groupe humain.

La reconnaissance suppose tout d'abord le droit d'accéder au droit, dans le cadre d'une authentique stratégie d'*empowerment*, mécanisme pro-actif par lequel les individus, les organisations ou les communautés diverses

---

15 V. P. Ricoeur (1995) *Le juste,* 199. Ed. Esprit; B. Edelman (1997) *La dignité de la personne humaine, un concept nouveau,* 185-188. Paris: Ed. Dalloz; M.L. Pavia (2000) (6è éd.), La dignité de la personne humaine, in: R. Cabrillac, M.A. Frison-Roche, T. Revet (dir.), *Libertés et droits fondamentaux,* 121-139. Paris: Ed. Dalloz.

16 V. E. Guigou (1999) Discours prononcé lors des XVèmes Assises de l'Inavem, multigraph., 2-3.

concernés acquièrent la maîtrise de leurs propres affaires.[17] A défaut, de nombreuses victimes demeurent méconnues, voire inconnues: par ignorance, défiance, perte de confiance, peur, éloignement, incapacité physique ou mentale. La Loi du 18 décembre 1998 favorise l'accès des victimes au droit et la résolution amiable des conflits. Ce même texte généralise la création des Maisons de justice et du droit, instrument privilégié de la justice de proximité qui convient bien aux victimes.[18] C'est dans le même esprit que toute plainte doit être enregistrée par les services de police judiciaire et transmise aux autorités de poursuites. L'inscription sur la main courante doit être réservée aux seuls faits non infractionnels. Le dépôt de plainte doit être le moins formel possible (simple lettre ou télécopie), quel que soit le lieu où se trouve la victime. Au cas de constitution de partie civile, aucune consignation préalable ne doit être exigée de la victime d'un acte grave.

La reconnaissance passe ensuite par l'accueil, tout aussi primordial, des victimes, à tous les stades de la prise en charge de la victimisation, de la révélation à l'exécution des décisions de justice: police, gendarmerie, hôpitaux, Urgences médico-judiciaires (U.M.J.), tribunaux, services d'aide aux victimes, services sanitaires et sociaux, mairies, compagnies d'assurance. Des locaux spécifiques doivent être disponibles, aménagés chaleureusement et des permanences doivent être organisées, aux plages horaires extensibles, y compris les fins de semaine et les jours fériés. La visite des salles d'audience doit également être systématisée; une place privilégiée étant réservée aux victimes lors de leur déroulement.

La reconnaissance passe alors par l'écoute des plaintes et des souffrances de la victime, généralement verbalisées avec beaucoup de difficulté. Compassion, empathie et attention s'imposent, car ce qui pourrait paraître banal à l'intervenant est toujours capital pour la victime. A défaut de pouvoir médiatiser les affects douloureux provenant du crime subi, les frustrations sont grandes et génératrices d'incompréhension de la part des victimes, animées alors par le doute du bien fondé de la démarche, de la gravité réelle des faits, ou envahies par le sentiment de « faire valoir » de la justice pénale surtout intéressée à collecter les preuves de la culpabilité de l'infracteur grâce, entre autres moyens, à leurs déclarations.

---

17 V. J. RAPPAPORT (1987) Terms of empowerment/exemplars of prevention : toward a theory for community psychology, *15 American Journal of community psychology* 121-145; D. DAMANT, J. PAQUET & J. BÉLANGER (2000) Analyse du processus d'empowerment dans la trajectoire de femmes victimes de violence conjugale à travers le système judiciaire, *33 Criminologie* 73-95.

18 L. 98-1163 relative à l'accès au droit et à la résolution amiable des conflits, *J.O.* du 22, 19343.

1.2. Droits à l'accompagnement

Accompagner, c'est se joindre à quelqu'un pour aller où il va, en même temps que lui. Il importe donc de placer la victime au centre de la prise en charge à laquelle elle a droit, car elle seule sait ce dont elle souffre, connaît la direction dans laquelle il faut chercher, ce que sont ses problèmes cruciaux et quelles expériences elle a vécu, voire même refoulé.[19]

L'accompagnement suppose que la victime soit entendue: elle doit être écoutée certes mais aussi crue dans ses déclarations. Et comprise si elle est étrangère. La recherche de la vérité est essentielle pour la victime et tout doit être mis en œuvre pour qu'elle y participe elle-même. Les réunions régulières et rapprochées avec les autorités diverses de prise en charge de son dossier la conforteront dans cette démarche, que le dossier avance ou non. La visibilité de son état de victime exige l'enregistrement des dossiers pénaux y compris sous le nom de la victime (pas seulement de l'infracteur) et la création systématique en leur sein d'une côte victime, de couleur particulière,[20] abondée par tous les éléments relatifs à sa reconnaissance. Dans ce même esprit, la victime s'estimera entendue lorsque tous les intervenants non seulement lui remettront les coordonnées du Service d'aide aux victimes le plus proche de son domicile mais encore, avec son accord, communiqueront au-dit service ses coordonnées voire même mandateront l'un d'entre eux pour l'accompagner tout au long du procès.

Si l'accompagnement consiste pour la victime à être reconnue et entendue, il implique le droit de n'avoir pas à répéter sans cesse, devant chaque interlocuteur, les circonstances de son affaire, les conditions de sa réparation. L'enregistrement des premières déclarations devrait être généralisé, à la manière des modalités prévues par la Loi du 17 juin 1998 concernant les mineurs,[21] à ces nuances près que la victime y consente et soit autorisée à retirer du dossier un enregistrement contre-productif ou incomplet.

L'accompagnement, c'est aussi le droit pour la victime à être informée des suites et des caractéristiques des contentieux qui seront activés: pénal, civil, administratif, disciplinaire. L'information porte également sur les droits dont elle dispose précisément pour faire aboutir ses demandes,

---

19 V. C.R. ROGERS (1961) *Le développement de la personne,* 10. Ed. Dunod.

20 V. en ce sens la Déclaration de la victime sur les conséquences du crime, de couleur jaune, utilisée par les tribunaux répressifs du Québec, R. CARIO (2001) *Victimologie. Les textes essentiels*, vol. 2, *o.c.*, 71 et s.

21 V. art. 706-52 *Code de Procédure Pénale*; V. not. D. RÉSERBAT-PLANTET (2000) L'audition filmée des mineurs victimes d'abus sexuels, *Les Cahiers de l'Actif* 284-285, 155-197.

relativement à la situation de l'infracteur et à sa sanction, relativement aux réparations qu'elle est en droit d'attendre, notamment devant la CIVI. La victime a le droit de connaître, en totale clarté et transparence, les potentialités réelles des démarches entreprises, les chances de succès, la durée moyenne des procédures, les recours dont elle dispose, comme ceux dont disposent divers organismes intervenant à la réparation de ses préjudices. Autant dans le cadre de poursuites pénales que dans celui de classements conditionnels, subordonnés à une mesure de médiation pénale notamment.

L'accompagnement doit consolider le droit de la victime à être protégée. Tout doit être mis en place pour qu'elle ne soit plus en contact avec l'infracteur et éviter la réitération de nouvelles infractions. Des visites régulières au domicile de la victime par les services de police ou de gendarmerie la rassurent efficacement. La victime doit également être protégée des médias. La publication de photographies représentant très concrètement la victime dans le drame qu'elle vient de vivre ne devrait avoir lieu, au minimum, qu'avec son plein consentement. L'accompagnement, c'est encore aider la victime. Elle a souvent besoin d'un secours financier ou matériel d'urgence, géré par les services d'aide aux victimes sur des fonds spécifiques, destinés à accompagner les petites choses de la vie quotidienne.

L'accompagnement suppose que des conseils soient prodigués aux victimes. Conseils sur les démarches à entreprendre pour faire cesser les troubles résultant de l'infraction. Conseils quant à la rédaction de dossiers auprès d'organismes divers: sécurité sociale, commission d'indemnisation des victimes d'infractions, assurances, employeur, aide sociale, aide juridictionnelle, administration pénitentiaire. L'accompagnement invite, dans ce même esprit, à orienter les victimes vers les services adéquats, chaque fois que le problème diagnostiqué sort du champ de la compétence propre de l'intervenant, quel qu'il soit, où qu'il se trouve, afin d'éviter toute victimisation secondaire. Le travail en partenariat, clairement établi par voie conventionnelle, est la solution idéale et réaliste à l'approche globale des souffrances de la victime. Grâce à cette stratégie d'intervention, elle demeure dans le réseau de l'aide aux victimes, en évitant le douloureux écueil de la répétition.

L'accompagnement c'est enfin et pour l'essentiel favoriser les droits de la défense de la victime, surtout dans les procédures rapides, dites « en temps réel ». Les conventions conclues entre barreaux et services d'aide aux victimes facilitent grandement les relations entre victimes et avocats. La systématisation de l'aide juridictionnelle au bénéfice des victimes est inévitable. Une défense de qualité assure à la victime d'être véritablement acteur du procès en lui permettant notamment: de réclamer -et recevoir effectivement- les différentes pièces du dossier pénal; de prendre connaissance des décisions prises et de leurs motivations (notamment en cas de classement sans suite, d'ordonnance de non lieu, de décision de relaxe ou d'acquittement); d'infléchir le cours de l'instruction, d'obtenir et le cas échéant contester les diverses expertises médicales, psychologiques et sociales destinées à fixer le plus exactement possible l'étendue de ses préjudices; d'être réellement partie à l'audience de jugement, d'être toujours convoquée -et avertie- des lieux, dates et heures des convocations diverses des audiences de jugement.

1.3. Droits à réparation

Réparer c'est reconnaître l'autre, sa place et ses droits en tant que personne. La réintégration de la victime, ou de ses proches, parmi les autres humains est un devoir communautaire absolument incontournable. L'indemnisation matérielle est nécessaire mais insuffisante au regard des traumatismes psychologiques et sociaux durables que l'infraction a générés: équilibre psychique fragilisé, statut social dévalorisé, activité professionnelle compromise, relations intersubjectives perturbées.

L'éparpillement actuel des contentieux, sans coordination véritable entre les différentes juridictions civiles, pénales et organismes payeurs, tout comme la prise en compte par la CIVI de la faute éventuelle de la victime, rendent urgente leur unification. Elle évitera encore les déconvenues ou malentendus provenant du caractère cumulable, ou non, des sommes versées (selon leur nature forfaitaire ou indemnitaire), comme des aléas de l'exécution de la décision de justice sur les intérêts civils (aujourd'hui toujours et anormalement à la charge de la victime), comme l'absence de contradictoire au cas de transaction avec les compagnies d'assurances.[22] Un traitement égalitaire des victimes doit également être respecté, quelle que soit l'origine de leurs victimisations (droit commun, attentats, accidents du travail, accidents de la circulation, aléas thérapeutiques notamment), que l'infracteur soit connu ou non, reconnu responsable ou non des faits dommageables commis intentionnellement ou non.[23] Le fonds de garantie,

22 V. not. L. MÉLENNEC (2000) De la main mise des compagnies d'assurances sur l'indemnisation des préjudices corporels et de la nécessité impérative de réformer la loi Badinter, *Gazette du Palais*, 28-29 juin, Doct., 47-52.

23 V. sur les délits non intentionnels, la Loi du 10 juill. 2000, *J.O.* du 11, 10 484, visant à endiguer la montée du risque pénal (non réelle) à l'égard des élus et des décideurs publics ou privés (distinction entre auteurs 'directs' et 'indirects'), art. 121-3 al. 3 *C. pén.*; V. M.F. STEINLÉ-FEUERBACH (2001) Les délits non intentionnels au regard de la Loi du 10 juillet 2000, 14 *Journal des Accidents et des Catastrophes (J.A.C.)*,

même s'il est une institution déjà performante, doit néanmoins devenir autonome, alimenté par la solidarité nationale (prélèvement sur les assurances de biens) et l'Etat (prélèvement sur les amendes pénales,[24] saisie du pécule de garantie des détenus non utilisé).

La réparation des préjudices doit être intégrale (préjudices économiques et préjudices extra-patrimoniaux) et effective, qu'il s'agisse de préjudices actuels ou futurs, directs ou par ricochet, quels que soient les revenus, sans plafond d'indemnisation. Elle doit être rapide, accompagnée de provisions immédiates et régulières, en fonction de l'évolution de la situation de la victime. En ce sens, l'accès à la CIVI doit être généralisé.

La diversité et l'ampleur des préjudices nécessitent le recours à l'expertise médico-légale, contradictoire ainsi que l'uniformisation des nombreux barèmes disponibles. Quant à l'expertise psychologique, elle doit être beaucoup plus largement entreprise, comme y invite dorénavant l'article 81-1 du Code de procédure pénale. Naturellement, elle ne peut consister qu'en la mesure de l'ampleur des traumatismes subis et en aucun cas en l'appréciation de la « crédibilité » des déclarations de la victime car, en cette matière aussi, le doute doit profiter à la victime. Un authentique droit aux soins doit être fermement consolidé, tant en ce qui concerne les blessures physiques (traitements médicaux et chirurgicaux, contraintes matérielles de la vie quotidienne) que les traumatismes psychologiques (au sens large)[25] dont souffrent les victimes d'un acte infractionnel ou d'un événement catastrophique. Les dangers de marginalisation, voire d'exclusion des victimes sont réels, à défaut de prises en charge spécifiques, dès la révélation des faits et aussi longtemps que les troubles persistent, aussi longtemps que le travail de deuil, de symbolisation des affects en provenance de l'infraction ne seront pas aboutis.

L'ensemble de ces droits à la reconnaissance, à l'accompagnement et à la réparation de tous les préjudices devraient recevoir une consécration constitutionnelle. La victime aura alors le sentiment d'être pleinement restaurée socialement. Il s'agit là du préalable absolument indispensable à l'avènement d'une authentique justice restaurative. Une telle orientation de notre système de justice pénale est salutaire. Si elle suppose une réelle et profonde mutation des mentalités, elle nous est aujourd'hui très accessible.

(http://www.iutcolmar.uha.fr); sur la décision de la culpabilité d'une personne non imputable, V. art. 349-1 nouveau *C.P.P.*

24 Ou encore institution d'une amende sur-compensatoire comme au Canada. V. sur ce point, la contribution de A. NORMANDEAU, in: BERNARD & CARIO, *o.c.* 79-103.

25 V. not. C. DAMIANI (1997) *Les victimes. Violences publiques et crimes privés*. Bayard Editions; J. AUDET & J.F. KATZ (1999) *Précis de victimologie générale*. Ed. Dunod; G. LOPEZ (1998) *Victimologie*. Paris: Ed. Dalloz.

A la condition de diversifier les contentieux pour focaliser la compétence du juge pénal sur les atteintes graves aux valeurs sociales fondamentales à la pérennité de l'être humain. La justice restaurative offre des perspectives prometteuses en ce sens car elle permet de concilier l'impératif de resocialisation de l'infracteur condamné avec celui de restauration sociale de la victime traumatisée par l'acte criminel.

2. L'avènement de la justice restaurative

Il est devenu banal de souligner qu'aujourd'hui encore des dysfonctionnements de tous ordres affectent nos systèmes de justice pénale: politique, éthique, scientifique, socio-culturel, financier, structurel ou fonctionnel... Pour ne pas être inévitables, ils rendent urgente la mise en place de modes beaucoup plus souples ou flexibles[26] de résolution des conflits,[27] favorisant la restauration sociale des protagonistes à l'infraction (2.1). Une telle souplesse dans l'intervention présente sans aucun doute des gages de célérité, de proximité, de moindre traumatisme pour les protagonistes, de moindre coût pour la communauté. Cependant, la mise en œuvre concrète d'une telle justice restaurative ne saurait heurter ni les principes caractéristiques d'un procès équitable, ni les libertés et droits fondamentaux de chacune des parties au conflit (2.2).

2.1. Eléments de définition de la justice restaurative

Depuis quelques années, au regard de l'échec des modèles répressifs classiques de neutralisation et, dans une moindre mesure, de resocialisation, de plus en plus d'auteurs appellent de leur vœux l'avènement (ou le rétablissement) d'une justice restaurative. Cette justice restaurative ne se crispe pas sur le passé de la faute, ne se cristallise pas sur la seule responsabilité pénale de l'auteur. Elle rééquilibre les priorités en réinvestissant, aux côtés de l'infracteur, la personne qui souffre de dommages particuliers. Par l'introduction du tiers, elle permet de socialiser le désir de vengeance de la victime comme la culpabilité de l'infracteur, lesquels deviennent alors réparateurs. En même temps qu'elle institue

26 V. J. Faget (1992) *Justice et travail social. Le rhizome pénal*, 8. Ed. Erès, Coll. Trajets.

27 V. sur ces aspects, les *Recommandations* du Conseil de l'Europe, not., *R(87)18* sur la Simplification de la justice pénale, 1988, 37 p.; *R(87)20* sur les Réactions sociales à la délinquance juvénile, 1989, 87 p.; *R(99)19* sur La médiation en matière pénale, 1999, 23 p.

chacun dans son rôle, opération symboliquement essentielle, elle tente de reconstruire l'avenir en associant à la réponse pénale un accompagnement psychologique et social des intéressés. En les plaçant au centre même du conflit qui les oppose, elle ne leur vole ni leur conflit, ni leur histoire.[28] Plus qu'un processus de règlement des conflits, c'est une dynamique régulatrice qui permet de les identifier et de les traiter dans leur globalité. En ce sens, la justice restaurative n'est pas vraiment une troisième voie: elle transcende plus positivement les modèles punitifs et réhabilitatifs traditionnels.

Par la justice restaurative, l'infracteur et la victime se réunissent, sous le contrôle bienveillant et protecteur des représentants de la société, pour « *décider ensemble de la meilleure façon d'aborder et de régler les conséquences du délit ainsi que ses répercussions futures* ».[29] En associant mieux les fondements des systèmes classiques (punition et resocialisation), en enrichissant les potentialités qu'ils recèlent (réparation), une telle philosophie de la justice favorise la restauration sociale du condamné et de la victime, en toute dignité et équité.

La justice restaurative les rend volontairement acteur du règlement et de la symbolisation de l'événement traumatique. Elle responsabilise l'infracteur qui prend connaissance des répercussions réelles de l'acte commis. Elle implique les victimes dans leur prise en charge par le système de justice pénale. Une telle reconnaissance des protagonistes à l'infraction restaure leur estime de soi par la conscience et l'acceptation d'une réparation équitable des dommages résultant de l'infraction. L'un comme l'autre ne subissent plus la loi pénale mais se l'approprient, sortant ainsi de l'isolement dans lequel la justice répressive les confine. Il devient alors possible d'envisager un traitement de restauration sociale afin de ne plus exposer ou être exposé à de nouveaux conflits intersubjectifs, groupaux ou sociétaux.

La justice restaurative réintroduit l'humanité après le basculement psychique provoqué par le passage à l'acte. Reconquête de la dignité, expression de la vérité, souci de l'autre, nomination et (re)apprentissage de l'interdit, respect de l'institution, atténuation du sentiment d'injustice subie sont encore à classer parmi les bienfaits de la justice restaurative. Sans nier que l'acte criminel est posé par l'infracteur de manière totalement illégitime, une telle réponse prend néanmoins en compte la vulnérabilité dans laquelle il se trouvait, dans un nombre important de cas, vulnérabilité susceptible non seulement d'en expliquer la réalisation mais encore de permettre la meilleure

28 V. N. CHRISTIE (1977) Conflicts as property, 17 *British Journal of Criminology* 1-15.

29 T. MARSHALL, cité in: J.J. LLEWELLYN, R. HOWSE, La justice réparatrice, *o.c.*, 8 ; V. également T. MARSHALL (1999) *Restorative justice. An overview.* London: Home Office.

adaptation possible de la sanction finalement prononcée à sa personnalité, aux besoins de la victime et à la préservation de l'intérêt général. Une telle approche se justifie d'autant plus que dans les crimes les plus sérieux, la plupart des protagonistes se connaissent et évoluent dans une forte proximité socio-culturelle. Cette vulnérabilité partagée distribue, dans de nombreuses affaires, les rôles -interchangeables- de criminel et de victime.[30]

Bien naturellement, la justice restaurative suppose un partenariat de tous les services impliqués dans la gestion pénale du conflit et dans l'accompagnement psychologique et social des victimes: police, justice, santé, protection sociale, aide aux victimes notamment. Plus que dans tout autre modèle de justice, la formation des intervenants est une clé fondamentale de la réussite des mesures mises en œuvre pour réintégrer en humanité les intéressés en particulier, pour restaurer l'harmonie sociale plus globalement.[31]

Sans aucun doute, la justice restaurative s'attache prioritairement à la prévention et, en cas d'échec, au traitement des victimisations d'origine pénale, dont l'inflation, caractéristique de notre société pénalisée,[32] peut laisser craindre, paradoxalement, un élargissement du contrôle social. Néanmoins, la redécouverte de pratiques régulatrices anciennes (les cercles de guérison et les cercles de sentence chez les Inuits ; les conférences du groupe familial chez les Maoris, par exemple),[33] comme l'invention de

---

30 V. E.A. FATTAH (1994) *The interchangeable roles of victim and victimizer*. Helsinki: HEUNI Papers, N°3, multigraph; R. CARIO, *Victimologie*, *o.c.*, vol. 1, 130 et s.

31 Sur la justice restaurative, V. not. J. BRAITHWAITE (1989) *Crime, shame and reintegration*. Cambridge Univ. Press: Cambridge; H. ZEHR (1990) *Changing lenses. A new focus for crime and justice*. Scottdale: Herald Press; H. BIANCHI (1994) *Justice as a sanctuary : toward a system of crime control*, Indiana Univ. Press; M. WRIGHT (1996) (2è éd), *Justice for victims and offenders. A restorative response to crime*. Waterside Press: Winchester; J. DIGNAN & M. CAVADINO (1998) Which model of criminal justice offers the best scope for assisting victims of crime ?, E.A. FATTAH & T. PETERS (eds), *Support for crime victims in a comparative perspective, Essays dedicated to Prof. F. McCLINTOCK*. Leuven: Leuven University Press; L. WALGRAVE (1998) (ed.), *Restorative justice for juveniles. Potentialities, risks and problems*, Leuven: Leuven University Press; L. WALGRAVE (1999) La justice réparatrice, 32 *Criminologie* 3-159; E.A. FATTAH (1999) Victim redress and victim-offender reconciliation in theory and practice, *35 Hokkaigakuen Law Journal* 155-182 ; E. FATTAH (2000) Du châtiment à la justice réparatrice : une évolution ?, 42 *Rev. Canadienne de Criminologie* 249-420 ; V. également *The restorative justice and mediation collection* sur le site de l'Office for Victims of Crime (OVC), Http://www.ojp.usdoj.gov/ovc.

32 V. not. A. GARAPON & D. SALAS (1997) *La République pénalisée*. Ed. Hachette; R. CARIO, *Victimologie*, volume 2-1, *oc.*, 22 et s.

33 V. M. JACCOUD (1999) *Criminologie*, 1, 79-105 ; J.E. COUTURE (2000-12) Les aînés et les guérisseurs : une collaboration fructueuse, *Forum*, 1, 38-39; de la même auteure,

réponses mieux adaptées à la civilisation contemporaine attestent de multiples variations restauratives pour répondre au crime.

2.2 Mise en œuvre concrète de la justice restaurative

Pour optimiste que pourra paraître le constat, les systèmes de justice pénale continentaux ne sont pas si éloignés de ce modèle restauratif, qu'ils (re)découvrent certes encore timidement. Des aménagements au procès pénal classique ont déjà vu le jour, en termes d'alternatives aux poursuites ou d'aménagements de la sanction pénale. En ce sens, la médiation pénale et la réparation pénale (à l'égard des mineurs) occupent désormais une place importante dans la régulation des conflits d'ordre pénal, non sans ambiguïté néanmoins, quant au contentieux concerné et quant au respect de principes fondamentaux de justice pénale lorsque ces mesures sont mises en place au stade des poursuites (a). D'autres mesures aujourd'hui disponibles mais d'utilisation beaucoup plus modeste, offrent encore de réelles potentialités restauratives, tant au stade présententiel qu'à celui du prononcé et de l'aménagement de la sanction, au plus grand profit des bénéficiaires (b).

a) La médiation pénale

Au même titre que d'autres formes de classements conditionnels,[34] laissées à l'opportunité du Parquet, la médiation pénale connaît, depuis quelques années, une vogue certaine. Ces alternatives aux poursuites, fortement supportées en France par le Ministère de la Justice, ont vocation à atténuer l'impact désastreux produit sur l'opinion publique par le taux de classement sans suite généralement observé: dans trois cas sur quatre.[35]
La médiation constitue, en théorie, un excellent procédé de régulation et de symbolisation des conflits. Son avènement dans notre système pénal repose surtout sur l'inaptitude de la justice à traiter les émotions. Le législateur

---

Justice réparatrice et violence, in: P. DUMOUCHEL (2000) (dir.), *Comprendre pour agir : violences, victimes et vengeances,* 183-206. P.U. Laval /L'Harmattan.

34 La Loi du 23 juin 1999 a opéré une classification de ces classements conditionnels, V. art. 41-1-1° *C.P.P.* (rappel à la loi), 2° (orientation vers une structure sanitaire, sociale ou professionnelle), 3° (régularisation de la situation de l'intéressé), 4° (réparation du dommage causé), 5° (médiation pénale). La même loi a introduit la composition pénale (art. 41-2 et 3 *C. P.P.*).

35 En 1999, par ex., sur 4 932 196 crimes, délits ou contraventions de 5ème classe ayant fait l'objet d'un procès-verbal de police judiciaire, d'une plainte ou d'une dénonciation, les Parquets ont procédé à 3 734 746 classements sans suite, soit un taux de 75,72 % (tous auteurs confondus); V. (2000) *Les chiffres-clés de la justice*, 16. Pub. Ministère de la Justice.

français a souhaité encadrer judiciairement la médiation des conflits d'ordre pénal en offrant au Procureur de la République la possibilité, préalablement à sa décision sur l'action publique et avec l'accord des parties, de décider de recourir à une médiation s'il lui apparaît qu'une telle mesure est susceptible d'assurer la réparation du dommage causé à la victime, de mettre fin au trouble résultant de l'infraction ou de contribuer au reclassement de l'auteur de l'infraction.[36] Cette même loi du 4 janvier 1993 a institué la médiation-réparation, ou réparation pénale, spécialement applicable aux mineurs, autour d'une formulation réparatrice volontairement plus imprécise mais dans un cadre de déclenchement nettement plus riche (au niveau du parquet, de l'instruction ou du jugement) et en l'assortissant d'un heureux suivi socio-éducatif.[37]

Les potentialités restauratives de la médiation pénale proviennent du contexte de justice négociée, plutôt qu'imposée, dans lequel elle s'inscrit. La place de la victime dans la régulation des conflits d'ordre pénal est très opportunément restituée et valorisée. Ce réinvestissement dans sa victimisation permet à l'intéressé(e) de communiquer son émotion, de la renvoyer à l'auteur de l'acte et d'envisager les modalités de son atténuation, voire de sa disparition. Par la mise en contact des protagonistes la violence se dissipe.[38] Par l'instauration du dialogue, les affects nés du conflit sont médiatisés par la victime et/ou ses proches.[39] La victime peut alors offrir au condamné une possibilité unique de pardon, vecteur trop négligé de la réconciliation.

La médiation pénale participe également à la responsabilisation de l'infracteur qui tout en réparant matériellement le mal causé, prend concrètement conscience de sa dimension psycho-affective relativement à la

---

36 V. nouvel art. 41-1 al. 1 *C.P.P.* introduit par la loi du 23 juin 1999; Assez curieusement, ces trois conditions sont dorénavant devenues alternatives, rendant ainsi possible, contre l'esprit même de la mesure initiale, l'extension du champ d'application de la médiation pénale.

37 V. art. 12-1 *Ord.* 2 fév. 1945 : « Le procureur de la République, la juridiction chargée de l'instruction de l'affaire ou la juridiction de jugement ont la faculté de proposer au mineur une mesure ou une activité d'aide ou de réparation à l'égard de la victime ou dans l'intérêt de la collectivité... » ; V. not. M. ALLAIX & M. ROBIN (1994) La genèse de la mesure de réparation pénale à l'égard des mineurs, in: M. VAILLANT (dir.), *De la dette au don. La réparation pénale à l'égard des mineurs*, 29-41. ESF Ed.; V. *Circ.* 11 mars 1993 (Nor Jus F 93 500.13 C K.2 n°1) relative à la mise en œuvre à l'égard des mineurs de la mesure de réparation pénale (pub. *De la dette au don*, *ibid.*, p. 217 et s.); M. VAILLANT (1999) *La réparation. De la délinquance à la découverte de la responsabilité.* Ed. Gallimard.

38 V. en ce sens B. CYRULNIK (1993) *Les nourritures affectives,* 144. O. Jacob.

39 S. ARNOUX & N. TERCQ, Les enjeux de la médiation pénale pour les victimes, in: R. CARIO (dir.), *La médiation: entre répression et réparation*, *o.c.*, 109-126.

personne victimisée ou, plus généralement, conscience de la réalité d'un trouble causé à la communauté. Une telle synergie permet à l'infracteur (majeur comme mineur) de « *découvrir que la loi symbolique échange est préférable à celle imposée par la force* ».[40]

Le rôle du médiateur apparaît alors réellement novateur au travers de la mission qui lui est confiée par l'autorité judiciaire. Il va tenter de dénouer le conflit en dynamisant la participation des parties afin qu'elles s'investissent personnellement dans la recherche des solutions. Par son aptitude à l'écoute, il doit les inciter à raconter le conflit, à se raconter. En provoquant l'expression de leur parole contradictoire, sans taire leur émotion, le médiateur rend possible l'apaisement des souffrances génératrices et consécutives de l'infraction. Il peut aussi inviter les protagonistes à agir sur leur environnement et à modifier leurs comportements respectifs pour éviter que de telles situations de conflit ne se renouvellent.

La médiation pénale offre encore à la régulation des conflits une autre justice,[41] plus humaine pour la victime et l'infracteur, plus consensuelle, plus flexible. Plus crédible, elle permet une réparation réelle, directe ou indirecte, du dommage causé par l'infracteur. Plus rapide, moins coûteuse, elle intervient au plus près des faits, au plus près des souffrances que l'acte a cristallisées. Plus pédagogique, elle donne du sens à l'intervention socio-pénale.

Vantée par tous, la médiation pénale connaît un succès certain en France. Les conditions de sa mise en œuvre soulèvent néanmoins quelques interrogations. Le parquet joue un rôle central à cet égard: il propose la mesure (obligatoirement pour les majeurs, très majoritairement chez les mineurs), délègue à un médiateur son déroulement et évalue les résultats obtenus, s'attribuant par là une mission juridictionnelle que ne lui reconnaît pas la loi. L'accord de l'infracteur ne semble toujours conforter les vertus de responsabilisation que recèle la médiation pénale, son acceptation ayant davantage pour objet d'éviter des poursuites pénales plus lourdes de conséquences. Le choix du médiateur, à la discrétion du parquet, ne constitue pas le meilleur gage d'impartialité et d'indépendance. Le contentieux traité atteste de petite délinquance, bien plus rarement de faits délictuels voire criminels contre les personnes ou les biens, anormalement exclus. Surtout, la médiation pénale ne recouvre pas exactement les besoins de la victime, en évacuant trop souvent les prises en charge psychologique et sociale. Le plus souvent, c'est la réparation indemnitaire (en nature ou par

---

40 V. J. SELOSSE, la réparation dans le champ éducatif, in: VAILLANT (1994) *o.c.*, 15-27 et spé. 27.

41 V. J.P BONAFÉ-SCHMITT (1992) *La médiation: l'autre justice*. Ed. Syros.

équivalent) qui est au cœur de la négociation, pas toujours conduite par des professionnels de l'aide aux victimes. Quand bien même d'aucuns s'en défendent en argumentant qu'il s'agit d'une délinquance assez banale, il demeure que les conséquences de l'infraction produisent des traumatismes plus ou moins importants, des difficultés sociales variables.

Comme le soulignent l'approche novatrice que développent précisément notre collègue Tony Peters et son équipe, la plupart des infractions graves peuvent bénéficier d'une médiation pénale. Deux programmes de médiation restaurative, en plus de la médiation pénale classique, sont actuellement expérimentés en Belgique. Le premier conduit le procureur, après avoir déclenché des poursuites pour infraction relativement grave, à inviter la victime et l'infracteur à une médiation. Par l'intermédiaire d'un médiateur (criminologue de formation) soucieux des intérêts de l'une comme de l'autre, les intéressés tentent, à l'occasion de rencontres directes ou non, de trouver une solution équitable au conflit qui les oppose. La seconde expérience est plus ambitieuse encore car elle se déroule en milieu carcéral. Reposant sur les mêmes objectifs, elle est mise en œuvre par un médiateur, en collaboration avec l'Administration pénitentiaire.[42] Dans un cas sur deux, ces médiations restauratives aboutissent à un accord écrit.

De tels programmes de médiation restaurative méritent d'être généralisés car ils présentent des bénéfices certains pour les protagonistes, en véritable position d'acteurs au sein du processus pénal décisionnel. La reconnaissance par l'infracteur et le système de justice pénale de toutes les conséquences de la victimisation et l'implication de la victime dans la régulation du conflit favorisent sa restauration individuelle et sociale. La responsabilisation de l'infracteur (qui n'échappe pour autant pas à la sanction pénale) relativement à l'interdit de l'acte posé comme à ses obligations de réparation est un levier fort de sa réinsertion sociale, d'autant plus que les efforts consentis sont de nature à rejaillir sur le quantum de sa condamnation dans le premier cas, sur l'individualisation de sa peine privative de liberté dans le second.[43]

A défaut d'évoluer vers de telles pratiques, on peut redouter que la médiation pénale, qui participe certes bien mieux que le droit pénal classique à la restauration du lien social blessé par l'infraction, ne soit justifiée que par l'unique crainte de la justice elle-même de voir échapper une part importante du contentieux pénal et, au-delà, de perdre de son autorité. A l'heure de la

---

42 V. dans le même sens, T. DE VILLETTE (2000) Dans un pénitencier du Québec: face à face victimes/agresseurs..., XII(1) *Rev. Porte ouverte*, 15 et s.

43 V. sur ces expériences innovantes not. T. PETERS & I. AERTSEN (1999) Approche restaurative des crimes et des délits en Belgique, 21 *A.P.C.* 161-179 ; T. PETERS, Victimisation, médiation et pratiques orientées vers la médiation, in: CARIO & SALAS, *o.c.*, vol. 1, 203-254; Http://www.enm.justice.fr.

tolérance zéro, l'extension du filet social semble dangereusement en marche, ce que confirme la pratique indiquant que la médiation pénale mord davantage sur les classements sans suite que sur les poursuites elles-mêmes.

b) Les sanctions restauratives

A bien y regarder, des sanctions véritablement restauratives existent également dans l'arsenal des mesures disponibles aux magistrats. Pour bien correspondre à la morphologie des infractions commises, elles sont trop rarement prononcées et insuffisamment encadrées dans leur exécution. Elles sont pourtant de nature à crédibiliser fortement la réponse pénale, aux yeux de tous. Le condamné voit ses efforts récompensés en effectuant réellement les engagements qu'il a pris (restitution, paiement des dommages et intérêts, activités compensatoires diverses, notamment). La victime, en recevant effectivement la réparation, plus ou moins négociée selon les mesures, est apaisée et rassurée, d'autant plus qu'elle bénéficie parallèlement de l'accompagnement psychologique et social que son état nécessite. La communauté sociale dans son ensemble garde confiance dans le système de justice pénale: l'interdit est puni tout en favorisant la (re)socialisation de l'infracteur (la nature et le quantum de la sanction dépendant ainsi du degré de responsabilisation qu'il manifeste); la victime est restaurée dans sa dignité de personne humaine et reçoit réparation des dommages, des traumatismes et répercussions sociales subis; l'harmonie sociale est rétablie et consolidée par la qualité de la réponse pénale qui offre aux intéressés les voies du retour au sein de la communauté humaine.

En ce sens, au stade présentenciel, le contrôle judiciaire peut être ordonné par le juge d'instruction si la personne mise en examen encourt une peine d'emprisonnement correctionnel ou une peine plus grave.[44] Cette mesure présente le premier avantage d'éviter le placement en détention provisoire de l'infracteur, normalement exceptionnel.[45] Le contrôle judiciaire offre surtout, embrassant par là une dimension socio-éducative, du sens à la réponse judiciaire en ce qu'il conduit à responsabiliser l'intéressé dès la commission de la transgression. Concernant les victimes, le contrôle judiciaire socio-éducatif présente un avantage supplémentaire majeur car, parmi les conditions imposées à l'auteur de l'acte, deux d'entre d'elles méritent attention. La première oblige l'infracteur à fournir un cautionnement dont le montant et les délais de versement, en une ou plusieurs fois, sont fixés par le juge d'instruction, compte tenu notamment des ressources de la personne

---

44 V. art. 137 et s., R. 17-1 et s. *C.P.P.*
45 V. art. 144 et s. *C.P.P.*

mise en examen.[46] La seconde l'amène à fournir un cautionnement ou à constituer, dans un délai, pour une période et un montant déterminés par le juge d'instruction, des sûretés personnelles ou réelles destinées notamment à garantir le paiement de la réparation des dommages causés par l'infraction, des restitutions et des amendes. Dorénavant, le juge d'instruction peut décider que les sûretés garantiront dans leur totalité les droits de la victime, le cas échéant par provision.[47]

Au stade du jugement, quelques sanctions sont de nature à renforcer la restauration de la victime. La dispense de peine peut-être prononcée en matière correctionnelle, lorsqu'il apparaît que le reclassement du coupable est acquis, que le dommage causé est réparé et que le trouble résultant de l'infraction a cessé.[48] La combinaison de cette mesure avec le contrôle judiciaire ou une mesure de réparation ordonnée en cours d'instruction à l'égard des mineurs est particulièrement heureuse. Dans les mêmes conditions, concernant plus spécialement les mineurs, la dispense de mesure[49] participe tout autant à la restauration du lien social rompu par l'acte de transgression posé par le mineur. Très judicieusement, le tribunal peut encore, après déclaration de culpabilité, ajourner le prononcé de la peine dans des situations qui récompensent l'investissement de l'infracteur dans la réparation du dommage qu'il a causé : lorsqu'il apparaît que le reclassement du coupable est en voie d'être acquis, que le dommage causé est en voie d'être réparé et que le trouble résultant de l'infraction va cesser.[50]

Le travail d'intérêt général présente aussi ces potentialités restauratives qui donnent du sens à la sanction. Il est prononcé à titre principal ou complémentaire pour les majeurs comme pour les mineurs. L'accord des intéressés est nécessaire et la possibilité de refuser la peine apparaît en ce sens, ici comme en matière de médiation-réparation, la condition de l'acceptation, donc de l'adhésion du condamné. Le T.I.G. remplit bien, en dépit de son aspect contraignant, un rôle de recomposition du tissu social.[51]

---

46 V. art. 138-11° *C.P.P.*

47 V. art. 138-15° *C.P.P.* modifié par la Loi renforçant la protection de la présomption d'innocence et les droits des victimes et l'art 142 nouveau *C.P.P.* qui généralise l'affectation des deux parties du cautionnement ou des sûretés constitués par la personne concernée.

48 V. art. 132-58 à 62 *C.P.P.* et 20-7 al. 1 *Ord. 1945* (mod. L. 1er juill. 1996).

49 V. art. 8 *Ord. 1945* mod. 1995; Comp. art. 132-59 *C.P.P.*; La liberté surveillée d'épreuve, décidée avant jugement sur le fond, procède du même esprit, V. art. 8 al. 8 et 19 al. 2 *Ord. 1945.*

50 Sur l'ajournement simple, V. art. 132-60 et s. *C. pén.* ; sur l'ajournement avec mise à l'épreuve, V. art. 132-63 et s. *C.P.P.*; art. 747-3 et s. *C.P.P.*

51 L'inconvénient majeur de la peine de t.i.g. réside en la sanction de la violation par le condamné des obligations l'accompagnant : emprisonnement de deux ans notam-

Il pourrait être effectué au bénéfice d'un Service d'aide aux victimes comme l'a proposé le Rapport Milliez. L'amende pourrait prendre une connotation restaurative si une partie de son montant était reversée soit au Fonds de garantie d'indemnisation des victimes d'infractions, soit aux Services d'aide aux victimes eux-mêmes (notamment pour assurer les aides matérielles d'urgence).

Les modalités d'exécution de la peine privative de liberté sont susceptibles de favoriser la perspective restaurative de la sanction. Le sursis avec mise à l'épreuve devrait conduire à imposer, parmi les conditions fixées par le juge, l'indemnisation de la victime en vue de réparer en tout ou partie, en fonction de ses facultés contributives, les dommages causés par l'infraction, même en l'absence de décision sur l'action civile.[52] Au cas de peine privative de courte durée (moins d'une année d'emprisonnement), une mesure de semi-liberté peut être ordonnée par le tribunal ou sollicitée par le juge de l'application des peines. Une telle opportunité est heureuse, si pour le moins le principe de proportionnalité est respecté, car l'intéressé continuera son activité professionnelle, ou en acquerra une, consolidant ainsi son insertion sociale. Par les produits du travail exercé, le condamné pourra plus effectivement indemniser la victime des sommes que le tribunal lui a allouées.[53]

Dans le cadre de l'octroi des mesures d'individualisation de la peine privative de liberté, le juge de l'application des peines doit dorénavant attacher la plus grande importance aux réels efforts développés par le condamné pour indemniser la victime. Il ne paraît en effet pas anormal d'en tenir compte pour l'octroi des réductions de peines supplémentaires, de la semi-liberté et du placement à l'extérieur, comme pour l'accès à la libération conditionnelle.[54] Tous ces aspects sont dorénavant introduits au « Plan d'exécution des peines », récemment mis en place dans les établissements pénitentiaires français.[55] Ils participent bien d'une sanction restaurative en ce qu'ils développent le sens de la responsabilité chez le condamné et assurent l'indemnisation de la victime.

Bien évidemment, parallèlement à ces sanctions appliquées au condamné, les victimes doivent toujours bénéficier d'un accompagnement psychologique et social de qualité, si leur situation le justifie. Mais leur prise en

---

ment (art. 434-42 *C.P.P.*.) ; V. également l'art. 132-57 *C. pén.* qui prévoit, de manière beaucoup discutable, que le TIG peut constituer l'épreuve assortissant une peine privative de liberté bénéficiant du sursis.

52 V. art. 132-40 et s. *C.P.P.*, spé. art. 132-45-5° et 13; art. 738 et s. *C.P.P.*

53 V. art. 132-25 et 26 *C.P.P.*; 723 et D 49-1 *C.P.P.*

54 V. art. 721-1 *C..P.P ;* 729 et s.*C.P.P.* et spé. 722-1 nouveau *C.P.P.*

55 V. art. D 116-1 et D 526 nouveaux *C.P.P.* (D. 13 déc. 2000, *J.O.* du 14, p. 19878).

considération dans l'exécution des peines doit s'arrêter là. Il n'apparaît pas du tout opportun de les associer davantage -en tout cas certainement pas de manière systématique- à l'octroi, au contenu et aux modalités d'application de ces sanctions. Ce serait les maintenir abusivement dans un « statut » de victime. Au même titre que leurs proches, les victimes possèdent le droit fondamental et légitime de se restaurer psychologiquement et socialement, sans se voir sans cesse rappeler les circonstances et conséquences de leur(s) victimisation(s) passée(s). Si le procès pénal a pleinement respecter leurs droits à la reconnaissance, à l'accompagnement et à la réparation, le travail de deuil est abouti ou en cours, pour douloureux qu'il soit. L'exécution de la peine demeure alors de la seule compétence des autorités judiciaires et pénitentiaires. Si les moyens dont disposent leurs services et les qualités professionnelles de leurs personnels respectifs sont à la hauteur de leur mission profondément humaine, ils sauront évaluer l'exacte dangerosité des intéressés et prendre les dispositions protectrices nécessaires au moment de la mise en œuvre des mesures d'individualisation.

Tournée vers l'avenir, la justice restaurative permet de rétablir les acteurs dans leur dignité, de les réconcilier dans une reconnaissance mutuelle de nature à (re)vitaliser l'esprit communautaire dans tous les lieux où vivent des êtres humains. Bien sûr, une telle justice restaurative doit demeurer prioritairement soucieuse de la prévention des victimisations, fonction première des sciences criminelles dans leur ensemble. En cas d'échec, la mise en place d'un authentique service public d'aide aux victimes s'impose, composé de professionnels spécialement formés et rompus à l'interdisciplinarité comme au partenariat.

Les convictions de Tony Peters ont fait école en ce sens et son inlassable investissement dans les programmes de formation universitaires nationaux (au sein de l'Université de Leuven) et régionaux (dans le cadre des programmes Erasmus/Socratès, du Certificat européo-canadien de victimologie et du récent *Master in European Criminology* qu'il dirige) - programmes auxquels il a toujours associé l'Université de Pau- est un autre aspect de son œuvre remarquable, toute entière dédiée à la juste cause des victimes.

PART II

ON REFORMING CRIMINAL JUSTICE

REPRESSIVE, RESTORATIVE AND REFLEXIVE CRIMINAL LAW

Beth Grothe Nielsen

Probably one of the most serious gaps in the system is the different perceptions of wrongdoing and how to best treat it.

In the non-Indian community, committing a crime seems to mean that the individual is a bad person and therefore must be punished.

The Indian community view a wrongdoing as a misbehaviour which requires teaching or an illness which requires healing.

Oji-Cree elder

Introduction

Modern "grand theories" on legal evolution and the relationship between law and society do not frequently include criminal law as an examplification. The absence of criminal law in theoretical socio-legal contexts may have something to do with the understanding of criminal law as a legal phenomenon having undergone no significant evolution since the good old days of the classical school. Specific theories on criminal law, on the other hand, are mainly concerned with questions like "What is punishment?", "Why do we punish?" and "How do we legitimize penal sanctions?".

Whether revenge, retribution or general and special prevention are plausible answers to one or all of these questions is highly debatable. However, a basic belief that a certain level of criminalization and punishment is a necessary tool for any society to keep itself together seems to be part of any theoretical justification.

What human acts and omissions are included in the criminal code (and other penal regulations) of a given country depends on diverse historical, political, social and economic factors. In 1984, Vagn Greve, a Danish professor of criminal law, asked whether time had come for a thorough revision of the

Danish Penal Code (Straffelov). He, himself, proposed the abolishment of some old delicts as well as the creation of new ones. At the same time he stated as a matter of course that, in modern criminal policy, not all interests otherwise worthy of protection should (or could) be protected by the legal system and less so by the criminal justice system.[1] A general revision of the Penal Code was not accomplished, however, and today, almost two decades later, different questions seem relevant.

First of all, it may be relevant to ask whether it is actually so obvious for contemporary politicians not to want to include in the penal legislation every interest worthy of protection. Do we rather see a political tendency to the contrary? Is there a tendency to consider almost every type of unwanted behaviour as targets for criminalization and/or increased penalization? Do the media and the politicians mutually reinforce the impression that people's fears can be diminished by legal regulation and their feelings protected by the criminal justice system? These questions have been tentatively answered in the affirmative by Nils Jareborg, a Swedish professor of criminal law.

According to Jareborg, *"the exaggerated belief in incarceration as a solution to social problems expressed by the public and those with political power is in itself a serious criminal policy problem*".[2] (unauthorized translation). Jareborg traces a development from what he terms "a defensive criminal law model", i.e. a model based on classical penal law with its aim of protecting the individual against abuse of power by other individuals as well as by state authorities, and towards what he calls "an offensive criminal law model", i.e. a model for solution of social problems. While the defensive model is characterized by legal principles and due process guarantees, the offensive model may best be described by its (practical) means and consequences.

The offensive criminal justice system is characterized by an increased use of criminalization of acts and behaviour directed against public authorities and the anonymous public and of acts and behaviour causing no actual harm but involving potential future danger. Moral guilt, according to this way of thinking, is sufficient justification for the introduction of new criminal provisions and the definitions of these new crimes are highly unspecific. Moreover, there is a tendency for certain groups of offenders to be treated like enemies rather than fellow human beings. Consequently, a threat of punishment is often the primary means rather than the last resort and it is often launched in relation to peripheral law and order transgressions rather than the

---

1 V. GREVE (1985) Er tiden moden til en ny straffelov? *Juristen*, 271-281.

2 N. JAREBORG (1995) Vilken sorts straffrätt vil vi ha? - Om defensiv och offensiv straffrättspolitik, in D. VICTOR (ed.), *Varning för straff. Om vådan av den nyttiga straffrätten*, 36. Stockholm, Fritzes.

most abominable acts. According to Jareborg, the penal code is implemented for "folk pedagogical" and paternalistic purposes. This leads to "over-criminalization" and extended use of incarceration which result in precarious strain on the justice system and the executive authorities, in weakening of due process principles, in less transparency and predictability, in more discretionary decision-making power to the police, in the use of "war language" by politicians, and in public and media demands for more effective crime prevention measures. More criminalization means more crime to combat. The common but unscientific belief in a direct relation between crime and punishment is logically tied to the assertion that harsher punishment will mean less crime and consequently a demand for harsher punishment will ensue.

According to Jareborg, this theory is supported *"by politicians in particular who want to stand out like warriors at the front of the battle against crime and who think they can do so by changing numbers in the law text by the stroke of a pen"*. (unauthorized translation). Experience will tell, however, that such changes (i.e. increased penal maxima) have no effect on the level of crime in a society. When that becomes clear in practice, the criminal justice system is accused of inefficiency - and the cries for "tough on crime" initiatives start all over again. According to Jareborg, *"the common sense superstition as to the importance of criminalization, harsh punishment, etc., will invariably lead to two things: failure and hypocracy or underachievement and symbolic legislation"*[3]. (unauthorized translation).

A couple of different questions, however, have to do with an emerging counter-movement. There seems to be a growing awareness of the fact that the classical criminal justice system is unable to protect personal and societal interests and to solve those problems which have already been defined as criminal. This awareness includes the experience that involving the criminal justice system in specific cases often adds to the problems, not only for the offender (and his or her family) but also for the victim (and his or her family). The questions to be asked are these: Do we need a completely different way of thinking, a new paradigm? And are there tendencies in that direction? Do we see an evolution in criminal law as a legal phenomenon after all?

In the following sections, the two sets of questions will be illustrated by Danish examples. In summary the questions are as follows: a) Do we experience a development from "defensive" to "offensive" criminal justice and is this in itself a criminal policy problem? b) To what extent are the unintended consequences of criminalization and punishment seen as criminal policy problems and are there traces of a shift of paradigm? Then, we will describe

---

3 JAREBORG, *o.c.*, 31.

the international restorative justice movement, and the last section will tie restorative justice as a theoretical legal form to a general socio-legal theory of reflexive law.

1. Criminalization and punishment as a criminal policy problem

In April 1994, The Danish Supreme Court ruled that a man who knew he was HIV-positive could not be convicted of intentional causing danger to several young women's lives by having had unprotected sexual intercourse with them. Politicians and the media expressed severe indignation of this "lacuna" in the Penal Code and exactly two months later an amendment was carried by Parliament (Folketinget) to the effect that a person who repeatedly exposes another to an infectious, incurable and deadly disease can be sentenced to max. 4 years of imprisonment. Legal experts warned against the speedy treatment of the bill (the Standing Penal Law Committee was not consulted) and the unspecific definition of the criminal act (e.g. "deadly" was explained in an appendix to the bill as "causing death within 10-15 years on average"). Professionals working with AIDS and HIV as a health problem criticized the bill from the point of view that criminalization would counteract voluntary HIV-testing. In 2001 the provision had to be amended again. In the meantime, life expectancy of HIV-positive people has been expanded because of new treatment possibilities and death will not as a rule occur within 10-15 years. Again, a specific case was the trigger.

In 1995, media coverage of the abduction and attempted rape by a young man (twice a sexual recidivist) of an 11-year-old girl in riding-outfit (this detail was salient to almost all commentators) resulted in new legislation including the extended possibility of indeterminate sentencing and the introduction of treatment programmes for sex offenders. Again, the amendment was hastened through Parliament and the Standing Committee was not consulted.

Another example of this tendency has to do with a "war" that broke out in 1996 between two groups of bikers: Hells Angels and Bandidos. In September, a minor rocket was fired by members of one biker group against the other group's "castle" by which attack others than bikers were endangered. Three weeks later a bill was passed by Parliament. This time the provision was criticized for criminalizing potential victims, viz. persons whose presence in particular houses with biker connection might attract an attack and thus put innocent neighbours and passers-by in danger too. A police warning to leave the house is a precondition for conviction. Non-compliance may lead to max. 2 years of imprisonment.

Violence among young men on Friday and Saturday nights in certain city quarters with many pubs, bars and discoteques continues to be high on the agenda of Danish politicians, especially right wing ones. Several times, they have succeeded in carrying through amendments by changing figures like Jareborg said, viz. by altering the maximum penalties in the Penal Code. Other types of violence, like for instance the domestic variety, do not get similar attention.

In general, the focus is much more on unwanted behaviour among children and youths than on socially damaging adult undertakings like corporate and white collar crime, tax evasion, environmental pollution, etc. One of the latest Danish innovations concerning criminalization of young persons' behaviour is the prohibition of wearing masks and hoods in connection with (lawful) demonstrations. According to the preparatory works of the law, this provision is meant to provide the police with better tools, before unrest and disorder erupt, to prevent violence, vandalism and other crimes. That is why the prohibition is not limited to include only participants in the demonstration but also spectators following the crowd. Even a person walking alone, if it can be established that he or she is on the way to a public meeting, procession etc. and found in possession of pieces of clothing that are deemed suitable for masking, may be punished. Masked persons may be arrested and searched on the spot and the relevant clothes confiscated. The police will not have to wait for disturbance or riot to occur or for the individual masked person to commit vandalism etc., and evidence of any further intent is not required.

To varying degrees, these examples show the tendencies described by Jareborg. The HIV-provision and the increased possibility of indeterminate sentencing of sex offenders are expressions of hasty legislation based on extreme single cases with morally blameworthy perpetrators from whom everybody can dissociate. There are no second thoughts as to the necessity and appropriateness of neo-criminalization or increase in the available sanctioning options. Legal initiatives related to specific cases of sexual misconduct are extremely well suited for the profiling of politicians as efficient and hard-hitting in the war against evil. It is a clear example of symbolic legislation.

The biker-provision and the prohibition of masks show the tendency to criminalize conduct which might involve future danger even if the individual situation does not develop into harming anybody or damaging anything. They are extreme examples of criminalization of remote harm or damage, the purpose of which is not primarily to prevent danger but to make police work easier and to promote law and order. They are characterized by providing the police -on the spot (the mask prohibition) or in advance (the biker-provision)- with the power to decide whether a particular conduct shall be punishable or not. The potential perpetrators -bikers, socalled autonomous groups or BZs, second generation immigrants and guest workers, street gangs, etc.- are well within the description by Jareborg of certain groups of youth being considered and treated like enemies rather than citizens. Neither the principle of legality nor due process considerations play any important role in this type of legislation.

The repeatedly increased level of punishment for violence indicates that the politicians actually hold an unscientific belief in a direct relation between a high level of penal sanctions and a low level of violence. In spite of a provable change in penal practice and the fact that, comparatively, many more cases of violence in Denmark than in other European countries end up with an unconditional prison sentence, the political right wing continues to demand harsher punishment. Lately, it has become legitimate to declare the purpose of punishment *not* to be the prevention of violence but to be the attention to the sense of justice of the victims and the public. Even the concept "revenge" has become accepted as "house-manners". In addition, the debate is almost exlusively concerned with violence among young men in public places (the so-called meaningless street violence). Consequently, there is a pattern of elderly middle-class men waging war against rootless youths without any visible association to the establishment. The paternalistic purpose and the untenable strain on the criminal justice system that Jareborg is talking about, are obvious aspects of the whole business.

These examples seem to justify the following answer to the first set of questions posed in the introduction: *Yes, there is a development from "defensive" to "offensive" criminal justice and the belief in criminalization, repression and punishment has become so strong as to constitute a criminal policy problem of its own.* But a reservation must be added: the new criminalizations and increased penalizations are mainly directed towards certain groups and certain interests. It is not a general tendency.

2. The unintended consequences of the criminal justice system as a criminal policy problem

When looking at the practical manifestations of the criminal justice system and at the conduct and self-perception of its professional agents, one might get the impression that the system is functioning in a social vacuum, uninterested in wider social issues and independent of the purposes and practices of other social institutions. Isolation from and independence of other functions in society being the very characteristics of a traditional criminal justice system, however, this impression is not surprising. This is how the system is supposed to be and made to work. There has never been any intention that the handling of a criminal case should include other considerations and concerns than the system-internal ones, i.e. those which are relevant and rational to the system itself. There are countless examples of the fact that referral of a case to criminal prosecution will cost resources and cause difficulties for the case management of other public authorities or put them off completely until the criminal case has come to an end. This is not a problem for the criminal justice system. It is a problem for these other authorities.

It is in the nature of things that police investigation, prosecution, conviction and incarceration cause difficulties for the offender. In a sense, he or she has got him- or herself only to blame for the situation. Whether the case creates other problems than the intended ones and whether other persons (e.g. family members) are hit by indirect consequences does not concern the criminal justice system.

A number of criminal cases have to do with one person having abused or invaded another person's physical or economical integrity. The background may be an existing conflict which triggers an assault or the assault may cause a situation which is now experienced as a conflict, at least by the person later to be defined a crime victim. The social reality in all its complexity, of which the single criminalized act often represents only a fragment -in the eyes of the combatants maybe even an inferior one- cannot be contained within the reality construction of the criminal justice system. The system will fragmentize and simplify the situation until one bite is left which may fit into a reality defined in advance. From a complicated set of circumstances a so-called *actus reus* which is consistent with a pre-defined actus reus in the Penal Code is constructed. The social event which a crime also represents is not understood in its specific context, i.e. in connection with a number of diverse human, cultural, social and economic events, situations, circumstances and conditions.

Time and again, it has been stressed in works on the functions of the criminal justice system that a criminal case is not between the offender and the victim as parties. It is between the offender -usually represented by an attorney- and the state represented by the prosecutor. The victim has been relegated to the side line and his or her only possible role it that of a witness. In other words: *"Victims are mere footnotes of the criminal justice process"*.[4] The very fact that the conflict is acted out within the confines of a criminal court often creates additional burdens and difficulties for the victim, economically as well as personally, and the conflict will often continue after the case. But

4 H. ZEHR (1990) *Changing Lenses.* Scottdale: Herald Press.

criminal justice including the system that administers criminal justice is different from almost any other type of legal justice in that it is not prepared for solving conflicts. The results of a criminal procedure, when a person is found guilty and sentenced to be punished, do not benefit anybody but may serve as a (temporary) satisfaction of an instinctive, emotional need felt by the victim and the public. Although the latest decade has seen significant attempts to alter the situation for the victim, this picture is basically still valid.

The following are examples of problems which may arise for the case management in other systems, the additional burdens which may be experienced by victims, the damage and harm which may not be repaired and the conflicts which may not be solved.

Children and adolescents are often hit especially hard by criminal justice decisions as a consequence of either their own behaviour, their victimization by others or their parents' crimes in general.

In Denmark, children below the age of 15 cannot be punished. In principle, therefore, the criminal justice system has nothing to do with cases of children's misbehaviour, be they ever so serious like murder for instance. The police, however, may arrest and detain a child to the extent necessary before the case is transferred to the social services authorities for further interference. The social services authorities alone have the competency and the criminal justice system cannot block appropriate measures.

Young persons between 15 and 18 are a different matter. With a few exceptions they are subject to the same rules as are adults when they have committed crimes. It is for the criminal justice agencies autonomously to decide whether and in what way other social institutions should be involved. The social services authorities have no power to force help and assistance if the criminal justice system decide on a prison sentence. There has alway been an ideological/political struggle between ideas of punishment and ideas of care when the issue is children and youths whose problems include their own transgression of rules and regulations. The very existence of an age of criminal responsibility (in Denmark: 15 years) contributes to the creation of a situation where a child below the age of 15 with serious social and personal problems (including his or her own "criminal" conduct) will mainly be considered a "victim" in need of care while that same child, as soon as he or she is 15, will almost automatically be regarded as an "offender" in need of punishment and correction, perhaps disguised as "consequential interference", confinement in a secure youth facility, etc. For instance, it is difficult for the criminal justice system to identify the 16-year-old rapist with the boy who was exposed to sexual abuse by his father during his entire childhood. The criminal justice system, according to its own rationale, decides what is to become of the young offender. The evaluation will rest first and foremost on the cricumstances of the rape and only secondly on his need for treatment.

Many children and adolescents are victims of violence and sexual abuse by adults who are close to them, be they parents and step parents or caretakers like teachers and sports coaches. During the last decade or so, sexual abuse in particular has got on the media and the political agenda. The common reaction -as mentioned above- is the creation of new crimes and increased levels of punishment. At the same time, a current adjustment takes place in the way these cases are handled by the criminal justice system. Due process and legal safeguards for the alleged perpetrator are put center stage, for good reasons. That is the way it has to be when the system is about punishment. Lately, the Danish Supreme Court ruled that the suspect is entitled to be present with his attorney in an adjoining monitor room while the police is videotaping an investigative interview with the child, if that videotape is later to replace the examination in chief of the child as a witness in court. At times, the debate on children's credibility and suggestibility has been extremely polarized and unpleasant and one result has been a reluctance to let a child have psychological treatment until after the investigation is completed, the decision about prosecution or discharge has been taken and a court hearing, if any, has taken place. Otherwise, defence attorneys will often claim that the child's testimony has been contaminated by the psychologist's preconceived opinion that this is a sexually abused child.

While the criminal justice system is reluctant to put too much weight on children's testimonies as the basis for conviction, at the same time it supplies a guilty person with strong incentives to denial. The actual consequences of a conviction as well as the formal legal guarantees are pulling in that direction. Punishment and incarceration are extremely frightening prospects to most sex offenders and very good reasons for not confessing. The rules of due process which include the right to silence and to lie without penal consequences (contrary to the position of a child witness) do not invite to telling the truth. In addition, the role of the defence attorney is to raise doubts about the guilt of the accused. Although there is supposed to exist a principle about the protection of the innocent *as well as* the conviction of the guilty, the criminal justice process is by and large the poorest legal process at all for fact finding, for reaching the material truth. In reality, the purpose of a criminal case is not to find the truth but to establish what can and cannot be proved. If the defendant does not plead guilty and there is reasonable doubt, he or she must be acquitted even if he or she did actually commit the crime. This is the difference between real guilt and legal guilt.

Consequently, the criminal justice system, if involved, frequently does not meet a child's need for the perpetrator to admit the abuse, to apologize and take full responsibility. It does the opposite. An even more serious problem, however, is the fact that many children and parents never come forward with their knowledge about abuse because they do not want the criminal justice system to be mobilized. Either they do not want the perpetrator to be punished or they do not want to live through a criminal case with all its unpleasant examinations, interrogations, etc. Moreover, many children have been intimidated to be silent by a reference to the very existence of the criminal justice system. That is true for cases of incest in the family as well as for cases of paedophilia in schools and children's institutions. Children are made to believe that they are the ones to be punished or to be responsible for the imprisonment of their fathers or caretakers.

Social services authorities, school and institution principals, etc., have problems too with the fact that sexual abuse of children is criminalized and they have mixed experiences with reporting cases to the police. Social services find themselves deprived of their ability to assist the child and the family when the police, the prosecutor and the court have taken over, and they often refrain from reporting. What is more problematic still is the fact that staff at children's institutions as well as parents and children themselves may decide not to involve the social services because they know or believe that these authorities will make immediate police reports. The result may be victimized children getting no help and boys in particular ending up becoming perpetrators of abuse, cf. the above mentioned almost automatic shift of attitude -and thereby treatment- of such boys when they reach the age of 15.

A different group of children who are hit hard by the unintended consequences of the criminal justice system are those with parents who are arrested, prosecuted, convicted and incarcerated for their own crimes. If both parents are involved or if it is the question of a single parent, as a rule, the children will be placed in an institution. A Danish research report shows that children experience to be treated as if the parents do not exist any more and that they do not have contact with the parents for a long time. The children become afraid that the parents do not care since they do not turn up. If one parent, typically the mother, is left behind while the other parent is in prison, she will face big problems. Because the income of the father, who is often the bread-winner, has disappeared the social services may have to step in. Public expenses to cover a child's placement in a children's institution, social aid to the maintenance of a home, etc., which are occasioned by the interference of the criminal justice system into a family's life are not incalculated in the total budget of the criminal justice system and thereby in the financial burden carried by the tax payers. The personal problems and psychological traumas which may result for children of incarcerated parents are totally ignored. In spite of the fact that "the social heritage" is a well established fact and methods to break it are discussed, the criminal justice system is by no means obliged or designed to include such considerations.

At best, adult victims do not profit either from the involvement of the criminal justice system, at worst they get further problems from the involvement. It has for a long time been realized that victims of rape often do not report to the police for fear of being distrusted and badly treated. Recently, however, a Danish legal expert pointed out that victims of economic and corporate crime may have the same reasons for not reporting. The criminal proceedings can be an ordeal which, in the end, will be of little help regarding the possibilities of economic compensation from the offender.

In many cases, it is not quite obvious who is the "victim" and who the "offender".[5] "Victim vs. offender" may be described as *"an arbitrary contradiction between artificial concepts"*.[6] One example concerning the sex offender who is or has been exposed to sexual abuse himself, i.e. the same person containing both aspects, has already been mentioned. The many cases of violence where it is more or less accidental who of two or more combatants will end up being labelled one or the other may highlight the point. The system, however, is based on the fiction that these labels are representing reality: "offender" is the one who was violent and "victim" is the innocent one. In actual fact, the latter may be the first to call the police and therefore in a better position to achieve victim status. Nevertheless, this is exactly the type of violence high on the political agenda in Denmark.

A rare exception from this pattern was heard in a Danish criminal court in 1999. A protracted disagreement between two neighbours about the property-line, the destruction of a tree, the presence of a wheelbarrow in the wrong place, the exchange of diverse personal insults, etc., culminated at Christmas time in a fist fight, a split eyebrow, a black eye and the summoning of the police. *Both* men were charged with violence, *both* men were fined 1.800 kr. and 1.500 kr. respectively, and in case of non-payment sentenced to lenient imprisonment for 6 and 5 days respectively. In addition, one man was made to pay damage (773,95 kr.). After consultation with their attorneys both men accepted the court's decision. A case like that gives rise to a couple of questions, among them whether it is reasonable to spend the resources of the justice system on a banal neighbour dispute only because the police was called

---

5 E. FATTAH (1994) *The Interchangeable Roles of Victim and Victimizer,* HEUNI Papers No. 3. Helsinki: HEUNI.

6 B.G. NIELSEN (1998) Forbryder vs offer: En kunstig modsætning mellem arbitrære begreber?, *Nordisk Tidsskrift for Kriminalvidenskab* 229-240.

and one or two ingredients of the dispute could be subsumed as crimes defined by the Penal Code. The basic issue, however, is whether the underlying conflict was solved. Contrary to many similar cases, the criminal justice system did not use the black and white labels of "victim" and "offender" but the muddier one of "they're in it together". This innovation might contribute to a de-escalation of the disagreement as opposed to what is often the case: an escalation because one of the combatants is deemed "right", the other one "wrong", and the ground is prepared for new clashes. But still the issue remains whether the conflict could have been solved in a way less expensive for society and more constructive for the concerned parties.

The answer to the second set of questions in the introduction will have to be: *The awareness of the inability of the criminal justice system to protect personal and societal interests and to solve problems which are habitually referred to crime policy initiatives, is sporadic, uncoordinated and as a rule implicitly expressed. There is a need for a general new way of thinking rather than for the introduction of new crimes and increased levels of punishment.*

3. Changing lenses - a shift of paradigm?

Throughout the Western world, during the last two or three decades, alternative models of tackling conflicts and problems, usually defined as crimes and met with punishment and repression, have emerged. In his book *Changing Lenses*, Howard Zehr, one of the pioneers in this development, describes the dichotomy between two different visions of the relation between crime and justice:[7]

- Retributive Justice: Crime is a violation of the state, defined by lawbreaking and guilt. Justice determines blame and administers pain in a contest between the offender and the state directed by systematic rules.
- Restorative Justice: Crime is a violation of people and relationships. It creates obligations to make things right. Justice involves the victim, the offender, and the community in a search for solutions which promote repair, reconciliation, and reassurance.

Denmark has been slow in grasping these new visions. Occasionally, however, a critical exposure of the first model, the model of retributive or repressive criminal law, is presented. In what he terms a *"meaningful dialogue about the purpose of criminal proceedings"*, a defence attorney describes the demand for understanding some elementary conditions having to do with

7 ZEHR, *o.c.*, 181.

"human intelligence and emotions".[8] As far as emotions are concerned, Larsen claims that we human beings have a disastrous desire for punishment which, behind all the nice explaining away, dictates the human behaviour that is displayed in the criminal justice system. Punishment is seen by Larsen as an emotionally conditioned reaction, provoked by an emotionally upsetting social behaviour, a reaction which may come from the victim him- or herself or from others on behalf of the victim and the rest of us. According to Larsen, this reaction can be described as a delayed aggression demanding its own victims and being vented in the penal measures. To make it perfectly clear what is at stake, Larsen borrows an expression from sex life in his labelling of the criminal proceedings as *"a ritualized attempt to evoke a social orgasm (which, in cases of victimless crime, is much like an autoerotic satisfaction)".*[9] (unauthorized translation).

It is unusual to meet one of the system's own agents putting the system as such to debate. As a rule, even defence attorneys seem satisfied to complain about a perceived lack of legal guarantees for the suspect/defendant and of "equality of arms" between the defence and the prosecutor. Visions and new ideas do not come up easily from inside the establishment. Neither have Danish politicians nor legal experts proposed any real paradigm shift. A pilot project concerning victim-offender mediation in so-called conflict resolution councils as a supplement to punishment in minor misdemeanour cases is the only relevant initiative so far.

The situation is different in many other countries, in Scandinavia and the rest of Europe, as well as in the USA and Canada. It is fair to speak of an international movement with various labels covering the same basic doubt, frustration, dissatisfaction and rejection regarding traditional penal measures as societal reactions to "violation of people and relationships". Concepts like "restorative",[10] "reparative", "transformative"[11] "reintegrative",[12] "peacemaking",[13] "healing" and other types of "non-retributive" or "non-repressive" justice are used.

The Canadian Church Council on Justice and Corrections, in a publication

8 B.U. LARSEN (1999) Noget om strafprocessens formål, *Juristen* 81-85.

9 *Ibid.*, 83.

10 B. GALAWAY & J. HUDSON (1996) (eds.), *Restorative Justice: International Perspectives.* Amsterdam: Kugler Publications.

11 R. MORRIS (1995) *Penal Abolition - the practical choice.* Toronto: Canadian Scholars Press Inc.

12 J. BRAITHWAITE (1989) *Crime, Shame and Reintegration.* Melbourne: Cambridge University Press.

13 H.E. PEPINSKY & R. QUINNEY (1991) (eds.), *Criminology as Peacemaking.* Bloomington/ Indianapolis: Indiana University Press.

from 1996, is asking for something called "satisfying justice". This publication which was produced with the support of the Correctional Service of Canada stresses the fact that Canadians are facing a crisis in the justice system: prison populations are soaring; costs are no longer affordable; yet people are feeling less safe and secure. What is needed is *"a response to crime that takes victims seriously and helps them to heal, a response that calls offenders to account and deals with them effectively, a response that "gets tough" on the causes of crime and does something about them"*.[14] The publication contains a convincing description of what is not satisfying justice and a listing of justice initiatives across Canada and abroad that attempt to repair harm, attend to related needs and avoid or significantly reduce the use of custody.

Being one of the trail-blazing countries Canada, in 1996, introduced additional sentencing goals in the Criminal Code (section 718.1), viz. "to contribute to (....) the maintenance of a just, peaceful and safe society (....) by one or more of the following objectives: (....) (d) to assist in rehabilitating offenders; (e) to provide reparation for harm done to victims and the community; and (f) to promote a sense of responsibility in offenders, and acknowledgement of the harm done to victims and the community". According to section 718.2(e) "all available sanctions other than imprisonment that are reasonable in the circumstances should be considered for all offenders (....)". In its decision R v. Gladue of 1999,[15] the Supreme Court of Canada interpreted section 718.2(e) as containing not only the traditional sentencing goals such as deterrence, denunciation and rehabilitation, but "new" restorative goals.[16]

The programmes, projects and services that are being launched under one of the above mentioned labels seem to have as a common characteristic that they try to give back the conflict behind the crime or caused by the crime to the directly involved parties (cf. "conflict as property"[17]), to minimize the damaging effects of the conflict itself or of the handling of the conflict and, at best, to create a basis for future peace and quiet between the parties and in the community. The initiatives may have more or less formal structure and varying degrees of interference and control by public authorities. They may be established by private and voluntary organisations or by justice agencies as alternatives to the criminal justice proceedings. Mediation is now integrated in

---

14 Church Council on Justice and Corrections (1996) *Satisfying Justice*. Ottawa: Church Council on Justice and Corrections.

15 R.v. GLADUE, 1999, 133 C.C.C. (3d) 385 (S.C.C.).

16 K. ROACH & J. RUDIN (2000) Gladue: The judicial and political reception of a promising decision, *Canadian Journal of Criminology* 355-388.

17 N. CHRISTIE (1977) Conflict as Property, 17(1) *British Journal of Criminology* 1-15.

many European (criminal) justice systems,[18] partly because of activities by the Council of Europe in its Recommendations Nos. R (85)11 and R (99)19. The same is true for meetings -or confrontations if you like- between victims and offenders, agreements between the parties on reparation and restitution, circle sentencing, family group conferencing, community sentencing panels and healing ceremonies, some of which are modelled on aboriginal peoples' conflict resolution traditions.

These options exist in particular when the victim is an individual like in cases of violence and sexual assault and a number of property crimes, i.e. the majority of penal law cases. However, according to their proponents, these ideas may be extended to situations where the victim is a corporation, an institution or society as such and to so-called victimless crimes, if only one starts thinking along untraditional lines.

"Restorative justice" seems be the established common denominator at present. Those advocating the ideas and the practical initiatives, however, often do not present a definition or theory of restorative justice. If they do, they do so primarily by saying what restorative justice is *not* rather than defining what it actually *is*. According to Bernd-Dieter Meier, professor of criminal law at the University of Hanover, this may be one of the reasons why there is much scepticism among criminal justice practitioners as far as restorative justice is concerned.[19] Meier quotes a definition by Tony Marshall: *"Restorative justice is a process whereby all the parties with a stake in a particular offence come together to resolve collectively how to deal with the aftermath of the offence and its implications for the future".*

This definition is criticized by Meier for not saying who is entitled to participate and especially for not clarifying how restorative justice can be destinguished from traditional, retributive justice. Instead of a definition describing the procedural character of restorative justice, Meier proposes to include in the definition what the offender is supposed to do. His own definition, therefore, reads as follows:[20] *"Restorative justice is the process whereby the offender voluntarily and autonomously accepts his or her responsibility for the offence and eliminates the consequences by positive, social-constructive activities".*

These *"positive, social-constructive activities" are contrasted with the "negative, social-destructive acts (i.e. the infliction of punishment), the*

---

18 I. AERTSEN & T. PETERS (1998) Mediation for Reparation: The Victim's Perspective, 6(2) *European Journal of Crime, Criminal Law and Criminal Justice* 106-124.

19 B.D. MEIER (1998) Restorative Justice - A New Paradigm in Criminal Law?, 6(2) *European Journal on Crime, Criminal Law and Criminal* Justice 125-139.

20 *Ibid.*

endurance of which is generally expected from the offender". Meier finds it important to distance oneself from the narrow conception that restorative justice is only relevant in cases of "conflict" between two individuals and he is critical of those authors who *"simply refer to Nils Christie's remarks of 1977 about 'conflict as property' - as if this referral alone would explain everything".*[21] According to Meier, the use of the word "conflict" is confusing in this relation. The definition must start from the fact that a crime has been committed which should be the background for restorative justice. By connecting to the criminal justice legislation, the rules of police investigation, due process and legal guarantees, etc., and the control by public authorities are retained. According to this view, restorative justice is not part a of civil law or an independent new legal discipline but a new branch of or extension to the criminal justice system.

The discussion about restorative justice as "an auxiliary arm to the police" or a brand new paradigm has been actualized in Norway where the "conflict resolution councils" were launched in 1981 as a pilot project under the auspices of the Ministry of Social Services but ended up recently as a regular part of the criminal justice reaction options. This development seems to be an example of the criminal justice system's ability to transform alternative ideas so they fit into the establishment and develop into "net-widening" rather than constitute a truly new, constructive creation. However, no matter how they are defined and how closely or loosely they are tied to the existing criminal justice system, the actual restorative justice programmes and projects represent ideas that mean a challenge to the primitive, repressive type of law that is contemporary criminal law.

4. Reflections on theories about law

Meier correctly points out that although the proponents of "restorative justice" are often speaking about a paradigm shift, their writings tend to be short of theory.[22] The movement is oriented towards practical issues and most of what has been written has to do with specific projects and programmes or criticism of them.[23] It turns out, however, that *"restorative justice"* has interesting traits

21 *Ibid.*

22 *Ibid.*

23 H. MESSMER & H.U OTTO (1992) (eds.), *Restorative Justice on Trial.* Dordrecht: Kluwer Academic Publishers; M.S. UMBREIT (1994) *Victim Meets Offender: The Impact of Restorative Justice & Mediation.* Monsey NY: Criminal Justice Press; GALAWAY & HUDSON, *o.c.*

in common with the theory on *"reflexive elements in modern law"* or a *"new 'evolutionary' stage of law ... in which law becomes a system for the coordination of action within and between semi-autonomous social subsystems"*, launched by Gunther Teubner in his attempt to develop a synthesis between the "neo-evolutionary theories about law" in the works of Jürgen Habermas and Niklas Luhman in Germany on the one hand, and Philippe Nonet and Philip Selznick in the USA on the other.[24] Teubner's theory on "reflexive law" evoked much interest and debate in Scandinavia in the 1980s and early 1990s. Internationally, the theory may since have been replaced by other (post-modernist) ways of explaining legal phenomena. Still it seems relevant as a framework for the development of an analysis of the differences and struggles between the two types of criminal justice: repressive and restorative/reparative, thereby creating the contours of a theory of "restorative justice" -embryonic as it must be in the present context. A brief introduction of the historic development of legal forms as Teubner sees it[25] is necessary.

In the traditional form, criminal law and the established criminal justice system are mainly repressive. *Repressive law* can be seen as the oldest form of law in the true sense of the law concept. Repressive law has developed during the transition from a segmented society based on kinship relations with no state structure as such, into a stratified society with a political order and institutionalized court procedures. Modern criminal law, moreover, has incorporated certain aspects of *autonomous law*, i.e. the form of law being developed in a functionally differentiated market society and characterized by legal professionalization, rule-orientation and due process principles (cf. Nils Jareborg's defensive criminal law model mentioned in the introduction). Now the role of the state is to guarantee the citizens' freedom from undue state intervention, to mark certain guidelines for behaviour in "the marketplace" and to establish law and order. In Denmark, this development which culminated around 1849 with the introduction of a democratic constitution has been called *"the happy moment of the 'Rechtstaat'"*.[26] However, the development did not stop by then. Especially from around the 1950s the interventionist welfare state has been implementing law as a means to achieve well defined social and economic goals. Such law will tend to include a solution or answer to societal

24 G. TEUBNER (1983) Substantive and Reflexive Elements in Modern Law, 17(2) *Law & Society Review* 239-285.

25 *Ibid.*

26 J. DALBERG-LARSEN (1988) Lige linjer, cirkler, trekanter eller spiraler i rettens og samfundets udvikling, in: A. BORN et al. (eds.), *Refleksiv ret,* 177. København: Nyt fra Samfundsvidenskaberne.

problems and must, therefore, be very general on the one hand and very detailed on the other. At the same time, there will be less emphasis on formal legal guarantees for the citizens and more emphasis on regulation of procedures for the decision-making authorities. This legal form has been known as *responsive law* and is legitimized by its orientation towards material goals cherished by a vast majority of citizens. Typical examples are environmental law and social services legislation. Responsive law, according to this theory, is the necessary form of law if a highly developed modern capitalistic market society of the welfare state variety is to function.

As already mentioned, contemporary criminal law can be described as repressive law with added aspects of autonomous law. Lately, however, responsive tendencies may be emerging. A Danish example could be the prohibition of the wearing of masks (cf. Nils Jareborg's offensive criminal law model) with its shortage of legality, absence of due process considerations and wide discretionary police authority. In addition, this piece of criminal legislation is directed towards a legitimate goal: the maintenance of law and order (by repressive means).

The question is whether this responsive form of law has actually made the welfare state work. According to many commentators, detailed regulation and state intervention into still more areas of life have contributed considerably to an increasing inability or unwillingness among people to solve their own problems. Feelings that state authorities are treating people as they choose seem widespread. The conflicts in society are not solved by more rules prescribing a given material result. Legal material regulation or criminalization of every social conflict does not constitute a road ahead. Therefore, formal legal frameworks for citizens' participation and self-government, negotiation mechanisms rather than objectives fixed in advance etc. are introduced. In Teubner's terminology, this tendency to formalize procedures for achieving - not pre-fixed material results but- results reflecting needs in other subsystems than the one in which the decision was taken, is called *reflexive law*. When Teubner coined his theory at the beginning of the 1980s, he saw only tiny traces of reflexive elements in modern law. In a way, his theory was primarily an attempt at the time to describe a necessary prospective type of law.

Jørgen Dalberg-Larsen, a Danish professor of legal theory, considers reflexive law primarily to be a legal form *"which can sustain a development towards (....) self-government rather than increased regulation by the market, (....) where the state endeavours to create a type of regulation that directs control away from itself and into the community. (....) Decisive for success may be partly whether the state will actually stand back and partly whether there are people out there to take over. (....) Experience suggests that the state and its many institutions have difficulty letting go of the power once bestowed on them. And there are many indications that the wish for self-government must come from the people if a situation of true self-government is to result".*[27] (unauthorized translation).

Today, almost twenty years after Teubner launched his theory on reflexive law, it may be stated that repressive criminal law has failed in a lot of respects, that it does not contribute to a decrease in society's level of conflict (on the contrary, rather) and that it must apparently give up when faced with "law and order" issues. The addition of responsive elements (and the ensuing abandonment of the positive aspects of autonomous law, e.g. the due process principles) that has emerged in Denmark, especially in the 1990s, has not been of much assistance. The conflict between the tendencies to increased penalization and new criminalizations on the one hand and a growing frustration of the impotence and unintended side effects of the criminal justice system on the other, should give rise to a thorough debate on how we as a society can and will tackle "the crime problem".

The international restorative justice movement represents a legal form much like Teubner's reflexive law. In combination with Dalberg-Larsen's remarks quoted just above on what may be accomplished by this legal form and his considerations and preconditions, the contours are appearing of a prolific new theoretical/analytical basis for -if not quite a shift of paradigm- then probably a new perspective on criminal law: a reflexive/restorative justice system. Accordingly, a definition could read as follows: *"A formalized legal framework for the establishment of an open communication between the perpetrator (of an infraction on another person's integrity or protected rights or on the protected rights of the community) on the one hand, and the victim (if an individual) as well as other persons with legitimate interests and representatives for the local community on the other, with the purpose to give the perpetrator incentives and possibilities to undertake relevant social-constructive activities, including the restoration of inflicted damages, and to give the victim means to start on a healing journey."* Or, with Teubner's words[28]: *"[A] system for the coordination of action within and between semi-autonomous social subsystems".*

---

27 DALBERG-LARSEN, *o.c.*, 190.
28 TEUBNER, *o.c.*, 242.

References

Aertsen, Ivo & Peters, Tony (1998) Mediation for Reparation: The Victim's Perspective, 6(2) *European Journal of Crime, Criminal Law and Criminal Justice* 106-124.

Braithwaite, John (1989) *Crime, Shame and Reintegration*. Melbourne: Cambridge University Press.

Christie, Nils (1977) Conflict as Property, 17(1) *British Journal of Criminology* 1-15.

Dalberg-Larsen, Jørgen (1988) Lige linjer, cirkler, trekanter eller spiraler i rettens og samfundets udvikling, in: Born, A. et al. (eds.), *Refleksiv ret*. København: Nyt fra Samfundsvidenskaberne.

Fattah, Ezzat A. (1994) *The Interchangeable Roles of Victim and Victimizer*, HEUNI Papers No. 3. Helsinki: HEUNI.

Galaway, Burt & Joe Hudson (1996) (eds.), *Restorative Justice: International Perspectives*. Amsterdam: Kugler Publications.

Greve, Vagn (1985) Er tiden moden til en ny straffelov?, *Juristen* 271-281.

Jareborg, Nils (1995) Vilken sorts straffrätt vil vi ha? - Om defensiv och offensiv straffrätts-politik, in: Victor, Dag (ed.), *Varning för straff. Om vådan av den nyttiga straffrätten*. Stockholm: Fritzes.

Larsen, Bent Unmack (1999) Noget om strafprocessens formål, *Juristen*, 81-85.

Meier, Bernd-Dieter (1998) Restorative Justice - A New Paradigm in Criminal Law?, 6(2) *European Journal on Crime, Criminal Law and Criminal Justice* 125-139.

Messmer, Heinz & Hans-Uwe Otto (1992) (eds.), *Restorative Justice on Trial*. Dordrecht: Kluwer Academic Publishers.

Morris, Ruth (1995) *Penal Abolition - the practical choice*. Toronto: Canadian Scholars' Press Inc.

Nielsen, Beth Grothe (1998) Forbryder vs. offer: En kunstig modsætning mellem arbitrære begreber?, *Nordisk Tidsskrift for Kriminalvidenskab* 229-240.

Pepinsky, Harold E. & Quinney, Richard (1991) (eds.), *Criminology as Peacemaking*. Bloomington/Indianapolis: Indiana University Press.

Roach, Kent & Rudin, Jonathan (2000) Gladue: The judicial and political reception of a promising decision, *Canadian Journal of Criminology* 355-388.

Teubner, Gunther (1983) Substantive and Reflexive Elements in Modern Law, 17(2) *Law & Society Review* 239-285.

Umbreit, Mark S. (1984) *Victim Meets Offender: The Impact of Restorative Justice & Mediation.* Monsey NY: Criminal Justice Press.
Zehr, Howard (1990) *Changing Lenses.* Scottdale: Herald Press.

THE VICTIM IN CRIMINAL LAW - ON THE WAY FROM AN OFFENDER-RELATED TO A VICTIM-RELATED CRIMINAL JUSTICE?

Frieder Dünkel

Introduction: A victim-related criminal policy - a new myth?

The crisis in the paradigm of resocialisation and the development of victimology as a scientific discipline have contributed to welcome improvements in the protection of victims, which, however, also entail certain dangerous aspects. For the movement towards the perspective of the victim has partially been accompanied by a move away from the offender. This has been coupled with ever intensifying general-preventive patterns of argument and an emphasis on "law and order" which culminated in the demand that the offender should be punished more severely, in particular in view of the injury suffered by the victim. As examples may be quoted the final report in 1982 of a commission set up by President Reagan, which demanded a relaxation of the requirements for ordering pre-trial detention, and the elimination of parole from prison under the "banner of victim protection".[1] The insights gained in the course of victimological research into the need for protecting the victim's interests have also stimulated tendencies to impose more severe sanctions on the offender as is shown clearly, e.g., by concepts such as "incapacitation" in the United States.

For this reason, a differentiated approach is called for. This approach should carefully take into account the implications of an intensified emphasis on the victim in both criminal law and criminal procedure. An expansion of the rights of victims might entail the withdrawal of the state and hence the "privatisation of criminal law", the effect of which would not necessarily always be to the benefit of the victim. The questions arising in the discussion on mediation projects as to the constitutionality of the procedure, the protection of victims (and offenders) against even indirect compulsion to participate in conciliation procedures[2] show that regarding a

1 See President's Task Force on Victims of Crime 1982, cited by Th. WEIGEND (1989) *Deliktsopfer und Strafverfahren*. Berlin: Duncker & Humblot.

2 See for a European comparison F. DÜNKEL (1986) Reparation and victim-offender reconciliation and aspects of the legal position of the victim in criminal procedures in a Western-European perspective, in: H.-J. KERNER, B. GALAWAY & H. JANSSEN (eds.), *Jugendgerichtsbarkeit in Europa und Nordamerika - Aspekte und Tendenzen*, 303-327. München: Deutsche Vereinigung für Jugendgerichte und Jugendgerichtshilfen; F.

future (European) victim-related criminal policy the issue is not only to conserve the constitutional principles that have developed in current criminal law and modern criminal procedure, but also to strengthen simultaneously the victim's interests with regard to compensation and the reconciliatory, conflict-solving dimension of criminal law.

1. The victim as initiator of crime control

In discussing the trends of the criminal justice system related to questions of privatisation, we might easily forget that in Europe it has been established by victimological surveys since the early 70s that the victim has a central role in initiating proceedings and in thus influencing the selection of crimes to be prosecuted. In Germany various studies of victimisation and victim reactions have shown that more than 90% of the offences classified as classical crimes are brought to the attention of the police solely by the victims as informants.[3] A representative poll of victims conducted in Baden-Württemberg in 1981 showed an overall complaint rate of 42%, ranging from 15% in the field of bodily assault without a weapon to 79% in the field of car theft.[4] This finding corresponds with earlier studies (which were also conducted in other countries), according to which only half of all offences are reported.[5] Another poll which was made in 1989 with law students in Germany,

DÜNKEL (1989) Täter-Opfer-Ausgleich und Schadenswiedergutmachung. Neuere Entwicklungen des Strafrechts und der Strafrechtspraxis im internationalen Vergleich, In: E. MARKS & D. RÖSSNER (eds.), *Täter-Opfer-Ausgleich, - Vom zwischenmenschlichen Weg zur Wiederherstellung des Rechtsfriedens,* 394-463. Bonn: Forum Verlag; F. DÜNKEL (1996) Täter-Opfer-Ausgleich. German experiences with mediation in a European perspective, 4 *European Journal on Criminal Policy and Research*, 44-66; See also H. MESSMER & H.-U. OTTO (1992) (eds.), *Restorative Justice on Trial. Pitfalls and Potentials of Victim-Offender Mediation - International Perspectives*. Dordrecht: Kluwer (NATO ASI Series); negative examples, once again, can be derived from the United States.

3 G. KAISER (1996) (3rd ed.), *Kriminologie. Ein Lehrbuch*. Heidelberg, Karlsruhe: C. F. Müller; EISENBERG, U. (2000) (5th ed.), *Kriminologie*. München: C. H. Beck.

4 H. ARNOLD (1986) Kriminelle Viktimisierung und ihre Korrelate. Ergebnisse international vergleichender Opferbefragungen, 98 *Zeitschrift für die gesamten Strafrechtswissenschaften* 1014-1058; H. ARNOLD & H.-J. ALBRECHT (1991) Research on Victimization and Related Topics in the Federal Republic of Germany – A Selection of Problems and Results, in: G. KAISER, H. KURY, & H.-J. ALBRECHT (Eds.), *Victims and Criminal Justice*, vol. 1, 20-36. Freiburg i. Br.: Max-Planck-Institut für ausländisches und internationales Strafrecht.

5 H.-D. SCHWIND (2001) (11th ed.), *Kriminologie. Eine praxisorientierte Einführung mit Beispielen*. Heidelberg: Kriminalistik Verlag.

Austria and Switzerland came to the same results with only half of the offences reported to the police. The ratio was considerably higher in the case of more serious offences like assault or burglary.[6]

The finding that more than 90% of crimes are brought to the attention of the police by complaints from among the population had created a criminal-theoretical sensation in the early 70s. One of the basic assumptions of the labelling-approach, namely, selective registration and sanctioning by the police and the public prosecutor according to social class of the complainant, had to be qualified considerably as a consequence. Subsequently, the interest shifted more strongly to the role of the victim, the process of deciding to inform and the practice of reporting crime. Studies conducted in England, Germany and the United States show that younger persons are less willing to report crimes than older persons, although they suffer victimisation more often. Members of lower social classes are more likely to report personal offences, whereas members of higher social classes are more likely to report property offences.[7] The seriousness of the offence and the extent of damage constitute the main motives for reporting. The closeness of victim-offender relationship plays a major role where personal offences are concerned. The closer this relationship is, the less likely it is that the offence will be reported. While the desire for compensation and the obligations with respect to private insurance companies are the main motives for reporting property offences the situation regarding offences against the person is quite different. Here a hopelessly disrupted victim-offender relationship often seems to offer no other solution than to seek official aid. A complaint constitutes the "last resort" of a disrupted relationship or of a conflict which can no longer be settled privately.[8] For this reason, in these specific cases, there is usually little willingness to participate in a mediation programme. On the other hand, the peacemaking dimension of mediation appears especially desirable in circumstances shaped by a personal relationship; positive experiences in numerous projects in Germany show that even such particularly difficult cases can be successfully settled.[9]

---

6 F. DÜNKEL, K. KRAINZ & M. WÜRGER (1991) Victimization and Incidence of Delinquency - An International Comparison - Results of a Survey of Law Students in the Federal Republic of Germany, Austria and Switzerland, in: KAISER, KURY & ALBRECHT, *o.c.*, 123.

7 G. KAISER, *o.c.*

8 VOSS, M. (1989) Anzeigemotive, Verfahrenserwartungen und die Bereitschaft von Geschädigten zur informellen Konfliktregelung. Erste Ergebnisse einer Opferbefragung. 72 *Monatsschrift für Kriminologie und Strafrechtsreform*, 34-51.

9 See the contributions in E. MARKS & D. RÖSSNER (1989) (eds.), *Täter-Opfer-Ausgleich - Vom zwischenmenschlichen Weg zur Wiederherstellung des Rechtsfriedens.* Bonn:

The most frequent reasons for not reporting are undoubtedly the presumed fruitlessness of the complaint, the opinion that it is a personal affair, fear of the police, and the expected great expenditure of time. However, the subjectively estimated low extent of damage ranks first.[10] The fact whether the victim is privately insured against burglary undoubtedly affects the decision to report the offence or not.[11] This explains the high complaint rates, in, e.g., the field of burglary or car theft of more than 70%, as the above-mentioned poll of victims in Baden-Württemberg showed.[12] In this respect, the victim fulfils an obligation to his insurer without having a direct interest as regards punishment. This finding is also confirmed by current surveys in Hamburg and North Rhine-Westphalia, according to which more than 75% of the victims questioned who were affected in particular by property offences were not interested in punishment. This may legitimise compensation (*Wiedergutmachung*) and mediation (*Täter-Opfer-Ausgleich*) strategies *instead* of penal sanctions.[13] Sessar even goes so far as to ask whether prosecution, rather than the renunciation of punishment, does not require legitimisation.[14] A survey conducted in North Rhine-Westphalia, e.g., showed the following distribution of motives for filing a complaint: 45% had a civil interest in compensation; 31% had sought immediate aid or thought they had an obligation to report the offence; only 24% expressed an interest in punishment. Of course this distribution varied according to the type of offence, the proportion of those desiring punishment being considerably higher in the cases of rape than in connection with property offences. The survey was linked to the acceptance of so-called diversion models, namely, the possibility that the public prosecutor might dismiss the charge and thus transgress the fundamental part of the principle of legality (the principle according to which it is mandatory for the public prosecutor to

---

Forum-Verlag (2nd ed. 1990); D. DÖLLING et al. (1998) *Täter-Opfer-Ausgleich in Deutschland. Bestandsaufnahme und Perspektiven*. Bonn: Forum-Verlag; see also F. DÜNKEL (1996) Täter-Opfer-Ausgleich, *o.c.*

10 See ARNOLD, *o.c.;* DÜNKEL, KRAINZ, & WÜRGER, *o.c.*; SCHWIND, *o.c.*

11 See SCHWIND, *o.c.*, 383: 90% of the victims who were insured reported a theft to the police in comparison to only 18% in the case when the victim had no insurance.

12 See G. KAISER (1996) *o.c.*, 562; in a representative German study in the mid eighties the proportion of reported car thefts and burglaries was more than 85%, see M. KILCHLING, (1995) *Opferinteressen und Strafverfolgung*. Freiburg i. Br.: Max-Planck-Institut für ausländisches und internationales Strafrecht.

13 See K. SESSAR, A. BEURSKENS & K. BOERS (1986) Wiedergutmachung als Konfliktregelungsparadigma ? 18 *Kriminologisches Journal* 86- 104.

14 K. SESSAR (1992) *Wiedergutmachen oder strafen; Einstellungen in der Bevölkerung und in der Justiz*. Pfaffenweiler: Centaurus-Verlag.

prosecute all offences). The prosecutor might couple the dismissal of the charge to the fulfilment of an obligation such as compensation or the payment of a fine. At present, almost 70% (1998: 69%,[15] the ratio has increased considerably since 1981, when it was "only" 41%) of the criminal proceedings under juvenile criminal law (pursuant to §§ 45, 47 JGG, Juvenile Justice Act) and about 44% of the proceedings under adult criminal law (pursuant to §§153 ff. StPO, Code of Criminal Procedure) are terminated on the basis that it would be opportune to do so. On the whole, about three fourths of all individual victims showed motives for reporting and expectations with regard to the proceedings and to punishment which appear to be compatible with the practice of diversion common in juvenile criminal law. 64% of the persons questioned stated that they did not want the offenders to be punished by a juvenile court and only 25% of the injured persons supported more repressive punishments.[16]

2. Penal-dogmatic approaches to avoid criminal proceedings: active penitence, compensation and reparation

In the previous section procedure-related possibilities of compensation and reparation and their acceptance by the public have been mentioned. Both the transgression of the principle of legality and an appropriate exercise of discretion by the public prosecutor are characteristic features of these procedural possibilities which are based on considerations of expediency.[17] However, substantive approaches which negate the criminal responsibility if the conflict is settled by mutual consent are also conceivable; this possibility might be of particular interest to countries where principle of legality is strictly applied such as Spain. Such penal-dogmatic starting points are contained in regulations relating to *tätige Reue* (*"active penitence"*), i.e. a voluntary act by which the perpetrator of a criminal attempt hinders the consummation of the offence. This legal concept in the German theory of criminal law, refers to the abandonment of the completion of the attempt to commit an offence and to the abandonment of the completed offence in the

---

15 W. HEINZ (2000) *Konstanzer Inventar zum Sanktionenrecht.* <www.uni-konstanz.de/rtf/kis/sanks2000.htm> .

16 See VOSS, *o.c.*, 40; see also KILCHLING, *o.c.*, 220, 227: 43% of the reporting victims required only compensation/reparation, 31% compensation and the punishment of the offender, and only 17% primarily the punishment of the offender.

17 P.J.P. TAK (1986) *The Legal Scope of Non-prosecution in Europe*. Helsinki: HEUNI; F. DÜNKEL (1989) *o.c.*, 394-463.

case of several specific crimes.[18] It applies to the causal hindrance of success in the case of a completed attempt or the removal of the effects of success, namely, restoration to the original condition through compensation and the like in the case of a completed offence. German criminal law decriminalises in this way certain offences such as arson, counterfeiting, hostage-taking, armed assault upon motorists and a number of crimes against the state. For the most part, the acts concerned are preparatory acts or crimes of attempt for which the law-makers have created extended possibilities for the offender to withdraw through active penitence or by paying compensation. This has become necessary because of the extent to which the definitions of crime have been extended to make attempts punishable as if they were completed crimes (so-called *"Unternehmensdelikte"*).

Interestingly the German Supreme Court (*BGH*) has changed his jurisprudence in the field of abandonment of the crime (*Rücktritt vom beendeten Versuch*) since 1982. The Court now claims for more extensive efforts by the offender in order to prevent the completion of the crime. So the offender has to prove "restitutive" efforts towards the victim (*"honorierfähige Umkehrleistung"*) and not only to withdraw from his criminal activities (see BGHSt 31, S. 46 ff.).

Lately there have been increased calls for an extension of the concept of active penitence not only to all completed crimes in the sense of *"Gefährdungs- und Unternehmensdelikte"* (in this respect, the pertinent literature relies on arguments by analogy), but also to all property offences and minor offences against the person (e.g., bodily injury). This is all the more so since the decisions of the courts have expanded penal protection considerably by recognising the endangerment of property as damage within the meaning of the crime of fraud and by shifting forward the moment of completion in the field of shoplifting, thus cutting off the possibilities of abandonment which exist otherwise in the field of attempt.

The criminal policy proposals in Germany to extend active penitence to other crimes like theft, fraud etc. are strongly influenced by the regulation of active penitence for property offences by § 167 of the Austrian Penal Code. According to this provision, an offender goes free if he has repaired the damage or has covenanted to do so before the offence comes to the knowledge of the prosecuting agencies. This regulation which dates from the ninetieth century has proved successful. Moreover, contrary to the fears often expressed in Germany, it has not led to the expected decline in the public's recognition of standards of conduct.

---

18 T. HILLENKAMP (1987) Möglichkeiten der Erweiterung des Instituts der tätigen Reue, in: H. SCHÖCH (ed.), *Wiedergutmachung und Strafrecht*, 81-113. München: Fink.

A comparable regulation exists in the Greek Penal Code (see Art. 379 Greek Penal Code).[19]

Regarding cheque fraud there are possibilities of a sort of active penitence which exempts from punishment, e. g., in Portuguese and French law,[20] in Italy the introduction of such a possibility of abandoning the completed offence within 60 days has been under discussion (the periods being comparatively shorter in Portugal and France with 30 and 10 days, respectively).

In Austrian law the concept of "lack of being punishable of the Act" in terms of § 42 of the Austrian Penal Code be mentioned in addition to active penitence where property offences are being taken into consideration. It is a further form of reversal of penalty which is connected with compensation. The sphere of application of this concept which was originally reserved for the judge was broadened considerably by the penal reform of 1987 which also granted the public prosecutor such decision-making powers. In this way the traditionally strict Austrian principle of legality was largely negated. Unlike active penitence, the decision as to whether the offender shall go free is still subject to the public prosecutor's or judge's discretion. The time limits go much further in that they take into account compensatory acts up to the date of trial. The scope of application is not restricted to property offences, rather, it concerns all crimes punishable with up to three years of imprisonment. Moreover, § 42 of the Austrian Penal Code requires merely the essential removal of the damage caused by the offence; forms of compensation other than material restitution are therefore permissible.

Furthermore, the 1988 reform of the Austrian Juvenile Justice Act recognised the positive results of mediation projects and conflict settlement in a procedural model which conceptualised punishment and criminal procedure as subsidiary to compensation (see §§ 7 and 8 of the Austrian Juvenile Justice Act, *JGG*).

In Switzerland a substantive regulation is under discussion which provides that there will be no prosecution or punishment if the offender has made every reasonable effort to pay damages or to perform another form of compensation so that the public interest in prosecution has become very small, or if he has made a special effort to make amends for the wrong he caused. Unlike the Austrian regulation which applies to property offences only, this provision, which is contained in the General Part of the Penal Code would create a compulsory exemption from punishment until the date of the

19 S.N. PATSOURAKOU (1994) *Die Stellung des Verletzten im Strafrechstsystem*. Bonn: Forum-Verlag.

20 See for an overview also on other forms of active penitence PATSOURAKOU, *o.c.*

judicial decision if the offender pays damages or at least makes a serious effort to do so.

The new Russian Penal Code of 1996 provides two forms of exemption from criminal responsibility. First of all a behaviour that formally could be defined as crime is not considered as such if the consequences are not "socially dangerous" and especially the offender has not caused a damage (see Art. 14.2). Repairing a damage can result to such a definition of a not socially dangerous offence, as Art. 77 provides that an offender can be exempted from criminal responsibility if changed circumstances give evidence that he is not socially dangerous anymore (see *Strafgesetzbuch der Russischen Föderation* 1998). Another form of exemption from criminal responsibility is provided by Art. 75 and 76 of the Penal Code: if the first time offender of a minor crime (punishable with a prison sentence of up to two years) sincerely regrets committing the offence, reports the offence himself and has averted the harmful consequences of the offence (see Art. 75.1 of the Russian Penal Code). Art 76 refers to the reconciliation of victim and offender and also provides for the exemption of criminal responsibility in the case of successful mediation/reparation. These provisions are, however, rather restricted and give only discretion whether to prosecute or not.

The new Lithuanian Penal Code of 2000 similarly provides for the exemption of criminal responsibility if the offender repairs the damage or arrives at a reconciliation with the victim. This applies not only to minor, but also to more serious offences (punishable with up to 6 years of imprisonment), however, recidivists are excluded.[21]

On the whole there is a clear need for substantive penal provisions to expand active penitence which exempts from punishment also in the realm of completed offences in the interest of a decriminalisation of petty offences on the one hand and the offender's resocialisation, as well as improved protection of victims on the other hand. This should be done independently of the prevailing rules of practice (principles of legality and expediency). Such provisions would take into account both the victim's interests in compensation which, as empirical studies have shown, are of central concern to the victim, and the interests of society as regards positive general prevention.

---

21 See F. DÜNKEL & G. SAKALAUSKAS (2001) Jugendstrafrecht und Jugendstrafrechtsreform in Litauen, 12 *DVJJ-Journal* 72-80.

3. Efforts of the Council of Europe to improve the position of the victim in the framework of criminal law and procedure

In 1985 the Committee of Ministers of the Council of Europe adopted the Recommendation No. R (85) 11 on the position of the victim in the framework of criminal law and procedure. It was stated that the objectives of the criminal justice system have traditionally been expressed in terms which primarily concern the relationship between the state and the offender and therefore the necessity to consider the fundamental function of criminal justice to meet the needs and to safeguard the interests of the victim was emphasised. It was seen as important to enhance the confidence of victims in criminal justice and to encourage their co-operation, especially in the capacity as a witness.

The recommendations differentiate improvements on the police level, in respect of prosecution and on the level of court proceedings including the enforcement stage after sentencing. At all stages of the procedure, the victim should be questioned in a manner which gives due consideration to his personal situation, his rights and his dignity.

Police officers should be trained to deal with victims in a sympathetic, constructive and reassuring manner. They should inform the victim about the possibilities of obtaining assistance, practical and legal advice, compensation from the offender and state compensation.

In some European countries the police have been advised by the Ministry of Interior to hand out leaflets or to give otherwise information to the victim. In France, since 1981, a whole range of about 140 victim-assistance schemes has been established which co-operate with the police (*bureaux d'aide aux victimes*, which are working as private organisations in the national association called *INAVEM*). In other countries, too, there is a growing movement of victim-assistance schemes (especially in England and Germany).

The Council of Europe recommends furthermore that the police should give as clear and complete a statement as possible on the injuries and losses suffered by the victim.

In all stages the rights to be informed about the outcome of the investigation (police), the final decision concerning prosecution and the date and place of court proceedings resp. the outcome of the trial should be guaranteed. In the case of non-prosecution the victim should have the right to ask for review by a competent authority, or the right to institute private proceedings.

At the court level it should be possible to order compensation by the offender to the victim. Legislation should provide that compensation may either be a penal sanction, or a substitute for a penal sanction or be awarded in addition to a penal sanction. The court should be informed about the victim's need for compensation and any compensation or restitution made by the offender or any genuine effort to that end.

In cases where the possibilities open to a court include attaching financial conditions to the award of a deferred or suspended sentence, of a probation order or of any other measure, great importance should be given –among these conditions– to compensation by the offender to the victim (to the legal provisions in some of the member states see below). If compensation is a penal sanction, it should be collected in the same way as fines and take priority over any other financial sanction imposed on the offender.

All state agencies involved in the investigation and trial of offences should give due consideration to the need to protect the victim from any publicity which unduly affect his private life or dignity. In special cases the trial should be held in camera.

The final statement of the recommendation asks the governments of the member states to examine the possible advantages of mediation and conciliation schemes and to promote and encourage research on the efficacy of provisions affecting victims.

In its commentary to the recommendation No. R (85) 11 the European Committee on Crime Problems clearly states that the desirable improvements for the victim must not be regarded as conflicting with other objectives of the system of justice, particularly criminal justice, such as upholding social norms, the rehabilitation of the offender and the possible reconciliation between the victim and the offender.[22]

The Recommendation No. R (87) 21 of 1987 emphasises the development of victim-assistance programmes. Victimisation surveys and other research should ascertain the victim's needs and victimisation rates in order to gather the necessary data to assist in the development of victim-assistance programmes. There should be general services designed to provide assistance to victims as well as services for special categories of victims or crimes like children, rape victims, victims of domestic violence, organised crime or racist violence.[23]

15 years after the Recommendation of 1985, Brienen and Hoegen published a vast evaluation report on 22 Western European member states concerning the implementation of the Recommendation on the position of victims in the framework of criminal law and procedure. This very valuable and comprehensive evaluation demonstrates on the one hand considerable

22 Recommendation R (85) 11, 16.
23 Recommendation R (87) 21, 6.

efforts to improve the position of the victim in many countries during the last years, on the other hand the researchers conclude that *"the overall rate of implementation of the guidelines of Recommendation (85) 11 is disappointing".*[24] The police provide victims with some general information about their rights and interests in 85% of the jurisdictions, but *"59% of the jurisdictions fail to train the police adequately on how to deal with victims."* Only *"in 18% of the jurisdictions, the victim stands a fair chance of being informed about the final decision concerning prosecution."* The top six jurisdictions that have improved best and have passed victim-oriented reforms are Belgium, England and Wales, France, Ireland, the Netherlands and Sweden. Best practices have been implemented in the Netherlands, England/Wales, Norway and Belgium and the best overall practice in relation to the standards set by the Recommendation has been achieved in England/Wales and the Netherlands. Germany takes "good scores" in legislation, but practice does not seem to be very effective concerning some of the guidelines (see below).

Further developments on the European level concerning victim issues refer to manifold activities and recommendations.[25] One of the topics was violence in the family, see the Recommendation No. R (90) 2 on social measures concerning violence in the family. Eight years later the Recommendation No. R (98) 1 on family mediation addressed the same problem. The Recommendation No. R (91) 11 concerning sexual exploitation, pornography and prostitution of, trafficking in, children and young adults should also be mentioned in this context. Recently it was followed by another more extended Recommendation on action against trafficking in human beings for the purpose of sexual exploitation, see the Recommendation R (2000) 11.

In 1999 the Committee of Ministers accepted the recommendation on Mediation in Penal Matters that encourages the member states to introduce restorative measures and proceedings at all stages of the criminal justice system. The Recommendation No. R (99) 19 emphasises that mediation should primarily be seen as an alternative to the criminal procedure and – according to good practices in many European countries (Belgium, England, Germany, France, Finland, etc.) could prevent formal proceedings to a great extend. The recommendation also claims for "fundamental procedural

---

24 M.E.I. Brienen & E.H. Hoegen (2000) *Victims of Crime in 22 European Criminal Justice Systems: The Implementation of Recommendation (85) 11 of the Council of Europe on the Position of the Victim in the Framework of Criminal Law and Procedure.* Nijmegen: Wolf Legal Productions.

25 See the overview at www.victimology.nl/onlpub/international/ce.html.

safeguards" (see Rule III.8.) that prevent abuses with respect of the presumption of innocence concerning the offender on the one hand and undue pressure to the victim (to participate) on the other. Therefore Rule II.1 emphasising the parties freely consent and IV.14. with regard to the basic facts that normally should be acknowledged by both parties).

Another important issue in many European countries has been the improvement the protection of victim witnesses. The Council of Europe dealt with that problem in its Recommendation No. R (97) 12 concerning intimidation of witnesses and the rights of the defence. Germany (as the Nordic countries before) passed new legislation on that issue in 1998 (see below).

The standing of victims in criminal proceedings was the topic of recent legislation of the Council of the European Union with its framework decision of 15 March 2001.[26] This framework decision provides numerous rules that are similar to the Council of Europe's Recommendations, e.g. concerning the rights of victims to be treated with respect for their dignity, to receive information (see Art. 4 of the framework), to be protected at the various stages of procedure, where specialised services and victim support groups should be involved (see No. 8 and 18 of the preamble and Art. 2, 8 and 13 of the framework). Art. 9 and 10 emphasise the importance of compensation in the course of criminal proceedings as well as of mediation schemes. Whereas the Recommendations of the Council of Europe are not binding legal rules (but rather "soft law" in the form of minimum standards), the Council Framework Decision imposes more pressure to the Member States by giving concrete deadlines for the implementation. In general the necessary provisions should be implemented by 22 March of 2002 (with the exception of Art. 5 and 6 on communication safeguards and specific assistance to the victim, which should be implemented by 22 March 2004 and Art. 10 on penal mediation that should be implemented by 22 March 2006).[27]

It is not surprising that the European initiatives are coinciding with global efforts to improve the position of victims in the criminal justice area. The United Nations repeatedly have passed important instruments concerning victims of crime. The most prominent one was the UN Declaration of Basic Principles of Justice for Victims of Crime and Abuse of Power of 1985,[28]

---

26 See Document 301F0220, published in *Official Journal* L 082, 22/03/2001, 0001-0004.

27 http://europa.eu.int/eur-lex/en/lif/dat2001/en_301F0220.html.

28 Helsinki Institute for Crime Prevention and Control affiliated with the United Nations (HEUNI): *Changing Victim Policy: The United Nations Victim Declaration and Recent Developments in Europe*. Helsinki: HEUNI 1989.

that were followed by a Guide for Policymakers on the Implementation of this Declaration in 1998 and a Handbook on Justice for Victims in the same year.[29] In a preliminary draft of the Vienna Declaration on Crime and Justice: Meeting the Challenges of the Twenty-first Century (A/Conf. 187/4) it is proposed that the Member States of the United Nations declare as follows: "25. We decide to introduce, where appropriate, national, regional and international action plans in support of victims of crime, including mechanisms for mediation and restorative justice, and we establish the year 2002 as a target date for States to review their relevant practices, to develop further victim support services and awareness campaigns on victim's rights and to consider the establishment of funds for victims, in addition to developing and implementing witness protection programmes."

The Commission on Crime Prevention and Criminal Justice recommended in April 2000 the adoption of a Draft Resolution for Basic Principles on the Use of Restorative Justice Programmes in Criminal Matters by the Economic and Social Council.

These and other initiatives on the UN and the European level clearly demonstrate the global consent on victims issues in general. However, the implementation by legislation and practice might be different, as the above mentioned review on 22 Western European jurisdictions of Brienen and Hoegen clearly demonstrates.

4. Survey of the victim's position in German criminal procedure

In Germany the "rediscovery of the victim"[30] was connected at first with attempts to introduce state compensation for victims of violent acts. This movement was brought to a conclusion with the enactment of the Victim Compensation Act of 1976. In the early 80s, the improvement of the status of the victim in criminal procedure became one of the focal points of discussions about criminal policy in West Germany.[31] With the *Erstes Gesetz*

---

29 See www.victimology.nl/onlpub/international/un.html.

30 See H. JUNG (2000) Zur Renaissance des Opfers – ein Lehrstück kriminalpolitischer Zeitgeschichte, 33 *Zeitschrift für Rechtspolitik* 59-163, w. further references to the historical development; for an international comparison see M. JOUTSEN (1987) *The Role of the Victim of Crime in European Criminal Justice Systems. A Crossnational Study of the Role of the Victim*. Helsinki: HEUNI (Helsinki Institute for Crime Prevention and Control affiliated with the United Nations, HEUNI); PATSOURAKOU, *o.c.;* BRIENEN & HOEGEN, *o.c.*

31 See H. JUNG (1981) Die Stellung des Verletzten im Strafprozeß, 93 *Zeitschrift für die gesamte Strafrechtswissenschaft* 1147-1176; P. RIEß (1984) Die Rechtsstellung des

zur Verbesserung der Stellung des Verletzten im Strafverfahren (First Law on the Improvement of the Position of the Victim in Criminal Proceedings) of 1987 –cited as Victim Protection Act below– the law-makers carefully tried to improve the gravest shortcomings of the earlier legal position without changing fundamentally the status of the victim.[32]

First one should make a few preliminary remarks on the criminal procedure in Germany to the extent that this seems necessary to understand the victim's position. Criminal procedure in Germany is strongly shaped by the fact that prosecution is a monopoly of the public prosecutor (there exists no so-called *Popularklage/actio popularis*, i. e. a collective action serving as a test case, as in Spain). The public prosecutor has to enforce the state's claim to punishment in accordance with the principle of legality, (which, admittedly, has been transgressed extensively by the principle of expediency, *Opportunitätsprinzip*). This already clearly shows that forms of private prosecution as they exist in the German Code of Criminal Procedure for petty offences such as insults, bodily injury and trespassing are conceptualised as exceptions to the principle. Although private prosecution grants the victim the right to seek the offender's conviction even where the public prosecutor has no interest in criminal prosecution, he is burdened with a considerable financial risk –as has been critically emphasised time and again– all the more so as existing empirical studies have shown that only 6% of the cases of private prosecution end in a conviction.[33] In the long run, the fact that actions are brought by only 10% of the victims referred to private prosecutions is a consequence of this. The shortcomings of the current procedure of private prosecution have led to the predominant opinion that it should be abolished.[34] This, however, does not apply to so-called conciliation proceedings ("*Schiedsmannverfahren*") which are connected with the private complaint in German law. They are an attempt at conciliation which in every case is required to precede the commencement of an action. Special arbitration agencies (e.g, in North Rhine-Westphalia and Hesse) and mediation committees at the local authority level (in the southern Federal States of Baden-Württemberg and Bavaria) were set up for this purpose. The conciliation proceedings have proved a success in that 50% of the private complaints are settled by mutual agreement as a result of this

---

Verletzten im Strafverfahren. Gutachten C für den 55. Deutschen Juristentag, In: *Verhandlungen des 55. Deutschen Juristentags*. München.

32 See H. JUNG (1987) Das Opferschutzgesetz, 27 *Juristische Schulung* 157-160; WEIGEND, *o.c.*

33 RIEß, *o.c.*; WEIGEND, *o.c.*

34 BRIENEN & HOEGEN, *o.c.*

form of conciliation. The rate of successful cases of conciliation was 60-70% in the federal states with special arbitrators (as a rule, they are respected laymen or citizens from the community) who act independently of the local government. A poll of the state ministries of justice revealed a decrease in conciliation proceedings by 31% between 1980 and 1987 although there has been a noticeable increase in the number of insults, bodily injuries and other crimes subject to private prosecution during the same period of time. This might be connected with an increased informal settling of conflicts already in the run-up to the conciliation proceedings and the aforementioned caution over private prosecution (in view of the financial risk and the anticipated fruitlessness of a possible private complaint).

It remains to be noted that conciliation proceedings in connection with offences subject to private prosecution are models of the form mediation should take. This form of mediation takes into account the constitutional scruples about such "privatisation" of criminal justice by making provision for a certain degree of formalisation and the intensive training of the arbitrators (at least where such arbitration procedures exist). From this angle, the demands for reform in Germany which are aimed at a general expansion of the conciliation procedure beyond the domain of private complaints seem to be justified.[35]

The second legal concept which is of importance with regard to the victim's status in criminal proceedings, namely, joint (auxiliary) prosecution ("*Nebenklage*"), is also exposed to considerable criticism. Originally, it merely referred to the independent joining of the victim of the charge in the case of an offence subject to private prosecution, which the Victim Protection Act of 1987 extended to the realm of serious violent crimes (particularly rape, homicide, murder etc., see §§ 395 ff. StPO, Code of Criminal Procedure). The joint prosecutor, that is the complainant, in general has the same rights as the public prosecutor and is entitled to appeal independently against the convicted person's acquittal. The Victim Protection Act, however, removed the possibility of appeal against the sentence imposed on the offender (see § 400 StPO), as the injured party was regarded as having a legitimate interest in seeing the offender convicted, but not, however, in the degree of punishment. In this respect, the legal status of the German joint prosecutor differs from the position of the private prosecutor in other countries in that the latter has rather extensive rights also in case the public prosecutor dismisses the charge or in the course of the

35 A concrete proposal was made by Arbeitskreis deutscher, schweizerischer und österreichischer Strafrechtslehrer (1992) *Alternativ-Entwurf Wiedergutmachung (AE-WGM)*. München.

trial.[36] From the German angle such a strong orientation to the victim (with regard to active rights) would be considered more likely to be harmful to the objectives of the criminal procedure (ascertaining the truth, protecting the victim through a fair trial, establishing legal peace etc., see below).

German legislation, like most other European legal systems, provides for civil claims for financial compensation within the framework of *criminal procedure*. This so-called adhesion procedure is of absolutely no importance in practice. Unlike the "action civile" which seems to be applied on a large scale in France, Belgium, Spain, Portugal and Finland, this procedure has not been accepted in Germany nor in Austria or Switzerland. Although the Victim Protection Act of 1987 has simplified this procedure (see §§ 403 ff. StPO) and offered the courts the possibility of delivering a basic or part judgement (a way of circumventing questions as to the extent of damage), a survey of the Federal Government by the individual Federal States showed that the adhesion procedure had not gained in significance.[37]

Unlike their Spanish or Portuguese and especially Dutch counterparts, the public prosecutor's office and the court are not required to use their official influence to work towards an assertion of civil claims. Moreover, because of the Code of Lawyers' Fees, the lawyers have no priority interest in the adhesion procedure (higher fees may be obtained in separate civil proceedings.[38]

On the whole, the victim's current possibilities of participating are not derived from a uniform concept of joining in the proceedings, rather, they evolved historically from very different roots and political currents.[39] The Victim Protection Act of 1987 is also a product of its lack of overall vision.

However, the similar pattern of development in other European countries shows this is a general problem of modern criminal proceedings and that the *"merely marginal status of the victim... is hence no accident of the history of procedural law, but the logical consequence of a de-privatisation of certain (serious) conflicts"*.[40]

36 H.H. KÜHNE (1998) (Ed.), *Opferrechte im Strafprozeß*. Ein europäischer Vergleich. Kehl et al.: Engel Verlag; BRIENEN & HOEGEN, *o.c.*

37 See for a critical empirical evaluation of the impact of the Victims Protection Act has been presented by M. KAISER (1992) *Die Stellung des Verletzten im Strafverfahren*. Freiburg: Max-Planck-Institut für ausländisches und internationales Strafrecht 262-279, 290.

38 BRIENEN & HOEGEN, *o.c.*

39 WEIGEND, *o.c.*

40 *Ibid.*

5. Victim protection in criminal proceedings in Germany

The exclusion of the victim from modern criminal proceedings manifests itself most clearly in the question of how victims should be protected in criminal proceedings. Until recently hardly any regulations existed in Germany that went beyond the protective regulations applying to witnesses in general. In this respect, the Victim Protection Act of 1987 has brought a number of improvements, in that questions concerning the personal sphere of life may only be asked during the examination of the witness if absolutely necessary (§ 68a StPO). This is intended to prevent the victims of sexual offences from being subjected to detailed interrogations as to their sexual life without a recognisable connection with the crime that is being tried. Moreover, it created the possibility of removing the accused from the court room if there is serious danger that the witness's health will be impaired if the accused is present during the interrogation. Finally, the law-makers broadened the provisions governing the exclusion of the public in order to protect the victim's personal rights and there were introduced improvements with respect to legal aid (free of charge) during the trial (see §§ 406f, 406g StPO, "*Opferanwalt*").

5.1. Changes introduced by the Victim Protection Act

The provisions governing the legal protection of personal rights introduced by the German reform conform with a general tendency that has also become evident in other European countries.[41] In summary the *Opferschutzgesetz* of 1987 introduced the following regulations:

- the possibility to refuse questions interfering in the private sphere of the victim (§ 68a StPO, Criminal Procedure Act; in this way the possibility to put questions to the victim e.g. about his sexual life can be restricted);
- the possibilty to temporarily exclude the accused while the victim is interrogated (§ 247 StPO);
- the exclusion of the public in order to protect the private sphere of the victim (§§ 171b, 172 GVG, Courts Organisation Act);
- the right of the victim to be informed about the outcome of the trial (§ 406d StPO);
- the right to look into the files of the trial (through an advocate, § 406e StPO);

41 KÜHNE, *o.c.*; BRIENEN & HOEGEN, *o.c.*

- the right to call on a victim's advocate, who has the right to participate at any interrogation of the victim, put questions at the trial etc. (§ 406f StPO);
- the right to call on a victim's advocate already before trial when the victim has the right to participate in a joint procedure on the side of the prosecutor (§ 406g StPO);[42]
- the obligation of the court to inform the victim about his rights (§ 406h StPO);
  the extension of the possibilities of the victim to join the prosecutor as an independent "subject" of the trial with his own rights to put questions and to present evidence etc. (§§ 395 ff. StPO), and to get legal representation by a lawyer (in case needed paid by the state, §§ 397, 397a StPO); the victim as a "joint prosecutor" has the same rights as the prosecutor with the exception that he/she cannot complain against the concrete sentence (§ 400 StPO);
- the extension of combining civil claims for compensation of material and immaterial losses with the penal trial (§§ 403 ff. StPO, so-called *Adhäsionsverfahren*);
- the consideration of mediation efforts shown by the offender when determining the sentence through the court (the central sentencing guideline of § 46 StGB, Penal Law, now explicitely refers to mediation and reparation/restitution);
- the execution of fines, which has to be of secondary importance when otherwise the offender's limited resources would endanger the compensation of the victim (§ 459a StPO).[43]

In this context reference should be made to a number of experiments in Germany in connection with the protection of victims in proceedings. E. g., according to the model of the social work in the professional office applied in the city of Tübingen, the victim's perspective is introduced into the procedure by means of a victim report of the social worker where serious violent crimes, in particular rapes, are involved.[44] Although the functions of the court aid are basically offender-related, consisting of inquiries into the offender's personality and social background which are made by social

42 The German criminal procedure follows the Continental-european model of an inquisitorial procedure where the judge plays an active role and the prosecutor has not the role of a party like in the Anglo-american adversatorial model; so e.g. he has also the duty to relate on evidence in favour of the accused.

43 M. KAISER (1992) *o.c.*

44 R.-D. HERING (1991) Court-Assistance and the Victim of Crime - The Opportunity of Social Services within the Justice System in Practice, in: KAISER, KURY & ALBRECHT, *o.c.*, vol.3, 115-125.

workers who are employed with the public prosecutor's office, the need to pay more regard to the victim's perspective, particularly where serious violent crimes are involved has arisen in Tübingen in connection with a project on mediation. In the court aid the victim, if he desires, will find a person to talk to about all his fears and insecurity with regard to the trial and assistance. The report of the court aid serves the public prosecutor and the court as a basis for a fair trial also with regard to the victimised witnesses. Finally, this report is considered a starting point for the accused for considering the harm the victim has suffered, which, in turn, is beneficial to the process of resocialisation.

A number of private victim assistance agencies have been set up since the mid 80s which assist the victims systematically. The best known is the Hanau model of victim assistance in Hesse which is applied on a large scale and generally accepted by the victims. In the meantime about 15 victim support schemes are joint under the umbrella of a National Victim Support Organisation (*Arbeitskreis der Opferhilfen*). The other very powerful private association for victims is the "Weisser Ring" (founded already in 1976) with more than 400 offices. It is somehow dominated by (ex-) police officers and raises considerable amounts of money for victim compensation.

The idea of victim assistance is systematically being put to practice by a first "*Zeugenhilfeprogramm*" (witness assistance programme) established in *Limburg* (Hesse) in 1988. This programme, initiated by the Ministry of Justice of Hesse, offers assistance by social workers before and during the trial. This project is also based on victimological findings on the special strain the witnesses and the victims are subject to during the trial. By giving the witnesses information about the course of procedure and all that is ahead of them, their fears may be alleviated in most cases.

While not so much experience has been gathered in this field in Germany so far, the idea of victims assistance programmes is much more widespread in the United States and –as mentioned above– in England; since 1981, the penal policy in France has also (with great success) triggered attempts to develop a network of victim-assistance schemes.

Because of the court's obligation to provide assistance there is a call in Germany for systematic providing for a report on victims. The experiment of Tübingen is seen as a model for such developments. Reports on victims should especially be given where it seems to be doubtful that the victim can stand the trial or he/she is likely not to say the truth (e.g. if the victim fears to be victimised by the offender for a second time).

The demand that the victim should be granted the right to call in a lawyer of his choice free of charge (in compensation for the current incidental action, see above) is to be considered under this aspect. The state, however, should pay the costs rather than the convicted person whose resocialization might be jeopardised by this.

5.2. Major improvements have been achieved by new legislation in the 90s.

Apart from the changes in legislation concerning restitution/compensation and victim-offender reconciliation programmes (see below), the legislator concentrated on more detailed strategies for victim's protection during the trial. The German constitutional court (*Bundesverfassungsgericht*) stressed that the German constitution guarantees the protection of witnesses at risk as a consequence of their duty to give evidence.[45] The Law of Criminal Procedure therefore has to provide for effective mechanisms. A witness is "at risk", when he or she has to fear for health, life, freedom of will or other constitutionally guaranteed freedoms and rights of him/herself or close persons. Mere disadvantages or difficulties in interpersonal relationships are not sufficient to justify the necessary precautions.

The German Code of Criminal Procedure still does not contain one specific section concerning witness protection. The provisions are scattered in the code, usually they are included in the regulations for the relevant part of the procedure in which they will have effect. The legislator tried to improve witness protection with the law against drug-trafficking and other forms of organised crime (*Gesetz zur Bekämpfung des illegalen Rauschgifthandels und anderer Formen der Organisierten Kriminalität*, OrgKG of 15 July 1992, BGBl. I 1302) of 1992. The central regulation is § 68 Code of Criminal Procedure (StPO) that deals with witness protection during the interrogation by the prosecutor and the judge. The witnesses' general duty to give evidence can be restricted e.g. concerning information on the witnesses identity or place of residence.

Important additions to those provisions were made in the Witness Protection Act *(Zeugenschutzgesetz)* of 1998. It concentrates not only on witnesses at risk but also on especially vulnerable witnesses such as children or young persons and contains several specific regulations:

- Further restrictions of the duty to give evidence are made when questions deal with dishonouring facts or go into intimate details (§ 68a StPO).
- the possibility of video-documentation of testimonies in addition to the conventional written protocols and their use in the trial (§§ 58a, 255a, 247a StPO);

45 See R. GRIESBAUM (1998) Der gefährdete Zeuge. Überlegungen zum Zeugenschutz im Strafverfahren, 18 *Neue Zeitschrift für Strafrecht* 433-441.

- simultaneous video-transmissions of interrogations by the judge, especially the interrogation of a witness that is not present in the court chamber (§§ 168e and 247a StPO);
- no cross examination of witnesses under 16 is allowed, questions can be put only by the jugde (§ 241a StPO)
- further regulations on counsels for witnesses (§ 68b StPO) and victims that are entitled to join the prosecution(§§ 397a, 406g);
- an extension of the group of victims entitled to join the prosecution (§ 395 StPO);
- more favourable regulations concerning the salary of lawyers acting as witness counsels.

The most important improvement of the Victim's Protection Act is the possibility to employ video-techniques during the interrogation of victims. This reform was proceeded by several serious cases of child abuse that shocked the public and attracted great attention of the media. In some of the trials the young victims were interrogated in presence of only one judge in accordance with the defence counsel (The so-called "Mainzer Modell" was introduced on a experimental way at the Regional Court, *Landgericht*, of Mainz.[46]) The interrogation was introduced into the trial by video-tape. The responsible judges tried to take into consideration scientific findings on post-traumatic stress symptoms and a possible second victimisation. The incorporation of the possibility of a simultaneous transmission during the trial (§ 247a StPO) in the Code of Criminal Procedure enables the court to such interrogations without the defendants consent. A presentation of video-tapes about interrogations of persons under 16 during the pre-trial proceedings is only admitted, when the defendant or his/her counsel had the opportunity to participate in that interrogation.

The now chosen form of video-interrogation takes into the consideration the critique[47] of several scholars and practitioners that feared a violation of the "principle of immediacy" (*Unmittelbarkeitsgrundsatz*), one of the fundamental principles of German procedural law. The drafts for the Victim's Protection Act originally had demanded to split the trial, so that the judge would have interrogated the witness face to face and his absence from court chamber would have been necessary.[48]

A more practical approach to the appropriate dealing with victims/witnesses under 16 is a handbook edited by the Federal Ministry of

---

46 See C. KEISER (1998) *Das Kindeswohl im Strafverfahren.* Frankfurt/M.: Lang.

47 G. PFEIFFER (2001) (3rd ed.), *Strafprozeßordnung. Kommentar* § 247a note 1. München: C. H. Beck.

48 See GRIESBAUM, *o.c.*, 433-441.

Justice *(Bundeseinheitliche Handreichung zum Schutz kindlicher Opferzeugen im Strafverfahren)*.[49] It is intended for the use by police, prosecutors, courts and social (youth) services and constitutes a set of standards for the proper treatment of possibly traumatised children. It also tries to standardise the differing practices in the different Federal States.

In 1998 a second law dealing with the interests of victims of crime was introduced, the *Opferanspruchssicherungsgesetz* (Act on Securing the Victim's Claims against the Offender). It is meant to improve the victim's status in the civil procedure in a specific case: If the offender gets any claims against third persons for the presentation of the crime in the media, the victim has the right to seize those earnings.

The efforts to improve on the victim's position in criminal law and the law of criminal procedure have not ceased since then. At the moment, two legislative initiatives deal with that problem. The first is a bill on "strengthening the rights of the victim" (*Gesetz zur Verstärkung der Verletztenrechte*, draft prepared by the Freie und Hansestadt Hamburg, Bundesratsdrucksache 507/99). It is an comprehensive approach to strengthen the rights of the victim in the proceedings and to enable him or her to participate more actively in the trial. The existing possibilities to sue financial compensation already during the criminal procedure that have almost no relevance in practice shall be improved.

The bill contains e.g. a provision on the duty to inform the witness not only of his or her duties to give evidence but also, that he or she has the right to object dishonouring questions (§ 68a StPO) or that under specific (further going than in the present legislation) circumstances the public (§ 171b StPO) or the defendant can be excluded from the trial (§ 247 StPO). The status of witness counsels that are not lawyers shall be improved. This is important e.g. for victim's support organisations that assist the victim during the trial.

The active participation of the victim shall be improved e.g. by the right to look at the case record by the victim himself without a lawyer. Victims shall have the right to be informed about the date of the trial. When entitled to join the prosecution he or she shall always have the right to be present during the trial.

Thirdly the bill contains provisions concerning definite agreements on restitution/compensation between victim and offender during the trial. Such an agreement shall be part of the official protocol of the trial and can be executed immediately.

49 See Federal Ministry of Justice 2000, obtainable at www.bmj.bund.de

The problems concerning the possibility of the victim to get financially compensated by the offender is also considered by the draft for the reform of the sanctioning system of the Penal Code (*Entwurf eines Gesetzes zur Reform des Sanktionenrechts*[50]) in several points. Important for the victims of crime is § 43a of the draft. The provision lays down that 10% of all fines shall be for the benefit of victim support. There are no further regulations, it is planned that the federal states must regulate in detail how the money is spent. It could go either to existing victim support schemes or to one single victim's fund. The provision would have considerable importance because more than 80% of all criminal sanctions are fines. It will certainly strengthen the victim support organisations and improve their work. Today such organisations exist in all federal states, but differ considerably in number, quality, organisational forms and funding. Only one federal state has incorporated support agencies in its social service (*Sachsen-Anhalt*), other states started own model projects or supported such institutions run by private organisations, such as safe houses for victims of domestic violence, psycho-social assistance for traumatised victims or organisations whose members e.g. accompany witnesses during the trial (see above).

Another reform project primarily deals with civil law aspects of domestic violence. Very often the battered woman in practice leaves the home (regularly together with the child or children) and gets help in one of the about 450 women's shelters in Germany, whereas the offending man stays in the flat. The new provisions of the Civil Law (§ 1361b Civil Code, *Bürgerliches Gesetzbuch*) being actually discussed provide that the man who has violated or threatened the woman, has to leave the home and that specific safeguards for the protection of the woman are guaranteed. The court can impose the prohibition to visit places where the victim regularly stays (not only the place where the victim lives, but also the working place etc.). The court can also prohibit telephone calls and other forms of molesting behaviour.[51] The draft provides a new penal offence for the case that the obligations of the court are not respected.

6. Active rights of the victim to join in the criminal procedure and limits of an expansion of the injured person's position

---

50 The draft of the Federal Ministry of Justice of 8 December 2000 can be obtained under www.bmj.bund.de, Gesetzesvorhaben.

51 See the draft of the Gewaltschutzgesetz of 13 December 2000; the draft can be obtained under www.bjm.bund.de, Gesetzgebungsverfahren

While the greatest possible protection of the victim against invasions of his private sphere by the proceedings is commonly accepted as desirable, all the more so as such provision has little or negative influence on the accused's position, the extension of active rights of the victim is more problematic. At any rate, for Germany as well as for most other European systems of criminal procedure, an expansion of the victim's "status as subject" would include a return to a adversary procedure. Active rights to codetermination as they exist in Germany only in connection with private and joint prosecutions can therefore hardly be generalised. The German law-makers did not provide for, e.g., an appeal against the sentence by the joint prosecutor with good reason. The Victim Protection Act of 1987, however, introduced a number of provisions which recognise to a certain degree the victim as an "independent litigant". For example, the right of the victim to be informed about the outcome of the proceedings was embodied in the law (see § 406d StPO). According to the empirical study by Shapland, Willmore and Duff[52] the need for information was of prime importance to the victims questioned in England. Moreover, the law grants the injured person the right to inspect files through a lawyer (see § 406e StPO). This "minimum stock" of general rights of the victim to join in the procedure may doubtless be termed adequate and corresponds to the recommendations of the Council of Europe mentioned above. More extensive rights, however, seem to be incompatible with state criminal proceedings as a primarily formalised conflict between the state and the accused, if one does not wish to change the balance that has developed between the defence and the prosecution to the disadvantage of the accused. This applies at least to the criminal procedure in Germany. In his comprehensive habilitation thesis Weigend[53] comes to the following conclusion: *"Every injured person can expect the state to protect him against avoidable infringements of his rights through the criminal procedure system. This demand, however, is restricted by the necessity of ascertaining the facts and allowing the unimpaired assertion of all possibilities of defence by the accused. There is no foundation for a right for the injured person to join actively in the proceedings with the aim of determining its course or outcome".*

By the example of German reform considerations there were demonstrated the difficulties current criminal law is having in redefining the injured person's status. Amongst others these difficulties result from the fact that criminal procedure is increasingly expected to re-establish legal peace, a

---

52 J. SHAPLAND, J. WILLMORE, & P. DUFF (1985) *Victims in the criminal justice system.* Aldershot: Dartmouth.

53 WEIGEND, *o.c.*

task it can accomplish only to a limited extent on account of its classical structure.[54] Direct interaction between the offender and the victim and the settlement of the conflict that has resulted from or had triggered the offence, appear to be appropriate for informal conciliation procedures (therefore mediation schemes regularly work before criminal proceedings take place,[55] however, they seem to be rather impracticable *within* the framework of the state criminal proceedings. As a consequence, the protection of the injured person's position in criminal proceedings is limited. Improvements are difficult as, almost inevitably they are coupled with a restriction of the ability of the accused to conduct his defence.

Victim-related reforms of the criminal procedure can hence consist only of a careful expansion of the active rights of the injured person. The institution of criminal proceedings should remain a task of the public prosecutor. The injured party, however, should be given the possibility of appealing against the withdrawal of prosecution (also in connection with discretionary decisions, see the recommendation No. R (85) 11, No. 7 of the Council of Europe). The victim, if he wishes, is entitled to a "prominent position as party to a procedure". Therefore the guarantee of the injured person's rights to information should go beyond the German rights that relate to the outcome of the proceedings.

Moreover one may doubt whether the injured party should be entitled to an independent appeal against the judgement. The forms of private and joint prosecution which exist in Germany (as in most European countries) ought to be abolished completely,[56] mainly because the purely retaliatory function of these forms of action is no longer appropriate to the criminal justice system of a welfare state. The protective functions of private and joint prosecutions, especially the consultation of a lawyer, can also be realised in other procedural forms. The conciliation procedure described above might be employed in cases of petty interpersonal crimes (as is currently the practice in the run-up to private prosecution), while the victim –as is the case in Germany– ought to be granted the right to consult a lawyer free of charge (a so-called victim attorney) in the course of the state criminal action where serious crimes are involved. This should apply especially to sexual offences and offences involving bodily injury and homicide.

---

54 K. SEELMANN (1989) Paradoxien der Opferorientierung im Strafrecht, *Juristenzeitung*, 670-676.

55 DÜNKEL (1996) Täter-Opfer-Ausgleich, *o.c.*

56 BRIENEN & HOEGEN, *o.c.*

7. Models of offender-victim compensation in criminal proceedings

Three basic models of material compensation in criminal proceedings are to be distinguished.[57]

Firstly, the connection of civil claims with criminal procedure as it exists in the countries like Belgium, Finland, France, Portugal or Spain in connection with the *action civile* and in Germany (Austria and Switzerland) with the so-called adhesion procedure (*Adhäsionsverfahren*). In chapter 5 it has been already pointed out the rather negative experiences made in Germany with regard to a very reserved practice of law. In countries with a more extensive practice (like Finland or France) the problems also appear to be evident considering the poverty of many offenders which seems to offer little chance that an executor title which has possibly been attained in the trial will be realised in practice. However, it seems to be remarkable that e.g. in Finland practically all civil claims are connected with the criminal trial.[58]

In a second model compensation is conceptualised as an independent penal sanction. This model is applied mainly in the common law jurisdictions that do not provide for adhesion procedures like England and Wales or Scotland in the form of the so-called compensation order[59] as well as in a great number of states of the United States. In Germany compensation is a possible criminal sanction for juveniles between 14-21 years of age. However, it is applied only in about 1-2% of all cases.[60] The English compensation order has gained greater importance; after all already in the eighties it has been imposed in 15% of the decisions of the Crown Courts. The average quantum of compensation payments imposed, however, has been rather low.[61]

---

57 DÜNKEL, Täter-Opfer-Ausgleich und Schadenswiedergutmachung, *o.c.*; F. DÜNKEL, (1996) Current Directions in Criminal Policy, in: W. MCCARNEY (ed.), *Juvenile Delinquents and Young People in Danger in an Open Environment*, 38-74, 216-222. Winchester: Waterside Press; BRIENEN & HOEGEN, *o.c.*

58 A. ESER & S. WALTHER (1996) (eds.), *Wiedergutmachung in Kriminalrecht. Internationale Perspektiven*, vol. 1. Freiburg: Max-Planck-Institut für ausländisches und internationales Strafrecht.

59 BRIENEN & HOEGEN, *o.c.*

60 F. DÜNKEL (1990) *Freiheitsentzug für junge Rechtsbrecher - Situation und Reform von Jugendstrafe, Jugendstrafvollzug, Jugendarrest und Untersuchungshaft in der Bundesrepublik Deutschland und im internationalen Vergleich*. Bonn: Forum Verlag; W. HEINZ (1997) Deutschland, in: F. DÜNKEL et al. (eds.), *Entwicklungstendenzen und Reformstrategien im Jugendstrafrecht im internationalen Vergleich* 3-65. Bonn: Forum Verlag; W. HEINZ (2000) *Konstanzer Inventar zum Sanktionenrecht*, *o.c.*

61 T. NEWBURN (1989) *The settlement of claims at the criminal injuries compensation board*. London: HMSO.

To the extent that compensation payments are imposed *in addition* to other sanctions (as, e. g., particularly in England), there are parallels to the regulations generally applied in numerous countries, according to which compensation is ordered as an obligation connected to other sanctions. The most far reaching possibility of "decriminalisation" is the absolute or conditional discharge when the offender has made reparation or is ready to do so. This may be applied only under the procedural principle of expediency (*Opportunitätsprinzip*), but even countries traditionally following the principle of legality, more and more open the floor for some discretion of the prosecutor (or judge) in order to cope with increasing numbers of petty crimes.

In Germany §§ 153 and seq. give the prosecutor the discretion to dismiss the case because of its petty nature or if the offender fulfils certain obligations. At first place § 153a StPO names the obligation of compensation. In 1993 the legislator has extended the scope of conditional discharge also to "medium" serious crimes. The (conditional) discharge is used very extensively as in the field of the Criminal Law for adults 44% of all cases are dropped.[62] The imposition of compensation orders in this context remains, however, rare. In practice, the obligation of compensation I used only in about 1% of the cases, whereas 98% are financial payments (*Geldbusse*) in favour of non-profit organisations or the state.[63]

Another possibility is the *connection* of compensation with a suspended prison sentence (probation, in some jurisdictions also with parole or conditional release). Such regulations exist, e.g., in Austria, Belgium, Germany, Denmark, the Netherlands, Portugal, Poland, Sweden and Switzerland. However, an international comparison shows that compensation as an obligation has not yet gained any central importance in any of these countries.[64]

In Swiss and Portuguese criminal law there exists the possibility of transmitting a fine paid to the state to the victim as a further model of compensation in criminal proceedings (see Art.60.2 of the Swiss Penal Code, Art. 129.3 of the Portuguese Penal Code). In Germany the above-mentioned Victim Protection Act of 1987 created the possibility of easy terms of payment being granted by the public prosecutor only when the collection of fines and costs of the proceedings endangered the payment of compensation (see § 459a StPO). An actual reform proposal of the Federal Ministry of Justice provides that 10% of fines shall be transferred to victims assistance

62 HEINZ, *o.c.*
63 HEINZ, *o.c.*
64 BRIENEN & HOEGEN, *o.c.*

organisations (see above under 6.). More far-reaching reform proposals such as the possibility of suspending fines on probation in case the offender undertakes to pay compensation (only in Austria) have not been able to gain acceptance so far.

Models of compensation as they exist in North American Federal Law and in Cuba deserve mention in this connection. Special state compensation funds have been set up which serve to pay the victim directly. The offender then has to pay his fine into these funds. However, the criticism of that such funds serve to destroy the personal relationship between the offender and the victim as regards compensation is justified.[65]

An international comparison of the course of development shows that the idea of compensation is increasingly being recognised and encouraged also in connection with judicial sanctions.

The reforms of Austrian juvenile and adult criminal law of 1988 and 1987 have already been mentioned. In France the regulations governing the deferment of the decision on the imposition of penalty in connection with an obligation to pay damages were expanded by the possibility of placing the accused under the supervision of a probation officer (Art.469-2 and 469-3 Criminal Procedure Act.[66] This is intended to encourage attempts at both reparation and a personal agreement between the offender and the victim under the guidance of social workers as has been realised in the project in St. Etienne.[67]

In England the Criminal Justice Act of July 1988 broadened the application of the compensation order by placing a special obligation on the courts to indicate expressly the reasons for no issuing a compensation order. In a circular the Home Office pointed out that a compensation order is sufficient as a sole sanction in certain cases (the statutory basis of this possibility was created in 1982) and that in every case it takes precedence over the fine. The Criminal Justice Act of 1991 and the *Crime and Disorder Act* of 1998 have extended the "restorative" approach by introducing the reparation order and the scope of compensating the victim.[68].

In the Netherlands the so-called Victim Act Terwee of 1995 introduced the compensation measure as an independent sanction. The Dutch legislator

---

65 SHAPLAND, WILLMORE & DUFF, *o.c.*

66 PATSOURAKOU, *o.c.*, 225.

67 See J.P. BONAFÉ-SCHMIDT, in: M. WRIGHT & B. GALAWAY (1989) (eds.), *Mediation and Criminal Justice. Victims, Offenders and Community*. London: Sage.

68 B. HUBER (1993) Großbritannien, in: A. ESER, & B. HUBER (eds.), *Strafrechtsentwicklung in Europa,* 4.1., 635-744. Freiburg: Max-Planck-Institut für ausländisches und internationales Strafrecht; B. HUBER, & Y. BRAUN (1999) Großbritannien, in: ESER & HUBER, *o.c.*, 1043-1164.

was following the example of the English compensation order.[69] On the other hand the traditional adhesion procedure was kept, although empirical studies demonstrated that there were many obstacles in the practical use of civil claims within criminal proceedings. Already in 1986, directives for the improvement of the victim's situation in criminal proceedings, which concern above all aspects of victim protection (victim-minded investigations etc) and victim assistance had brought improvements in the field of compensation in that the police and the public prosecutor's office are urged to carry out more intensive investigations also with regard the extend of damage. This approach has largely been extended by the Victim Act Terwee in 1995 and several Guidelines for the police and prosecutors in order to extend the victim's possibility to get compensation.[70]

Current German law –especially criminal justice for juveniles, as mentioned above– offers many opportunities for arranging or considering damage compensation and mediation. Juvenile prosecutors may waive prosecution if reformatory measures have already been implemented or introduced (§ 45 II JGG, Juvenile Justice Act). The 1990 reform act explicitly equates mediation with such a reformatory measure. Significantly, the legislator already recognises sincere efforts by juveniles to resolve conflicts or to provide restitution. This arrangement protects juvenile and 18-20 years old young adult offenders if the victim of the crime refuses to co-operate. Successful damage restitution more frequently leads to a dismissal because of "reduced culpability" (pursuant to § 45 I JGG or § 153 StPO in adult criminal law). Under the same conditions that apply for juvenile prosecutors, juvenile court judges may waive prosecution to enable subsequent consideration of mediation efforts by the young offenders. Peculiarities associated with German juvenile law concern the material losses restitution, as well as mediation and the judge's order or precept (as an independent sanction; see §§ 15, 10 JGG). Adult criminal justice until recently lacked such means for judges to respond. Both juvenile and adult criminal justice provide for damage compensation in conjunction with a suspended term of detention in a remand home or imprisonment (the same applies for release on probation.[71] Restitution as a juvenile court sanction remains quite limited: in 1998 less than 2% of the sanctions imposed on convicted juveniles involved a restitution order. Providing mediation as a

---

69 BRIENEN & HOEGEN, *o.c.*

70 *Ibid.*

71 For a summary, F. DÜNKEL, & D. RÖSSNER (1989) Law and Practice of Victim/Offender Agreements, in: WRIGHT & GALAWAY (eds.), *o.c.*, 152-177; DÜNKEL, (1996) Täter-Opfer-Ausgleich, *o.c.*, 44-66; RÖSSNER/KRAUS in: DÖLLING et al., *o.c.*

court sanction in juvenile justice (see § 10 I No. 7 JGG) was rightly criticised for violating the voluntary principle of mediation efforts. In practice mediation as a juvenile court educational directive is not used,[72] because suitable cases are dealt in an informal proceeding (diversion in the sense of § 45 II JGG, see above) before a court trial and therefore do not enter the level of formal court proceedings.[73]

The first pilot projects concerning juvenile law began in 1985. In the late 1980s, about twenty major projects existed, including a few dealing with adult criminal law.[74] Mediation covers a broad scope for an individual measure (especially for the 1990 legal reform). In the early 1990s, 224 institutions in a nation-wide survey (of the old Federal states) indicated that they had already implemented or that they had concrete plans to implement mediation.[75] Among juvenile welfare departments, 60% subsequently implemented mediation. 85% of the institutions worked with juveniles or young adults. A growing range of projects catered to adults over 21. In a later poll concerning the year 1995 Wandrey and Weitekamp reported 368 mediation projects, i.e. an increase of 68% since 1992. The case numbers increased even more, from about 2,100 to 9,000 in 1995, i.e. by 78% within three years. On the other hand the authors comment that most projects practise mediation only rarely and as an additional "ad-hoc-approach" to other educational measures mostly in the field of juvenile justice.[76] The projects working with adults over 21 increased to 28% of all mediation schemes.

Recently, another poll conducted by the department of Criminology at the University of Greifswald at the assignment of the Federal Ministry of Justice revealed that mediation was available virtually everywhere in the old Federal states (and also in the new ones, since the reunification of Germany) during

---

72 RÖSSNER/KRAUS, *o.c.*

73 F. DÜNKEL (1996) Täter-Opfer-Ausgleich, *o.c.*

74 B. BANNENBERG (1993) *Wiedergutmachung in der Strafrechtspraxis*. Bonn: Forum-Verlag; R.D. HERING & D. RÖSSNER (1993) *Täter-Opfer-Ausgleich im allgemeinen Strafrecht*. Bonn: Forum-Verlag; E. MARKS, K. MEYER et al. (1994) (eds.), *Wiedergutmachung und Strafrechtspraxis*. Bonn: Forum-Verlag; C. PFEIFFER (1997) (ed.), *Täter-Opfer-Ausgleich im Allgemeinen Strafrecht*. Baden-Baden: Nomos-Verlag; DÖLLING et al., *o.c.* See F. DÜNKEL & J. ZERMATTEN (1990) (eds.), *Nouvelles tendances dans le droit pénal des mineurs - Médiation, travail au profit de la communauté et traitement intermédiaire*. Freiburg: Max-Planck-Institut für ausländisches und internationales Strafrecht; F. DÜNKEL (1996) Current Directions in Criminal Policy, *o.c.*; F. DÜNKEL (1996) Täter-Opfer-Ausgleich, *o.c.*

75 J. SCHRECKLING et al. (1991) *Bestandsaufnahme zur Praxis des Täter-Opfer-Ausgleichs in der Bundesrepublik Deutschland*. Bonn: Bundesministerium der Justiz.

76 See WANDREY/WEITEKAMP, in: DÖLLING, *o.c.*

the period 1993/94. 70% of the youth welfare departments surveyed in the old Federal states and 88% in the new ones reported that either social workers at the juvenile welfare departments or private juvenile aid services offered mediation. This option is available in about three quarters of all youth welfare districts (74%) in the context or rather as a strategy before criminal punishment (diversion). Nearly half of all juvenile welfare departments (48%) offered mediation by their own services. An additional 11% provided this service in conjunction with or alongside a private service, and in 14.5% of the cases mediation was implemented exclusively by a private service.[77] The numbers of mediation projects are still increasing. A recent survey in the new Federal states revealed 128 projects in 1997, whereas in 1994 "only" 48 have been working.[78] So Wandrey and Weitekamp[79] are right to state that mediation in Germany is still "booming". On the other hand there is a danger that mediation will play more or less the role of an additional educational/rehabilitative sanction within the traditional juvenile or adult criminal justice system and not be a step towards real restorative justice. The annual cases dealt by the youth authorities or specialised projects remain rather limited. In 1993/94 half of the youth welfare departments of the local communities dealt with no more than 7-8 cases a year.[80]

Notwithstanding the limited prospects for quantitative growth, mediation and damage compensation play a central role in crime policy also in the Criminal Law for Adults. Accordingly, a team of German, Swiss and Austrian criminal law scholars and the leading expert[81] at the 59th Assembly of German Legal Scholars in 1992 have suggested transforming restitution in general criminal justice into an independent track (with priority) in addition to punishment and therapeutic measures.[82] Voluntary and full damage restitution (§§ 1, 2 AE-WGM) should be the preferred response to minor and moderate crime (e. g. prison sentences up to one year; § 4 AE-WGM). In

---

77 See F. DÜNKEL, B. GENG & W. KIRSTEIN (1998) *Soziale Trainingskurse und neue ambulante Maßnahmen in der Bundesrepublik Deutschland.* Bonn: Bundesministerium der Justiz.

78 R. STEFFENS (1999) *Wiedergutmachung und Täter-Opfer-Ausgleich im Jugend- und Erwachsenenstrafrecht in den neuen Bundesländern.* Mönchengladbach: Forum-Verlag.

79 DÖLLING et al., *o.c.*

80 With no differences between East and West Germany, see DÜNKEL, GENG & KIRSTEIN, *o.c.*

81 H. SCHÖCH (1992) Empfehlen sich Änderungen und Ergänzungen bei den strafrechtlichen Sanktionen ohne Freiheitsentzug? Gutachten C zum 59. Deutschen Juristentag. München: C. H. Beck.

82 Arbeitskreis deutscher, schweizerischer und österreichischer Strafrechtslehrer; SCHÖCH, *o.c.*

cases incurring a sentence of more than a year, a compulsory sentence reduction should apply. Elsewhere, the court will waive the penalty and merely find the offender guilty. If a victim is unavailable or unwilling to settle, symbolic acts of restitution (community service, payment of fines to non-profit organisations) to restore the legal order may also be applied (§ 2 AE-WGM). While the 59th Assembly of German Legal Scholars basically agreed with these suggestions, it rejected restitution as a "third track of sanctions" as well as compulsory exemption from penalty in the event of active remorse in accordance with the Austrian example (§ 167 Austrian Penal Code). The group advocated expanding restitution through existing arrangements in criminal procedure (§§ 153, 153a StPO) as optional means for adjusting the proceedings (NJW 1992, pp. 3021). The group also rejected the suggestion to implement community service as an independent sanction.

As part of the 1994 act to eradicate organised crime, the legislator changed these demands for reform only slightly upon implementing § 46a of the StGB. If the offender "through his efforts to reach a settlement with the injured party (mediation) has compensated entirely or partially or has genuinely tried to atone for his act, or if the restitution requires considerable individual service or sacrifice on his part to compensate the victim fully or mostly, the court may (...) reduce the punishment" or – in the event of acts incurring up to one year of imprisonment – waive punishment entirely. The (possible) importance of this rule may be explained by the fact that about 90% of all prison sentences in Germany are in the range of up to one year. § 46a StGB is becoming more and more important and the High Courts repetitively agree to appeals that claim that the court has not taken enough care to reparative efforts of the offender (as a mitigating circumstance or precondition to waive punishment.[83] Although the idea of mediation in Germany is strongly attached to the criminal justice system, the trend towards restorative justice cannot be denied.[84]

---

83 STEFFENS, *o.c.*

84 See F. DÜNKEL (1996) Täter-Opfer-Ausgleich. *o.c.*; for general aspects of restorative justice see B. GALAWAY & J. HUDSON (1996) (eds.), *Restorative Justice: International perspectives.* Monsey/New York: Criminal Justice Press; L. WALGRAVE (1998) (ed.), *Restorative justice for juveniles: potentialities, risks and problems.* Leuven: Leuven University Press; G. BAZEMORE & L. WALGRAVE (1999) (eds.), *Restorative juvenile justice: repairing the harm of youth crime.* Monsey/New York: Criminal Justice Press; M. WRIGHT (2001) *Restorative Justice. Selected reading list*, International Victimology Website (www.victimology.nl).

8. State victim compensation

Although material and immaterial compensation by the offender to the victim is a welcome development, the problem that the victim may be left empty-handed because of the offender cannot be detected or caught (or is not able to pay compensation) has not been solved. In this respect, a need for state victim compensation schemes still exists. The situation is especially serious for victims of violent crimes, particularly if their earning capacity has been reduced and if they shall remain disadvantaged or injured for a relatively long period, also by the mental affect of the crime. The Council of Europe emphasised the need for legal provisions governing state compensation for victims of violent crimes, amongst others, in its resolutions of 1977 and again in 1985. The General Assembly of the United Nations has also stressed this particular aspect in the 1985 resolution on victim rights. In fact, most European countries created relevant provisions in the course of the 70's (England already in 1964; see for a comprehensive overview *Greer* 1996). In the 80's Belgium and Luxembourg introduced state victim compensation schemes and Switzerland introduced some principle rule into its Constitution. In 1984, Spain introduced a claim to damages against the state only for victims of terrorist violent crimes (see Art. 24 et seq.), in 1995 a more general law was passed. The reform in France (of 1990) extended the scope of victim compensation. Now all victims of violent acts without any restriction and even victims of property crimes (if they are in need of financial help) can get state compensation. Germany extended the scope of state victim compensation in 1993 also for (especially European, but under certain circumstances also other) foreigners that have been victimised in Germany (see sect. 1 (5-7), 2 (1) OEG.[85].

However, the systems of compensation and the prerequisites for claims differ considerably. Most countries created a single form of compensation from a victim fund, whereas victim compensation in Germany as well as in Austria is conceptualised as a regular monthly pension based on the system of pensions and related benefits to war victims.[86]

So far, the empirical studies of the legal reality of state victim compensation have been conducted mainly in England, the Netherlands and

---

85 E. KUNZ, & G. ZELLNER (1999) *Opferentschädigungsgesetz. Kommentar*. München: C. H. Beck.

86 See F. DÜNKEL (1985) Victim Compensation and Offender Restitution in the Federal Republic of Germany. A Western-European Comparative Perspective, 9 *International Journal of Comparative and Applied Criminal Justice* 29-39; D. GREER (1996) (ed.), *Compensating Crime Victims. A European Survey*. Freiburg: Max-Planck-Institut für ausländisches und internationales Strafrecht.

West Germany.[87] They have made evidence not only to the shortcomings of the legal provisions, but also to the practical application of the relevant laws. A study conducted in England, e.g., showed that only 39% of the victims had knowledge of the existence of regulations relating to state victim compensation. Accordingly, an application had been filed only rarely, although the proportion of positive decisions relative to the number of applications appears to be comparatively high – 83%. But nevertheless, only half of the victims questioned expressed satisfaction with the compensation procedure and the payments received. This has led to some improvements and a new Criminal Injuries Compensation Act in 1995 with a considerable impact on the number and rate of positive awards.[88]

The proportion of notices of compensation was clearly lower in the Netherlands than in England. In 1986 only 20% of the victims who were injured considerably (and who ware basically entitled to assert a claim) are estimated to have filed an application. Here, too, the reason stated is an insufficient knowledge of the state compensation scheme. In accordance with the findings of the English survey, the victim poll showed that the victims would prefer compensation by the offender to state victim compensation. The situation in the Netherlands has improved, however, in the last years. The application rate increased to about 25% (in some years even more) and the government in 1993 has changed the law in order to speedy up the procedure of awarding compensation.[89]

The rather negative assessment of the English and Dutch researchers of the practice of state victim compensation has been confirmed by a study in Germany. However, this is partially due to the particularly restrictive German legislation, according to which, e.g., only victims whose earning capacity has been reduced by at least 25% are entitled to assert a claim. Injuries to health of up to 6 months are not compensated. Moreover, compensation may be denied in case of slight contributory negligence. In view of these restrictive conditions it is small wonder that less than 10% of the victims of violent crimes submit requests with the pension offices. The decentralised decision-making structures account for which the proportion of positive decisions made in 1984 ranging between 9% in Berlin and 38% in Hesse is particularly problematic. The victims expressed discontent not only

---

87 See B. VILLMOW & B. PLEMPER (1989) *Praxis der Opferentschädigung*. Pfaffenweiler: Centaurus; B. VILLMOW (1991) Victim Compensation in some Western Countries, in: KAISER, KURY & ALBRECHT, *o.c.*, vol. 2, 175-193.

88 See ZEDNER in A. ESER & S. WALTHER (1996) (eds.), *Wiedergutmachung in Kriminalrecht; internationale Perspektiven,* vol. 1. Freiburg: Max-Planck-Institut für ausländisches und internationales Strafrecht.

89 See GROENHUIJSEN/VAN DER LANDEN, in: ESER & WALTHER, *o.c.*, vol. 1, 81-86.

on account of the rejected applications but also because of the length of proceedings which was felt to be especially burdensome. Recent statistics collected by the private organisation "*Weisser Ring*" and concerning also the new federal states of the former GDR demonstrate continuing differences in the rates of successful applications. It is estimated that only 11% of possible applicants submit an application to the competent boards. In the year 2000 about 46% of the applications were successful, which is a considerable increase in comparison to the research conducted in the 80s (see above). In most cases only a lump sum for the medical care was granted, whereas a pension because of diminished earning capacities etc. was the exception (18%). The rate of successful applications ranged from 25% in Saar, 27% in Baden-Württemberg and Schleswig-Holstein up to 54% in Thuringia, 59% in Rhineland-Palatinate and even 95% in North Rhine-Westphalia.[90]

On the whole, state victim compensation is as much in need of improvement as ever. The shortcomings of the statutory regulations and of their implementation is compensated for only in part by private victim support organisations. In Germany, for all that, the so-called "*Weisser Ring*" has devoted itself to the financial compensation of victims at considerable financial costs. This initiative seems only questionable in that victim assistance has been –at least to some extent– connected with a repressive form of penal policy that was oriented to "law and order".

Summary final remarks

The question touched by the subject matter of this paper, namely, whether the current trend is coupled with a change in tendency away from the offender perspective towards the victim perspective cannot be settled finally. We must contrast the justified concern with improving the victim's situation especially in criminal proceedings with the danger that the accused's legitimate rights to defend himself will be impaired. A new balance needs to be found which makes criminal procedure and the enforcement of state claim to punishment unnecessary in wide realms of property offences and beyond. In this respect, the trend in criminal law towards "privatization" and to divert appropriate cases to forms of restorative justice ought to be encouraged. However, as the German example shows, it would be appropriate and necessary for constitutional reasons to maintain a private settlement of conflicts that is closely connected with state justice and to guarantee a

90 WEISSER RING (2001) *Staatliche Opferentschädigung – oft nur ein Lippenbekenntnis*. MEDIEN-INFO, Weisser Ring e. V. Mainz (www.weisser-ring.de).

measure of control to ensure a fair conciliation procedure. This may be achieved by using professional social workers as arbitrators, through supervision by the public prosecutor's office or the court with regard to the course and the outcome of conciliation procedures.[91]

Improvements in the injured party's position in state criminal proceedings ought to be regarded with the utmost reserve to the extent that they concern active rights of the victim to participate in and influence the course of proceedings, as they normally place the accused in an poorer position. Victim impact statements as used in the USA and wide influence on sentencing and parole through the interfering victim do not fit to the culture of continental European justice systems. We have to remember that the peace making function of the classic criminal procedure has been reached by excluding revenge and establishing the state power for guaranteeing a rational and fair trial that is based on the relation of the state and the offender. The victim was widely excluded not in order to diminish its rights, but to take off the burden to prosecute by himself. That is why active rights of the victim are somehow paradoxical to the classic criminal procedure with its aims of different forms of prevention.[92] (see *Seelmann* 1989). Taking the concrete interests of the victim for compensation into account has another risk: when concretising the suffering and damage the question of victim precipitation may arise and contribute to mechanisms of "blaming the victim". In Germany in the 80s some scholars claimed for a specific interpretation of crimes like fraud, embezzlement or theft in cases where the victim has facilitated or otherwise contributed to the crime. The so-called victimo-dogmatic theory, however, has been rejected as this is not the area of defining (and decriminalising) certain criminal behaviour, but of the sentencing decision[93].

The question of an improved victim protection in proceedings is to be judged differently; in this connection, invasions of privacy and other burdensome procedural arrangements might be avoided more than is currently the practice in order to avoid a secondary victimisation of the victim. In this area much has been achieved in the last decade, especially concerning child victims of sexual abuse etc. (see the reforms in Sweden, Norway, Germany etc.)

---

91 See the proposal of Arbeitskreis deutscher, schweizerischer und östereichischer Strafrechtslehrer, *o.c.*

92 K. SEELMANN (1989) Paradoxien der Opferorientierung im Strafrecht, *Juristenzeitung* 670-676.

93 C. ROXIN (1997) (3rd ed.), *Strafrecht Allgemeiner Teil*, vol. I. München: C. H. Beck.

We can do more justice to the idea that both criminal proceedings and punishment should be used only as last resort by restricting the state claim to punishment to behaviour which is particularly harmful to society and which calls for a state reaction for general preventive purposes (especially with regard to the illustration of standards in terms of so-called positive general prevention). For those reasons we should not demand a shift in paradigm but emphasise a criminal policy which is directed to both the offender and the victim and which adheres to the idea of prevention and to the elementary legal guarantees that are coupled with a formalised procedure.

References

Materials of the Council of Europe

- European Convention on the Compensation of Victims of Violent Crimes of 24 november 1983.
- Explanatory report on the European Convention on the Compensation of Victims of Violent Crimes. Strasbourg 1984.
- European Committee on Crime Problems: Recommendation No. R (85) 11 on the position of the victim in the framework of criminal law and procedure and report of the CDPC. Strasbourg 1985.
- Council of Europe (ed.), Assistance to victims and prevention of victimisation. Recommendation No. R (87) 21 and explanatory memorandum. Strasbourg 1988.
- Council of Europe (ed.), Mediation in penal matters and explanatory memorandum. Recommendation No. (99) 19. Strasbourg 1999.

References

Arbeitskreis deutscher, schweizerischer und österreichischer Strafrechtslehrer (1992) *Alternativ-Entwurf Wiedergutmachung (AE-WGM)*. München.

Arnold, H. (1986) Kriminelle Viktimisierung und ihre Korrelate. Ergebnisse international vergleichender Opferbefragungen, 98 *Zeitschrift für die gesamten Strafrechtswissenschaften* 1014-1058.

Arnold, H., Albrecht, H.-J. (1991) Research on Victimization and Related Topics in the Federal Republic of Germany – A Selection of Problems and Results, in: Kaiser, G., Kury, H., Albrecht, H.-J. (eds.), *Victims and*

Criminal Justice, vol. 1, 20-36, Freiburg i. Br.: Max-Planck-Institut für ausländisches und internationales Strafrecht.

Bannenberg, B. (1993) *Wiedergutmachung in der Strafrechtspraxis*. Bonn: Forum-Verlag.

Bazemore, G., Walgrave, L. (1999) (eds.), *Restorative juvenile justice: repairing the harm of youth crime*. Monsey/New York: Criminal Justice Press.

Brienen, M. E. I., Hoegen, E. H. (2000) *Victims of Crime in 22 European Criminal Justice Systems: The Implementation of Recommendation (85) 11 of the Council of Europe on the Position of the Victim in the Framework of Criminal Law and Procedure*. Nijmegen: Wolf Legal Productions.

Dölling, D., et al. (1998) *Täter-Opfer-Ausgleich in Deutschland. Bestandsaufnahme und Perspektiven*. Bonn: Forum-Verlag.

Dünkel, F. (1985) Victim Compensation and Offender Restitution in the Federal Republic of Germany. A Western-European Comparative Perspective, 9 *International Journal of Comparative and Applied Criminal Justice* 29-39.

Dünkel, F. (1986) Reparation and victim-offender reconciliation and aspects of the legal position of the victim in criminal procedures in a Western-European perspective, in: Kerner, H.-J., Galaway, B., Janssen, H. (eds.), *Jugendgerichtsbarkeit in Europa und Nordamerika - Aspekte und Tendenzen*, 303-327. München: Deutsche Vereinigung für Jugendgerichte und Jugendgerichtshilfen.

Dünkel, F. (1989) Täter-Opfer-Ausgleich und Schadenswiedergutmachung. Neuere Entwicklungen des Strafrechts und der Strafrechtspraxis im internationalen Vergleich, in: Marks, E., Rössner, D. (eds.), *Täter-Opfer-Ausgleich*, 394-463. Bonn.

Dünkel, F. (1990) *Freiheitsentzug für junge Rechtsbrecher - Situation und Reform von Jugendstrafe, Jugendstrafvollzug, Jugendarrest und Untersuchungshaft in der Bundesrepublik Deutschland und im internationalen Vergleich*. Bonn: Forum Verlag.

Dünkel, F. (1996) Current Directions in Criminal Policy, in: McCarney, W. (ed.), *Juvenile Delinquents and Young People in Danger in an Open Environment* 38-74, 216-222. Winchester: Waterside Press.

Dünkel, F. (1996) Täter-Opfer-Ausgleich. German experiences with mediation in a European perspective, 4 *European Journal on Criminal Policy and Research* 44-66.

Dünkel, F., Kirstein, W., Geng, B. (1998) *Soziale Trainingskurse und neue ambulante Maßnahmen in der Bundesrepublik Deutschland.* Bonn: Bundesministerium der Justiz.

Dünkel, F., Krainz, K., Würger, M. (1991) Victimization and Incidence of Delinquency - An International Comparison - Results of a Survey of Law Students in the Federal Republic of Germany, Austria and Switzerland, in: Kaiser, G. et al. (eds.), *Victims and Criminal Justice,* vol. 2, 123-172. Freiburg: Max-Planck-Institut für ausländisches und internationales Strafrecht.

Dünkel, F., Rössner, D. (1989) Law and Practice of Victim/Offender Agreements, in: Wright, M., Galaway, B. (eds.), *Mediation and Criminal Justice* 152-177. London: Sage.

Dünkel, F., Zermatten, J. (1990) (eds.), *Nouvelles tendances dans le droit pénal des mineurs - Médiation, travail au profit de la communauté et traitement intermédiaire.* Freiburg: Max-Planck-Institut für ausländisches und internationales Strafrecht.

Dünkel, F., Sakalauskas, G. (2001) Jugendstrafrecht und Jugendstrafrechtsreform in Litauen, 12 *DVJJ-Journal* 72-80.

Eisenberg, U. (2000) (5th ed.), *Kriminologie.* München: C. H. Beck.

European Forum for Victim/Offender Mediation and Restorative Justice (2000) (ed.), *Victim/offender mediation in Europe: making restorative justice work.* Leuven: Leuven University Press.

Eser, A., Kaiser, G., Madlener, K. (1990) (eds.), *Neue Wege der Wiedergutmachung im Strafrecht.* Freiburg: Max-Planck-Institut für ausländisches und internationales Strafrecht.

Eser, A., Walther, S. (1996) (eds.), *Wiedergutmachung in Kriminalrecht; internationale Perspektiven,* vol. 1. Freiburg: Max-Planck-Institut für ausländisches und internationales Strafrecht.

Fattah, E. A. (1991) *Understanding Criminal Victimization.* Scarborough/Ontario: Prentice-Hall.

Galaway, B., Hudson, J. (1990) (eds.), *Criminal Justice, Restitution, and Reconciliation.* Monsey/New York: Criminal Justice Press.

Galaway, B., Hudson, J. (1996) (eds.), *Restorative Justice: international perspectives.* Monsey/New York: Criminal Justice Press.

Greer, D. (1996) (Ed.), *Compensating Crime Victims. A European Survey.* Freiburg: Max-Planck-Institut für ausländisches und internationales Strafrecht.

Griesbaum, R. (1998) Der gefährdete Zeuge. Überlegungen zum Zeugenschutz im Strafverfahren, 18 *Neue Zeitschrift für Strafrecht* 433-441.

Heinz, W. (1997) Deutschland, in: F. Dünkel et al. (eds.), *Entwicklungstendenzen und Reformstrategien im Jugendstrafrecht im internationalen Vergleich,* 3-65. Bonn: Forum Verlag.

Heinz, W. (2000) *Konstanzer Inventar zum Sanktionenrecht.* <www.uni-konstanz.de/rtf/kis/sanks2000.htm> .

Helsinki Institute for Crime Prevention and Control affiliated with the United Nations (HEUNI) (1989) *Changing Victim Policy: The United Nations Victim Declaration and Recent Developments in Europe.* Helsinki: HEUNI.

Hering, R.-D. (1991) Court-Assistance and the Victim of Crime - The Opportunity of Social Services within the Justice System in Practice, in: Kaiser, G., et al. (eds.), *Victims and Criminal Justice*, vol.3, 115-125. Freiburg: Max-Planck-Institut für ausländisches und internationales Strafrecht.

Hering, R. D., Rössner, D. (1993) (eds.), *Täter-Opfer-Ausgleich im allgemeinen Strafrecht.* Bonn: Forum-Verlag.

Hillenkamp, T. (1987) Möglichkeiten der Erweiterung des Instituts der tätigen Reue, in: Schöch, H. (ed.), *Wiedergutmachung und Strafrecht,* 81-113. München: Fink.

Huber, B. (1993) Großbritannien, in: Eser, A., Huber, B. (eds.), *Strafrechtsentwicklung in Europa 4.1,* 635-744; Freiburg: Max-Planck-Institut für ausländisches und internationales Strafrecht.

Huber, B., Braun, Y. (1999) Großbritannien, in: Eser, A., Huber, B. (eds.), *Strafrechtsentwicklung in Europa 5.2*, 1043-1164. Freiburg: Max-Planck-Institut für ausländisches und internationales Strafrecht.

Janssen, H., Kerner, H.-J. (1985) (eds.), *Verbrechensopfer, Sozialarbeit und Justiz*. Bonn: Eigenverlag der Deutschen Bewährungshilfe.

Joutsen, M. (1987) *The Role of the Victim of Crime in European Criminal Justice Systems. A Crossnational Study of the Role of the Victim.* Helsinki (Helsinki Institute for Crime Prevention and Control affiliated with the United Nations, HEUNI).

Jung, H. (1981) Die Stellung des Verletzten im Strafprozeß, 93 *Zeitschrift für die gesamte Strafrechtswissenschaft* 1147-1176.

Jung, H. (1987) Das Opferschutzgesetz, 27 *Juristische Schulung* 157-160.

Jung, H. (2000) Zur Renaissance des Opfers – ein Lehrstück kriminalpolitischer Zeitgeschichte, 33 *Zeitschrift für Rechtspolitik* 159-163.

Kaiser, G. (1996) (3rd ed.), *Kriminologie. Ein Lehrbuch.* Heidelberg, Karlsruhe: C. F. Müller.

Kaiser, G. (1989) (8th ed.), *Kriminologie. Eine Einführung in die Grundlagen*. Heidelberg.

Kaiser, G., Kury, H., Albrecht, H.-J. (1991) (eds.), *Victims and Criminal Justice,* vol. 1-4. Freiburg: Max-Planck-Institut für ausländisches und internationales Strafrecht.

Kaiser, M. (1992) *Die Stellung des Verletzten im Strafverfahren*. Freiburg: Max-Planck-Institut für ausländisches und internationales Strafrecht.

Keiser, C. (1998) *Das Kindeswohl im Strafverfahren.* Frankfurt/M.: Lang.

Kerner, H.-J., Hassemer, E. et al. (1994) (eds.), *Täter-Opfer-Ausgleich auf dem Weg zur bundesweiten Anwendung?* Bonn: Forum-Verlag.

Kerner, H.-J., E. Marks et al. (1990) Täter-Opfer-Ausgleich im Jugendstrafrecht, 37 *Bewährungshilfe* 169-176.

Kilchling, M. (1995) *Opferinteressen und Strafverfolgung*. Freiburg i. Br.: Max-Planck-Institut für ausländisches und internationales Strafrecht.

Kühne, H.-H. (1988) (ed.), *Opferrechte im Strafprozeß. Ein europäischer Vergleich.* Kehl et al.: Engel Verlag.

Kunz, E., Zellner, G. (1999) *Opferentschädigungsgesetz. Kommentar*. München: C. H. Beck.

Marks, E., Meyer, K., et al. (1994) (eds.), *Wiedergutmachung und Strafrechtspraxis.* Bonn: Forum-Verlag.

Marks, E., Rössner, D. (1989) (eds.), *Täter-Opfer-Ausgleich - Vom zwischenmenschlichen Weg zur Wiederherstellung des Rechtsfriedens.* Bonn: Forum-Verlag (2nd ed. 1990).

Marshall, T., Merry, S. (1990) *Crime and Accountability. Victim/Offender Mediation in Practice*. London: HMSO.

Messmer, H., Otto, H.-U. (1992) (eds.), *Restorative Justice on Trial. Pitfalls and Potentials of Victim-Offender Mediation - International Perspective.* Dordrecht: Kluwer (NATO ASI Series).

Newburn, T. (1989) *The settlement of claims at the criminal injuries compensation board*. London (HMSO).

Patsourakou, S.N. (1994) *Die Stellung des Verletzten im Strafrechstsystem*. Bonn: Forum-Verlag.

Pfeiffer, C. (1997) (ed.), *Täter-Opfer-Ausgleich im Allgemeinen Strafrecht*. Baden-Baden: Nomos-Verlag.

Pfeiffer, G. (2001) (3rd ed.), *Strafprozeßordnung. Kommentar*. München: C. H. Beck.

Rieß, P. (1984) *Die Rechtsstellung des Verletzten im Strafverfahren. Gutachten C für den 55. Deutschen Juristenta,* in: Verhandlungen des 55. Deutschen Juristentags. München: C.H. Beck.

Roxin, C. (1997) (3rd ed.), *Strafrecht Allgemeiner Teil*. vol. I. München: C. H. Beck.

Schöch, H. (1992) *Empfehlen sich Änderungen und Ergänzungen bei den strafrechtlichen Sanktionen ohne Freiheitsentzug? Gutachten C zum 59. Deutschen Juristentag*. München: C. H. Beck.

Schreckling, J., et al. (1991) *Bestandsaufnahme zur Praxis des Täter-Opfer-Ausgleichs in der Bundesrepublik Deutschland*. Bonn: Bundesministerium der Justiz.

Schwind, H.-D. (2001) (11th ed.), *Kriminologie. Eine praxisorientierte Einführung mit Beispielen*. Heidelberg: Kriminalistik Verlag.

Seelmann, K. (1989) Paradoxien der Opferorientierung im Strafrecht, *Juristenzeitung* 670-676.

Sessar, K. (1992) *Wiedergutmachen oder strafen; Einstellungen in der Bevölkerung und in der Justiz*. Pfaffenweiler: Centaurus-Verlag.

Sessar, K., Beurskens, A., Boers, K. (1986) Wiedergutmachung als Konfliktregelungsparadigma ? 18 *Kriminologisches Journal* 86- 104.

Shapland, J., Willmore, J., Duff, P. (1985) *Victims in the criminal justice system*. Aldershot: Dartmouth.

Steffens, R. (1999) *Wiedergutmachung und Täter-Opfer-Ausgleich im Jugend- und Erwachsenenstrafrecht in den neuen Bundesländern*. Mönchengladbach: Forum-Verlag.

Strafgesetzbuch in der Russischen Föderation (1998) *Deutsche Übersetzung von Friedrich-Christian Schroeder und Thomas Bednarz. Einführung von Friedrich-Christian Schroeder*. Sammlung ausländischer Gesetzbücher in deutscher Übersetzung. Freiburg i. Br.: Max-Planck-Institut für ausländisches und internationales Strafrecht.

Tak, P.J.P. (1986) *The Legal Scope of Non-prosecution in Europe*. Helsinki (HEUNI).

Villmow, B. (1991) Victim Compensation in some Western Countries, in: Kaiser, G. et al. (eds.), *Victims and Criminal Justice*, vol. 2, 175-193. Freiburg: Max-Planck-Institut für ausländisches und internationales Strafrecht.

Villmow, B., Plemper, B. (1989) *Praxis der Opferentschädigung*. Pfaffenweiler: Centaurus.

Voß, M. (1989) Anzeigemotive, Verfahrenserwartungen und die Bereitschaft von Geschädigten zur informellen Konfliktregelung. Erste Ergebnisse einer Opferbefragung, 72 *Monatsschrift für Kriminologie und Strafrechtsreform* 34-51.

Walgrave, L. (1998) (ed.), *Restorative justice for juveniles: potentialities, risks and problems*. Leuven: Leuven University Press.

Weigend, T. (1989) *Deliktsopfer und Strafverfahren*. Berlin: Duncker & Humblot.

Weisser Ring (2001) *Staatliche Opferentschädigung – oft nur ein Lippenbekenntnis*. MEDIEN-INFO, Weisser Ring e. V. Mainz (www.weisser-ring.de).

Wright, M. (2001) *Restorative Justice. Selected reading list*. International Victimology Webside (www.victimology.nl).

Wright, M., Galaway, B. (1989) (eds.), *Mediation and Criminal Justice. Victims, Offenders and Community*. London: Sage.

CONSTITUTIONAL CHANGE, DEVOLUTION AND CRIMINAL JUSTICE IN SCOTLAND

Peter Young

One of Tony Peters' main contributions to penology and the sociology of punishment lies in his promotion of comparative analysis. His work demonstrates an abiding interest in how criminal justice systems differ, the role culture plays in this and of our collective need to be aware of this if we are to understand and explain. Moreover, Tony is one of those fortunate souls whose academic interests combine with, indeed are further developed, by his personal ones. Tony (and Maggie) likes to travel –he has been a distinguished visitor in many universities, including the University of Edinburgh, where I first met him. I have moved on now to work in another small country, Ireland, but my contribution to his Festschift is on a theme– change, and about a country – Scotland, that I know continue to intrigue him.

Introduction

My paper is about change in the Scottish criminal justice system. While, Scotland, exists on the periphery of Europe and its criminal justice system is relatively small and in some senses quaint –for example, it contains such exotics as three verdicts in jury trials– what is happening there has a wider importance. Scottish society and its criminal justice system are undergoing a quiet revolution, or, at least, they have the potential for this. This process of change is only just under way and things could go in different directions. At the moment, however, Scotland presents scholars with a rare thing, a case study of a criminal justice system in a western democratic society that is subject to new and sudden forces that threaten to transform its institutions dramatically. In this sense, then, what one sees in Scotland comes close to approximating a natural experiment, the very thing, as social scientists, we ought to study.

1. Constitutional Contexts

At the core of the process of change are the wide ranging constitutional changes associated with devolution. The Scotland Act 1998, established a new parliament in Scotland. By itself this is of great significance not least because it transferred responsibility for all matters related to criminal justice from the old Parliament in Westminster to the new one in Edinburgh. Beyond this, however, the Act introduced another change and this was the absorption into domestic Scottish law of the European Convention on Human Rights (ECHR), the implications of which were reinforced by the Human Rights Act 2000.

These developments need to be examined separately. The place to start, however, is to consider their joint effect. Taken together they amount to what could be called a "double reconstitutionalisation" of Scots criminal law and the criminal justice system. This is readily apparent in the case of the Parliament. One can observe a new constitutional structure in the making. New committees and ministries have emerged to regulate many aspects of social life, including the criminal justice system. It would be a mistake, however, to limit the analysis to these institutional developments alone. This is because, I contend, the ECHR is of constitutional significance in its own right. By itself, I suggest, the ECHR has placed the Scottish criminal justice system in what amounts to a new political framework that, importantly, appears to be working independently from the institutional arrangements introduced by devolution. The ECHR has had this effect, because, I suggest, it is based upon a distinctive and different theory of the relationship between the citizen and the state than has prevailed historically in Scotland. Traditionally, the Scottish system has given priority to the values of pragmatism and flexibility and while individuals were accorded what may be called "process rights", it has lacked the type of strong rights culture that is inherent in the ECHR. The ECHR gives citizens strong rights claims that the state must, by law, recognise and it is this which is a new element.

It is difficult to exaggerate both the constitutional importance of this strong rights culture and the suddenness and sharpness of its impact in Scotland. For example, while it is known that the Crown Office (the administrative headquarters of the Public Prosecutor) had put in place a team to prepare for the ECHR, it is clear, given how events have unfolded, that the effects of the Convention have been surprising. Indeed, it has become something of a spectator sport in Scotland to observe its serendipitous effects. As shall be seen, temporary sheriffs, one of the mainstays of the Scottish criminal justice system, were effectively dismissed over night, evidence in routine moving traffic offences was declared unconstitutional and the seizure of criminal assets has been judged to violate the terms of the Convention. Furthermore, it is anticipated that one of the sacred cows of the Scottish system, the unique Children's Hearing, may well have to be substantially modified to accommodate the Convention.

So, the Scottish criminal justice system has been subject to a double-re-constitutionalisation, both of profound importance. Now, what I want to do in this paper is first to describe in more detail each of these constitutional developments. I then want to consider the relationship between them, for I believe it can be argued that they have the potential to pull in different directions. Finally, I want to speculate on how far each of these developments will affect the Scottish criminal justice system by reflecting on what could turn out to be barriers that will place limits on at least some of possible effects.

2. Human Rights and the Scottish Criminal Justice System

Let's begin our examination of the two strands of constitutional development by examining the impact of the ECHR. The place to start is examining its impact on the internal workings of the criminal justice system.

It should be said that there is always a specific element to the impact of human rights and that this will vary from case to case. The basis for human rights challenges in Scotland, however, flows from the Scotland Act 1998, which absorbed the ECHR into domestic law. Section 57 holds, for example, that all members of the Scottish executive must act in a way compatible with the ECHR. The effects of this absorption can be shown by briefly examining two actual cases mentioned above in passing, that of the temporary sheriffs and that of evidence in moving traffic cases.

The rights issue met with in the case of temporary sheriffs related to the Lord Advocates' traditional power to recommend judicial appointments. Temporary sheriffs had for sometime been one of the main stays of the Scottish criminal justice system. Temporary sheriffs were appointed by the Lord Advocate to hear criminal and civil cases and were employed on a yearly basis. Temporary sheriffs heard about 25% of the criminal cases that passed through the Scottish criminal justice system. It was held, however, by the High Court of Justiciary on the basis of a challenge made in a specific case by a defence agent, who argued that a conviction of his client by a temporary sheriff was unconstitutional as the temporary sheriff had been appointed to his position by a party to the prosecution, the Lord Advocate, and that was clearly against the provisions of the Convention; there is a conflict of interest and thus a question of procedural fairness. The High Court upheld the appeal and held that the power of the Lord Advocate to appoint temporary sheriffs violated Article 6 (1) of the ECHR.[1] This had the potential to unsettle all the decisions made in the past by temporary sheriffs but the core question related to the traditional power of the Lord Advocate to make recommendations on judicial appointments which now clearly was in violation of the Convention and thus could not stand. The solution has been to remove the Lord Advocate from the appointments process and to consider setting up a Judicial Appointments Board.

In this case, there is a clear constitutional implication as the fabric of the existing constitutional structure of Scotland has been changed. This contrasts, however, with another example mentioned above - the use made of evidence in certain moving traffic cases.

The Road Traffic Act 1988 (section 172(3)) conferred upon the Police a power to require the owners of cars to supply the name of the person driving it, if, for example, a speed camera recorded the car as exceeding the speed limit. The High Court was asked, again on the basis of an appeal against conviction raised in a specific case, if this provision of the Act violated the Convention.[2] The Convention asserts a right against self-incrimination yet this provision required an accused to incriminate his or herself. The Court upheld the appeal on convention grounds as the provision of the Road Traffic Act were seen (again) to violate section 6 (1) of the ECHR.

On the surface, there appear to be no constitutional implications in this example as contrasted to the first, although, clearly, it does leave the police with a headache. This is not, however, true. While no immediate or specific constitutional implications followed from the case, there are still nevertheless constitutional issues in the background which were fundamental to the decision. In this example, the Court has seen itself as being in the position where it had to reason from a basis in which the relationship between citizens and the prosecuting authorities was held to have changed because of the incorporation of the Convention. To put this a different way, this second example shows that, even in very routine and low level matters, the incorporation of the ECHR turns the criminal court, in effect, into a constitutional one.

Criminal law, of course, has always been rooted in a constitutional framework and thus there has always been the potential for a criminal case to raise a constitutional issue. The position that obtains now, at least for the

1 STARRS v RUXTON (2000) *Scots Law Times* 42-74.
2 BROWN v STOTT (2000) *Scots Law Times* 379-398.

foreseeable future, is, however, qualitatively different. At the moment, constitutional questions have moved from the background very much more to the foreground. This has resulted in criminal courts having to be more aware of them and, increasingly, to make decisions which proceed more explicitly in terms of constitutional reasoning. The result is a substantial alteration in the criminal justice landscape.

This may be no bad thing but it is clearly different. The question arises, therefore, of why the ECHR has had this impact?

The reason for this, I suggest, is that human rights do two closely related things; first, the consideration of human rights as part of domestic law introduces a new vocabulary in which decision makers are required to think about matters. Notice, I say required; human rights considerations are no longer matters which public authorities or members of the public can take or leave. They now provide, in Scotland, one of the key discourses or conceptual frameworks for thinking about what the term "justice" consists of in the phrase, "criminal justice". Indeed, in a very direct way, human rights fix that notion in a way which is quite new to the Scottish criminal justice system. Traditionally, the Scottish criminal justice system has emphasised flexibility as a core normative value; the idea of a just decision was evaluated in this light.[3] The continuing common law basis of Scottish criminal law has ensured this as has the closely related very wide discretion in decision making enjoyed by all the key actors in the criminal justice system, the gate keepers, the procurator fiscal (the public prosecutor), the judiciary, that has for so long been a prominent feature, especially when it is viewed in a comparative light.

This tradition of flexibility and pragmatism has a much diminished role in human rights discourse. The incorporation of the ECHR and the Human Rights Act allocate a much lower place in the hierarchy of values to this tradition. Rights are now be at the centre; rights are a key organising concept and thus central to how we think about criminal justice.

Many of the long existing modes of thinking in Scotland will, in consequence, have to be modified or dropped. It follows that the traditional flexibility and pragmatism of the criminal justice system will come increasingly to be the subject of critical analysis and, indeed, increasingly come to be constrained. Key decision-makers will be expected to be able to give reasons for their decisions if they are called upon to do so and this will, undoubtedly, hedge the exercise of their discretion.

---

3 P. YOUNG (1997) *Crime and Criminal Justice in Scotland*. Edinburgh: The Stationery Office.

Beyond the realm of decision making there are other important changes to record. There are, for example, very likely to be demands to closely specify the substance of criminal law. Scotland's is the only system of criminal law in Europe that retains a common law basis; by human rights standards this is deficient as it means that the crimes people may be charged with are too vague. The common law crime of breach of the peace, for example, covers behaviour that ranges from "ordinary" drunkardness to serious rioting and there is a corresponding range of penalties available to the court from fines to life imprisonment. (There exists a project to codify Scottish criminal law and at the same time make it human rights proof. Once again, there are advantages and disadvantages to this but, for present purposes, the existence of the code project is direct evidence of the fundamental changes that are on the doorstep).

There are other, more hidden, but very important aspects of the criminal justice system that are likely to be effected by human rights. It remains to be seen, for example, how human rights considerations will affect the relationship between offenders and victims. Now, it is the case that the European Court on Human Rights has set out the rights of victims and sees them as coming within the scope of the Convention. But there is a more subtle issue at stake here. A strong human rights culture has the potential to change the relative balance between the rights of victim and offender in a way which may reverse the policies most governments now follow with respect to victims. As a matter of policy, governments have shifted the balance between victim and offender over the last decade in favour of the victim. A strong human rights culture may bring about a partial reverse of this. The key relationship at the heart of the ECHR is the relationship between the offender and the state. The primary rights the Convention protects are the rights of the offender. It is not clear how victims' rights fit into the balance here.

The other key area which may be affected by human rights is the relationship between different types of discourse articulated within the criminal justice system. For example, it has been argued that western criminal justice systems are undergoing a substantial change in the types of justifying ideology that underpin them. Feeley and Simon, for instance, contend that we are witnessing the emergence of what they call "actuarial justice" - a way of conceiving of offenders in terms of the "risk" different categories of offenders pose to the public.[4] Feeley and Simon argue that the growth of risk as the governing concept of penal discourse is, in turn,

4 M. FEELEY and J. SIMON (1994) Actuarial Justice: The Emerging New Criminal Law, in: D. NELKEN (ed), *The Futures of Criminology*. London: Sage.

associated with the development of post-modernism and they suggest, therefore, that there is an emerging new type of penal system in which the older ways of talking about justice – punishment, responsibility, treatment - will be marginalised.

While Feeley's and Simon's argument is not without its critics,[5] their argument does pick up on key developments in most western penal systems. There is substantial evidence that risk and danger, as organising concepts, are increasingly used as a justifying ideologies in decision making at various stages of the penal system (there is an argument, however, about how far these developments go).[6]

The development of a strong individual rights culture adds a complication to this picture. There is an inherent tension between decision making based on calculations of risk and danger and decision making based on rights. On the one hand, the vocabulary of risk and danger is one which quickly but silently moves consideration away from more traditional conceptions of individuals possessing rights and being held responsible for the actions they perform. If a person constitutes an unacceptable risk, which poses a danger to the public, then there is a tendency to allow this to override the rights the individual possesses. The ability to assert certain basic rights, however, remains as a counter-balancing force. For example, there is an increasing tendency to write parole licences in such a way as to create a clash with a rights based conception of individual liberty. This comes out most clearly in the case of those offenders who are seen to pose the highest risk, the sex-offenders. It may be desirable, for instance, from a risk and danger point of view to write a licence which substantially impairs the offenders freedom of movement and freedom of association - not to mix with children, not to see his/her children, not to go to certain places e.g. playgrounds. This immediately creates a tension with Articles of the ECHR which are aimed at maximising the freedom of the individual. Now, the European Court has recognised that if it can be shown that an offender poses a continuing and substantial risk and danger, then his/hers Convention rights can be overridden. The very fact, however, that there now exists a clear charter which has the force of law and in terms of which an offender can launch a

---

5 See D. GARLAND (1995) Penal Modernism and Postmodernism, in: T. BLOMBERG and S. COHEN (eds.), *Punishment and Social Control*. New York: Aldine de Gruyter Publishing.

6 See, in the case of Scotland, P. YOUNG (1999) Towards a Rational Penal Policy for Scotland?, 5(1) *The Scottish Journal of Criminal Justice Studies* 45-56; MCARA (1999) The Politics of Penality: An Overview of the Development of Penal Policy in Scotland, in: DUFF, P. and HUTTON, N. (eds.), *Criminal Justice in Scotland*. Aldershot: Ashgate

challenge, in itself, will tend, I argue, to change the behaviour of the body making the decision.

So, while, it is the case that risk and danger are emerging as justifying ideologies, as Feeley and Simon contend, the extent of their impact will be limited by appeals to rights. A tension will exist both between competing principles and competing broader social forces. At the level of decision making in specific cases, there will be tensions between risk/danger and rights. At the more general level of policy there will be tensions between different objectives. At the most broad level, there will be tensions created between the forces of post-modernism and modernism. For, if Feeley and Simon are right in associating risk and danger with the emergence of post-modernity, it seems equally reasonable to argue that the development of a strong rights culture marks strong the continuing influence of that which is suppose to be in retreat - modernity.

So, the incorporation of the ECHR into the Scottish criminal justice system amounts to more than the absorption of another piece of European culture into the UK. It creates by itself a new constitutional context within which the system has to work. It is clear, that at this moment, it is this strand of re-constitutionalisation that is having the greater impact. Change in the Scottish system is being driven more by rights than it is by devolution. At present, the Scottish system is at a point of transition where one constitutional tradition by which the criminal justice system was embedded is being replaced by another. As was seen above, it is in such contexts that the processing of routine cases leads to constitutional debate and change that is led by Courts rather than parliaments. One result of this is the creation of a high degree of uncertainty in the criminal justice system, where many practitioners, as it were, sit around trying to double guess where the effects of the next human rights…

3. Devolution and Criminal Justice in Scotland

While it may be possible at the moment to account for change in the criminal justice system mostly in terms of the impact of human rights, it would be wrong to ignore the new institutional structures introduced by the Scotland Act. These can be very briefly described.

Whereas previously Scottish legislation had to pass through the Parliament in Westminster, the Scotland Act has made criminal law and punishment matters within the sole jurisdiction of the newly created Scottish Parliament. From one point of view, of course, this new arrangement can be seen to amount just to a recognition, de jure, of a pre-existing de facto situation in which the criminal justice system of Scotland was seen essentially to be a matter for Scottish ministers and the Scottish Office. The Act of Union (1707) guaranteed that the Scottish legal system would remain separate and independent and, certainly, from the time at which the Scottish Office and the Secretary of State for Scotland emerged, home affairs were largely left to these two institutions, together with those whom they chose to consult, to run. But the creation of a Parliament in Edinburgh ought to be seen as more than this, at least in potential, for two reasons. First, as Walker argues, the fact that previously Scottish legislation had to pass through Westminster meant that it tended to be squeezed, as it, often, was given only perfunctory consideration due to lack of time.[7] Second, because of this, Scottish business tended not to receive extended scrutiny. The new Parliament, working with different procedures and considering just Scottish affairs, ought to change this. New institutional structures have been created to this end. There is, for example, a new Department of Justice which brings together operations which were previously spread over several departments within the then Scottish Office. There is a Minister of Justice, who is also Deputy First Minister and there is an all party Committee on Justice and Home Affairs which until very recently was convened by a Scottish National Party Member of the Scottish Parliament.

There are other proposals being actively discussed which would also change the formal constitutional structure in which the criminal justice system is embedded. There is, for example, as was indicated, a good prospect of a Judicial Appointments Board being established and a consultation paper on a national Scottish Police force may well be issued in the near future.

The question that arises is whether these new constitutional arrangements are bringing about the type of closer scrutiny that the previous ones did not or achieved only to a limited extent. It is, of course, too early to say but it is possible to observe already a growing sense of frustration that the rate of change is slow and that the new structures have yet to deliver the type of scrutiny that they were designed to achieve. Why?

The answer lies in part, I contend, in the relationship between the new Parliament and the already existing structures of government, particularly the power of the civil service, that the Parliament inherited.

As was said, before the creation of the new Parliament, Scottish home affairs were largely a matter for a fairly small group of individuals. I have

---

7 N. WALKER (1999) Situating Scottish Policing, in: P. DUFF and H. HUTTON (eds.), *Criminal Justice in Scotland.* Aldershot: Ashgate.

described the pre-existing constitutional arrangements, as an example of "administrative devolution".[8] By this I mean that decision making affecting the running of the criminal justice system in Scotland was left, to a fairly small policy making network. Overlapping and quite small circles of decision makers - ministers, civil servants, senior judiciary, some academics, Conventional of Scottish Local Authorities, Directors of Social Work. This policy making network operated through Edinburgh, not Westminster and this is why, in addition to the reasons adduced by Walker, that the criminal justice system of Scotland remained relatively insulated from Westminster Parliamentary scrutiny.

The advantages of these arrangements are fairly obvious. Administrative devolution resulted in a fairly small group, "owning" the criminal justice system in Scotland and shaping policy to suit their conceptions. To put this in Weberian terms, this was akin to a patrimonial bureaucracy. These arrangements, of course, sometimes brought about good things, like the Children's Hearing system and the position where, during the period of the previous Conservative governments 1979-1997, there was in essence, except for the two years of the last Secretary of State for Scotland, a different and much less punitive penal policy in Scotland than in England and Wales. Yet, as Weber argued, bureaucracy and democracy exist in tension as they work on different logics.

Devolution has the potential to change this. It could alter very substantially the control of the close knit policy making network over criminal justice matters. Power elites, however, have a developed ability to continue the exercise of their influence under new arrangements and it is not inconceivable that with a few alterations at the edge this may happen.

4. The Limits of Reform

In this section I want very briefly to reflect on what may be called the limits to reform and change, and to consider the relationship between the two constitutional developments I have described.

I want to do this by making use of the work of Lord Kames, one of the leaders of the first Scottish Enlightenment. In his Historical Law Tracts (1792), Kames drew a distinction between what we would now call private law and criminal law. He argued that both types belong to what he called "the great river" of law that flows through the culture of a society and are connected to "the manners of the people" but, importantly, he says, in

8 P. YOUNG (1997) *o.c.*

different ways. Private law, he suggested, is refined and in some ways rather distantly related to manners. This is because of the jobs we give private law to do. He contends, these jobs are very often complex and technical; for example, the regulation of financial transactions or the sale of property and, Kames suggests, these types of tasks can only be properly taken care of if the law is also complex and technical in nature. It follows, therefore, he says, that private law must be relatively insulated from emotion and from manners.

Criminal law, by contrast, is different. It is not concerned with regulating complex and technical behaviour, Kames argued, because its central task is to respond to acts which violate morality. Criminal law, thus, according to Kames, is not at all insulated from emotion. Rather, he says, criminal law reflects, "the rude manners of the people".

Kames is making two points here. His argument is one of the first statements of what is now a commonplace and very general thesis - that the law is a product of certain cultural and institutional arrangements and thus at any point in time, law reflects, more or less closely, this background. This, I think, is an argument that most scholars would accept even if they may wish to qualify it both in form and substance in significant respects. As important as this general argument is, it is not the most interesting thing that Kames says. His second, more specific thesis concerning criminal law is clearly more significant and relevant.

The importance of Kames' more specific thesis lies in his contention that the criminal law - and its attendant institutions of the criminal justice and penal systems - are deeply embedded, not just in culture but also, and more significantly, in a deeper set of emotional ties. Kames is saying that the criminal law appeals to a "deep structure" of sensibilities and this is why it is so closely connected to "the rude manners of the people". Now, of course, by "rude", Kames did not mean lacking in politeness (although, quite clearly, this is a meaning he could not have ruled out); rather, "rude," in this context means, I think, manners which are not mediated by a veneer of constraints which arise from the requirements of daily interaction. In addition, "rude" means, I suggest, common or shared. So, for Kames, the criminal law of a country differs from its civil or private law, precisely because it reflects more immediately aspects of that country's deep culture, its underlying sentiments.

I want to build on Kames' argument because it is directly relevant to the argument of this paper. First, a somewhat indirect connection; let us remember that Kames was writing at a period in this nation's history that was as significant as I have argued the present and immediate future may be.

He was writing at a time of fundamental change and one of Kames's objectives was, in the midst of this, to establish some notion of continuity and of identity. Kames, was saying, look to the criminal law because it is there that the deep culture and values of a nation reside. This does not mean Kames was resisting change. He was all in favour of it; he was, to use an ambiguous phrase of the moment, a great "moderniser". He thought that change would occur but that it would be given direction by the exercise of reason which he saw as a naturally progressive force. But reason and emotion exist in tension and his point was that, if one repository of a nation's cultural and political identity is its criminal law, then this constitutes in itself a force with a certain momentum. Kames was not saying that change can only happen slowly (although, I do think he probably thought this); he was saying be aware of what is at stake in attempts to reform criminal justice – it is always more than you think.

This last thought provides the direct link to the present. Kames seems to me to correctly identify what may be called the "conundrum of change" in criminal justice. Change in the criminal justice system both threatens more and feeds off more than its immediate object - it has ramifications far beyond the boundaries of the system and it is these wider challenges that test the limits of the process. Importantly, attempts to change the criminal justice system, Kames is saying (and this is the conundrum), need to fit in with the deep structure of moral sentiments which with it both resonates and which provide it with its moral legitimacy. To put this more directly, Kames is saying that the criminal law of a country retains its moral bind only to the extent that it appeals to a deep sense of tradition and culture. Reform and change thus - and this is an obvious thing to say but nevertheless seems also to be forgotten - is a moral project in which the basis of legitimacy is provided not by the wishes and desires of the reformer (although they are relevant to judgements others may make) but primarily by its successful appeal to the sentiments of the wider community. Now there is reciprocal effect here, in the sense that actions can change, over time, the structure of moral sentiments but perhaps only slowly.

What has all this abstraction to do with the changes occurring in the criminal justice system that I sketched earlier? The crucial question put very broadly is whether the changes which are under way will find legitimacy.

As I hinted above this is a complex issue. There is deep seated support for devolution but the same can not be said with such certainty about human rights. Indeed, there may be some senses in which certain aspects of human rights may corrode that which has the sort of appeal to the deep structure of sentiments of which Kames spoke. The likely challenges to the Children's

Hearing system may again be taken as an example in point. It will become increasingly difficult to justify the Hearing System in terms of the educational or welfare ethos upon which it was founded. This ethos created a system in which due process considerations play a minor role. The Children's Hearing is not a criminal court, it does not settle questions of innocence or guilt by an adversarial or inquisitorial procedure, there is no right to legal representation and thus it falls short of many of the requirements of the ECHR. Yet, it is seen by many to "work" as an institution that dispenses "justice", albeit of a different sort.

There is another deeply rooted aspect of the Scottish criminal justice system that may be challenged by the ECHR. This is the ideal of "community" as providing one of the deep structures of much Scottish criminal law. It is an idea that runs through many aspects of the Scottish system, including relatively new and somewhat tangential areas such as crime prevention. The idea of community has long played a key role in the distinctive civic culture of Scotland as has the notion of communities democratically debating how to organise their own shape. I am not (?) suggesting that Scotland is an example of primitive communism or that socialist ideas flourish there in a particularly fertile soil. Rather, my argument is more rooted in developments in policy which stretch back some way.

Hume, in his Commentaries, almost in passing, points out that long prison sentences in Scotland where by no means as common in his day as they were in England (early nineteenth century). He provides a rather off hand explanation of this. Hume says this is not because Scots judges are more lenient than English ones, but because the idea of individual liberty has never been so highly valued in Scotland. Rather, the uniqueness of Scottish social structure gave priority to the values associated with community and it was these values that the criminal law was intended to uphold. In this context, depriving an individual of his or her liberty as a punishment has a lesser appeal as compared, for example, to banishment from the community, a punishment often used in Scotland.

Conclusion

There is a relevance in this to my subject matter. I think before the coming of devolution there was a view that it would allow all things traditionally understood as Scottish to flourish and perhaps nowhere more so than in the criminal justice system, that most Scottish of all institutions. The creation of a Parliament, for instance, quite clearly has the potential to bring the community in touch with its criminal law. The incorporation of human rights, however, pushes the system in another direction. There is always a balance between recognising the demands of the community and the rights of the individual, but the incorporation of human rights swings this balance decidedly in favour of the latter at the expense of the former. The result is constitutional developments, both of great significance and importance, which may be pulling in opposite ways - they are certainly in tension. My ex-colleagues Chris Himsworth and Colin Munro begin their commentary on the Scotland Act by hinting that devolution may revive an "auld song". My view is that there are grounds for doubting this. We may not be seeing the continuation of a system but be at a point where it is about to pass away.

References

Feeley, M. and Simon, J. (1994) Actuarial Justice: The Emerging New Criminal Law, in: D. Nelken (ed), *The Futures of Criminology*. London: Sage.

Garland, D (1995) Penal Modernism and Postmodernism, in: T. Blomberg and S. Cohen (eds.), *Punishment and Social Control*. New York: Aldine de Gruyter Publishing.

Himsworth, C and Munro, C. (1998) *The Scotland Act. 1998*, Greens, Edinburgh: Greens.

McAra, L. (1999) The Politics of Penality: An Overview of the Development of Penal Policy in Scotland, in: Duff, P. and Hutton, N. (eds.), *Criminal Justice in Scotland*. Aldershot: Ashgate.

Walker, N. (1999) Situating Scottish Policing, in: P. Duff and H. Hutton (eds.), *Criminal Justice in Scotland*. Aldershot: Ashgate.

Young, P. (1997) *Crime and Criminal Justice in Scotland*. Edinburgh: The Stationery Office.

TOUGH JUSTICE: SOUTH AFRICAN STYLE?

Dirk van Zyl Smit

Introduction

It is easy to analyse changes in criminal justice systems in terms that overemphasise the impact for good and for evil of wider political developments. Nowhere is the risk of doing this greater than in South Africa, where the undoubted virtue of the replacement of the old minority government by a government elected by majority suffrage and operating within the framework of a constitution that includes a justiciable Bill of Rights was hailed as a panacea for a range of social problems. When these problems stubbornly refuse to go away, or even get worse, as crime seems to many to have done, the danger is that the initial analysis will be revised drastically and criminal justice strategies will be adopted that reflect despair about the continued existence of the evil rather than a real appreciation of what has been achieved. The antidote to such major oscillations is, I suggest, to pay close attention to the evolution of penal ideas and of penal practices, for these are not identical to major political developments. Such an understanding offers a firmer basis for evaluating penal policy and perhaps even intervening in it.

In June 1997 I undertook a careful analysis of the evolution of criminological ideas in the South African transition up to that point.[1] It noted that the transition to democracy was a triumph for both legal reformism and a radical criminology imbued with strong communitarian ideals over the conservative, racially based approaches to crime that had dominated South Africa for most of the century. For legal reformists the Constitution with its justiciable Bill of Rights, guaranteeing in some detail the rights of all accused persons on trial and in prison, was a considerable triumph. An attempt was then being made to develop these constitutional principles, through strategic litigation that would extend constitutional rights by challenging existing laws or by introducing new laws that met constitutional norms. Both strategies were initially very successful. For legal reformists there were major victories when the existing laws enabling the imposition of the death penalty[2] and of corporal punishment[3] were struck down by the

1 D. VAN ZYL SMIT (1999) Criminological Ideas and the South African Transition, 39 *British Journal of Criminology* 198-215.
2 S v MAKWANYANE and another 1995 (3) SA 391 (CC).

Constitutional Court and a start was made with new legal frameworks for the police,[4] for juvenile justice,[5] for sentencing,[6] and for prisons.[7]

For radical criminologists the strategy was to insert communitarian ideas into criminal justice policy and to a lesser extent into legislation as well as to work directly with communities in order to enable them to deal with their 'own' crime problems. They too were successful. Criminal justice policy was cast in communitarian terms and various pilot projects to encourage the development of community justice initiatives were developed. Perhaps most spectacularly of all, the Truth and Reconciliation Commission's work could be seen and indeed was presented as a giant initiative in restorative justice.[8]

In spite of these major developments the analysis concluded on a somewhat pessimistic note. It suggested that in a climate in which there seemed to be a real increase in serious crime, and where there was certainly a massive increase in popular punitiveness, both the legal reformist and the communitarian tendencies were likely to come under threat. Legal reformism would be faced with the fact that the enforcement of extensive constitutional rights of those labelled as criminal could lead to the undermining of the legitimacy of the Constitution itself. At the same time attempts to deal with serious crime in the community would not pay much attention to constitutional due process, or would be ineffective, or both. The interesting question then was how the elected government would respond to pressures for it to intervene and how the courts and the communities would respond to any new initiatives.

We now know some of the answers:

At the legislative level the primary response of the government has been to water down the first wave of constitutionalising legislation, while at the same time to push through the harshest possible new criminal justice legislation that it thinks it can get away with in constitutional terms.

---

3 S v WILLIAMS 1995 (3) SA 632 (CC).

4 The South African Police Services Act 68 of 1995.

5 The South African Law Commission has produced a comprehensive report on juvenile justice, including draft legislation: *Report on Juvenile Justice,* Pretoria, South African Law Commission, 2000. The Government has not yet acted on this report. Attempts to ensure that juveniles are not detained in adult prisons in the mean time have been singularly unsuccessful: J. SLOTH-NIELSEN and L. MUNTINGH (1999) Juvenile Justice Review 1998, 12 *South African Journal of Criminal Justice* 65-80.

6 See South African Law Commission, *Report on a New Sentencing Framework.* Pretoria, South African Law Commission, 2000.

7 The Correctional Services Act 111 of 1998, which for the largest part had still not been brought into effect by July 2001.

8 H. ZEHR (1997) Restorative Justice: When justice and healing go together, *Track Two* 20.

Conversely, talk of community justice has continued but there have been only patchy legislative initiatives to involve communities significantly in the formal criminal justice system or to incorporate their informal processes into the overall crime prevention strategy.

At the more concrete level of how the formal system is administered there has been a general decline in efficiency as measured in terms of crime reported and successfully processed through the system. Some of the failures, most notably escapes from custody and the failure to bring prominent offenders to book, have elicited a great deal of public comment but such failures have been reflections of the general administrative malaise. The responses to these shortcomings have been new administrative initiatives using techniques often consciously borrowed from abroad, particularly from the USA but also from the UK and elsewhere, coupled with a great deal of tough talk and, occasionally, in the field of correctional services in particular, specific steps to make life harder for offenders.

Finally, to complete this brief introductory overview, the continued rhetorical support for community anti-crime initiatives and the failure either to regulate or incorporate them in the formal system, combined with the perceived failures of the formal system have had significant negative effects. Data are hard to come by, but these self-help community initiatives appear to have become more prevalent and certainly have become more brutal as the first idealistic flush of extending due process to them has been replaced by a desperate, ends-justifying-all-means fear of crime.

1. The Clogged Criminal Justice System

There are many examples that could be used but to illustrate recent tendencies. This paper concentrates on those that impact most on the prison system. First, however, it is necessary to mention that the poor performance of the criminal justice system as a whole has had an enormous impact on the shape of the prison population.

At the court level the most noticeable change has been that, in spite of a more or less constant number of cases being fed into the system by the police, the number of prosecutions undertaken and of convictions resulting from them have declined dramatically. Convictions are particularly interesting; they declined from 362 500 in 1992/3 to 218 400 in 1995/6.[9] The most recent research shows that conviction rates have continued to decline:

---

9 South African Institute of Race Relations, *Fast Facts*, May 1998.

from 39.2 percent in 1996 to 36 percent in 1999.[10] Moreover, the long-term trend is for a declining percentage of those that are convicted to be sentenced to terms of imprisonment. One may have thought that this would lead directly to a decline in the prison population but this has not been the case. There are two reasons for this: the lesser reason was a gradual increase in the length of the prison terms imposed on those actually sentenced to imprisonment. Secondly and more importantly, there has been a great increase in the time that cases take to be completed and therefore an enormous increase in the numbers of awaiting trial prisoners.[11]

At the end of May 2001 there were 169 451 persons detained in South African prisons. Of these 115 975 were sentenced and 53 210 were unsentenced. The official capacity of the system was 102 048.[12] This meant that the average occupancy level was 166.5 per cent. In reality, the overcrowding in individual prisons was much higher, because it is impossible to have an optimal distribution of prisoners across the system. The results in the prison system have been as predictable as they have been depressing. Overcrowding at this level has meant that there have been training programmes of various kinds for fewer prisoners. Particularly spectacular has been the increase in unsentenced prisoners; on 30 June 1976 there were 15 139, which included a number of political opponents of the government who were being detained without trail.[13] On 30 June 1996, although detention without trial had been abolished, there were 28 047,[14] and by January 2000 the number had risen to 61 563. In other words, whilst in the twenty years between 1976 and 1996 the number of such prisoners did not quite double, they more than doubled in the three and a half years from mid-1996 onwards. Since then the number has declined slightly through the emergency measures such as releasing prisoners who cannot pay small amounts of bail, but such ad hoc interventions are not sustainable in the long run. In practice in South Africa, as elsewhere, less is done for unsentenced prisoners than sentenced prisoners. But it is the sheer mass of such prisoners that has led to persistent reports that some unsentenced prisoners are not

---

10 See M. SCHÖNTEICH (2001) *Lawyers for the People: The South African Prosecution Service,* 100. Pretoria: Institute for Security Studies.

11 For details of these tendencies, see D. VAN ZYL SMIT, Change and Continuity in South African Prisons, in: R WEISS and N. SOUTH (1999) (eds.), *Comparing Prisons. Towards a Comparative and International Penology,* 401-427. Amsterdam: Gordon and Breach.

12 These figures were conveyed privately to the author by the Department of Correctional Services.

13 Department of Prisons (1977) *Report on the Department of Prisons for the period 1 July 1975 to 30 June 1976*, 22. Pretoria: Government Printers.

14 See source in: VAN ZYL SMIT, note 12 above.

getting what they are entitled to in terms of the minimum daily exercise periods, for example.[15]

The cause of the overcrowding seems to lie in the first instance in administrative decline; it is not because more cases are coming before court. In some instances, it is true that the newly constitutionalised rights of accused persons have contributed to longer trials. More accused persons are represented by lawyers now, for example, than was the case in the past. However, neither the legislature nor the courts have moved decisively in the criminal justice area to use the Constitution in appropriate ways to deal with the massive overcrowding problems caused by the numbers of prisoners awaiting trial. Thus, to take a straightforward example: the constitutional provision that "every accused person has a right to a fair trial, which includes ... [amongst other things] the right to have their trial begin and conclude without unreasonable delay"[16] has not been applied strictly. The Constitutional Court has considered the matter of undue delays,[17] but it has not given very clear guidance on what this right means, nor has it dismissed a case on grounds of undue delay.

2. Legislative Toughness

Most symptomatic of an interaction between the legislature and the courts in contributing to an increase in the number of prisoners has been the recent history of pre-trial release of suspects in South Africa. Both the interim Constitution of 1993[18] and the 'final' Constitution of 1996[19] have recognised the rights of suspects in this regard. In the current 1996 form the relevant constitutional provision reads:

"Everyone who is arrested for allegedly committing an offence has the right... to be released from detention if the interests of justice permit, subject to reasonable conditions."[20]

---

15 See in general, S. PETE (1998) The Politics of Imprisonment in the Aftermath of South Africa's First Democratic Election, 11 *South African Journal of Criminal Justice* 51-83.

16 Section 35(3)(d) of the 1996 Constitution. See note 19 below.

17 SANDERSON v Attorney-General, Eastern Cape 1998(1) SACR 227 (CC); Wild and another vHoffert 1998(2) SACR 727 (CC).

18 The Constitution of the Republic of South Africa Act 200 of 1993. The Constitution came into force after the first democratic elections in April 1994.

19 The Constitution of the Republic of South Africa Act 108 of 1996. The 1996 Constitution is currently in force. All references in the text are to this Constitution unless otherwise indicated.

20 Section 35(1)(f) of the 1996 Constitution. Cf. also section 25(2)(d) of the interim 1993 Constitution.

This provision may appear to be a conventional due process guarantee of individual liberty. However, it needs to be given effect by the ordinary criminal procedure legislation. One would have thought that the existing legislation would have to be liberalised to bring it into line with the new constitutional order. In fact, in 1995 already, the Criminal Procedure Act, inherited from the old regime, had been amended to make it harder for an accused person to get bail.[21] In 1997 the legislature went intervened even more drastically.[22] It further restricted the power of the courts to grant bail by setting out a long list of grounds which, if present, would compel the court to find that it was not "in the interests of justice" to grant bail. These provisions although strict were constitutionally relatively uncontroversial, but two further provisions seemed unlikely to pass constitutional muster. They were the stipulations that bail can be denied if their is the likelihood, in exceptional circumstances, "that the release of the accused will disturb the public order or undermine the public peace or security"[23]; and the requirement that unless "exceptional circumstances", presumably additional to those listed grounds, were present, persons accused of certain serious offences were automatically to be refused bail.[24] In the event, in June 1999 the Constitutional Court dismissed all the challenges to the bail legislation, without as much as a reference to the massive problem of rapidly growing numbers of awaiting trial prisoners.[25] The basis for the decision was that, while the court accepted that these two provisions did infringe the right to be released from detention, they were saved by the general limitations clause of the Constitution, which allows a right in the Bill of Rights to be limited by "law of general application to the extent that the limitation is reasonable and justifiable in an open and democratic society based on human dignity, equality and freedom...".[26] Interestingly, the Court emphasised that it was the extraordinary crime situation that required these limitations.[27] It did so, however, without considering specific evidence on the overall crime

21 The Criminal Procedure Amendment Act 75 of 1995.

22 The Criminal Procedure Second Amendment Act 85 of 1997.

23 Section 60(4)(e) of the Criminal Procedure Act 51 of 1977 as amended by the 1997Criminal Procedure Second Amendment Act.

24 Section 60(11) of the Criminal Procedure Act 51 of 1977 as amended by the 1997 Criminal Procedure Second Amendment Act.

25 S v DLAMINI; S v DLADLA and Others; S v JOUBERT; S v SCHIETEKAT 1998 (2) SACR 51 (CC).

26 Section 36 of the 1996 Constitution.

27 *S v* DLAMINI (note 25 above) at 80e.

problem or on how the drastic restrictions on personal liberty that it was endorsing would assist in addressing that problem.[28]

In the area of parole, too, the predictable effect of new legislation is to increase the prison population. The history briefly was that the existing parole system was widely criticized. Its effect was that most prisoners were released by a complicated and somewhat secretive parole procedure after they had served about a third of their sentences. An independent inquiry suggested to the government that they simplify the procedure by making all prisoners eligible for parole after they had served half their sentences. The government enacted this legislation in 1997 but added a rider that allowed the courts to order that offenders who had "been sentenced to more than two years imprisonment not be released after they had served two-thirds of their sentences".[29] In 1998 this non-parole period was increased to a possible four-fifths for offences subject to the newly enacted mandatory minimum sentences.[30] It is worth emphasizing that although all this parole legislation has passed into law it has not yet been brought into effect, so that prisoners are still being released relatively early. Once again, however, the whole legislative process has been completed without serious consideration of the problems of prison overcrowding.

Finally in regard to legislation, in 1997 a 'temporary' law was enacted that introduced mandatory minimum sentences whilst more fundamental sentencing reform was being considered. It compels courts to impose life sentences and other drastic terms for various defined serious offences unless "substantial and compelling circumstances" can be found for departing from the prescribed minima.[31] This law came into effect on 1 May 1998 and was to be in force for only two years, after which its life could be extended by Parliament on an annual basis until new legislation could be tabled. Its operation has been extended and it is still in force, with no indication yet of when proposals by the South African Law Commission for more comprehensive sentencing reform will be considered. Initially its effect on prison numbers was limited because it applied only to offences committed after it had come into effect and cases were taking very long to come to

---

28 See in general, J. SARKIN, E. STEYN, D. VAN ZYL SMIT, and R. PASCHKE (2000) Individual liberty in crisis? Reflections on the decision of the Constitutional Court in *S v Dlamini; S v Dladla and Others; S v Joubert; S v Schietekat,* 16 *South African Journal on Human Rights* 292-312.

29 Parole and Correctional Services Amendment Act 87 of 1997.

30 Section 73(6)(b)(v) of the Correctional Services Act 111 of 1998.

31 Criminal Law Amendment Act 105 of 1997.

court.[32] Although courts may find grounds from departing from the prescribed minima there can be little doubt that the legislation will increase the length of the sentences for the most serious crimes and thus have the effect of increasing the prison population in the long run. Indeed the recent increase in the number of sentenced prisoners suggests that its effects are now being seen. The mandatory sentencing legislation is another example of a law passed without any attempt to consider its impact on the rest of the system. Indeed, and here is the crime control rub; in the period before the most recent general election phase the Government lumped together its bail, parole and sentencing legislation as representing its 'tough on crime' policies.[33]

South African judges like judges in England[34]and those in the federal system in the United States of America[35] who have faced similar changes have attempted to resist such innovations at a political level. Like their English counterparts the South African judges have historically been strongly against mandatory sentences, both because they limit their powers and because they genuinely believe that mandatory sentences produce unjust results in individual cases.[36] This belief is strengthened amongst the South African judiciary because they correctly perceive mandatory sentences as a device used by the old regime to get the courts to enforce the government's will on its political opponents. Moreover, the new South African Constitution gives the judiciary greater powers to resist such injustices by striking down unconstitutional legislation.[37] However, in spite of all these

---

32 South African Law Commission (2000) *Research Paper 17: An Empirical Quantitative and Qualitative Study of the Sentencing Practices of the South African Criminal Courts, with particular emphasis on the Criminal Law Amendment Act, 105 of 1997.* Pretoria: South African Law Commission.

33 "ANC rolls out its stars to kick-start election." 5 November 1998, *Cape Times,*.3.

34 I. DUNBAR and A. LANGDON (1998) *Tough Justice: Sentencing and Penal Policies in the 1990s.* London: Blackstone.

35 A. ANTHONY DOOB (1995) The United States Commission Sentencing Guidelines: If you don't know where you are going, you might not get there, in: C. CLARKSON and R. MORGAN (1995) (eds.), *The Politics of Sentencing Reform,* 199-250. Oxford: Oxford University Press.

36 See D. VAN ZYL SMIT (2000) Mandatory Sentences: A conundrum for the new South Africa? 2 *Punishment and Society* 197-212 for full references for claims made in this paragraph.

37 The judicial response to the constitutionality of the 'temporary' mandatory sentencing legislation has been cautious. Both the Supreme Court of Appeal and the Constitutional Court have held that it is in fact constitutional as it allows the courts some discretion See *S v Malgas* 2001 (1) SACR 469 and *S v Dodo* 2001 (1) SACR 594(CC) respectively. While these decisions are technically correct, they underline the relative powerlessness of the courts.

advantages the judges failed at the political level to prevent the introduction of a range of mandatory minimum sentences.

In the courts too the South African judiciary has not struck back effectively. Their interpretation of the "substantial and compelling circumstances", which allow them to depart from these prescribed sentences, has thus far been uncertain. Either they have grumbled about the new law in their judgments but enforced the minima nevertheless, or they have departed from them but given reason for doing so that rightly enrage feminists and other pressure groups that are looking for judicial recognition of the harm done by offenders. All this has been done by imposing, even in cases where they depart from the minima, such heavy sentences that the number of sentenced prisoners is likely to increase drastically.[38]

3. Administered Toughness

Not all changes have been legislative. The calls for being tough on crime and the real pressures to accommodate rapidly growing numbers of prisoners have not left the prison system unaffected. There has been much tough talk from the side of the authorities, about housing prisoners in disused gold mines,[39] for example, but little of this has transpired thus far. Two developments that are not unique to South Africa are the introduction of so-called C-max (super-high security) prisons in various forms and a rapid move towards implementing private prisons. A word on each of these:

C-max has received a great deal of publicity in South Africa,[40] but as yet there has been no scholarly study of it. What seems to be happening is that a very restrictive, very secure regime is being applied within the old Pretoria Central Prison both to prisoners who are difficult to handle and to those who might be threatened by others on the outside or on the inside. A small number of awaiting trial prisoners is included in the approximately 100 prisoners held in C-max in Pretoria Central. This appears to be a direct response to the public perception that many prisoners escape. In fact, escape

---

38 For a summary of this jurisprudence, see S. TERBLANCHE (2001) Aspects of minimum sentence legislation: judicial comments and the courts jurisdiction, 14 *South African Journal of Criminal Justice* 1-19.

39 "Disused mine may become prison" 23 August 1996, *Cape Times* 3. See also Dirk van Zyl Smit "South Africa," in: D VAN ZYL SMIT and F. DÜNKEL (2001) (eds.), *Imprisonment Today and Tomorrow: International Perspectives on Prisoners' Rights and Prison Conditions,* 606. The Hague: Kluwer Law International.

40 See for example, "Life in C-Max, SA's own Hi-tech Dungeon", 22 March 1998 *Sunday Insight* 15.

rates are relatively low and most notorious escapes of prisoners are from police holding cells rather than prisons. Other C-max prisons have been announced but, to the best of my knowledge, none has yet come into operation. Public criticism of C-max has focussed somewhat sensationally on rights abuses, with a maybe-they-deserve-it undertone. More informed comments, whilst not denying some abuses such as unnecessary isolation, have pointed to the expense involved in providing secure but relatively benign treatment for such a small group of prisoners in a system where most abuses are sins of omission brought about by a lack of resources.

Private prisons are likely to be the story for the short-term future.[41] The policy decisions have been taken and the legislative framework enacted. American companies and British bureaucrats are vying for influence. At the moment the Department of Correctional Services is allowing only limited outside scrutiny of its processes, but that may change. Although the first two private prisons have now been operating for a short period, the usual questions about the short- and long-term effects of privatisation are still open. One simply does not know whether conditions in private prisons will be harsher than what we have had hitherto; but their introduction is a way of expanding prison that certainly does not bode well for a significant move away from imprisonment.

A more worrying development has been the sudden announcement of a reduction in the substantive privileges of prisoners, particularly the entitlement of most grades to watch television.[42] The step was presented as a security related exercise - apparently the risks presented by TV sets were suddenly discovered - but the not so subtle message to the public was that prisoners would now be treated more harshly in prison as well.

4. Judicial Responses

The penal reform lobby in South Africa is weak and, paradoxically, the new government is relatively well isolated from pressures from outside the country. Imagine the outcry if the minority regime had suggested housing the same dangerous prisoners down mines! A lot therefore depends on how the courts will interpret prison law. The illiberal decision of the Constitutional Court in the recent bail case and the decline of the authority of

41 J. BERG (2000) *Private Prisons: International Experiences and South African Prospects*, M.Soc.Sci. thesis, University of Cape Town.

42 The policy change is outlined in *Strydom v Minister of Correctional Services and others* 1993 (3) BCLR 342 (W) at 346A.

the judiciary generally as reflected in its inability to influence the passage of mandatory minimum sentencing legislation are signs of declining influence. Their significance should not be overstated, however. The Constitution itself stresses that everyone who is detained, including every sentenced prisoner, has specified rights, amongst which is a right to conditions that are consistent with human dignity, including a right to exercise and the provision, at state expense of adequate accommodation, nutrition, reading matter and medical treatment.[43] This catalogue of rights has been clarified and extended by the 1998 Correctional Services Act, which, notwithstanding some modifications that the original design underwent in the course of the legislative process, must still be seen as part of the post-election phase of amending existing legislation to reflect liberal constitutional values. Most sections of the Act have not yet come into force almost three years after it was passed by Parliament, but even in its absence the courts have adopted some strong pro-rights interpretations of prisoners' constitutional and other rights. Thus the Cape Division of the High Court has ruled that an aids sufferer is constitutionally entitled to adequate medical treatment even where the State could not provide such treatment to indigent people on the outside.[44] The Transvaal Division has ruled in equally difficult circumstances that the prison authorities could legally be compelled to provide electric wiring that they had undertaken to prisoners to install, so that they could use electrical appliances to which a privilege system entitled them.[45] Even the Constitutional Court has weighed in; holding that the right of prisoners to vote could not be removed by administrative rulings that made it impossible for them to do so.[46] So far so good: but will the courts and particularly the Constitutional Court be prepared to use their powers to take decisions that would compel the government to divert more resources to meet its constitutional obligations? Will the Constitutional Court rule that existing overcrowding is unconstitutional, for example, and be prepared to draw the consequences of requiring massive further expenditure or the release of prisoners. It is worth a try, but I believe that it will not do so.

43 Section 35(2) of the 1996 Constitution.
44 Van Biljon v Minister of Correctional Services 1997(4) SA 44 (C).
45 Strydom v Minister of Correctional Services 1993 (3) BCLR 342 (W).
46 August and Another v Electoral Commission and others 1999 (3) SA 1 (CC).

Conclusion

Is it desirable to think of developing liberal penal policy solely on the basis of what the courts may do to intervene? That constitutional courts can play a role in shaping, indeed in altering permanently, the way prisons are run, is obvious from the German experience prior to the enactment of 1976 *Strafvollzugsgesetz* and perhaps now again with the recent decision of the German Federal Constitutional Court on remuneration for prison labour. [47]

In times of perceived crisis, such as that engendered by the current fear of crime in South Africa, however, the full import of a rights-based approach is often overlooked. Yet even in such circumstances hard-fought gains can be protected. Thus, even in the United States of America where the emphasis on the constitutional rights of prisoners has declined, the influence of earlier rights-based decisions remains significant. The prisons in Texas, for example, may hold more inmates than ever before, but they will never again be managed in the way they were prior to the detailed orders made on constitutional grounds by the courts of that State.[48]

It must be recognised, however, that, when confronted by a particular case, courts often tend not to focus on the system as a whole. We have seen in South Africa how they have ignored the impact of overcrowding even where they themselves could have influenced it directly by ruling differently on bail and on the right to a speedy trial. In pointing out the unintended consequences of judicial decisions, scholars have a key role to play.

It is not desirable to restrict such intervention to a critique of the judgments of the courts. South African criminal justice in general and the prison system in particular are now in the phase where major legislative or even policy changes to implement constitutional standards directly are unlikely. In this sphere the function of scholars who intervene in debates about penal policy must be one of damage limitation. It is still possible that the clamour for harsh crime control measures can be met with reasoned argument that points out the shortcomings of such measures and suggest alternatives that may be equally effective without destroying the prospects of a more humane penal system that was one of the ideals of the new South African order.[49]

---

47 B VerfGE of 1 July 1998: see (1998) 47 Zeitschrift für die gesamte Strafrechtswissenschaft 242 ff.

48 See M.M. FEELEY and E. L. RUBIN (1998) *Judicial Policy and the Modern State: how the courts reformed America's prisons.* Cambridge: Cambridge University Press.

49 See the perceptive comments of the late SIR LEON RADZINOWICZ in his autobiography published in 1999: *"Today the Republic of South Africa, like many other newly born states, presents, at least in the criminal sphere, a disjunction between aspirations and*

practice. The recently adopted Constitution, which aims to inculcate a 'human rights culture' is firmly grounded on what I have described as the socio-liberal doctrine in criminal policy. Capital punishment was abolished even though murder, violent criminality and many other forms of serious criminal activities have all risen drastically. Indeed, the maintenance of public order is fragile. I believe it will take some twenty years – providing that political and economic circumstances evolve in the right direction – before the new republic is endowed with a system of criminal justice faithful to the sprit of the new Constitution.": L. RADZINOWICZ (1999) *Adventures in Criminology*, 410. London and New York: Routledge.

"GOOD CORRECTIONS"

Ole Ingstrup

Introduction

"Human beings are human beings wherever they live. Concern for their suffering from hunger, other deprivation and disease does not end because those so afflicted are on the other side of an international frontier. This is the case even though no elementary truth is so consistently ignored or, on occasion, so fervently assailed."

These are the words of John Kenneth Galbraith, Paul M. Warburg Professor Emeritus of Economics at Harvard University. They are part of the first chapter of his very insightful little book from 1996, *The Good Society* with the subtitle "The Human Agenda".

Professor Galbraith sees a need to describe and define the good and achievable society and argues that otherwise *"there is no chance for the better society"*. He also states that *"to identify and urge the good and achievable society may well be a minority effort, but better that effort than none at all. Perhaps, at a minimum, the comfortable will be afflicted in a useful way.*"[1]

I do not pretend to be a John Kenneth Galbraith, nor is this a book. This is an article to honour my long time friend Professor Tony Peters and to thank him for his significant contribution to better criminal justice policy thinking and analysis – and for his wonderful friendship. It is also an attempt to outline my views on what good correctional systems, including community based sanctions, probation, incarceration and conditional release in a civilized and/or dignified society ought to look like.

This article has that in common with *The Good Society* by John Kenneth Galbraith "that it intends to send a couple of messages to the apathetic elites in modern societies" and at least provide a framework for future discussions or better dialogue about corrections – about "good corrections".

This is not science – it is policy or perhaps more politics, albeit politics supported by research, and the traces from a long career in corrections. It is an invitation to politicians and to criminal justice practioners to engage in a dialogue about corrections with a useful purpose and with results that are likely to contribute to the overall quality of life in society. I have deliberately

1 J. K. GALBRAITH (1996) *The Good Society: the Humane Agenda*, 152. London: Sinclair-Stevenson.

chosen the word dialogue to describe what is needed: the two Greek roots, *dia* and *logos* suggesting "meaning flowing through" as opposed to "debate" which means "to bed down", and discussion with the same root as "precaution" and "concussion" which means "to break things up".[2]

The following pages contain my opening statement in the dialogue which I hope will take place. This dialogue as I see it is essential to any progress in corrections. I hope for a dialogue which will take place inside such international, professional fora as The International Corrections and Prison Association which some of us created a few years ago exactly for that purpose. I also hope that dialogues will take place among responsible politicians and journalists and among the public at large, in service clubs and in schools.

In our media intense world, in the "sound bite universe", catastrophising and playing strongman is both easier and apparently more rewarding than it is to show balance and thoughtfulness. A dialogue on corrections therefore does not have an inviting and fertile environment in which to unfold. And it shows! One of the characteristics of the political attitudes towards corrections in most developed countries appears to be that politicians have placed themselves –and thereby their administrators and advisors– in a next to hopeless position.

On the one hand, the politicians are promising "tough and unsentimental measures against criminals" in order to satisfy a –mostly perceived or media created– need on the part of the public to see "justice to be done" to those who violate the laws of the land. Super jails are being built to show that governments are determined and committed to delivering on those promises. Legislative packages are arriving at parliamentary doorsteps at frequent intervals in order to address –often non existing– problems by introducing longer sentences, fewer conditional releases, lower age limits for criminal responsibility and even expansions of what is to be considered a criminal act. The money, which could never seem found to be address the social conditions which have been proven over and over again to lead to crime in the first place, seem to be falling from heaven when the need is a punitive one.
In the same category falls the ill placed arguments that offenders must serve long sentences and their rights and privileges must be kept to a minimum in order to show respect for the victims of their crimes.

On the other hand, our politicians are also promising the citizens that the system of corrections will –and certainly should– transform the offenders

2 See J. Jaworski and B.S. Flowers (1996) *Synchronicity – the Inner Path of Leadership,* 110. San Francisco: Berret-Koehler.

into law abiding citizens and they tend to underscore this view by entertaining the "who did not do what he/she was suppose to do?" type of question when an offender re-offends seriously while on conditional release. I have never heard a politician –or for that matter even a thoughtful journalist– ask questions about accountability for crimes committed by offenders because they were not conditionally released.

The obvious problem with this line of arguments is that the two objectives are incompatible. We know that longer, harsher punishment will lead to more crime – not less. We do not get safer streets and safer homes through that type of intervention. What we do get is slightly unsafer streets and unsafer homes.

I am not saying that the criminal justice policy field has opened both the goal side and the professional strategy side to public debate, but it certainly is one of the hardest hit areas in that category of politics and policy. Anything similar in the health policy area would be unthinkable.

No matter how complex the situation may be, we still need to strive for high performance in the field of corrections and what follows is my best suggestion to the world of correctional politicians, researchers and administrators with respect to a framework and some definitions of what constitutes "good corrections".

The framework, which I will be using in the following, is based on the ideas in *The Three Pillars of Public Management* written for public management in general by Paul Crookall and myself.[3] Studying some of the best public service organizations in the world let us to the conclusion that one of the keys to the success of these organizations was that they have an ongoing, open and vigorous dialogue –a socratic dialogue– in three main areas: aim, character and execution.

1. Aim

A good correctional service knows its direction.

A good correctional system knows where it is going. It knows its mission and it is also clear about its operating values. It is a system driven by results and based on values. This sounds pretty simple and straightforward. – It is not!

The fact that corrections in many countries has become a political football makes it very difficult to decide upon an unambiguous mission.

---

3 O. INGSTRUP & P. CROOKALL (1998) *The Three Pillars of Public Management*. Montreal & Kingston (Canada): McGill-Queen's University Press.

Mission meaning the ultimate goal the direction for a never-ending journey of improvements the organizational North Star or Southern Cross for leadership navigation. The fact that we still do not seem to have a generally agreed upon understanding of the relationship between criminal justice policy, penal law, the purpose of sentencing and the purpose of corrections does not make matters any easier.

Having said that, good corrections still need to be defined in order to be achieved. Like the good and achievable society needs to be defined in order to give a chance to improve the existing society, so do the individual parts of a good society need to be defined in order to enable those responsible for the individual areas to make useful changes.

In addition to the political difficulties already mentioned and the theoretical uncertainties, corrections are still an area of societal life where no agreements exists as to what corrections is suppose to accomplish. The international community of corrections –as reflected in the membership of the International Corrections and Prisons Association– seem to be divided into at least three groups. The largest group is a group of States and Nations who have not even considered the question. The second group of States and Nations seem to prefer or accept a primarily punitive system for which "serving time under tough and severe conditions" is the factual but most often not explicitly stated mission. The third group is leaning towards a mission dominated by ideas of rehabilitation, reintegration and assisting offenders getting on with their lives. One should remember though that in most countries where the importance of mission is recognized, there seldom appears to be total agreement on what it ought to be. Denmark is a particularly good example where the central correctional administration has decided on a model of reintegration and crime prevention for their mission which is now also enshrined in the newly past Danish Corrections Act from the year 2000. At the same time one of the really good Danish warden (head of an institution) continues to argue loudly, repeatedly and publicly that attempts to reduce recidivism is not even part of the business of corrections.

The trend seems to be that more and more correctional systems go the way of developing a mission statement and in it include a prominent reference to crime prevention, reintegration or rehabilitation. As a matter of fact, I do not know of one single system which has a mission statement with no reference to this family of concepts. My suspicion is that is simply too embarrassing to put out a mission statement which reflects a "punitive only" philosophy, and that it is a great deal easier to be punitive in speeches and policy without making an unequivocally clear statement to that effect.

One of the first mission statements to see the light of day in the area of corrections was developed by the federal Correctional Service of Canada in 1988. The strategic approach to corrections in Canada was inspired by a serious crisis in the Service prior to 1988 and the mission clearly reflects the conviction that corrections best contribute to society by helping and encouraging offenders to become law-abiding citizens. Corrections as crime prevention are a key in this directional statement which in its entirety reads:

> *"The Correctional Service of Canada as part of the criminal justice system and respecting the rule of law contributes to the protection of society by actually encouraging and assisting offenders to become law-abiding citizens while exercising reasonable safe secure and humane control".*[4]

To achieve "good corrections" to simply state the expected outcome, the results dimension (that is the mission) is not sufficient. It appears that results driven and value-based organizations tend to perform better than other types of organizations. An overall mission statement must be supported by a number of organizational values which have to be defined and communicated as sharply and as vigoursly as the mission statement itself.

In the Correctional Service of Canada we identified the following five core values:

> *"Core value 1: We respect the dignity of individuals, the rights of all members of society and the potential for human growth and development.*
>
> *Core value 2: We recognize that the offender has the potential to live as a law-abiding citizen.*
>
> *Core value 3: We believe that our strength and our major resource in achieving our objectives is our staff and that human relationships are the cornerstone of our endeavour.*
>
> *Core value 4: We believe that the sharing of ideas, knowledge, values and experience, nationally and internationally, is essential to the achievement of our mission.*
>
> *Core value 5: We believe in managing the service with openness and integrity and we are accountable to the Solicitor General."*[5]

Getting the results definition and the values right is critical to success. It also ensures some measure of stability in the evolution of the organization. In the case of the Correctional Service of Canada, the mission and values and the accompanying long term (strategic) objectives have remained intact over a

---

4 Mission Statement of the Correctional Service of Canada (see website: www.csc-scc.gc.ca)

5 INGSTRUP & CROOKALL, *o.c.*

period of thirteen years. During that time both a conservative and a liberal government have been in power and nine different individuals served at the ministerial level of responsibility. This suggests that if the work is thoroughly done, there is no reason to fear that major changes to the mission and values would be requested by incoming ministers. A clearly described, realistic and research based correctional "universe" gives any minister, any government in charge, the opportunity to lead both by changing the framework and by setting priorities within the existing framework.

Without "good leadership", "good corrections" is not possible. Good leadership means in its deepest manifestation, the kind of leadership which is most likely to move the organization towards its mission and doing this in a way that clearly and visibly respects the defined values of the organization.

What constitutes good leadership may vary from place to place. However, research conducted by Crookall and myself supports the findings of others that universally valid and significant elements in leadership include: the ability to listen, a desire to involve others and the skill required to delegate without abdicating responsibility. Also, leadership is not "a thing" vested in the CEO but a dispersed phenomena. Leaders must demonstrate a commitment to their employees and in all they do in consistency with the mission and values; there must be consistency among the leaders of an organization and perhaps most importantly, there must be absolute consistency between the leaders' words and their deeds. They must walk the talk. Furthermore, they must take the long view and they must demonstrate leadership beyond borders.

The third, and in this context the final, element in the area of direction setting which must be solidly in place, is accountability. "Good corrections" cannot be achieved and certainly not be sustained, without the ability on the part of the organization to clearly explain how and to what extent the organization is making progress relative to both its mission and its values. One cannot have that an organization is making progress on its mission if the ongoing performance measurements and the performance indicators are not related to that mission. Measuring, for instance, the number of staff training days and costs says little about the success of safely reintegrating offenders into society. The Canadian Auditors General have repeatedly pointed to the need in the Public Service of Canada to strengthen its accountability frameworks at the departmental level to ensure better coordination between performance measures and the overall purpose mission of the department. In his recently published overview report covering the last ten years, the Auditor General –by the way!– notes that the Correctional Service of Canada is one of only three departments where that kind of accountability exists. I'm personally convinced that there exists a very close connection between the extremely focused accountability system of the Correctional Service of Canada and the fact that the Service has been able to reduce rates of recidivism substantially.

2. Character

A good correctional service has character.

A clear, well communicated and truly driving mission and a good set of values, focused leadership of high caliber and an accountability system adjusted to the directional statement, provides corrections with aim. However, more is needed to deliver "good corrections". The system must pay attention to its "character", including "people", "communications" and "trust".

A correctional service will most often employ many people, and as the system evolves and becomes more sophisticated, more and more different professions will be represented on staff. For a correctional service to be a good correctional service, efforts must be made to seek out and retain the very best people for all of the jobs. It is not enough to *say* that "our employees are our most important resource" or "we want to be the employer of choice". The organization, and especially its leadership, must consistently and visibly make the employees feel that they indeed are being treated as "the most important resource" or as the "employee of choice".

The interplay between the areas of "leadership" and the "people area" is obvious. It is worth noting that a comprehensive Danish study of personnel issues includes amongst its findings that most of the significant reasons for employees leaving the public service seems to be "bad leadership".

The best organizations in the world understand the importance of good people policies and practices and they have such policies and practices in place to guide them in such areas as selection, assessment, training and development, promotion and demotion. This is particularly important for corrections where the environment is often harsh, basically unfriendly and more often than not littered with frustrating and disappointing experiences. These realities call for an extra effort to be made just to level the playing field.

It is part of the character of a good correctional organization that communications occur at a high level and in a systematic manner. Communications is no longer an after thought. It is no longer the cooler based chatting. It is no longer on a need to know basis.

Communications appears to be an ongoing and universal challenge. Organizations never seem to get it quite right. The best in the world, however, seem to consistently improve and continue to struggle for further improvements in this area. They have recognized the significance of communications and they apply a multitude of strategies in order to get the best out of it.

One key element seems to be to identify those with whom to communicate. Mapping out the hundreds or thousands of lines of ongoing or occasional communications. It is an integral part of this mapping process to determine the nature of the relationship, criteria for success in the relationship and also to assign responsibility and accountability to someone for taking care of the relationship.

Most correctional leaders and senior managers are surprised by the extent and complexity of organizational networks once they are properly understood and made manageable, especially when the network mappings include those relationships which should exist, but do not exist.

I have personally found it rewarding to think in terms of a number of networks: "internal relationships (within the service itself)", "networks external to the service but internal to government", "Networks external to government but national in nature" and "international networks".

Each of those areas are or ought to be, huge and constantly expanding. One dimension which regularly seems to be underemphasized in corrections is the horizontal dimension, i.e. the relationship with other departments. It is relatively obvious, for example, that the role and characteristics of corrections is poorly understood and appreciated in the international community even in the international law enforcement community. Sadly the situation often does not seem to me much better at the national level. Legislation is routinely passed in one sector of criminal justice with no appreciation for other sectors, most notably corrections. Correctional services are often guilty of the same sins, often acting unilaterally without consulting their counterparts internationally or without the necessary appreciation of the horizontality of most issues such as health, security, minority groups, rehabilitative programming, social control and research to mention just a few. It appears that correctional organizations themselves must redouble their efforts in order to take their rightful place in the community of government organizations. In some places, governance structures constitute a further impediment to good lateral communications. Another hurdle to overcome, another obstacle over which a communications bridge must be built.

Literally thousands of communications strategies are in use and this is not the place to even begin talking about these issues let alone assessing their value. Suffice it to state that communication absolutely must be open, prompt, to the point and brutally honest. I say this recognizing that often almost anything else would seem to be so much easier and expedient.

Corrections, which wants to strive for excellence, must invest considerable effort in its world of communications. If that area fails, the organization and its CEO, will loose standing inevitably among peers and in the world external to the public service. That in itself will make the pass to excellence even more exhausting to climb.

Many organizations, including correctional organizations, find it difficult -even embarrassing– to discuss the issue of trust in and around their organizations. They seem to feel that discussing trust becomes too "up close and personal". And yet, based on my own studies and experience at the organizational level, I have no hesitation in stating that trust is key to good leadership, management and collaboration. Trust is a lynch pin in the effective and efficient operation of well performing organizations. Employees and partners alike who feel that they have to devote a considerable amount of time covering their backs are not effective employees and partners. The absence of trust creates more than uncertainty. It is the main reason why people will be "looking after themselves", good ideas will not be shared, bad news will be held back as long as possible, staff morale will plummet, absenteeism will soar, good people will be looking for employment elsewhere and an indefinable negative aura will become more and more visible. An untrusting environment is a poisonessnous environment.

If trust is not there, it must be generated. If trust is there, it must be sustained and nurtured. Ensuring that the organizational character includes trust, is first and foremost a leadership responsibility. However, by definition, all members of the organization must share in that responsibility in order to meet this critical objective.

Within the context of a good correctional service, one can look at trust from a variety of perspectives.

One such aspect of trust is personal trust. Personal trust concerns the degree to which people may trust others to say what is true. There is no hidden agenda. Simply put, people are trustworthy. Ethical behavior is often included in this area. With respect to leaders, there seems to be one more dimension. It would appear that trustworthiness, on the part of leaders, must be combined with their ability to trust others in order for those leaders themselves to be fully trusted. Leaders, who carry long lists of items to check on, may be as truthful as can be but they will still not enjoy the full trust of their employees and therefore, will not benefit from their full energy and ingenuity either.

Another aspect of trust is a professional trust. Professional trust involves a trust that the organization and its individual members know what they are doing and that they are good at it. In corrections, lives literally depend on that trust being justified and for correctional leaders one of their important tasks is to ensure that all the members of the service meet standards sufficiently high to warrant trust in them and in the organization and as a consequence to solidify external trust by letting the world know about the competency level of correctional staff. Again, leaders must also ensure that their employees and subordinates confidently may trust their leaders' ability to lead and to manage, over and above their ability, to engage meaningfully and competently in discussions about correctional subject matters.

A third aspect of trust is a political trust. The politicians responsible for good governance –the government– and especially those who have a direct responsibility for corrections, must be confident that their correctional agency is performing competently and with integrity and is moving performance at a reasonable pace towards a mission which is compatible with the government's overall political agenda. Without that kind of trust, a correctional agency will be less and less able to pursue its mission, more and more external mechanisms will be imposed, internal self-confidence will be lost the, level of energy and creativity will diminish – and soon there will be good and visible reasons not to trust the organization. This was the way in which Correctional Service of Canada was perceived by many in 1987/88.

Finally, a good correctional service must enjoy public trust. Public trust is about the degree to which the public at large –often influenced through the media– feel that they can trust their correctional agency to do what corrections is supposed to do.

This area of trust is, at best of times, very difficult even to sustain. The media often seems to be driven by identifiable incidences. – An offender on conditional release commits a serious offence and the whole system is being questioned. It is remarkable that the fact that an offender is not found by the police influences public trust significantly less than when a released offender reoffends. This simple fact allows the police to enjoy a great deal more public confidence than what is the case with respect to corrections even if correctional success rate generally are superior to the clearance rate by the police.

Whether this is fair or not is immaterial. What it entails is a fact that the building and sustaining of public trust is a task of great significance in good corrections.

3. Execution

A good correctional service knows how to get things done.

Without "aim" and "character", as discussed earlier, there will be no "good corrections". However, more still is required. Collectively the members of the service must have the skills to translate ideas, attitudes, creativity, energy and intellectual insights into well-directed actions that produce results as defined by the mission.

In order to get things done, leaders need to know how to lead and managers need to know how to manage. Very few are born leaders or managers. Even fewer are born as the best leaders and managers that they can become. As in all types of other trades, people need education and exposure to organizational life in order to eventually master the art of leadership and management. Leadership and management in corrections – and for that matter in public service in general– is no exception to that rule.

Unfortunately, leadership and management training and development is frequently not a high priority in most organizations, certainly not in public service organizations. Developing leaders and managers frequently is something that happens a long time after the individual has been staffed into his/her position of authority. During the many hours of my life that I spent traveling by air, I often felt very good about the fact that the airlines seem to take a different approach to the training and development of their pilots than most organizations take with respect to their leaders and managers. I particularly like the fact that pilots tend to have been trained before they take up their duties on the flight deck and not at some later point in time.

It is part of being a good manager that the person is capable of identifying problems and opportunities, that the person is capable of seeing solutions or ways of capitalizing on opportunities for improvement. Furthermore, leaders and managers must know which tool or strategy to apply and how to handle the tool. Those people must also know how to maintain a tool, to keep it sharp, and must be able to see the difference between a new solid tool on the market and yet another slick gadget that looks good and promising but which does not match the kind of problems that the organization is dealing with.

In good corrections, leaders and managers do master the areas just mentioned and those abilities exist at all managerial level throughout the organization. Off the shelf tools are rarely found in the toolboxes of high performing organizations. Their tools are either tailor made to fit their problems and opportunities or they are adjusted versions of the "brand names".

The management toolbox in corrections has two major components: the management tools are in one compartment and the correctional tools are in the other compartment. Especially with respect to the correctional tools the International Corrections and Prisons Association has created a "best practices institute" through which members have access to tools that have worked well in order jurisdictions.

In any event, the leaders and managers toolbox must be in good shape in order for good corrections to happen.

Teamwork –sophisticated teamwork– also seems to be essential ingredients in good corrections. It appears that well performing organizations (also outside of corrections) display a very mature attitude towards teams and teamwork. They tend to use teams primarily when the task is one which requires a high level of creativity and/or a relatively high level of skills from different professional areas. Teams should be given broad mandates and, when appropriate, short timeframes. Routine tasks are usually not carried out in teams.

It does not appear that letting those team members who have developed the ideas be part of the implementation process increases the likelihood of success in the implementation. "Implementers" are often individuals with a different personality from those who are natural choices for the idea development phase.

The need to work in teams and to manage teams and team processes will likely grow, not diminish. The fact that more and more governments realize that good horizontal working relationships among departments is a key to success, entails that teamwork will be in high demand to get the job. Teamwork may often be most useful when circumstances are difficult, time frames are short and multi-disciplinary and/or multi-cultural perspectives are required.

Understanding how to best work in teams and how to get the best from teams, may very well be one of the most significant keys to success in the future organization including the "good correctional organization".

Corrections is not an area, which, generally speaking, has been known as a fast moving area of any public service. There is movement, of course, in the field of corrections but often, lack of significant movement, is more obvious than the opposite. A couple of correctional services, on the other hand, have actually placed themselves at the cutting edge of public administration.

It seems obvious that correctional organizations and institutions with any ambition to serve their governments and country well, will have to adopt an organizational style of aggressive and decisive, goal-oriented improvement.

An organization, which is not improving, is decaying. Constant change is part of what makes an organization good and the only way in which constant change becomes constant improvement is when the mission is clear and present in the minds of people and when the organization is comfortable with relatively high pace of change.

In "good corrections", therefore, the mastery of change management and organizational adaptation becomes key. I am not thinking of the kind of change, which is merely political opportunisms and conflict avoidance. What I do have in mind is a kind of change, which accommodates both a ministerial agenda and a professional, knowledge-based correctional agenda.

Leaders in good correctional organizations must understand how to create a change prone and change willing organization. They must also understand the nature of change and not least the art of comforting employees affected by change. They must learn to deal effectively with the ever present pressure to lower the pace or bring change to an end altogether.

Often processes of renewal and change take longer and move more slowly than leaders had hoped for. In those cases, blaming the "implementing classes" for resistance to change, counterproductive foot dragging and the like, is not uncommon. This tendency to lay blame somewhere is itself, a factor, which tends to slow down the process and certainly a factor, which is likely to generate less enthusiasm for the continued process of change.

Conclusion

I have made an attempt to set the framework for a constructive dialogue in the area of corrections. Each national system can add and substract, or they can try to fill the framework, with meaningful substance. The only thing they cannot do is to stay as a spectator on the sideline of the correctional playing field while claiming that they make an optimal contribution to their society.

THE TRANSFER OF COMMUNITY SANCTIONS AND MEASURES FROM A EUROPEAN PERSPECTIVE

Anton van Kalmthout

During his long career as a criminologist and professor at the Catholic University of Leuven, Tony Peters has made an intensive effort in word and deed to seek different ways to approach the phenomenon of crime and how to respond to it. Even before the concept of restorative justice was introduced as a new term in the theory of criminology, his work and opinions could already be distinguished from the prevailing opinions because he was one of the first to work towards a re-evaluation and improvement of the victim's position, both within and outside criminal proceedings, and towards other forms of criminal sanctions. Thanks in part to the pioneering work of Tony Peters, many initiatives relating to diversion, compensation of the victim, mediation and non-custodial or community sanctions have meanwhile developed into recognised forms of response and are now, at home and abroad, an important component of the modern instruments of penal policy.

Introduction

Initiatives relating to diversion, victim compensation, mediation and non-custodial or community sanctions possess two main features. On the one hand, they are characterised by an increased attention for preventive measures, aimed at removing the breeding grounds on which criminal behaviour can thrive. On the other hand, they display new forms of response that do not center on retribution and suffering, but give the sanction a more positive objective. This can be seen clearly when the current sanction systems in Europe are compared with those of forty years ago. This comparison shows that in practically all countries, the simple, surveyable sanction system with imprisonment, fine and conditional or suspended sentence as its core sanctions has disappeared. The list of penalties and measures has been expanded with the addition of a series of such non-custodial sanctions as probation, community service, compensation and restitution, victim-offender mediation or community mediation, withdrawal of licences, training courses, cognitive-behaviour-oriented learning and training programmes, treatment programmes (especially for drug and sex offenders), supervision and attendance orders, placement in probation hostels or day centres, intensive supervision or probation orders, curfew orders, house arrest and electronic monitoring, deferment of sentence with supervision, family custody, controlled freedom, combination orders (consisting of a combination of two or more of these sanctions) and many others. The possibilities to apply these new sanction modalities in the European criminal justice systems are just as diverse as their manifestations. They are manifested mainly as a principal penalty or measure or as a condition attached to a conditional or suspended sentence, imposed after trial by the sentencing judge. In addition, there is a growing tendency to apply variations of these judicial sanction modalities as well in the pre-trial and post-trial phases. In the pre-trial phase, they can be applied as a front-door sanction by the police, public prosecutor or investigating judge. As a back-end sanction, they can be applied in many countries in the post-trial phase by a specialised sentencing judge or by the prison authorities.

Characteristic of all these new sanction and enforcement modalities is that they demand an active attitude and cooperation from the offender/defendant in his/her resocialisation and re-integration process. In order to influence and stimulate this process, these sanctions are no longer enforced in total institutions, but in open, free society. In this respect these sanctions and measures differ essentially from traditional penalties. Many of these new sanctions and measures (in particular community service, social training courses and victim-oriented sanctions) need society's involvement. After all, that is why they are called community sanctions or community-based sanctions. According to Recommendation No R (92) 16 of the Council of Europe, this should mean "sanctions and measures which maintain the offender in the community and involve some restriction of his/her liberty through the imposition of conditions and/or obligations, and which are implemented by bodies designated in law for that purpose".[1]

The real value and meaning of a community sanction or measure, however, should not be sought in the fact that the offender can remain in the community during the enforcement of the sanction, but in the fact that these new sanctions and measures can contribute to re-integrating offenders into society. This is done by stimulating and improving offenders' sense of responsibility and their social skills by confronting them with the consequences of their offending behaviour and by asking them to perform resocialisation activities. Because the emphasis is put on the offender's inclusion rather than exclusion from society, it means that the involvement and commitment of the community -in particular the local institutions, local authorities and volunteers- are indispensable.

1 European Rules on Community Sanctions and Measures, Recommendation No. R (92) 16 and Explanatory Memorandum, Council of Europe, Strasbourg 1992, Appendix 1.

1. Re-integration and the principle of equality

One of the reasons that community sanctions have expanded enormously in Europe is the assumption that these community based sanctions are more effective in preventing offending than those provided in institutions. This is expressed concisely in de mission statement of CEP (Conférence Européenne de la Probation), the European collaborative venture of national probation organisations, that states: *"a society built on the principles of social inclusion provides the best protection for communities from the harm and distress caused by crime"* and that *"the social exclusion of offenders through incarceration reduces the chances of their effective re-integration and increases the risk of their re-offending"*.[2]

Effective re-integration and social inclusion also mean that in the statutory rule, or in the imposition and enforcement of the community sanctions, no barriers should be put up that make it de facto impossible to achieve this objective or hinder its achievement. However, the different statutory rules and sentencing practice have serious shortcomings in this respect. In my contribution to the recent publication *Crime and Criminal Justice in Europe*, I mentioned a number of factors that, up to now, have prevented the breakthrough of community sanctions in most countries. These factors range from lack of clarity as to the nature and objective of the particular community sanction, inconsistencies in the statutory rules, defective infrastructure, lack of mutual compatibility and commensurability to the exclusion of certain categories of offenders who, given the nature of the crime, should not be excluded.[3] Therefore, where the envisaged reduction of the unconditional custodial sentence is concerned, community sanctions have achieved their objective only to a very limited degree. In that regard, the picture is much less rosy than the statutory rules, with their wide range of community sanctions, suggest. Statistics concerning the number of unconditional prison sentences imposed during the last decade, especially in countries where these community sanctions have been applied on a very large scale, show that there has been no major reduction in prison sentences, neither in the prison population. In fact, the contrary is the case if we take into account the enormous increase in prison

---

2 A. VAN KALMTHOUT and J. DERKS (2000) *Probation and Probation Services. A European Perspective*, 571. Nijmegen.

3 A. VAN KALMTHOUT (2000) Community sanctions and measures in Europe: a promising challenge or a disappointing Utopia?, in: *Crime and Justice in Europe*, 121-135, 126-135. Strasbourg: Council of Europe.

capacity in such countries as England, Wales, France and the Netherlands during the last decade. Positive exceptions to this are Canada and Finland, where the number of offenders under community supervision, in particular probation or community service, is rising faster than the number of people in prison. Nevertheless, in general, the share of most community sanctions and measures developed during the past decade is seldom more than 1% of all sentences imposed.

But also in those countries where some community sanctions have undergone a successful development in terms of quantity (England and Wales, France, the Netherlands, Finland, Switzerland), it is striking that the concept of social inclusion instead of exclusion explicitly or implicitly does not apply to certain categories of offenders. One of these categories concerns foreigners who don't live in the country in which they have committed their crime. As a result of increasing tourism, movement of employees across borders and international exchanges in the field of sports or education, more and more mostly relatively young people are coming into conflict with the police and the law of a country other than that in which they live. The offences committed do not usually differ from those committed by contemporaries from that country. Frequently committed offences are: shoplifting, drunk driving, car theft, being a public nuisance, public violence, selling or buying drugs, particularly soft-drugs.

However, when we look at the sentencing and prison statistics, we can conclude that the category of foreign offenders is underrepresented by far among those who are sentenced to a community sanction. On the other hand, they represent a larger part of the prison population, which is to be expected in a quantitative sense.

There are different reasons for this. The first is that to the extent that community sanctions are actually used as an alternative to prison sentences, they are in principle only imposed on 'normal, decent' national offenders or less serious criminals who lead a more or less stable life. Rule 20 of the European Rules prohibits discrimination in the imposition and implementation of Community Sanctions and Measures (CSMs) on the basis of, amongst other things, ethnic origin or nationality. However, this rule seems to be very difficult to comply with, considering that many community sanctions require the offender to live under relatively stable conditions and to be capable of fulfilling the demanding obligations attached to a community sanction. Offenders who are not citizens of the country where the offence was committed are underrepresented amongst those sentenced to a community sanction because formal regulations or sentencing practice exclude them from the application of a community sanction.

Nor do most probation services give any priority to foreign offenders, because the objectives of re-integration and resettlement are in principle limited to the national society. The national probation services do not usually concern themselves with offenders who return to their own countries after serving their sentence. A reasonable interpretation of the rehabilitation principle in Article 10 of the International Covenant on Political and Civil Rights, however, tells us that the obligation of resocialisation and re-integration also extends to foreign offenders who stay only temporarily, usually only for a short time, in another country and commit an offence there.

This does not mean that the re-integration and resocialisation must be aimed at the society in which the sentencing takes place. That would not only make little sense, but would also be virtually impossible to implement, in view of the often considerable social, economic and cultural differences. Where custodial sentences are concerned, this is now widely understood. Precisely to enable a successful re-integration, important international conventions have been drawn up that allow foreign offenders to serve their prison sentence in their own country, such as the European Convention on Mutual Assistance in Criminal Matters, de European Convention on the supervision of conditionally sentenced or conditionally released offenders, the European Convention on the international validity of criminal judgements and the Convention on the transfer of sentenced persons.

Although these conventions are far from being satisfactorily complied with and applied, they are not without significance in principle because they emphasise that a sentence should be served as far as possible in the country where a person lives, works or studies. Here, too, it can be said that we are still at the very beginning of a route in which the principle of serving a sentence in one's own country is not the exception, but the rule.

2. Transfer of community sanctions: the current situation

The question that is becoming more and more topical is whether, in any case at European level, more attention and energy should be devoted to the possibility, in addition to imprisonment, the fine and the suspended sentence with conditions, to enforce a community sanction in a country other than the one in which it was imposed. Now that community sanctions have been recognised in so many jurisdictions as a real alternative to traditional sanctions such as imprisonment, fines and suspended sentence with conditions, and their viability has been demonstrated in several countries, that question can no longer be avoided. In some countries the number of community sanctions meanwhile approaches the quantity of prison sentences and community sanctions largely determine the quality of the probation service. This is to the advantage of both the offender and society.

The question is whether it is time to enable the enforcement of community sanctions also in countries other than where they were imposed. It is, after all, unfair and contrary to the ban on discrimination and the resocialisation principle to exclude a foreign offender from a community sanction, only because he or she does not live in the sentencing country. It is also contrary to the spirit of the Treaty of the European Union, which has precisely removed the boundaries between states and provides for free trade and free movement of persons. Nor is it in line with this Treaty and the European spirit to punish nationals of European countries by a prison sentence for similar crimes committed outside the national borders, when a community sanction would suffice in their own country.

For these reasons, therefore, the judicial authorities and probation services in the border area between the Netherlands, Belgium and Germany have taken a few initiatives to facilitate the enforcement in the offender's country of residence of a community sanction imposed on a foreigner by the Public Prosecution Service or court. This does not receive much publicity, because such a practice is not based on any treaty or other statutory provision, and would not benefit from publicity that could nip such initiatives in the bud.

On the other hand, it does not satisfy one's sense of justice that these informal initiatives are only incidental in nature and are not open to all potentially eligible foreign accused and sentenced persons.
The reason why the procedure for the transfer of community sanctions remains limited for the time being to informal agreements between authorities in the aforementioned border areas is that current instruments for judicial cooperation in criminal matters are inadequately equipped for the transfer of community sanctions. This is has different causes.

One of them is the diffuse nature of the term community sanctions and measures, which according to the definition of the European Rules on Community Sanctions and Measures (ERCSM) include all sanctions and measures "which maintain the offender in the community and involve some restriction of his liberty through the imposition of conditions and/or obligations, and which are implemented by bodies designated in law for that purpose". This definition does not, as most European Conventions on judicial cooperation in criminal matters require, limit the community sanction or measure to final decisions given by a court or a judge after trial, but includes the community sanctions that are applied before or instead of a decision on a sanction, as well as ways of enforcing a prison sentence outside a prison establishment. Particularly for these front-door and back-door modalities, a wide variety of which exist in different countries, the existing European Conventions do not offer the possibility to transfer their enforcement to another country.

But the community sanctions imposed by the court after trial are usually not suitable either for transfer to another country. The applicable European Conventions were enacted in a period when community sanctions did not yet exist and restrict the possibility of transfer to the sentences that, until several decades ago, were considered as the core sanctions of all European penal systems: custodial sanctions, suspended sentences, financial sanctions such as fines and forfeiture, and the withdrawal of certain rights. The same is true of the Benelux Treaty on the enforcement of judicial decisions in penal matters of 1968.[4] Although community sanctions are often applied as an alternative to unconditional custodial sanctions or as an alternative to fine default detention, they themselves cannot be classified as custodial sanctions or fines. The characteristic of these sanctions is, after all, that they attempt to avoid a custodial sanction by not depriving the accused/sentenced person of his or her liberty, but only limiting it and attaching conditions to such limitation of liberty that are aimed at re-integration and resettlement. Because this does not involve pure deprivation of liberty or a purely financial sanction, the literal wording of the conventions does not permit a transfer to another country. But even if the community sanctions, by way of a broad interpretation, could nevertheless be classified as custodial sanctions, this would not provide a solution without amendment of the Treaty criteria, because practically all treaties limit the transfer to custodial sanctions of at least 6 months. Community sanctions are usually sanctions imposed as an alternative to short-term prison sentences.

3. Transfer of community sanctions in the near future: Utopia or promising challenge?

The issue of the transfer of the enforcement of community sanctions has become topical, since the European Council placed this theme on the political agenda for the first time during the recent EU summit in Tampere. Article 31 (a) TEU foresees that common action on judicial cooperation in criminal matters shall include "facilitating and accelerating cooperation between competent ministries and judicial or equivalent authorities of the Member

4 *Bulletin of Treaties*, 1969, 9.

States in relation to (....) the enforcement of decisions". This idea was developed further during the Special European Council on Justice and Home Affairs Matters in Tampere on 15/16 October 1999. Based on the results of that consultation, in July 2000 the Commission of the European Communities presented a comprehensive proposal to the Council and the European Parliament to arrive at a system of mutual recognition of final decisions in criminal matters.[5] This plan entails abolishment of the 'request principle', which is typical of the current judicial cooperation in criminal matters and in practice constitutes a serious obstacle to the already existing possibilities for the transfer of sentenced persons. The request principle does, after all, allow the requested sovereign state the freedom to decide whether or not to honour the request. Sometimes, as stated in the document of the European Commission, the rules on compliance are rather strict, not leaving much of choice; on other occasions, the requested state is quite free in its decision. In almost all cases, the requesting state must await the reply to its request before it gets what its authorities need in order to pursue a criminal case. Another argument that, precisely where the transfer of community sanctions is concerned, makes a strong plea for replacement of the request principle by the principle van mutual recognition is that the request principle, as experience has taught in the past decades, is coupled with unnecessary bureaucratic rigmarole, is time consuming and leaves the authority imposing the sanction uncertain as to whether the intended transfer of enforcement will actually take place. A judge will not be quick to impose a community sanction on a foreign accused person without knowing beforehand whether it can actually be enforced in the other country. The request principle may still be defensible when heavy custodial sentences are concerned, but it is unrealistic to require this rule to apply to the transfer of relatively light sanctions as well, such as community sanctions, imposed for relatively minor offences.

Replacement of the 'request principle' by the principle of mutual recognition, certainly where community sanctions are concerned, has the undeniable advantage that in more cases than now, foreign offenders will also be able to profit from less radical forms of sanctions than the customary custodial penalties. In the words of the European Commission: "Mutual recognition should thus ensure not only that sentences are enforced, but also that they will be served in a way that protects individual rights. For example,

---

5 Commission of the European Communities, Communication from the Commission to the Council and the European Parliament, Mutual recognition of Final Decisions in Criminal Matters, Brussels 26.7.2000, COM (2000) 495 final.

enforcement in another Member State should also be sought when it permits a better social reintegration of the offender".[6]

Although, particularly with respect to community sanctions, the pursuit of the mutual recognition of final decisions in a European context should be evaluated positively, it is questionable whether the transfer of community sanctions within Europe can be realised this way in the short term. The Commission's document itself mentions many obstacles that could stand in the way of this, such as the need to establish a European registry of criminal sentences passed, including the development of common European multi-language forms that could be used to request information on existing criminal records. Another problem is that the current community sanctions in the different Member States are so diverse that without far-reaching harmonisation measures, mutual recognition and the transfer of sentences based on it will remain an illusion. The question is whether States will be prepared to harmonise, precisely in the area of penal sanctions. This is even more true for community sanctions than for the prison sentence and the fine, for which there are more similarities than differences in the statutory frameworks of the Member States. In respect of community sanctions, however, there is an unbridled proliferation of manifestations, extra-judicial and judicial sanction and enforcement modalities, application and exclusion criteria, conversion rates in the event of non-compliance, that even of the States were willing, harmonisation at national level, let alone European level, seems to be a utopian idea. The recently published book *Probation and Probation Services, A European Perspective* shows how immeasurably great these differences are. In some countries, community sanctions are applied strictly as an alternative to the unconditional prison sentence, in others, on the contrary, such as England and the Netherlands, community sanctions are considered sanctions *sui generis* that also extend to the territory of the fine, the suspended sentence with conditions or other non-custodial sanctions.

4. Is there another way?

In view of the complexity and dissimilarity of the national sanction systems, their diverse penal policy and dogmatic starting points and sovereign states' traditional resistance to the harmonisation of what is considered national criminal law heritage, it can be assumed that, for the time being, the European Commission's aim to enable transfer of the enforcement of community

---

6 COM (2000) *o.c.*, 2.

sanctions in Europe through the mutual recognition of final decisions in criminal matters will remain an illusion. The plan, that concerns all final decisions in criminal matters, is too ambitious for this purpose and much too comprehensive, and will come up against a complex structure of sanction systems in general and of community sanctions in particular. This is also evident from the reservations the European Commission itself attaches to its proposal. It does, after all, assert: "Whereas in principle mutual recognition of alternative sanctions should follow the same guidelines as that of custodial or pecuniary penalties, it seems legitimate, due to the wide range of types and modalities of measures that could fall within that category, to leave more discretion to the Member States concerned. Each of them could ask for the transfer but the requested Member State would not be obliged to consent.".[7]

In spite of this, possibilities exist nevertheless, along a less ambitious pathway, to give an initial impetus to the transfer of community sanctions. This would be possible if the idea is abandoned that the relevant Convention must include all penal sanctions or even all community sanctions, as endorsed by the European Commission. Looking at the reality of contemporary criminal justice in the European countries, one must conclude that at present only three community sanctions play a more than marginal role in the criminal justice system: the conditional or suspended sentence, compensation to the victim and the community service order. The first does not need any new regulation for the time being, because its transfer is already provided for in the European Convention on the supervision of conditionally sentenced or conditionally released offenders. The second, compensation to the victim is less suitable for a regulation that makes transfer possible because a sentence in the state where the victim lives, in other words the state where the offence was committed, is more logical than transfer to the state where the offender lives. This would not be in the victim's interest.

Community service remains. Here too, an objection to the transfer of its enforcement could be that this sanction is partly characterised by a restorative element, compensation to the community. However, contrary to compensation to the victim, such compensation to the community is usually more abstract and symbolic in nature. The efforts made in the context of a community service order do not benefit the local community, who have been injured by the offence, because the assumption is that community service is implemented in or in the vicinity of the place where the accused/sentenced person lives, and that is often a different place from where the offence was committed. When the potential benefit for the community against whom the offence was directed

---

7 COM (2000) *o.c.*, 16.

must be balanced against the benefit of permitting the offender to render the community service in the Member State where he or she is socially integrated, much can be said for tipping the balance in favour of the latter. Two more arguments can be given for this. The first is not opting for community service if transfer to the country where the offender lives is not possible, but for precisely an unconditional prison sentence. In that case as well, the injured community will not profit from the potential benefit of a community service. The second argument is that, precisely in a unifying Europe, the community element in the term community service should be interpreted broadly, in the sense that there would not be much objection if community could include the European Community.

The fact that the term community does not have to be interpreted in such a limited sense that it only means the community against whom the offence was directed is evidenced by two regulations that make the transfer of certain community sanctions possible to a limited extent in (parts of) Europe. The first is the Convention between the Scandinavian countries Denmark, Finland, Iceland, Norway and Sweden relating to the enforcement of sentences.[8] Initially limited to prison sentences, fines and conditional sentences, in 1996 this cooperation was also extended to the enforcement of community service .[9]

The second example is the Powers of Criminal Courts (Sentencing) Act 2000 of the United Kingdom, that provides the basis for the transfer of community service orders, probation orders and combination orders imposed in England on offenders residing in Scotland or Northern Ireland.[10] In both regulations, the term community is interpreted more broadly than the community against whom the offence was committed.

Both regulations are therefore important because they limit the possibilities for transfer to a few community sanctions for which it would be sensible to transfer enforcement to a different country. England is the country with the most varied and comprehensive sanction system of all European countries. The number of sanction modalities that can be classified as community sanctions has more than 20 manifestations. The fact that, nevertheless, only three of them are eligible for transfer of enforcement has to do with, on the one hand, the nature of the sanction which, in many cases, makes transfer undesirable, such

---

8 Justitsministeriet (1963) *Cirkulære om samarbejde med Finland, Island, Norge og Sverige angænde fuldbyrdelse af straf m.v.* Copenhagen: Justitsministeriet.

9 Justitsministeriet (1996) Skrivelse angænde Cirkulære om samarbejde med Finland, Island, Norge og Sverige angænde fuldbyrdelse af straf m.v., May 1996, *Journal* no. 4.k, 95-1330-20. Copenhagen: Justitsministeriet.

10 HMSO, Powers of Criminal Courts (Sentencing) Act 2000, (www.legislation.hmso.gov.uk/acts2000/00006).

as the compensation order, and, on the other hand, with the circumstance that the sanction concerned does not have a comparable equivalent in the country of transfer and thus cannot be enforced there.

The same reasons that convinced the Scandinavian and English legislature to limit the transfer of the enforcement of community sanctions to a community service, probation or combination order should also be the starting point for a regulation that would enable transfer in a European context. The transfer of community sanctions to countries where there is no comparable equivalent will remain a dead letter in practice and will impede the transfer of sanctions that could be eligible, such as a probation, community service or combination order.

Another reason to limit the efforts made for the transfer of community sanctions to these three modalities for the time being is that support for this can be found in the already existing European Convention on the supervision of conditionally sentenced or conditionally released offenders. The basic principle of this Convention, the supervision of the offender to facilitate the good conduct and re-adaptation to social life of the offender and to keep a watch on his behaviour is also a fundamental aspect of the probation and community service order. In that respect, this Convention is also the most suitable framework in which to include these two community sanctions. Supervision, guidance and control by the probation service is just as essential a part of the probation, community service and combination order as it is of the conditional sentence and conditional release. Insofar as probation and community service orders in national justice systems have the legal structure of a condition of a conditional sentence or conditional release, all of them are already within the scope of this Convention. The problem is, however, that in different countries, such as England, the Netherlands, Norway and Portugal, the probation and/or community service order are not in the nature of a special condition but are included as a separate principal penalty in the Penal Code. The first step that should be taken is therefore to expand the Convention, in accordance with the Scandinavian and English example, by other legal manifestations of both sanctions. Following the example of the English Sentencing Act, it would also be advisable to include a provision in this adjusted European Convention entailing that a transfer is ruled out if, before imposing such a probation or community service order, the court cannot be certain that suitable arrangements can be made for the enforcement and supervision of the community sanction by the probation service in the state where the offender resides.

The consequence of using the European Convention on the supervision of conditionally sentenced or conditionally released offenders as a legal basis for the transfer and enforcement of probation and community service is that not all legal modalities applied to community service are eligible for transfer. The Convention, after all, excludes modalities that are not based on a court decision, as well as sentences that are pronounced in absentia. This objection is not decisive, because only a few states allow the imposition of community service by a non-judicial authority or imposition in absentia. The interests of an offender who wishes to be eligible for a sanction that can be served in his or her own social environment are not harmed when the condition is attached to the sanction that he or she must consent to it in person and before the court.

Weighing the pros and cons against each other, the modest option endorsed here to limit the transfer of the enforcement of community sanctions for the time being to probation, community service and combination orders is more realistic and easier to implement in practice than the ambitious plan of the European Commission to regulate the transfer of the enforcement of community sanctions via mutual recognition of all final decisions in criminal matters. It would be better to test the possibility of this first on a modest scale under an existing Convention, whereby the exchange of the 'request principle' for that of mutual recognition would not have to face serious objections. A convention limited to the transfer of the enforcement and supervision of suspended sentences, probation and community service offers more possibilities for this than the Conventions intended for the transfer of heavier sentences. On the basis of the experience thus gained, it could be considered at a later stage whether expansion by other community sanctions is possible and desirable, whether or not with replacement of the 'request' principle by the concept of mutual recognition.

THE STATUS OF CRIMINOLOGY IN THE FRAMEWORK OF THE CRIMINAL SCIENCES[1]
In particular, the relationships between Criminology and Criminal Law

Isidoro Blanco Cordero
Mª Isabel Sánchez García de Paz

1. Coincidences and divergences with respect to the study of the Science of Criminal Law and Criminology

The objective of this contribution to the *Festschrift* for Professor Tony Peters, is the examination of the origins and consolidation of Criminology as an autonomous discipline in the framework of the criminal sciences, as a separate science from Criminal Law.

Criminology and Criminal Law Science are two disciplines that have a mutually intense relationship at the very least. On the one hand, Criminal Law Science cannot dispense absolutely of the reality to which are applied the legal norms that integrate it. However, the knowledge of such reality is not just the task of Criminal Law Science but relates to a large extent to Criminology (and other social sciences). The Sciences of Criminal Law and Criminology coincide, principally, in respect of their object of knowledge. Both sciences study the offence, the offender, the Criminal Law, the criminal sanctions.[2] However, their approach and more precisely their method of knowledge, is clearly different. While Criminal Law Science has a purely normative nature and is faced with knowledge of the object described from a legal perspective, using the technical-legal method, Criminology, as a causative-explanatory science, employs the empirical method, inductively, as typical of the natural sciences.[3] The scientific and systematic study of the norms concerning the offence -and its consequences, that is to say, the penalty and the safety measures- is the task of Criminal Law Science; its object of study is the positive Criminal Law in force. Criminology is defined on the other hand, as an empirical and interdisciplinary science that has as object of study the crime,

---

1 We like to thank Beth Sargent, Laura Sánchez Sargent and Christopher Sargent for their assistance in the translation of this article

2 See A. BERISTAIN IPIÑA (1986) *Ciencia penal y Criminología*, 38. Madrid.

3 See G. KAISER (1988) (2ª ed.), *Kriminologie. Ein Lehrbuch*. 1. 4 y 5, nº 14 ss, Heidelberg; y A. GARCIA-PABLOS DE MOLINA (1999) *Manual de Criminología. Introducción y teorías de la criminalidad*, 41 y 47 ss. Madrid; A. GARCIA-PABLOS DE MOLINA (1994) (2ª ed.), *Criminología. Una introducción a sus fundamentos teóricos para juristas*, 21 ss. Valencia, characterizes the criminological method as "empirical and interdisciplinary".

the offender, the victim and the social control of deviant behaviour.[4] Kaiser defines it as the orderly set of empirical knowledge (based then, on the experience), on the offence, the offender and the possible antisocial behavioural controls. Consequently, offence, offender and social control of the offence constitute the objects of this discipline, to which should be added, as Kaiser indicates, the studies directed to the protection of the victims (Victimology) and crime prevention.[5]

The multidisciplinary character of Criminology[6] is also notable. As opposed to the approaches that have granted Criminology a single meaning, individual or social, Naucke indicates how at present there exists in the criminological investigation the trend to gather the designated "theories of criminality" *"to conceptualize the punishable fact as a multifactorial event"*.[7] In the first place, it is understood that Criminology integrates criminal Anthropology, that considers the individual factors -biological and psychological- of the offence. Within it are located biology and criminal psychology. In the second place, criminal sociology is also part of criminological study, that investigates the social causes of the offence, elaborating different theoretical models that connect it with a defective socialization process or with a defective social structure.

2. Relationships between the Science of Criminal Law and Criminology. A historical perspective

The relationships between Criminology and the Science of Criminal Law -also called Criminal Dogmatic- during the short history of the existence of both, has been stormy. The object of investigation of Criminology was, until the 1930's, the Criminal Law in force in a given place. This is the era of dominance of the philosophical trend of legal positivism. This doctrine denies

---

4 See GARCIA-PABLOS DE MOLINA (1999) *o.c.*, 41 ss.

5 See G. KAISER (1988) *Introducción a la Criminología*, translation J.A. Rodríguez Nuñez, 7ª ed., 25 ss., Madrid; and also, *Kriminologie. Ein Lehrbuch*, *o c.* § 1. 1, nº 1. In Spain, GARCIA-PABLOS DE MOLINA marks as objects of the Criminology the offence, the offender, the victim and the social control, in *Manual de Criminología, o.c.*, 41 y 61 ss. and, of the same author, *Criminología. Una introducción a sus fundamentos teóricos para juristas*, *o.c.*, 26 ss.

6 S. WALKLATE (1988) *Understanding Criminology. Current theoretical debates,* 2. Buckingham, Philadelphia: Open University Press, emphasizes the multidisciplinary character of the Criminology.

7 See W. NAUCKE (1978) Las relaciones entre la Criminología y la Política Criminal, translation E. Bacigalupo, 5 *Cuadernos de Política Criminal* 95 ss., cfr. 97.

the scientific character of legal study of the offence and proposes its substitution by perspectives of sociological or anthropological character, that has been designated "sociological-naturalist positivism".[8] It is the start of the scientific stage of Criminology whose beginning is dated around the end of the 19th century with criminological positivism, concretely, with the Italian *Scuola Positiva* that headed Lombroso, Garófalo and Ferri.[9]

Also meaningful in the origins of criminological Science is the so-called "*jungdeutsche Kriminalistenschule*", the young German criminal school, headed by Franz von Liszt. This German author presents fundamental postulates in his inaugural lesson at the University of Marburg (1882), designated afterwards "Program of Marburg". Among them, stands out the "global Science of Criminal Law" (*gesamte Strafrechtswissenschaft*), which should form part, in addition to Criminal Dogmatic, with its deductive and abstract method -the dogmatic method- of other sciences that permit the empirical knowledge of the "causes" of the offence and of the effects of penalties, as criminal anthropology, criminal psychology and criminal statistics.[10] And lastly, the Science of Criminal Policy, that considers the appropriateness of the Criminal Law in force -as means- for the struggle against the offence -as end-; it assumes a critical reflection of the Criminal Law in force, and the formulation of reform criteria based on the criminological data and Criminal Policy principles.

The subsequent evolution of the work of von Liszt reveals his ideology suffers a weakening of the scientific character of the legal method.[11] This causes sciences such as Criminology, Penology and Criminal Policy to displace the Science of Criminal Law, the Dogmatic, trying to substitute for it. In spite of this, Criminology was not in that era a totally independent science, that annulled completely the legal study of Criminal Law. The positivist Criminology extracted its data, in an exclusive way, from individuals found in jails and madhouses, that is, those that already had been selected by the

---

8 See J.M. SILVA SÁNCHEZ (1992) *Aproximación al Derecho Penal contemporáneo,* 46. Barcelona.

9 About the origins of the criminological science, see KAISER, *Introducción a la Criminología, o.c.*, 41 ss.

10 See F. von LISZT (1905) Die Aufgaben und die Methode der Strafrechtswissenschaft, *Strafrechtliche Vorträge und Aufsätze*, tomo II, Berlin, reprinted Berlin, 1970, 284 ss.

11 In this sense, S. MIR PUIG (1982) (2ª ed.), *Introducción a las bases del Derecho penal,* 222. Barcelona; también L. MORILLAS CUEVA (1989) Anotaciones sobre la Ciencia del Derecho Penal, in: J.L. DE LA CUESTA, I. DENDALUZE Y E. ECHEBURÚA (eds.), *Criminología y Derecho Penal al servicio de la persona. Libro - Homenaje al Profesor Antonio Beristain*, 585 ss, 592. San Sebastián.

criminal system.[12] There is, in this sense, a relationship of methodological dependency between both disciplines. Criminology in this instance granted legitimization to the prevailing criminal system and was committed with the inspired ideology of the Criminal Law of the era.[13]

During the 1930's the Science of Criminal Law recovers with firmness the adoption of its own method, the dogmatic method, that removes it from the sociological and anthropological disciplines to which it had been united with precedence.[14] Arturo Rocco exposed the guidelines of the dogmatic method in Italy[15] in his famous speech delivered at the University of Sassari the 15 of January of 1910,[16] in the sense that the Dogmatic consists of the interpretation and systematizing of the positive law.[17] In Germany, Karl Binding in 1922 was already supporting the need of opting for a positivist-normativist method, limited to the study of the norms with a rejection of any reference to ends or values.[18] Both authors represent the defence of the postulates of the purer legal positivism in the area of the Science of Criminal Law. This trend results in a total separation of the Criminal Dogmatic from the rest of the criminal disciplines to which it was connected, generating its isolation in Europe. This isolation is maintained until the present time.[19] The political and social situation of the era influenced this evolution in a notable manner, with a Europe in which the authoritative regimes were proliferative, that did not absolutely incite the elaboration of empirical investigations on social reality and its more relevant problems.[20]

---

12 See A. BARATTA (1981) Criminología y dogmática penal. Pasado y futuro del modelo integral de la ciencia penal, in: S. MIR PUIG (1981) (ed.), *La reforma del Derecho penal II. Jornadas hispano - alemanas sobre la Reforma del Derecho Penal,* 25-26 ss. Bellaterra.

13 *Ibídem*, 27.

14 See A. BARATTA (1992) Criminología y dogmática penal. Pasado y futuro del modelo integral de la ciencia penal, *Política criminal y reforma del Derecho Penal* 28.

15 See A. ROCCO (1933) Il problema e il metodo della Scienza del Diritto penale, *Opere giuridiche, vol. I, Scritti giuridici varii*, 263 ss. Roma (*El problema y el método de la Ciencia del Derecho penal*, reprinted of the 3ª edition, Santa Fe de Bogotá, Colombia, 1999).

16 J.M. SILVA SÁNCHEZ (1992) *Aproximación al Derecho Penal contemporáneo,* 51, nota 43, Barcelona, emphasizes that Bettiol, in his book *Diritto penale*, 12ª ed. (Pettoelo Mantovani), Padova 68, says that the speech took place in year 1908.

17 ROCCO, *o.c.*, 263 ss. (297), emphasizes that the Criminal Law Science includes the exegetical investigation, the dogmatical and sistematical and the critical investigation. With respect to the last one, being value judgments, this author concludes that it is not a scientific knowledge of the law (309 ss).

18 See K. BINDING (1965) *Die Normen und ihre übertretungen. Band I. Normen und Strafgesetze.* Neudruck der 4. Auflage (Leipzig, 1922), Aalen.

19 BARATTA, *o.c.*, 29.

20 *Ibídem.*

While the Criminal Dogmatic reaches a high degree of development in Europe, in Great Britain and in the United States[21] different evolutionary lines are followed. The investigations that have as a goal the offence in its socio-cultural context are decisively influenced by the fruitful development of criminal sociology beyond the 1930s.[22] One of its consequences is the takeoff of Criminology -particularly of criminal sociology as one of its integrating parts-, that is disentailed to a large extent from the Science of Criminal Law.

Sociological theories of criminality reach their summit. These theories design various theoretical explanation models of the offence as a social phenomenon, that is, theories that try to isolate the variables that influence it in a sociological key.[23] From the methodological point of view, the most important datum is the change of the object of investigation of Criminology and of the Criminal Dogmatic. As compared to the previous era in which there was a relationship of "methodological dependency" between Criminology and the Science of Criminal Law, now Criminology has as object of investigation the "criminal system" as a whole -not understood as a mere collection of norms-, from the criminal legislator to the execution of the penalty, as well as the instances and official and unofficial mechanisms of social reaction. The Criminal Dogmatic belongs equally to that criminal system, and therefore also constitutes the object of study of Criminology.[24]

An illustrative example of the described trend is offered by "Critical Criminology", "New Criminology"[25] or "Radical Criminology",[26] that focus on the study of the criminal system in a critical sense, that tends to assume a critical speech as compared to official Criminal Policy.[27] At present the

---

21 J. Lilly, F. Cullen, R. Ball (1995) *Criminological Theory. Context and consequences* 37. London: Sage, explain that in United States emerged in the 20th century a competing and powerful vision of crime: "a vision suggesting that crime, like other behaviour, was a social product". See also, S. Jones (1998) *Criminology,* 5/6. London: Butterworths.

22 Baratta, Criminología y dogmática penal. Pasado y futuro del modelo integral de la ciencia penal, *o.c.* , 30.

23 See a exposition of this theories in Garcia-Pablos De Molina, *Manual de Criminología, o.c.*, 461 ss.

24 Baratta (1992) *o.c.*, 43; E. Bacigalupo Zapater (1982) Relaciones entre la dogmática penal y la criminología, 66 *Derecho penal y ciencias sociales* 53 ss.

25 See I. Taylor, P. Walton, J. Young (1973) *The new criminology. For a social theory of deviance*. London: Routledge & Keagan Paul.

26 About the use of these names see L. Munoz Gonzalez (1989) La criminología 'radical', la 'nueva' y la criminología 'crítica': matizaciones y precisiones en torno a sus nombres, 2 *Eguzkilore. Cuaderno del Instituto Vasco de Criminología*, Extraordinario, octubre, 267 ss. See also, about the transition from de Classical Criminology to the so-called Critical Criminology, Baratta (1981), *o.c.*, 28 ss.

27 As says P. Stangeland (1998) La criminología europea: entre la utopía y la burocracia.

scientific character of Critical Criminology, which rejects in a forceful way empirical methodology, is questioned because it does not appear to base its affirmations on documental analysis or on to statistics.[28]

The empirical method has been used since the end of the seventies by the so-called "institutional or administrative Criminology", with scientific analysis of the penitentiary systems, of minors protection, therapies for drug addicts, new police performance methods and, fundamentally, with the development of crime prevention projects.[29]

The divisions that took place at the beginning of the 1980's in critical Criminology provoked the emergence of a movement in England designated as "new realist" or "left realism"[30] that developed the so-called realist Criminology[31] (also developed in the United States, during the time of President Reagan, the so-called Right Realism, which *"is not in itself a discrete theory, but an overall conservative view of crime"*[32]). This direction enjoys at present great diffusion, since, according to its supporters, it is a trend that accepts the more positive of each one of the previous theories and trends. Thus, it has inherited the predilection for the empirical investigation methods of the positivist movement, and the interest in social control from critical Criminology, understanding criminality as an interaction between those who make and impose the norms and those who violate them, so that it is necessary to analyze both sides of the coin.[33]

Finally, with the division of the Critical Criminology, has also emerged a trend that agglutinates numerous critical criminologists who propose the abolition of the criminal system.[34] Others prefer to speak of the need of adopting a minimal Criminal Law, whose fundamental mission would be the defense of the Human Rights.[35] Most recently other trends can be emphasized

---

Esbozo para una criminología realista en España, 1 *Revista de Derecho Penal y Criminología* 207-219, 208, the most outstanding contribution of the Critical Criminology is the amplification of the topics of study.

28 *Ibid*, 210.

29 *Ibid.*, 211/2.

30 As says E. LARRAURI (1991) *La herencia de la criminología crítica*, 197. Madrid: Siglo XXI.

31 See R. MATTHEWS, J. YOUNG (1992) (eds.), *Issues in Realist Criminology*. London: Sage.

32 As says JONES, *o.c.*

33 STANGELAND, *o.c.*, 211/2.

34 L. HULSMAN, J. BERNAT DE CELIS (1982) *Sistema penal y seguridad ciudadana: Hacia una alternativa*, translation S. Politoff. Barcelona; J. BERNAT DE CELIS (1984) La abolición del sistema penal contra la reforma, in: A. BERISTAIN (ed.), *Reformas penales en el mundo de Hoy*. Madrid.

35 The best representative of this movement is A. BARATTA (1985) Principi del diritto penale minimo. Per una teoria dei diriti umani como oggeti e limiti della legge penale, 3/3 *Dei*

such as Republican Criminology,[36] Feminist Criminology or Constitutive Criminology.[37]

3. Contributions of Criminology to the Science of Criminal Law. Questioning some of its postulates.

The exposed evolution of the method and the object of study of Criminal Law Science and Criminology has produced a fruitful collection of reciprocal contributions. The modest objective of this study is to try to point out the advances produced in the Science of Criminal Law as a consequence of its intensive relationship -denied on occasions- with Criminology. The large scientific innovations produced in the various criminal sciences have had some incidence, more or less direct, on legal perspectives.[38] Even some of the criminological theories exposed that cast doubt on various postulates of the Science of Criminal Law, have on occasion provoked substantial changes in the Criminal Law theories.

3.1. Questioning of the postulate of freedom as the basis of culpability

Thus, criminological theories have questioned the culpability principle typical of Criminal Law, understood as the normative approach based on the "power to act of other manner" of the subject in the concrete situation, which is based on the postulate of free discretion or will as human quality. However the free will is scientifically indemonstrable. Criminology developed by the Italian positive school, under the influence of the designated criminological positivism, denied the free human will, and was pronounced on the contrary in favour of a determinist conception of the person. The human behaviour would have in their opinion, a causally given character by the interaction of multiple factors of biological, psychological as well as social order.[39] In comparison to this, it has been maintained by the jurists that the free discretion or will, that is, the indeterminate character of the human behaviour is the basis of culpability, in spite of its scientific indemonstrability.

Delitti e delle Pene.

36 The best representative is J. BRAITHWAITE (1998) Reducing the Crime Problem: A not So Dismal Criminology, in: P. WALTON & J. YOUNG (eds.), *The New Criminology Revisited,* 47 ss. Great Britain.

37 Cfr. J. LEA (1998) Criminology and Postmodernity, in: WALTON & YOUNG, *o.c.*, 163 ss.

38 E. BACIGALUPO ZAPATER (1982) Relaciones entre la dogmática penal y la criminología, *Derecho penal y ciencias sociales* 53 ss., 54.

39 See LARRAURI, *La herencia de la criminología crítica*, *o.c.*, 91.

Most recently the modern subcultural theories have studied thoroughly the decisive influence that social factors have on some occasions in the criminal behaviour. They understand that criminal behaviour is learnt and that the differential contact between delinquent groups and persons not delinquent is a generating criminality factor. Theories such as "differential association", proposed by E.H. Sutherland,[40] have made clear that a unique value system does not exist, other value systems exist in addition to the official system as subcultures, and that the individual is not free to choose to participate or not in a given subculture. Thus, the learning of the values of a system different than the dominant, or of deviance models, remains out of the power of decision of the individual.[41]

Also during the sixties, the Marxist direction of Criminology and the so-called "new Criminology" tried to emphasize the responsibility of the capitalistic system on the production of the offence, until the point of perilously approaching pure determinism.[42] This direction was shaded during the seventies, indicating that the person was free, though the economic causes can play a causing role in some offences, but not the most important.[43] This has had a direct influence in the area of Criminal Law, that has evolved to an understanding of culpability in a more individual and concrete way, that takes into account the real biopsychological features and, of course, the social conditionings of the subject in the moment of valuing his acts and the possibility to adjust his behaviour to the norm.[44]

3.2. Questioning of the equality principle of Criminal Law

In Criminal Law a fundamental principle is the principle of equality. Criminal Law is equal for all and is applied in an equal way to all persons. This principle, however, has been seriously doubted by the "labeling approach" theory. According this theory, the deviation and the offence do not have an ontological nature - they do not exist at the margin of official mechanisms of

---

40 See E. SUTHERLAND and D. CRESSEY (1955) (5e ed.), *Principles of Criminology.*

41 BARATTA (1992) *o.c.*, 30.

42 LARRAURI, *La herencia de la criminología crítica, o.c.*, 175.

43 *Ibídem.*

44 J.L. DE LA CUESTA ARZAMENDI (1994) El legado genético y el principio de culpabilidad. Algunas conclusiones provisionales, *Volumen II El Derecho ante el Proyecto Genoma Humano,* 63 ss, 67, Madrid, says that this affirmation derives from the equality principle that has to respect every democratic State, which tries to avoid to treat equally what is unequal; the best representative in Spain of this trend is A. TORIO LOPEZ (1988) Indicaciones metódicas sobre el concepto material de culpabilidad, *Cuadernos de Política Criminal* 759 ss.

definition and selection. These social instances of control (policeman, attorney-general's office, judicature) are those which define that a given act is criminal. Consequently, the offence is not a "fact" but a "social construction", that requires an act and a social reaction. Criminality is a social status that characterizes an individual when the criminal label is awarded to him with success by the official instances that have the power of definition of the offences. This theory originates from the fact that the criminal quality of a behaviour is not material or ontological, but the product of an attribution process or stigmatization by the instances of social control (policeman, attorney-general's office, judicature). It is the typical society which generates the criminality that it then represses, because criminality is the result of the confluence of various factors that end in the labeling of an individual as delinquent.

The labeling approach has emphasized that the possibilities of being labeled are disparately distributed in society. Criminality is not an exceptional phenomenon but a regular phenomenon that appears in all the social areas. Consequently, what is decisive is the selection that the authorities carry out. The authorities, then, distribute the stigmas and create the criminality, and they make it, generally, reproducing the social inequality schemas. They do not detect the criminality, but create or configure it, especially in attention to social status. The equality principle is therefore questioned in the measure to which the minority, which is considered delinquent, is the consequence of a highly selective and unequal process within the population.[45]

3.3. The crisis of the postulate of resocialization as the goal of prison penalties

The theories of criminality group a set of criminological theories characterized by the understanding that the offence is a phenomenon conditioned first of all, by social nature factors. As we will see, some of their contributions have had an important influence in the Science of Criminal Law.

The sociological positivism that impregnates the criminal conceptions of von Liszt around the end of the 19th century emphasizes special prevention as the purpose of Criminal Law and, of the prison as the main penalty of the criminal system. The ideas elaborated by the theories of criminality, that propose the creation of a progressive system directed to achieve the social readaptation of the condemned, his resocialization - as one of the aspects of special prevention[46]-, have prevailed in the execution of prison penalties.

---

45 BARATTA (1981) *o.c.*, 35.

46 See G. ROMERO BARRANQUERO (1987) Teorías de la Criminalización, Derecho Penal y

However, multiple criminological investigations questioning the principle of resocialization, have recently been carried out.[47] From the empirical point of view it has been revealed that the prison does not actually fulfill the resocialization goal.[48]

According to the theoretical point of view, there are three fundamental critiques formulated against the postulate of resocialization as the end result of prison. In the first place, it is said that resocialization can not be reached through penitentiary treatment. The impossibility of an "education for freedom in conditions of absence of freedom" is emphasized, as well as the desocialization effects of prison. The prison provokes negative effects on the inmates[49] that can carry even to the depersonalization of the individual, something that clashes with the idea of resocializatión.[50] In second place, it has rejected the excesses that have led to the "absolutizing" of the goal of resocialization, that have lead to the end of the general prevention of the penalty or of reference to the committed fact in some States, and is centered exclusively on the criminal prognosis to decide on the nature, duration and conditions of the penalty.[51] This has supposed damage to the fundamental rights of the individual, whose maximum expression has been the setting-up in the United States of "indeterminate judgment", in which a very wide penal framework is fixed, and the decision to set the prisoner free is left up to administrative organisms, integrated by technical personal. The intention of

---

Política Criminal, *Anuario de Derecho Penal y Ciencias Penales* 135 ss, 137/8.

47 In this sense, T. PETERS (1993) El futuro de las prisiones: los valores esenciales, 6 *Eguzkilore. Cuaderno del Instituto Vasco de Criminología*, extraordinario 101-109, 102 ss.

48 Widely, about the problems that the resocialization poses, see A. ESER (1974) Resozialisierung in der Krise? Gedanken zum Sozialisationsziel des Strafvollzuges, *Festschrift für K. Peters*, 505 ss. Tübingen; S. MIR PUIG (1994) ¿Qué queda en pie de la resocialización?, *El Derecho Penal en el Estado social y democrático de Derecho*, 141 ss; F. MUÑOZ CONDE (1979) La resocialización del delincuente, análisis y crítica de un mito, *Cuadernos de Política Criminal* 91 ss; A. GARCIA-PABLOS DE MOLINA (1979) La supuesta función resocializadora del Derecho Penal: utopía, mito y eufemismo, *Anuario de Derecho Penal y Ciencias Penales* 645 ss; B. MAPELLI CAFFARENA (1984) Desviación social y resocialización, *Cuadernos de Política Criminal* 311 ss; SILVA SANCHEZ (1992) *o.c.*, 29 ss.

49 The negative effects of total institutions were emphasized in the classical work of E. GOFFMAN (1961) (edition of 1991) *Asylums. Essays on the social situation of mental patients and other inmates*. Penguin Books.

50 And even a "negative socialization", as says J.L. DE LA CUESTA ARZAMENDI (1993) La resocialización: objetivo de la intervención penitenciaria, *Papers d'estudis i formació. Nuevas formas de delincuencia. Núcleo familiar y dinámicas de separación*, diciembre de 1993, nº 12, 9 ss., 14.

51 See SILVA SANCHEZ (1992) *o.c.*, 29; DE LA CUESTA ARZAMENDI (1993) *o.c.*, 15.

this is to lengthen the necessary prison time to obtain the resocialization of the subject. However, the experience has demonstrated the existence of an excessive authoritarianism and the incompatibility of this system with the humanity principle and the guarantees of State Law, by reason of the uncontrolled arbitrariness of the administrative institutions, the "scarce reliability" of the criteria followed by these to accept a favorable prediction and even the infringement on the principle of proportionality.[52] In third place, the modern criminological theories have indicated that resocialization is not the appropriate means for crime prevention. Concretely, as we have already said, the labeling approach has made clear that the condition of "criminal" is not a quality of behaviour, but a consequence of the application of norms and sanctions that others apply to the offender. The deviant is the person to whom the label has been applied with success; the deviant behaviour is what the instances of control define as diverted. Criminality is not typically characteristic of certain acts or individuals. Because of this, the individualized penitentiary treatment of the offenders directed to resocialization can hardly be the suitable way to crime prevention.[53] It is not legitimate to try to resocialize the inmates without acting on the root of the problem, trying first to resocialize society.[54]

3.4. The development of alternatives to prison

The critiques of prison and its resocialization goal by Criminology, starting in the sixties and seventies, resulted in proposals of alternatives to prison.[55] These new alternatives were intended to offer other possibilities to contact with the jail and to avoid its desocializing effects, derived by offenders in the criminal system,[56] and to limit the use of the prison, since that constitutes the main form of obtaining the resocialization goal.[57] Institutions such as

---

52 Cfr. T. WEIGEND (1978) Entwicklungen und Tendenzen der Kriminalpolitik in den USA, *Zeitschrift für die gesamte Strafrechtswissenschaft* 1083 ss. (1115 ss.): en la doctrina española SILVA SANCHEZ (1993) *o.c.*, 30; DE LA CUESTA ARZAMENDI (1993) *o.c.*, 15. To all this is added the practice of coactive interventions that attempt directly against the individual rights, arriving even to practice experiments with the inmates without therapeutic purpose; see B. MAPELLI CAFFARENA (1983) *Principios fundamentales del sistema penitenciario español*, 256. Barcelona; DE LA CUESTA ARZAMENDI (1993) *o.c.*, 15.

53 DE LA CUESTA ARZAMENDI (1993) *o.c.*, 14.

54 DE LA CUESTA ARZAMENDI (1993) *o.c.*, 14.

55 LARRAURI, *La herencia de la criminología crítica*, *o.c.*, 210.

56 LARRAURI, *La herencia de la criminología crítica*, *o.c.*, 210.

57 See J. CID MOLINE, E. LARRAURI PIJOAN (1997) (coord.), *Penas alternativas a la prisión*, 11. Barcelona.

probation, community service order, the days-fine, electronic monitoring, etc., have been used in legislations of European countries.[58] The book that Schur published in 1973, entitled *Radical non intervention*, advocating non-intervention or intervention less stigmatized, has been an important step in the discovery of alternatives to prison.[59]

However, in spite of the presumable beneficial effects of the alternatives, that were avoiding the negative aspects of prison, the 1980's strengthened in Critical Criminology a hard criticism against this approach. The works in 1984 of Scull[60] and of Foucault,[61] and of Cohen in 1985[62] were the beginning of an era of critiques on alternatives to prison.[63] In the first place, it was questioned whether the alternatives served to channel the individuals out of the criminal system. In spite of the existing alternatives, the inmate population was not declining. Furthermore it was criticized that the alternatives were applied to persons that normally would not be condemned to the prison penalty.[64] In second place, as said Foucault and Cohen, the alternatives were supposing a greater social control, an amplification of the power of punishing, an amplification of the criminal net, that is, they were implying a more intrusive control.[65] But a cautious reaffirmation of the alternatives to prison takes place in the decade of the nineties. The new English realists propose to evaluate each concrete case, evaluating which of the alternative works, with whom and in what conditions.[66]

In any case, as it has been said, nowadays theoretical and practical investigations are accomplished in which the victim is included in the search

---

58 See CID MOLINE & LARRAURI PIJOAN, *o.c.*, 14/5, for the most frequent alternatives in comparative law. A large study can also be seen in A. SOLA DUENAS, M. GARCIA ARAN, H. HORMAZABAL MALAREE (1986) *Alternativas a la prisión. Penas sustitutivas y sometimiento a prueba*. Barcelona.

59 See E. SCHUR (1973) *Radical non intervention: rethinking the delinquency problem*. Nueva Jersey.

60 A. SCULL (1984) *Decarceration*. Nueva York.

61 M. FOUCAULT (1986) *Vigilar y castigar. Nacimiento de la prisión*, 5ª edición de España.

62 S. COHEN (1988) *Visiones de control social. Delitos, Castigos y Clasificaciones*, translation Elena Larrauri, Barcelona.

63 See LARRAURI, *La herencia de la criminología crítica*, *o.c.*, 210 ss.

64 About these critiques see LARRAURI, *La herencia de la criminología crítica*, *o.c.*, 210 ss; CID MOLINE & LARRAURI PIJOAN, *o.c.*, 18/9.

65 See LARRAURI, *La herencia de la criminología crítica*, *o.c.*, 210 ss; CID MOLINE & LARRAURI PIJOAN, *o.c.*, 19.

66 See LARRAURI, *La herencia de la criminología crítica*, *o.c.*, 212. CID MOLINE & LARRAURI PIJOAN, *o.c.*, 21 ss., accept a proporcionalist model for the alternatives, which has as fundamental objective to reduce the use of the prison, while the individualistic model considers that the alternatives have rather a rehabilitative objective.

for imaginative alternatives, as the victim-offender mediation.[67]

3.5. The rediscovery of the victim: the development of Victimology

The rediscovery of the victim has supposed the emergence in the framework of Criminology of a new discipline, designated Victimology,[68] which aims to systematize the empirical knowledge related to the victim of the offence. Victimology, as integrated in Criminology,[69] uses the same empirical and interdisciplinary method. Victimology is defined[70] as the part of Criminology that tries to emphasize the perspective of the victim of crime.[71] Among its

---

67 See G. VARONA MARTINEZ (1998) *La mediación reparadora como estrategia de control social. Una perspectiva criminológica.* Granada: Comares.

68 See T. PETERS (1988) Consideraciones teóricas sobre la victimología, 2 *Eguzkilore. Cuaderno del Instituto Vasco de Criminología* 107-133, 109 ss; also, about the birth and evolution of the victimology A. BERISTAIN IPINA (1994) *Nueva Criminología desde el Derecho Penal y la Victimología*, 196. Valencia; GARCIA-PABLOS DE MOLINA, *Criminología, o.c.*, 40 ss; L. RODRIGUEZ MANZANERA (1988) *Victimología. Estudio de la víctima*, 9 ss. México; G. LANDROVE DIAZ (1990) *Victimología*, 19 ss. Valencia; J. BUSTOS RAMIREZ, E. LARRAURI PIJOAN (1993) *Victimología: presente y futuro (hacia un sistema penal de alternativas)*, 9 ss. Barcelona; E. NEUMAN (1994) *Victimología. El rol de la víctima en los delitos convencionales y no convencionales*, segunda edición, 23 ss. Buenos Aires; M. HERRERA MORENO (1996) *La hora de la víctima. Compendio de victimología*, 63 ss. Madrid; J.M. TAMARIT SUMALLA (1994) *La reparación a la víctima en el Derecho penal. Estudio y crítica de las nuevas tendencias político-criminales*, 116 ss. Barcelona.

69 PETERS, *o.c.*, 110 y 130, says that the victim has been converted progressively into one of the fundamental development poles of the Criminology, while the trend towards an independent science of victimology is minoritarian today.

70 See JUNG, Viktimologie, in: G. KAISER, H.J. KERNER, F. SACK, H. SCHELLHOSS (1993) (3ª ed), *Kleines kriminologisches Wörterbuch*, 582 ss, 582. Heidelberg.

71 Cfr. JUNG, Viktimologie, *o.c.*, 582 ss; J. SCHNEIDER (1975) *Viktimologie. Wissenschaft vom Verbrechensopfer.* Tübingen; in Spain, A. GARCIA-PABLOS (1989) Hacia una "redefinición" del "rol" de la víctima en la criminología y en el sistema legal, *Estudios penales en memoria del Prof. A. FERNANDEZ ALBOR* 307 ss., Santiago de Compostela; A. BERISTAIN IPINA (1990) (ed.), *Victimología*, VIII Cursos de verano de San Sebastian; A. BERISTAIN IPINA (1994) *Nueva Criminología desde el Derecho Penal y la Victimología*, Valencia; A. BERISTAIN IPINA (1981) Desde la victimología hacia la reforma del Código Penal, *Cuadernos de Política Criminal* 5 ss.; A. BERISTAIN IPINA, El Código penal de 1995 desde la victimología (I y II), *La Ley* de 4 y 5.6.97; A. BERISTAIN IPINA (1997) Jóvenes, víctimas, cárceles y valores humanos en los medios de comunicación, 32 *Actualidad Penal*; A. BERISTAIN IPINA (1998) *De los delitos y de las penas en el País Vasco*, Madrid; M. POLAINO NAVARRETE (1989) Victimología y criminalidad violenta en España, *Estudios penales en memoria del Prof. A. FERNANDEZ ALBOR,* 571 ss.; Santiago de Compostela; G. LANDROVE DIAZ (1990) *Victimología.* Valencia; M.A. SORIA VERDE (1993) Desarrollo histórico de la victimología, in: M.A. SORIA VERDE (comp.), *La víctima: entre la justicia y la delincuencia" (Aspectos psicológicos, sociales o jurídicos de la victimización,* 13.

main areas of study can be mentioned the victimization processes -interesting especially in connection with violent and sexual crimes-, interviews with the victims, treatment programs of the victim and the position of the victim in criminal justice.[72]

The perspective of the victim starts to be underlined in the decades prior to World War II. In this sense, Beristain indicates that it *"can be said that the current Victimology was born as reaction to the macro victimization of World War II"*[73]. Its official birth can be ciphered in 1979 with the celebration of the Third International Symposium of Victimology, in Münster (Germany), that provides impulse to multiple publications and congresses.[74] Between the pioneer projects in this field can be cited one in 1948 of H.v. Hentig, entitled *The Criminal and his Victim*. From this moment starts the development, at domestic and international level, of an aid legislation to the victims, in the sixties and seventies, that is intensified from the decade of the eighties on.[75]

The Science of Criminal Law in recent years, by influx of this new criminological trend attentive to the victims of offences, has developed an approach that pays attention to the behaviour of the victim.[76] It is the designated "Victimodogmatic", and takes into account, in dogmatic elaboration, the empirical investigations of Victimology, those which emphasize that the behaviour of the victim can be a co-cause of the causation of the offence.[77] It is emphasized that some victims contribute with their behaviour to the damage of the protected social value, in this way, being co-responsible for it.[78] The Victimodogmatic has to determine if the intentional or

---

Barcelona; P.A. LANZAROTE MARTIN (1994) La víctima del delito y el sistema jurídico penal: ¿hacia un sistema de alternativas?", *Poder Judicial* 34; J.L. DIEZ RIPOLLES, F.J. GIRON GONZALEZ-TORRE, P. STANGELAND, A.I. CEREZO DOMINGUEZ (1996) *Delincuencia y víctimas*. Valencia.

72 See JUNG, Viktimologie, *o.c.*, 584.

73 See A. BERISTAIN (1994) *o.c.*, 235 ss. Valencia; GARCIA-PABLOS DE MOLINA, *Criminología. Una introducción a sus fundamentos teóricos para juristas, o.c.*, 40 ss.; M.A. SORIA VERDE, Desarrollo histórico de la victimología, *o.c.*, 13 ss.; G. KAISER (1993) Viktimologie heute, in: *Festschrift für Schüler-Springorum*, 3 ss. Köln.

74 Cfr. BERISTAIN 1994) o.c., 236.

75 Ibid., 237.

76 See J. DE VICENTE REMESAL (1997) La consideración de la víctima a través de la reparación del daño en el Derecho penal español: posibilidades actuales y perspectivas de futuro; JESÚS-MARÍA SILVA SÁNCHEZ (ed.), *Política criminal y nuevo Derecho penal. Libro Homenaje a Claus Roxin*, 137 ss., 174. Barcelona.

77 SILVA SANCHEZ, *Aproximación al Derecho Penal contemporáneo, o.c.*, 99.

78 J.M. SILVA SANCHEZ (1993) La consideración del comportamiento de la víctima en la teoría jurídica del delito. Observaciones doctrinales y jurisprudenciales sobre la 'victimodogmática', *La victimología, Cuadernos de Derecho Judicial,* 13 ss, 16. Madrid: Consejo

negligent behaviour of the victim of the offence influences or not the criminal responsibility of the offender, and if so, in what measure. This has given place, for example, to the formulation of the discussed and criticized "victimological principle", which states that the conduct of the offender stops being criminally relevant due to its atypical character, when the victim has not behaved in a self-responsible way and permits the production of damage to the protected social value, when this could be have been avoided since it was in his/her own area of responsibility.[79] Victimological arguments are used to solve problems of the General Part of Criminal Law. Thus, for example, for the determination of the efficiency area of the cause of justification of the consent; or for the exclusion or limitation of the right to self-defense when there is a previous provocation of the victim.[80]

But Victimology also has emphasized that in many cases the victim of the offence does not obtain compensation for the damage suffered, in spite of the condemnation of the offender, fundamentally by his/her insolvency.[81] Trying to find ways to give response to the needs of the victim, trends emerge that propose, as a third route, to give content to reparation to the victim,[82] near the

---

General del Poder Judicial

79 See B. SCHÜNEMANN (1986) Zur Stellung des Opfers im System der Strafrechtspflege. I, *Neue Zeitschrift für Strafrecht (NStZ)* 193 ss, and II, *Neue Zeitschrift für Strafrecht* 439 ss; SILVA SÁNCHEZ (1993) *o.c.*, 25 ss; M. CANCIO MELIA (1998) *Conducta de la víctima e imputación objetiva en Derecho penal. Estudio sobre los ámbitos de responsabilidad de víctima y autor en actividades arriesgadas*, 235 ss. Barcelona. This principle is built in a deductive way based on the principles that limit the *ius puniendi* of the State, concretely in those of de subsidiarity and fragmentariety.

80 See C. ROXIN (1997) *Strafrecht. Allgemeiner Teil. Band I. Grundlagen. Der Aufbau der Verbrechenslehre, 3. Auflage* § 14.III, nº 15. München says that the Victimodogmatic begins to project its influence in the Dogmatic and offers a wide information about other victimological developments (nº 16 ss.); J.M. SILVA SANCHEZ (1989) ¿Consideraciones victimológicas en la teoría jurídica del delito? Introducción al debate sobre la Victimodogmática, *Criminología y Derecho Penal al servicio de la persona, Libro-Homenaje al Profesor A. Beristain,* 633 ss. San Sebastián.

81 See A. GARCIA-PABLOS DE MOLINA, La resocialización de la víctima: víctima, sistema legal y política criminal, *Criminología y Derecho penal al servicio de la persona. Libro-Homenaje al Profesor Antonio Beristain,* 193 ss. (195), San Sebastián; G. LANDROVE DIAZ (1990) *Victimología,* 40. Valencia; SILVA SANCHEZ (1993) *o.c.*, 16.

82 Professor Tony Peters is a fervent defender of reparation as high-priority and fundamental value toward which must be guided the penal justice administration, see T. PETERS & A. NEYS (1994) La pena considerada desde una perspectiva de la reparación, 8 *Eguzkilore. Cuaderno del Instituto Vasco de Criminología* 165-195, 185 ss; also, T. PETERS & I. AERTSEN (1995) Mediación para la reparación: presentación y discusión de un proyecto de investigación-acción, 8 *Eguzkilore. Cuaderno del Instituto Vasco de Criminología* 129-146.

penalties and to the safety measures, assigning it the typical ends of Criminal Law. At the same time, it is emphasized the convenience of attending to extra judicial conciliation processes between the victim and the offender with the objective of solving the conflict generated in certain offences.[83]

6. *The contribution of Criminology to the discussion "criminalization versus decriminalization"*

We have already referred to the criminological trends that propose a minimal Criminal Law and even the abolition of Criminal Law.[84] However, in the present, these trends face the demands of movements that request a greater utilization of the Criminal Law basically in areas such as terrorism, organized crime, the environment, the economy, drugs, domestic violence, sexual violence, etc.[85] A wide decriminalization with the objective of reducing the intervention of the State in the private life of the citizens is requested from Critical Criminology, but at the same time the growing utilization of Criminal Law to sanction the offences of the powerful[86] is recovered. In reality, Criminal Law is not criticized, but the way in which its applied can be unequal and against the oppressed classes.

In fact, particularly since the 1980's, the use of the *ius puniendi* is the object of a strong discussion in which groups with different criminal-political directions are apposed. Various progressive social groups demand the resource to Criminal Law to protect the values that they claim.[87] Ecologist movements request the criminal sanction of the conduct against the environment, anti-racism movements the criminalization of racial discrimination, unions the criminalization of the conducts against labour laws, feminist movements the escalation of criminal repression of offences against the women, etc. In reality, it is intended to impose a form of society that reflects the values of these groups. The creation of a purely symbolic

83 Cfr. J.M. SILVA SÁNCHEZ (1990) La víctima en el futuro de la dogmática, in: A. BERISTAIN & J.L. DE LA CUESTA (eds.), *Victimologia*, 229 ss, 231/2. San Sebastián; VARONA MARTINEZ, *o.c.*

84 The Critical Criminology did not pay attention excessively to the study of the function of the Criminal Law, although it verified that it was a "class instrument" that was used to protect the interests of the powerful (LARRAURI, *La herencia de la criminología crítica, o.c.,* 216).

85 G. KAISER (1992) La función de la criminología con respecto a la política legislativa penal, 6 *Eguzkilore. Cuaderno del Instituto Vasco de Criminología* 181 ss, 183.

86 LARRAURI, *La herencia de la criminología crítica, o.c.*, 216/7.

87 LARRAURI, *La herencia de la criminología crítica, o.c.*, 216/7; LARRAURI, Las paradojas de importar alternativas a la cárcel, *o.c.*, 56.

legislation[88]is therefore proposed.

The penal doctrine has emphasized this trend in the criminal legislation elaborated in the last years.[89] The legislator uses Criminal Law to satisfy social demands that require a rapid solution to certain problems, trying at all times, to obtain from this a political profitability.[90] This is appreciated clearly in criminality areas such as domestic violence,[91] terrorism,[92] drugs consumption, environment[93] or sexual violence,[94] that have a very large impact in the society, and therefore require of the public powers a rapid reaction. The public powers answer with the most profitable instrument from the political point of view, Criminal Law; the increase in criminal repression is erected as the solution to the problems.[95] The root of the social problems is not at all analyzed in depth through programs of social character. The existence of serious social situations is clear, but this does not mean that it will be necessary to resort to Criminal Law as means for its solution, furthermore, the scarce efficiency that criminal response has to curtail them [96] is patent.

Conclusion: Criminal Policy as liaison between Criminology and the Science of Criminal Law

As we have been saying, Criminology, as an empirical science that provides data on the criminal phenomenon and the various instances of social control, has questioned some postulates of Criminal Law. However, the Science of Criminal Law does not accept directly the empirical results derived from criminological investigation. This acceptance is produced necessarily through

---

88 See DIEZ RIPOLLES (1998) Exigencias sociales y política criminal, 85 *Claves de razón práctica* 48 ss. Exigencias sociales y política criminal, 50.

89 See W. HASSEMER, Winfried (1991) Derecho penal simbólico y protección de bienes jurídicos, translation Elena Larrauri, en 51 *Nuevo Foro Penal* 17 ss. (also in *Pena y Estado. Función simbólica de la pena*, 1, 1991, 23 ss.); DIEZ RIPOLLES (1998) *o.c.*, 85 ss.

90 DIEZ RIPOLLES (1998) *o.c.*, 50.

91 See S. EDWARDS (1991) La función simbólica del Derecho Penal: violencia doméstica, 1 *Pena y Estado*, 83 ss.

92 See I. BERDUGO GOMEZ DE LA TORRE, Sobre la función simbólica de la legislación penal antiterrorista española, 1 *Pena y Estado* 91 ss.

93 See J. BUSTOS RAMÍREZ (1991) Necesidad de la pena, función simbólica y bien jurídico medio ambiente, 1 *Pena y Estado* 101 ss; W. PAUL, Megacriminalidad ecológica y Derecho ambiental simbólico, 1 *Pena y Estado* 111 ss.

94 DIEZ RIPOLLES (1998) *o.c.*, 50/1.

95 *Ibid.*, 51.

96 G. KAISER (1992) La función de la criminología con respecto a la política legislativa penal, 6 *Eguzkilore. Cuaderno del Instituto Vasco de Criminología* 181 ss, 185.

the contributions of other criminal sciences i.c. Criminal Policy, that therefore is a link between both.[97]

Around the sixties and the beginning of the seventies,[98] the critique to the Criminal Dogmatic due to its *"systematical excesses and to its purely formal comprehension"*[99] was strengthened. The great differences between the theory that elaborates the Dogmatic and the reality to which it is intended to apply is critically emphasized, basically by its pretension of "coherence", in spite of going against the "rationality of the solution".[100] The dogmatic postulates are not always suitable to solve the problems of application of the law that emerge in practice. The abstract and deductive method of the Dogmatic does not have in mind the concrete problem to which Criminal Law is applied and it does not know the reality this impacts.[101] A great "approximation to the reality" on the side of the Science of Criminal Law [102] is necessary. In order to achieve this, it is required that Criminal Dogmatic reacts against its traditional reticence to take into account the advances produced in other sciences,[103] and devote greater attention to the not-legal sciences and, concretely, to Criminology (together with the History, the Psychology, the Sociology, etc.).[104]

This crisis of Criminal Dogmatic coincides with what is the known as the "reappearance of Criminal Policy" that is observed after World War II. Its more meaningful development took place in the 1960's in Germany with the works of Roxin and Hassemer.[105] As Roxin stressed, it is necessary to guide Criminal Dogmatic with the Criminal Policy positions.[106] The most problematic issue resides in determining which are the principles of the Criminal Policy and how Criminal Dogmatic is guided to them.[107] Criminal

97 De La Cuesta Arzamendi (1989) *o.c.*, 78; Silva Sanchez (1992) *o.c.*, 98, refers to the "bridge" of Criminal Policy through it must pass the collaboration between Dogmatic and Criminology.

98 As says Silva Sánchez (1989) *o.c.*, 46.

99 De La Cuesta Arzamendi (1992) *o.c.*, 75.

100 See W. Hassemer (1984) *Fundamentos del Derecho penal*, translation Francisco Muñoz Conde y Luis Arroyo Zapatero, 26. Barcelona; De La Cuesta Arzamendi (1989) *o.c.,* 75.

101 As says Silva Sánchez (1992) *o.c.*, 47.

102 De La Cuesta Arzamendi (1989) *o.c.*, 75.

103 As says Silva Sánchez (1992) *o.c.*, 47.

104 De La Cuesta Arzamendi (1989) *o.c*, 76.

105 *Ibid.*, 76/7.

106 See C. Roxin (1972) *Política Criminal y Sistema de Derecho Penal*, translation F. Muñoz Conde, Barcelona.

107 J.M. Silva Sánchez (1997) Política criminal en la dogmática: algunas cuestiones sobre su contenido y límites, in: J.M. Sánchez (ed.), *Política Criminal y Nuevo Derecho Penal (Libro Homenaje a Claus Roxin),* 17 ss. (19). Barcelona.

Policy fulfils a "political function" in the sense that it guides criminal legislation, either in its creation or in its application,[108] to the fulfillment of certain ends.[109] It provides the necessary reference to the goals and values that have to inspire Criminal Law. But these goals and values that emphasize Criminal Policy can not be deduced exclusively from the abstract principles dictated by reason, but in this valorous context should be integrated the empirical data that Criminology provides.

The Criminal Policy is a "valorous science" that has its own autonomy.[110] This takes into account that the data that Criminology offers of reality is "valued"[111] by Criminal Policy based on political legal principles (for example, those of humanity, proportionality, equality, freedom, etc.).[112]

Recapitulating, the contributions of criminological science to the Science of Criminal Law have to pass through the sieve of Criminal Policy first. This, as we have been saying, values the empirical data that Criminology (also other social sciences)[113] provides, so that the resulting value judgments will serve, on the one hand, as inspired from the subsequent legislative reforms (*de lege ferenda*)[114] and, additionally, for the setup of a legal theory of the offence not merely conceptual and formal, but "opened" to the reality to which it is applied.[115] In this way it will be possible to surpass an exclusively formal criminal science and to formulate a critical Dogmatic,[116] typical of a democratic State that is the headline of the *ius puniendi*, of the power to punish, but that is subjected to limiting principles. It is the duty of the Dogmatic to protest if the Criminal Law in force adapts or not to these principles.[117]

---

108 In this sense, J.M. SILVA SANCHEZ, Reflexiones sobre las bases de la política criminal, in: J. CEREZO MIR/ R.F. SUÁREZ MONTES, A. BERISTAIN IPIÑA/ C.M. ROMEO CASABONA (editores), *El nuevo Código Penal: presupuestos y fundamentos. Libro Homenaje al Prof. Dr. D. A. Torío López*, 209 ss, 212/3, makes a distintion between the *praxis* of Criminal Policy and theoretical Criminal Policy. The first one is composed of empirical activities, directed to the protection of the individual and of the society avoiding crime. The second one is composed of theoretical principles which have to give to this *praxis* a rational basis.

109 As says SILVA SÁNCHEZ (1992) *o.c.*, 48.

110 As says SILVA SÁNCHEZ (1992) *o.c.*, 9.

111 MIR PUIG (1982) *o.c.*, 306.

112 As says J.M. SILVA SANCHEZ (1992) *o.c.*, 98.

113 See J.L. DIEZ RIPOLLES (1990) *Los elementos subjetivos del delito. Bases metodológicas*, 313/4. Valencia.

114 *Ibid.*, 315, nota 26.

115 See MIR PUIG, *Introducción a las bases del Derecho Penal*, *o.c.*, 306; SILVA SÁNCHEZ (1992) *o.c.*, 99.

116 See DE LA CUESTA ARZAMENDI , *o.c.*, 76.

117 BACIGALUPO ZAPATER, Relaciones entre la dogmática penal y la criminología, *o.c.*, 70.

All things considered, it is really difficult to translate the empirical knowledge to the legislative plan. It is clear that the results that are obtained from the criminological investigations are not always unidirectional, but on occasion we find ourselves before conclusions that, if not totally different, are touched by differences. As a consequence of this, the collaboration between the Science of Criminal Law and Criminology encounter large difficulties nowadays. The legislator chooses, on some occasions, the scientific results or parts of them, that he considers more in concordance with the decision that previously he/she has taken. The empirical results would be, as is asserted by some authors, *"an argument between arguments"*.[118] But this does not mean that the legislator has to dispense the empirical knowledge in the elaboration of criminal legislation. It is necessary that the legislators accept the criminological results and integrate them in his/her decision process.[119]

The need for being based on empirical knowledge is evidenced, not only in the great importance it has for Criminal Policy discussion prior to the development of criminal legislation, but also in the moment of its application, to control the success of a given criminal measure by verifying if the objectives, both Criminal and Political, set by the legislator have been fulfilled or not.[120]

References

Bacigalupo Zapater, Enrique (1982) Relaciones entre la dogmática penal y la criminología, *Derecho penal y ciencias sociales* 53 ss.

Baratta, Alesandro (1981) Criminología y dogmática penal. Pasado y futuro del modelo integral de la ciencia penal, in: S. Mir Puig (ed.), *La reforma del Derecho penal II. Jornadas hispano - alemanas sobre la Reforma del Derecho Penal*, 25 ss. Bellaterra.

Baratta, Alesandro (1985) Principi del diritto penale minimo. Per una teoria dei diriti umani como oggeti e limiti della legge penale, *Dei Delitti e delle Pene*, vol. III, nº 3.

Baratta, Alesandro (1992) Criminología y dogmática penal. Pasado y futuro del modelo integral de la ciencia penal, *Política criminal y reforma del*

---

118 KAISER, La función de la criminología con respecto a la política legislativa penal, *o.c.*, 183.

119 See H. SCHULER SPRINGORUM (1989) Sobre la relación entre criminología y política criminal, *Cuestiones básicas y estrategias de la política criminal*, 1 ss., 17. Buenos Aires (translation of the german version "Zum Verhältnis von Kriminologie und Kriminalpolitik", *Gedächtnisschrift für Peter NOLL*, Zurich, 1984, 141 ss.).

120 KAISER (1992) *o.c.*, 189/190.

Derecho Penal 28 ss.

Berdugo Gomez De La Torre, Ignacio, Sobre la función simbólica de la legislación penal antiterrorista española, 1 *Pena y Estado* 91 ss.

Beristain Ipiña, Antonio (1981) Desde la victimología hacia la reforma del Código Penal, *Cuadernos de Política Criminal* 5 ss.

Beristain Ipiña, Antonio (1986) *Ciencia penal y Criminología*. Madrid.

Beristain Ipiña, Antonio (ed.) (1990) *Victimología*, VIII Cursos de verano de San Sebastian.

Beristain Ipiña, Antonio (1994) *Nueva Criminología desde el Derecho Penal y la Victimología*. Valencia.

Beristain Ipiña, Antonio, El Código penal de 1995 desde la victimología (I y II), *La Ley* de 4 y 5.6.97.

Beristain Ipiña, Antonio (1997) Jóvenes, víctimas, cárceles y valores humanos en los medios de comunicación", 32 *Actualidad Penal*.

Beristain Ipiña, Antonio (1998) *De los delitos y de las penas en el País Vasco*. Madrid.

Bernat De Celis, Jacqueline (1984) La abolición del sistema penal contra la reforma, in: A. Beristain (ed.), *Reformas penales en el mundo de Hoy*. Madrid.

Binding, Karl (1965) *Die Normen und ihre übertretungen. Band I. Normen und Strafgesetze*. Neudruck der 4. Auflage (Leipzig, 1922), Aalen.

Braithwaite, John (1998) Reducing the Crime Problem: A not So Dismal Criminology, in: P. Walton and J. Young (eds.), *The New Criminology Revisted*, 47 ss. Great Britain.

Bustos Ramirez, Juan/Larrauri Pijoan, Elena (1993) *Victimología: presente y futuro (hacia un sistema penal de alternativas)*. Barcelona.

Bustos Ramirez, Juan (1991) Necesidad de la pena, función simbólica y bien jurídico medio ambiente, 1 *Pena y Estado* 101 ss.

Cancio Melia, Manuel (1998) *Conducta de la víctima e imputación objetiva en Derecho penal. Estudio sobre los ámbitos de responsabilidad de víctima y autor en actividades arriesgadas*. Barcelona.

Cid Moline, J./Larrauri Pijoan, E. (1997) (coord.), *Penas alternativas a la prisión*. Barcelona.

Cohen, Stanley (1988) *Visiones de control social. Delitos, Castigos y Clasificaciones*, traducido al castellano por Elena Larrauri. Barcelona.

De La Cuesta Arzamendi, J.L. (1989) Presupuestos fundamentales del Derecho penal, 3 *Eguzkilore. Cuaderno del Instituto Vasco de Criminología* 55 ss.

De La Cuesta Arzamendi, José Luis (1994) El legado genético y el principio de culpabilidad. Algunas conclusiones provisionales, *El Derecho ante el*

Proyecto Genoma Humano, Volumen II, 63 ss. Madrid.
De La Cuesta Arzamendi, José Luis (1993) La resocialización: objetivo de la intervención penitenciaria, *Papers d'estudis i formació. Nuevas formas de delincuencia. Núcleo familiar y dinámicas de separación*, diciembre de 1993, nº 12, pgs. 9 ss. (14).
De Vicente Remesal, Javier (1997) La consideración de la víctima a través de la reparación del daño en el Derecho penal español: posibilidades actuales y perspectivas de futuro, in: J.M. Silva Sánchez (ed.), *Política criminal y nuevo Derecho penal. Libro Homenaje a Claus Roxin*, 137 ss. Barcelona.
Diez Ripolles, José Luis (1990) *Los elementos subjetivos del delito. Bases metodológicas*. Valencia.
Diez Ripolles, José Luis (1998) Exigencias sociales y política criminal, 85 *Claves de razón práctica* 48 ss.
Diez Ripolles, J.L., Giron Gonzalez-Torre, F.J., Stangeland, P., Cerezo Dominguez, A.I. (1996) *Delincuencia y víctimas*.Valencia.
Edwards, S. (1991) La función simbólica del Derecho Penal: violencia doméstica", 1 *Pena y Estado* 83 ss.
Eser, Albin (1974) Resozialisierung in der Krise? Gedanken zum Sozialisationsziel des Strafvollzuges, *Festschrift für K. Peters*, 505 ss. Tübingen.
Foucault, M.(1986) *Vigilar y castigar. Nacimiento de la prisión*, 5ª edición de España.
Garcia-Pablos De Molina, Antonio (1979) La supuesta función resocializadora del Derecho Penal: utopía, mito y eufemismo", *Anuario de Derecho Penal y Ciencias Penales* 654 ss.
Garcia-Pablos De Molina, Antonio (1999) *Manual de Criminología. Introducción y teorías de la criminalidad*. Madrid.
Garcia-Pablos, Antonio (1989) Hacia una "redefinición" del "rol" de la víctima en la criminología y en el sistema legal, *Estudios penales en memoria del Prof. A. Fernandez Albor*, 307 ss. Santiago de Compostela.
Garcia-Pablos De Molina, Antonio (1989) La resocialización de la víctima: víctima, sistema legal y política criminal, *Criminología y Derecho penal al servicio de la persona. Libro-Homenaje al Profesor Antonio Beristain*, 193 ss. Donostia-San Sebastián.
Garcia-Pablos De Molina, Antonio (1994) (2ª ed.), *Criminología. Una introducción a sus fundamentos teóricos para juristas*. Valencia.
Garcia-Pablos De Molina, Antonio (1996) *Criminología. Una introducción a sus fundamentos teóricos para juristas*. Valencia.
Goffman, Erving (1991) *Asylums. Essays on the social situation of mental*

patients and other inmates, (1961) se cita la edición de 1991, de Penguin Books.
Hassemer, Winfried (1984) *Fundamentos del Derecho penal*, translation Francisco Muñoz Conde y Luis Arroyo Zapatero. Barcelona.
Hassemer, Winfried (1991) Derecho penal simbólico y protección de bienes jurídicos, translation Elena Larrauri, 51 *Nuevo Foro Penal* 17 ss. (también se encuentra en 1 *Pena y Estado. Función simbólica de la pena* 23 ss.).
Herrera Moreno, Myriam (1996) *La hora de la víctima. Compendio de victimología*. Madrid.
Hulsman, Louk, Bernat De Celis, Jacqueline (1982) *Sistema penal y seguridad ciudadana: Hacia una alternativa*, translation S. Politoff. Barcelona.
Jones, Stephen (1998) *Criminology*, London: Butterworths.
Kaiser, Günther (1988) (2ª ed.), *Kriminologie. Ein Lehrbuch*. Heidelberg.
Kaiser, Günther (1988) *Introducción a la Criminología*, translation J.A. Rodríguez Nuñez, 7ª ed. Madrid.
Kaiser, Günther (1992) La función de la criminología con respecto a la política legislativa penal, 6 *Eguzkilore. Cuaderno dèl Instituto Vasco de Criminología* 181 ss.
Kaiser, Günther (1993) Viktimologie heute, *Festschrift für Schüler-Springorum* 3 ss., Köln.
Landrove Diaz, Gerardo (1990) *Victimología*. Valencia.
Lanzarote Martin, P.A. (1994) La víctima del delito y el sistema jurídico penal: ¿hacia un sistema de alternativas?, *Poder Judicial*. 34.
Larrauri, Elena (1991) *La herencia de la criminología crítica*. Madrid: Siglo XXI (3th. edition 2000).
Larrauri, Elena (1991) Las paradojas de importar alternativas a la cárcel, *Anuario de Derecho Penal y Ciencias Penales*, 45 ss.
Lea, John (1998) Criminology and Postmodernity, in: P. Walton & J. Young (eds.), *The New Criminology Revisted,* 163 ss. Great Britain.
Lilly, J. Robert/Cullen, Francis T./Ball, Richard A. (1995) *Criminological Theory. Context and consequences*. London: Sage.
Liszt, Franz von (1970) Die Aufgaben und die Methode der Strafrechtswissenschaft, *Strafrechtliche Vorträge und Aufsätze*, tomo II, Berlin, 1905, reprinted Berlin.
Mapelli Caffarena, Borja (1983) *Principios fundamentales del sistema penitenciario español*. Barcelona.
Mapelli Caffarena, Borja (1984) Desviación social y resocialización, *Cuadernos de Política Criminal* 311 ss.
Matthews, Roger/Young, Jock (1992) (eds.), *Issues in Realist Criminology*.

London: Sage.

Mir Puig, Santiago (1982) (2ª ed), *Introducción a las bases del Derecho penal*. Barcelona.

Mir Puig, Santiago (1994) ¿Qué queda en pie de la resocialización?", *El Derecho Penal en el Estado social y democrático de Derecho*, 141 ss. Barcelona.

Morillas Cueva, Lorenzo (1989) Anotaciones sobre la Ciencia del Derecho Penal", in: J.L de la Cuesta, I. Dendaluze & E. Echeburúa, *Criminología y Derecho Penal al servicio de la persona. Libro - Homenaje al Profesor Antonio Beristain*, 585 ss. San Sebastián.

Muñoz Conde, Francisco (1979) La resocialización del delincuente, análisis y crítica de un mito", *Cuadernos de Política Criminal*, 91 ss.

Muñoz Gonzalez, Luz (1989) La criminología 'radical', la 'nueva' y la criminología 'crítica': matizaciones y precisiones en torno a sus nombres, 2 *Eguzkilore. Cuaderno del Instituto Vasco de Criminología,* Extraordinario 267 ss.

Naucke, W. (1978) Las relaciones entre la Criminología y la Política Criminal, translation E. Bacigalupo, 5 *Cuadernos de Política Criminal* 95 ss.

Neuman, Elias (1994) *Victimología. El rol de la víctima en los delitos convencionales y no convencionales*, segunda edición, reestructurada y ampliada, 23 ss. Buenos Aires.

Paul, W., Megacriminalidad ecológica y Derecho ambiental simbólico", 1 *Pena y Estado* 111 ss.

Peters, Tony (1988) Consideraciones teóricas sobre la victimología, 2 *Eguzkilore. Cuaderno del Instituto Vasco de Criminología* 107-133.

Peters, Tony (1993) El futuro de las prisiones: los valores esenciales, 6 *Eguzkilore. Cuaderno del Instituto Vasco de Criminología*, extraordinario, 101-109.

Peters, Tony/Neys, Achille (1994) La pena considerada desde una perspectiva de la reparación, 8 *Eguzkilore. Cuaderno del Instituto Vasco de Criminología* 165-195.

Peters, Tony/Aertsen, Ivo (1995) Mediación para la reparación: presentación y discusión de un proyecto de investigación-acción, 8 *Eguzkilore. Cuaderno del Instituto Vasco de Criminología, extraordinario*, 129-146.

Polaino Navarrete, M., (1989) Victimología y criminalidad violenta en España, *Estudios penales en memoria del Prof. A. FERNANDEZ ALBOR*, 571 ss. Santiago de Compostela.

Rocco, Arturo (1999) Il problema e il metodo della Scienza del Diritto penale", *Opere giuridiche, vol. I, Scritti giuridici varii*, Roma, 1933, pgs.

263 ss. (*El problema y el método de la Ciencia del Derecho penal*, reprinted of the 3th edition, Santa Fe de Bogotá, Colombia).
Rodriguez Manzanera, Luis (1988) *Victimología. Estudio de la víctima*. México.
Romero Barranquero, Gladys (1987) Teorías de la Criminalización, Derecho Penal y Política Criminal, *Anuario de Derecho Penal y Ciencias Penales*, 135 ss.
Roxin, Claus (1972) *Política Criminal y Sistema de Derecho Penal*, translation F. Muñoz Conde. Barcelona.
Roxin, Claus (1997) *Strafrecht. Allgemeiner Teil. Band I. Grundlagen. Der Aufbau der Verbrechenslehre, 3. Auflage*. München.
Schneider, J. (1975) *Viktimologie. Wissenschaft vom Verbrechensopfer*. Tübingen.
Schüler Springorum, H. (1989) Sobre la relación entre criminología y política criminal, *Cuestiones básicas y estrategias de la política criminal*, 1 ss. (17) Buenos Aires, (translation of the german versión "Zum Verhältnis von Kriminologie und Kriminalpolitik", *Gedächtnisschrift für P. NOLL*, Zurich, 1984, pgs.141 ss.).
Schünemann, Bernd (1986) Zur Stellung des Opfers im System der Strafrechtspflege I, *Neue Zeitschrift für Strafrecht (NStZ)*, 193 ss, y II, *Neue Zeitschrift für Strafrecht* 439 ss
Schur, E. (1973) *Radical non intervention: rethinking the delinquency problem*. Nueva Jersey.
Scull, A (1984) *Decarceration*. Nueva York.
Silva Sanchez, Jesús-María (1989) ¿Consideraciones victimológicas en la teoría jurídica del delito? Introducción al debate sobre la Victimodogmática, in: *Criminología y Derecho Penal al servicio de la persona, Libro-Homenaje al Profesor A. Beristain*, 633 ss. San Sebastián.
Silva Sanchez, Jesús-María (1990) La víctima en el futuro de la dogmática, in: Antonio Beristain y José Luis de la Cuesta (eds.), *Victimología*, 229 ss. San Sebastián.
Silva Sanchez, Jesús-María (1992) *Aproximación al Derecho Penal contemporáneo*. Barcelona.
Silva Sanchez, Jesús-María (1993) La consideración del comportamiento de la víctima en la teoría jurídica del delito. Observaciones doctrinales y jurisprudenciales sobre la 'victimo-dogmática', *La victimología, Cuadernos de Derecho Judicial, Consejo General del Poder Judicial*, 133 ss. Madrid.
Silva Sanchez, Jesús-María (1997) Política criminal en la dogmática: algunas cuestiones sobre su contenido y límites, in: J.M. Silva Sánchez (ed.),

Política Criminal y Nuevo Derecho Penal (Libro Homenaje a Claus Roxin), 17 ss. Barcelona.
Silva Sanchez, Jesús-María (2000) Reflexiones sobre las bases de la política criminal, in: J. Cerezo Mir/ R.F. Suárez Montes, A. Beristain Ipiña/ C.M. Romeo Casabona (editores), *El nuevo Código Penal: presupuestos y fundamentos. Libro Homenaje al Prof. Dr. D. A. Torío López,* 209 ss.
Sola Dueñas, Angel/Garcia Aran, Merecedes/Hormazabal Malaree, Hernán (1986) *Alternativas a la prisión. Penas sustitutivas y sometimiento a prueba.* Barcelona.
Soria Verde, M. A., "Desarrollo histórico de la victimología", M. A. Soria Verde (comp.) (1993) *La víctima: entre la justicia y la delincuencia (Aspectos psicológicos, sociales o jurídicos de la victimización*). 13 ss. Barcelona.
Stangeland, Per (1998) La criminología europea: entre la utopía y la burocracia. Esbozo para una criminología realista en España", 2(1) *Revista de Derecho Penal y Criminología* 207-219.
Sutherland, E.H., Cressey, D.R. (1955) *Principles of Criminology*, 5 ed.
Tamarit Sumalla, J.M. (1994) *La reparación a la víctima en el Derecho penal. Estudio y crítica de las nuevas tendencias político-criminales*. Barcelona.
Taylor, Ian, Walton, Paul, Young, Jock (1973) *The new criminology. For a social theory of deviance*. London: Routledge&Keagan Paul.
Torio Lopez, Angel (1988) Indicaciones metódicas sobre el concepto material de culpabilidad", *Cuadernos de Política Criminal*, 759 ss.
Varona Martinez, Gema (1998) *La mediación reparadora como estrategia de control social. Una perspectiva criminológica*. Granada: Comares.
Walklate, Sandra (1988) *Understanding Criminology. Current theoretical debates*. Buckingham, Philadelphia, Open University Press.
Weigend, Thomas (1978) Entwicklungen und Tendenzen der Kriminalpolitik in den USA, *Zeitschrift für die gesamte Strafrechtswissenschaft* 1083 ss.

PART III

ON DEVELOPING RESTORATIVE JUSTICE

RESTORATIVE JUSTICE - ANSWERS TO QUESTIONS THAT NOBODY HAS PUT FORWARD

Hans-Jörg Albrecht

Throughout the 1980s the topics of reparation, restitution, compensation, victim-offender-mediation or reconciliation, and finally restorative justice, received considerable attention in most Western European countries.[1] Tony Peters –an outstanding scientist in the field of criminology, criminal justice and crime policy– has covered the topic of restorative justice in many of his writings.[2] Although Tony Peters sees a great potential in restorative justice – as well as in its core elements like mediation and restitution– the question of how big this potential actually is has to be seriously and critically explored.

Introduction: Why has Restorative Justice Become so Attractive?

The objective of this contribution is to explore the question of the potential of restorative justice. Indeed, in the past twenty years numerous experiments with restitution and victim-offender-mediation have been carried out. Reparation/compensation, as well as victim-offender-reconciliation practices, were introduced as sole sanctions, non-prosecution conditions or sentencing rules, in virtually all criminal justice systems, in particular in juvenile criminal law.[3] The most important questions have been left open, both from the viewpoint of criminal law as from the viewpoint of theoretical criminology and social theory. These basic questions shall be dealt with in the following remarks. Some of the less fundamentally oriented but policy related questions which will be addressed at the outset are: why did restitution and mediative practices all of sudden receive so

1 See, for example, The European Forum for Victim-Offender Mediation and Restorative Justice (2000) (ed.), *Victim-Offender Mediation in Europe. Making Restorative Justice Work*. Leuven: Leuven University Press.

2 T. PETERS (2000) Victim-Offender Mediation: Reality and Challenges: in: The European Forum for Victim-Offender Mediation and Restorative Justice, *o.c.*, 9-15.

3 See for Germany, H.-J.KERNER (1999) *Opferrechte/Opferpflichten. Ein Überblick über die Stellung der durch Straftaten Verletzten im Strafverfahren seit Inkrafttreten des Zeugenschutzgesetzes.* Mainz: Weisser Ring; for European and international accounts see The European Forum for Victim-Offender Mediation and Restorative Justice, *o.c.*

much attention since the 1980s? Why did victim-offender mediation/reconciliation and restitution/ compensation develop into policies aimed at establishing restorative justice schemes together with full alternatives, or at least completely different approaches, to the traditional criminal justice system? Different answers can be found to those questions. First of all, the victim perspective has to be taken into consideration. As early as the 1970s it was claimed[4] that the victims of crime had been marginalized in the criminal process which -since the emergence of modern criminal law and modern criminal procedure sometime in the 19th century-centered upon the offender (and the criminal offence of course). Indeed, focussing the process and procedure on the core tasks of establishing criminal guilt and responsibility, and punishing the offender (while discarding most of the issues related to compensation and the future relationship between the victim and the offender) corresponded to mainstream criminal legal theory. From the 19th century onward, prevention, pursued either through individual or general deterrence, through rehabilitation or incapacitation, developed into sentencing and punishment goals that legitmized State criminal law for at least a century.

When rehabilitative efforts (and prevention by means of criminal law) failed to produce significant effects on crime and recidivism rates, the vacuum left behind[5] during the 1970s and 1980s could be easily filled with a new rationale for society's response to the offender, namely restitution and compensation to the victim.[6] Though the vacuum was not filled by „deterrence", as Christie has suggested,[7] it was produced (and consequently filled up) by what may be considered a drastic move away from the empirical justification of punishment (such as individual or general prevention), as well as a move back to or towards a normative justification of criminal penalties. Theories on the proportionality of punishment and on punishment's role in the validation of norms (concepts that are substantively empty but logically convincing) replaced the old and naive thinking of criminal law and penal sanctions as social instruments or as technologies in the organization of societies. By considering the victim of crime, a major step towards an expressive, politicized and rather simple crime policy was

---

4 See E. WEITEKAMP (2000) Research on Victim-Offender Mediation. Findings and Needs for the Future, in: The European Forum for Victim-Offender Mediation and Restorative Justice, *o.c.*, 99-121.

5 N. CHRISTIE (1995) *Grenzen des Leids*, 36-37. Münster: Votum-Verlag.

6 H. JUNG (2000) Zur Renaissance des Opfers - ein Lehrstück kriminalpolitischer Zeitgeschichte, 33(4) *Zeitschrift für Rechtspolitik* 159-163.

7 CHRISTIE, *o.c.*, 36-37.

implemented which then developed into a process of communication on how best to produce safety and reduce feelings of unsafety.[8]

An answer is also provided by cost-benefit-considerations arguing that the financial burden of the criminal justice system, especially corrections, could be reduced by introducing pre-trial restitution as an alternative to regular criminal proceedings and criminal penalties, and by using mediation as a process by which cases could be diverted from criminal, civil, and administrative courts.

Evidently restitution appeals to desires, hopes and ideas that can be easily accepted and agreed upon by virtually everyone. It appeals to the community and creates, in fact, a (scientific) community or an identity group[9] to which one can choose to belong. This is the restorative justice or mediation group that provides its members with values, morals and a good fiend (the traditional criminal law). Among those acceptance-generating ideas that fuel the demands for replacing traditional criminal procedure and criminal penalties by a system of mediation and restitution is the concept of consensus itself. It is also the prospect of a peaceful neighbourhood, permanent (and successful), characterized by mediation of conflicts, by patterns of direct human interaction that produce intimate feelings, by participation in political procedures and decision-making, as well as a conception of socialized and altruistic men (and women of course).[10] Restorative justice concepts fit also well into communitarian ideologies which evidently appeal to the homeless former social democrats and socialists who are looking for new political and, particularly, ideological havens (that can be partially found in „republican theories“[11]). Essentially, this amounts to recycling the thinking of standard liberal and social democratic parties of some forty years ago. Then, mediative restitution is not only perceived as a mere alternative to traditional criminal sanctions but essentially as a procedural alternative to the traditional model of criminal procedure based as it is upon confrontation and conflict, as means and ends at the same time,[12] with an underlying assumption that participation in the

8 M. DINGES and F. SACK (2000) Unsichere Grossstädte? in: M. DINGES and F. SACK (eds.), *Unsichere Grossstädte? Vom Mittelalter bis zur Postmoderne,* 9-66. Konstanz: Konstanzer Universitäsverlag; R. HEFENDEHL (2000) Wie steht es mit der Kriminalitätsfurcht und was hat der Staat damit zu tun? 33(2) *Kritische Justiz* 174-187.

9 E. HOBSBAWM (1994) *The Age of Extremes.* London: Michael Joseph.

10 S. LEVRANT (1999) Reconsidering Restorative Justice: The Corruption of Benevolence Revisited?, 45(1) *Crime & Delinquency* 32-71.

11 J. BRAITHWAITE and Ph. PETTIT (1990) *Not Just Deserts: A Republican Theory of Criminal Justice.* Oxford: Oxford University Press.

12 CHRISTIE , *o.c.*, 98.

process of mediation is more important than the resolution of the conflict). Some partisans of restorative justice even resort to religious-sounding (and pre-enlightenment) elements such as „healing ceremonies", therapeutical approaches, for example, family group conferences.[13] This comes close to those conventional basket-shopping approaches which promise anything to anybody.[14] It could certainly be seen as some significant expression of (deliberately upheld) vagueness which leaves the consequences and the ultimate content of restorative justice unclear and hidden.

It is rather interesting that the new attractiveness of restitution, with its focus on the consequences of criminal behaviour and the impact the offence has had on the victim, emerged in a time period when actual developments in criminal law and criminal legislation were pointing to a growing importance of so-called offences of endangerment. Moreover, family group conferences, „healing" ceremonies and compensation, as well as mediation processes, are being promoted in times when the rational offender, organized crime and criminal networks, and market economy approaches are gaining momentum in explaining relevant segments of the criminal subcultures of industrial (and other) societies. Offences of endangerment focus on the risk which was created by human behaviour and partially takes up the idea that modern societies should at least avoid certain consequences totally, because restitution or reparation in such cases wouldn't make (much) sense (for example, environmental disasters, nuclear waste consequences or hazardous and dangerous medicaments). But one has to consider, too, that the idea of restitution matches what today's mainstream thinking, insofar as cooperation and coordination are concerned, ranks among high-valued principles. Furthermore, the development of criminal law and criminal sanctions display increasingly administrative, civil and consensual elements, as in many criminal justice systems summary procedures, not including elements of conflict and confrontation, far outnumber full criminal trials.

When looking at what is perceived under the label of restorative justice it comes rather close to what emerges as modern trends in criminal procedure and criminal justice at large. However, there are obviously difficulties in defining what restorative justice is. As Braithwaite[15] has put it: *„Restorative Justice is most commonly defined by what it is an alternative to."* While the alternative sofar amounts evidently to nothing, it is not too difficult to

---

13 WEITEKAMP, *o.c.*

14 LEVRANT, *o.c.*

15 J. BRAITHWAITE (1999) Restorative Justice: Assessing Optimistic and Pessimistic Accounts, in M. TONRY (ed.), *Crime and Justice: A Review of Research*, vol. 25, 4. Chicago/London: The University of Chicago Press.

identify some of the significant ingredients of restorative justice. First, a conflict is needed. Second, conflicts are to be mediated (not through a judge though, but through professional „mediators" who have aquired (somewhere) a basic knowledge in how to mediate conflicts and to restore peace (a new profession mostly staffed by social workers and others formerly involved in rehabilitative techniques). Third, there is extensive room and a great need for debates and discussions (or discourse and exchange of arguments). Fourth, there is restitution or restoration (of property loss, dignity, a sense of security, democracy, empowerment, equality and finally even something like harmony![16] Finally, humans are needed who respond to all that by way of feeling shame, the need of mediation and the desire to participate in mediation processes. However, what would be needed beyond this is regularly left aside, that is a de-modernized and de-industrialized society, as well as a society which is based on belief and the search for harmony.

While in principle no objections can be raised against implementing restitution as an additional option in the context of criminal law, conflicts evidently arise when one raises the central question of how far restitution can be extended as an alternative to criminal procedure and criminal law. Or when one asks whether signs said to indicate the emergence of restorative justice in post modern societies actually represent alternatives to the conventional system of justice, including conventional criminal sanctions. In fact, it seems somewhat strange when the US and England are cited simultaneously to provide evidence of an „explosion" of (conventional) criminal penalties and repressive crime policies[17] and on the strength of the restorative movement.[18] Certainly, both analytical results cannot be drawn from the same set of information. This example of how data and information are treated provides ample evidence that criminology in some places is still understood as a „professing" science.

On the one hand, it is argued that criminal penalties and criminal procedure could be replaced by mediation and restitution, especially through mediative restitution. On the other hand, restitution is understood as a middle-range, or even short-range, concept which should be developed within the framework of criminal law but has to be adapted, in any case, to the structure made up by the criminal law, penal sanctions and sentencing

16 *Ibid.*, 6.

17 I. TAYLOR (1999) *Crime in Context: A Critical Criminology of Market Societies.* Cambridge: Polity Press.

18 WEITEKAMP, *o.c.*

goals. It is obvious that restitution can be made to fit any position in the field of criminal justice. In rehabilitative or offender-centered perspectives, restitution offers a concept of learning and communication promising positively valued experiences. Furthermore, restitution is associated with the opportunity to provide assistance to the victim with the consequences of the crime. For the partisans of crime victims, the focus is on compensation and on strengthening victims' rights. The criminal law perspective may be based on the idea of (positive) general prevention. When inserting restitution in the line of criminal sanctions, it could be argued that the severity of the sanction should be reduced when the offender has „surrendered" by offering compensation, and in so doing has expressed acceptance of the social norm that he or she has transgressed, and has consented to the consequences of criminal liability. If control is the core element of criminal justice goals, then, restitution may be combined with various types of supervision (as can be shown, for example, in the English criminal law reforms of the 1990s and in the new trends in intermediate sanctions in general).[19] Even a classic retributive theory of criminal law may be compatible with the concept of restitution if the victim of crime is provided with aggressive statutory procedural rights and if restitution is backed up by a powerful statutory basis. Then, restitution or compensation clearly conveys the message that the offender has to pay for the crime he or she has committed and, as such, fits well into post modern expressive criminal policies. Critical approaches to criminal justice, especially abolitionism, may use restitution as an alternative procedure which moves the conflict away from criminal law and towards re-privatization and de-professionalization of social problems and finally to a reallocation of competence and power in solving social conflicts.

1. Restorative Justice and Theory

After all that, it should not come as a surprise that restorative justice is not derived from a homogenous theoretical framework (as can be observed with respect to other crime policy concepts) but consists of ideological elements which can be made to fit various criminal policies. It consists also of an

19 H.J. ALBRECHT and A. VAN KALMTHOUT (1997) Intermediate penalties in Europe: Developments in the conception and use of non-custodial sanctions, 6 *CEP Bulletin* 1-6; H.J. ALBRECHT (1999) Penal Policies and Criminal Sanctions: A Look at Developments and Trends in Europe, in: R. HOOD (ed.), *The Changing Face of Crime and Criminal Policy in Europe*, Occasional Paper No. 19, 1-23. Oxford: University of Oxford, Centre for Criminological Research.

interpretation of history which evidently is a serious misinterpretation of the historical evolution of criminal justice, criminal law, as well as the concepts of crime, deviance and punishment.[20] It is true such a transformation took place. But it was not a transformation from a wrong done to another individual to a wrong done to the State or the King. Actually, this type of wrongdoing did not change at all. Today personal crime is still a wrong done to another person, and there is no doctrine that maintains otherwise. The transformation was from a wrong that caused harm not only to an individual (victim) but, to varying degrees, to societey at large. Modern societies are societies structured through norms (in a modern sense). Therefore, the meaning of crime and deviance had also to be extended from the factual consequences suffered by a personal victim to a (normatively conceived) loss of trust, experienced by all those relying on normative structures.

The atheoretical nature of restitution and restorative justice becomes especially evident when one tries to relate restitution to crime theories. It seems rather evident , for example, that the concepts of restitution, compensation or mediation do not fit into economic theories of crime. By reducing the costs of criminal behaviour to a mere compensation of the damage or the losses caused, the costs of such behaviour will never outweigh the potential benefits. Costs of criminal behaviour may outweigh its benefits only if the costs exceed the mere elimination of the acquired benefits. Stress theories of crime are not consistent with restitutive considerations either. It is clear that situations of anomie, and the ensuing attractiveness of criminal behaviour or other types of deviance, are not touched by restitution. In fact, successful strategies of restitution re-establish the point of departure, namely, the stress produced by the conflict between the goals to be attained and the insufficient means of the individual. Thus, from the perspective of anomie theories, the individuals' options in responding to anomic stress would be restricted to resignment behaviour. It is obvious, therefore, that the concept of restitution does not consider social structures and social inequality. From the perspective of control theory, the concept of restitution does not receive support either. As control theory suggests, emotional and rational bonds provide restraints that keep the individual away from crime. It is not clear why restitution or mediation should have some impact on bonding. Rational and emotional ties between

20 See BRAITHWAITE, *o.c.*, 2, who insists that sometime at the end of the „Dark Ages“ crime was transformed into a felony against the king instead of a wrong done to another person.

the individual and society are either well-established, serving as efficient protective shields against deviant impulses, or have not developed at all (or not to a sufficient degree) which, in turn, creates unrestricted opportunities to deviate from social norms. Obviously, in terms of theory nothing speaks in favour of the integration of restituton or mediation as independent variables.

Sofar, labeling theory may actually be the approach best-suited to the restitutive and ultimately restorative response to criminal behaviour and to offenders. Labeling considerations seem to figure rather prominently in the reasoning of partisans of restitution and mediation. They argue that mediation provides a major challenge to everyday theories of crime and criminals, herewith creating obstacles in the way of assigning negative roles, as well as adopting deviant roles. The question must then be raised: which consequences may be the result of restitution that factually and efficiently do restrict stigmatization and labeling? In answering the question it should be pointed out that such consequences may lead to the complete powerlessness of the victim. As creating, and firmly establishing, a monopoly of criminal sanctions by means of criminal law and criminal trials has led to the exclusion of the victim (and of the public) from the process of punishment, only informal sanctions will remain as the sole powerful means of responding to the offender. If as a result of this type of informal sanctions the potential for stigmatisation is reduced or eliminated altogether, the end result would actually be the complete powerlessness of the victim.

Another theory that is sometimes invoked in relation to restitution or restorative justice is learning theory. This is because restitutive mediation is believed to provide learning opportunities for the offender (and for the victim). It is claimed that through mediation the offender may learn about the victim's interests, attitudes and fears. Such changes in the perception and attitudes of the offender may lead to the building up of obstacles against reoffending as he becomes aware of the victim as a subject, as an individual and as a human being. In such a perspective, mediative restitution is related to the theory of neutralization, and is also suggestive of certain psychoanalytical concepts.

Another perspective of mediative restitution refers to abolitionism. Within the abolitionist perspective, restitution and mediation are seen as means of private resolution of conflicts and as potential substitutes to criminal law and the criminal process. The basis of such claims may be seen in a theory of social exchange that refers to the capability and the interests of citizens to take care privately and immediately of those situations of conflict, disorder or unstability which result from a criminal offence.

Furthermore, abolitionist approaches promise positive outcomes of massive reduction in the power of the State to intervene in social conflicts. Furthermore, the radical abolitionist perspective claims other advantages of informal, private resolution of conflicts, advantages which are allegedly too restricted in systems of social control based on penal law. Findings of survey research pointing to public acceptance of restitution as a sole response to offences and offenders, and public dissatisfaction with penal law-based social control are offered in support of those claims. The radical abolitionist perspective is extended by emphasizing active participation of the offender, the victim and the public in the formulation of social and criminal policy. Decentralization, privatization and informal justice based in the community serve as the key concepts of this perspective. The basic idea underlying abolitionism is that a system of informal restitution may replace the criminal process and criminal penalties. It is evident, however, that the meaning of conflict which actually is a key concept in such a theory of restorative justice, is neither made explicit nor is explained properly.

2. What does „Conflict" Mean?

Obviously, the presence of a criminal offence seems to suffice in assuming a conflict.[21] The term conflict thus becomes a "black box" which can hide something as trivial as shoplifting, but also something as serious as civil war type violence. Referring to "conflict" is, undoubtedly, a reminder of the historical process by which the State centralized and monopolized the power to impose sanctions and to use violence, essentially the emergence of modern criminal law. During the (pre-monopolization) period harmful actions and conflicts were actually regarded as private disputes between the doer and the sufferer. Dealing with the conflict required an evaluation of behaviour to decide whether it is wrong or justified. The same conflict occurred (between individuals) as far as violent responses towards the perpetrators were concerned. These reactions or sanctions also related to the basic problem, whether certain behaviour could be labelled as „crime" or as a justified act. When the monopoly of violence was successfully implemented within the modern state a distinction was made between different types of conflicts. We may, today, differentiate between the following conflicts.

---

21 CHRISTIE, *o.c.*, 98.

1. The conflict that may be hidden and efficient in those conditions which are relevant to the emergence of the crime.
2. The conflict that may be produced by the impact of the crime, in terms of material and other damages affecting the victim (or others like, for instance, the State).
3. The conflict that may be a result of the meaning of the criminal offence in terms of disrespect for the norm, non-acceptance and therefore de-validation of the social norm itself.
4. The conflict that may result from the infliction of punishment on an offender, as punishment itself may be percieved as unjust, unjustified and deviant or wrong.

It is obvious that the problems embedded in points 3. and 4. must be resolved in order to allow offender-related and victim-related conflicts (and problems) to become visible.

From the perspective of criminal law and sociology of law, penal norms and penal procedures are the response to the problem of norms and punishment. These institutions are not a response to those individual conflicts which may occur between the offender and the victim. By centralizing the power to punish and by monopolizing the use of violence, conflicts between offenders and victims were not taken away (or stolen) but certain means and procedures were set up to cope with such conflicts. This is an enormous difference, though. Victims were deprived of certain responses to alleged crime and deviance, responses that included violence and punishment. Contrary to what Christie[22] has suggested, victims were never robbed of their conflicts. It is not the conflicts that were taken away but only certain ways of dealing with such conflicts. Notions such as „Conflicts as properties" and „Stealing conflicts" conjure seductive images of settings where immediate conflict resolution (between involved parties) seemingly played a role. In so doing, sometimes rather distorted histories of primitive societies, which seemingly managed to deal with crime and deviance by means of compensation and restitution, are put forward. The implication is that, on the road to modern societies, somewhere, somehow, sometime, this positive potential of compensation and mediation, as well as the victim as an actor of criminal justice, got lost.[23]

By establishing an exclusive (and excluding) link between a centralized criminal justice system and the offender, both parties (or individuals), the

---

22 CHRISTIE, *o.c.*
23 WEITEKAMP, *o.c.*, 99.

offender and the victim, gained certain advantages.[24] Centralization and the monopoly of (criminal) punishment provided benefits for both, the offender and the victim. This is because the immediate conflict resolution was characterized by the imminent risk of escalation which was limited only by the resources available to both parties and their alliances.[25] But today, the norm itself doesn't lead to conflicts anymore, at least if basic criminal norms are considered. Today the potential of such conflicts becomes evident only marginally in the field of political criminal law, economic and environmental offence statutes where organized (and organizable) interests are involved. The dispute today is no longer about the justification of punishment or the right to consider punishment itself as a deviant or criminal act. Today, the problem of punishment, as viewed in this perspective, may be considered solved.

But what is then the meaning of conflict, especially the meaning of a conflict which can be dealt with by restitution or mediative restitution. The meaning of points to an understanding of a criminal offence which is either regarded as a consequence of a basic problem in the interactions between offender and victim, or as a cause of conflict in terms of a dispute on the type and the amount of what should be compensated. It should be emphasized here that the concept of criminal law was never meant to pursue such problem solving and that, for that matter, the criminal law should never pursue such goals.

There is another misunderstanding which consists of assuming that criminal punishment aims at individual and general prevention (or deterrence).[26] If, today, the norm problem and the punishment problem may be regarded as solved, the question which may be put forward has to do only with how far punishment may be reduced or modified without affecting norm validation and without provoking a revival of the punishment problem. Sometimes it is argued that the dark field of crime may serve as an example that the restitution model works in informal settings. And sometimes, even war crimes and dealing with the aftermath of terrorist

---

24 T. v. TROTHA (1983) Limits to Pain. Diskussionsbeitrag zu einer Abhandlung von Nils Christie, 15(1) *Kriminologisches Journal* 34-53.

25 See G. SPITTLER (1980) Streitregelung im Schatten des Leviathan. Eine Darstellung und Kritik rechtsethnologischer Untersuchungen, 1(1) *Zeitschrift für Rechtssoziologie*, 4-32; O. BRUNNER (1984) *Land und Herrschaft. Grundfragen der territorialen Verfassungsgeschichte Österreichs im Mittelalter*. Darmstadt: Wissenschaftliche Buchgesellschaft, for what remains as the best historical account of what actually happened when a monopoly of violence was established

26 CHRISTIE, *o.c.*, 36, for his argument about the „twin ideologies" of treatment and general deterrence.

regimes,[27] as well as economic and environmental crimes, are used as examples in outlining the potential of restorative justice.[28] In fact, there is something in the field of control of economic and environmental crimes, in particular, which comes close to dispute resolution, argumentative discourses, bargaining and ultimately to achieving the goal of replacing criminal punishment and the criminal process through mediation. The problem here may be discussed in terms of conflicting perspectives, perspectives provided by the criminal law approach to the control of the environemnet or economy, on one hand, and (existing) administrative models of control on the other. Although the overall goal, that is the protection of the natural environment or the protection of particular economic conditions, underlies both the criminal law and administrative law, the means which have been elaborated to achieve this goal are basically different. Administrative control of the environment, for example, is based upon the consideration that compliance-achieving mechanisms of enforcement of environmental laws should preferably be based on voluntary action and persuasion or positive incentives, but not on coercion and criminal sanctions. This model relies heavily on cooperation and bargaining.[29] Moreover, administrative decision-making in general is characterized by wide discretionary powers. These discretionary powers concern permitting or prohibiting polluting activities in the commercial and industrial system. The rationale for empowering administrative agencies to use discretion lies in the goals pursued in environmental administrative law. Administrative decision-making is characterized by the pursuit of two differing and conflicting goals: protection and preservation of the natural environment on the one hand, and economic or commercial use of the environment on the other. From the perspective of environmental administrative agencies, invoking the criminal law is apt to destroy an indispensable positive relationship between the administration and industrial clients. In this perspective, short-term benefits in terms of successful criminal prosecution of environmental offences would be exchanged for long-term benefits in terms of achieving the goal of future compliance with the objectives of administrative law. It is therefore evident that the conflict perspective underlying the processing of certain environmental or economic offenders through the justice system, and the attempt to achieve compliance

27 M.A. DRUMBL (2000) Sclerosis. Retributive Justice and the Rwanda Genocide, 2(3) *Punishment & Society* 287-308.

28 J. BRAITHWAITE, *o.c.*, 7.

29 G. RICHARDSON, A. OGUS and P. BURROWS (1982) *Policing Pollution. A Study of Regulation and Enforcement.* Oxford: Oxford University Press.

with legal provisions (and therefore prevention) by means of criminal sanctions, is not part of the efficiency calculation of environmental administration. This is true at least as far as highly organized fields of behaviour such as industry and commerce are concerned. It is even argued that in those fields aggressive or militant prosecution should be rejected and, occasionally one even hears, that criminal prosecution of environmental offences is counterproductive. Given this perspective, the use of criminal law evidently results in a zero-sum game likely to increase the problem of non-compliance as well as to aggravate the problem of other legal conflicts between companies and administrative authorities. For the criminal justice system (or the State or moral entrepreneurs or other interested groups), the reasons to play the zero-sum game are clearly at hand, too. The definition of a criminal offence requires a categorical either/or decision.[30] Leaving the definition un-decided would mean jeopardising universal acceptance of norms and neutralizing their capacity to create and to preserve structural trust in societies. However, what is constitutive of those developments – as is the case for all those situations where states resort to amnesties and ultimately to the option of refraining from criminal punishment (for example, responses to criminal activities by the State in the past and approaches like the „Truth and Reconciliation" commissions in South-Africa) is that the basic problem or question of what is wrong or right, and of who is powerful enough to answer that question is not yet resolved. It could well be that an attempt to find such an answer would result in escalation, instability and disorder, ultimately situations that are worse than what could be expected from not insisting on the validity of normative expectations. It should be stressed here that we do not know much about the positive and negative consequences of such immediate and informal handling of criminal offences. It is evident, however, that besides the formal system of control, informal mechanisms have to take over a certain share of criminal offences. Handling all deviant acts or criminal offences by the criminal justice system is neither economically feasible nor a functional option. Furthermore, it is equally evident, that just because informal handling of criminal offences without resorting to the criminal justice system already exists, this does not necessarily mean that those criminal offences which are being reported to criminal justice authorities could be handled informally as well. Moreover, it is not known whether informal and immediate conflict resolution yields, on average, as satisfying results as

30 K.-L. KUNZ (1990) Commentary, in: G. KAISER and H.-J. ALBRECHT (eds.), *Crime and Criminal Policy in Europe*, 47. Freiburg: Max-Planck-Institute.

formal processing of cases and offenders. We may assume that successful conflict resolution is dependent on the availability of formal procedures and a potential of coercion. The always available threat to resort to criminal law may support informal procedures and push towards mediation. But in those fields where, for different reasons, criminal law may not be used or accessed, compensation and mediation will not be the regular consequence of a "natural" development of conflicts. Historical research,[31] theoretical approaches to norms and punishment[32] and ethnological studies[33] clearly demonstrate the tremendous potential of escalation that is embedded in conflicts which are to be mediated without the (efficiently implemented) monopoly of violence. And yet, the lack of recognition and acknowledgement of historical literature and ethnological research still can be clearly seen in the restorative justice literature. The problems which become visible with family violence, violence in the drug scene or in other marginal social settings point to the fact that efficient obstacles on the way of making use of formal procedures and criminal law normally do not lead to acceptable outcomes.

3. Policy Conflicts and Alternatives to Restorative Justice

The concept of restorative justice touchs several policy strategies which have to be discussed in terms of their interrelationships. These policy strategies concern:

- the concept of decriminalization and, of substitutes to criminal law in terms of civil and administrative law,
- the concept of depenalization,
- diversion,
- alternative criminal penalties,
- victim compensation,
- the concept of rehabilitation, and
- most recently, the confiscation of the proceeds of crime.

Here, problems of compatibility of perspectives are concerned. Furthermore, problems of redistribution of resources and, evidently, of costs emerge. Therefore, the analysis has to be extended to the question whether these

31 BRUNNER, *o.c.*

32 T. v. TROTHA (1980) Die Dominanz von Rechtsnormen in der Organisation sozialen Verhaltens, 1(2) *Zeitschrift für Rechtssoziologie* 141-164; v. TROTHA (1983) *Limits to pain*, *o.c.*; T. v. TROTHA (1983) *Recht und Kriminalität*. Tübingen: Mohr.

33 SPITTLER, *o.c.*

different perspectives can be harmonized. When attempting an integrative approach it is evident that the effects of implementing restorative justice may be assessed from the perspective of other interests and policy options as negative side effects. Regarding victim compensation and mediative restitution, the problem concerns whether the offender's or the victim's perspective should be ranked higher, whether the primary goal of restitution should be to compensate the victim or rather to rehabilitate the offender. Regarding restitution and confiscation of criminal proceeds, the problem may turn out to be whether the primary objective should be to strip the offender of the illegal profits, or whether restitution to the victims of the crime should be the overriding goal. Finally, the implementation of restitutive concepts in the framework of current criminal law must address the question of whether decriminalization, in the sense of replacing the criminal law with administrative or civil law, is obsolete and devalued. From the perspective of diversion, net-widening and intensification of criminal law may turn out to be problems. This is true especially for those types of offences and offenders for whom, up till now, unconditional dismissals were rather routinely used (and for whom shaming, as well as stigmatizing procedures as suggested sometimes by restorative justice partisans, could indeed serve as harsh penalties).[34] One must consider, not only net-widening and intensification of the response to the offender, but also the intensification of the search for information in the context of criminal law. The concept of restorative justice evidently relies on types of information and data that go beyond the traditional and rather restricted (to establishing a criminal offence) information used for criminal law purposes. These types of information concern the economic and social circumstances, the (co-)responsibility of the victim (e.g. with respect to damage-reducing activities), and finally information on the readiness to co-operate and the expectations of the community, etc.. From the perspective of rehabilitation - which for a long time aimed to alleviate the financial consequences of certain types of crimes (as well as criminal procedures) for the offender - the problem is whether successful attempts to reduce the financial burden placed on offenders could also be perceived as successful from the perspective of restitution. This is why the financial capability of offenders figures prominently in the discussion of restitutive or restorative concepts. Although victim surveys and analyses of official crime data support, on the surface, the assumption that the average damage caused by criminal

34 See the analysis of J. PRATT (2000) The Return of the Wheelbarrow Man; Or, the Arrival of Postmodern Penalty?, 40(1) *British Journal of Criminology* 127-145.

offences does not preclude successful restitution (seen from the quantitative dimension), this is true only when considering well-integrated populations of offenders. But it is well-known from research on the collection of fines, for example, that even very low amounts may cause considerable hardship to the population of unemployed or, in other respects, marginal offenders. Finally, one has to ask whether a concept of restitution which, due to structural reasons, consists of symbolic action (such as community service) could be considered as economically (and otherwise) rational as are fines and simplified criminal procedures.

Concluding Remarks

Restorative justice partisans are surfing on waves of criminal justice trends which have created plenty of small nishes for compensation, restitution or restorative justice style decision-making and have in fact produced now and then the kind of community service, mediation or compensation „bubbles" which have attracted a lot of attention but have not contributed to change the character of criminal law and criminal justice.[35] In fact, criminal justice everywhere, and independent of family conferencing and victim-offender-reconciliation, compensation Schemes rely on: firstly, ordinary (though often simplified and adapted to administrative convenience) processing of criminal cases; and then, secondly, on the conventional criminal sanctions which after all -when considering fines and suspended sentences- meet all the demands that can be put forward both from crime theory positions and from basic rights positions (proportionality and least intrusive intervention principle).

The trends in criminal justice which seemingly support restorative justice thinking, and sometimes, practices concern:

- simplification and streamlining of criminal procedure,
- elements of an administrative justice, as well as
- elements of an enforcement-dominated justice;

while pursuing interests such as

- compensation to the victim and reparation of the loss of trust created by the crime,
- reduction of stigma and and other negative effects of labeling, as well as
- saving resources.

35 ALBRECHT & VAN KALMTHOUT, *o.c.*; ALBRECHT, *o.c.*

What has also become evident in recent criminal justice trends is the dominance of the implementation of law over the creation of law and the neglect of the basic principle of division of power in organizing criminal justice. Conditions of modern societies obviously require flexibility and informality in the administration and enforcement of law (and with that create also conditions which allow and sometimes even demand mediation, compensation, etc.). Modern legislation has responded to such needs by actually entrusting police and prosecutors with more and more discretionary powers that have changed considerably the relationship between the creation and application or implementation of law. Today, it seems that in many areas it is no longer the legislative bodies which decide on penalization of behaviour but the police and prosecution services. It is here where the executively-determined law poses numerous questions on the relationships between the executive power and parliaments.

The conditions that obviously are linked to those needs, which in turn have provoked trends in informal, flexible and „out of court" settlements of criminal cases, can be broken down into different concepts. One of these concepts refers to modernization. The concept of modernization switches the focus to the basic mechanisms of societal integration and, herewith, to the role of formal control systems and the function of criminal law in modern and complex societies. Part of the process of modernization refers to certain developments in the fields of crime and criminal justice which pose new challenges to criminal law and particularly to the system of criminal sanctions. Challenges to criminal justice reform in modern societies are found in several fields.

Among the crime phenomena that place new strains on criminal justice systems mass crime and mass delinquency rank rather high. Furthermore, organized crime, transnational and cross-border crimes and new crimes like, for example, economic and environmental crimes have been placed on the policy agenda.[36] Mass crimes and complex crimes have led to problems of capacity and overload and have contributed to a significant trend towards the simplification and streamlining of basic criminal law and criminal procedure. Organized, economic and other types of rational crime have led to an ongoing search for measures likely to improve clearing rates and to

36 A. FARKAS (1993) Stand und Tendenzen der Strafrechtsreform in Ungarn, in A. ESER, G. KAISER and E. WEIGEND (eds.), *Von totalitärem zu rechtsstaatlichem Strafrecht. Kriminalpolitische Reformtendenzen im Strafrecht osteuropäischer Länder*, 43-53. Freiburg: Max-Planck-Institute.

overcome problems of collecting and processing evidence which have created a notorious field of concern in virtually all criminal justice systems.

Then, the complexity of criminal cases has increased dramatically with certain types of economic, environmental and transnational crimes that place new and hitherto unknown demands on the procedural, legal and technological expertise of criminal prosecution and criminal courts. Finally, with all that, the costs of criminal justice have increased dramatically, too. This reminds us of the point that when criminal law and criminal sanctions implement basic principles and standards they are likely to produce costs. Reform of the criminal law and the system of criminal sanctions therefore is associated with the question of how much of the gross national product should be devoted to crime prevention and criminal justice, and how criminal justice resources should ultimately be distributed and allocated. New types of offenders who are partially linked to new crime phenomena like, for example, the rational offender, the minority offender and criminal organizations or corporate criminals, will have to be considered. For such types of offenders the basic approach adopted in criminal justice systems during the 1960s and 1970s, namely rehabilitation and re-integration focussed on the individual offender, has come under considerable criticism. Socio-economic changes in modern societies point also towards new demands. Societies undergo major changes with black markets and the shadow economy representing new social and economic realities and producing new precarious groups out of which, and for whom, crime policy and criminal justice reform have to be developed. The victims then reappeared in the picture together with their needs and their expectations from the criminal justice system in terms of compensation and restitution. Besides the victim, the public's role, more specifically the community's role in crime control, as well as the private sector's potential in crime control, in justice administration and in penal corrections have become important issues in crime policy debates.

While all that has contributed to the rather precarious trend of de-formalizing criminal justice, it is evident that this same trend is favorable to the creation of conditions that allow for mediation and compensation as an answer to capacity and legitimacy problems. However, this does not provide an empirically proven need for an alternative to criminal law and punishment, nor does it provide for a theoretically plausible response to the basic questions and problems to which modern criminal law was meant to provide the answers and the solutions.

References

Albrecht, H.-J. (1999) Penal Policies and Criminal Sanctions: A Look at Developments and Trends in Europe, in: R. Hood (ed.), *The Changing Face of Crime and Criminal Policy in Europe*, Occasional Paper No. 19, 1-23. Oxford: University of Oxford, Centre for Criminological Research.

Albrecht, H.-J. and van Kalmthout, A. (1997) Intermediate penalties in Europe: Developments in the conception and use of non-custodial sanctions, 6 *CEP Bulletin* 1-6.

Braithwaite, J. and Ph. Pettit (1990) *Not Just Deserts: A Republican Theory of Criminal Justice*. Oxford: Oxford University Press.

Braithwaite, J. (1999) Restorative Justice: Assessing Optimistic and Pessimistic Accounts, in: M. Tonry (ed.), *Crime and Justice: A Review of Reserach*, vol. 25, 1-127. Chicago/London: The University of Chicago Press.

Brunner, O. (1984) *Land und Herrschaft. Grundfragen der territorialen Verfassungsgeschichte Österreichs im Mittelalter*. Darmstadt: Wissenschaftliche Buchgesellschaft.

Christie, N. (1995) *Grenzen des Leids*. Münster: Votum-Verlag.

Dinges, M., Sack, F. (2000) Unsichere Grossstädte? in: Dinges, M., Sack, F. (eds.), *Unsichere Grossstädte? Vom Mittelalter bis zur Postmoderne*, 9-66. Konstanz: Konstanzer Universitäsverlag.

Drumbl, M.A. (2000) Sclerosis. Retributive Justice and the Rwanda Genocide, 2(3) *Punishment & Society* 287-308.

Farkas, A. (1993) Stand und Tendenzen der Strafrechtsreform in: Ungarn, in, Eser, A., Kaiser, G., and E. Weigend (eds.), *Von totalitärem zu rechtsstaatlichem Strafrecht. Kriminalpolitische Reformtendenzen im Strafrecht osteuropäischer Länder,* 43-53. Freiburg: Max-Planck-Institute.

Hefendehl, R. (2000) Wie steht es mit der Kriminalitätsfurcht und was hat der Staat damit zu tun? 33(2) *Kritische Justiz* 174-187.

Hobsbawm, E. (1994) *The Age of Extremes*. London: Michael Joseph.

Jung, H. (2000) Zur Renaissance des Opfers - ein Lehrstück kriminalpolitischer Zeitgeschichte, 33(4) *Zeitschrift für Rechtspolitik* 159-163.

Kerner, H.-J. (1999) *Opferrechte/Opferpflichten. Ein Überblick über die Stellung der durch Straftaten Verletzten im Strafverfahren seit Inkrafttreten des Zeugenschutzgesetzes*. Mainz: Weisser Ring.

Kunz, K.-L. (1990) Commentary, in: Kaiser, G. and H.-J. Albrecht (eds.), *Crime and Criminal Policy in Europe,* 47. Freiburg: Max-Planck-Institute.

Levrant, S. (1999) Reconsidering Restorative Justice: The Corruption of Benevolence Revisited?, 45(1) *Crime & Delinquency* 32-71.

Peters, T. (2000) Victim-Offender Mediation: Reality and Challenges, in: The European Forum for Victim-Offender Mediation and Restorative Justice (ed.), *Victim-Offender Mediation in Europe. Making Restorative Justice Work,* 9-15. Leuven: Leuven University Press.

Pratt, J. (2000) The Return of the Wheelbarrow Man; Or, the Arrival of Postmodern Penalty? 40(1) *British Journal of Criminology* 127-145.

Richardson, G., Ogus, A. and P. Burrows (*1982) Policing Pollution. A Study of Regulation and Enforcement.* Oxford: Oxford University Press.

Spittler, G. (1980) Streitregelung im Schatten des Leviathan. Eine Darstellung und Kritik rechtsethnologischer Untersuchungen, 1(1) *Zeitschrift für Rechtssoziologie* 4-32.

Taylor, I. (1999) *Crime in Context: A Critical Criminology of Market Societies*. Cambridge: Polity Press.

The European Forum for Victim-Offender Mediation and Restorative Justice (2000) (ed.), *Victim-Offender Mediation in Europe. Making Restorative Justice Work*. Leuven: Leuven University Press.

v. Trotha, T. (1983) Limits to Pain. Diskussionsbeitrag zu einer Abhandlung von Nils Christie, 15(1) *Kriminologisches Journal* 34-53.

v. Trotha, T. (1983) *Recht und Kriminalität*. Tübingen: Mohr.

v. Trotha, T. (1980) Die Dominanz von Rechtsnormen in der Organisation sozialen Verhaltens, 1(2) *Zeitschrift für Rechtssoziologie* 141-164.

Weitekamp, E. (2000) Research on Victim-Offender Mediation. Findings and Needs for the Future, in: The European Forum for Victim-Offender Mediation and Restorative Justice (ed.), *Victim-Offender Mediation in Europe. Making Restorative Justice Work,* 99-121. Leuven: Leuven University Press.

SOCIETAL DEVELOPMENT, QUALITY OF LIFE AND RESTORATIVE JUSTICE

Otto Driedger

Introduction

Restorative Justice is an initiative toward a major paradigm shift from the present approach to keeping the peace in society and is the basis for an examination of the existing criminal justice system. In this essay the intention is to discuss the restorative justice paradigm, particularly the way it impacts societal development and the quality of life in society as well as its potential for enhancing the quality of life. In order to do this, it is necessary to clarify the concepts used in this essay.

Societies are in a constant state of flux and change. The rapid and substantive change resulting from technologies related to computerization is well documented. Globalization is causing profound changes in communities, nation states, economics, labour and human interaction. How do societies adapt to this rapid change? What are the symptoms of creative positive response, and what are the symptoms of difficulty in coping with change?

Sociological studies have shown that in well-functioning communities when there is a sudden, massive change, the community suffers from fragmentation, social problems and disintegration. When a large mine, factory or other enterprise locates near an existing small town or village, problems of alcoholism, family disunity, promiscuity, crime, etc. become much more severe and the community can become partially or totally dysfunctional. The rapid change in the world today is leading to many societies becoming increasingly dysfunctional while others appear to be finding ways of coping with change in positive ways.

In this essay, the term "societal development" is used to refer to the ways in which societies are able to respond to change in a positive, developmental way that enhances, rather than diminishes, the quality of life for the community and its members. In order to refer to the enhancement of the quality of life, the term "human-centred" is used. Much of the focus in globalization and computerization is centred on economic development, technology, organizations, profit and well-being of global structures and systems with their elites. It is then assumed that this is good for everyone, that the benefits permeate all of society. The principle of human-centred development challenges us to examine societal well-being in the first instance, in terms of the well being of the people.

The word "sustainable" is used to highlight the importance of conceptualising all development within a positive, enduring framework. This is frequently not a consideration in economic development priorities, but must be incorporated if there is to be long-term well-being, or "sustainable, human-centred development". The concept "sustainable, human-centred development" is used to enhance our understanding of the terms "societal development" and "quality of life". Credit for the development of the term goes to Yussuf Kly.[1]

"Restorative Justice" is used very broadly in a variety of contexts, including victim-offender mediation, healing and sentencing circles, and community policing. It incorporates diverse philosophic orientations from the Maori of New Zealand, John Braithwaite, Nils Christie, Ezzat Fattah, Christian formulations such as those of Howard Zehr, and many others.

1. Violence and Victimization

Violence and victimization are pervasive elements of human history. Mythology, classical literature and historical records are replete with those themes. For example, much of children's literature is a reflection of what is considered "acceptable" and "unacceptable" violence. There are also examples of blaming victims of violence for not taking adequate precautions for self-protection.

The book *Violence in Canada* published in 1978 is an examination of violence in our society. One chapter addresses issues of violence and the social structure as reflected in children's books from 1850 to 1970. It states: "*The message communicated in the literature which children read is that physical violence is an appropriate act, given the motive and the script*".[2] In their review it was established that *"a 50 page book is likely to include about seven violent acts and a 150 page book about 21 violent acts"*.

In subsequent discussions, the authors present some important and interesting findings.

"It may be that the high incidence of violence in these books occurs as a vehicle to expose and punish those who use violence. Several of our findings suggest that this is not (italics in the text) the case. In fact, the implicit message is that violence is something which is effective in solving seemingly insolvable

1 For a more extensive discussion of the term, see his book: Y. Kly (1997) *Societal Development and Minority Rights*. Ottawa, Canada: Clarity Press Inc.

2 M. A. B. Gammon (1978) *Violence in Canada*. Toronto: Methuen.

problems when violence is portrayed as a means of achievement, it tends to be given the stamp of social approval by the authors of these books. But when it is portrayed as an expression of emotion, it is depicted as illegitimate. Overall, in answer to the question of whether the high frequency of violence in children's books is part of the social control process restricting violence, the evidence suggests the opposite. Specifically, the violence in these stories is typically carried out to achieve some end or solve some problem".[3]

Members of our society are socialized into a mentality that accepts violence as a tool for problem solving and for advancing one's agenda. An example from Canadian history would be the hanging of Louis Riel in 1874. He was a Metis leader who wanted to advance the well-being of the metis people in Western Canada. The Canadian Government saw this as a threat to its idea of Nation building. The concept of nation building in Canada changed radically in the past 125 years. Canada is now seen as a pluralist and multicultural society. In 2001 the highway route between Regina and Saskatoon is being named the Louis Riel Trail.

For a long time now crime victims have been the ignored segment of the criminal justice system. But in the past few decades, much theoretical work has been done on victims and victimization within the field of criminology by persons such as Ezzat Fattah and is well documented.

Violence and victims have been analysed extensively from a psychosocial perspective. They have also been examined extensively in theological circles that are committed to non-violence and peace making. The work done by Rene Girard and others provides insight into the nature of violence and victimization from an anthropological and theological perspective.

Girard's thesis is that violence is a universal human characteristic. This violence is based on the deep-seated human orientation of "mimetic desire". Mimetic desire *"should be understood as claiming that individuals develop their desires by contagiously picking them up from -or patterning them after-other people, something that often occurs unconsciously.'*[4] One example used is that of a small child who, when it sees another child having a good time with a toy, will want that toy even though it may have been playing with a number of other toys. The desire to have what another has is imitative rather than reflecting the objective value of the item.

"This mimetic desire leads to conflict, violence and often disintegration in society. The task then becomes one of regulating this violence in human

---

3 GAMMON, *o.c.*

4 W.M. SWARTLEY (2000) *Violence Renounced.* Telford, Penn./Scottdale, Penn.: Pandora Press/Herald Press.

societies".[5] In order to protect themselves, communities find ways of dealing with this violence. Historically, societies have resolved this, Girard contends, by establishing scapegoats on which the violence of the community can be focussed and thus bringing peace to the community. This scapegoat phenomenon has been formalized into religious rituals of sacrifice, initially of humans, then of animals as surrogates. The phenomenon however is not limited to religious ritual. Many societies have and do scapegoat minorities based on race, ethnicity, sexual orientation, gender, etc.

Laws and regulations are another way by which societies address issues of conflict and violence. Implementation takes many forms, which can differ from society to society. Custom, taboos and ejection from or rejection in the community are effective ways in ancient societies and smaller communities.

The criminal justice system provides the response for controlling violence. It is the controlled violence (and power) of the State that is used as the means of responding to violence or death resulting from mimetic desire when it erupts into violence or death.

In the introduction I referred to the increasing fragmentation of society in this era of rapid change. In countries where there is a high and increasing incarceration rate, such as the USA and the Russian Federation, public panic leads to heightened demands for escalation of punishment and incarceration. This results in a downward spiral which, in the words of some American criminal justice professionals6 could bankrupt the country. The contention by the documentary commentator is that change from the high incarceration rates is bound to occur, not because of a change in attitudes toward reintegration and rehabilitation of offenders, but because the system will become so expensive that alternative measures will be needed.

2. Restorative justice as a paradigm shift

The restorative justice paradigm is not actually a shift to a new way, but rather a return to patterns that were used in many societies in their early development. There are records of mediation processes, healing circles, conflict resolution models, etc. which developed as alternatives to the scapegoat phenomenon and

---

5 *Ibid.*

6 A&E Documentary Video: *Behind Bars*. Produced by 44 Blue Productions, Inc. and Actuality Productions, Inc. for A&E Network. Executive Producers Gerald W. Abrams and Rasha Drachkovitch. Directors/Writers Lasta Drachkovitch and Rob Engelhardt. Host /Narrator Bill Kurtis. A&E Supervising Producer Gayle Gilman, A& E Executive Producer Michael Cascio.

the patterns of sacrifice discussed earlier. In spite of this, Girard would argue that violent patterns of resolution used by the State, often in close cooperation or even in concert with the religious order, inevitably won out as the pattern of conflict resolution.

Serious attempts to find an alternative model have gained momentum in the past few decades. There appears to be a number of factors that have led to this momentum.

First, research initiatives in victimology have moved victim issues to centre stage so they are being addressed with the gravity they deserve, along with traditional concerns for offenders. Prior to this focus on victims in research and writing, the only recourse victims had was to become vocal in demanding greater punishment for offenders. This increased the spiral of punitive response and led to further alienation and fragmentation. Victimology set the stage for addressing victim issues in such a way that they could be examined and explored in a more productive way.

Second, the mounting attention given to the views of aboriginal communities in many countries is important. It is being increasingly recognized that current criminal justice responses to aboriginal involvement in crime are counterproductive. Recognition of aboriginal spirituality, patterns of community conferencing (as in New Zealand) and healing, talking and sentencing circles in Canada have contributed greatly to seeking alternative patterns of response.

2.1. Social and theological reform

Since late in the 19th century, and particularly since the 1930's, social democratic societies have recognized the need for and have pushed for social reform. Such initiatives recognized the importance of the social context and of the enhancement of the well-being of all members of society as the basis for social cohesion and as a means of preventing alienation and violence. This movement led to social reform in many sectors of society, including criminal justice. In the criminal justice system, it took the form of a re-focus from penology to corrections to rehabilitation and reintegration of the offender rather than punishment and retribution. It was found that such initiatives were important contributors to the humanization of corrections and the reintegration of offenders, but they did not alter the basic assumptions of the system. Scandinavian and some other West European countries demonstrated the positive results of this initiative to the greatest extent.

Initiatives by Christian communities have also played an important role in this shift. Programs such as Victim - Offender mediation have contributed to the momentum. Theological writings about the basic principles of Christianity -love, reconciliation and forgiveness- have repositioned many in the Christian community as a counter force to the punitive approaches by some of the fundamentalist religious groups. Other religions such as Buddhism and Baha'i also have a strong religious/philosophic orientation to peace and reconciliation.

All the initiatives identified above have contributed greatly to a serious consideration of the paradigm shift to what is presently referred to as Restorative Justice.

Restorative Justice should not be seen as one monolithic singular thrust, but as a set of principles and approaches that lead to restoration of people, relationships, communities and societies.

The response to societal conflict and criminality by the existing criminal justice systems and by means of sanctioned State violence reinforces control and containment and contributes to the fragmentation and alienation in society. The many faces of Restorative Justice on the other hand, are initiatives to reinforce positive and re-integrative forces in society. Reconciliation, healing, conflict resolution are all designed to establish societal cohesion based on the broader understanding of social justice and the well being of all.

2.2. Aboriginal approaches

Canadian aboriginal approaches to criminal activity view such actions in the broader context of community and society. They recognize that criminal activity is largely a result of the fragmentation and disintegration that have occurred in their communities through the great migrations of Europeans and others to North America. In their profound sense of humour, they observe that their immigration policy prior to the coming of the Europeans was the reason why they now have so many problems. In order to address the present high level of crime and community disintegration, First Nations in Canada are taking a multi-faceted approach.

In the late 1960's, when aboriginal communities began organizing and taking greater control of their own destiny, they were clear on some of the basic issues. Their analysis led them to recognize that aboriginals were demoralized, disconnected, alienated and had a poor self image. There was a high drop-out rate from schools, much alcoholism, family and community violence and hostility. The hostility was frequently turned inwards on their own people, and would occasionally erupt against other Canadians mainly when they were intoxicated.

In response, in Saskatchewan for example, in the late 1960's, aboriginal Indian leaders developed a culture college. The aim was to rediscover their history, their spirituality, their stories and their roots. Much of this heritage was unknown to younger aboriginals since they had been forced to attend residential schools where they could neither speak their own languages, nor continue their own spirituality or culture since the objective of Canadian society was to integrate and "civilize" the aboriginal population. The culture college collected artefacts, recorded and documented oral history of the elders who were still around, developed "culture camps" where youth were brought to learn and experience the life and culture of their heritage. They re-established sweat lodges, native dances, drums and music, the use of sweet grass and tobacco for spiritual ritual purposes.

The history of the Canadian West was rewritten so that aboriginals were no longer identified as savages and heathen. Information on historic battles and conflicts was reformulated so that it reflected history more accurately. The history books used in Canadian schools originally depicted aboriginals as horse thieves and savages who massacred innocent victims, and scalped persons taken hostage in battles. No wonder aboriginal students dropped out of school!

There was active lobbying by the Departments of Education to adopt changes in the curriculum that would reflect history more accurately. Archaeological sites were developed and historic conflicts and battle sites were developed in a way that would reflect the quality of life of the original peoples of the prairies. These initiatives were important steps in the development of a positive identity for aboriginals. Native people who were successful in sports, business, education and other areas of endeavour were also highlighted as role models for children and youth.

Although many initiatives have been taking shape the depth of disintegration is so great in the aboriginal community, that social problems and criminal activity are pervasive. The existing criminal justice system has been overwhelmed by the sheer numbers of aboriginals coming into the system. Correctional institutions have a disproportionately high percentage of aboriginal inmates.

The initiatives referred to above are seen as a long term action that will re-establish a positive equilibrium between aboriginal societies and the larger Canadian society.

Aboriginal organizations have accurately shown that the existing criminal justice system further fragments and alienates them and their communities. As a result, alternative direct action to deal with criminality is being developed. Their approach is one that adapts their traditional ways of dealing with conflict to the current situation. The historic pattern was that when issues required resolution in the community, the elders and the members of the community would sit in a circle and discuss matters of importance. "Talking circles" were used for many purposes, and would turn into "healing circles" when there was hurt, hostility or damage done by one party to another. This pattern has been used to develop sentencing circles that are an adaptation of the traditional to the Canadian system.

When a circle was used a specific process was followed although the process differed from one community to the next. Sweet grass would be burned and an elder would say prayers. If the matter was concluded successfully, a peace pipe would be handed around the circle and each person would smoke. This was a way of demonstrating commitment to the agreement. The process demonstrates the major objective of resolving issues whether criminal or not, in a way that would enhance, strengthen or re-establish community well-being . This is in sharp contrast to the indiscriminate use of the Canadian criminal justice system. The harshest results of the Canadian Criminal Justice system can be seen in the way it was implemented in the Northern parts of Canada.

Frequently, when there were criminal offences in the north, the investigation was done by the Royal Canadian Mounted Police who would fly in if there was no local detachment. Often there was no police detachment as the communities were much too small. When a court date was set, the judge, prosecutor and defence lawyer would fly in on the same plane, hold court, announce the verdict and pronounce the sentence. If the sentence was prison, the offender would be flown out to serve the sentence in a prison far from the community. The process was entirely alienating for the community, for the offender and also for the victim. It further fragmented the community and alienated its members thus reinforcing the fragmentation and alienation of which the criminal activity was only a symptom.

The paradigm shift to a restorative justice perspective enhances sustainable human-centred community (societal) development. This is particularly important in marginalized and minority groups, but also important for society in general.

The Maori experience in New Zealand, is another example of the shift to the use of family and community building as the basis of dealing with criminal and deviant behaviour.

Many minority groups and sub-groups in most societies have community-based ways of dealing with unacceptable behaviour. Providing the patterns do not violate societal laws, such patterns of regulation are accepted in democratic societies because they actually enhance societal cohesion.

In pluralist societies societal cohesion occurs at many levels. It is important to find many ways of enhancing the quality of life and the well being of citizens because of the plethora of fragmenting elements. To have a pattern of response to crime that assists in societal cohesion rather than accentuating fragmentation and alienation is very useful. There is evidence that aboriginal initiatives are having a profoundly beneficial effects on community cohesion and, as a result, a reduction in fragmentation and alienation is occurring.

3. Reformulation of the existing world view

There is one additional important element that must be considered in addressing issues of restorative justice vis-à-vis societal development and human well-being.

The 20th Century can be described as the century in which the paradigm of analysis was polarized: Left/Right, Socialism/Capitalism, Totalitarian/ Democratic, Atheistic/"God fearing". The primary context for analysis however, was the Socialist/Capitalist and Left/Right. With the end of the cold war, the move toward globalisation and localization, and advanced technological developments such as computerization, the old context of analysis proved to be inadequate.

The European Centre for Social Welfare Policy and Research in Vienna, Austria, has been engaged in developing fresh patterns of analysis that reflect the changing world. In the book *Shifts in the Welfare Mix*,[7] researchers in the Centre formulate a context for analysis that has already been used effectively by the Centre in issues related to children (*Childhood Matters*), seniors (*Care for the Elderly* and *Payments for Care*), local service (*Healthy Public Policy at the Local Level*) and an analysis of industrial shifts and responses (*The Social Construction of an Industry*).

There have also been more theoretical writings, which provide a context for their developing models for analysis such as "Balancing Pluralism" and "General Political Exchange". Although an extensive discussion is beyond the scope of this paper, a basic understanding of the model will be helpful in advancing our comprehension of the connections between restorative justice, societal development and human well being. The model initially had three polar points but was subsequently modified to include four points. It stipulates that there are four crucial foci that have a major impact on the well-being of people in society.

One, is the role of the (mixed market) economy; the second, is the role of the State; the third, is the Household (referred to as Household rather than Family due to the range of patterns of basic units); and the last, is the

7 A. EVERS, H. WINTERSBERGER (1990) (eds.), *Shifts in the Welfare Mix*, European Centre for Social Welfare Policy and Research, Vienna. Frankfurt am Main/Boulder, Co: Campus Verlag/Westview Press.

community. Underlying this model are the value assumptions of society. The value assumptions will have a primary influence on the balance between the four elements. The question then, is not "are you left or right, socialist or capitalist?", but "what is the nature of the mix to address the well being of society and its citizens - assuming that their well being is the concern?" If well-being of the citizens is not the primary concern, the model can clearly identify that as well.

The Scandinavian countries are members of the Centre, and they have made important contributions to the development of the model. They have for decades attempted to blend the best of socialism and capitalism. In the references to the work done by the Centre on seniors and children, comparative work was done between countries using this model.

There have been additional initiatives in using the model. A graduate student, Brenda Stinson at the University of Regina reformulated the model for use in examining initiatives in the Canadian aboriginal community and developments in the Ukraine following the major changes in the last decade of the twentieth century in that country. The model has not been restructured for application in the field of criminal justice, although it would lend itself well to such an application.

The dominance of the State in criminal justice is clear. The restorative justice paradigm is a radical shift of balance toward the community and the household. It is also well known that poverty; poor housing and inadequate support services are important correlates of crime. Therefore, major work needs to be done in examining justice services and the restorative justice initiatives in the light of the Welfare Mix model.

The next logical step is to address the criminal justice system.

4. The criminal justice system

Each segment of the criminal justice system has been experimenting with alternatives to current practices. One of the early books documenting such initiatives is the book by Tutt, *Alternative Strategies of Coping with Crime*. In it are many examples of alternatives being developed, particularly in the corrections field.

In the area of juvenile delinquency the alternative paradigms that were in use in Massachusetts and Saskatchewan are discussed. In Massachusetts, the assumption was that the current system could not be reformed because new initiatives would always be subverted by the system, so a new model was substituted.[8] The Saskatchewan model was an alternative pattern of dealing with youth under age 16 through the Family and Child Welfare rather than through the criminal justice system.[9]

Both models have since been abolished. Canadian law changed in such a way that Saskatchewan no longer had the flexibility to use an alternative model. The Young Offenders' Act in Canada moved the juvenile system back strongly into the traditional criminal justice system. It then developed possibilities of diversion from the system in recognition of the need for alternatives. The tragedy was, that the context and orientation of services to youth reverted to the existing adult criminal justice model. Current changes from the "Young Offenders Act" to the "Youth Criminal Justice Act" complete the transition back to the Criminal Justice model. The paradox is that in adult criminal justice legislation and policy Canada is moving to a restorative justice model while in youth justice it is reverting to a criminal justice model.

There were also examples of alternatives to adult corrections. In other segments of the criminal justice system, experimentation with alternatives developed later. Community policing gained momentum in the 1980's and '90's. Law reform has a long history and legal aid developed in the 1970's, but initiatives in alternative paradigms in the court process, such as sentencing circles, only developed in the 1980's and gained some momentum in the 1990's. These initiatives however, are still in the very early stages and judges who experiment with alternatives are still on the periphery, and are often marginalized.

Serious questions arise with regard to incorporation of restorative justice initiatives into the criminal justice system. On the one hand, it is encouraging to see alternative initiatives being incorporated in a way that humanizes the system and makes it more responsive to human development and well being. On the other hand, if all initiatives in restorative justice are co-opted into the system without a basic switch and commitment to the assumptions underlying restorative justice, one ends up with a more humanized system, which is good, but with no basic change in the philosophical approach. This would mean that creative development of alternatives would be strictly confined to the limits of the present system.

This pattern is already emerging in some jurisdictions. In Saskatchewan, Canada, for example, the provincial Government has accepted restorative justice as an important perspective and new approaches are being developed. The Restorative Justice Division of the Government, however, has a

8 N. Tutt (1978) *Alternative Strategies for Coping with Crime.* Oxford/London: Blackwell/Martin Robertson.

9 *Ibid.*

proscriptive approach to understanding restorative justice, which inhibits flexibility and creativity in developing alternatives based on the value assumptions of restorative justice.

If a jurisdiction were serious about experimentation with restorative justice as a paradigm shift, it would have to develop an approach that would be at arm's length from the existing criminal justice system, and not under the control of that system. If this initiative is not taken and if restorative justice simply takes the form of modifications to the existing system, then restorative justice becomes merely a continuation of the initiatives referred to in Tutt's book, that is alternative strategies within the existing system, and not an alternative paradigm/system.

Even under such circumstances, this author could not see the restorative justice paradigm operating as the sole model, but would prefer to see it operating as a parallel system with the current system of criminal justice. There are encouraging developments in New Zealand and Canada along those lines. However, in Canada it appears that present developments are closely tied to the existing system. Hopefully, it will still be possible for parallel systems to develop.

Restorative justice developments in the Non Governmental Organization (NGO) sector is another pattern that is gaining momentum and is frequently overwhelmed by requests for service. This indicates that there is substantial positive response to the alternative approaches. The funding however, cannot be done only on a volunteer basis if these initiatives are to become a solid parallel system.

5. Societal development, human well-being and restorative justice

In this essay we have identified the fragmentation in societies and a criminal justice system that further alienates and fragments communities and people. The justice system is beginning to recognize its negative impact. Experimentation with alternative measures and approaches has occurred in the past several decades. Some jurisdictions have begun to use restorative justice terminology, others have incorporated some of its concepts and principles and some have "co-opted" restorative justice.

Restorative justice is based on principles of healing, reconciliation, taking responsibility for actions and behaviour and addressing issues that affect offenders, victims and the community.

Maslow's hierarchy of needs identifies the importance of access to basic necessities, satisfying interpersonal relationships, recognition and self-fulfilment as essential and fundamental to human well being.

Stinnett and DeFrain,[10] in the research they did for their book *Secrets of Strong Families* identify six basic strengths for strong families. These are: Commitment, Appreciation, Communication, Time together, Spiritual Wellness, and Coping with Crises and Stress. They suggest that these factors form the "Circle of Power" for families. Similarly, healthy communities require social cohesion, concern for the well being of all members of the community, fairness, structure and vision. Restorative justice builds on the strengths of people and communities and as a result enhances both societal development and human well-being.

Conclusion: Potential for the future

Restorative justice is not only a justice issue, but also an issue of enhancement of the quality of life.

The possibilities and potential for future development and growth of restorative justice alternatives are great. The benefits to societies developing such approaches will enhance positive societal development, improve the quality of life for citizens and families and strengthen communities and the society. It can enhance positive identity for minorities, and be inclusive of minorities as citizens and as legitimate communities in the context of the larger societal identity.

Increasing mobility and communication in the era of globalisation means that Nation States are becoming multicultural and Nation States themselves are changing in their roles and degree of control in the light of power blocs such as the EC, NAFTA and multinational corporations. Many multinational corporations have greater resources and power than most Nation States. In our present kind of world, a justice model that is inclusive, that enhances societal cohesion and respects human dignity whether victim or offender, holds a great deal of promise.

10 N. Stinnett and J. DeFrain (1976) *Secrets of Strong Families.* New York: Berkley Books.

References

A&E Documentary Video: *Behind Bars*. Produced by 44 Blue Productions, Inc. and Actuality Productions, Inc. for A&E Network. Executive Producers Gerald W. Abrams and Rasha Drachkovitch. Directors/Writers Lasta Drachkovitch and Rob Engelhardt. Host /Narrator Bill Kurtis. A&E Supervising Producer Gayle Gilman, A&E Executive Producer Michael Cascio.

Evers, A., Farrant, W., Trojan, A. (1990) (eds.), *Healthy Public Policy at the Local Level,* European Centre for Social Welfare Policy and Research, Vienna. Frankfurt am Main/Boulder, Co: Campus Verlag/Westview Press.

Evers, A. Pijl, M., Ungerson, C. (1994) (eds.), *Payments for Care*, European Centre Vienna. Aldershot, England: Ashgate.

Evers, A., Wintersberger, H. (1990) (eds.), *Shifts in the Welfare Mix*, European Centre for Social Welfare Policy and Research, Vienna. Frankfurt am Main/Boulder, Co: Campus Verlag/Westview Press.

Gammon, Mary Alice B. (1978) *Violence in Canada.* Toronto: Methuen.

Girard, Rene (1978) *Things Hidden since the Foundation of the World.* Stanford California: Stanford University Press.

Kenis, Patrick (1992) *The Social Construction of an Industry*, European Centre for Social Welfare Policy and Research, Vienna. Frankfurt am Main/Boulder, Co: CampusVerlag/Westview Press.

Kly, Y.N. (1997) *Societal Development and Minority Rights*. Ottawa, Canada: Clarity Press Inc.

Kraan, Robbert J., Baldock, John, Davies, Bleddyn, Evers, Adalbert, Johansson, Lennarth, Knapen, Martin, Thorslund, Mats, Tunissen, Catherine (1991) *Care for the Elderly,* European Centre for Social Welfare Policy and Research., Vienna. Frankfurt am Main/Boulder, Co: Campus Verlag-Westview Press.

Stinnett, Nick and DeFrain, John (1976) *Secrets of Strong Families.* New York: Berkley Books.

Swartley, Willard M. (2000) *Violence Renounced.* Telford, Penn/Scottdale, Penn: Pandora Press/Herald Press.

Tutt, Norman (1978) *Alternative Strategies for Coping with Crime.* Oxford/London: Blackwell/Martin Robertson.

Qvortrup, Jens, Bardy, Marjatta, Sgritta, Giovanni, Wintersberger, Helmut (1994) (eds.), *Childhood Matters.* Aldershot, England: Ashgate.

RESTORATIVE JUSTICE AND CRIME REDUCTION: ARE POLICY-MAKERS BARKING UP THE WRONG TREE?

Jim Dignan

Introduction

Restorative justice approaches have experienced a phenomenal growth over the last quarter of a century and, as the contributions to this volume attest, their influence now extends far beyond the criminal justice system.[1] Nevertheless it is within the criminal justice system that restorative justice approaches have made the greatest impact to date, by shaping the development of mainstream criminal justice policies in a growing number of countries around the world, particularly though by no means exclusively, with regard to juvenile offenders. Although there are many factors that have contributed to the remarkable expansion of restorative justice initiatives in recent years, one of the principal reasons for their appeal to criminal justice policy-makers lies in their perceived potential to contribute to a crime reduction strategy by reducing the rate of reoffending.

In this short essay I will briefly chart the changing fortunes of the restorative justice movement in England and Wales and will set out the theoretical claims that help to explain its growing attraction for penal policy-makers before reviewing the current state of the empirical evidence from around the world. Even though it is too soon to reach a definitive conclusion with regard to restorative justice's potential to contribute to lower reconviction rates, I will nevertheless argue that the current emphasis by penal policy-makers on this particular aspect of restorative justice may be misplaced. For however effective restorative justice interventions with individual offenders might prove to be, the scope for achieving significant reductions in overall levels of offending is likely to be severely limited by the many operational constraints to which restorative justice processes and, indeed, all forms of criminal justice interventions are subject. As for the policy implications to be drawn from this analysis, I will suggest that this is not an argument for policy-makers to lose interest in restorative justice-inspired reforms of the existing criminal justice system, nor its potential

1 J. DIGNAN (with K. LOWEY) (2000) *Restorative Justice Options for Northern Ireland,* Research Report No. 10. Belfast: Criminal Justice Review Commission/Northern Ireland Office.

contribution to the goal of crime reduction. However I would argue that this latter potential is more likely to be realised by harnessing the theoretical insights that underpin restorative justice approaches in the criminal justice sphere to the development and evaluation of much broader social crime prevention strategies that are themselves informed by restorative justice principles. I will conclude by examining some tentative developments in English social policy in recent years that might be consistent with such an agenda even though the connection with restorative justice principles appears to have been overlooked, and despite the fact that no attempt has yet been made to measure or even assess their crime reductive potential.

1. The changing fortunes of the restorative justice movement in England and Wales

During the mid 1980s, criminal justice policy makers in England and Wales showed a brief flicker of interest in the approach that has subsequently become known as restorative justice by funding and evaluating a small number of experimental victim offender mediation and reparation schemes. The initiative was practitioner-led rather than theory-driven and, perhaps for that reason, little emphasis was placed on its crime reduction potential, either in the aims of the schemes or in the Home Office funded short-term evaluation studies that were conducted in the early days of the initiative.[2] Government interest in the approach proved short-lived, however, following a succession of critical early research studies[3] and disagreements both within the Home Office and between the Home Office and those responsible for the experimental schemes over the role that mediation and reparation might play within the criminal justice system.[4] Several of the schemes themselves continued to eke out a somewhat precarious existence on the margins of the criminal justice system in spite of these setbacks but their influence on mainstream criminal justice policies remained insignificant.

---

2 T.F. MARSHALL and S. MERRY (1990) *Crime and Accountability: Victim-Offender Mediation in Practice*. London: HMSO.

3 See for example, G. DAVIS, J. BOUCHERAT, J. and D. WATSON (1988) Reparation in the Service of Diversion: The Subordination of a Good Idea, 27 *Howard Journal of Criminal Justice* 127-262; G. DAVIS, J. BOUCHERAT and D. WATSON (1989) Pre-court Decision-making in Juvenile Justice, 29 *British Journal of Criminology* 219-35.

4 G. DAVIS (1992) *Making Amends: Mediation and Reparation in Criminal Justice*. London and New York: Routledge.

Shortly after the 1997 general election, however, the prospects for restorative justice were transformed following the adoption of a radical new agenda for dealing with youth crime.[5] The key features of this new agenda for present purposes consisted of the incorporation of a new statutory 'principal aim' for the youth justice system, which is to prevent offending by children and young persons,[6] the creation of a new institutional framework based on multi-agency youth offending teams in each local authority area with responsibility for co-ordinating services and delivering youth justice interventions,[7] the creation of a new national agency –the Youth Justice Board– to monitor the operation of the youth justice system, promote good practice, set national standards and advise the Home Secretary on how the system is functioning,[8] and the promotion of an evidence-based culture that is intended to both inform and monitor youth justice practice.

A number of new measures for dealing with crime committed by young offenders were also introduced at around the same time, several of which are informed at least to some extent by the philosophy of restorative justice.[9] They include, firstly, a new set of diversionary 'admonitory' measures, known as 'reprimands' and 'final warnings',[10] that have now replaced the long-standing and non-statutory practice of cautioning of offenders under the age of 18. The reprimand is seen as a less formal measure that is aimed

5 J. DIGNAN (1999) The Crime and Disorder Act and the Prospects for Restorative Justice; *Criminal Law Review* 48-60; M. CAVADINO, I. CROW and J. DIGNAN (1999) *Criminal Justice 2000*. Winchester: Waterside Press.

6 Section 37 of the Crime and Disorder Act 1998.

7 Section 39 of the Crime and Disorder Act 1998.

8 Section 41 of the Crime and Disorder Act 1998.

9 The term 'restorative justice' is not restricted to a particular approach or programme, and it may be helpful to think of a continuum of approaches, from those with a relatively narrow perspective – with regard to the participants who are eligible to take part, the type of process they favour and the particular goals they adopt – to those in which the perspective is much broader. For further discussion see J. DIGNAN and P. MARSH (2001) Restorative Justice and Family Group Conferences in England: Current State and Future Prospects, in: A. MORRIS and G. MAXWELL (eds.), *Restorative Justice for Juveniles: Conferencing, Mediation and Circles*. Oxford: Hart Publishing.

10 Sections 65 and 66 of the Crime and Disorder Act 1998. These and the other youth justice measures that were introduced by the Crime and Disorder Act were initially piloted before being 'rolled out' nationally in June 2000. For results of the pilot evaluation see S. HOLDAWAY, N. DAVIDSON, J. DIGNAN, R. HAMMERSLEY, J. HINE and P. MARSH (2000) *New Strategies to Address Youth Offending: the National Evaluation of the Pilot Youth Offending Teams,* RDS Occasional Paper No. 69. London: Research, Development and Statistics Directorate.

at first time non-serious offenders. The final warning was originally envisaged as a more formal measure suitable for offenders who have already been reprimanded, or whose offences are too serious for a reprimand. In addition to being warned, young offenders are also assessed by the youth offending team to see if they might benefit from a 'rehabilitation' or 'change' programme, the contents of which are intended to address their offending behaviour, but which could include some form of reparation for either the victim or the community. Before the national introduction of these new warning measures the Thames Valley police had already replaced their old-style police cautions with a new-style of 'restorative cautioning' process that was strongly influenced by the police-led conferencing procedures developed in Australia and elsewhere.[11] Just before the youth justice reforms were 'rolled out' nationally in June 2000, the Home Office issued new guidelines for reprimands and final warnings,[12] which encouraged the new youth offending teams to make more systematic use of this kind of restorative justice approach when delivering both reprimands and final warnings.

The new-style reprimands and warnings were originally envisaged as a two-rung pre-prosecution tariff, the idea being that offenders would normally be given at most one reprimand, then one (final) warning before being prosecuted. Since their introduction, however, a second set of restorative justice-inspired measures has been introduced[13] that will effectively add an additional rung to this pre-prosecution tariff for most young offenders. When dealing with offenders aged 10-17 who plead guilty and are convicted for the first time youth courts will be obliged to impose a

---

11 R. YOUNG and B. GOOLD (1999) Restorative Police Cautioning in Aylesbury: from Degrading to Reintegrative Shaming Ceremonies?; *Criminal Law Review* 126; R. YOUNG (2000) Integrating a Multi-Victim Perspective through Restorative Justice Conferences?, in: A. CRAWFORD and J. GOODEY (eds.), *Integrating a Victim Perspective within Criminal Justice*. Aldershot: Ashgate; R. YOUNG (2001) Just Cops doing Shameful Business?: Police-led Restorative Justice and the Lessons of Research, in: MORRIS and MAXWELL, *o.c.*

12 Home Office (2000) *The Final Warning Scheme: Guidance for Youth Offending Teams.* London: Home Office. Also available on-line at: http://www.homeoffice.gov.uk/cdact/yotguide.htm

13 Under the Youth Justice and Criminal Evidence Act 1999. Like the youth justice reforms introduced under the Crime and Disorder Act, these new measures are also being piloted and will be evaluated over 18 months, commencing in March 2000 before a national roll-out that is expected to commence in 2002. For the first interim report of the pilot evaluation see NEWBURN et al. (2001) *The Introduction of Referral Orders into the Youth Justice System*, RDS Occasional Paper No. 70. London: Research, Development and Statistics Directorate.

new sentencing disposal known as the 'referral order'.[14] The effect will be to assign the case to a newly created 'youth offender panel' that will consist of three members: one representing the local youth offending team; the other two drawn from a panel of community volunteers.

The aim of the panel is to provide a forum away from the formality of the court, in which the young person, the family and, where appropriate, the victim of an offence, will be able to reflect on the offence and its consequences. The panel's rôle will be to encourage the parties to agree a contract that will include reparation for either the victim or the community and a programme of activity that is designed to prevent further offending. It is important to note that where a young person is referred to a youth offender panel this will constitute the only sentence that may be imposed for the relevant offence, which means that it cannot be combined with any other disposal.[15] The government has indicated that it expects the work of the youth offender panels to be governed by the principles 'underlying the concept of restorative justice': defined as 'restoration, reintegration and responsibility'.[16] Moreover, once a young person has satisfactorily completed the agreement, the panel (not the court) discharges the referral order, the effect of which will be to purge the offence, which will be regarded as spent for the purposes of the Rehabilitation of Offenders Act. This underlines the extent to which the new referral order procedure is intended to reflect restorative justice thinking. It also represents a significant shift towards a more socially reintegrative approach and stands in marked contrast to the open-ended form of stigmatic shaming that has long characterised more conventional forms of retributive punishment.

For young offenders who *are* prosecuted and convicted, the Crime and Disorder Act 1998 expanded the range of existing sentencing disposals by introducing a third set of measures that also incorporate some elements of a restorative justice approach.[17] They include, firstly, the reparation order, which requires young offenders (aged between 10 and 17) to undertake some form of reparation either to their victim (provided the latter consents) or to the community at large. This is envisaged as a routine low-tariff 'entry-level' disposal for young offenders, since the courts are required to

---

14 The only exceptions relate to offenders who are dealt with by means of an absolute discharge, or those for whom the court decides to impose a custodial sentence.

15 DIGNAN & MARSH, *o.c.*

16 Home Office (1997) *No More Excuses – A New Approach to Tackling Youth Crime in England and Wales*. Cm 3809. London: Home Office.

17 J. DIGNAN (1999) The Crime and Disorder Act and the Prospects for Restorative Justice, *o.c.*; HOLDAWAY et al., *o.c.*

give reasons for *not* imposing a reparation order. A second new disposal is the Action Plan Order, which comprises a three month supervised programme of intensive and highly focused community intervention that is intended to combine 'punishment, rehabilitation and reparation'.[18] This is a higher tariff penalty than the reparation order, and is intended to be used for young offenders whose offending is serious enough to warrant a 'community punishment', as opposed to a lower tariff financial or warning penalty. Finally, the Crime and Disorder Act also amended the existing supervision order by enabling courts to impose an additional requirement that offenders should make reparation either to their victim or the community at large.[19]

Cumulatively, these developments represent a significant shift in direction for the youth justice system in England and Wales, which is now much more strongly influenced by restorative justice principles than seemed likely as recently as five years ago. Nor is the change in direction confined to young offenders. In 2001 the government committed funds for the development and evaluation of three separate innovative restorative justice programmes aimed at adult offenders and their victims. One of the schemes involves a mediation-based restorative justice programme and is operated by a voluntary sector organisation.[20] A second scheme involves post-conviction conferences between victim, offender and their supporters or, alternatively, indirect victim-offender mediation, for adult offenders who are sentenced at one magistrates' court covering two boroughs in the Inner London area. The scheme is being developed by a statutory agency and a not-for-profit organisation[21] and makes use of an existing sentencing disposal known as the deferred sentence, which enables courts to adjourn a case for up to six months before passing sentence, thereby enabling it to have regard to the offender's conduct (including the making of reparation) in the meantime. The third scheme, which is also the most complex, involves a series of random allocation experiments[22] being carried out in at least six sites at many stages of the criminal justice process (including offenders who are serving a custodial sentence) with both adults and young

---

18 Home Office guidance issued in 1998 stated unequivocally that 'reparative activity should be one of the requirements of the Action Plan Order wherever possible' (para. 3.10).

19 Section 71.

20 REMEDI, which will be operating in the South Yorkshire area.

21 The Inner London Probation Service and the National Association for the Care and Resettlement of Offenders, respectively.

22 The same methodology is being used in the RISE experiments, described below.

offenders and using different kinds of facilitators. This scheme involves a number of different criminal justice agencies in London, Sunderland and Thames Valley, and is being co-ordinated under the auspices of the Justice Research Consortium.

The principal reason for the dramatic revival of government interest in restorative justice over the last few years relates to its perceived relevance for the government's Crime Reduction Strategy, which was published on 29 November, 1999. This wide-ranging strategy was linked to a three-year £250 million programme, the aim of which is to take an evidence-based approach to reducing crime in England and Wales. With the exception of the police-funded Thames Valley restorative conferencing initiative, all of the above developments, both in the youth justice and adult offender spheres, are linked to the Crime Reduction Programme, funding for which was agreed by the Treasury because of its perceived relevance for crime reduction. Not surprisingly, therefore, one of the primary objectives for each of the ongoing evaluation studies that have been commissioned to date in respect of the three main sets of restorative justice initiatives[23] is to examine the impact of restorative justice on levels of reoffending. Although each of the evaluations has adopted a much broader focus encompassing a variety of other aims apart from crime reduction, the fact remains that government support for restorative justice on such a significant scale would almost certainly not have been forthcoming but for its perceived potential in contributing to a reduction in reoffending. In the next section I will briefly examine the basis for this perception and (without wishing to pre-empt the outcome of the ongoing English evaluations) will also summarise the limited empirical evidence that is currently available relating to the effect of restorative justice interventions on reoffending and recidivism rates.

23 Namely: i) the new youth justice interventions introduced under the Crime and Disorder Act, for which the reconviction study is still ongoing, even though the 'final report' on the piloting process has now been published (HOLDAWAY et al., *o.c.*); ii) the referral order evaluation (which has so far published an interim evaluation: (T. NEWBURN, G. MASTERS, R. EARLE, S. GOLDIE, A. CRAWFORD, K. SHARPE, A. NETTEN, C. HALE; S. UGLOW and R. SAUNDERS (2001) *The Introduction of Referral Orders into the Youth Justice System*, RDS Occasional Paper No. 70. London: Research, Development and Statistics Directorate) and iii) the 3 schemes for adult offenders, which are to be evaluated by a team based at Sheffield University, under the direction of Professor Shapland.

2. Assessing restorative justice's potential to reduce levels of reoffending

The theoretical grounds for surmising that restorative justice interventions could reduce reoffending levels are chiefly derived from John Braithwaite's now well-known theory of reintegrative shaming.[24] The theory posits that conventional criminal justice responses to crime tend to stigmatise offenders, not just the offences they have committed. This has the effect of excluding them (either literally or metaphorically) from the community and, as a result, makes it more difficult for them to lead law-abiding lives as responsible members of that same community. Conversely, it argues that restorative justice interventions which rely on techniques for shaming offenders 'reintegratively' within a community of care are more likely to avoid these negative consequences. They do so, firstly, by mobilising sentiments of shame around the misdeeds for which an offender is responsible rather than the offender as a person, and then by seeking to re-engage or strengthen the offender's ties with the rest of the community once the shaming process is at an end.

The theory of reintegrative shaming also draws indirect support from the work of Tom Tyler[25] and others who have demonstrated that people who feel they have been fairly treated by the criminal justice system are more likely to obey the law in future than those who don't. Sherman's[26] findings - that offenders who experienced formal criminal justice interventions were more likely to reoffend than those diverted to informal processes, especially when the court process made the offender more defiant of conventional society – are consistent with Tyler's work. So, too, even more relevantly, are the more recent RISE findings that offenders who are randomly assigned restorative justice conferences are much more satisfied with the procedural fairness of their treatment than those who are randomly allocated to court proceedings.[27]

---

24 J. BRAITHWAITE (1989) *Crime, Shame and Reintegration.* Cambridge: Cambridge University Press.

25 T. TYLER (1990) *Why People Obey the Law.* New Haven: Yale University Press.

26 L. SHERMAN (1993) Defiance, Deterrence and Irrelevance: A Theory of the Criminal Sanction, 31(4) *Journal of Research in Crime and Delinquency* 445-73.

27 L. SHERMAN, H. STRANG and D.J. WOOD (2000) *Recidivism Patterns in the Canberra Reintegrative Shaming Experiments (RISE).* Canberra: Centre for Restorative Justice, Australian National University. Available on-line at: http://ww.aic.gov.au/rjustice/rise/recidivism/index.html

Studies that have sought to directly assess the impact of restorative justice interventions on recidivism rates, however, have mainly tended to produce inconclusive or equivocal findings. As Kurki reports, attempts to measure the impact of victim offender mediation on levels of recidivism rates to date have mainly been confined to youth programmes, and most of these have shown that mediation neither decreases nor increases recidivism. Of half a dozen U.S. studies using matched control groups, only one[28] found a statistically significant reduction in reoffending following mediation, but offenders in this study were only tracked for one year, and only limited controls were employed.[29] The only study cited by Kurki to use random sampling showed no difference in reoffending between mediation and court cases.[30]

The effect of family group conferencing on recidivism rates has been more intensively studied to date, though the results are still mixed and fail to consistently support the hypothesis generated by Braithwaite's theory of reintegrative shaming. The first study on conferencing that set out to measure the impact of restorative justice on recidivism rates using a random allocation methodology[31] involved the Bethlehem police-led conferencing initiative.[32] The Bethlehem study was confined to first-time juvenile offenders who were arrested for relatively minor misdemeanour and summary offences. Recidivism rates were monitored over a twelve-month period beginning with the arrest that preceded the adjudication or conference. However, the study concluded that (as with the majority of victim offender evaluations) the conferencing process had no independent effect on a person's propensity to reoffend. Although there was a difference in recidivism rates between the conference and control groups, this was felt

---

28 W.R. NUGENT and J.B. PADDOCK (1995) The effect of victim-offender mediation on severity of reoffense, 12(4) *Mediation Quarterly* 353-67.

29 Matching on the basis of offence type and admission of guilt; see J. DIGNAN (2000) *o.c.*

30 R.C. DAVIS, M. TICHANE and D. GRAYSON (1980) *Mediation and Arbitration as Alternatives to Prosecution in Felony Arrest Cases: An Evaluation of the Brooklyn Dispute Resolution Centre.* New York: Vera Institute of Justice.

31 Cases were randomly assigned to courts (control group) or conference (treatment group) irrespective of an offender's willingness to participate in a conference. Since participation was voluntary, however, this generated a third category of cases in which the conference did not take place because either victim or offender declined to participate.

32 P. MCCOLD and B. WACHTEL (1998) *Restorative Policing Experiment: The Bethlehem Pennsylvania Police Family Group Conferencing Project.* Pipersville, Pa: Community Service Foundation.

to be a product of the offender's positive attitude towards conferencing rather than the conferencing process itself.[33]

A second study that has also measured the impact of police-led conferencing processes on recidivism rates for different groups of offenders using a random allocation methodology[34] is the large-scale Reintegrative Shaming Experiment (RISE) being conducted in Canberra. Recidivism rates were monitored over a 12-month period from assignment to the programme (or control group) in respect of four different categories of cases involving offenders of different ages. They comprised 'drink driving' cases (all age groups); violent offences (involving offenders under 30 years of age, so not confined to youth offenders only); juvenile shoplifting (restricted to offenders under the age of 18) and other juvenile property crime (also restricted to offenders under the age of 18).

The preliminary findings showed a marked reduction in recidivism rates in respect of the violent offence group comprising youths and younger adults who were assigned to diversionary conferences, for whom the net rate of reoffending was 38 per cent lower than the control group assigned to court. While this was significant at the 0.16 level, however, it does not satisfy the more stringent tests for statistical significance at the 0.1 or 0.05 levels that are conventionally insisted upon. The two categories of juvenile property offences (involving personal victims or retail store victims respectively) showed no differences in offending rates between the conference groups and court (control) groups. The any-age drink driving group who were assigned to conferences registered a slightly higher reoffending rate compared with the control group, though it was felt that this might have been attributable to an 'incapacitative effect' resulting from the power of the court (but not conferences) to suspend driving licences in such cases.[35]

A third study that has investigated the impact of police-led conferencing on recidivism rates for juvenile offenders charged with minor offences (assault, trespass, criminal mischief, shoplifting and theft) in Indianapolis is the only one so far to show a statistically significant reduction in recidivism

---

33 *Ibid.*

34 The random allocation methodology used for the RISE project differed from the Bethlehem study (note 14 above) in that cases were assigned to either treatment or control group only after the offender had indicated that they would be willing to take part in the project.

35 SHERMAN, STRANG & WOOD, *o.c.*

rates.[36] Although the study used a similar random allocation technique, however, the comparison group consisted of offenders who were referred to other court-ordered diversion programmes (including victim offender mediation), so no conclusions can be drawn about the relative effectiveness of restorative justice approaches as opposed to conventional criminal justice processes.[37]

As yet there have been no comparable studies using random allocation (or even matched control) techniques to measure the impact on recidivism rates in respect of the rather different style of family group conferencing that is practised in New Zealand.[38] This is not surprising since it would be difficult if not impossible to undertake such a study within a system in which restorative justice approaches have been 'mainstreamed' as part of the regular criminal justice system. Instead, the approach that has been adopted there has involved interviews together with a sophisticated statistical analysis of the reconviction records of a sample of those who had taken part in a family group conference between 1990-1.[39] The findings suggest that aspects of the conference itself – notably a sense of remorse, active participation in the conference decision-making process, meeting the victim and perceiving the conference outcome to be fair – were key factors in accounting for reductions in reoffending.[40] While these findings are

---

36 E. McGarrell, K. Olivares, K. Crawford and N. Kroovand (2000) *Returning justice to the community: the Indianapolis Juvenile Restorative Justice Experiment.* Indianapolis: Hudson Institute.

37 For those who successfully completed the conferencing programme, recidivism rates after six months (measured in terms of new arrests) were 46 per cent lower than for the control group, which is significant at the 0.05 level.

38 The New Zealand model of family group conferencing differs from the Australian variant in a number of important respects. In particular, it is legislatively prescribed as a 'mainstream' response to youth offending, does not use police facilitators nor the 'scripted' approach that is associated with the Australian variant and does not involve victims in the decision-making process that culminates in the 'action plan' for the offender. See Morris et al. (1993) Giving Victims a Voice: A New Zealand Experiment, 32(4) *The Howard Journal* 304-21; J. Dignan, *o.c.*

39 G. Maxwell and A. Morris (1999) *Understanding Reoffending.* Wellington: Institute of Criminology, Victoria University of Wellington; G. Maxwell and A. Morris (2001) Family Group Conferences and Reoffending, in: Morris and Maxwell, *o.c.*

40 The South Australia Juvenile Justice Evaluation (SAJJ) also found that young people who were remorseful in the conference or who agreed with the outcome were less likely to offend K. Daly and H. Hayes (2001) Restorative justice and conferencing in Australia, *Trends & Issues in Crime and Criminal Justice No. 186.* Canberra: Australian Institute of Criminology.
http://www.aic.gov.au/publications/tandi/tandi186.html. K. Daley (forthcoming) Mind the Gap: Restorative Justice in Theory and Practice, in: A.E. Bottoms, J. Roberts and

clearly in line with Braithwaite's theory of reintegrative shaming, they are also subject to the same caveat as the Bethlehem findings referred to earlier: that they may be a product of the offender's positive attitude towards conferencing rather than the conferencing process itself.

On the basis of the evidence that has been reviewed so far, and despite some promising early indications, it would perhaps be unrealistic to expect restorative justice initiatives to produce massive reductions in reoffending compared with conventional criminal justice responses. It is, of course, possible that the mixed results to date reflect implementational shortcomings and deficiencies in evaluative research techniques[41] as opposed to limitations in the theory and practice of restorative justice approaches themselves. But even when due allowance is made for these possibilities, it would be wise to exercise caution when assessing the potential for restorative justice initiatives to make a significant contribution to a given crime reduction strategy by reducing reoffending rates. The need for caution stems from the multiple operational constraints to which restorative justice responses to crime are inevitably subject.

3. Constraints on restorative justice's capacity to reduce reoffending levels

Whatever advantages restorative justice responses to crime may offer (with regard to offenders, victims and the wider community) compared with conventional responses, they are nevertheless subject to a number of operational constraints that are likely to severely limit their capacity to reduce overall offending levels. Some of these constraints are common to all forms of criminal justice-based approaches, but it is still worth emphasising them because they are all-too-frequently overlooked. Other constraints are specific to restorative justice approaches, at least as currently conceptualised.

One unpalatable but undeniable operational constraint to which restorative justice approaches are no less subject than other criminal justice responses stems from the fact that the vast majority of offences do not result in an offender being apprehended and dealt with at all. The 'rate of attrition'

A. von Hirsch (eds.), *Restorative Justice and Criminal Justice: Theory and Conflict.* Oxford: Hart Publishing.

41 L. Kurki (forthcoming) Evaluation of restorative justice practices, in: Bottoms, Roberts and von Hirsch, *o.c.*

within the criminal justice system is such that of all offences against individuals and their property that are committed in England and Wales each year, only just over two in every hundred result in a conviction.[42] This has serious implications for restorative justice's capacity to deliver whatever potential benefits it might theoretically be capable of, including its capacity to prevent further crime by reducing recidivism rates.

Quite apart from the operational limits to which all forms of criminal justice interventions are subject, restorative justice processes such as victim offender mediation and conferencing are also subject to additional procedural or functional constraints. The most fundamental limiting principle relates to the need for informed consent on the part of victims and offenders. But this raises an important question regarding the extent to which parties, particularly victims, may be willing to participate in informal restorative justice processes; and what should happen in cases where they are unwilling to do so.[43]

Although very high victim participation rates have been reported for some Australian police-led conferencing initiatives,[44] other studies have reported much lower levels of victim participation. They include the early New Zealand evaluations of family group conferencing, where victims attended only half the conferences[45] and also the Bethlehem police-led conferencing project, where the victim participation rate was 42 per cent.[46]

---

42 G. BARCLAY and C. TAVARES (1999) *Digest 4: Information on the Criminal Justice System in England and Wales*. London: Home Office Research, Development and Statistics Directorate. The figure rises to three in every hundred if offences resulting in a caution are also included. Of the offences that are recorded by the British crime survey, fewer than half are reported to the police, fewer than one quarter are recorded by the police and only just over one in twenty are cleared up.

43 J. DIGNAN (2001) Reparation Orders, Ch. 5, in: B. WILLIAMS (ed.), *Reparation and Victim-Focused Social Work*. London: Jessica Kingsley (forthcoming).

44 Notably the Canberra RISE experiment, for which the reported rate of victim participation is 85 per cent: J. BRAITHWAITE (1999) Restorative Justice: Assessing Optimistic and Pessimistic Accounts, 25 *Crime and Justice: A Review of Research* 1; and also the Wagga Wagga conferencing evaluation, which reported a victim participation rate exceeding 90 per cent: D.B. MOORE and T. O'CONNELL (1994) Family Group Conferencing in Wagga Wagga: A Communitarian Model of Justice, in: C. ALDER and J. WUNDERSITZ (eds.), *Family Conferencing and Juvenile Justice*. Canberra: Australian Studies in Law, Crime and Justice, Australian Institute of Criminology.

45 G. MAXWELL and A. MORRIS (1996) Research on Family Group Conferences with Young Offenders in New Zealand, in: J. HUDSON, A. MORRIS, G. MAXWELL and B. GALAWAY (eds.), *Family Group Conferences: Perspectives on Policy and Practice*. Sydney: Federation Press and Criminal Justice Press.

46 MCCOLD and WACHTEL, *o.c.*

However, the victim participation rate for most restorative justice-style processes in England and Wales has been lower still, and in most cases has been less than 10 per cent. For example, Umbreit and Roberts[47] reported that of all referrals to two English Victim Offender Mediation Projects (Coventry and Leeds) during 1993, only 7 per cent participated in direct (face to face) mediation. Likewise, of the reparation orders made under the Crime and Disorder Act 1998 during the piloting phase, only 9 per cent involved direct mediation between victims and offenders.[48] A similarly low rate of victim participation has also been reported in relation to the new youth offender panels.[49] Provisional and as yet unconfirmed reports indicate that the levels of victim participation in the police-led Thames Valley restorative cautioning project are also likely to be much closer to those encountered in other restorative justice processes in England and Wales than to its Australian or North American counterparts.

Such figures are a matter of concern partly because they raise serious doubts about the proportion of criminal cases in which a fully participatory restorative justice process would present a viable alternative to the regular criminal justice system, at least in jurisdictions such as England and Wales. But they are particularly disappointing if participation on the part of victims is indeed one of the factors that is associated with lower reconviction rates following restorative justice interventions, as suggested by some of the reconviction studies referred to above.

The fact that victim participation figures in England and Wales are significantly lower than those recorded in other jurisdictions suggests that they may possibly be the result of implementational problems, and there is certainly some evidence to support this, at least with regard to the more recent restorative justice initiatives. The evaluation of the pilot youth offending teams set up under the Crime and Disorder Act 1998 identified a number of implementational problems relating to the victim consultation process that it established.[50] One problem was a degree of cultural resistance on the part of some youth offending team staff who were reluctant to accept that their responsibilities also extended to addressing the needs of victims. A second problem was linked to the defective consultation procedures that were adopted in one of the pilots (leaving the onus on victims to take the

47 M. Umbreit and A. Roberts (1996) *Mediation of Criminal Conflict in England: An Assessment of Services in Coventry and Leeds.* St. Paul, MN: Centre for Restorative Justice & Mediation, University of Minnesota.

48 Holdaway et al., *o.c.*

49 See above Newburn et al, *o.c.*

50 Dignan (2001) *o.c.*; Holdaway et al., *o.c.*

initiative if they wished to take part in any form of direct reparation). A third factor is related to the tension between the 'victim-focused' aspects of the reforms and the desire to speed up the processing of youth justice cases. This made it impossible to consult victims before the young offender was dealt with for the offence, which meant that it was unclear whether mediation or some other form of direct reparation might be feasible at the time of sentence.

A fourth and final problem, which has almost certainly become more acute since the pilot phase ended, involves conflict of a different kind, between the youth justice provisions and a quite separate piece of legislation that was enacted at the same time, to strengthen the protection of personal data against unauthorised disclosure. Because of the increasingly restrictive way in which the Data Protection Act of 1998 has been interpreted, the police in many parts of the country are now refusing to disclose victim contact details without consent even to bodies such as Victim Support, youth offending teams and agencies that are contracted by the latter to deliver restorative justice interventions including mediation and conferencing. This places the onus on the police not only to identify the appropriate victim, but also, in effect, to initiate the consultation process itself, since a victim's willingness to consent to being approached by some other organisation to discuss the possibility of mediation or reparation will clearly be influenced by what they have been told this might entail. It also raises serious doubts as to whether the police have the time and inclination - let alone the training and experience - that might be required to discharge this sensitive task.

While there may be some grounds for suspecting that implementational failings could be partly responsible for the extremely low victim participation rates in relation to some of the more recent restorative justice initiatives in England and Wales, it would be unwise to press this argument too far. For, as Umbreit and Roberts[51] have shown, victims in England and Wales appeared much less willing to take part in victim offender mediation schemes than their counterparts in North America even before the latest restorative justice initiatives were introduced. And even if victim participation rates could be raised to levels achieved in other jurisdictions, this would still be unlikely to silence the doubts of those[52] who have

51 UMBREIT and ROBERTS, *o.c.*

52 A. ASHWORTH (2000) Assessing the Restorative Justice Paradigm, Paper presented at the Restorative Justice Symposium, University of Cambridge, 6-8 October 2000.

questioned the extent to which restorative processes might be capable of replacing the conventional criminal justice system.

Elsewhere I have argued that the concept and practice of restorative justice could be reformulated in such a way that it might provide the kind of 'replacement discourse' that Andrew Ashworth[53] himself has called for.[54] Even if one accepts this argument, however, the fact remains that there are limits to the extent to which *any* form of criminal justice-based response can be expected to significantly reduce levels of offending.[55] This is partly, as we have seen, because so few offences result in a criminal conviction, but also because criminal justice-based approaches of whatever kind, and however holistic they may be, are unlikely to be able to address the complex social, economic and cultural factors that chiefly influence crime rates.[56]

4. Policy implications: revisiting restorative justice's crime reduction potential

What policy implications are to be drawn from the above analysis? The first lesson is that policy makers need to retain a sense of realism about the crime reduction potential of restorative justice initiatives in the criminal justice sphere, and to accept that there may be other sound reasons for supporting such developments even if the hoped-for reduction in recidivism rates does not materialise or turns out to be more modest than might have been anticipated. For example, most evaluations to date – whether of victim-offender mediation programmes or family group conferences - have shown that compliance rates are high, and that both victims and offenders are satisfied with both process and outcomes.[57] These are important and valuable benefits in themselves irrespective of any impact on reoffending rates. A second lesson is that if restorative criminal justice initiatives are to deliver lower reconviction rates policy makers need to be prepared to commit adequate resources to support the reintegrative outcomes that may be negotiated in the course of a conference. Where an offender agrees to

---

53 A. ASHWORTH (1997) Sentenced by the Media, 29 *Criminal Justice Matters* 14-15.

54 J. DIGNAN (forthcoming) Towards a systemic model of restorative justice: reflections on the concept, its context and the need for clear constraints, in: BOTTOMS, ROBERTS and VON HIRSCH, *o.c.*

55 See also BRAITHWAITE (1989) *o.c.*

56 K. ROACH (2000) Changing punishment at the turn of the century: restorative justice on the rise, *Canadian Journal of Criminology* 249-80.

57 KURKI, o.c.

take part in a drug rehabilitation programme or anger management course during the course of a restorative justice conference, for example, funding has to be provided to ensure that such facilities are available when and where they are needed or the restorative justice intervention is most unlikely to succeed.

The third and potentially most valuable policy message for criminal justice policy makers who are interested in crime reduction is to reinforce the penological reality that this is unlikely to be achieved by reforming the criminal justice system, even if those reforms are influenced by the philosophy of restorative justice. However, it also raises the question whether the plethora of restorative criminal justice initiatives that have been developed in recent years represent the only or indeed the most effective contribution that restorative justice thinking could make in the pursuit of crime reduction. A more promising approach might be to apply the same theoretical insights that have stimulated these developments to the development and pursuit of a social crime prevention strategy that does address the various social, economic and cultural factors that are known to influence levels of offending.[58]

Thus, we know from the criminological literature[59] that young people are particularly at risk of offending if their relationships with family or school are tenuous or disaffected. The period of transition from school to work is also a time during which the risk of offending is likely to be higher. Rates of offending are likewise known to be higher for both men and women who are unemployed, and also for those who are otherwise economically or socially disadvantaged. Moreover, crime is disproportionately committed by those who are rootless, and who live in urban areas that are characterised by high levels of residential mobility. Most of these factors are symptomatic of various forms of social exclusion.

This suggests that social policy measures which aim to tackle the problem of social exclusion directly, are far more likely to have significant crime reductive effects than are punitive measures (even where they take the form of restorative justice interventions) that are aimed at individual offenders. Within the spheres of economic, employment, housing, child care and educational policy measures that are designed to foster 'social

---

58 J. DIGNAN (1999) Restorative Crime Prevention in Theory and Practice, 123 *Prison Service Journal* 2-5.

59 See esp. J. GRAHAM and B. BOWLING (1995) *Young People and Crime*. London: Home Office; D. FARRINGTON (1996) *Understanding and Preventing Youth Crime*. York: Joseph Rowntree Foundation/York Publishing Services.

inclusion' seem likely to provide a far more effective form of crime prevention. For if Braithwaite's analysis is accurate, a society in which all citizens are genuinely valued and treated accordingly will be a more cohesive society, and also a more pluralistic one, which accepts a variety of cultures and subcultures.[60] Such a society would seem to be less likely to suffer from problems of crime, which have their roots in social dislocation, fragmentation, insecurity and alienation.

Interestingly, a number of measures have been adopted in England and Wales over the last five years that are consistent with the development of a more socially integrative approach. Indeed, a number of 'social crime prevention' measures have been adopted as part of the Crime Reduction Programme that was referred to above. They include the 'On Track' programme, which is a long-term initiative that is aimed at children who are perceived as being at risk of getting involved in crime.[61] Twenty two On Track projects are located in high deprivation areas in England, each covering around 2,000 children. Within each area approximately £0.5m p.a. is being invested to develop a range of non-stigmatising evidence-based preventive services for children aged between 4-12 and their families. Inter-agency co-operation is being developed in order to identify children at risk at an early stage. The range of services includes parent training, home school partnerships, structured pre-school education, home visiting and family therapy.

A second initiative that is being funded under the Crime Reduction Programme is the Youth Inclusion Programme, which comprises 70 projects that seek to reduce offending, truancy and exclusion in disadvantaged neighbourhoods by providing targeted support and assistance to the 13-16 year olds who are most at risk. The programme is being evaluated by 7 teams of regional university-based evaluators whose activities are being co-ordinated by a private sector consultancy firm. A complementary programme also aims to reduce offending by improving schools' management of pupils' behaviour and reducing levels of truancy and school exclusion. Although the impact of these social crime prevention initiatives on levels of offending is being evaluated, it is a matter of regret that those responsible for their development and evaluation appear to have made no

60 M. CAVADINO, I. CROW and J. DIGNAN (1999) *Criminal Justice 2000*. Winchester: Waterside Press.

61 The initiative was launched in December 1999 and, although it was subsequently incorporated into the separately administered Children's Fund Programme it continues to be evaluated by a team of academic researchers on behalf of the Home Office.

connections with the current restorative justice debate, despite its obvious relevance. Nevertheless the evaluations themselves should provide the first indications, in an English context, whether the adoption of these kinds of socially inclusionary policies that are broadly compatible with a restorative crime prevention strategy, are capable of reducing levels of offending.

Unfortunately, the same cannot be said of a second category of socially inclusive policies that have also been adopted since 1997, but which fall outside the ambit of the Crime Reduction Programme, despite their equally obvious potential to significantly reduce overall crime levels. One example is the 'New Deal' package that was introduced in 1997 with the aim of reducing unemployment of the young, the disabled, lone parents and those released from prison. The government claims that the 'New Deal' package has contributed to a steady reduction in unemployment levels that are now lower than they have been for over a quarter of a century. Although the claims are controversial since some of the reduction in unemployment is likely to have been accounted for by the continuing strength (until recently) of the domestic economy,[62] it does seem highly probable that a reduction in long-term unemployment in particular could succeed in reducing crime levels. As far as I am aware, however, no attempt is being made by any government department to assess its crime reduction impact.

A second example comprises a range of various initiatives that have been associated with the creation of the Social Exclusion Unit, which was set up within the Cabinet Office to co-ordinate policy-making on specified cross-cutting topics. These include school exclusions and truancy, rough sleeping, teenage pregnancy, youth at risk and deprived neighbourhoods. The broad aims of the Unit have been to prevent social exclusion happening in the first place; reintegrating those who become excluded back into society; and delivering basic minimum standards to everyone (Social Exclusion Unit, no date). The Social Exclusion Unit has also claimed a number of successes: for example reductions in the number of school exclusions and in the proportion of children in homes where no one is in work, and the introduction of a £550m Sure Start programme designed to ensure that 100,000 children are ready to learn by the time they reach primary school. Once again, however, there is no evidence that the Unit itself or any other agency is seeking to audit the impact of these policies on crime levels. This

---

62 An independent report recently estimated that the New Deal for Young People has reduced long-term youth unemployment by 45,000; R. RILEY and G. YOUNG (2001) *The macroeconomic impact of the New Deal for Young People*, National Institute for Economic and Social Research (NIESR), Discussion paper 184.

is all the more ironic in view of the Unit's professed emphasis on the link between economic and social policy, and the need for joined up implementation of policy that crosses departmental boundaries.

As with the crime reduction programme initiatives, this omission represents a missed opportunity to assess the crime reduction potential of a social crime prevention strategy that is clearly highly compatible with a restorative justice approach even if it is not directly influenced by it. If the analysis contained in this paper is correct, social policy-makers may have erred in devoting so much attention to the evaluation of restorative criminal justice initiatives that are unlikely to yield significant crime reduction dividends while neglecting the opportunity to evaluate a range of social crime prevention measures that are compatible with a potentially much more promising restorative social justice strategy.

References

Ashworth A. (1997) Sentenced by the Media, 29 *Criminal Justice Matters* 14-15.

Ashworth, A. (2000) Assessing the Restorative Justice Paradigm, Paper presented at the Restorative Justice Symposium, University of Cambridge, 6-8 October 2000.

Barclay, G. and Tavares, C. (1999) *Digest 4: Information on the Criminal Justice System in England and Wales.* London: Home Office Research, Development and Statistics Directorate.

Braithwaite, J. (1989) *Crime, Shame and Reintegration.* Cambridge: Cambridge University Press.

Braithwaite, J. (1999) Restorative Justice: Assessing Optimistic and Pessimistic Accounts, 25 *Crime and Justice: A Review of Research* 1.

Cavadino, M., Crow, I. and Dignan, J. (1999) *Criminal Justice 2000.* Winchester: Waterside Press.

Daley, K. (forthcoming) Mind the Gap: Restorative Justice in Theory and Practice, in: A.E. Bottoms, J. Roberts and A. von Hirsch (eds.), *Restorative Justice and Criminal Justice: Theory and Conflict.* Oxford: Hart Publishing. (Forthcoming).

Daly, K. and Hayes, H. (2001) Restorative justice and conferencing in Australia, *Trends & Issues in Crime and Criminal Justice No. 186.* Canberra: Australian Institute of Criminology. http://www.aic.gov.au/publications/tandi/tandi186.html

Davis, G., Boucherat, J. and Watson, D. (1988) Reparation in the Service of Diversion: The Subordination of a Good Idea, 27 *Howard Journal of Criminal Justice* 127-262.

Davis, G., Boucherat, J. and Watson, D. (1989) Pre-court Decision-making in Juvenile Justice, 29 *British Journal of Criminology* 219-35.

Davis, G. (1992) *Making Amends: Mediation and Reparation in Criminal Justice*. London and New York: Routledge.

Davis, R.C., Tichane, M. and Grayson, D. (1980) *Mediation and Arbitration as Alternatives to Prosecution in Felony Arrest Cases: An Evaluation of the Brooklyn Dispute Resolution Centre.* New York: Vera Institute of Justice.

Dignan, J. (1999) The Crime and Disorder Act and the Prospects for Restorative Justice, *Criminal Law Review* 48-60.

Dignan, J. (1999) Restorative Crime Prevention in Theory and Practice, 123 *Prison Service Journal* 2-5.

Dignan, J. (2001) Reparation Orders, Ch. 5 in: B. Williams (ed.), *Reparation and Victim-Focused Social Work.* London: Jessica Kingsley (forthcoming).

Dignan, J. (forthcoming) Towards a systemic model of restorative justice: reflections on the concept, its context and the need for clear constraints, in: A.E. Bottoms, J. Roberts and A. von Hirsch (eds.), *Restorative Justice and Criminal Justice: Theory and Conflict*. Oxford: Hart Publishing. (Forthcoming).

Dignan, J. (with K. Lowey) (2000) *Restorative Justice Options for Northern Ireland,* Research Report No. 10. Belfast: Criminal Justice Review Commission/Northern Ireland Office.

Dignan, J. and Marsh, P. (2001) Restorative Justice and Family Group Conferences in England: Current State and Future Prospects, in: A. Morris and G. Maxwell (eds.), *Restorative Justice for Juveniles: Conferencing, Mediation and Circles*. Oxford: Hart Publishing.

Farrington, D. (1996) *Understanding and Preventing Youth Crime.* York: Joseph Rowntree Foundation/York Publishing Services.

Graham, J. and Bowling, B. (1995) *Young People and Crime,* London: Home Office.

Holdaway, S., Davidson, N., Dignan, J., Hammersley, R., Hine, J. and Marsh, P. (2000) *New Strategies to Address Youth Offending: the National Evaluation of the Pilot Youth Offending Teams,* RDS Occasional Paper No. 69. London: Research, Development and Statistics Directorate.

Home Office (1997) *No More Excuses – A New Approach to Tackling Youth Crime in England and Wales*. Cm 3809. London: Home Office.

Home Office (2000) *The Final Warning Scheme: Guidance for Youth Offending Teams*. London: Home Office. Also available on-line at: http://www.homeoffice.gov.uk/cdact/yotguide.htm

Kurki, L. (forthcoming) Evaluation of restorative justice practices, in: A.E. Bottoms, J. Roberts and A. von Hirsch (eds.), *Restorative Justice and Criminal Justice: Theory and Conflict*. Oxford: Hart Publishing. (Forthcoming).

McCold, P. and Wachtel, B. (1998) *Restorative Policing Experiment: The Bethlehem Pennsylvania Police Family Group Conferencing Project*. Pipersville, Pa: Community Service Foundation.

McGarrell, E., Olivares, K., Crawford, K. and Kroovand, N. (2000) *Returning justice to the community: the Indianapolis Juvenile Restorative Justice Experiment*. Indianapolis: Hudson Institute.

Marshall, T.F. and Merry, S. (1990) *Crime and Accountability: Victim-Offender Mediation in Practice*. London: HMSO.

Maxwell, G and Morris, A. (1996) Research on Family Group Conferences with Young Offenders in New Zealand, in: J. Hudson, A. Morris, G. Maxwell and B. Galaway (eds.), *Family Group Conferences: Perspectives on Policy and Practice*. Sydney: Federation Press and Criminal Justice Press.

Maxwell, G. and Morris, A. (1999) *Understanding Reoffending*. Wellington: Institute of Criminology, Victoria University of Wellington.

Maxwell, G. and Morris, A. (2001) Family Group Conferences and Reoffending, in: A. Morris and G. Maxwell (eds.), *Restorative Justice for Juveniles: Conferencing, Mediation and Circles*. Oxford: Hart Publishing.

Moore, D. B. and O'Connell, T. (1994) Family Group Conferencing in Wagga Wagga: A Communitarian Model of Justice, in: C. Alder and J. Wundersitz (eds.), *Family Conferencing and Juvenile Justice*. Canberra: Australian Studies in Law, Crime and Justice, Australian Institute of Criminology.

Morris, A., Maxwell, G.M. and Robertson, J.P. (1993) Giving Victims a Voice: A New Zealand Experiment, 32(4) *The Howard Journal*, 304-21.

Newburn, T., Masters, G., Earle, R., Goldie, S., Crawford, A., Sharpe, K., Netten, A., Hale, C., Uglow, S. and Saunders, R. (2001) *The Introduction of Referral Orders into the Youth Justice System*, RDS

Occasional Paper No. 70. London: Research, Development and Statistics Directorate.
Nugent, W.R. and Paddock, J.B. (1995) The effect of victim-offender mediation on severity of reoffense, 12(4) *Mediation Quarterly* 353-67.
Riley, R. and Young, G. (2001) *The macroeconomic impact of the New Deal for Young People*, National Institute for Economic and Social Research (NIESR), Discussion paper 184.
Roach, K. (2000) Changing punishment at the turn of the century: restorative justice on the rise, *Canadian Journal of Criminology* 249-80.
Sherman, L. (1993) Defiance, Deterrence and Irrelevance: A Theory of the Criminal Sanction, 31(4) *Journal of Research in Crime and Delinquency* 445-73.
Sherman, L., Strang, H. and Wood, D.J. (2000) *Recidivism Patterns in the Canberra Reintegrative Shaming Experiments (RISE)*. Canberra: Centre for Restorative Justice, Australian National University. Available on-line at:
http://ww.aic.gov.au/rjustice/rise/recidivism/index.html
Social Exclusion Unit (no date), *Preventing Social Exclusion*. Available on-line at: http://www.cabinet-office.gov.uk/seu/index/publishe.htm
Tyler, T. (1990) *Why People Obey the Law*. New Haven: Yale University Press.
Tyler, T. R., Boeckmann, R.J., Smith, H.J., and Huo, Y.J. (1997) *Social Justice in a Diverse Society*. Boulder: Westview Press.
Umbreit, M. and Roberts, A. (1996) *Mediation of Criminal Conflict in England: An Assessment of Services in Coventry and Leeds*. St. Paul, MN: Centre for Restorative Justice & Mediation, University of Minnesota.
Young, R. and Goold, B. (1999) Restorative Police Cautioning in Aylesbury: from Degrading to Reintegrative Shaming Ceremonies?, *Criminal Law Review* 126.
Young, R. (2000) Integrating a Multi-Victim Perspective through Restorative Justice Conferences?, in: A. Crawford and J. Goodey (eds.), *Integrating a Victim Perspective within Criminal Justice*. Aldershot: Ashgate.
Young, R. (2001) Just Cops doing Shameful Business?: Police-led Restorative Justice and the Lessons of Research, in: A. Morris and G. Maxwell (eds.), *Restorative Justice for Juveniles: Conferencing, Mediation and Circles*. Oxford: Hart Publishing.

RESTORATIVE JUSTICE: THE BASIC IDEA, AND PRACTICE IN THE UNITED KINGDOM

Martin Wright

Tony Peters is a great internationalist; for example, I am told that he learnt Spanish simply because he felt that it would be useful in communicating with Spanish colleagues. He has been one of the driving forces behind the European Forum for Victim/Offender Mediation and Restorative Justice, which has helped to develop links between many European countries. The Forum has worked to encourage links with countries in Eastern Europe, among which Poland has taken a leading part in developing restorative justice. Partly as a result, I have been fortunate to be invited to speak in Poland, and therefore I should like to contribute to this volume a revised version of a previously unpublished paper to a seminar on 'Victim/offender mediation in adult cases', in Popowo, near Warsaw, in September 1998.

Introduction

'Restorative justice' ("sprawiedliwość naprawcza") is a relatively new term, and different people have different understandings of what it means. Looking for common ground, because that is what mediators do, I want to say that in many ways restorative justice is common sense. When I looked in a dictionary, I found that Polish is a very rich language, in which these words can be translated in different ways. It appears that 'common sense' is "zdrowy rozsgdek", healthy and sensible, or "chtopski rozum", the way ordinary people understand things. 'Common ground' is "rzecz wspólna", something held jointly. I am going to suggest that the idea of restorative justice can be described as 'common' in the sense of: "gminny", shared by the community; "codzienny", everyday; "zwykty", usual or customary, and "ogólony", universal.

It is a new idea; but it is also a very old one. Some of the ideas derive from anthropology, the study of communities of ordinary people in other countries, including Africa, New Zealand and Canada.[1] It includes the idea of compensation, which, I understand, was introduced in the Polish Penal

1 N. Christie (1977) Conflicts as property, 17(1) *British Journal of Criminology*, 1-15; M. Wright (1996) (2nd ed.), *Justice for victims and offenders: a restorative response to crime.* Winchester: Waterside Press.

Code of 1932 (Article 62 § 2), in the context of a conditionally suspended sentence (and I do not know how much it was used); but restorative justice is a wider concept, as we shall see. The Penal Code of 1969 also allowed it inter alia in the context of conditional discontinuance of prosecution (Article 28 § 2 and 3), and I understand that in privately prosecuted offences an attempt at mediation was required; about two-thirds of these cases were discontinued, often accompanied by reconciliation. Polish readers will be aware that the Penal Code which came into force on September 1st 1998[2] allows courts to take account of positive results of victim/offender mediation (Article 53 § 3; Articles 60 § 2 and 66 § 3 are also relevant). Compensation for damage is also, of course, a basic principle of civil law; and it is possible to settle a civil claim without going to court. This is another idea which has a place in restorative justice; indeed in Austria, the term used for victim/offender mediation is 'out-of-court offence resolution'.

1. Everyday responses to crime

May I ask readers for a moment to put all their knowledge and experience of the criminal justice system on one side; imagine that you are taking a blank sheet of paper, and writing down how you would expect a society to respond when one of its members commits a crime against another.

1.1. Help for victims

The first priority, I suggest, is to help the victim to recover (I am simplifying, of course; as we know, in many cases either there is no individual victim, or a person who is maltreated turns on their persecutor so that in a sense both are offenders and both are victims). Victims should be offered help and support, the processes of justice should be explained to them and they should be kept informed of the progress of their case. They want those processes to ease their pain, not to add to it. They would like the harm that they have suffered to be acknowledged, both on behalf of the community and if possible by the offender him/herself. They would like

2 In 1970 to 1982 privately prosecuted criminal cases comprised between one-fifth and one-quarter of all criminal cases in Poland. In 1978, for example, there were almost 30000 private criminal cases, of which judges discontinued about 20 000, and in one-third of these, the reason for discontinuance was reconciliation: A. RZEPLINSKI (1984), private communication.

some assurance that action will be taken to reduce the likelihood of others experiencing the same.

Results over the past twenty years in several countries have shown that many victims would welcome the opportunity to speak to the offender, face-to-face or at least indirectly, to see what he looks like, let him know their feelings about the effect his actions have had on them (and often on their families), to ask questions, and take part in discussing what form the reparation should take, which we will look at later. Restorative justice is a voluntary process, so victims do not have to use it, and it deals only with reparation, so that they do not have the burden of responsibility for influencing punishment.

1.2. Holding offenders accountable

Secondly, what should happen to offenders? A common feeling (in any of those senses of the word 'common') is that offenders should be held accountable and answerable, and should make reparation of some sort. People want this to 'cost' the offender at least some effort, even if he has no money with which to pay compensation. In addition, most people would agree that a minority of serious offenders have to be restrained, but with the minimum necessary use of force; imprisonment would be used only for those who are seriously likely to cause serious harm.

The restorative justice process allows them to speak in their own words: they do not have lawyers to speak for them and they are not limited to answering lawyers' questions. They have the opportunity to say why they committed the offence: this does not mean making excuses, but explaining so that the victim can understand. It is an uncomfortable experience for them, but it ends positively by enabling them to make a new start: by making reparation they can earn reintegration and re-acceptance into the law-abiding community.

You may be wondering whether the 'common ground' includes the idea that offenders should be punished. The short answer is that although many people believe this, there is also a widespread feeling that punishment doesn't achieve much, and even that it is wrong for the state to inflict punishment on its citizens unless it can be shown that it is effective;[3] so I do not think this can be included in the common ground.

Having mentioned punishment, I should define it: in this paper 'punishment' does not refer to all types of sentence or sanction, but only to

---

3 M. WRIGHT (1999) *Restoring respect for justice*. Winchester: Waterside Press.

those which are intended to cause pain or unpleasantness. As the Norwegian criminologist Nils Christie has said: imposing punishment within the institution of law means the infliction of pain, intended as pain.[4] For clarity, I will use the word 'sanctions', which may be punitive, rehabilitative, retributive, or restorative. No distinction is made here between 'restorative', `reparative' and 'making amends'.]

Often punitive sanctions are only used because of a feeling that 'something' should be done. People recognize that any good effects of prisons are usually outweighed by harmful ones; but they feel that rehabilitative sanctions pay too much attention to the needs of the offender, and ignore the harm he has caused to the victim. Restorative sanctions provide a third way, a different 'something'. Prisons are part of the problem, not part of the solution, and evidently this is recognized in Poland: it is reported that the prison population has been reduced from 100 000 in the 1980s to 66 500 in 1995 and 56 700 in 1996 (149 per 100 000 population), and the new penal code introduced on September 1st 1998 was expected to reduce it still further. In England and Wales, unfortunately, the trend is the other way: in 1993 we had 41 500 prisoners, and the number rose rapidly until in 1998 it appeared to level off at about 65 000 (128 per 100 000 population). Most worrying is that the number of young men aged 15 to 17 in prison in England increased by 28 per cent in one year (mid-1996 to mid-1997); since male young offenders have a reconviction rate of 76 per cent, the courts are storing up trouble for us by sending so many to prison. I hope that Poland will be able to continue to release resources for community sanctions by reducing the numbers held in prisons; and I wish that the British government would do the same. Unfortunately, by 2000 the Polish trend was upward again: to 70 000, or 191 per 100 000, with 10 to 30 per cent overcrowding, partly because the time served before conditional release has been substantially increased.[5] This is not the place to mention the United States of America, Russia or Belarus, which are far and away at the bottom of this lamentable league table.[6]

If a more constructive (reparative) sanction were available, many people would prefer this, as national and international public opinion surveys have

---

4 N. CHRISTIE (1982) *Limits to pain*. Oxford: Martin, Robertson.

5 Dziennik Polski, 8 June 2001, 3.

6 Penal Reform International and International Centre for Prison Studies (1998) *Newsletter: Penal Reform Project in Eastern Europe and Central Asia*, No. 1. PRI, Unit 114, The Chandlery, 50 Westminster Bridge Road, London SE1 7QY, England; V. STERN (1998) *A sin against the future: imprisonment in the world*. London: Penguin.

shown.[7] In England, in a survey of victims of a range of crimes, 49 per cent said they would have accepted the chance to meet the offender to agree on a way in which he could make a repayment for what he had done, and a further 20 per cent would like such an agreement without a meeting, 69 per cent in all; the proportion was higher for property offences, lower for violent ones.[8] In Germany, a survey of the general population found that for a range of offences, the great majority wanted restitution; only 21 per cent wanted punishment without consideration of restitution (but this proportion was higher for the more serious offences).[9] In Britain the proportion wanting offenders to be imprisoned has been increasing, but there is also evidence that the public is largely misinformed about crime and sentencing; and when people are informed of the available sentences, more want compensation and fewer want prison.[10] In short, although there are many people who want offenders to be punished, many others want more constructive sanctions.

What do offenders themselves want? Probably the only generalization one can make is that they want to feel fairly dealt with. Most want to avoid punishment, although there are some who accept it as the only available way of demonstrating regret (or as a way to show how tough they are). Others would like the victim to know that they regret what they have done: but few would spontaneously meet face-to-face to apologize, it is a daunting prospect.

1.3. Involving the community

What does the community want? Insofar as it has a collective voice, probably (like the victims themselves) it wants victims to be supported if they need it, for example through Victim Support and compensation for crimes of violence. Unless the offender has any money, compensation for property crimes probably has to be left to private insurance, except for victims with the lowest incomes who can be helped by the state social security system in those countries where there is one. It wants offenders to make amends. Many people, when they think about it, recognize that it is

---

7 M. WRIGHT (1989) What the public wants, in: M. WRIGHT and B. GALAWAY (eds.), *Mediation and criminal justice: victims, offenders and community*. London: Sage; STERN, *o.c.*

8 M. MAGUIRE and C. CORBETT (1987) *The effects of crime and the work of victim support schemes*, 223-231. Alderschot: Gower.

9 K. SESSAR (1992) *Wiedergutmachen oder Strafen: Einstellungen in der Bevölkerung und der Justiz - ein Forschungsbericht*. Centaurus.

10 M. HOUGH and J ROBERTS (1998) *Attitudes to punishment: findings from the British Crime Survey*, Home Office Research Study 179. London: Home Office.

desirable to reintegrate offenders and provide them with the opportunity to make reparation, for example through community service, or training or treatment programmes that will help them to be reaccepted into the community and avoid future offending. It must however be admitted that members of the community will sometimes have to be persuaded to provide the necessary time and money to enable this to happen.

The community can be involved in several ways. The management committee of the mediation service can include people from outside the criminal justice system. Mediators may be trained lay people (volunteers or paid for each session). Mediation may develop into conferencing, which brings in the families of the victims and offenders (who are also members of the community). I will say more about lay mediators and conferencing later. Lastly, the community in the form of local welfare services or independent non-governmental organizations (NGOs) can provide the support needed by victims recovering from crimes and by offenders making reparation.

Although I have no evidence for this, I believe that most people would prefer a maximum of individual autonomy and community action and a minimum of intervention by the state.[11] But there may be some inconsistency in people's attitudes: they want things done for them, but they don't want to pay for it. There are essentially three ways of providing care for the elderly, assistance to victims, support for parents and children, mediation, and similar services: they can be provided by the state and paid for from tax revenues; or by NGOs and paid for by charitable donations; or by individuals. These can of course be combined; an NGO can receive government money, for example. In Britain much of this work is done by NGOs: they employ almost half a million paid workers (half of them part-time or on a casual basis, and a quarter educated to degree level), almost 2 per cent of the total UK workforce; there are also more than 3 million volunteers. Many individuals simply act on their own, for example by caring for an elderly relative or adopting a child; but others work voluntarily in their spare time with an NGO, which provides training and supervision, and this is a method which can be used in restorative justice. For people who do not want to offer their services in this way, or cannot spare the time, but do not want to pay taxes either, donations to NGOs provide a way to ensure that people with special needs are cared for. In Britain, some NGOs are largely funded by the national or local government (that is, the taxpayer); but they also have to put much effort into raising funds from charitable foundations and the general public.

---

11 J. BRAITHWAITE and P. PETTIT (1990) *Not just deserts: a republican theory of justice*. Oxford: Clarendon.

1.4. Learning lessons for crime reduction

I believe that most people, if asked, would also agree that the response to crime should include preventive measures. Sometimes 'prevention' is used as if it were synonymous with 'deterrence': 'Punish people and they will stop committing crimes'. This has not proved very effective. As McGuire and Priestley[12] say in their review of 'what works': "*The notion that punishment can reduce the rate of crime in society is little more than an irrational and unfounded hope.*" I mean a crime prevention strategy: that information should be passed back from the agencies that deal with crimes to those responsible for crime policy, to improve the strategy for tackling crime. It is often said that the 'criminal justice system' is not a system, because its parts do not interact with each other in a planned way. A further principle, then, is that it should be a system: that is, if the state is intervening in people's lives, it should study the cases that it deals with, providing feedback of information to the crime prevention agency both from the point of view of 'situational crime prevention': security (locks, alarms, Neighbourhood Watch, and so on) and of 'social crime prevention': reducing pressures towards crime (for example by providing the right education, work, recreation and nurture for young people, persuading them to avoid drugs, and enabling them to make something of their lives). As one writer has put it, "*Instead of asking how effective our programmes are in controlling people and crime, we should be trying to find out what is so lacking in the lives of our neighbours that they see no alternative but a life of crime and violence*".[13] Deterrence depends on detection rather than on punishment; crime prevention is a matter for the whole community, not only for the courts.

This aspect is not yet well developed, but a new British law, the Crime and Disorder Act 1998, has provided an opportunity by requiring all local authorities and police chiefs to draw up a strategy for crime prevention. Information from conferences about factors which increase the pressures and opportunities for crime would be useful in designing such a strategy.

---

12 J. McGuire, and P. Priestley (1995) Reviewing "What works", past, present and future, in: James McGuire (ed.), *What works: reducing re-offending. Guidelines from research and practice*. Chichester: Wiley.

13 R. Elias (1993) *Victims still: the political manipulation of crime victims.* Newbury Park, CA: Sage.

2. Criminal and restorative justice: comparisons and contrasts

2.1. Restorative justice: two keynote ideas

Restorative justice is based on the idea that the response to crime should be to make good the harm, as far as possible, and not, as hitherto, to inflict further harm on the offender. That achieves nothing except to add to the total amount of harm in the world,[14] and many offenders are already disadvantaged. As much as possible of the making good should be done by the wrongdoer (provided, of course, that he is caught). There is a common feeling among people in general and victims in particular that some good should come out of the harm, even if the harm itself cannot be undone.

Two particular ideas distinguish restorative justice. One is that the process is an essential part of the response: it is constructive, perhaps even therapeutic. The other is reparation.

2.2. The criminal justice process

Let us look first at conventional criminal justice: the process is geared to producing a result, and the effect on the participants is merely incidental, and often painful. It aims only to answer the question 'Did the accused commit a criminal offence?' and if so, the court decides what sanction to use: the process is seen as incidental to this aim, and if it is painful for the victim, that is an unfortunate necessity. It has been criticized for not giving recognition to victims: they are not kept informed of the progress of the case, and (in the English adversarial system at least) they usually have little or no place in the process, but are sometimes re-victimized when giving evidence in court. The defence lawyer first attempts to discredit them as witnesses; if he fails, and the accused is convicted, the lawyer tries to minimize the offender's responsibility; meanwhile the offender is often a passive spectator at his own trial. The victim, also, has no part in English criminal proceedings if he or she did not witness the crime, or if the offender pleads guilty; there are however initiatives to keep victims informed and to enable them to give information to the court about the extent of the harm they have suffered.

---

14 M. WRIGHT (1992) Victim/offender mediation as a step towards a restorative system of justice, in: H. MESSMER and H.-U. OTTO (eds.), *Restorative justice on trial: pitfalls and potential of victim/offender mediation - International research perspectives,* 525. Dordrecht: Kluwer.

2.3. The restorative process

I do not want to make unfair comparisons, and it is right to point out that some of these activities of lawyers take place when the accused denies guilt, whereas restorative justice comes into operation only when the accused has admitted the act or been convicted. In England, 8 out of 10 defendants plead guilty in magistrates' courts, and more than half in the Crown Court. But from that point onwards, restorative justice asks different questions: 'How did he harm the victim?' 'Does he understand the effect on the victim?' 'What would the victim like him to do to make up for it?' The process itself helps to heal, by giving the victim the opportunity to express feelings and ask questions. encouraging the offender to repair the harm. Offenders, instead of facing officers of the law, can meet the people who have been harmed and answer them. This process, unlike a conventional trial, enables the victim and the offender to communicate; the offender can understand the hurt he or she has caused to the victim, his own family and the community, and make reparation. Consequently, further punitive action is not needed or justified, because from then on it is a question of deciding what the offender can do for the victim and for his own reintegration. This may require him or her to make some form of reparation, as an outward and visible sign of remorse and understanding.

The process has been called victim/offender mediation, but in Britain we are beginning to use a new verb, 'conferencing' (which also has the advantage of being shorter!). Victim/offender mediation usually takes place between one victim and one offender, with mediators, but they may be supported by, for example, a parent or a Victim Support worker. Conferencing is basically a similar idea, but the offender and victim are encouraged to bring their extended families, or perhaps a teacher or youth leader with whom the offender has a good relationship. The more people are present, the more ideas can be put forward to enable the offender to be reintegrated into the community. The offender may realize that he has hurt his own family, as well as the victim; but he may also find unexpected support, from a sympathetic victim, or from an uncle or grandparent with whom he had lost touch. The supporters may be helpful for a vulnerable victim, such as a child or an elderly person; if the victim does not wish to take part at all, he or she may agree that they can speak on the victim's behalf. We do not yet know when it is better to use one-to-one mediation, and when to choose a conference; we need research and experience.

It needs an act of faith for social workers and probation officers to let people make decisions about their own lives, but they often produce imaginative solutions that the social workers would never have thought of. The idea has been developed from the tradition of family group conferences among the Maori of New Zealand, and a similar concept, circle sentencing or peacemaking circles, is being used among Indigenous communities in Northern Canada;[15] but the idea is being extended to larger cities.

The outcome of a conference may appear 'soft' compared with a conventional punishment, but taking part in a conference (in person, not represented by a lawyer) is in fact a difficult and demanding experience.[16] Mediation sessions are an uncomfortable experience for offenders. They have to accept facts about themselves, their behaviour and their future which they preferred not to think about; but it is not punishment, according to the definition I am using, because the unpleasantness is not the aim, but a side-effect, and because the realization and reparation are matched by what Professor Braithwaite calls 'public gestures of reacceptance' - or at least they should be if the community fulfils its side of the implied contract.

2.4. Reparation

The second distinctive idea of restorative justice is reparation. This includes the legal principle of compensation, in which a value is placed on the loss or harm, and the offender pays it.[17] But reparation is a wider concept. It is often symbolic. The offender may have little or no money; the loss may be covered by insurance; the value of the goods stolen may be sentimental rather than monetary; or it may be difficult to put a monetary value on the harm, for example the fear caused by a burglary or robbery, or the inconvenience of having a car stolen. As an alternative to compensation, reparation may take the form of work by the offender for the victim (especially a corporate victim - a 'legal person' - such as a school or a shop); if the victim does not want that, the offender can do work for the community. Thirdly, what many victims want is action which will make it less likely that the offender will re-offend. This is for the sake of the victim and other potential victims, but it is also for the sake of the offender: many

---

15 See for example B. STUART (2001) Guiding principles for peacemaking circles, in: B. GORDON and M. SCHIFF (eds.), *Restorative community justice: repairing harm and transforming communities*. Cincinnati, OH: Anderson.

16 J. BRAITHWAITE (1998) *Restorative justice: assessing an immodest theory and a pessimistic theory*. Canberra: Australian Institute of Criminology: webmaster@aic.gov.au

17 In the British Crime and Disorder Act 1988, however, 'reparation' refers only to work for the victim or the community; compensation is dealt with by a separate 'compensation order'.

victims have shown concern and empathy for the offender, and want to help him to make better use of his life. There is not a fixed line dividing victims from offenders; sometimes the victim or a member of their family has committed offences in the past, and they do not want to see another young person making the same mistakes (in England, almost one third of the male population has a criminal conviction by the age of thirty). Therefore, victims will want the offender not only to apologize but to show that he is sorry and is making a real effort to avoid offending again, by taking part in a programme that will help him with any problems and pressures that led him into crime. He may agree to avoid certain places, or to stay at home after a certain time. He may need work skills (in some cases literacy), social skills such as anger management, or therapy for addiction to alcohol, drugs or gambling. Therefore the community (for example the local authority or non-governmental organizations) have to provide these programmes.

In preparing this paper, I asked some co-ordinators of mediation services for examples of reparation agreements. One said she had dozens of examples; she gave me two which she had seen that same morning:

- The victim of an assault said he did not want to meet the offender, but knew that the latter's aggressive behaviour was due to alcohol problems and the break-up of a relationship. What the victim wanted was to know that the offender was receiving and accepting help with those difficulties.
- Teenagers had been roughly teasing smaller children who were playing in the street, and this made them frightened and upset. The parents of the younger children wanted the teenagers to understand what the experience had been like for the victims; it was arranged that they would help with a play project for young children in the summer holidays. They did this, and the play project organizer praised their work warmly.

Another mediation service told me:

- A burglar wanted to apologize to his victims, the couple whose house he had burgled, who agreed that he could write to them from prison (he was serving a three-year sentence). He wrote and said that he had been trying to imagine how they felt when they discovered the burglary; he had done it because he needed money for drugs. Like many offenders, he came from a disturbed background. They wrote back, and said they were willing to meet him face-to-face. He said afterwards that he nearly didn't go through with it because he was so ashamed; their letters had been so kind, and showed that they were thinking about him. At the meeting he said that he would go to a drug rehabilitation centre, and would find new friends. They asked what he would do if he met his old friends again; he said 'I wouldn't go back with them, because I would be thinking about you, and wouldn't want to let you down'.

- A young man broke into a school for children with special needs, looking for things he could sell so that he could buy drugs. As he broke a window and climbed over a table, he broke some models made by the children - which had been difficult for them, because of their disabilities. When he was told about the effect on the children, he was very sorry, and spent a long time making some models to replace the ones he had broken.

Other examples include helping to start a youth club (an example of social crime prevention), taking a young person with muscular dystrophy out in a wheelchair, and working for elderly people under supervision: shopping, painting or gardening. One service said that the most usual reparation is simply an apology.

Often the offender needs remedial education, job training, or other forms of rehabilitation or therapy, and if he commits himself to a suitable programme, this way of making things right is an acceptable form of reparation for many victims. The essential factor in these stories, and many others like them, is that the reparation was what the victims and the offenders themselves wanted, not what a social worker or judge had imposed upon them. They also involve an element of rehabilitation, but (unlike what happens in the conventional system) the victim is involved in planning what is best for the offender, and the offender is motivated by his concern for someone else, or by the knowledge that someone else is concerned about him.

The community has to play its part by making such programmes or work available; and when the offender cannot repair the full extent of the damage (or is not caught), the community should do what it can to make up the shortfall, for example if the national health service does not cover all medical costs.

After drawing this optimistic picture I will make a disclaimer: restorative justice is an ideal, and I am aware that ideals are not always achieved. The full form of restorative justice, with participation by both victims and offenders, is not possible or appropriate when the offender is not caught, or denies the act of which he is accused, or shows no sign of regret; or when the victim does not wish to take part. But there are partly reparative measures that can be used, for example the offender can make reparation to the community if the victim does not wish to be involved. A second point: mediators are not perfect, and not every case will be handled in the best possible way (the same is perhaps true of lawyers!). But it is a strong process, ordinary people have common sense, mediators can be trained and supervised, and research results are encouraging, as I will describe later.

2.5. How restorative justice achieves conventional aims

People accustomed to conventional criminal justice may say 'That's all very well, but what about the traditional aims: individual deterrence, general deterrence, containment and retribution?' The first two depend chiefly on the likelihood of being caught, which is just as great in a restorative system. But restorative justice does not rely on fear; it recognizes that there are other, more effective ways of influencing human conduct: incentives to good behaviour, a process which helps to increase understanding, and a comprehensive crime prevention strategy.

The third aim is to contain people who are very likely to commit further serious offences. With restorative justice, will we be able to abolish prisons? No, but in a fully restorative system they will only be used when necessary for protection of public; non-custodial methods of control will be used when possible, such as disqualification from specified activities (driving a car, managing a commercial firm, working with children, going near the place where a certain person lives). People subject to control would also be required to make reparation as far as their circumstances allowed.

Fourthly, court sentences are supposed to express collective denunciation and retribution for actions which are not acceptable. Restorative justice achieves these aims in a different way. It attaches importance to the actual harm, rather than the fact that a rule has been broken, and it shows this by requiring the offender to make reparation. Then it reinforces the collective values by reintegrating the offender into the community which upholds them.

Finally, conventional justice either blames offenders and punishes them, or it tries to understand their behaviour and to rehabilitate them. Restorative justice recognizes that many offenders come from disadvantaged backgrounds, but it does not regard that as an excuse for their actions; they have still caused harm to another person or to the community. In conventional rehabilitation, a social worker helped the offender because he needed it; the offence and the victim were often left out of the picture, and the offender could use his deprived upbringing or the unfairness of society as an excuse for his actions. In restorative justice, he is required to recognize how his actions affect other people (often from a similar background to his own); it is for their sake, as well as his own, that he co-operates with the educational or therapeutic programme.

2.6. How restorative justice works

In England victim/offender mediation or conferencing can be used at any stage of the criminal justice process. An offence can be referred by police, by prosecutors (who have not yet started to use this method in England, but they have in Scotland), by writers of pre-sentence reports, by courts, after sentence, or before release from prison. If the two parties know each other, for example in a dispute between neighbours which has led to an assault or criminal damage, they can go to a community mediation service (if there is one) instead of the police. If I were recommending a new system, I should propose a three-level process, with two more possibilities as safeguards (Appendix I):

- the least serious offences would be discontinued by the police or prosecutor (depending on their powers in the country concerned), with an informal or formal warning. If an offence arises from a dispute, the case can be referred to a community mediation service.
- more serious offences would be referred to the mediation service for mediation or conferencing.
- the most serious cases, and those where the offender denied the act, would be prosecuted in court. After a finding of guilt the case would be referred to the mediation service (just as at present the court asks for a pre-sentence report). The court would then endorse the agreement reached by the parties, or in some cases would reduce or add to it.

The two safeguards are that:

- cases can also be referred by the Victim Support service, in countries where there is one, because this process is for victims as well as for offenders;
- they can be referred at any later time, if one of the parties requests it and the other agrees. Mediation can take place when the offender is in prison, if the victim is willing to travel or the prison will release the prisoner for a day. It can take place while the accused is remanded in custody awaiting trial, if he does not deny the act of which he is accused. Or 'shuttle diplomacy' can be used, with the mediators acting as go-betweens. For example:
  - A woman's husband left her; a man who lived in the same street knew this, climbed into her house at night, and tried to rape her. She managed to talk him out of it, and called the police. He was sent to prison. When he was due to come out, she did not want to meet him but wanted to know what he would do; although he did not apologize for what he had

done, he asked the mediators to tell her that he was going to live in another town, and she was reassured.

2.7. *The process of mediation*

Preparation and screening of participants. In the 'more serious' cases both the victim and the offender should be visited, so that they understand the process and can give informed consent. The mediators should confirm that the accused does not deny the act.[18] Physical and emotional safety are important considerations; in case of doubt, the mediators would recommend that the case should not go ahead. These questions are not necessarily related to the offender's criminal record or the seriousness of the current offence; it may be the victims of the more serious offences who have the most questions to ask and feelings to express. Both victims and offenders have been helped by mediations where the offender is serving a life sentence for murder, or (in the USA) is on 'Death Row'. Cases where the offender has committed repeated violence, including domestic violence, or where the victim is vulnerable or a child, raise complex issues; it would be advisable not to attempt mediation in such cases until considerable thought has been given to them, and until experience has been gained from other types of case.

At this stage the mediators will consider who should take part in the mediation or conference. They will also take steps to ensure that victims and offenders understand the process; have given consent to taking part voluntarily; and are aware that at any stage of the process the victim can leave, or the offender can choose to go to courts instead. One concern in England is that for some victims it could be stressful even to be asked to decide whether to take part. The more mediation is a normal part of the process (as in Austria and New Zealand), the less difficult this decision will be.

The proceedings at the meeting or conference are not exactly the same everywhere, but a typical procedure would be:

- Offender is asked to say what he did (this sets the scene and confirms that the offender admits the act)
- Victim expresses feelings, asks questions
- Other participants contribute
- Outcome agreed: reparation (as defined above), apology, or no further action except the mediation itself

---

18 He might still have a legal defence, such as provocation or honest mistake; if this were not resolved through mediation, the defence would still be available if the case came to court.

- Community finds resources to enable offender to complete reparation

These agreements are not ordered by the court. They are enforced mainly by persuasion. If the offender fails to pay compensation, the case could be looked at again to see whether, for example, the offender's circumstances had changed. In the last resort the victim could ask the mediation service to help him or her to sue for damages in a civil court (small claims court), but this rarely happens.

For the 'most serious' offences there would be:

- Court appearance, then
- Procedure as above if offender does not deny act
- Return to court: agreement approved or modified by judge

In this case the agreement can be included in the court's sentence, and is enforced in the same way as other sanctions such as fines.

If possible the meeting should take place in a neutral place: not the home of either of the participants, nor the premises of an organization that works mainly with victims or offenders. It can normally be arranged quite quickly, but there should not be pressure on the victim to decide before they are ready.

The way it works can be shown by an example.

USC as an example of restorative Justice working!

3. A case history from Coventry

Coventry Cathedral was bombed during the second world war, and rebuilt in a modern style; only the old spire remains. It has some fine examples of modern art, including a large tapestry by the artist Graham Sutherland. The cathedral has been the focus of many initiatives to promote reconciliation between the people of England and Germany. But recently one young man was caught (with others) vandalizing a chapel in the cathedral, breaking an ancient icon, setting fire to an old bible and drawing swastikas. He was horrified to find that news of his actions had reached national and international news. You can imagine what would have been the conventional response: the church has been desecrated, we must make an example of this young man to give a clear message that this cannot be tolerated. He would have been sent to prison, and would have come out more angry than before.

But the local victim/offender service found that the priest responsible for the cathedral building would be willing to meet the offender; he had spoken to the cathedral staff and they were willing that he should, as an act of reparation, work there on Saturday afternoons, and the young man was willing to do it; so the judge deferred the sentence for three months, and told the young man that he should start saving up, because he would have to pay compensation.

They met, with mediators, and the priest explained how hurtful the damage was to people who used and loved the cathedral; then for the next few Saturdays the young man came to help prepare the cathedral for the Sunday services, cleaning the stone floor, polishing the wood and brass. On one occasion the great tapestry had to be taken down to be cleaned, and the priest explained its symbolism; he pointed to a human figure, which looks very small when seen from the ground, but is actually life-size, and to demonstrate this he allowed the young man to lie down on it to measure himself against it - perhaps the only person ever to do so. He was also allowed to play Scott Joplin on the cathedral organ.

Cathedral staff and volunteers explained the significance of the cathedral furnishings, and the co-ordinator of the mediation service accompanied him to the cathedral in her own time on Saturdays to make sure he went there. In talking to him she found that he had left home and was not rebelling against the church, but against his over-strict parents who had become born-again Christians. This shows that the work was not the only important thing: the relationship with other people was also significant. This means an investment of time, so adequate resources are vital if a programme like this is to succeed.

When the case came back to court the priest wrote to the court saying he was satisfied with what the young man had done, and did not require any compensation; but the judge made a compensation order. So the priest invited the young man to choose what to do with the money; they agreed to buy a pair of candlesticks for the chapel which had been damaged, the young man himself ordered them and paid for them, and attended the service at which they were consecrated. He did not become a Christian, but said that he now respected the beliefs of members of the church; he went back to live with his parents, has a good job, and has not offended again.

4. The administration of restorative justice

In England some victim/offender mediation services are operated by independent non-governmental organizations (NGOs), and this is the model I prefer, precisely because it is independent. Independence is a relative term, however; some services are limited by lack of funds; and because they are independent, they have to work hard to build links with the official system. The NGO can be established by social workers, probation officers, police, court (judge or prosecutor), education, health, Victim Support, mediators, and other capable members of the local community: business people, trades unionists, lawyers, church people, or other NGOs. For some of these professionals, this will be a new role: not working face-to-face with clients, but creating and managing an organization. Another method is multi-agency co-operation. In any case management should involve some of these agencies, some of whom can also share the funding, and should include at least one representative of the mediators. If the service is managed by only one agency, such as the probation service, at least it should have an advisory committee to supervise the programme.

Who are the mediators? Should they be lay people or professionals? One of the advantages of mediation is the opportunity it offers for involving 'ordinary' members of the community, as well as professionals such as social workers and lawyers. Their entry requirement to the training course is common sense; they have obtained their qualification from the 'university of life', and their 'special subject' is the area where they live. Whether they are professionals or lay people, they need specific training as mediators; this is mainly practical ('learning by doing') and is followed by an assessment including an interview and a role-play; some may not, in the end, have the qualities needed to be mediators. In some mediation services they work as volunteers, because they believe that there is an advantage in being able to tell the participants that they are offering their skills free for the benefit of the community. It also makes a difference to the cost of using two mediators for each session, which is widely regarded as good practice. They also receive support and supervision from the co-ordinator (administrator). In other services, after a probationary period, they are paid for each session; this may make it possible to attract lay people who need the money, and is an incentive to come to regular in-service training, which is essential to exchange experience and keep mediators' skills from becoming rusty. In England a 'National Vocational Qualification' in practical skills is available in many fields of work, and mediation is about to be added to the list.

'Professional' is a word with two meanings. It can mean a service provided by trained people, of a recognized standard, with a procedure for complaints if that standard is not met. In that sense mediation by lay mediators can and should be professional. But it can also mean people who earn their living by such work, and in some ways it would be better if mediation did not become 'over-professionalized', with academic entry requirements: another career opportunity for the middle class. If members of other professions such as law or social work want to mediate, it is important that they should be trained specifically in mediation, because training in other disciplines is different. Trainers of mediators may however be professional in this sense, provided that they have had personal experience in mediating; and perhaps we need a new profession of mediation administrator, which requires a wide range of skills. I believe that if the service is to flourish, administering it should be the administrator's only job, so that he or she has a strong incentive to make it succeed; it should not be done in time left over from another job.

5. Safeguards

Any process involving people's lives needs safeguards, both for the clients and the practitioners. I will suggest five principal ones: clearly defined aims, standards, training, accreditation, and monitoring of performance. I should add that these are ideals which are still far from being completely achieved in Britain; they are a 'counsel of perfection'.

The first priority is to define the primary aim, in general terms, and the measurable objectives by which this aim can be achieved. This is also essential before mediators can be trained, and before `success' can be measured. If we take the view that, although individuals are important, the community is even more important, we might define the primary aim as: to restore community harmony at least to its level before the harmful act was committed.

The objectives would be:

- to help the victim to recover
- to show the offender that his action was wrong because it harmed someone else
- to enable him (or require him) to make amends, and
- to reintegrate him into the community
- to ensure that the community made it possible for the offender to make reparation and be reintegrated in this way, and
- to draw any lessons for crime prevention strategy and pass them to the relevant authorities.

To do this the service should:

- offer both victim and offender the opportunity to communicate, face-to-face or indirectly; it would be for them, not the service, to decide how to use this: to agree about reparation, to give and receive an apology, or simply to ask and answer questions and express feelings

- follow-up the participants, to ask whether the process was helpful. They should be asked at the time of the mediation whether they agree to the follow-up, which may re-awaken memories of painful experiences.

Other people may not define the aims and objectives in quite the same way; the important thing is that they should be defined so that the project knows where it is going, and that they should be based on the restorative principle of healing. This aim and these objectives would be the basis for standards, training of mediators, accreditation, and monitoring.

The next safeguard is that there should be standards, both for mediators and for mediation services. For example, Mediation UK has published Practice standards[19] and there are Standards for restorative justice compiled by the Restorative Justice Consortium;[20] in Germany the Service Bureau for Victim/Offender Mediation and Conflict Resolution has issued standards, usefully divided into 'Essential' and 'Desirable'.[21] Mediation UK's Directory of mediation and conflict resolution trainers also includes a code of practice for trainers, and guidelines for making contracts with them.

Examples of standards for a mediation service are: independence, record-keeping, monitoring, and the satisfaction of 'customers'. Mediators should make sure that clients are aware of their rights, especially the right to leave the mediation process at any time; legal advice should be available, but lawyers' participation in mediation sessions is not recommended. Standards should also include 'equal opportunities': the principle that all clients, staff and mediators should be treated equally, regardless of gender, religion, ethnic background, skin colour, and similar characteristics. There should be a complaints procedure, for clients, staff and lay mediators, and they should be informed of it; it should of course include mediation at an early stage. Each service should have a procedure for passing on suggestions for crime prevention policy.

For mediators, standards include respect for all people, confidentiality (except as required by law or with the agreement of the parties), neutrality, and evaluation of their own work and each other's after each session.

---

19 Mediation UK (1998) Practice standards for mediators and the management of mediation services. Mediation UK, Alexander House, Telephone Avenue, Bristol BS 1 4 BS. Mediation UK (1998) Directory of mediation and conflict resolution trainers. Mediation UK, as above.

20 Restorative Justice Consortium (1998) *Standards for restorative justice*. RJC, co SBL, Room 9, Winchester House, 11 Cranmer Road, London SW9 6EJ, England.

21 Servicebüro für Täter-Opfer-Ausgleich und Konfliktschlichtung (1995) *Standards: ein Handbuch für die Praxis des Täter-Opfer-Ausgleichs. Servicebüro*, Aachener Strasse 1064, D-50858 Köln, Germany.

The third safeguard is adequate training of all concerned: mediators, co-ordinators (administrators), and trainers themselves; when it becomes possible, trainers should have direct experience of acting as mediators.

Fourthly, to assess whether these standards are being followed, there should be regular accreditation for these categories of people and for mediation services. In those cases which go to court after mediation, the court will assess whether an agreement is unreasonable from the point of view of the victim or the offender.

Last but not least, the participants in every case should be followed up (with their permission) after a stated period of weeks or months, to find out about their well-being, and to collect statistical information about the effect of the process on them.

Let us have a look at some research findings. In accordance with the objectives I have listed, the criteria for evaluation concentrate on the effects on the victim and the offender. Several studies have found a high proportion of satisfaction among victims; the exception is New Zealand, where in the early days of conferencing not enough attention was paid to the needs of victims,[22] but changes have now been made. In England, nearly all those who took part in mediation felt that it was important to them to receive answers from the offender, to tell him the effects of the crime, and to receive an apology; the proportion that attached importance to restitution was lower.[23] After mediation, fewer American victims were upset about crime or afraid of being re-victimized by the offender.[24] Large-scale Australian research into conferencing found that more offenders felt ashamed of what they had done, and had increased respect for the police, than those who went to court. After a conference fewer victims felt angry with offenders than before it, and the proportion who felt sympathy for them almost doubled.[25]

Does mediation reduce crime? Although, as I have said, this is not a primary objective, it is a legitimate question. We need at least to know that crime does not increase. In the United States, 18 per cent of offenders who

---

22 A. MORRIS, G. M. MAXWELL and J.P. ROBERTSON (1993) Giving victims a voice: a New Zealand experiment, 32(4) *Howard Journal* 304-321.

23 M.S. UMBREIT and A.W. ROBERTS (1996) *Mediation of criminal conflict in England: an assessment of services in Coventry and Leeds.* Centre for Restorative Justice & Peacemaking, School of Social Work, University of Minnesota, 1404 Gortner Ave, 105 Peters Hall, St Paul MN 55108-6160, USA, e-mail: rjp@tlcmail.ch.umn.edu.

24 M. UMBREIT (1994) *Victim meets offender: the impact of restorative justice and mediation.* Monsey, NY: Criminal Justice Press.

25 L.W. SHERMAN and H. STRANG (1997) *RISE working papers: the reintegrative shaming experiments for restorative community policing.* Canberra: Research School of Social Sciences, Australian National University.

took part in mediation were reconvicted within one year, compared to 27 per cent of those who did not. The difference, however, is not statistically significant.[26] As we know, reconvictions are not a reliable measure of re-offending. In addition, there could be a self-selection effect: since participants are screened for suitability, and mediation is voluntary, those who are selected for mediation and agree to take part may be the ones who are less likely to re-offend anyway. But there are no signs that recidivism is higher. There are other short-term advantages, and there may be long-term ones as well.

6. Conclusions

I have tried to show that the idea of restorative justice is not a new one, and in many ways it is common sense. Common sense, however, must be accompanied by correct facts, clear thinking and research, because without them, it can easily be confused with prejudices. Common sense told people that the sun revolved around the earth until the more accurate research of Copernicus proved otherwise. I am glad that Poland is also playing an active part in this new revolution. Here is a way of responding to crime in which we begin by helping the victim. The old common sense said that crime is wrong because it breaks the law, and people who break the law will be hurt by agents of the state, if they are caught. The new common sense tells us that crime is wrong because it hurts someone else, whether the offender is caught or not; if he is caught, he will be shown this, and there will be an opportunity for the victim, if he or she wishes, to ask for explanations and to make him understand. Then he will not be harmed further, but will be given the opportunity to make reparation to the victim and the community. He will be expected to do what he can to avoid making more mistakes, with the help of any people or organizations in the community who can contribute. I believe that by responding to criminal acts in this way we can not only restore, but also strengthen, the community and its resistance to crime.

26 UMBREIT and ROBERTS, *o.c*

References

Braithwaite, John (1998) *Restorative justice: assessing an immodest theory and a pessimistic theory*. Canberra: Australian Institute of Criminology. (webmaster@aic.gov.au)

Braithwaite, John, and Philip Pettit (1990) *Not just deserts: a republican theory of justice*. Oxford: Clarendon.

Christie, Nils (1977) Conflicts as property. 17(1) *British Journal of Criminology*, 1-15.

Christie, Nils (1982) *Limits to pain*. Oxford: Martin, Robertson.

Elias, Robert (1993) *Victims still: the political manipulation of crime victims*. Newbury Park, CA: Sage.

Hough, Michael, and Julian Roberts (1998) *Attitudes to punishment: findings from the British Crime Survey*, Home Office Research Study 179. London: Home Office.

Maguire M. and C. Corbett (1987) *The effects of crime and the work of victim support schemes*, 223-231. Alderschot: Gower

McGuire, James, and Philip Priestley (1995) Reviewing "What works", past, present and future; In: James McGuire (ed.), *What works: reducing re-offending. Guidelines from research and practice*. Chichester: Wiley.

Mediation UK (1998) *Practice standards for mediators and the management of mediation services*. Mediation UK, Alexander House, Telephone Avenue, Bristol BS 1 4 BS.

Mediation UK (1998) *Directory of mediation and conflict resolution trainers*. Mediation UK, as above.

Morris, Allison, Gabrielle M Maxwell and Jeremy P. Robertson (1993) Giving victims a voice: a New Zealand experiment. 32(4) *Howard Journal*, 304-321.

Penal Reform International and International Centre for Prison Studies (1998) *Newsletter: Penal Reform Project in Eastern Europe and Central Asia*, No. 1. PRI, Unit 114, The Chandlery, 50 Westminster Bridge Road, London SE1 7QY, England.

Restorative Justice Consortium (1998) *Standards for restorative justice*. RJC, co SBL, Room 9, Winchester House, 11 Cranmer Road, London SW9 6EJ, England.

Rzepliński, Andrzej (1984) Private communication.

Servicebüro für Täter-Opfer-Ausgleich und Konfliktschlichtung (1995) *Standards: ein Handbuch für die Praxis des Täter-Opfer-Ausgleichs. Servicebüro*, Aachener Strasse 1064, D-50858 Köln, Germany.

Sessar, Klaus (1992) *Wiedergutmachen oder Strafen: Einstellungen in der Bevölkerung und der Justiz - ein Forschungsbericht*. Centaurus.

Sherman, Lawrence W, and Heather Strang (1997) *RISE working papers: the reintegrative shaming experiments for restorative community policing*. Canberra: Research School of Social Sciences, Australian National University.

Stern, Vivien (1998) *A sin against the future: imprisonment in the world*. London: Penguin.

Stuart, Barry (2001) 'Guiding principles for peacemaking circles; in: Gordon Bazemore and Mara Schiff (eds.), *Restorative community justice: repairing harm and transforming communities*. Cincinnati, OH: Anderson.

Umbreit, Mark (1994) *Victim meets offender: the impact of restorative justice and mediation*. Monsey, NY: Criminal Justice Press.

Umbreit, Mark S, and Ann Warner Roberts (1996) *Mediation of criminal conflict in England: an assessment of services in Coventry and Leeds*. Centre for Restorative Justice & Peacemaking, School of Social Work, University of Minnesota, 1404 Gortner Ave, 105 Peters Hall, St. Paul MN 55108-6160, e-mail: rjp@tlcmail.che.umn.edu.

Wright, Martin (1989) What the public wants; in: Martin Wright and Burt Galaway, eds. *Mediation and criminal justice: victims, offenders and community*. London: Sage.

Wright, Martin (1992) Victim/offender mediation as a step towards a restorative system of justice; in: H. Messmer and H.-U. Otto (eds.), *Restorative justice on trial: pitfalls and potential of victim/offender mediation - international research perspectives*. Dordrecht: Kluwer.

Wright; Martin (1996) (2nd ed.), *Justice for victims and offenders: a restorative response to crime*. Winchester: Waterside Press.

Wright, Martin (1999) *Restoring respect for justice*. Winchester: Waterside Press.

Appendix I: How restorative justice can be used

(1) Least serious offence: Discontinue (with or without a Warning)

(2) More serious offence

- police
  - accused admits act or `does not deny'
    - conference
      - agreement; apology, reparation, etc.
        - (no further court involvement)
          - mediation service monitors agreement
      - conference does not reach agreement
        - court imposes sentence* (reparative if possible)
  - accused denies guilt
    - court
      - convicts
        - conference
          - conference does not reach agreement (see above)
          - agreement
            - court accepts agreement or adds to it or reduces it
              - mediation service monitors agreement
      - finds not guilty

* victim or offender can request mediation after sentence (sentence is not affected)

(3) Most serious offence

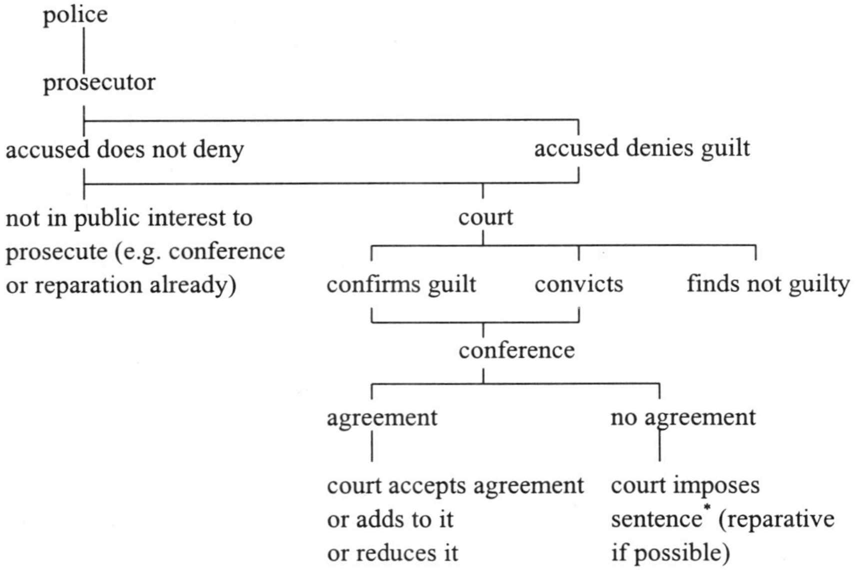

* victim or offender can request mediation after sentence (sentence is not affected)

ANSWERS TO ATROCITIES. RESTORATIVE JUSTICE AS AN ANSWER TO EXTREME SITUATIONS[1]

Nils Christie

Introduction

Confronted with small damages, such as against property or honour, it is not complicated to argue for mediation and restoration. The situation becomes more difficult when we are confronted with serious crimes as killing or rape. In this article I want to go even one step further and ask: what is the situation when we are confronted with the most extreme of damages, with atrocities as those from World-War II or other later horrors. Would it still be possible to think of responses other than punishment? To grasp the multitude of possibilities, I will suggest a scale of possible answers; from total amnesia, then silence, truth-seeking, punishment and restoration, and at the other end of the scale amnesty; that is where authorities officially declare that amnesia is to take place.

1. Amnesia

It is obvious that none of us could have survived with a memory of all the traumatic events we might have remembered. It would have meant an extremely heavy burden. We do not register all writings on those walls we pass. And if we do register, we remember only a fragment. It is also obvious that we are highly selective in what we see, in what we store, and in what we re-call. What is abortion to the doctor might be perceived as killing by the priest. To some women it might be a moment of great relief, to others the utmost of sin, hidden behind stonewalls in the mind.[2] We perceive

1 Thanks to Hedda Giertsen, Ragnhild Hennum, Kristin Hobson and Lill Scherdin for helpful comments. This article is a further elaboration of a plenary presentation at the 35th Biannual Congress of the International Institute of Sociology, Krakow 11-16 July 2001. For an example of damaging results of not penetrating the past, see M. LOS and A. ZYBERTOWICZ (2000) *Privatizing the Police-State. The Case of Poland*. GB: Basingstoke.

2 "The mind", a term which significantly enough means just memory, or in old-Norse "minne".

selectively, we remember selectively, we recall selectively. We construct. We are human beings.

I was a child in an occupied country during World War II. Did the usual things. Followed the rules: Never fraternise with a German soldier or a Norwegian Nazi-member. There were big signs in streetcars and buses announcing that it was strictly forbidden, and punishable by imprisonment, to remain standing in the carrier if there was an empty seat next to a soldier. So, I was a good Norwegian and remained standing. Nevertheless, I cannot remember from the time it happened that the Jews were deported, I can not remember one single comment about it in my generally patriotic circles. The Jews were apprehended by the ordinary Norwegian police. Since they were too many, one hundred ordinary taxies were used for transporting them to the ship that brought them to Germany. I suppose the drivers soon forgot that episode in their life. When the few survivors came home from the camps, they came to a country that, to some extent, has forgotten that they ever had been there. And their property was mostly gone. It was not until 1996 that they -or mostly their children and grandchildren- got a decent compensation.

2. Silence

Silence is the next, and probably the most common, answer to atrocities. Silence, because there is nobody around to listen. Isolation of the victim is one of the major features in social systems where illegitimate violence is applied. The mechanism can be observed in cases of battered women. Husbands in such cases tend to isolate both wife and children, see to it that they have no close friends or relatives near by. Kids are not allowed to take friends home. There is nobody to tell. Or may be nothing to tell. The dinner was not ready when he came home that day or the meat was not quite tender. May be the husband had reasons for his anger. The wife's intellectual need for an explanation is reverted towards her own deficiencies and silences her protest. To change this, it is essential that she comes out of the isolation, gets access to an audience that will not strengthen her man's definition of the situation.

It was a similar situation in concentration camps. Those unable to see themselves as enemies of the oppressors seemed to be worse off than militant opponents defending a cause. They had nothing to say, except that it was all a terrible misunderstanding. But most prisoners struggled to break the silence, to convey the truth to those outside the camps. The milk-bucket from the ghetto in Lodz is a moving example. Lodz is a big industrialised city roughly halfway between Krakow and Warsaw. Throughout all the turmoil in the ghetto, a newspaper was printed there every day in three copies. A few days before the last transport left in 1944, one copy of all the volumes was hidden in a bucket, buried, regained after the war, and then published in the terrible/wonderful book by Lucjan Dobroszycki,[3] *The Chronicle of the Lodz Ghetto 1941-1944*. Here also the victims got a voice.

There is no end to attempts by oppressors to silence their victims. Nor are there ends to the continuous struggles to break the silence. To me, Mauricio Rosencoff is a prime example. He is from Uruguay. For eleven years he - and ten other men - were kept under complete isolation by the military junta of the country. International attention prevented their killing, but not their torture and the totality of their isolation. In periods, they got nearly no water. To survive, they had to drink their own urine. To survive as human beings, nearly all of them engaged in some sort of artistic activity. The one who did not turned insane, just as intended by the junta. Mauricio Rosencoff wrote poetry in his head. At one stage, he got hold of a piece of pencil and little by little he was able to smuggle out his poems on small bits of paper. When he was released, he found he had become a famous poet in Uruguay. They treated us like dogs, said Mauricio. But we did not bark back. At a seminar in Oslo on torture Mauricio took part. So did a man who had acted as a torturer in Uruguay. One day this man was given the task to work on a person from his own street. He saw a man like himself, and fled the country. After the seminar, Mauricio and the former torturer went out for a coffee.

3. Seeking the truth

From the situation of battered women, newspapers in milk-buckets, and seminars on torture, it is only a small step to the Truth Commission of South Africa and the numerous similar commissions in Latin America.[4] There is nothing mysterious here, only systematic attempts to break the silence combined with a thrust in the strength of truth. Bishop Tutu was central in creating an arena for exposure. People, who had been subjected to unbelievable degradations, in the form of physical and mental pain, were given the opportunity to tell their tales. They could do so eye to eye with

---

3 L. DOBROSZYCKI (1984) *The Chronicle of the Lodz Ghetto 1941-1944*. New Haven and London: Yale University Press.

4 For a perceptive discussion of Truth Commissions, see B.A. MISZTAL (2001) Legal Attempts to Construct Collective Memory, 1 *Polish Sociological Review* 133.

their oppressors. And what is essential, independently of all the critique that has also hit the commissions. They were given the opportunity to concentrate on what they had seen, what they had experienced, and not on the matter of revenge, particularly not on the task of getting anybody formally sentenced.

Some of this was also an essential element in the situation of the oppressors. Mostly they appeared before the Truth Commission as an alternative to being brought before a penal court. When they talked, they talked under stress. And they had much to defend, self-respect, honour. But they had agreed to break the silence, to participate, to expose what they knew. And they could talk in a context that was not determined by legal constraints.

3.1. Did they tell the truth?

We will never know. But we are able to compare two systems. We can compare the Truth-Commissions to the ordinary penal courts, and ask: "what type of information comes out of these two social systems, what sort of answers to atrocities do they produce"?

3.2. Several elements are clearly different.

First, the goals of the whole operation are basically different. Penal law is oriented towards finding responsibility, or guilt. This produces consequences for the pattern of thinking within the institution. Penal law is built upon dichotomies, guilty or not guilty. A decision of "half guilty" does not count. It is the decision of either/or that counts. Truth Commissions are, in a way, relieved from the dichotomies. They can think in continuums; it was bad what he did, awful, but certain acts were OK. If the total picture was of a character that made him "guilty", that is not central to the description.

Within penal law it has also to be a personalised guilt. Not a "system-guilt", not a historical development, but the behaviour of one specific person. Once more we see that Truth Commissions have more to play with, greater possibilities for raising questions closer to a sociologically oriented understanding of the phenomenon.

In addition to decisions on guilt, the essence of the penal process is delivery of pain. In much writing on penal law this is camouflaged; pain and sufferings are not elaborated upon. The system is filled with euphemisms; prisons are called institutions. In my country prison cells are called rooms, prisoners are called inmates, guards are called "betjenter" which literally means those who serve other people. Nonetheless, even in countries without torture and capital punishment, we know that delivery of pain is an essential part of the whole operation. And pain makes this a serious matter. Most states develop mechanisms to control it. The emphasis on equality is one such mechanism. Equal pain for equal crimes. But crimes are seldom equal, and offenders are rarely identical twins. Central to penal law is therefore the striving towards ways of handling the differences, particularly by reducing the number of factors to be taken into consideration. This is primarily done through elaborate systems of training or socialisation into what sort of information is accepted as "relevant information". Legal training is to large extent training in relevance, or to be more precise, in irrelevance. Many among us have been in situations where we were told by our lawyers that what we think of as our best arguments in a legal conflict should not be mentioned at all in court. The judge would think we were out of our mind, and that the lawyer was a bad one by bringing in what to us was the essence of the case. Again, it is probably necessary in a legal system to have established some sort of agreement on relevance. But this is not necessarily good for exposure of the total story of what happened.

Compared to this, the Truth Commissions stand in a more free position. It is an arena for exposure, for complaints, for emotional displays, and also for denials. But the central point is the exposure of what happened, not a decision about delivery of pain later on.

For the purpose of preventing errors in the delivery of pain, the penal law arrangements when they are functioning properly -and sometimes they are not- are probably the best that can be invented. But when it comes to a more thorough exposure of what happened, my preliminary conclusion will be that Truth Commissions -if they are functioning properly, and again sometimes they are not- probably are better instruments than penal courts.[5]

4. Justice done

But of course, penal courts are not meant only for the exposure of atrocities. They are instruments for the implementation of justice. One element in that justice is to let the guilty ones receive the intended pain. The question here is

5 One reservation: This is an ideal-typical picture. Some Truth Commissions have worked under highly unfavourable conditions, politically and/or economically. They have thereby experienced trouble, as penal courts in the same situation also would have experienced.

simply: How is it possible to avenge atrocities of such type, avenge evil acts of a quality and quantity not encountered in ordinary life?

Not far from Krakow is Auschwitz and next to it is the major death-camp: Birkenau. Where the railway-tracks end in Lager Birkenau, the gallows were raised after World War II and it was there that they hanged the Commander.[6]

I have never been able to understand it. One life against one and a half million! One broken neck against all those who suffocated, starved to death, or were plainly killed in that camp. To me, the execution became a sort of denigration of the 1.5 million victims. The worth of each became just 1.5 millionth of the worth of the Commander!

But what else could be done? So asked my Polish colleagues when far back in time I exposed my doubt. And I had no answer, except this: Maybe a trial had to be carried out. Day after day survivors would have to reveal what happened. All sorts of victims would have to express their despair, rage and wish for vengeance. The Commander would also express his position, his reasons then, and now, in front of the survivors and his judges.

But then, how would the judge, if he were a free judge and not only an executioner hired by the rulers, decide in the end? One possibility, and that would be my preference, is that he should so address the Camp Commander: *"You have clearly done it. You have administered death to more than a million human beings. You are guilty. Your acts are morally repulsive to an extent above what can be imagined. We have heard it. All in the civilised world will get to know about your horrible acts carried out at this horrible place. No more can be said and done. Go away in shame."*

But of course, I know that could not happen. I had, in the beginning of the 1960s long talks with professor Batawia in Warsaw. He was professor in forensic psychiatry, and had carried out long conversations with the commander of one of the large concentration camps. I have forgotten which one, it was probably Rudolf Höss. We compared notes. I had worked in the same field, interviewing guards who tortured and killed in Nacht und Nebel (Night and Fog) -camps in the North of Norway. We found that we had two common experiences. First, none of us had met any monsters from the camps. Bad news for those hoping to find beasts behind the atrocities; by and large there were no monsters. Secondly, neither the Polish, nor the Norwegian society was particularly interested in getting acquainted with our results. Batawia was flatly forbidden to publish and my small articles were

6 This is as I remember it. In the book X. (1985) *Auschwitz*, 188. Warsaw: Interpress, I find that Rudolf Höss was hanged April 1947 outside the building from where he had governed the camp.

ignored. It was not until a new generation had grown up that I was able to publish the whole report in the form of a book. Too close in time to the atrocities, it was not an analysis that was asked for, only revenge.

5. The execution of an idea

Nonetheless, they might have been right, those who hanged the commander. They did not only hang the commander, but a whole system. His broken neck symbolised a broken idea. It was the nazi-ideology that was hanged in those gallows. Societies need clear and fast answers when their most fundamental values have been under attack such as in the nazi area.

I agree, of course I agree, how could I not. But nonetheless, in a little corner of my sociological conscience lurk some doubts. We kill the commander, yes. We even killed the major initiators after Nuremberg. We exterminate the evil ideas and their major carriers, swiftly, unanimously. We make it crystal-clear that certain acts, genocide and extermination of unwanted minorities, are crimes so abhorrent that no mercy is possible. My only doubts are: Do we thereby hit the whole target? By hanging the commander and also those bosses in Nuremberg, a good feeling of accomplishment is created, vengeance, often called justice, is carried out, but at the same time, the discussion of related phenomena is efficiently closed.

The commander was guilty, and from a legal standpoint he certainly deserved his punishment. Nonetheless, at the same time he also functioned as a scapegoat, as did his chiefs who were hanged in Nuremberg. Behind them were some untamed forces, protected by the penal actions against their carriers. Atrocities met with individual punishments may prevent the development of a fuller understanding of those forces and of the phenomena in general. It was not until 1989 that we got through the deep layers of understanding of the concentration camps with Zygmunt Bauman's book on "Modernity and the Holocaust".

By hanging commanders, and while the judges in Nuremberg focused on finding personal guilt for atrocities, other phenomena were left in peace, left to grow. Three themes were not discussed in Nuremberg:

- Dresden
- Hiroshima and Nagasaki
- The Gulag's

Dresden was made into a no-town in less than 24 hours, and with at least 135 000 victims. Later it was difficult to find rational military reasons or justifications for their extinction.

Hiroshima and Nagasaki were made into churchyards with one atom bomb to each town. The reasons behind these mass-killings of civilians seem unclear; no one -even if they tried- got the question up in Nuremberg or before any other international court. It has been difficult to find rational military reasons for what happened. A better founded hypothesis seems to be that the dropping of the bombs was intended as a sign of warning to the USSR, a glorious introduction to the cold war.

And then the Gulag's. Of course they could not be discussed in Nuremberg with a prominent Russian among the judges. But while they decided on death in Nuremberg, the Gulag's bulged.

6. Preventing atrocities

By hanging the individuals most closely related to the atrocities we re-establish certain standards. We teach everybody a lesson. Mass-killers will end in the gallows. Maybe we are preventing other people from going into the service of evil forces.

These are the conventional arguments for all severe punishments. And I am afraid they have even less validity here than in more ordinary cases. Perpetrators of this type of evil acts see themselves as servants of states, most often of national states surrounded by aggressors. Or they are just functionaries, as Adolph Eichman was in his office. Or they may see themselves as soldiers in an inevitable and also just war, as when secret forces from Israel kill or kidnap persons far outside the borders of the Middle East. In my country, we shot the chief-traitor Vidkun Quisling after World War II. It is unreasonable to think that this will influence the next potential traitor. The situation will be another, the cause will be another. And the next person in will, while he acts, see himself as an obvious winner. It is the bandits on the other side who will be brought to court.

7. International penal courts

The Nuremberg court was clearly a court established by the winners. It was a military court, and international only in the sense that the four judges came from the four major countries that defeated Germany. And it was a court deciding over an enemy that had suffered total defeat.

In more recent attempts to establish international standards, this has, to some extent, changed. Some courts have gone international. The

International Criminal Tribunal for Former Yugoslavia in The Hague is the most recent example. The International Criminal Court will come into being when 60 countries have ratified the Statute. Up till now, only 36 have done so. These are, or will be, civil courts with judges and prosecutors from several different countries. This represents long steps forward, compared to Nuremberg. But some basic problems with penal courts remain.

While I was preparing this essay, Yugoslavian authorities came under enormous pressure to send Milosevic to The International Criminal Tribunal for Former Yugoslavia in The Hague. Milosevic was at this point in prison in Belgrade, waiting for trial.[7] If the government agreed to send him to The Hague, it would receive money from the West to rebuild the country. If they only brought him to court at home, they would receive nothing. They sent him, and received next day a promise for money: 11,9 billion dollars against one person: Milosevic. It happened on June 28th, the very same day Serbs memorise the catastrophy in a war against the Turks in the 14th Century. The prosecution made the claim to get Milosevic to The Hague before the NATO-war against Yugoslavia had come to an end. It seems probable that those claims prolonged the war. After the war, the prosecutor's claims created considerable internal instability in the country. The president of Yugoslavia was strongly against the deportation. The Supreme Court of Yugoslavia had not finished their discussion on the legality of the case. The same turmoil, for the same reasons, took place in Croatia.

In addition to these concrete problems that we witness in the Balkans these days, there are three principal problems that mar international courts of the type we see in The Hague:

First: Western legal order emphasises justice values such as being sentenced by equals and according to laws passed by elected representatives. But even within the most tranquil among national states, those values are not always adhered to. Or maybe I should rather say: They are never fully realised. Jury-members, as well as judges, are nearly always older, better educated, and from more prominent class-background than those they are called upon to judge. Laws are mostly better suited to control the poor than the rich, and to control those without power than those with power, and they are made by and for the more successful citizens of the population. With international courts or tribunals, it is even more difficult to play according to the basic rules of the game. It will not be a drama according to national laws, it will not be a trial carried out by national judges, and it will not be trial by an ordinary jury. In my little country, 80 000 collaborators were convicted

7 Milosevic might be a bad man, and also be found guilty. I have no opinion on that.

after World War II. Of course no nazi-members served as prosecutors, jury-members or judges. They were by definition not worth listening to. The winners decide the aftermath of wars. There was never much talk about Genocide when Europe colonised Africa and America. And it was only recently that claims were made by Africans or Indians for Truth-Commissions. This break with normal procedure is both inevitable and wanted when a dictator from a terror-regime is brought before the international court. But it becomes a challenge to the legitimacy of the international court in cases where the suspect comes from a more ordinary functioning state.

Second: Values of impartiality and fairness are emphasised in Western legal systems. Equality is here an important element: equal results in equal cases, equality not only in what *comes out* of court, but also in what goes in. Again, this is an ideal not always adhered to in national courts. It might sometimes prove less risky to steal the bank than rob the cashier. But again, international courts have extraordinary problems. Large and powerful states, and small states with good connections to the large ones, are obviously better protected against being brought before international courts than small states without power and/or with miserable connections to the great powers. It was the total losers that were hanged in Nuremberg. As to later developments, it is difficult not to express a certain surprise at not having been able to register any call for the former president Tudjman of Croatia in The Hague. When the International Criminal Court comes into being, new problems will arise. Turks might be expected there due to their treatment of Kurds. Suharto might be a suitable candidate from Indonesia. Some might even expect Kissinger in one of those courts one day, and may be also Ariel Sharon for both old and new acts, rather than being claimed only by Belgian courts. Some Russian generals might also be asked to come to answer for their methods in Chechnya. It is not without interest that none of the nations these prominent persons come from has ratified the Statute creating the International Criminal Court.

The third problem with the international courts is the question of relevance. I have already discussed this problem. To create equality, lawyers have strong wishes to eliminate what shall be discussed in courts, to concentrate on certain elements. But international courts are close to international politics. Sharon will claim that his state was in danger and demand that his acts be seen as an answer to this danger. Milosevic will, if he decides to defend himself before the court, claim it to be illegal. He will probably say that the Kosovo-Albanians were trained and supported by the CIA, and that the whole NATO-operation was intended to weaken

Yugoslavia and give access to territories further East in Europe. It is therefore NATO, not he, that ought to be on trial. But courts are badly suited to handle such statements. They will retreat to statements of relevance and, just as in ordinary court cases, will not open up for what the accused persons see as their most important arguments. But thereby they also expose their basic weakness in telling us what happened.

I have no definite answers to the problems raised here. What I cannot hide, and will not hide, is scepticism regarding international penal law as the answer to atrocities. Penal law creates always restrictions on the flow of information, and is therefore not the best instrument in clarifying what happened. International penal law is inevitably the law of the winners, and is therefore of dubious utility in attempts to create social peace. It is an instrument to describe parts of what happened in the past. But we need systems that look forward. We need instruments that both clarify the past, and help the future. Systems for restoration might be one answer.

8. Restoration

But can restoration take place after years of oppression, after years of killings and rape, or even serious attempts of genocide? Of course not completely. Husbands are killed; those raped are left with their scars and may be also with children intentionally forced on them by the enemy. Or they are, as travellers in my country - it is a gypsy-related group - brought in a situation where they are sterilised, or their children are taken to unknown addresses by the authorities. These evil acts can never be undone.

Particularly complicated in Europe just now is a situation like the present one in Kosovo: with highly deplorable Serbian acts, with highly deplorable Western interference, and also with highly deplorable Kosovo-Albanian acts. Before the bombing, there were 1 300 international peace-observers in Kosovo. They were withdrawn, so that the bombing may commence. Most observers seem to agree that 13 000 international peace-observers would have kept the peace in Kosovo, and thus prevented bombs and the flight of 800 000 civilians. To day, there are 45 000 soldiers in the province.

There are two ways to address the Kosovo-conflict. One is the usual penal way; kill the killers, or hurt them. The second is to help the conflicting parties meet and create an arena where they can tell their stories, expose their grievances, and then slowly, may be after many, many attempts, come to some sort of common understanding of what happened, and what might be done in an attempt to alleviate the situation.

8.1. The utmost of naiveté?

Not quite. A very strong influence on modern penal policy these days stem from native traditions in New Zealand, Australia, and from native Indian culture, particularly in Canada, and also in the USA. It has become clear how heavily native youngsters are over-represented in modern prisons. Thereby the need for returning to the old ways of coping with conflicts has been exposed. These old ways are based on mediation. In relatively egalitarian societies far away from central authorities, it is close to obvious that punishment might lead to civil war, just as punishments on the international arena without one central power can lead to a renewal of old conflicts and warfare. In such societies, it becomes essential to restore the situations and thereby preserve social systems. Restore is an Old-Norse term. It means, literally, to rise up once more those wooden stocks – staur - that have fallen down, or more poetically, to rebuild the house. These activities represent a negation of ideals from penal law. If blame and shame is to be applied, it has to be in the form of re-integrative shaming. If an offender is clearly defined, emphasis is put on how he or she can repair the damage, materially or symbolically, and not on how that offender can be made to suffer. Restorative meetings of this type are, in many ways, a further development of Truth Commissions.

8.2. Not possible in the Balkan-region?

I heard that statement in Tirana, the capital of Albania, some years ago. It was a huge meeting with hundreds of participants. The theme was how to get blood-vengeance come to a stop. Impossible, said several participants. We are too proud; therefore the rules of blood-vengeance have to be obeyed. Then rose a huge, white-haired man, who I later learned had served as a general in the guerrilla against the Italian occupants, and later in the army. But that was far back in time. Now he said: I have been imprisoned for so many years under Hoxha (the former ruler of Albania). Now it is over. I feel no hatred. Albanians are not that way; they are not a peculiar sort. The discussion immediately came to an end. The project on mediation is by now well established in Albania.

8.3. Not possible when monsters are behind the atrocities!

Having worked with crime and punishment most of my life, I have to confess that I have never met any monster. I could not find them among the killers in concentration camps, nor have I met anyone later. There are people I dislike, but none that is completely impossible to reach, at least for some important seconds. My basic supposition is that most people are like most people. We have all been infants and cared for. We have had, as Cooley sees it, a common experience of being nursed by someone. This common experience is what makes it possible for us to understand the plot in the Greek dramas written 2000 years ago, as well as the persons behind recent atrocities.

8.4. But when the acts are unbelievable such as Genocide?

Many nations are based on genocide, my own included. Norway made an attempt to exterminate the Sami people and their culture to the best of our abilities. But in the 1990s the remaining Sami's got their own Parliament. It was as compensation for a particularly ugly destruction of one of their major salmon-rivers. Quite recently the University of Oslo, which is my university, has also given back to the Sami a whole assembly of sculls. It was the physical anthropologists who had them exhibited for years not far away from my office. Several of them had been executed for sorcery, some for opposition against Norwegian authorities. I admit that these sins are old and small-scale compared to the white man's behaviour in Africa or America. But they are not small for the Sami population, confronting what they might have seen as Norwegian monsters.

What I am trying to say is that atrocities are common phenomena. It is important for our understanding of them that their answers are not monopolised as a property of one nation or one category of victims. They are general features of human history, a part of our destiny. Most nations have been involved, as victims or as perpetrators, most often as both. This makes it important to include atrocities into the normality of abnormality. We must find ways of both prevention and reaction to atrocities where we mobilise the ordinary stock of knowledge on how to handle social conflicts.

Conclusion: The importance of not having answers

My major conclusion from attempts to find answers to atrocities is that there are no easy answers in individual cases, and maybe no good answers in general. This sounds negative, and is intended so. To pretend to have answers might be counterproductive. There are many vested interests behind claims of having the good answers. So much is launched as answers to atrocities, which actually increase the chances for further atrocities. Penal action might strengthen certain nations, or forces within those nations, but weaken others. They might also carry the seeds for new atrocities. International courts, deviating so much from the ordinary ideals for courts, may prevent a deeper understanding of the forces behind mass-scale killings. A conclusion that there are no good answers to atrocities is not a heroic one. It is not one that will initiate strong actions, or immediately create new barricades against evil forces. But may be an admittance of the non-existence of good answers is a foundation to build peace on. If the hunt for good answers is a vain one, we are forced back to ordinary ways of handling conflicts. Particularly we have to tap experience from peace-research and civil ways of handling conflicts. We have to live with sorrow and misery in the shadow of atrocities. But -if you forgive me for expressing my own morality- we must at the same time also try out some old-fashioned ways of solving conflict, restore - and forgive, may be even before the culprits have moved so far as to ask for it. We do not want amnesia. But after all has been brought to the surface, imprinted into all minds and all human history, we might in the end have no better final solution than amnesties.

References

Bauman, Zygmunt (1989) *Modernity and the holocaust.* Cambridge: Polity Press.

Dobroszycki, Lucjan (1984) *The Chronicle of the Lodz Ghetto 1941-1944.* New Haven and London: Yale University Press,

Loz′, Maria and Andrzej Zybertowicz (2000) *Privatizing the Police-State. The Case of Poland.* GB: Basingstoke.

Miszal, Barbara A. (2001) Legal Attempts to Construct Collective Memory, 133 *Polish Sociological Review* 1.

X. (1985) *Auschwitz.* Warsaw: Interpress.

UNIVERSITY, JUSTICE AND THE CHURCHES BEFORE THE VICTIMS OF TERRORISM[1]
Commentary on Restorative Justice

Antonio Beristain

This contribution is dedicated to the to the generous Professor and friend Tony Peters, as a small symbol of great respect and deep gratitude for his teaching, especially in Spain and Latin America.

Introduction

In Spain three institutions look after the victims of terrorism. A recurrent topic in research such as this one, deals with the institutions that ought to be created in order to solve the problems caused by terrorism. This contribution takes a more hopeful, optimistic path. It will be on the subject of the positive achievements we already enjoy, in order to get to know them better, develop them further and get the most out of them.

When facing the present tragedy of terrorism I would like to look at reality from a different point of view, aiming at getting to know the other face of the moon.

In short, the first part will bring together some objective data about the phenomenon of ETA's terrorism in Spain. The second part will discuss the appropriateness of the establishment in some universities of a professorship of victimology, with its own fundamental principles, its specific themes, its methods of research and instruction in terrorism, and with a commitment to its victims. The third part is about a specific innovation, something similar to exile, confinement and deportation, that is at the same time very different, more effective and also more humane, namely article 57, which was recently introduced in the Spanish penal code. Lastly I will point out to the fact that some sector -a very small one- of the churches has, or will have to, rediscover the parable of The Good Samaritan, which demands and achieves too much both in favour of the victims and against terrorism. Are the huge damages and prejudicial consequences that terrorism produces reversible?

---

1 These pages summarize my report to the *International Conference on "Countering Terrorism Through Enhanced International Cooperation"* organized for The International Scientific and Professional Advisory Council of the United Nations Crime Prevention and Criminal Justice Programme (Courmayeur, Mont Blanc, 22-24 September, 2000), with some updates and bibliographical references.

1. Objective data about the phenomenon of terrorism in Spain

Table 1: Murders and kidnappings of ETA in Spain (1968-2001)[2]

Murders

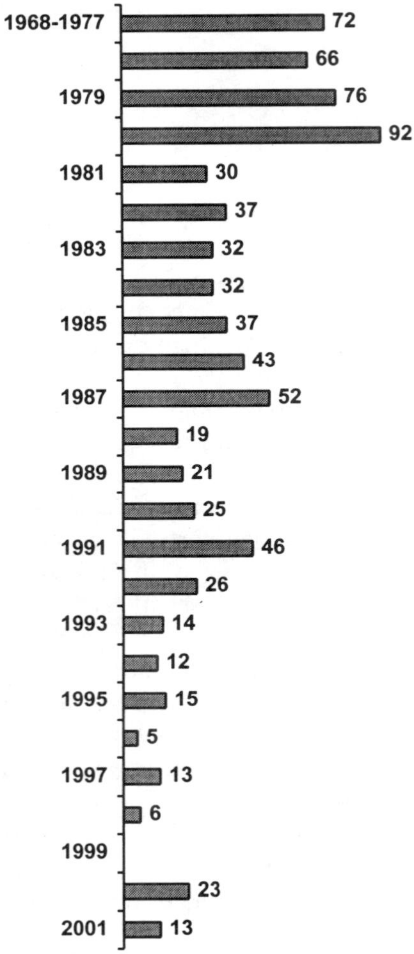

Total 807

Kidnappings

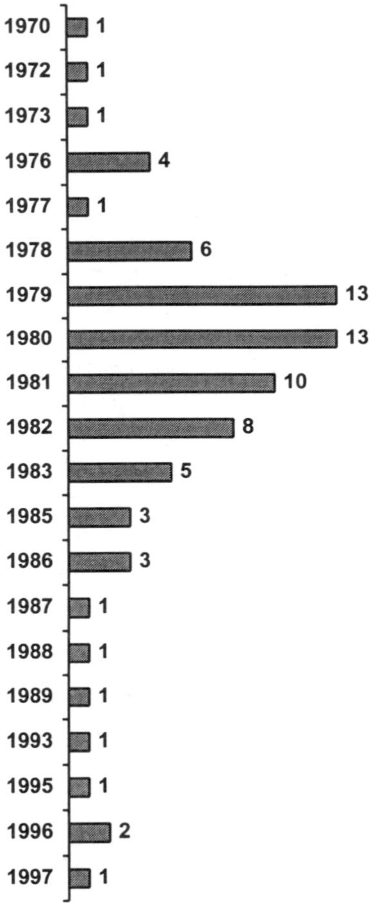

Total 77

2 Source: Ministerio del Interior de España (http://www.mir.es). There were no murders in 1999.

2. A New and Innovative Professorship at the University

Last August took place in Montreal, Canada, the 10th International Symposium of the World Association of Victimology. Among the participants were experts on the subject coming from all over the world. The various subjects tackled in papers, forums, workshops, visits to institutions, etc. made it clear to me that nowadays any university of significance must have a professorship of victimology.

Figure 1: Main topics of victimology as presented at the 10th International Symposium on Victimology, Montréal, 2000.

1. THEORETICAL AND CONCEPTUAL ISSUES ON VICTIMOLOGY
2. VICTIM ASSISTANCE PROGRAMMES
3. COMPENSATION AND RESTITUTION PROGRAMMES
4. LAWS CONCERNING VICTIMS-VICTIMS IN CRIMINAL JUSTICE PROCESS
5. VICTIMS'BILLS OF RIGHTS
6. RESEARCH AND POLICY
7. VICTIMIZATION BY VIOLENCE:
   a. International Terrorism Victims
   b. Homicide Victims and their Families
   c. Sexual offences
8. ACCIDENT VICTIMS-WORK; ACCIDENTS, TRANSPORTATION ETC.
9. VICTIMS OF ABUSE OF POWER
10. HOLOCAUST& GENOCIDE VICTIMS
11. KIDNAP VICTIMS AND FAMILIES
12. ENVIRONMENTAL & NUCLEAR VICTIMS
13. VICTIMIZATION OF SPECIAL GROUPS:
    a. The Aged
    b. Missing and Runaway Children and Adolescents
    c. Women
    d. Children
    e. Handicapped and Retarded
    f. Minorities- Ethnic, Gays, etc.
    g. State and Institutional reaction to people inflicted with AIDS

Such a creation would provide a place to deal with the new subjects of knowledge and research, a source of information about terrorism and, above all, a means of exploring the new paradigms in this field. Our penal code, criminology or criminal politics are no longer enough. We need to introduce a new vision within the university; a new and innovative professorship.

3. Restorative Justice creates a new norm that goes beyond banishment

> *"The concept of restorative justice is not restricted to a concrete method, a programme or a technique, but goes rather in the direction of a new paradigm or global vision, "changing lenses", the development of another view, not only of the social or criminal-justice reaction that must follow a crime, but also and primarily of the nature of the crime itself."*
>
> Tony Peters and Ivo Aertsen[3]

In this section we should probably discuss the new laws that many countries are promulgating in the field of victimology. We will not deal with them, though; as such discussion would largely exceed our assigned space. For information on the UN draft resolution on restorative justice programmes in criminal matters the reader is referred to a very useful and informative website (*www.restorativejustice.org)*.

We will just make a statement about a new rule, extremely appropriate, that will surely yield much benefit in criminal policy, namely article 57 of the penal code currently in force in Spain. This section, according to the Public General Act of Parliament of the 9th June 1999, enables judges and the courts to efficiently protect the victims and also to ensure that the perpetrators of some offences are neutralized and re-socialised. Terrorist crimes are without doubt included among the offences mentioned above. The article empowers judges and courts to set some new and effective specific obligations. They do have, for instance, the authority to forbid the criminal to approach the victim, whether directly or indirectly victimised by him, to communicate with the victim, or to return to the place where the crime was committed. The ban can last up to five years.

Such a rule should be introduced in other countries' penal codes.

---

3 T. Peters & I. Aertsen (2000) Towards 'Restorative Justice': Victimisation, Victim Support and Trends in Criminal Justice, in *Crime and Criminal Justice in Europe,* 45. Strasbourg: Council of Europe.

4. Religions re-discover the Good Samaritan

"We hardly need to be reminded after the recent storms that there are victims of floods and high winds-which in some strange theological perspective are termed by the insurance industry as acts of God!"

Frederic McClintock[4]

As I have shown in this same forum, a couple of years ago, some people and religious institutions, when driven by fanaticism, or because of their rejection of the values of law and justice, can become etiological factors of terrorism. When they are not, they can and must contribute to overcoming it all over the world.[5]

Unfortunately, nowadays some theologians and some ecclesiastical corporations, in Spain as well as abroad, leave a lot to be desired when acting, talking or writing about the terrorism of ETA and its victims. As far as I have been informed, very seldom indeed do they refer directly or indirectly to those victims.[6]

Karl Rahner, an excellent theologian, made this very regrettable omission in Germany. He never talked nor wrote about the Nazi holocaust. I mention this here so that we may consider the following point: Is there something hidden in some sectors of Christianity, that allows for such a tragic oblivion of the myth of Abel and of the parable of the Good Samaritan (St. Luke's Gospel, chap. X).

It is the religion's faculty and duty to contribute most positively to the overcoming of terrorism all over the world. Theologians are in fact compelled to encourage the development of positive and constructive values such as a basic attitude of "linkedness" to be acquired vis à vis: (1) themselves, (2) others, (3) materials, (4) the group-society-the cultural world, (5) the natural world-the totality of life.[7] They also have to encourage

---

4 F. McClintock (1998) Prologue: Victims and Criminal Justice, in E. Fattah and T. Peters (eds.) *Support for crime victims in a comparative perspective, A collection of essays dedicated to the memory of Prof. Frederic McClintock*, 13-19. Leuven: Leuven University Press.

5 A. Beristain (1998) *Criminología y Victimología. Alternativas Re-creadoras al delito.* Bogota, Colombia: ed. Leyer; A. Beristain (1998) *De los delitos y de las penas desde el Pais Vasco.* Madrid: Dykinson.

6 A. Beristain (1998) *De los delitos y de las penas desde el Pais Vasco, o.c.*, 139.

7 J. Deklerck and A. Depuydt (1998) An ethical and social interpretation of crime. Through the concepts of 'linkedness' and 'integration-disintegration'. Application to

the development of compassion and fraternity, particularly towards the victims of violent criminal organisations.

Figure 2: The concept of 'linkedness'[8]

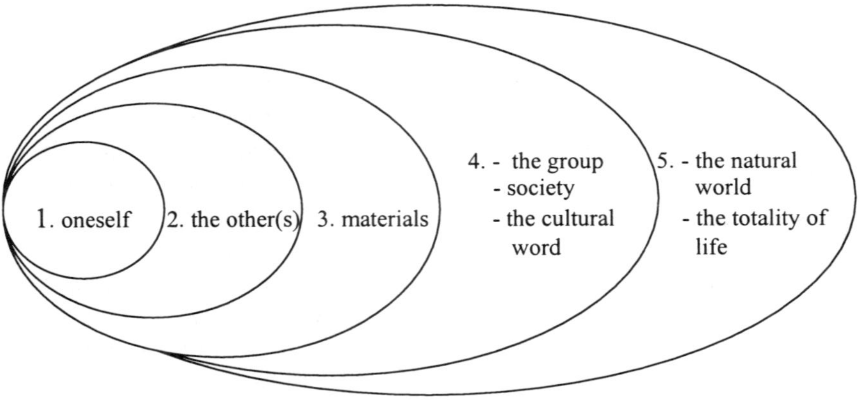

It would also be praiseworthy were they to foster the growth of an evangelical value: recreating the power of a fraternal nature within each person. Man and woman can turn new all things. This difficult recreating dimension was scientifically shown by Pierre Teilhard de Chardin. Following this same idea of the need for a drastic renovation in all human things, I dare to ask religions to overcome the pessimistic points of view of some specialists, such as Jankelevitch, Sanchez Ferlosio, V. Camps, etc., when they assert that guilt – Cain's mark – together with the macrovictimization of terrorism are irreversible. In the light of the great religions, I wonder if terrorist victimizations are, somehow and in some sense, reversible.

It would therefore be suitable to place the parable of the Good Samaritan as the keystone of an international human means to overcome terrorism.

---

restorative justice, in L. WALGRAVE (ed.), *Restorative Justice for Juveniles. Potentialities, Risks and Problems*, 137-156. Leuven: Leuven University Press.

8 Source: DEKLERCK and DEPUYDT, *o.c.*

References

Juan Avilés Farre (2000) Violencia terrorista y conflicto político en el País Vasco, N°XXII *Cuadernos de la Guardia Civil. Revista de Seguridad pública* 111-118.

Antonio Beristain (2000) *Victimología. Nueve palabras clave.* Valencia: Tirant lo Blanch.

A. Beristain (2000) Protagonismo de las víctimas en la ejecución penal, 37 *Actualidad penal* 9-15 octubre, 785-799.

A. Beristain (1999) *Nuevas soluciones victimológicas.* México: Centro de Estudios de Política Criminal y Ciencias Penales.

A. Beristain (1998) *Criminología y Victimología. Alternativas Re-creadoras al delito.* Bogotá: Colombia: ed. Leyer.

A. Beristain (1998) *De los delitos y de las penas desde el Pais Vasco.* Madrid: Dykinson.

M. E. I. Brienen and E. H. Hoegen (2000) *Victims of Crime in 22 European Criminal Justice Systems. The Implementation of Recommendation (85) 11 of the Council of Europe on the Position of the Victim in the Framework of Criminal Law Procedure,* Nijmegen: Wolf Legal Production. (Spain, in 839-879, with bibliography).

J. Deklerck and A. Depuydt (1998) An ethical and social interpretation of crime. Through the concepts of 'linkednees' and 'integration-disintegration'. Application to restorative justice, in: L. Walgrave (ed.), *Restorative Justice for Juveniles. Potentialities, Risks and Problems,* 137-156. Leuven: Leuven University Press.

V. Garrido, P. Stangeland, S. Redondo (1999) *Principios de Criminología,* 659-681. Valencia: Tirant lo Blanch.

A. Gaudreault and T. Peters (2000) (eds.), *La Victimologie: quelques enjeux,* 33(1) *Criminologie. Acta criminológica.*

Myriam Herrera Moreno (1996) *La hora de la víctima. Compendio de Victimología.* Madrid: Edersa.

G. Jauregui (2000) ETA: orígenes y evolución ideológica y política, in: A. Elorza (coordinator) *La historia de ETA*, 211-260. Barcelona: Planeta.

G. Landrove Diaz (1998) *La moderna Victimología.* Valencia: Tirant lo Blanch.

Reyes Mate (1991) *La razón de los vencidos.* Barcelona: Anthropos.

F. McClintock (1998) Prologue: Victims and Criminal Justice, in: Ezzat Fattah and Tony Peters (eds.), *Support for crime victims in a comparative perspective, A collection of essays dedicated to the*

memory of Prof. Frederic McClintock, 13-19. Leuven: Leuven University Press.
E. Neuman (1995) *Victimología supranacional. El acoso de la soberanía.* Buenos Aires: ed. Universidad.
T. Peters and I. Aertsen (2000) Towards 'Restorative Justice': Victimisation, Victim Support and Trends in Criminal Justice, in: *Crime and Criminal Justice in Europe,* 45. Strasbourg: Council of Europe.
L. Rodriguez Manzanera (1996) *Victimología. Estudio de la víctima.* México: ed. Porrúa.
Jon Sobrino (1999) *La fe en Jesucristo. Ensayo desde las víctimas.* Madrid: Trotta.
E. Viano (1999) La vida diaria y la victimación, *Victimología*, 7-35. Argentina: Córdoba, Centro de asistencia a la víctima del delito.
M. Walter et al. (1999) *Täter-Opfer-Ausgleich aus der Sicht von Rechtsanwälten.* Bonn: Bundesministerium der Justiz.

THE SOUTH AFRICAN TRUTH AND RECONCILIATION COMMISSION. TOWARDS RESTORATIVE JUSTICE IN THE FIELD OF HUMAN RIGHTS.

Stephan Parmentier

During the last decade of his academic career at the K.U. Leuven, Tony Peters has paid extensive attention to the newly emerging paradigm of restorative justice. By doing so, his interests closely reflect the developments in criminology itself, from its long-time focus on issues of penology, to a broader perspective for the victims of crime, before seeking a new balance between the interests of offenders and victims, and those of the community and the society at large. Tony has always been an "explorer of the scientific field", noticing new developments before others and keen on examining their strengths and weaknesses. His attitude to academic matters, constructive and critical at the same time, has constituted the inspiration for this contribution. Its aim is to discuss the application and the applicability of the notion of restorative justice in the field of human rights, thereby exploring new and interdisciplinary horizons for the ever dynamic discipline of criminology, and thus paying tribute to a great scholar and a remarkable colleague.

Introduction

During the nearly three years of its operational existence (1995-1998), the Truth and Reconciliation Commission of South Africa (TRC) has attracted an enormous amount of attention from many observers world wide, including activists, policy-makers, academics, the press, and ordinary citizens. Literally dozens of books and hundreds of articles and papers have seen the light of day, describing and analysing various aspects of the Commission's work. If most of the comments and the debates have centred around the notion of truth, far less attention was paid to the second key notion in the Commission's name, that of reconciliation. Yet, the TRC has extensively dealt with this notion right from the start of its voluminous Report,[1] and on several other places. Moreover, the Report has struck many an observer by making the link between truth and reconciliation on the one hand, and restorative justice on the other hand. The concept of restorative

1 Truth and Reconciliation Commission of South Africa (1998) *Report*, 5 volumes, vol. 1, 106-110. Cape Town: Juta & Co (hereafter: Report).

justice, however, stems from a very different background, as it has emerged in the field of criminology and criminal justice during the 1990s of the past century. Since that time, it has gained widespread appreciation and enthusiasm as an alternative paradigm for bringing together offenders and victims of common crimes, in order for them to restore their relationship through measures other than retributive or rehabilitative. Can the work of the TRC, with its focus on gross violations of human rights committed by groups of perpetrators against groups of victims, be viewed as a form of restorative justice? This question lies at the heart of the present contribution.

Linking the work of truth commissions in the field of human rights and the perspective of restorative justice in cases of ordinary crime has not attracted much attention thus far, neither from the angle of human rights studies, nor from the viewpoint of criminology. Given the scarcity of specific writings, the prime objective of the present contribution is to explore the intersection between these two distinct perspectives. As a result, the text contains two parts: the first briefly presents the major objectives of the TRC, seeking truth and promoting reconciliation, and its institutional design; the second and larger part examines these features from the perspective of restorative justice, with particular reference to the preliminary draft elements of a declaration of basic principles on the use of restorative justice programmes in criminal matters as adopted by the United Nations in 2000.

1. Seeking truth and promoting reconciliation: objectives and institutional framework of the TRC.

The Truth and Reconciliation Commission of South Africa (TRC) was formally established in late 1995, and held its first meeting on 16 December of that year.[2] As the title of the Promotion of National Unity and Reconciliation Act No 34 (the Act) of 19 July 1995 indicated, the overall objective of the Commission was "to promote national unity and reconciliation in a spirit of understanding which transcends the conflicts and divisions of the past (...)" (section 3,1). In this respect, the Commission has to be seen *"as part of the bridge-building process designed to help lead the nation away from a deeply divided past to a future founded on the recognition of human rights and democracy".*[3] The following paragraphs offer a brief overview of the historical context, the exact mandate of the Commission, and its institutional framework.

2 Report, *o.c.*, vol. 1, 44-45.
3 Report, *o.c.*, vol. 1, 48 ff.

1.1. Historical background

It should be noted that the first call for a truth commission came from the African National Congress (ANC), before the first democratic elections of 1994.[4] In the fall of 1992, and following an idea by one of its prominent intellectuals, Kader Asmal, the ANC entrusted a commission of enquiry with the task of investigating allegations of human rights violations in some of its camps-in-exile. Around the same period, when it became clear that the white government wished to introduce far-reaching provisions of amnesty for members of the outgoing elite, the ANC launched an appeal for a commission that would investigate not only its own abuses but also those of the government. It was an attempt to make sure that the serious human rights abuses of the past would not go unacknowledged, and that some form of accountability be installed, though of a non-judicial nature.[5] This format served both parties well, in the general context of this "negotiated transition".[6] As a result, the choice for a truth commission already appeared in the Postamble to the interim Constitution of 1993.

In spite of its predominant role in the first years of the new democracy, it is clear that the TRC did not serve as a unique mechanism to deal with the legacy of the Apartheid's regime. For much of 1996, a number of criminal trials were instituted against high-ranking officials of the former regime. Particularly the proceedings against Eugene de Kock, colonel and former commander of the secret police assassination unit, and against Magnus Malan, general and former minister of defence, attracted close attention.[7] How and to which extent these ongoing trials have impacted on the position of the TRC is not fully clear. However, it seems that the determination of the criminal justice system to prosecute certain crimes generated sufficiently strong threats to spur many -mainly whites- to work with, and even to appear before, the truth commission, thereby preferring public exposure and shame

---

4 Report, *o.c.*, vol. 1, 49 ff.

5 See, i.a.: A. BORAINE, J. LEVY and R. SCHEFFER (1997) (eds.), *Dealing With the Past. Truth and Reconciliation in South Africa*. Cape Town: Institute for Democracy in South Africa (IDASA). Acknowledgement and accountability are crucial in every type of political transition, see: N. KRITZ (1995) (ed.), *Transitional Justice. How Emerging Democracies Reckon with Former Regimes*, 3 vols. Wash. D.C.: US Institute of Peace.

6 L. HUYSE (1996) Justice after Transition: On the Choices Successor Elites Make in Dealing with the Past, in: A. JONGMAN (1996) (ed.), *Contemporary Genocides: Causes, Cases, Consequences*, 187-214. Leiden: PIOOM.

7 P. HAYNER (2001) *Unspeakable Truths. Confronting State Terror and Atrocity*, 100-102. New York: Routledge; also: K. ASMAL, L. ASMAL and R.S. ROBERTS (1997) (2nd ed.), *Reconciliation Through Truth. A Reckoning of Apartheid's Criminal Governance*. Cape Town/Oxford/New York: David Philip/James Curry/St.Martin's Press.

over the risk of being held liable in a criminal court. It demonstrates that these mechanisms are not necessarily mutually exclusive when addressing gross violations of human rights of the past, but that they can also be complementary to one another. The existence, or even the strong likelihood, of criminal prosecutions may enhance an avoidance strategy in favour of non-judicial proceedings as those of a truth commission.

1.2. The mandate

Against this general background, the TRC was expected to reach very ambitious objectives. The Act namely instructed the Commission with a fivefold task (art. 3,1 and 3,2): (1) to establish a picture of the gross human rights violations covered; (2) to facilitate the granting of amnesty for specific acts and under specific conditions; (3) to grant victims an opportunity to relate their own accounts, and to recommend reparation measures for them; (4) to compile a comprehensive report; and (5) to make whatever recommendations in view of the overarching objective.

This list being a mixture of objectives and competences, it seems more useful to focus on the two essential components of the Commission's name, namely truth and reconciliation. In its final Report, the Commission proved very well aware of the complexity of both concepts and the fact that they can interpreted in a variety of ways. Concerning the first, the Report distinguishes between four notions of truth:[8] (1) factual or forensic truth, meaning the evidence obtained and corroborated through reliable procedures; (2) personal and narrative truth, meaning the many stories that individuals told about their experiences under Apartheid; (3) social or dialogue truth, established through interaction, discussion and debate; and (4) healing and restorative truth, meaning the truth that places facts and their meaning within the context of human relationships. Also the concept of reconciliation received substantive attention, by distinguishing four different levels:[9] (1) the individual level of coming to terms with painful truth, e.g. after exhumations and reburials of beloved ones; (2) the level of specific victims and their perpetrators; (3) the community level, when addressing the internal conflicts inside and between local communities; and (4) the national level, by focussing on the role of the state and non-state institutions. In the course of its activities, the Commission tried to clarify the relationship between these various notions, by consistently repeating that truth constituted the road to reconciliation. Particularly the passages on reconciliation have allowed the Commission to make the link with the notion of restorative justice, which is broadly interpreted in the Report as

8 Report, *o.c.*, vol. 1, 110-114.
9 Report, *o.c.*, vol. 1, 106-110.

"restoring civil and human dignity" for all South Africans.[10] This restorative process was first of all directed to the victims, who were given maximum possibilities to tell their stories and who received recognition for their severe victimization. But the TRC also paid attention to restoring the dignity of the perpetrators, by trying to understand their motives and the social and political structures they operated in, without excusing the violations they committed. To establish their accountability was seen as part of the quest for understanding, within the broader framework of restorative justice.

Despite the relatively wide consensus in political and legal circles in South Africa about the value of a truth commission to deal with the horrors of the past through other means than by criminal prosecution, the idea of a truth commission did not remain unchallenged. In 1996, the Azanian Peoples Organisation (AZAPO) and a number of families, including that of Steve Biko, challenged the constitutionality of the amnesty provisions that made any further criminal and civil proceedings in court impossible. In its judgment, the Constitutional Court rejected the complaint and held that the granting of amnesty was consistent with the constitution, as it *"might assist in uncovering the truth about the past, thus assisting in the process of reconciliation and reconstruction"*.[11]

1.3. Institutional framework

To give effect to its mandate, the TRC received specific competences. It was entitled to investigate a number of gross violations of human rights expressly mentioned in the Act (section 1(1)(ix), i.c. the killing, abduction, torture, or severe ill-treatment of persons, in the period between 1 March 1960 and 10 May 1994. Other gross violations, such as forced removals of people from their homes, were excluded from its mandate. Given the origins of the idea, it was clear that the violations of both parties -the former regime and the former "freedom fighters"- should be investigated. This also extended the geographical competence of the Commission to other countries, such as Mozambique. The TRC operated by means of three committees.

Best known is the Human Rights Violations Committee (HRVC), under the charismatic chairmanship of Bishop Desmond Tutu, and entrusted with the

---

10 *Ibid.*, 125-131. In the report, restorative justice is specifically defined as a process, which: (a) seeks to redefine crime (from breaking laws to violations against human beings); (b) is based on reparation (as it aims at the healing and the restoration of all concerned); (c) encourages victims, offenders and the community to be directly involved in resolving conflict; and (d) supports a criminal justice system that aims at accountability of offenders, and the full participation of victims and offenders.

11 The Azanian Peoples Organisation, Ms NM Biko et al., in the Constitutional Court, Case No CCT 17/96. See: Report, *o.c.*, vol. 1, 174-178.

investigative aspect.[12] This committee gathered over 21.000 written statements from victims all over South Africa, relating to over 37.000 violations of human rights. Innovative in comparison to all preceding truth commissions, the committee organized more than 75 widely attended public hearings of different sorts: hearings where victims, and offenders, had an opportunity to tell their individual stories; hearings to focus on specific events, such as mass killings; institutional hearings with specific sectors of society, such as the legal and medical professions, the media, and business; special hearings, e.g., on women and children; and hearings with political parties.

An absolutely unique feature of the TRC was (and is) its Amnesty Committee (AC), in charge of dealing with individual applications for amnesty.[13] Under very strict conditions, including the full disclosure of all relevant facts, could persons receive amnesty for acts associated with political objectives within a specific period of reference. In June 1998, already more than 7.000 applications for amnesty had arrived. Until this very moment, this committee is still processing all remaining applications.

The power of the third committee, the Reparation and Rehabilitation Committee (RRC), was limited to making recommendations to the government on matters of reparation and rehabilitation.[14] It made use of this competence in an extensive way, by recommending reparation measures at various levels: individual reparations; symbolic reparations, and legal and administrative matters; community rehabilitation programmes; and institutional reforms. During the whole process, the committee also dispensed urgent and interim reparations to persons in need of, e.g., medical, psychological or material help.

2. Towards restorative justice in the case of human rights violations.

This brief overview of the Truth and Reconciliation Commission in South Africa clearly demonstrates an emphasis on promoting reconciliation, between victims, offenders, communities, and society at large. This key notion of reconciliation also occupies a prominent place in the developing paradigm of restorative justice in criminology. The central question therefore is to which extent the work of the TRC can be viewed as a form of restorative justice, as will be discussed in the following paragraphs.

12 Report, *o.c.*, vol. 1, 140-151.

13 Report, *o.c.*, vol. 1, 153-157.

14 Report, *o.c.*, vol. 5, 170-195.

2.1. Different approaches to restorative justice

Few concepts have been quoted more frequently in criminology during the last decade than the concept of restorative justice. At the same time, few concepts cover a more diversified meaning that this one, which has been called "relatively vague"[15] and seems to remain "somewhat fluid".[16] Looking for a meaning that is widely accepted and that can serve as the starting base for our analysis, is obviously no sinecure. At present, it seems that two main types of approaches may serve as points of departure.

A first approach is to search for specific definitions of restorative justice, an exercise that proves far from easy. When Paul McCold recently asked 29 experts about their concept of restorative justice, he was forced to conclude that the wide divergence of opinions precluded the adoption of any consensual definition on the matter.[17] As a result, the expert group finally adhered to the existing definition suggested by Tony Marshall, which is more and more internationally accepted, to the effect that:

> *"[R]estorative justice is a process whereby all the parties with a stake in a particular offence come together to resolve collectively how to deal with the aftermath of the offence and its implications for the future."*[18]

While this definition can be regarded as a milestone in the field of restorative justice, it has not remained without criticism.[19] For some, it portrays restorative justice as too limited a practice, because of its strong emphasis on the process of communication between the parties, at the neglect of the aspect of restoring the harm done and the practices undertaken to that effect. Others argue that the definition is too broad, because its limited attention for the outcomes of restorative practices opens the door for punitive or repressive outcomes to be subsumed under the same heading. Many other definitions are of course possible. Some say that *"restorative*

---

15 L. WALGRAVE (1994) Beyond Rehabilitation: In Search of a Constructive Alternative in the Judicial Response to Juvenile Crime, 2(2) *European Journal on Criminal Policy and Research* (Special Issue on the Juvenile Justice System) 57-75, 62-67.

16 J. TREPANIER (1998) Restorative Justice: A Question of Legitimacy, in: L. WALGRAVE (ed.), *Restorative Justice for Juveniles. Potentialities, Risks and Problems for Research*, 55-73. Leuven: Leuven University Press.

17 P. MCCOLD (1998) Restorative Justice - Variations on a Theme, in: WALGRAVE, *o.c.*, 19-53.

18 T. MARSHALL (1996) The Evolution of Restorative Justice in Britain, 4(4) *European Journal on Criminal Policy and Research* (Special Issue on Restorative Justice and Mediation) 21-43, 37.

19 For a concise and perceptive overview, see: I. AERTSEN (2001) *Slachtoffer-daderbemiddeling: een onderzoek naar de ontwikkeling van een herstelgerichte strafrechtsbedeling*, doctoral dissertation in criminology, 235-240. Leuven: Catholic University of Leuven, Faculty of Law.

justice is every action that is primarily oriented toward doing justice by repairing the harm that has been caused by a crime".[20] For others, restorative justice is *"a response to crime that focuses on restoring the losses suffered by victims, holding offenders accountable for the harm they have caused, and building peace within communities"*.[21] The wide diversity of definitions has prompted Ezzat Fattah to state that restorative justice can be viewed in many ways, as *"a movement, a paradigm, a model, an approach, a concept, an alternative. Clearly Restorative Justice means different things to different people"*.[22]

This multitude of definitions of restorative justice also clearly illustrates the major problems with this approach: it is essentially based on constructing categories of inclusion and exclusion, what is covered by the notion and what is left out. Determining the dividing line between the two is often subjected to a wide margin of appreciation, that stems from a more or less coherent view on the objectives and the functioning of the traditional criminal justice system.

While the search for definitions is predominantly present in academic debates and writings, a more pragmatic approach is reflected in recent documents of international organisations. In April 2000 the Tenth UN Congress on Crime Prevention and the Treatment of Offenders in Vienna adopted a draft declaration of Basic Principles on the Use of Restorative Justice Programmes in Criminal Matters, which were subsequently adopted in the form of a resolution by the UN Economic and Social Council (see annex).[23] The text is heavily influenced by draft versions produced by the Working Party on Restorative Justice, a group of large NGOs dealing with

---

20 G. BAZEMORE and L. WALGRAVE (1999) Restorative Juvenile Justice: In Search of Fundamentals and an Outline for Systemic Reform, in: G. BAZEMORE & L. WALGRAVE (eds.), *Restorative Juvenile Justice: Repairing the Harm of Youth Crime*, 45-74. Monsey: Criminal Justice Press.

21 As presented on the extensive website: www.restorativejustice.org (last consulted 6 November 2001)

22 E. FATTAH (1998) Some Reflections on the Paradigm of Restorative Justice and Its Viability for Juvenile Justice, in: WALGRAVE, *o.c.*, 389-401, 393; along the same lines: T. PETERS and I. AERTSEN (2000) Towards 'Restorative Justice': Victimisation, Victim Support and Trends in Criminal Justice, in: *Crime and Criminal Justice in Europe*, 35-46, 45. Strasbourg: Council of Europe.

23 Preliminary draft elements of a declaration of Basic Principles on the Use of Restorative Justice Programmes in Criminal Matters, ECOSOC Res. 2000/14, adopted on 27 July 2000 (hereafter: preliminary draft elements or draft declaration) (www.restorativejustice.org); for an interesting discussion of the draft declaration, see: J. NADEAU (2001) *Critical Analysis and Practical Application of the United Nations Declaration of Basic Principles on the Use of Restorative Justice Programs in Criminal Matters*, M.A. Paper in European Criminology. Leuven: Catholic University of Leuven, Faculty of Law, partly available on the website mentioned.

crime prevention and criminal justice, and is also inspired by Recommendation R(99)19 concerning mediation in penal matters, adopted by the Committee of Ministers of the Council of Europe on 15 September 1999.[24] In December 2000, the UN Secretary General asked all member states, as well as a number of NGOs, for their views and observations on the text, with special attention to the question whether an international instrument on restorative justice would be useful. The country responses were discussed very recently, at an expert meeting in Canada in October 2001.

It is noteworthy that the draft declaration does not contain any formal definition of restorative justice as such, an omission that, according to Daniel Van Ness, was quite intentional for two reasons.[25] The first is that the text does not address the theory of restorative justice *"at the level of vision, public policy or a comprehensive system"*, but is explicitly directed to particular programmatic expressions of restorative justice. More convincing, however, is the second reason, namely that in the absence of a general agreement on restorative justice, the drafters of the text considered it unwise to include any particular definition. The text first of all refers to a "restorative justice programme", meaning "any programme that uses restorative processes or aims to achieve restorative outcomes" (element 1). These two pillars are clearly distinguished. The former relates to processes whereby all parties "affected by a crime actively participate together in the resolution of matters arising from the crime, often with the help of a fair and impartial third party", as exemplified by mediation, conferencing and sentencing circles (element 3). The second pillar, restorative outcomes, comprises agreements reached as the result thereof, and explicitly includes restitution, community service, and other programmes with an objective of reparation for victims and the community and reintegration of victims and offenders (element 2).

Rather than defining restorative justice, the draft declaration enumerates various conditions under which restorative justice programmes can and should actually work. These include, i.a., the availability of restorative justice programmes at all stages of the criminal justice process, the voluntary character of restorative justice processes, the establishment of clear guidelines and standards governing the use of restorative justice programmes, the importance of procedural safeguards in such processes, the issue of confidentiality, the importance of follow-up and implementation of

---

24 See: D. VAN NESS (2001) Proposed UN Basic Principles on Restorative Justice, draft text, 18 p.,1-4; available on the website: www.restorativejustice.org (last consulted 6 November 2001).

25 *Ibid.*, 5.

agreements, the skills required for facilitators, and the importance of evaluation research. Through this focus on the working conditions of restorative justice programmes, the draft declaration may be seen to mark the start of a more "conditional" approach to the problem of a common understanding of restorative justice. Here lies its major strength, and also the reason why we will use it as our frame of reference for a further analysis of the work done by the Truth and Reconciliation Commission in South Africa.

2.2. Types of crimes as object of restorative justice

Before doing so, however, it is unavoidable to address the issue of the object of restorative justice. This perspective has gained widespread attention as a new model of bringing together offenders and victims of so-called "common crimes", in order for them to restore their relationship with one another and with society. Restorative justice programmes have traditionally handled property offences, such as ordinary theft by juveniles, burglary and related offences. In recent years, many programmes seem to receive an increasing number of cases of violence against persons, which may also include such serious offences as rape and even homicide.[26] As many common crimes tend to involve only two parties, the offender and the victim, a good deal of procedures have been tailored to that one-to-one relationship and are of an individual nature, such as the victim-offender mediation programmes. In more recent procedures, a larger number of persons can be present to support one or more of the parties, as is typically the case in family group conferences.

Yet, all of these aspects are fundamentally different when dealing with gross violations of human rights, such as genocide, mass killings, disappearances, extra-judicial executions, ethnic cleansing, widespread torture, systematic rape, destruction of villages, and forced removals. These offences are typical illustrations of "political crimes", a broad category of offences often divided into two main sections: one comprises the crimes committed by people against the state, designed to protest, change, or bring down the existing establishment; the other part encompasses the crimes committed by the state against people, in order *"to sanction those who threaten or appear to threaten the establishment (...), or in order to maintain and enhance the existing political and economic systems"*.[27] Other examples of political crimes include forms of terrorism and aggression, espionage,

26 H. ZEHR (2001) Restorative Justice, in: L. REYCHLER and T. PAFFENHOLZ (eds.), *Peace-building. A Field Guide*, 330-335. Boulder, Co: Lynne Rienner Publishers.

27 See: S. BROWN, F.-A. ESBENSEN and G. GEIS (1991) *Criminology. Explaining Crime and Its Context*, 667 ff. Cincinnati, OH: Anderson Publishing Co.

collaboration with foreign powers and treason, and various sorts of assassinations. Despite the many differences, political crimes have several elements in common, namely the political motives of the offender, the political object of the offence, and the political context within which it is committed.[28] Political offences, particularly when committed by the state against people, are often not prosecuted because of general amnesty legislations precluding further legal action. In such frame, truth commissions tend to be presented as "a third way", developing collective procedures of accountability to escape from situations of outright impunity.[29]

In the following paragraphs, we will explore whether the South African Truth and Reconciliation Commission can be regarded as a form of restorative justice in the case of political crimes, and of gross violations of human rights in particular. At this stage, it can already be mentioned that no procedure to deal with gross violations of human rights can avoid paying attention to two major aspects. One lies in the nature of the crimes, which are often of an extreme violence, going back to deeply rooted conflicts in a given society that continue to generate a general "culture of violence". The second aspect relates to the number of victims affected, since gross violations often imply mass victimisation as a result of actions committed by groups of state agents or by state-supported groups.

With these *caveats* in mind we will discuss the work of the TRC, using the draft declaration of basic principles as our frame of reference. After considering the general concepts of the text, we will look at the main conditions for the use and the operation of restorative justice programmes. In the end, we will pay some attention to the role of the facilitators and to the continuing development of restorative justice programmes.

2.3. General concepts

While avoiding any hard definitions of restorative justice, the draft declaration does indicate that restorative justice programmes use restorative

---

28 As indicated in the Norgaard principles, reproduced in the South African *Government Gazette* of 7 November 1990.

29 On impunity and accountability, see, i.a.: N. KRITZ (1996) Coming to Terms with Mass Atrocities: A Review of Accountability Mechanisms for Mass Violations of Human Rights, 59 *Law and Contemporary Problems* 127-152; M. MINOW (1998) *Between Vengeance and Forgiveness. Facing History after Genocide and Mass Violence.* Boston: Beacon Press; D. ORENTLICHER (1991) Settling Accounts: The Duty to Prosecute Human Rights Violations of a Prior Regime, 100 *Yale Law Journal* 2537-2615; N. ROHT-ARRIAZA and L. GIBSON (1998) The Developing Jurisprudence on Amnesty, 20 *Human Rights Quarterly* 843-885; C. VILLA-VICENCIO (2000) Why Perpetrators Should not Always be Prosecuted: Where the International Criminal Court and Truth Commissions Meet, 49 *Emory Law Journal* 101-118.

processes or aim to achieve restorative outcomes. The notion of "restorative process" comes strikingly close to Marshall's definition mentioned above.[30] His general idea of "parties with a stake in a specific offence" is replaced here by three specific categories of persons, namely victims, offenders, and other individuals or community members affected by a crime (element 3). It is not difficult to identify these three categories in the context of the South African TRC. First of all, thousands of written statements from direct and indirect victims of the Apartheid regime were recorded and presented to the Commission at large; and hundreds of victims exposed their experiences in an oral manner before the Human Rights Violations Committee (HRVC). Although the number of alleged perpetrators was substantially lower, several dozens of them decided to appear in person before the same committee, while many thousands of offenders sent in their application for amnesty to the Amnesty Committee (AC). It should be noted that, unlike restorative justice programmes for common crimes, those regarded as perpetrators in the context of the TRC were never legally designated as offenders or suspects, but participated on the basis of their willingness to provide information about the human rights violations of the past. Finally, all of the public hearings, in large cities and in small villages, took place before audiences of community members virtually all affected by the political violence and the human rights violations; moreover, large portions of South African society, such as the media, the academic world and also the political parties, became quite interested, and sometimes actively involved, in the momentum created by the TRC process.

The crux of a restorative process, however, namely that the parties "actively participate together in the resolution of matters arising from the crime", poses more problems in the case of the TRC. If this passage is to be understood in a minimalist sense, namely that victims and offenders were physically present in the same public space at the same moment, then it applies specifically to the hearings of the HRVC and of the AC. If, however, the idea of active participation also requires some psychological or moral disposition on behalf of the parties, which coincides with the underlying philosophy of restorative justice, then the TRC process displays a mixed picture at least. There is no doubt that some victims have succeeded in receiving a personal sense of "healing" by telling their story and knowing the truth, despite the often brutal realities referred to. There is no doubt that some victims and offenders, by actively working together to unveil the general patterns of political violence affecting their dramatic past, may have achieved some degree of reconciliation between them. The amnesty proceedings in particular have been, and still are, the prime forum for such

30 Along the same lines: VAN NESS, *o.c.*, 6.

experiences, because offenders are legally obliged to disclose all relevant information and to express remorse in a public setting. However, despite the frequent optimistic accounts of such healing experiences, it is not difficult to argue that many hearings have only witnessed offenders wishing to justify their past behaviour on a variety of grounds, and victims being left with a sense of disarray, bitterness, anger or despair. Moreover, there is little evidence of the types of reconciliation reached at the level of communities and at the national level. This mixed picture is further illustrated by the fact that the TRC has not organised any of the three examples of restorative processes explicitly listed in the draft declaration, i.c. mediation, conferencing, and sentencing circles.

These critical comments should not obfuscate another reality, namely that were this provision of the draft declaration to be applied to truth commissions outside of South Africa, all of them would fall short to an even larger degree. The reason is simple. Of the four other truth commissions labelled by Priscilla Hayner as "illustrative", none held any public hearings or organised amnesty proceedings that could have provided a common forum for the active participation of victims, offenders, and the community at large.[31] Their conclusions were all based on written documents and on oral statements from many victims, and from occasional offenders.

According to the draft declaration, restorative justice programmes can also be based on a second pillar, namely "restorative outcomes", meaning agreements reached as the result of a restorative process (element 2). Also this element is open to several interpretations. To the extent that such agreements can remain limited to a common understanding of the crime by the parties, the TRC has definitely produced results. As suggested above, several hearings have most likely increased the understanding of victims, offenders and the community at large of what has happened and why it did. Furthermore, at a more general level, nobody can loose sight of the voluminous final report, which for the first time details a specific part of South Africa's horrendous past and thus offers an institutionalised memory of mass victimisation that is widely agreed to in various sectors of society. If agreements, however, should also entail written agreements that provide for concrete measures to overcome the consequences of the crime, then the TRC does not seem to have achieved a great deal. The only outcomes with tangible (and legal) consequences are the decisions of the Amnesty Committee: granting amnesty is to be seen as an agreement to wipe out the offender's responsibility before court, while refusing it reflects an agreement not to do so. It remains, however, difficult to define these decisions as the

31 These are the truth commissions in Argentina, Chile, El Salvador, and Guatemala. See: P. HAYNER (2001) *o.c.*, Ch. 4, 32-49.

result of a restorative process, because they rest on the sole interpretation of the committee members and do not require any consent on the part of the victims affected.

The results are equally meagre with respect to the examples of restorative outcomes listed in the draft declaration, i.c. restitution, community service and any other programme or response designed to accomplish reparation of the victim and community, and reintegration of the victim and/or the offender. The explanation is simple, as the TRC did not possess any legal competences to order restitution of property, to impose community service or to organise programmes for the reintegration of victims or offenders. One exception concerns the area of reparations, as the Reparation and Rehabilitation Committee (RRC) did grant urgent interim reparation to certain categories of victims in need, thus producing tangible outcomes for them. Moreover, it formulated a substantial number of recommendations in which more outcomes have been suggested. They focus on reparations provided by the state authorities for the victims recognised in the TRC report, with a view of promoting the rehabilitation for victims, for offenders, and for the community. Encouraged by these recommendations, many victims have tried to move beyond their individual cases and to bring their claims for reparation to the collective level, by starting victim support groups, by seeking support with larger NGOs, or by lobbying directly with government agencies. Thus far, it seems that very few concrete results have been achieved. Moreover, as these victim strategies have largely remained unilateral, without concertation with the other parties affected by the said crimes, they can hardly be seen to result from a restorative process.

With regards to reparations for victims, the South African story is not very different from the stories of other truth commissions: overall, it seems quite difficult for truth commissions to produce or to encourage restorative outcomes of this type. If this appears to be the general "rule", there are two exceptions to it: in Chile, the families of the disappeared and killed have received life-long state pensions, medical benefits and educational benefits for their children; in Argentina, sometimes significant lump sums of money were given to the families of the disappeared and killed, and to those imprisoned for political reasons or forced into exile.[32]

2.4. The use of restorative justice programmes

After the general definitions, the draft declaration goes on to list a number of basic conditions that programmes should comply with in order to fall within

32 See: HAYNER (2001) *o.c.*, 170-182 and 314-317.

the scope of restorative justice, the most important aspects of which will be discussed.

First of all, restorative justice programmes should be available "at all stages of the criminal justice process" (element 6). This provision is to be seen in a broader context since the drafters were realistic in acknowledging that restorative processes and/or outcomes are not always possible (element 10). In those circumstances, criminal justice officials are instructed to encourage offenders "to take responsibility vis-à-vis the victim and affected communities". How does the TRC comply with these provisions ? Given the political compromise, the Commission was set up as a non-judicial body, outside of any judicial context, and the cases and testimonies presented, in oral and in writing, were in no way referred by any police or court services. Within this framework, the Commission has consistently encouraged victims to tell their stories and perpetrators -whites, blacks and others- to assume responsibility for their crimes of the past. There seems to be little evidence, however, that offenders have responded to this intention on a wide scale, with the exception of the amnesty proceedings, which entailed direct legal consequences for those who did take responsibility. This is not to describe the truth commission process as completely detached from the criminal justice system. It is not impossible that information obtained through the written submissions and the public hearings, e.g. concerning the planning and the preparation of police and army operations, could very well serve as background materials for instituting criminal proceedings in court in the coming years. In that sense, even if non-judicial by nature, the TRC could in some instances be seen to serve a "proto-judicial" function.

A second condition relates to "the free and voluntary consent of the parties" in entering the restorative process, and the possibility of withdrawing this consent and leaving the process at any time (element 7). The TRC process has arguably been based on the voluntary participation of all the parties to present their viewpoints, the victims, the offenders and other individuals or community members. It should be noted that particularly the victims have seized with both hands this unique opportunity to express their viewpoints and their emotions in a public forum, to the extent that the HRVC became sometimes overburdened with requests for oral testimonies and had to restrict access. The obvious exception to the rule of voluntary participation are the Commission's legal powers of *subpoena*, search and seizure, in order to oblige certain witnesses and perpetrators to be questioned by the Commission, as well as to produce more evidence.[33] Furthermore, the idea of voluntary participation on the part of the offenders requires further nuance. As several criminal cases against high-ranking officials of the

33 Report, *o.c.*, vol. 1, 54.

Apartheid regime were already underway in 1996, there is little doubt that some offenders experienced varying degrees of moral or even political pressure to collaborate with the TRC. If this could not be interpreted as an admission of guilt (element 8) in the case of the HRVC, it definitely could be seen as an escape strategy in the case of the amnesty proceedings. The draft declaration extends the voluntary character to all agreements arrived at by the parties. However, this provision hardly applies in the case of the TRC, in the absence of any agreements or obligations strictly speaking.

To take into consideration disparities with respect to "power imbalances and the parties' age, maturity or intellectual capacity", as well as "threats to any of the parties' safety", is another condition expressed in the draft declaration (element 9). Strong emphasis is hereby put on the appreciation of the parties themselves as to whether the restorative processes or outcomes are suitable, without, however, leaving that decision to them.[34] In the course of the TRC, the problem of disparities between parties has indeed come to the forefront, but in another way as suggested in the draft declaration. Instead of being based on age, maturity or intellectual capacity, the differences between victims and offenders were predominantly based on their social and economic position. The vast majority of victims who submitted written statements and testified in the HRVC's public hearings were black and living in underprivileged, sometimes outright poor, conditions. While a large proportion of white offenders, and victims alike, visibly belonged to the middle class, with all the characteristics attached to such position. The Commission was therefore facing the challenge to balance social, economic (and partly linguistic) disparities when organising the process of statement taking and when conducting the hearings, and put substantial efforts into it. All in all, the issue of balancing has appeared less important here than in other restorative processes, for the simple reason that the TRC process was largely open-ended and did not include direct mediation or conferencing sessions with a view of reaching concrete agreements between the parties. Following the provisions of the Act, the Commission also organised an extensive witness protection programme.[35]

2.5. The operation of restorative justice programmes

The third part of the draft declaration lists various conditions pertaining to the actual operation of restorative justice programmes.

A first point of attention concerns the establishment of guidelines and standards to govern the use of restorative justice programmes (element 11).

---

34 VAN NESS, *o.c.*, 7.
35 Report, *o.c.*, vol. 1, 387-391.

According to the draft declaration, these guidelines and standards should address several issues, i.c. how to refer cases to restorative justice programmes and how to secure their follow-up afterwards; the skills and assessment procedures of the facilitators; the general administration of restorative justice programmes; and the standards of competence and ethics governing their operation. These provisions are particularly important in the informal and flexible settings of many restorative justice programmes, which increase the parties' ability to look for responses to the crime that are tailored to their needs, but may also jeopardise certain individual rights and interests.[36] In such contexts, clear standards and the transparency of standards are of utmost importance. The TRC for its part has operated in a context that was fundamentally different: it was established by law, it was governed by strict legal rules, and it became the subject of extreme public scrutiny from very diverse angles. Thus far, no single truth commission has received more public attention and offered more transparency than the South African one. Following its own deliberate policy, the HRVC organised many public hearings, while also the amnesty hearings were in principle open to the public and were presided by a magistrate in order to secure maximum impartiality. Given the TRC's nature, the need for standards for referring cases did not come into play, nor did the issue of their follow-up after the restorative process. In relation to latter aspect, the Commission did pay attention to whatever needs that arose out of its own process: many persons received psychological assistance following a hearing or a testimony that revived the brutalities of the past;[37] in some cases, urgent reparations were provided.

A further condition relates to the procedural safeguards in restorative justice programmes (element 12). The draft declaration explicitly mentions the following issues, which are often regarded as problematic in processes of restorative justice: the right for parties "to legal advice before and after the restorative process and, where necessary, to translation and/or interpretation"; the duty to inform parties "of their rights, the nature of the process and the possible consequences of their decision" to participate; and the absence of any unfair means to force victims or offenders to participate. The application of these rules to the TRC process does not pose any specific problems. All parties who expressed an interested in participating in the HRVC and the AC hearings were clearly briefed by staff members about the nature of the process, about their rights and about the consequences of their presence and of the information that they would provide. The right to legal advice was more extensive than suggested in the text of the draft declaration,

36 VAN NESS, *o.c.*, 8.
37 Report, *o.c.*, vol. 1, 146.

as all parties, particularly offenders, disposed of all freedom to the legal advice of their choice, not only before and after the hearings, but even during. Indeed, in some hearings the alleged offenders brought their lawyers, and allowed them to be actively engaged in the question-and-answer sessions. Furthermore, translation has never been an issue in the TRC process, quite on the contrary. The Commission spent considerable efforts and funds to secure that all statements and all testimonies were given in the language of choice of the person concerned, to allow a maximum freedom of expression.[38] As to the matter of forcing victims or offenders to participate in the Commission's work by unfair means, no accounts have come to the forefront that could lead to hard conclusions of the sort.

The situation is obviously different in relation to the condition that discussions in restorative processes should be "confidential and should not be disclosed subsequently, except with the agreement of the parties" (element 13). If this provision can encourage the exchange of information among the parties in private settings relating to common crimes,[39] the TRC adopted an opposing view in relation to the gross and massive human rights violations. Disseminating the information obtained to the audience present and to the public at large proved far more important than keeping that information confidential between the parties and respecting their privacy. This policy not only applied to the HRVC hearings, but also to the amnesty proceedings, although in the latter it was (and is) possible to conduct the hearings *in camera*.

One condition deals with the legal consequences of agreements arising out of restorative justice programmes (element 15), and states that "judicial discharges (...) should have the same status as judicial decisions or judgements and should preclude prosecution in respect of the same facts (*non bis in idem*)". While this provision is not applicable to most of the TRC activities, it bears substantial relevance for the amnesty process. The decision to grant amnesty precludes any further criminal or civil action in court against the party concerned, as spelled out in the Act.

Finally, the draft declaration discusses two conditions that relate to the absence of agreements or the failure to implement agreements (elements 15 and 16). In such situations, cases have to be referred back to the criminal justice authorities, who should take a decision about the further proceedings without delay. Also these conditions are less relevant for the TRC process, in the absence of any referrals whatsoever between the Commission and the justice system. The situation is somewhat different with relation to the Amnesty Committee, because a decision to refuse amnesty opens the door

38 Report, *o.c.*, vol. 1, 146-147.

39 Van Ness, *o.c.*, 9.

for subsequent proceedings in court against the party concerned. However, as such actions do not originate with the AC, it is not possible to talk about any cases being referred to the criminal justice system.

It is clear that the conditions set in the draft declaration for the operation of restorative justice programmes have had less weight in the TRC process. Aimed at collecting information about the past and at exposing that collective picture of mass victimisation to the parties and to the nation, the various processes have always been quite open-ended and have not entailed concrete agreements between the parties concerned. That is, with the exception of the amnesty proceedings, in which the required procedural safeguards seem to have been closely followed.

2.6. Other conditions

The draft declaration is aware of the fact that the success (or the failure) of restorative justice programmes is very much dependent on the precise role played by the facilitators, meaning "a fair and impartial third party whose role is to facilitate the participation of victims and offenders in an encounter programme" (element 5). To assume their roles adequately, these facilitators have to comply with several conditions (elements 17-20): be recruited "from all sections of society"; be able "to demonstrate sound judgement and interpersonal skills"; perform their task in an "impartial manner, based on the facts of the case and on the needs and wishes of the parties"; provide "a safe and appropriate environment"; and receive initial and in-service training.

While restorative justice programmes for common crimes may allow for these roles to be collected in one person, or a handful of persons, a complex process as the TRC inevitably comprised "multiple" roles, spread over a large number of people. Statement takers reached out to often remote places in the countryside to record the stories of victims of Apartheid, in their own language, and to "translate" these into reliable documents for the Commission's use. Researchers unearthed large piles of information, from individuals victims and their relatives, from community organisations and international NGOs, from government sources and international governmental organisations, in order to look for individual histories and for systematic patterns of human rights violations. Other staff members of the Commission assumed the task of briefing the parties, victims and offenders, coming to public hearings or to amnesty proceedings, about the process and about their rights; sometimes they also provided psychological support for those in need of it. Apart from these hidden, and sometimes anonymous faces, there were the actual members of the Truth and Reconciliation Commission, who constituted the public faces of the South African model to the country and to the rest of the world. Each of these categories, in their own capacities, contributed to facilitating the participation of victims and offenders in the encounter programme that the TRC has been, not so much geared towards achieving concrete outcomes between the parties, but focussing mostly on the process. It would require further research to know if all of these staff people complied with each and every standard listed above. At this stage, the information available offers no indications to the contrary. It is true that in the course of Commission's life, the National Party no longer considered several members impartial, and demanded in court for an unconditional apology and that they act in accordance with the Act. After urges from the judge, however, the matter was settled between the parties.[40]

The draft declaration finishes off by emphasising the continuing development of restorative justice programmes (elements 21-23). This means first of all that criminal justice authorities and administrators of restorative justice programmes need to have regular consultations "to develop a common understanding of restorative processes and outcomes" and to increase their use. On top of that is expressed the need for research and for evaluation of restorative justice programmes to assess their restorative outcomes, and to verify how they serve as an alternative to the criminal justice process. The text concludes that this research should provide very useful information that may lead to adapting and modifying restorative justice programmes over time to better fulfil their functions. By including these elements, the draft declaration clearly adopts an "expansive" view on developing existing and new forms of restorative programmes,[41] which can be fostered through self-reflection, scientific evaluation, and adaptation.

How these elements can relate to the Truth and Reconciliation Commission in South Africa is anything but clear. Given its non-judicial nature, there seems to have been no reasons for regular consultations between the heads of the TRC and the criminal justice system, certainly not in view of developing a common understanding of restorative processes and outcomes. This is far from saying that the Commission remained locked in its ivory tower, because there have been multiple consultations with other bodies in society, political circles, economic actors, and non-governmental organisations, aiming at explaining the whole process and asking for their collaboration. It is clear that the TRC has been a unique endeavour, which by its nature cannot become part of the regular criminal justice system. Despite the enormous wealth of information on the work of the Commission, the number of true evaluation studies have remained surprisingly limited.[42] In

---

40 Report, *o.c.*, vol. 1, 190-191.

41 VAN NESS, *o.c.*, 12.

42 For an exception, see: HAYNER (2001) *o.c.*

the coming years, such evaluations seem absolutely crucial, not only to look back at this past process, but also to provide valuable lessons for dealing with political (and with common) crimes in South Africa in the future, e.g. in relation to the recommendations on reparations for victims. Evaluation research, moreover, is indispensable for other parts of the world, that are increasingly using the TRC as their prime point of reference for dealing with similar types of crime.[43]

Conclusion

The South African Truth and Reconciliation Commission has attracted world wide attention for the way is has tried to deal with the horrendous legacy of Apartheid. As the result of a political compromise, and in a context of a negotiation transition to democracy, the Commission was set up as a non-judicial body with the objectives to seek the truth and to promote reconciliation. During three years of intensive work, from 1995 to 1998, the TRC took thousands of written statements, conducted many hearings with hundreds of victims and offenders, and produced an impressive Report that can serve as a collective memory of its past for South Africa's future generations.

Can the work of the TRC be viewed as a form of restorative justice?, was the central question of this contribution. The answer to this question obviously depends to a large extent upon the notion of restorative justice that is used. Because the many definitions of restorative justice all create strict categories of inclusion and exclusion, we decided to look for another approach. This approach was found in the preliminary draft elements for a draft declaration of basic principles on the use of restorative justice programmes in criminal matters, as approved by the UN in 2000. The strength of this text lies in the fact that, instead of defining restorative justice, it lists a fair number of conditions that restorative justice

---

43 See, e.g., the panel on "Restorative Principles in Response to State-Sanctioned Crime: Truth and Reconciliation Commissions", organised during the ancillary meetings of the Tenth UN Congress on the Prevention of Crime and the Treatment of Offenders, Vienna, Austria, April 2000 (www.restorativejustice.org). In the literature, i.a.: P. HAYNER (1997) International Guidelines for the Creation and Operation of Truth Commissions: A Preliminary Proposal, 59 *Law and Contemporary Problems* 173-180; J. SARKIN (1999) The Necessity and Challenges of Establishing a Truth and Reconciliation Commission in Rwanda, 21 *Human Rights Quarterly* 767-823; N. SPRINGER (forthcoming) *Setting Up A Truth Commission in the Middle of the Conflict. A Case Study of Colombia.* Leuven: Catholic University of Leuven, Law and Society Institute.

programmes have to comply with. Our exploratory analysis of the work of the TRC from the angle of the draft declaration has produced a mixed picture: a large number of aspects of the Commission's work squarely relate to restorative justice as conceived in the text, other aspects clearly do not comply, still others are doubtful, and a handful of elements of the draft declaration does simply not apply to the TRC.

Aspects that can be seen in accordance with the draft declaration are the following: several parties, victims, offenders and/or other individuals or community members came together to consider the impact of the political crimes committed in the past; some victims received reconciliation at the personal level; some victims and perpetrators established forms of reconciliation between them; all parties could enter the process with their free and voluntary consent, and they could also leave it at any time; the Commission put substantial effort in paying attention to the social and economic disparities between the parties participating in the processes; it also organised a witness protection programme; in the absence of any agreements or restorative outcomes, the Commission encouraged the offenders to assume responsibility for the violations of the past (particularly prominent in the amnesty proceedings); all parties had the right to legal advice before, after and even during the process; they were all offered translation; they were all informed of their rights and of the nature of the processes they entered; there were no indications of unfair means to oblige parties to participate; in the case of the amnesty proceedings, the decisions to grant amnesty precluded any further criminal or civil legal action against the persons concerned; the facilitators of the TRC seem to have broadly recruited and to have acted impartially; they have tried to produce a safe environment for the parties; and they received the necessary training.

Several important aspects, on the other hand, clearly do not meet the standards of restorative justice programmes as conceived in the draft declaration: the TRC process was not intended for parties working together in the "resolution" of matters arising from the political crimes of the past, but was designed to try to understand these matters; as a result, the processes were not concluded by any agreements binding upon the parties to deal with the consequences of gross and massive violations of human rights (with the exception of the amnesty proceedings); evidently, the TRC did not comply with the condition of confidentiality, as its aims lay in publicity.

A couple of aspects have remained unclear and would require further research: the existence of consultations between those responsible for the TRC and those responsible for the criminal justice system, with a view to develop a common understanding of restorative justice; any studies conducted to provide a thorough evaluation of the TRC process, particularly in respect of reconciliation within communities and at the national level; and the way in which lessons can be drawn from the TRC for other forms of conflict management in South Africa, and in other parts of the world.

Finally, some elements of the draft declaration are simply not applicable to the TRC: given its non-judicial nature, the type of processes offered by the Commission were not available at all stages of the criminal justice system; there were no cases referred to the Commission, and no cases referred back to the criminal justice system in the case of non-agreement; failures to implement agreements could not arise; and the TRC cannot undergo any changes in the future because its mandate has lapsed (with the exception of the Amnesty Committee that is still dealing with applications).

This brings us to a final point, namely the relationship between the TRC and the criminal justice system. While both mechanisms serve their proper purposes in addressing gross human rights violations of the past, it is clear that they are not mutually exclusive. On the one hand, it can be argued that the probability of criminal prosecutions has led some offenders to cooperate with the Commission. On the other hand, the work of the TRC has generated a wealth of information that may be of further use when instituting criminal or civil proceedings in court against some perpetrators in the future. The coming years will make clear in which way the work of the TRC and the regular courts can be complimentary.

Let us finish off with the words of Howard Zehr, the famous scholar in restorative justice, who back in 1997 looked upon the Truth and Reconciliation Commission in a critical, yet constructive, manner: *"The TRC process is flawed, opportunities have been missed, but the importance of this undertaking -not only for South Africa, but for the world- must not be underestimated. It is "a bold step on an uncharted path."* [44]

References

Aertsen, I. (2001) *Slachtoffer-daderbemiddeling: een onderzoek naar de ontwikkeling van een herstelgerichte strafrechtsbedeling*, doctoral dissertation in criminology. Leuven: Catholic University of Leuven, Faculty of Law.

44 H. ZEHR (1997) Restorative Justice. When justice and healing go together, 6 (3/4) *Track Two* (Special Issue on Truth, Reconciliation and Justice), also available on website: ccrweb.ccr.uct.ac.za/two (last consulted 6 November 2001).

Asmal, K., Asmal, L. & Roberts, R.S. (1997) (2nd ed.), *Reconciliation Through Truth. A Reckoning of Apartheid's Criminal Governance*. Cape Town/Oxford/New York: David Philip/James Curry/St.Martin's Press.

Bazemore, G. and Walgrave, L. (1999) Restorative Juvenile Justice: In Search of Fundamentals and an Outline for Systemic Reform, in: Bazemore, G. and Walgrave, L. (eds.), *Restorative Juvenile Justice: Repairing the Harm of Youth Crime*, 45-74. Monsey: Criminal Justice Press.

Boraine, A., Levy, J. and Scheffer, R. (1997) (eds.), *Dealing With the Past. Truth and Reconciliation in South Africa*. Cape Town: Institute for Democracy in South Africa (IDASA).

Brown, S., Esbensen, F.-A. and Geis, G. (1991) *Criminology. Explaining Crime and Its Context*. Cincinnati, OH: Anderson Publishing Co.

Fattah, E. (1998) Some Reflections on the Paradigm of Restorative Justice and Its Viability for Juvenile Justice, in: Walgrave, L. (ed.), *Restorative Justice for Juveniles. Potentialities, Risks and Problems for Research*, 389-401. Leuven: Leuven University Press.

Hayner, P. (1994) Fifteen Truth Commissions - 1974-1994. A Comparative Study, 16(4) *Human Rights Quarterly* 597-655.

Hayner, P. (1997) International Guidelines for the Creation and Operation of Truth Commissions: A Preliminary Proposal, 59 *Law and Contemporary Problems* 173-180.

Hayner, P. (2001) *Unspeakable Truths. Confronting State Terror and Atrocity*. New York: Routledge.

Huyse, L. (1996) Justice after Transition: On the Choices Successor Elites Make in Dealing with the Past, in: Jongman, A. (1996) (ed.), *Contemporary Genocides: Causes, Cases, Consequences*, 187-214. Leiden: PIOOM.

Kritz, N. (1995) (ed.), *Transitional Justice. How Emerging Democracies Reckon with Former Regimes*, 3 vols. Washington D.C.: United States Institute of Peace.

Kritz, N. (1996) Coming to Terms with Mass Atrocities: A Review of Accountability Mechanisms for Mass Violations of Human Rights, 59 *Law and Contemporary Problems* 127-152.

Marshall, T. (1996) The Evolution of Restorative Justice in Britain, 4(4) *European Journal on Criminal Policy and Research* (Special Issue on Restorative Justice and Mediation) 21-43.

McCold, P. (1998) Restorative Justice - Variations on a Theme, in: Walgrave, L. (ed.), *Restorative Justice for Juveniles. Potentialities, Risks and Problems for Research*, 19-53. Leuven: Leuven University Press.

Minow, M. (1998) *Between Vengeance and Forgiveness. Facing History after Genocide and Mass Violence*. Boston: Beacon Press.

Nadeau, J. (2001) *Critical Analysis and Practical Application of the United Nations Declaration of Basic Principles on the Use of Restorative Justice Programs in Criminal Matters*, M.A. Paper in European Criminology. Leuven: Catholic University of Leuven, Faculty of Law.

Orentlicher, D. (1991) Settling Accounts: The Duty to Prosecute Human Rights Violations of a Prior Regime, 100 *Yale Law Journal* 2537-2615.

Peters, T. and Aertsen, I. (2000) Towards 'Restorative Justice': Victimisation, Victim Support and Trends in Criminal Justice, in: *Crime and Criminal Justice in Europe*, 35-46. Strasbourg: Council of Europe.

Roth-Arriaza, N. and Gibson, L. (1998) The Developing Jurisprudence on Amnesty, 20 *Human Rights Quarterly* 843-885.

Sarkin, J. (1999) The Necessity and Challenges of Establishing a Truth and Reconciliation Commission in Rwanda, 21 *Human Rights Quarterly* 767-823.

Springer, N. (forthcoming) *Setting Up A Truth Commission in the Middle of the Conflict. A Case Study of Colombia*. Leuven: Catholic University of Leuven, Law and Society Institute.

Trépanier, J. (1998) Restorative Justice: A Question of Legitimacy, in: Walgrave, L. (ed.), *Restorative Justice for Juveniles. Potentialities, Risks and Problems for Research*, 55-73. Leuven: Leuven University Press.

Truth and Reconciliation Commission of South Africa (1998) *Report*, 5 volumes. Cape Town: Juta & Co.

Villa-Vicencio, Ch. (2000) Why Perpetrators Should not Always be Prosecuted: Where the International Criminal Court and Truth Commissions Meet, 49 *Emory Law Journal* 101-118.

Walgrave, L. (1994) Beyond Rehabilitation: In Search of a Constructive Alternative in the Judicial Response to Juvenile Crime, 2(2) *European Journal on Criminal Policy and Research* (Special Issue on the Juvenile Justice System) 57-75.

Walgrave, L. (1998) (ed.), *Restorative Justice for Juveniles. Potentialities, Risks and Problems for Research*, A selection of papers presented at the International Conference in Leuven, May 12-14, 1997. Leuven: Leuven University Press.

Zehr. H. (1997) Restorative Justice. When justice and healing go together, 6 (3/4) *Track Two* (Special Issue on Truth, Reconciliation and Justice), also available on website: ccrweb.ccr.uct.ac.za/two

Zehr, H. (2001) Restorative Justice, in: Reychler, L. and Paffenholz, T. (eds.), *Peace-building. A Field Guide*, 330-335. Boulder, Co: Lynne Rienner Publishers.

Appendix: Preliminary draft elements of a declaration of basic principles on the use of restorative justice programmes in criminal matters.

I. Definitions

1. "Restorative justice programme" means any programme that uses restorative processes or aims to achieve restorative outcomes.
2. "Restorative outcome" means an agreement reached as the result of a restorative process. Examples of restorative outcomes include restitution, community service and any other programme or response designed to accomplish reparation of the victim and community, and reintegration of the victim and/or the offender.
3. "Restorative process" means any process in which the victim, the offender and/or any other individuals or community members affected by a crime actively participate together in the resolution of matters arising from the crime, often with the help of a fair and impartial third party. Examples of restorative process include mediation, conferencing and sentencing circles.
4. "Parties" means the victim, the offender and any other individuals or community members affected by a crime who may be involved in a restorative justice programme.
5. "Facilitator" means a fair and impartial third party whose role is to facilitate the participation of victims and offenders in an encounter programme.

II. Use of restorative justice programmes

6. Restorative justice programmes should be generally available at all stages of the criminal justice process.
7. Restorative processes should be used only with the free and voluntary consent of the parties. The parties should be able to withdraw such consent at any time during the process. Agreements should be arrived at voluntarily by the parties and contain only reasonable and proportionate obligations.
8. All parties should normally acknowledge the basic facts of a case as a basis for participation in a restorative process. Participation should not be used as evidence of admission of guilt in subsequent legal proceedings.
9. Obvious disparities with respect to factors such as power imbalances and the parties' age, maturity or intellectual capacity should be taken into consideration in referring a case to and in conducting a restorative process. Similarly, obvious threats

to any of the parties' safety should also be considered in referring any case to and in conducting a restorative process. The views of the parties themselves about the suitability of restorative processes or outcomes should be given great deference in this consideration.

10. Where restorative processes and/or outcomes are not possible, criminal justice officials should do all they can to encourage the offender to take responsibility vis-à-vis the victim and affected communities, and reintegration of the victim and/or offender into the community.

III.Operation of restorative justice programmes

11. Guidelines and standards should be established, with legislative authority when necessary, that govern the use of restorative justice programmes. Such guidelines and standards should address:

(a) The conditions for the referral of cases to restorative justice programmes;

(b) The handling of cases following a restorative process;

(c) The qualifications, training and assessment of facilitators;

(d) The administration of restorative justice programmes;

(e) Standards of competence and ethical rules governing operation of restorative justice programmes.

12. Fundamental procedural safeguards should be applied to restorative justice programmes and in particular to restorative processes:

(a) The parties should have the right to legal advice before and after the restorative process and, where necessary, to translation and/or interpretation. Minors should, in addition, have the right to parental assistance;

(b) Before agreeing to participate in restorative processes, the parties should be fully informed of their rights, the nature of the process and the possible consequences of their decision;

(c) Neither the victim nor the offender should be induced by unfair means to participate in restorative processes or outcomes.

13. Discussions in restorative processes should be confidential and should not be disclosed subsequently, except with the agreement of the parties.

14. Judicial discharges based on agreements arising out of restorative justice programmes should have the same status as judicial decisions or judgements and should preclude prosecution in respect of the same facts (*non bis in idem*).

15. Where no agreement can be made between the parties, the case should be referred back to the criminal justice authorities and a decision as to how to proceed should be taken without delay. Lack of agreement may not be used as justification for a more severe sentence in subsequent criminal justice proceedings.

16. Failure to implement an agreement made in the course of a restorative process should be referred back to the restorative programme or to the criminal justice authorities and a decision as to how to proceed should be taken without delay. Failure to implement the agreement may not be used as justification for a more severe sentence in subsequent criminal justice proceedings.

IV. Facilitators

17. Facilitators should be recruited from all sections of society and should generally possess good understanding of local cultures and communities. They should be able to demonstrate sound judgement and interpersonal skills necessary to conducting restorative processes.
18. Facilitators should perform their duties in an impartial manner, based on the facts of the case and on the needs and wishes of the parties. They should always respect the dignity of the parties and ensure that the parties act with respect towards each other.
19. Facilitators should be responsible for providing a safe and appropriate environment for the restorative process. They should be sensitive to any vulnerability of the parties.
20. Facilitators should receive initial training before taking up facilitation duties and should also receive in-service training. The training should aim at providing skills in conflict resolution, taking into account the particular needs of victims and offenders, at providing basic knowledge of the criminal justice system and at providing a thorough knowledge of the operation of the restorative programme in which they will do their work.

V. Continuing development of restorative justice programmes

21. There should be regular consultation between criminal justice authorities and administrators of restorative justice programmes to develop a common understanding of restorative processes and outcomes, to increase the extent to which restorative programmes are used and to explore ways in which restorative approaches might be incorporated into criminal justice practices.
22. Member States should promote research on and evaluation of restorative justice programmes to assess the extent to which they result in restorative outcomes, serve as an alternative to the criminal justice process and provide positive outcomes for all parties.
23. Restorative justice processes may need to undergo change in concrete form over time. Member States should therefore encourage regular, rigorous evaluation and modification of such programmes in the light of the above definitions.

RESTORATIVE JUSTICE IN SPANISH POPULAR TALES

Gema Varona Martínez

Two years ago I started a research project on popular tales and criminal justice for the ethnological and anthropological section of a Basque cultural institution. Due to several reasons, the project was never fully developed. When I received the kind invitation to participate in this book through Professor José Luis de la Cuesta, I felt both delighted and grateful. This represented a very special opportunity to honour and thank Professor Tony Peters. Many years ago, without knowing each other, I admired him as a guest lecturer at the Basque Institute of Criminology in San Sebastián. Then I met him during his sabbatical year, while I was an Erasmus student in Leuven. At the end of 1997, he was too kind to be on the jury of my Ph.D. thesis. Before and after that, we met in Spain and abroad on several occasions. On some of those occasions he was accompanied by his wonderful wife. Now, through calm writing, I am trying to recover the above-mentioned project, which I believe contains some beauty that I would like to offer to Professor Peters to express how grateful I am to him.

Introduction

Recent researches on culture and society have shown the construction of popular culture and its influences upon criminal policy, and vice versa. Popular tales represent stories about -more or less universal- fears and hopes and their study goes beyond the connections between literature and justice, in order to head to reflections within the area of Criminology. Tales express people's perceptions of social order with all their inherent ambivalences. They offer a human sense to the quest of reality, archetypes or models of behaviour. This article examines the survival of penal mythology through popular tales in the 21st century Spain. After a brief introduction, a criminological search begins for traces of restorative justice by means of content analysis of Spanish popular tales.

The context of my study differs from what I usually work on, but recent interest in the interplay between culture and criminal justice attracts me.[1]

1 F. BAILEY and D. HALE (1998) (eds.), *Popular Culture, Crime & Justice*, 16. Belmont: West/Wadsworth; J. FERRELL and C. R. SANDERS (1995) (eds.), *Cultural Criminology*. Boston: Northeastern University.

From structuralism, through Marxist and semiotic theories, to feminism, elements of the construction of popular culture -today mass culture- have been subject to systematisation attempts, as well as attempts to identify its effects on social policies. As an oblique research route to criminal justice, these studies offer an original perspective to analyse aspects that usually go unrecognized in ordinary life as we listen to music, read a newspaper, a journal, a comic, watch television, go to the cinema, listen to the radio, or work and play with computers. The question relies on integrating everyday life studies within the theoretical framework of reality and identity construction processes and seeing how this affects criminal policy. This brief article is only a tentative approach to point out guidelines for further research.

Nowadays popular culture seems to change too fast to deserve scientific concern. This is the case of my topic: popular tales. Whether so-called popular tales, stories of long ago by definition, have an actual influence on today's worldviews is questionable. One of my hypotheses relies upon the existence of cultural sediments. This means that the mass media and the entertainment industry -let's think for example about Disney[2]- do not occupy the whole space of tales[3] yet. Some itineraries for old traditions and customs can be detected. These traditions and customs express values, standpoints of thinking and world understanding that are constantly adapting to new times. As Bailey and Hale argue,[4] humans have always shared stories on good and evil, murder and revenge... and some contemporary formulas to tell us these stories are rooted in remote times and folklore. Tales retain their sense to illustrate fears and hopes, more or less universal. Their study goes beyond connections between justice and literature to head to considerations within the area of Criminology and Anthropology of Law, and more specifically of restorative justice.

In this article, I shall first concentrate on the significance of popular tales for the study of criminal mythology. Then I shall limit my content analysis to several Spanish popular tales. This will allow me to reflect on restorative justice and to reach some conclusions about its relation to popular culture and the difficulties in its implementation.

---

2 Cf. E. SMOODIN (1994) *Disney Discourse: Producing the Magic Kingdom.* New York: Routledge.

3 In Spain there is a rebirth of tales publications and storytellers in local culture houses. Cf. about the renaissance of "urban tales" in the Internet society, MARTOS NÚÑEZ, ELOY and VÍCTOR M. DE SOUSA Trindade (1997) (coords), *La casa encantada. Estudios sobre cuentos, mitos y leyendas de España y Portugal. Seminario interuniversitario de estudios sobre la tradición.* Mérida: Junta de Extremadura.

4 BAILEY, *o.c.*

1. The Mythology of Crime and Criminal Justice in popular Tales

Several criminologists have written about criminal mythology.[5] Fattah's reflections on the fascination, sensationalization, dramatization and glamorization of crime can be pointed out. Crime has always been a topic for literature and it has become a commodity in the entertainment market of today's societies.[6] Monestier argues that there is nothing as mythological as news about crimes.[7] Sometimes reality copies or even surpasses fiction. In newspapers criminal events are simplified in such a manner that they come to resemble novels and tales. In any case, art and science have always tried to reflect reality in different ways, ways that produce thoughts on what is real, true, likely or credible.[8]

The term *popular tale* implies a myriad of forms. Among myths, tales, romances and legends similarities can be found.[9] Tales are defined by three key elements: they report a fantastic happening; are brief and simple; and have moral and entertaining ends. Popular tales are properly oral narratives through which people express their perceptions of nature, social order, personal wishes and needs, with all their ambivalences and implications for criminal justice. As part of oral tradition, tales vary constantly.

Greek, Latin and Biblical myths, without forgetting the Oriental origin of the oldest tales, should be seen as oral stories, finally written down, long before popular tales spread in Western Europe.[10] A myth is a traditional narrative on memorable and paradigmatic actions of extraordinary characters -heroes or gods- within a prestigious and essential time. Symbolically, myths also offer a human sense to reality: "some images that stuck in the collective memory, and survived in tradition, because without doubt they answer

---

5 E.A. FATTAH (1997) *Criminology - Past, Present and Future. A Critical Overview*. London: St. Martin's Press; See J. KATZ (1988) *Seduction of Crime*. New York: Basic Books. From the point of view of mass media, Cf. V.E. KAPPELER, M. BLUMBERG and G.W. POTTER (1995) *The Mythology of Crime and Criminal Justice*. Prospects Heights, Il.: Waveland. In the origins of Spanish Criminology, cf. Q. SALDAÑA (1914) *Los orígenes de la Criminología*. Madrid: Victoriano Suárez

6 Considering the birth of detective stories, it has been argued that lowest classes have always preferred fiction beyond their everyday tragedies. Other studies signalise that this premise is also true for middle and higher classes, even if in a different language.

7 A. MONESTIER (1992) *Los grandes casos criminales*. Madrid: del Prado.

8 P. FEYERABEND (2001) *La conquista de la abundancia. La abstracción frente a la riqueza del ser*. Barcelona: Paidós.

9 MARTOS NÚÑEZ, ELOY and DE SOUSA TRINDADE, *o.c.*

10 J.C. COOPER (1986) *Cuentos de hadas. Alegorías de los mundos internos*. Málaga: Sirio.

fundamental questions of human beings and their anxiety about life mysteries and social challenges".[11] According to Wasserziehr,[12] dreams, tales and myths share archetype characters of human beings, which make a certain understanding among cultures easier.[13] However, in tales the identification with archetypes seems stronger and they reveal more poetry, fiction and, especially in the case of fairy tales, more magic and happy endings.[14] Conversely, as already mentioned, in the line of realism, in tales many main persons are ordinary people, and are neither gods nor great warriors.

Tales as oral narratives, in which women played a great role at home, started to be written mainly in 19th century Europe. This task was carried out mostly by men,[15] as part of romanticism. In the process of writing, many changes occurred. Yet, more or less traditional values were kept. One of the well-known collections of that time is the fairy tales written by the Grimm brothers, notwithstanding the previous *Contes de Fées* of Charles Perrault.

Gabriela Wasserziehr has studied Jung's analytical Psychology in connection to the symbolic content of Grimms' fairy tales as part of the universal collective subconscious (1996). In her view, tales function as a self-representation of human psyche or as a bridge between the unconscious and the conscious. In them, we can discover models of conduct to guide us for personal fulfilment. Envy or hunger for power represents evil and they can be interpreted within dialectics of regeneration. For his part, Bettelheim has approached tales from the perspective of Psychoanalysis by showing their pedagogical value which allows them to raise existential problems and to differentiate between good and evil.[16]

2. Content Analysis of Several Spanish Popular Tales and their Connections to Restorative Justice

According to Wasserziehr,[17] symbolism is used in tales as a non-explicit language. The door for new interpretations always remains open and this contributes to their magic, mystery and attractiveness. In this article, I propose their reinterpretation within the context of Criminology and

11 C. GARCIA GUAL (1997) *Diccionario de mitos*. Barcelona: Planeta.

12 WASSERZIEHR, GABRIELA (1996) Los cuentos de hadas para adultos. Una lectura simbólica de los cuentos de hadas recopilados por J. y W. Grimm. Madrid: Endymion.

13 COOPER, *o.c.*

14 *Ibid.*, 14.

15 For several exceptions, see during the 18th century the work of Madame de Beaumont.

16 B. BETTELHEIM (1978) *Psicoanálisis de los cuentos de hadas*. Barcelona: Crítica.

restorative justice. Tales are fiction and, at the same time, metaphors of a complex and variable reality. Those metaphors can be modestly studied through the scientific method. Therefore, a recent criminological search for the significance of tales[18] joins those of Psychology, Literature, Folklore,[19] and Anthropology.[20] [21]

Methodologically, I will use the theoretical groundwork of several sociologists and anthropologists from the standpoint of cultural Criminology[22]. After connecting diverse Anthropology and Sociology of Law literature, I will point out the relation of popular culture to legal culture. Following the classical definition by Friedman,[23] legal culture expresses people's values and attitudes towards law, in a broad sense, that affects their behaviour. Popular culture influences those values.

Technically, my qualitative research is based on a selection of Spanish popular tales, the design of a questionnaire to collect data and content analysis. A selection was made through literary sources. Within the same specialized publisher, two works were chosen. The first is a two-volume compilation by the writer José María Guelbenzu.[24] It contains 117 tales from different regions that show cultural differences within Spain. The second selected source is the work by the writer Felipe Alfau,[25] published in English in 1929 in the United States. It assembles ten tales. As part of my qualitative research, this selection was not intended to be representative either of Spanish popular culture or of Spanish popular tales, if both are understood as a monolithic whole.

The questionnaire to collect the data identifies several elements in each tale: the kind of emerging conflict and the way it is managed; the values being promoted; the context of violence, if any; the genre and characteristics

17 G. WASSERZIEHR, *o.c.*

18 G. MUELLER, (1986) The Criminological Significance of the Grimm's Fairy Tales, in: R. B. BOTTIGHEIMER (ed.), *Fairy Tales and Society-Illusion, Allusion, and Paradigm*. Philadelphia: The University of Pennsylvania.

19 V. PROPP (1974) *Las raíces históricas del cuento*. Barcelona: Fundamentos.

20 A. IÑARRA (1994) *El asesinato en la cultura popular vasca*. Irún: Iralka.

21 IÑARRA has studied murder in Basque popular culture: *"Tales that deal with this subject invite us to think on this crime and report on the way it should be valued; moreover they reflect social thoughts on the fact and its effects. Through this oral expression between storyteller and audience, a message is sent, together with certain values, so that it is accepted, rejected or criticized"* (*o.c.*, 26-7).

22 I understand cultural Criminology as a shared sphere of Anthropology of Law and Sociology of culture.

23 L. FRIEDMAN (1969) Legal Culture and Social Development, 4 *Law & Society* 29-44.

24 J.M. GUELBENZU (1998) (ed.), *Cuentos populares españoles*, 2 vols. Madrid: Siruela.

25 F. ALFAU (1995) *Cuentos españoles de antaño*. Madrid: Siruela.

of victims and aggressors; the sense of responsibility; the type of social control, and so forth.

The content analysis develops the hypothesis raised by Guelbenzu,[26] namely that most Spanish popular tales share the following three characteristics:

1. Miracles come as a solution to life problems. Many times, the character that provides the hero with the "magic object" to fulfil his task belongs to heaven in a catholic sense. On the other hand, the devil appears sometimes as the bad character. In my analysis, I found the presence of faith and trust in providence. But even when miracles happen, active participation and personal effort are quite important.
2. Wit is valued beyond belief. This idea, however, does not emerge that clearly from my analysis. For example, reception of elderly wisdom appears as a key element for change. Moreover, I agree with Martín Garzo in that, in many popular tales, wisdom of the poor and the powerless is stressed: they know things about life that the rich and powerful ignore. They teach us: "To be conscious of their suffering and needs, but also to collect from their hands the gift of otherness. Because we receive all we are from others' hands".[27].
3. Imagination is limited by realism. In contrast to the belief in miracles, realism is expressed in misery conditions of some characters and cruelty situations. Some tales follow the biblical dictum "an eye for an eye". Bad characters are demonised in such a way that few tales end in reconciliation. Even in fairy tales, the initial victimisation of the hero (humiliation and desperation) is equalized in the end by his final revenge.[28] Writers like Gustavo Martín Garzo have stressed that in tales (1988: 14): "It's surprising to think of the materials this house is built upon. Terrible crimes, treasons, fragmented bodies, blood signs, alternate with golden birds, wonderful virtues, unsuspected allies, hearts that miss a beat. Because this is the wonder of tales, they do not lie to us about how the world is. They offer children a shelter, while letting them observe the contradictory and naked reality".

In most tales, conflicts do not clearly correspond to crimes in a formal or legal sense. Therefore, we cannot always talk properly of "offenders" or "victims". Results of my content analysis show that the prevalent kind of

---

26 J.M. GUELBENZU (1998) (ed.), *Cuentos populares españoles*, 2 vols. Madrid: Siruela.

27 G. MARTIN GARZO (1998) El pájaro de oro, *El País*, November 22nd, p. 14. All translations from Spanish into English are my own responsibility. I do my best to have them make sense within the context of the full text where they are integrated. For those belonging to tales, this consideration justifies their subsidiary inclusion in footnotes.

28 M. TATAR (1987) *The Hard Facts of the Grimms' Fairy Tales*. Princeton, NJ.: Princeton University Press.

conflicts in popular tales is as old as humanity. They have to do with passions and partners/love relationships; authority, power and socio-economic differences; vanity, excessive pride; and envy. Of course, popular tales do not reflect present day conflicts that are brought about by drugs, multicultural society and technology (its use in arms, ways of travelling, computers, etc.).

Values such as friendship, loyalty, self-confidence, perseverance, courage, leadership, generosity, empathy, peace, tolerance and kindness are promoted. Nonetheless, as partly mentioned above, characters also use lies, astuteness, tricks and violence.

Violence is an integral part of the tales[29] and this is clear in the Spanish popular tales studied here. However, distinctions should be made. The kind of violence presented in the selected tales has nothing to do with male or group violence. In general, it is a theatrical violence,[30] different from today's *gore* and *snuff* movies. It does not provoke scandal; it is not morbid or pathological. Horrible happenings occur (manslaughter, murder, torture, etc.), but in a context where they have a sense and are removed from everyday life. Violence in the tales I analysed is part of a ritual of *just deserts*, coercion and/or determinism. It is not carried out by formal social control agencies, but by informal ones. It is usually inflicted by fantastic characters that resemble natural forces. The sphere of violence alternates between the private or domestic domain and the abuse of "public" power. Even if in old societies violence was more accepted, I did not find a promotion of violence in popular tales, as we find it in some of today's popular culture manifestations. In any case, visual or oral violence has always being attractive to audiences, perhaps as a way of catharsis or clash with routine life, where that kind of happening is generally exceptional.

In rare occasions characters are animals or trees, mainly with a human past. The kind of "offenders" presented in the selected tales is usually minors or juveniles, although the concept of minor/juvenile has been extended today. I also discovered the intervention of elderly people that show the importance of intergenerational relations. The main characters are males and females alike, without a previous criminal career or mental health problems and with what is now called multiple intelligence: they have both bad and good qualities that help explain their tragedies and their ways of overcoming

---

29 S. THOMPSON (1972) *El cuento folklórico*. Caracas: Biblioteca de la Universidad Central.

30 Cf., in relation to detective stories, the statement that death or murder means spectacle, not really tragedy, but that they are necessary elements to bring the whole plot or storyline; R. GUBERN (1982) (ed.), *La novela criminal*. Barcelona: Tusquets.

them. Many times, "victims" and "offenders" are two sides of the same coin. Their situation is interchangeable. I cannot draw conclusions as to the risks of victimisation associated with belonging to a certain ethnic group, social status, age, gender or occupation. The kind of original victimisation might be related to Tittle's theory of control balance: their living and dying conditions are determined by their being objects of social forces beyond the scarce control they can exercise. On the other hand, I found something akin to what early victimologists described as “guilty” or “deserving” victims.

There is a prevailing belief in the possibility of reparation, together with supernatural punishment. In reparation, rituals and symbols contain an important meaning. Usually, the main character begins some kind of risky travelling that will finally provoke a constructive change for his person and circumstances.

The idea of community is marked by the past and here I see a reinforcement of stereotypes of good and bad people (for example, Arabs are among the bad, which is not surprising in view of our history). The good will be rewarded; the bad will be punished, sometimes with oppression or stigmatizing shame.

Analytical dimensions[31] in selected tales show the following four groups of beliefs or images in relation to fundamental questions for humanity:

1. Human beings' behaviour is not so different from that of animals. It can be aggressive, and yet, at the same time, it is social. However, human beings are not totally free. Besides, as we will mention below, some tales make distinctions -some people are considered superior in certain ways-.
2. Social order exists but it is constructed of conflict and cooperation in a dialectic manner. There is no concept of civil society, but of small communities that hardly change.
3. Criminal law is not present. In its place there are more or less informal controls that work. There is a common understanding of what a violation of social order means as evidence of both integration and deviance.
4. There is room for individuals' free decisions but sometimes they cannot escape an external determinism (they are not influenced by biological or psychological given characteristics, but by macrosocial conditions or supernatural forces). At the end, characters might have good luck, but first they have to look for it. Uncertainty of a happy ending always exists. In fact, some stories describe very bad outcomes.

---

31 These analytical dimensions are taken from Einstadter and Henry's study on criminological theories. W. EINSTADTER and H. STUART (1995) *Criminological Theory. An Analysis of its Underlying Assumptions*. Fort Worth: Harcourt Brace College.

When popular tales are deeply studied, complicated messages are uncovered. It could not be any other way. If they yield metaphors of reality, this one is multiple, complex and contradictory. That is why science is needed, even if it cannot offer exact answers.

In Spanish popular tales, we do find the dichotomy of good and bad, together with revenge appraisal -somehow influenced by an old negative interpretation of Catholicism-. Yet, restorative justice elements also appear in the promotion of values such as:

- The need for communication and empathy *("...tú nunca te diste cuenta de mi presencia, porque siempre estabas mirando para arriba y yo no me atrevía a hablarte")*[32].
- The good handling of conflicts by mediators as catalysts (they are usually fantasy characters or elderly people).
- The symbiosis between what we call reality and fiction in order to interpret the past to construct a peaceful future.
- Interdependence, and
- The need for a change of lenses, even if, at first, its promoters are taken as mere Utopians *("Hay arco iris... Tú no lo ves por falta de costumbre")*.[33]

Conclusion

Popular culture, with its constant changes and contradictions, offers a bridge between the past and the future. Oral tradition in the form of popular tales is a method of social control that has been replaced by the modern mass media and the entertainment industry. However, many of their old archetypes in relation to criminal justice remain in our subconscious, even if they are constantly adapting to new times.

Despite the deep changes that once turned the oral world into a written one, and are now turning the written world into a more and more visual one, popular tales survive in our collective memory, with their inherent transformations. As part of reality, they awaken criminological interest with their archetypes of crime and criminal justice. This interest combines Ethnology,[34] social History, cultural Anthropology, social Psychology,

32 ALFAU, *o.c.*: "You never realised about my presence, because you were always looking up, and I did not dare to talk to you."

33 ALFAU, *o.c.* : "There is a rainbow... you do not see it because you are not used to it".

34 Interdependence between Ethnology and Criminology is reflected in Spain in the work of famous ethnologists, like BARANDIARAN and CARO BAROJA, collected in the Basque

Literature, etc. in what recent studies consider one of the most promising research lines. This requires, as Tatar expresses,[35](1987: xix-xx) points out, the palaeontologist's love for the remote, the historian's appetite for facts, the psychologist's curiosity for causes, and the anthropologist's passion for the understanding of cultural differences. To that I would like to add the criminologist's interdisciplinary endeavour for explaining the complexity and relativity of crime, criminalisation and victimisation. The concept of crime entails a great symbolic component that involves values such as good and evil, human responsibility, victimisation, restoration, retribution, etc. These values appear in the penal codes of the 21st century as a manifestation of the Enlightenment reason that could not rid itself completely of myths. Those myths implicate positive and negative values for the sake of restorative justice. Among the negative ones, stereotypes of crime and criminal justice are found that render the development of victim-offender mediation and the like quite difficult in Spanish culture. In Einstein's words, disintegration of prejudice is far more difficult than atomic disintegration.

When talking of Spanish culture as an explanation for the lack of "success" of restorative justice in my country,[36] I would rather think of professional interests and of social control interplay. Here it is important to recall the idea of Spanish civil society beyond a community, as Crawford has suggested in the case of France (2000). But, even within Spain, there are many variations from one region to another and, for example, the challenge for the Basque Country is to find routes for restorative justice in the context of terrorist macrovictimisation. What seems clear is that popular culture influences legal culture and vice versa. Hopefully, further studies will illuminate this issue, by considering, as well, what popular culture means in societies that are becoming more and more multicultural.

Today's quest for globalisation is to try to create new institutions that respond to the needs of an interrelated world. Those institutions, such as mediation in the criminal sphere, can only succeed if they are able to adapt to the new conditions of the political, economical and cultural spheres. We cannot go back to the kind of community reflected in popular tales, but there are several ideas I would like to take as points of departure for further critical discussion and comparative research:

Institute of Criminology Journal *Eguzkilore*. In my work, Ethnology is taken in a recent meaning as a strategy for cultural research within comparative studies on a small scale.

35 M. TATAR (1987) *The Hard Facts of the Grimms' Fairy Tales*. Princeton, NJ.: Princeton University Press.

36 G. VARONA (1998) *La mediación reparadora como estrategia de control social. Una perspectiva criminológica*. Granada: Comares.

1. Intergenerational relations and interdependence to construct links of open identity and solidarity. Community can be understood as communication, daily living and participation in the definition and reaction to problems.
2. Trust and hope. Decisions as individuals and together as groups can be made, such as the Forum for Victim-Offender Mediation and Restorative Justice, to influence conditions of living, without ingenuousness and without resignation. Out of a tragedy, capacity to overcome victimisation, trust in self-transformation and improvement are possible, given certain individual, group and structural conditions. As it is said in a tale: *"... de la unión de luz y oscuridad ha surgido el ocaso".*[37]

Epilogue

Motherhood has revived my interest in popular tales and their educative role. Now that life is so different from what I imagined years ago, being an Erasmus student in Leuven, I recognize my debt to my *maestros* and Professor Peters is one of them.[38] Because Professor Peters has taught me to ask questions and to find ways of reaching my own answers, with the risk of being mistaken and with the advice of knowing that, many times, answers live far away from their questions. Something apparently so simple has helped me as a Criminology researcher and probably much more as a human being. Thank you Professor Peters for sharing your humanity with me "once upon many many times...". As in the *Rainbow* tale of the painting master, Professor Peters: *"Siempre se las arreglaba para poner de relieve pequeños detalles y sombras de color que pasaban desapercibidos a la mirada corriente. Siempre les daba consejos bien fundados que les servían de mucho para hacer progresos en su trabajo. Pero la mayor parte del tiempo les hablaba de otros muchos asuntos que no tenían relación con la pintura, y al cabo de algún tiempo los alumnos se dieron cuenta de que estaban aprendiendo cantidad de cosas importantes".*[39]

---

37 ALFAU, *o.c.*, 26: "Sunset, with its beauty, is born out of unity of light and darkness."

38 Together with Professors Antonio BERISTAIN and JOSÉ LUIS DE LA CUESTA.

39 ALFAU, *o.c.*, 26: "He always managed to underline small details and color shadows that are not perceived by an ordinary look. He always gave them well-founded advices that really help them to make progress in their work. But most of the time, he told them about many other matters not related to painting, and after a while students realised they were learning lots of important things".

References

Alfau, Felipe (1995) *Cuentos españoles de antaño*. Madrid: Siruela.

Bailey, Frankie and Donna Hale (1998) (eds.), *Popular Culture, Crime & Justice*. Belmont: West/Wadsworth.

Barandiaran, José Miguel (1988) El juicio que han merecido algunos crímenes en nuestro entorno. El País Vasco, 2 *Eguzkilore* 33-6.

Bettelheim, Bruno (1978) *Psicoanálisis de los cuentos de hadas*. Barcelona: Crítica.

Camarena, Julio and Maxime Chevalier (1995) *Catálogo tipológico del cuento folklórico español*, vol. 1, Cuentos maravillosos. Madrid: Gredos.

Caro Baroja, Julio (1979) *Ensayos sobre la cultura popular española*. Madrid: Dosbe.

Cooper, J. C. (1986) *Cuentos de hadas. Alegorías de los mundos internos*. Málaga: Sirio.

Crawford, Adam (2000) Contrasts in Victim-Offender Mediation and Appeals to Community in France and England, in: D. Nelken (ed.), *Contrasting Criminal Justice. Getting from Here to There*. Aldershot: Ashgate.

Dueso, José (1997) *Diablos*. Roger: Donostia-San Sebastián.

Einstadter, Werner and Stuart Henry (1995) *Criminological Theory. An Analysis of its Underlying Assumptions*. Fort Worth: Harcourt Brace College.

Fattah, Ezzat A. (1997) *Criminology - Past, Present and Future. A Critical Overview*. London: St. Martin's Press.

Ferrell, Jeff and Clinton R. Sanders (1995) (eds.), *Cultural Criminology*. Boston: Northeastern University.

Feyerabend, Paul (2001) *La conquista de la abundancia. La abstracción frente a la riqueza del ser*. Barcelona: Paidós.

Friedman, Lawrence (1969) Legal Culture and Social Development, 4 *Law & Society* 29-44.

Garcia Gual, Carlos (1997) *Diccionario de mitos*. Barcelona: Planeta.

Garner, James Finn (1994) *Politically Correct Bedtime Stories. Modern Tales for Our Life & Times*. New York: Macmillan.

Gubern, Román (1982) (ed.), *La novela criminal*. Barcelona: Tusquets.

Guelbenzu, José María (1998) (ed.) (2.ª ed), *Cuentos populares españoles*, 2 vols. Madrid: Siruela.

Iñarra, Aitxus (1994) *El asesinato en la cultura popular vasca*. Irún: Iralka.

Kappeler, V. E., M. Blumberg and G. W. Potter (1995) *The Mythology of Crime and Criminal Justice*. Prospects Heights, Il.: Waveland.

Katz, J. (1988) *Seductions of Crime*. New York: Basic Books.

Klotz, Volker (1970) Weltordnung im Märchen, 81 *Neue Rundschau* 73-91.

Martin Garzo, Gustavo (1998) El pájaro de oro, *El País*, November 22nd, 14.

— 2001. La cuesta de la Maruquesa, *El País*, April 15th, 10.

Martos Núñez, Eloy and Víctor M. de Sousa Trindade (1997) (coords), *La casa encantada. Estudios sobre cuentos, mitos y leyendas de España y Protugal. Seminario interuniversitario de estudios sobre la tradición.* Mérida: Junta de Extremadura.

Monestier, Alain (1992) *Los grandes casos criminales*. Madrid: del Prado.

Mueller, Gerhard O. W. (1986) The Criminological Significance of the Grimm's Fairy Tales, in: R. Bottigheimer (ed.), *Fairy Tales and Society-Illusion, Allusion, and Paradigm*. Philadelphia: The University of Pennsylvania.

Propp, Vladimir (1974) *Las raíces históricas del cuento*. Barcelona: Fundamentos.

Quintano, A. (1955) *La Criminología en la literatura universal. (Ensayo de propedéutica biológico-criminal sobre fuentes literarias*). Bosch: Barcelona.

Saldaña, Quintiliano (1914) *Los orígenes de la Criminología*. Victoriano Suárez: Madrid.

Smoodin, Eric (1994) *Disney Discourse: Producing the Magic Kingdom*. New York: Routledge.

Tatar, Maria (1987) *The Hard Facts of the Grimms' Fairy Tales*. Princeton, NJ. Princeton University Press.

Thompson, Stith (1972) *El cuento folklórico*. Caracas: Biblioteca de la Universidad Central.

Tittle, Charles R. (1995) *Control Balance: Toward a General Theory of Deviance*. Boulder: Westview.

Varona, Gema (1998) *La mediación reparadora como estrategia de control social. Una perspectiva criminológica*. Granada: Comares.

Wasserziehr, Gabriela (1996) *Los cuentos de hadas para adultos. Una lectura simbólica de los cuentos de hadas recopilados por J. y W. Grimm*. Madrid: Endymion.

SELECTED BIBLIOGRAPHY OF TONY PETERS (SINCE 1980)

1. Books and monographs

& J. Goethals (1993) (eds.), *De achterkant van de criminaliteit. Over victimologie, slachtofferhulp en strafrechtsbedeling.* Antwerpen: Kluwer Rechtswetenschappen, 391 p.

& A. Neys, F. Pieters en J. Vanacker (1994) (eds.), *Tralies in de weg.* Leuven: Universitaire Pers Leuven, 425 p.

& C. Fijnaut, J. Goethals, T. Peters & L. Walgrave (1995) (eds.), Changes in society, crime and criminal justice in Europe, Vol. I: Crime and insecurity in the city, 324 p.; Vol. II: International organised and corporate crime, 278 p. The Hague: Kluwer Law International.

& E. Fattah (1998) (ed.), *Support for crime victims in a comparative perspective. A collection of essays dedicated to the memory of Prof. Frederic McClintock.* Leuven: Leuven University Press, 256 p.

2. Articles in books and scientific journals

& J. Van Kerckvoorde en L. Van Outrive (1980) Vijftig jaar criminologie onderwijs: een groei naar zelfstandigheid, *Panopticon* 197-212.

& J. Goethals (1981) De legitimiteitscrisis van de vrijheidsberoving, *Streven* 316-327 en 364-365.

(1981) Mesures de substitution aux peines privatives de liberté, in : *Actas del XXIX Curso Internacional de Criminologia*, 689-702, Pamplona, Fundación de Carranza 689-702.

(1985) Derechos humanos y aislamiento celular, in: Beristain, A. y. de la Cuesta, J.L. (eds.), *Los derechos humanos ante la criminologia y el derecho penal*, 279-317. Serv. editorial Universidad del Pais Vasco.

(1985) In search of the criminal. Utility or inutility? The desirability and dangers of TV-programmes, in: Vigh, J. (ed.), *Proceedings of the international conference on social defence and crime prevention*, Budapest, 341-354.

& C. Eliaerts en S. Snacken (1985) Le juge face au problème des courtes peines de prison, in: *La criminologie au Prétoire*, Colloque du 50ième Anniversaire, Ecole des Sciences Criminologiques Léon Cornil, 31-46. Bruxelles: Story Scientia.

& C. Eliaerts (1986) Considérations sur le tribunal de l'application des peines (avant-projet R. Legros), XLVI(3) *Annales de Droit de Louvain* 147-167.
& J. Detienne en G. Houchon 1986) Conseil Surpérieur de la politique pénitentiaire, Rapport sur les travaux, avis de grandes options de politique pénitentiaire 1978-1982, *Revue de Droit pénal et de criminologie* 693-699.
& S. Snacken en C. Eliaerts (1987) Le juge face au problème des courtes peines de prison, 2 *Revue Internationale de Criminologie et de Police Technique* 176-182.
(1988) Consideraciones téoricas sobre la Victimologia, 2 *Eguzkilore. Cuaderno del Instituto Vasco de Criminologia* 107-133.
(1988) Victimologie, in *Manuel des services policiers*, IXE - 9/1 13-55.
& L. Dupont (1988) Reclassering, hulpverlening en strafrechtspleging in België, in: C. Fijnaut (ed.), *Reclassering: Horizon 2000, Ontwikkelingen in strafrecht en samenleving en de rol van de reclassering*, 177-200. Arnhem: Gouda Quint.
& R. De Graef en J. Dewit (1988) Les mesures post-pénitentiaires de contrôle social et le patronage, in: F. Tulkens (ed.), *Généalogie de la défense sociale en Belgique (1880-1914),* 143-168. Gent : Story Scientia 143-168.
& L. Dupont (1989) Criminal justice and social welfare in Belgium, in: *Criminologia y Derecho Penal al servicio de la persona, Libro Homenaje al professor Antonio Beristain*, 133-146. San Sebastian, Instituto Vasco de Criminologia.
(1989) Criminaliteitspreventie en onveiligheid, in: *Publieke opinie, onrustgevoelens en de rol van de media. Handboek voor politiediensten,* IXF2 115-139.
& J. Vervaele (1990) Aperçu historique et importance actuelle de l'Union Internationale de Droit Pénal. Notions sur le système de sanctions pénales, 61 *Revue Internationale de Droit Pénal, Association Internationale de Droit Pénal* 239-253.
& C. Fijnaut en L. Walgrave (1990) Politie, gevangeniswezen en jeugdrecht in België, 9 *Justitiële Verkenningen* 74-94.
(1990) Criminología y victimología, in: A. Beristain Ipiña (ed.), *Victimología,* VIII *Cursos de Verano en San Sebastian - I Cursos Europeos*, 97-104. Servicio Editorial Universidad del País Vasco.
& J. Goethals (1991) Victimas de Violencia. Analisis descriptivo de Crimines callejeros y Robos con Allanamiento de Morada en Bélgica, 1 *Revista de Derecho Penal y Criminología* 131-179.

& J. Goethals (1991) Victims of violence: a descriptive analysis of streetcrime and burglary in Belgium, in: G. Kaiser, H. Kury and H.J. Albrecht (eds.), *Victims and Criminal Justice*, Max Planck Institut für Aüslandisches und Internationales Recht, 52(1) Kriminologsiche Forschungsberichte 611-653.

& W. Meyvis (1991) Cinq ans d'aide sociale aux justiciables en Communauté Flamande, in : Ph. Mary (ed.), *L'Aide sociale aux justiciables*, 217-243. Bruxelles, Bruylant.

& L. Dupont (1993) Justicia Criminal y Asistencia Social en Belgica, in: R. Bergalli (ed.), *Sistema Penal y intervenciones Sociales*, 63-89. Barcelona, Hacer Editorial.

& J. Van Kerckvoorde (1993) Belgium in the second international crime survey, in: A. Frate, U. Zvekic and J.J.M. Van Dijk (eds.), *Understanding Crime: Experiences of crime and crime control*, 441-454. Rome: UNICRI.

(1993) Bemiddeling, herstel en strafrechtspleging, 2 *Panopticon*, 96-107.

& J. Van Kerckvoorde (1993) De Internationale Crime Survey. Een voorstelling van de resultaten voor België, *Panopticon* 338-352.

& G. Kellens en J. Van Kerckvoorde (1993) L'Enquête Internationale de victimisations vue de Belgique, 9/10 *Revue de Droit Pénal et de Criminologie* 825-839.

& A. Neys en P. Young (1993) Prisons in Europe, *European Journal of Crime, Criminal Law and Criminal Justice* 350-371.

& J. Van Kerckvoorde (1994) Profession criminologue: La situation en Belgique, in: R. Cario, A.M. Favard. et R. Ottenhof (eds.), *Profession Criminologue*, Collection Criminologie et Sciences de l'Homme, Actes du XVIIIième Congrès de l'Association Française de Criminologie, Toulouse, 45-62 Editions érès.

& A. Neys (1994) La pena desde la reparación, 8 *Eguzkilore, Cuaderno del Instituto Vasco de Criminologia* 165-195.

& I. Aertsen en L. Van Garsse (1995) Is there an incompability between insurance and mediation?, 3(2) *European Journal on Criminal Policy and Research* 106-112.

& I. Aertsen (1995) Restorative Justice: in search of new avenues in dealing with crime, in: C. Fijnaut et al. (ed.), *Changes in Society, Crime and Criminal Justice in Europe*, vol. 1, 311-342. The Hague, Kluwer Law International.

& A. Neys (1996) La peine considerée dans une perspective de réparation, 1 *Revue Internationale de Criminologie et de Police Technique* 3-29.

(1996) Probleemoplossing en herstel als functies van de straf, *Panopticon* 555-569.
& I. Aertsen (1997) Herstelbemiddeling in slachtofferperspectief, *Tijdschrift voor Criminologie* 372-383.
(1998) Victimización: analisis del problema, reacciones sociales y penales. Los estimulos para un enfoque victimológico en la criminologia, 16 *Victimologia* 7-69.
& I. Aertsen (1998) Mediation for Reparation: The Victim's Perspective, 6(2) *European Journal of Crime, Criminal Law and Criminal Justice* 106-124.
& I. Aertsen (1998) Mediation and Restorative Justice in Belgium, 6 *European Journal of Criminal Policy and Research* 507-525.
& I. Aertsen (1998) Reparation through mediation: the victim's perspective, in: E. Fattah and T. Peters (ed.), *Support for crime victims in a comparative perspective. A collection of Essays dedicated to the Memory of professor Frederick McClintock,* 229-251. Leuven: Leuven University Press.
& S. Snacken, G. Kellens, G. De Coninck, K. De Jaegher, K. Lauwaert, E. Maes, E. Stassart, H. Tubex en H. Verhoeven (1999) Fondements pour une politique judiciaire cohérente axée sur la réparation et sur la victime, in: B. Van Doninck, L. Van Daele en A. Naji (eds.), *Le droit sur le droit chemin?*, 113-160. Brussel, Academia Bruylant.
(2000) Slachtofferschap, bemiddeling en herstelgerichte praktijken, in: B. Raeymaekers en A. Van De Putte (eds.), *Krachten voor de toekomst, Lessen voor de eenentwintigste eeuw*, 332-366. Leuven: UPL/Davidsfonds.
& I. Aertsen (2000) Towards 'Restorative Justice': Victimisation, Victim support and trends in criminal justice, in: *Crime and Criminal Justice in Europe*, 35-46. Strasbourg, Council of Europe Publishing.
(2000) Victimisation, mediation et pratiques orientées vers la réparation, *Annales Internationales de Criminologie* 135-175.
(2001) Victimisation, médiation et pratiques orientées vers la réparation, in: R. Cario et D. Salas (eds.), *Oeuvre de justice et victimes*, 203-254. Paris: L'Harmattan.

3. Research reports

& C. Eliaerts, J. Goethals en C. Jacobs (1984) *Solitary confinement in prisons: the legal standards and the practices. A preliminary report about Belgium for Amnesty International*, Leuven, 74 p.

& S. Christiaensen, L. Dupont en J. Goethals (1987) *Diefstal met geweld of bedreiging. Achtergronden, verschijningsvormen en beheersbaarheid,* Onderzoeksrapport K.U.Leuven, Deel I (74 p.), Deel II (46p.), Deel III (143p.), Samenvatting (38 p.).

I. Aertsen, T. Peters en L. Van Garsse (auteurs), Peters, T. (promotor) (1994) *Project Herstelbemiddeling*, Onderzoeksrapport, Leuven, 87 p.

I. Aertsen en L.Van Garsse (auteurs), T. Peters (promotor) (1996) *Tussen dader en slachtoffer: de bemiddeling in de praktijk*, Onderzoeksrapport, Leuven, 137 p.

& L. Dupont en G. Smaers (1996) *Rechtsbescherming van gedetineerden*, Brussel: DWTC, 242 p.

& J. Vanacker (ed.) (1997) *Van oriëntatienota naar penaal beleid?,* K.U.Leuven, Onderzoeksgroep Penologie en Victimologie, Doc. 1, p. 86, I86 en II 133.

I. Vandeurzen, H. Verhoeven, A. Verstraete en J. Willemsens (auteurs), T. Peters (promotor) (1999) *Slachtoffer- en herstelgerichte detentie: visie en activiteiten,* Verslag, Leuven, 93 p.

S. Christiaensen, I. Vandeurzen en H. Verhoeven (auteurs), T. Peters (promotor) (2000) *Herstelgerichte detentie: van actie-onderzoek naar beleidsvoering*, Leuven, 171 p. + 4 bijlagen.

NOTES ON THE CONTRIBUTORS

Hans-Jörg Albrecht studied law at the universities of Tübingen and Freiburg (Ph.D., 1979) (Germany). In 1991, he obtained the *venia legendi* for criminal law, juvenile criminal law, criminology, and prison law. H.-J. Albrecht was a research fellow at the Max Planck Institute from 1977 until 1991, when he started to lecture criminal law and criminology at the University of Konstanz. In 1993 he was offered the chair for criminal law, juvenile criminal law and criminology at the University of Dresden where he stayed for 4 years, until he assumed his current position as director at the Max Planck Institute for Foreign and International Criminal Law in Freiburg/Germany. He teaches criminal law, criminal justice and criminology at the University of Freiburg, and was recently appointed as a guest professor at the China University of Political Science and Law, Beijing, and at Hainan University. Albrecht's research interests cover various legal, criminological and policy topics ranging from sentencing theory, juvenile crime, drug policies, environmental crime and organised crime, evaluation research and systems of criminal sanctions. He has published, co-published and edited various books, among them volumes on sentencing, day-fine systems, recidivism, child abuse and neglect, drug policies, research on victimisation, etc. He is the editor-in-chief of the journal *Monatsschrift für Kriminologie und Strafrechtsreform* and of the *European Journal of Crime, Criminal Justice, and Criminal Law*, and a member of the editorial board of *Déviance et Société*, *Criminal Justice* and the forthcoming *Crime and Criminal Justice in Europe*.

Antonio Beristain Ipiña, S.J., is a professor emeritus at the University of the Basque Country (Spain), is founder (1978) and former director (1978-2000) of the Basque Institute of Criminology (San Sebastian). He holds a Doctorate *honoris causa* of the University of Pau and the Pays d'Adour (France), and received the Hermann Mannheim Award for Comparative Criminology (1993), the Medaille al Mérito Social Penitenciario (1994) and the Gran Cruz de San Raimundo de Peñafort (2001). He has a special interest and is working in the area of penal policy, corrections and victimology, and has visited various universities in Europe and the Americas. A. Beristain has published 28 books and more than 300 articles in Spain and abroad, and he gave conferences in a great number of universities in Europe and America.

Isidoro Blanco Cordero studied law (Lic., 1991; Doctor 1996) and criminology (Diplom., 1990; Master, 1995) at the University of the Basque Country (Spain). He currently teaches criminal law at the Faculty of Law of the University of Vigo (Spain). The author has been a research fellow at the Max-Planck-Institut für Ausländisches und Internationales Strafrecht und Kriminologie (Freiburg, Germany), at the Institute of Human Rights of DePaul University (Chicago, USA) and at the Institute of Criminal Law and Criminology of the University of Salzburg (Austria). His research interests include money laundering and organized crime, corruption and international criminal law.

Robert Cario est professeur de Sciences criminelles au sein de l'Université de Pau et des Pays de l'Adour et dirige le DESS Droit des victimes, unique à ce jour en France. Depuis de nombreuses années, il est responsable de programmes d'échange européens (Erasmus, Tempus, Socratès, Leonardo). Il a présenté dans ce cadre de nombreuses conférences auprès d'universités européennes. Il est l'auteur de plusieurs ouvrages dont: *Femmes et criminelles*, Ed. Erès (1992); *Jeunes délinquants. A la recherche de la socialisation perdue*, Ed. L'Harmattan (2è éd., 2000); *Introduction aux sciences criminelles. Pour une approche globale et intégrée du phénomène criminel* (3è éd., 2001); *Victimologie. De l'effraction du lien intersubjectif à la restauration sociale* (2è éd., 2001).

Nils Christie is professor of criminology, Faculty of Law, University of Oslo (Norway). He is the author of numerous scientific articles and twelve books, some of them published in a great number of languages. Among them are *Limits to Pain* (Oslo University Press, 1981) and *Crime Control as Industry. Towards Gulags, Western Style ?* (Routledge, revised and enlarged edition, 2000). Most of his writing has been in the field of crime and crime control, but he has also published books on education, drugs and on alternative communities, villages for extraordinary people, by many called mentally retarded. N. Christie has been member of Royal Commissions in Norway on the organisation of the police, on dangerous criminals and on educational matters. He has been the president of the Scandinavian Council for Criminology, and for many years director of the Institute for Criminology and Penal Law in Norway. He has served as a member of the National Criminal Justice Commission in Washington (which published the report *The Real War on Crime*, ed. Steven Donziger). N. Christie is member of the Academy of Science in Norway (Oslo) and in Sweden (Lund), and is honorary doctor in Copenhagen and Sheffield. He has worked as a visiting professor in Berkeley, Jerusalem and Oxford, and also given lectures in a great number of other universities. His particular interest during the last years has been an analysis of the development of prison figures in industrialised countries, as well as the analysis of mediation.

José Luis de la Cuesta studied law (Lic., 1977) at the University of Valladolid and at the University of the Basque Country (Ph.D., 1981), and criminology at the University of Madrid (Diplom., 1979). Other studies and research were conducted at the University of Edinburgh (U.K.), the Max Planck Institut (Freiburg, Germany), the K.U. Leuven (Belgium), the U.C. Louvain (Belgium), and DePaul University (Chicago, USA). He is professor of criminal law of the University of the Basque Country, and director of the Basque Institute of Criminology, and has been visiting professor of the K.U. Leuven (Belgium), the Université de Pau et des Pays de l'Adour (France) and the Université de Paris XII (France). He is deputy of the secretary general of the International Association of Penal Law and chief editor of the *Revue Internationale de Droit Pénal / International Review of Penal Law*. J.-L. de la Cuesta is also a member of the Board of Directors of the International Society of Criminology and of the Istituto Internazionale di Scienci Criminali (Siracusa, Italy). His publications in collective books and scientific reviews deal with topics like penitentiary law, sanctions and alternatives, penal law protection of the environment, terrorism, drug offences, victims and the law, young offenders, organized crime, penal responsibility of corporations, torture, etc.

Jim Dignan holds an LL.B. (Manchester) and an M.A. (Sheffield). He teaches in the fields of criminal justice, criminal process, legal systems and penology at Sheffield University. His current research and publications include the fields of penal and criminal justice policy, comparative penology and restorative justice policy. He is involved in a number of empirical evaluation projects, i.a. for the Home Office, investigating both policy and practice-based initiatives within the spheres of criminal justice reform and the prevention of criminality.

Otto H. Driedger studied social work (M.S.W., 1958) at McGill University, Montréal (Canada), sociology (B.A.) at Bethel College, Kansas (USA), theology (BchE) at the Canadian Mennonite Bible College, Winnipeg (Canada). He holds a Doctorate *honoris causa* (2000) of the Zaporozhye State University (Ukraine) and another one (2001) of the Academy of Arts and Sciences (Odessa, Ukraine). O. Driedger is currently teaching at the University of Regina (Canada) in Human Justice and Social Work, teaching one month annually at Zaporozhye and as a teaching faculty member of Socium, Odessa, Ukraine. His areas of research and writing include social policy, restorative justice and human service education.

Frieder Dünkel studied law at the universities of Heidelberg and Freiburg/Germany (second state examination, 1976). His Ph.D. in 1979 dealt with an empirical research on the effectiveness of therapeutic treatment in prisons. From 1979 until 1992 he worked as a researcher at the Max-Planck-Institute of Foreign and International Penal Law, Criminological Unit, in Freiburg (together with Prof. Günther Kaiser). The subject of his *Habilitation* (1989) was on juvenile imprisonment and other forms of deprivation of liberty in an international comparison. Since 1992 he teaches criminology, penology, juvenile justice, criminal procedure and penal law at the university of Greifswald in the north-east of Germany. The research at the chair (department) of criminology covers a wide range of empirical studies in juvenile criminology, penology, prisons and alternative sanctions, alcohol and drunk driving, drug policy etc. (see www.uni-greifswald.de/~ls3). He has widely published in these areas (20 books and 260 articles), and is the co-editor of the journal *Neue Kriminalpolitik* since 1989 and has organised many international conferences.

Ezzat A. Fattah is the founder of the School of Criminology at Simon Fraser University in Vancouver (Canada), where he is an emeritus professor. He is the author, co-author, editor, co-editor of over a dozen books and has published over ten dozen book chapters, articles, and papers in scholarly journals. E. Fattah is one of the pioneers in victimology, having published in the discipline as early as 1966 and is a strong proponent of restorative justice. Among his recent books are: *Criminology, Past, Present and Future*; *Understanding Criminal Victimization*; *Towards a Critical Victimology*; *The Plight of Crime Victims in Modern Society*; and *From Crime Policy to Victim Policy*. He is a fellow of the Royal Society of Canada, a Doctor *honoris causa* from the University of Liège

(Belgium), and is an elected member of the Board of Directors of the International Society of Criminology.

Arlène Gaudreault détient un baccalauréat (1973) et une maîtrise en criminologie (1988) de l'Université de Montréal (Canada). Depuis 1994, elle enseigne la victimologie à l'Université de Montréal. En octobre 2000, elle était professeure-invitée à l'Université de Pau et des Pays de l'Adour (France) dans le cadre du Diplôme d'études supérieures en victimologie. Elle a contribué au développement de plusieurs programmes dans le champ de la victimologie au Québec et au Canada. Elle est présidente de l'Association québécoise Plaidoyer-Victimes depuis 1988. En août 2000, elle a co-présidé le Xe Symposium international de victimologie à Montréal.

Marc Groenhuijsen graduated in law (1980) at the University of Utrecht (The Netherlands) and received his Ph.D. (1985) at the University of Leiden (The Netherlands) with a thesis on restitution for victims of crime in the criminal justice process. Since 1987, he holds a chair in criminal law and criminal procedure at Tilburg University (The Netherlands). For many years, he has served as chairperson of the Dutch National Association for Victim Assistance and the European Forum for Victims Services, respectively. He has published widely on various topics in victimology and restorative justice.

Ole Ingstrup studied law (Master's, 1966; Ph.D., 1970) at Aarhus University (Denmark) where he subsequently taught law and criminology. The author has been guest lecturing at several universities such as Aarhus University, Copenhagen University, Queen's University, Toronto University, Université de Montreal, Sam Houston State University, K.U. Leuven, Universitaet Greifswald and the University of Western Australia. The author has also been visiting professor to the UN Asia and Far East Institute for the prevention of crime and the treatment of offenders (Tokyo, Japan). He has served as commissioner of the Correctional Service of Canada and is currently research fellow at the School of Business at Queen's University, and a visiting scholar at the Faculty of Arts and Science at Queen's University. His research interests include management and leadership.

Beaty Naudé obtained her MA (1976) and D.Litt. et Phil. (1980) in criminology with distinction at the University of South Africa (UNISA), where she was head of the Department of Criminology at her retirement in 1999. She is currently emeritus professor and research fellow in criminology at UNISA, is a founder member and the past president of the Criminological Society of South Africa and currently serves on the scientific boards of the International Society of Criminology and the *British Journal of Criminology*. She is the author and co-author of 114 scientific publications and conducted a number of victims of crime surveys in Southern Africa in collaboration with the United Nations Institute for Criminal Justice Research Institute (UNICRI) in Rome. In 1998 she was awarded for one of her publications the Butterworth prize for the most useful and best-motivated law reform proposal concerning crime victims. Her research interests are victim surveys, victims of commercial crimes, organised crime, crime prevention and restorative justice.

Beth Grothe Nielsen studied law (cand.jur., 1972; lic.jur. (eq. Ph.D.), 1981) at the University of Copenhagen (Denmark). She currently teaches criminal law, criminology and victimology at the Institute of Law at the University of Aarhus (Denmark) and criminology at the Department of Sociology at the University of Aalborg (Denmark). She has been visiting professor at the Law Faculty, University of Reykjavik (Iceland) and member of the Accreditation Panel for Sex Offender Treatment Programmes at the Correctional Service of Canada. She has written extensively on child sexual abuse in the family, treatment of sex offenders, victims in the criminal justice system and juvenile justice. Her research interests include incest discourse, restorative justice and criminal policy in general.

Stephan Parmentier studied law (Lic., 1983; Ph.D., 1997), political sciences (Cand., 1982) and sociology (Lic., 1987) at the K.U. Leuven (Belgium), and sociology (M.A., 1987) at the University of Minnesota-Twin Cities (U.S.A.). He currently teaches sociology of crime and law, and human rights at the Faculty of Law of the K.U. Leuven and is the director of its Law and Society Institute. S. Parmentier has been a visiting scholar at the University of Stellenbosch (South Africa), and a visiting professor at the International Institute for Sociology of Law in Oñati (Spain), where he has also served as member of the Board. He is currently the editor-in-chief of the *Flemish Yearbook on Human Rights*, and his research and publications relate to transitional justice and human rights (particularly criminal prosecution and truth commissions), the administration of (criminal) justice, and asylum law and policy.

Georges Picca is Doctor in Law, and associate professor in criminology and penal law at the University Paris X (France). He served as legal adviser of the Ministry of Justice for prison system, and as judge at the Supreme Court of Cassation (Paris). He is currently the secretary general of the International Society for criminology, and has written several books and researches in criminology, penology and criminal policy.

Isabel Sánchez García de Paz studied law (Lic., 1987; Doctor 1993) at the University of Valladolid (Spain). He currently teaches criminal law at the Faculty of Law of the University of Valladolid (Spain). The author has been a research fellow at the Max-Planck-Institut für Ausländisches und Internationales Strafrecht (Freiburg, Germany), the Department of Criminology at the Faculty of Law of the University of Edinburgh (United Kingdom) and at the Institut of Criminal Law and Criminology of the University of Salzburg (Austria). Her research interests include juvenile delinquency, white-collar crime, international criminal law and organized crime.

Anton van Kalmthout studied Law (LL.M., 1978; Ph.D., 2001) at the K.U. Nijmegen and the K.U. Tilburg (The Netherlands) and Classics (M.A., 1972) at the K.U. Nijmegen (The Netherlands) and the K.U. Leuven (Belgium). He currently teaches criminal law, criminal procedure and comparative criminal law and migration law at the Faculty of Law of the K.U. Tilburg. The author is since 1998 honorary professor at the State University of Krasnoyarsk (Russian Federation), where he teaches comparative criminal law. His research interests include penitentiary law, comparative criminal law, migration law and sentencing issues.

Dirk van Zyl Smit studied law (B.A., 1970; LL.B., 1972) at the University of Stellenbosch (South Africa) and criminology (Ph.D., 1981) in Edinburgh (Great Britain). He has been professor of Criminology at the University of Cape Town since 1982. Since January 2000 he also holds a half-time chair as professor of Comparative and International Penal Law at the University of Nottingham

(Great Britain). He has advised the new South African government on prison and sentencing legalisation, and a great deal of his work has been in the area of comparative criminal justice. His most recent publication in this area is *Imprisonment Today and Tomorrow: International Perspectives on Prisoners' Rights and Prison Conditions* (edited with Frieder Dünkel, 2001). He has recently completed a study of the jurisprudence of life imprisonment.

Gema Varona Martinez studied law (Lic., 1992; Ph.D., 1997) and criminology (Dipl., 1991) at the University of the Basque Country, and sociology of law (M.A., 1995) at the International Institute for Sociology of Law in Oñati (Spain). She has been a visiting researcher at the K.U. Leuven (Belgium), HEUNI (Finland), the Max-Planck-Institut (Germany) and the University of Cambridge (U.K.). She currently teaches criminology and sociology of law at the Institute of Criminology of the Basque Country. G. Varona is the author of books about human rights and immigration, restorative justice, and legal cultures in relation to juries. Her research interests include the police and women in the criminal justice system.

Martin Wright studied modern languages (M.A., 1954) at the University of Oxford, and obtained a Ph.D. in criminology (1990) at the London School of Economics (U.K.). He has been librarian at the Institute of Criminology, University of Cambridge, director of the Howard League for Penal Reform, and policy officer for Victim Support. He is currently a visiting research fellow at the School of Legal Studies, University of Sussex (U.K.). He was a founder member of Mediation UK, and is currently vice-chair of the Restorative Justice Consortium and a member of the board of the European Forum for Victim/Offender Mediation and Restorative Justice. He is a volunteer mediator in Lambeth, South London. His publications include *Making good: prisons, punishment and beyond* (1982), *Justice for victims and offenders: a restorative response to crime* (2nd ed., 1996), and *Restoring respect for justice* (1999).

Peter Young is director of the Institute of Criminology, Faculty of Law, University College Dublin (Ireland). Previously, he worked in the Faculty of Law, University of Edinburgh where he was a founder member and then director of the Centre for Law and Society; he was also vice-dean and head of the Edinburgh School of Law. P. Young has published widely on the sociology of punishment and criminal justice, including *The Power to Punish* (with D. Garland) and *Crime and Criminal Justice in Scotland*. His current research interests are in long-term changes in punishment and comparative rates of crime; his study of crime rates in Ireland, *Crime in Ireland*, written with Emma Clare and Ian O'Donnell is to be published shortly.

SAMENLEVING, CRIMINALITEIT EN STRAFRECHTSPLEGING

5. A. Neys, T. Peters, F. Pieters en J. Vanacker (red.),
Tralies in de weg. Het Belgische gevangeniswezen: historiek, balans en perspectieven
1994, xxviii-425 p., ISBN 90 6186 654 5, BEF 1.450 - 35,94 €
6. S. Parmentier en T. Peters (red.),
Detentie doorgelicht. Het Belgisch rapport van het Europees Comité voor de Preventie van Foltering
in voorbereiding
7. W. Van Laethem, T. Decorte en R. Bas,
Private politiezorg en grondrechten. De methoden van private bewaking en opsporing en de grondrechten van de mens
1995, xxii-357 p., ISBN 90 6186 679 0, BEF 1.750 - 43,39 €
8. J. Van Kerckvoorde
Een maat voor het kwaad? Over de meting van criminaliteit met behulp van officiële statistieken en door middel van enquêtes
1995, xii-362 p., ISBN 90 6186 697 9, BEF 1.250 - 30,98 €
9. L. Walgrave (red.),
Confronterende jongeren
1996, 272 p., ISBN 90 6186 782 7, BEF 1.250 - 30,98 €
10. C. Fijnaut en R. Verstraeten,
2 delen: Het strafrechtelijk onderzoek inzake de "bende van Nijvel". De rapporten ten behoeve van de Parlementaire Onderzoekscommissie belast met een onderzoek van de noodzakelijke aanpassingen van de organisatie en werking van het politie- en justitiewezen op basis van de moeilijkheden die zijn gerezen bij het onderzoek naar de "bende van Nijvel"
1997, 2 delen, 1204 p., ISBN 90 6186 850 5, BEF 2.500 - 69,98 €
A. Masset,
L'enquête criminelle sur les "tueurs du Brabant". Enquête parlementaire sur les adaptions nécessaires en matières d'organisation et de fonctionnement de l'appareil policier et judiciaire, en fonction des difficultés surgies lors de l'enquête sur les "tueurs du Brabant"
1998, 204 p., ISBN 90 6186 852 1, BEF 750 - 18,59 €
Volumes 10a + 10b + 10c: BEF 3.000 - 74,36 €
11. L. Dupont (red.),
Op weg naar een beginselenwet gevangeniswezen
1998, 293 p., ISBN 90 6186 919 6, BEF 1.250 - 30,98 €
12. L. Walgrave (ed.)
Restorative Justice for Juveniles. Potentialities, Risks and Problems for Research
1998, 407 p., ISBN 60 6186 920 X, BEF 1.600 - 39,67 €

13. E. Fattah and T. Peters (eds.)
Support for Crime Victims in a Comparative Perspective
1998, 256 p., ISBN 90 6186 927 7, BEF 1.250 - 30,98 €
14. C. Fijnaut, D. Van Daele en F. Verbruggen (red.)
De uitdaging van de georganiseerde misdaad in België. Het antwoord van de overheid
1998, 371 p., ISBN 90 6186 931 5, BEF 1.500 - 31,18 €
15. C. Fijnaut en D. Van Daele (red.)
De hervorming van het openbaar ministerie
1999, 454 p., ISBN 90 6186 937 4, BEF 1.700 - 42,15 €
16. J. Goethals, A. de Boye en C. Fijnaut
Criminaliteit en onveiligheidsgevoelens in de Limburgse ex-mijngemeenten
1999, 160 p., ISBN 90 6186 983 8, BEF 950 - 23,55 €
17. C. Fijnaut, B. de Ruyver en F. Goossens (red.)
De reorganisatie van het politiewezen
1999, 277 p., ISBN 90 6186 989 7, BEF 1.800 - 44,63 €
18. L. Walgrave
Met het oog op herstel. Bakens voor een constructief jeugdsanctierecht
2000, 178 p., ISBN 90 5867 015 5, BEF 950 - 23,55 €
19. L. Vandekerckhove
On Punishment. The Confrontation of Suicide in Old-Europe
2000, 182 p., ISBN 90 5867 024 4, BEF 1.295 - 32,10 €
20. The European Forum for Victim-Offender Mediation and Restorative Justice (ed.)
Victim-Offender Mediation in Europe. Making Restorative Justice Work
2000, 382 p., ISBN 90 5867 035 X, BEF 1.600 - 39,66 €
21A. C. Fijnaut, D. Van Daele en S. Parmentier
Een openbaar ministerie voor de 21ste eeuw
2000, xx-266 p., ISBN 90 5867 052 X, BEF 1.450 - 36 €
21B. D. Van Daele
Het openbaar ministerie en de afhandeling van strafzaken in Duitsland
2000, 358 p., ISBN 90 5867 078 3, BEF 1.500 - 37,18 €
22. L. Dupont en F. Hutsebaut (red.)
Herstelrecht tussen toekomst en verleden. Liber Amicorum Tony Peters
2001, 606 p., ISBN 90 5867 180 1, BEF 2.057 - 51,00 €
23. E. Fattah, S. Parmentier (eds.)
Victim policies and criminal justice on the road to restorative justice
2001, 460 p., ISBN 90 5867 181 X, BEF 1.412 - 35,00 €

Drukkerij en Binderij
SCHEERDERS van KERCHOVE
9100 ST.-NIKLAAS